*Resources and Development*

*The Wisconsin Seminar on Natural Resource Policies
in Relation to Economic Development and
International Cooperation, 1977–1978*


co-sponsored by

University of Wisconsin-Madison
Organization of Arab Petroleum Exporting Countries (OAPEC)
Arab Fund for Economic and Social Development (AFESD)
Kuwait Fund for Arab Economic Development (KFAED)

# Resources and Development

Natural Resource Policies
and Economic Development
in an Interdependent World

*Edited by*

Peter Dorner
Mahmoud A. El-Shafie

THE UNIVERSITY OF WISCONSIN PRESS
CROOM HELM LONDON

Published in the United States and Canada by
The University of Wisconsin Press
114 North Murray Street
Madison, Wisconsin 53715
ISBN 0-299-08250-4

Published in the United Kingdom, the Continent of Europe, India, and Australia by
Croom Helm Ltd
2-10 St John's Road, London SW 11
ISBN 0-7099-0382-0

First printing 1980
Printed in the United States of America

For LC CIP information see the colophon

# Contents

# Contributors

**Peter Dorner**
Professor of Agricultural Economics and the Land Tenure Center, University of Wisconsin-Madison, and Seminar Co-Chairman

**Mahmoud A. El-Shafie**
United Nations Chief Planning Advisor, UN Development Program, Damascus, Syria, and Seminar Co-Chairman

**I. H. Abdel-Rahman**
Senior Advisor to the Prime Minister of the Arab Republic of Egypt and Consultant to OAPEC (March–July 1978)

**Abdulaziz Al-Wattari**
Assistant Secretary General, OAPEC, Kuwait (September–October 1977, August 1978)

**Richard B. Bilder**
Professor of Law, University of Wisconsin-Madison

**Edgar L. Feige**
Professor of Economics, University of Wisconsin-Madison

**M. Sarwat Montassir**
Industrial Consultant and Director, Investment Promotion—International Consultants, Cairo, Egypt (January–July 1978)

**Raymond J. Penn**
Professor Emeritus of Agricultural Economics, University of Wisconsin-Madison

**Vincent C. Rideout**
Professor of Electrical and Computer Engineering, University of Wisconsin-Madison

**John E. Ross**
Professor of Agricultural Journalism and Environmental Studies, University of Wisconsin-Madison

**John Steinhart**
Professor of Geophysics and Environmental Studies, University of Wisconsin-Madison

**George Tomeh**
Senior Advisor to OAPEC on International Relations, Kuwait

Except where noted parenthetically, all contributors participated in the Seminar throughout the 1977–78 academic year. Usameh F. Jamali, Head of Energy Studies, OAPEC, Kuwait, also participated in the Seminar in October and November 1977.

# Student Participants

David M. Blau
Carel C. DeWinkel
Adel S. Elmaghraby
Sami Haddad
Donald Hertzmark
Humoud B. Humoud
Mohamed K. Mansour
William M. McCalla
El-Saudi A. Mohamed
Ali A. Naas*
Jan I. Ondrich
Mohamed O. A. Osman
Said M. Seif El-Yazal
Fouad J. Shamesaldin*


John E. Bielefeldt, Seminar Editor
Olivia L. Naeseth, Secretary

*Ali A. Naas, Legal Officer of the OAPEC Staff, and Fouad J. Shamesaldin, Economic Researcher, Ministry of Oil, Iraq, were enrolled at the University of Wisconsin-Madison as special students and devoted full time to the work of the seminar. All others were degree candidates in various University departments and part-time participants in the Seminar.

# Foreword

I am pleased and honored to be asked to introduce this significant book. It contains the contributions of the senior participants of the Seminar on both theoretical and practical aspects of the technical, economic, legal, and policy problems, issues, and prospects of developing and using natural resources in economic development and international cooperation.

The idea of the Seminar originated with a proposal submitted by the University of Wisconsin's Institute for Environmental Studies. In February 1976, Professor John Ross, Associate Director of the Institute, and Professor Raymond J. Penn presented the proposal to representatives from the Arab co-sponsors. The theme of their proposal was international policies in relation to natural resources, and subsequent discussions resulted in revision of the original outline in order to concentrate more clearly on natural resources in relation to economic development and international cooperation.

It was clear from the beginning that the Seminar should be multidisciplinary and should include senior and student participants from the countries of the co-sponsoring organizations. It was agreed that the Seminar should be a joint project, supported by all the co-sponsors, but that participants should be free from any official obligations pertaining to their positions or affiliations with the co-sponsoring institutions. It was felt that this approach would give the Seminar participants maximum opportunity to debate freely these many complex problems and issues.

The paramount place of natural resources in relation to economic development and international cooperation needs no illustration in today's world: because natural resources provide the means for personal and national wealth, their possession and management are often the main area for international conflict and confrontation. The theme of the Seminar is all the more significant because it does address the problems of natural resources in the context of national and regional development, supported by a system of international cooperation, as the only alternative to confrontation. The basic issues of resources, development, and cooperation are not new. They have been debated in many forums, especially since the first United Nations Conference on Trade and Development held in Geneva in 1964. They have been studied by academic institutions, international organizations, professional groups, and associations such as the Club of Rome. They have also been discussed in political forums such as the so-called North-South dialog and, of course, in the United Nations and its specialized agencies.

However, in many of these last forums the discussions were often constrained either by conflicting political positions or by the narrowness of the scope within which the discussions were conducted. In many cases assertions of conflicting positions were dominant. Sometimes the discussions focused too much, perhaps, on how the world should be and disregarded contemporary realities. Often the developing countries tended to talk to themselves, as did the developed countries.

It is the hope of the co-sponsors that the informal and professional approach followed by the participants in this Seminar has succeeded in making a fresh contribution toward better understanding of the nature and scope of natural resource policies in relation to economic development and international cooperation. The reader should be able to make his or her own judgment on whether the Seminar participants have succeeded in this respect.

Because the Seminar devoted a great deal of deliberation to the concept and structure of international cooperation and interdependence, it is relevant to ask why nations find it necessary to cooperate with each other. Is it because some of them are no longer able to dominate the others, or is the world graduating to a higher level of universal cooperation and human brotherhood? After all, powerful nations historically have tended to compete for those parts of the world which they could dominate. In other words, do nations turn to the concept of cooperation only when they realize that domination can no longer accomplish their objectives? Do we see a tendency for cooperation among nations of unequal power? Can the world enjoy genuine cooperation and interdependence without containing domination by and dependence on the powerful nations of the world? When talking about cooperation and interdependence are we really saying that we want to move away from where we are to what we want? Is this a value judgment or a global necessity?

The term "cooperational confrontation" is sometimes used to suggest that confrontation can take place only among nations of some equality in power, so that it may be necessary to have some confrontation as a prerequisite for true cooperation. In this regard, the developing countries must seek to achieve regional cooperation among themselves as a precondition for effective cooperation with the advanced industrial countries.

The Arab co-sponsors of the seminar have great interest in natural resources, economic development, and international cooperation. Several of their member countries are significant oil exporters. Their most important and depletable natural resources are now used as a bridge over which the world is passing in an energy transition from oil to coal, to nuclear power, and to renewable sources of energy. The main challenge for the future of these countries is managing their depletable resources in a way that will allow their societies to develop and join in the passage over the bridge to the world of renewable energy sources. They must at all costs avoid being left behind on the other side of the bridge or collapsing with it. All the Arab countries depend on imports for their domestic food supplies. They all depend on the import market for capital goods and for many manufactured and semimanufactured consumer goods. They are also heavily dependent on foreign markets for many kinds of professional skills and technical know-how.

With all these structural dependencies the Arab countries, like the rest of the developing countries, frequently suffer from a steady flow of real resources in favor of the developed countries. This flow takes the form of adverse terms of trade and monetary fluctuations, and even a brain drain in the case of some Arab countries. These trends tend to perpetuate a global resource-distribution problem in which most of the world's resources are consumed by a few industrial countries with less than one-third of the world's population.

Although the Arab oil-exporting countries are often portrayed as the world's wealthy, it is significant to note that the gross domestic product of Italy is greater than that of all the Arab countries combined. The twenty-one Arab countries combined (including the oil exporters), with about 120 million people, earn less than Italy with only 50 million inhabitants and a standard of living that is not among the highest in Europe. Yet Italy has a developed infrastructure, a highly literate population, and an advanced industrial society whose value cannot be readily measured in monetary terms.

Oil provides capital for investment but it also tends to create some conditions which make development more difficult to achieve. In an under-developed economy, oil quickly creates excessive monetary expansion, rapid rural migration to crowded urban areas, and rapid deterioration of the traditional forms of production with correspondingly rapid and heavy dependence on imports. The result in many cases is integration of consumer sectors in the oil-exporting countries with producing sectors of the advanced industrialized countries. Thus oil can become the main vehicle for widening the gap between the newly developed consumer and service sector which feeds on oil and the indigenous resources and skills of the economy.

All these problems face the Arab countries in general and the oil exporters among them in particular, and it is natural that the Arab co-sponsors of the Seminar are very much interested in the kinds of problems and issues covered by this book. In fact, the Arab Fund for Economic and Social Development (AFESD) and the Kuwait Fund for Arab Economic Development (KFAED) are fully engaged in providing financial and technical assistance to developing countries. Although the Arab Fund limits its assistance to its member countries, the Kuwait Fund extends aid to both Arab and non-Arab developing countries.

The third Arab co-sponsor is commodity-oriented, but it too is in essence a development organization. The Organization of Arab Petroleum Exporting Countries (OAPEC), consisting of only ten Arab countries, is concerned with promoting policy coordination and development of members' domestic hydrocarbon sectors, along with those sectors' integration within the rest of the economy where local resources permit. OAPEC also encourages and supports joint development projects in the field of hydrocarbons and related activities.

In conclusion, I wish to express the hope that the results of this Seminar, as partly conveyed in this book, will be of interest and assistance to researchers, students, and policy-makers dealing with the complex global problems of natural resources, economic development, and international cooperation. The co-sponsors would be very much pleased if their contribution in supporting this Seminar could give rise to more intensive research and international debate on the problems raised in this book. It is hoped that the concept of a multidisciplinary and multinational approach organized on a regional basis will gain wide acceptance in the formulation and conduct of future research. This could be the first step toward achieving greater international cooperation in other fields.

ALI A. ATTIGA
Secretary General—OAPEC

*Kuwait*
*November 1978*

# Preface

This volume is the work of the senior participants, with research assistance from the students, of the Wisconsin Seminar on Natural Resource Policies in Relation to Economic Development and International Cooperation. It is written to provide a multidisciplinary perspective for national and international efforts, both private and public, aimed at some of the most pressing problems of our time. The economic, legal, social, political, and technological issues inherent in the subject matter are not only complex; they are also controversial. There is little professional consensus about most of them. Neither academia nor political bodies consider them settled matters, and political action will certainly continue to put these issues into new perspectives. Consequently, we wish to make clear that these chapters represent their authors' views and are not to be interpreted as representing complete agreement among contributors to this volume or among Seminar participants in general. Likewise none of the views are to be attributed to the co-sponsoring organizations.

Participants in the Seminar represent a broad range of academic disciplines and wide experience in professional public service with national and international organizations. Although consensus on the difficult policy issues discussed during the Seminar sessions was not always achieved, all of the participants did find the Seminar a true learning process and none emerged after the year-long deliberations without major additions to, and reformulations of, ideas previously held. It is our hope that readers of this volume will find it of equal value.

The breadth of the issues investigated and the participants' backgrounds also presented problems of communication. In writing this volume the authors agreed to keep technical language to a minimum and to write for a more general audience. No doubt specific sections will still seem too technical for some, while they may strike experts in the field as not technical enough. Our objective has been to avoid where possible technical language without sacrificing precision of expression.

The co-chairmen of the seminar were selected and mutually agreed upon by the co-sponsoring organizations in the Middle East and by the Chancellor of the University of Wisconsin, Madison. Other participants were selected by the two co-chairmen in consultation with the Chancellor and the co-sponsoring organizations.

The Seminar met in formal sessions at Madison three times weekly during the 1977–78 academic year. We were fortunate to have University of Wisconsin faculty members from a variety of fields address the Seminar on their research in issues of resources, development, and international cooperation. A number of invited speakers from the United States, the Middle East, and elsewhere also addressed the Seminar, and their remarks were most helpful in establishing guidelines and delineating problems for further analysis. At other sessions, Seminar participants themselves presented views and analyses for the day's discussion. In the first week of March 1978, the Seminar held a three-day session at the headquarters of the Organization of Arab Petroleum Exporting Countries in Kuwait.

This volume attempts an integration of the great amount of material studied, discussed, and produced by Seminar participants. Three volumes of proceedings have been printed. Volume I contains all the formal papers presented by invited speakers. Volumes II and III contain the working documents developed by Seminar participants and the editor's summaries of individual sessions.

As co-chairmen, speaking for all participants, we wish to express our deep appreciation to the organizations and the individuals who made it possible to hold the Seminar and to get this book and the proceedings into print. We wish to thank the co-sponsoring organizations for their financial and intellectual support: the Organization of Arab Petroleum Exporting Countries; the Arab Fund for Economic and Social Development; the Kuwait Fund for Arab Economic Development; and the University of Wisconsin-Madison, its Graduate School, and its Institute for Environmental Studies. We are grateful to the staff of the Institute for all the logistic and administrative support it provided to the Seminar. The Seminar was greatly enriched by the active and energetic participation of the students, and by the wisdom that other University of Wisconsin faculty members and invited speakers shared with the Seminar participants. We are deeply grateful for their assistance.

We express our sincere thanks and appreciation to Ms. Olivia Naeseth, Head Secretary and Office Manager, who kept the Seminar and its participants on schedule. In addition to managing the office affairs for this rather complex enterprise, she did much of the typing of manuscripts for the several publications as well as typing all correspondence. For her very capable and always goodnatured performance under, at times, rather hectic conditions, we are deeply grateful. We are also most appreciative of the very meticulous manuscript typing for both the proceedings and for this volume by Ms. Jeanne Zwaska. We are indebted to these two people for their excellent work and cooperation.

Finally, we wish to acknowledge our great debt for the high professional standards and quality of work of the Seminar's Editor, John Bielefeldt. Without his very skillful assistance neither this nor the Proceedings volumes would have been possible. His summaries of each Seminar session were extremely useful in keeping participants supplied with a concise and focused record of the Seminar's work. His comprehension of all the complex substantive issues discussed by Seminar participants was an invaluable asset for helping to improve the organization and the readability of this volume. We are all deeply grateful for the many ways in which he helped authors individually and as a group.

To all of the above, as well as to the Staff at OAPEC for the excellent planning and arrangements which made our session in Kuwait a most pleasant and successful experience, we express our deep gratitude and appreciation.

PETER DORNER
MAHMOUD A. EL-SHAFIE

Seminar Co-Chairmen

*Madison, Wisconsin*
*December 1978*

*Resources and Development*

*Peter Dorner*

# Introduction

The stock resources that fueled the industrial revolution and fed the growth of industrial economies are now recognized to be finite and nonrenewable, and with the realization of that fact has come an awareness that the institutional structures which emerged from that revolution and guided the development of economies around the world are no longer adequate. There is an urgent need for policies which can redirect and reshape those institutional structures. To design and implement such policies, in the light of the growing conflicts of interest among nations and groups of nations, constitutes a challenge to the leadership—intellectual, economic, political, and moral—in all national and international agencies and organizations.

In the past decade, consciousness of resource scarcity and its effect on the development of the world's economies has been heightened by a combination of several circumstances. Chief among these were sharp increases in the price of petroleum, accelerating prices for grains and other food products after several poor harvests in various parts of the world, high rates of inflation and mounting indebtedness, and a growing concern about unfavorable environmental consequences of continued economic growth. The impact of these factors on global economic development has been startling and significant. For the first time since World War II (indeed, in the modern era) the industrial nations have been made painfully

3

aware of the fact that even in times of peace they were not fully in charge of their own policies, that they were increasingly dependent on natural resources owned and controlled by others, and that, where they had once dealt with dependent colonies, they were now dealing with states which enjoyed varying degrees of independence and which were seeking to take full control over their resources and their own economic and political development. The developing countries are faced with an urgent need for vast amounts of capital and for natural resources of all kinds, and competition for both capital and natural resources has been intensified. As natural resources, or at least several strategic ones, have seemed to be getting scarcer and have certainly been getting more costly, the demand for them has promised to grow ever more rapidly. And even resources that seem abundant now may very well become increasingly scarce and costly as a result of continued economic growth in the wealthier nations and accelerated development efforts by the poorer nations of the world.

Compounding the problem, of course, is the fact that natural resources are distributed very unevenly among the countries of the world, and there is often little relationship between the location of strategic resources and population densities or between resources and developmental aspirations and current levels of living and consumption patterns. Consequently, substantial quantities of most natural resources or their immediate products move in international trade. There is a renewed and growing concern over the terms on which these natural resources and resource commodities are traded for other goods, such as manufactures, capital goods and equipment, technical skills and services, etc.

Although the problems of resources and development have become increasingly interrelated and global in scope, most past studies have confined their analyses to particular aspects of these issues. The Wisconsin Seminar on Natural Resource Policies in Relation to Economic Development and International Cooperation, out of which this volume grew, attempted to treat these problems within a comprehensive, multidisciplinary framework. The main concern of the Seminar was with more equitable, humane, and efficient modes of development, both within and among nations, given the constraints of finite natural resources, ecosystems with poorly measured yet definite limits for absorbing the shocks and the by-products of growing populations and geometrically expanding resource use, and political systems that have so far attempted to resolve pressing social problems by inducing rates and kinds of economic growth that cannot be sustained indefinitely. Each of the individual chapters in this volume was designed to address a specific aspect of these overarching global issues, and all were guided by the three central themes of the Seminar and the volume—natural resource policies, economic development, and international cooperation.

Our primary purpose in dealing with these themes in this volume was to achieve some insight into, and clarification of, the policy questions and issues they pose for nation-states and international organizations. We have undertaken to consider them not in isolation or from the perspective of a single discipline, but in the context of their global interrelatedness. Policy must deal with all the complex global aspects of the issues raised by these concerns, and policy makers cannot afford to ignore the intricate interrelationships among them. Policy cannot be shaped in isolation; it requires a comprehensive view of the conditions and events in the real world and a recognition of the demands and aspirations of the people in that world. Obviously, all the phases of these complex issues cannot be treated in anything approaching a definitive way in one volume. Nor do we make any claims to having "solved" any of these complicated policy questions. While each chapter (and especially the final one) provides some general policy recommendations, this volume is essentially exploratory, concerned with a realistic examination of policy alternatives. There is, we are convinced, no single objective truth about the policy measures best suited to deal with these global issues.

Indeed, in reviewing the vast literature on various aspects of these issues, one is struck by the wide divergence in conclusions and positions that emerge from different analyses. On the one hand are the conclusions projecting doom and catastrophe and instilling fear, and on the other, the positions of unqualified and unfounded optimism, frequently based on blind faith in future technological developments. The "truth" (or a workable compromise) may lie somewhere within the broad spectrum of possibilities encompassed by these extremes. One should recognize, however, that there are many valid reasons why serious students of these complex issues will reach conclusions that vary widely.

Because policy deals with the future it is always necessary to make certain assumptions and estimates about many behavioral variables and their interactions. Projections of past trends of resource use and environmental degradation do indeed lead to a gloomy outlook for the future. But some analysts counter that increasing scarcity of finite resources will be reflected in higher prices and costs which will curb consumption, stimulate technological developments to economize on the scarcer resources, and in fact induce people to change their consumption habits. The contention here is that sheer physical projections of resource availabilities ignore the most fundamental resource—human knowledge and intelligence. Science, it is suggested, has changed emphasis and direction in the past, and it can (indeed it must) do so in the future. And although any new course in science and technology will inevitably be disruptive of some human values, the creations of science and technology also provide new options, new alternatives, and new value possibilities. Future developments in science and technology cannot be foreseen. If they could, we would not need research. There is always an element of faith with respect to the future constructive uses of science and technology, but human experience throughout history has shown the creativity of human intelligence in dealing with the physical universe and in shaping and reshaping behavior, institutions, and techniques in living within that physical universe. Has the modern era locked man into patterns of growth and dependence in which this demonstrated capacity for creative adaptation has been weakened? Differing assumptions about some of these intangibles can lead to divergent views about future prospects and appropriate policies.

One of the basic and inescapable problems in treating the global issues of natural resource policies and economic development is that of time. No serious student would contend that there are *no* physical limits to natural resources of the earth, or that there are no limits on the earth's ultimate capacity to support biological systems. But how close are we to approaching such limits and how much time can be allowed in planning to adjust to them? Assumptions vary widely, as do policy prescriptions rooted in these different assumptions.

At one extreme are prescriptions for "zero growth" in the economies of the current industrial countries. Such no-growth policies could relieve pressure on finite resources and permit the developing nations to grow and at least provide the goods and services needed to satisfy the basic needs of their people, hundreds of millions of whom are desperately poor. But no-growth economies in the industrial countries, or even very low rates of economic growth, would also have major effects on the economies of developing nations which depend on the markets of the industrial countries. At the other extreme are assumptions and accompanying policy prescriptions for rates of growth throughout the foreseeable planning period similar to those of the past 20 to 30 years. Resource scarcities, according to this position, have been predicted throughout history, but new sources of supply have been found, substitutes have been developed, and technology has been created to make more efficient use of resources that are becoming scarcer or more expensive. To be sure, there may be problems of environmental pollution and destruction, but they have been known to occur in the past even without the technological developments and the population pressures of the present. Problems of this sort, it is maintained, should be approached not by no-growth policies but by measures designed to internalize costs so that those responsible for detrimental effects on the environment are required to pay for restoring it. Appropriate cost allocations would provide the incentives necessary to avoid many of the current processes of environmental degradation. Between these extreme positions lies a wide range of possible opportunities and restraints, and the choice of paths over which the nations of the world will move toward the future will be to a large extent determined by the assumptions with which they begin.

Another issue that depends on assumptions about human adaptability and about the time span under consideration and likewise leads to diverse policy prescriptions is the issue of growth in human populations. Rhetoric to the contrary notwithstanding, and with a few exceptions, most nations are concerned with population growth. Advocacy of population control and of movement toward zero growth in numbers seems ubiquitous. Although there seem to be few defenders of continued rapid growth in population, the Third World nations where population growth (and often current density as well) is highest remind the industrial nations that growth in numbers is only one side of the population question. The other side is rates of use and levels of consumption of natural resources by the wealthier populations in the industrial countries. The majority of the world's people live in the developing countries, but the minority living in the developed industrial countries consumes a highly disproportionate amount of the natural resources moving in international trade.

The contrast seems clear. One view suggests that only by controlling population numbers and growth rates can the poor of this world hope to improve their status and physical well-being. The other view holds that although population control is often necessary in practice and accepted in principle, there will be insufficient resources for the poor to improve their position unless the rich control their levels and rates of growth of resource consumption.

Differing analyses and prescriptions are grounded not only in differing assumptions, but in differing political realities and power relations among nation states. A common view of people in the industrial countries is that they never got anything for nothing: they worked hard for what they got; let others do likewise. Yet in the minds of many, there is an uneasy feeling that the industrial countries have gained disproportionate advantage from their leadership in science and engineering and the multitude of techniques for "conquering and controlling" nature. Moreover, there is a feeling of near certainty by many in the developing world that the industrial states' advantage and current high levels of material consumption are the direct result of colonization and exploitation, over many years, of the developing world. Divergent policy prescriptions are not purely analytical matters of assumptions and empirical conclusions, but also matters of interpretation of history and of political relations among equally sovereign yet not equally powerful nation states.

A further complication results from the fact that in any discussion or evaluation of policy for the future it is never quite clear to whom prescriptions are addressed. Individuals are all, to a degree, trapped by their own culture and its institutions. Yet the changes that must occur will indeed be based on the decisions of millions of individuals and families—whether reducing the number of births, lowering rates of resource use and consumption, adopting new values and pursuits to displace resource-intensive styles of living, and so forth. However, inducing the changes necessary in the decisions of tens of millions of individuals so that those decisions will move society in a new and consistent direction can be achieved only by restructuring national institutions and incentive systems, and not by merely appealing to individuals to change their ways voluntarily. People do live and act at the local level, but their alternatives and opportunities are shaped significantly by events at the regional, national, and international levels.

Even policies devised and implemented at the level of the sovereign nation-state are inadequate to meet the problems. Just as the physical environment links all people of the globe in an intricate web of interrelationships, so too do increasingly complex economic and political interrelationships and interdependencies both expand and restrict the possibilities for action on the part of nations. In a simpler era when life's functions were provided for on a smaller scale and with something closer to self-sufficiency at local levels, resource use and conservation issues could be more readily encompassed by local action. Natural resources are imbued with a "public interest." With ever greater complexity and scale of mutual dependencies, however, the concept of the public in defining that "public interest" has come to include ever larger numbers over increasingly wide geographic areas. Some of these issues cannot be resolved at the national level, but require international cooperation, negotiation, and agreement.

The way in which the world is now structured institutionally does not provide enough feedback to discipline powerful decision makers, be they private or public, to make their acts consistent with the larger (sometimes global) public interest. Decisions and actions taken by economically powerful private interests or nations may have widespread and costly consequences for people in remote parts of the globe, yet those who make the decisions may be unaware of the far-reaching influence of their own acts. Even if they are aware of these consequences, they do not feel their real costs. It is only as these costs (which are now widely diffused) are reflected back and borne by the private firm or the nation which incurred them that the self-interest of that firm or nation will be enlisted for the promotion of the wider public (or international) interest. The incentives and sanctions created to induce more responsible and responsive actions promoting the larger public interest will be transmitted to smaller organizational units throughout the system and will eventually serve to redirect the actions of millions of individuals at the local level. In earlier and simpler times, incentives and sanctions could be devised and changed at the local level. In today's complicated world of mutual dependencies and disparate economic, military, and political powers held by ever larger decision-making units, this process of reconstructing institutions and incentives must include first and foremost those powerful actors who help by their decisions to shape the opportunity structure of individuals the world over.

It is this entire context of interwoven issues, uncertainties, and dilemmas which defines the ground for the chapters in this volume. In the chapters that follow, divergent views and their underlying bases are by no means absent. Different assumptions from different disciplines and experiences of the authors serve both to enrich the content and to assure the exploration of a wide range of prospective policy directions.

Although individual chapters were written from the disciplinary and intellectual perspectives of their authors, writing began only after a year of deliberative meetings and was finished only after another six months of individual critique, redrafting, group critique, and revision. Even though the authors of the volume have made a long effort to understand and address the issues in a comprehensive manner, conceptual and analytical integration must necessarily be incomplete: the subject is too broad and the problems too intricate for a truly interdisciplinary analysis. There is no single body of theory which encompasses all the strategic variables. The theoretical and historical connections among natural resources and resource policies, economic development, and national and international concerns are combined with empirical evidence as available and useful. For many of the questions, however, evidence is sparse and sometimes contradictory.

The chapters have been grouped under four general headings: Natural Resources, Economic Development, International Cooperation, and Analytical and Policy Redirections. It was the judgment of the authors that natural resource policy issues, as they are affected by growth in numbers, consumption levels, and the accumulation of human knowledge, must be related to the questions addressed in each chapter and not treated in isolation. For that reason, and because other literature on the subject is very extensive, population questions are not treated in a separate chapter. Growth in numbers of people and growth in human knowledge obviously underlie the issues and concerns discussed in this volume, and a recognition of population problems and human potentialities permeates all chapters. Some implications arising from the ever-expanding number of the world's peoples are treated within the general framework of the volume, and more specifically addressed in the analysis in Chapter 3 of carrying capacity and environmental limits, and in the discussion in Chapter 9 of world food production and agricultural resources. The fundamental role and potential of the human resource and the opportunities foregone by neglecting its development are highlighted in the final chapter.

Chapters 1 through 7 focus on the physical and economic dimensions of natural resources. In Chapter 1, the editors outline some of the key resource issues as they relate to economic development in the international setting, with a brief review of the growing consciousness of natural resource scarcity, the historical shifts in resource use and developmental paths, definitional and conceptual issues, and the nature of the public interest in natural resources. A brief summary of the nature and magnitude of natural resources moving in international trade is given, and the resource-related interest in a new international order is outlined.

Chapters 2 and 3 deal with physical dimensions of natural resource scarcity—the potential availability of mineral resources, and the environmental limits to resource use. Any discussion of natural resource issues must first address the state of knowledge about potential sources, identified reserves, and current supplies of the resources themselves. Although this seems a reasonably straightforward question, there are major differences in assumptions as to what is being measured and how to measure it. There are also fundamental differences in the definition of a resource, not only notably between physical scientists and many economists, but also among physical scientists or among economists themselves, and differences in the use of the concepts of carrying capacity and environmental limits. Moreover, different assumptions about future developments in technology as well as about the time span under consideration lead to varying conclusions; it is hardly surprising that policy makers become confused when there is such variation in the information provided by professional analysts. Physical and biological scientists and engineers are steadily accumulating knowledge, crucial to intelligent planning, regarding technological and physical possibilities and limits. Chapters 2 and 3 present a current understanding and some present estimates of such limits.

Access to reliable information on physical potentialities and limits is critical for planning purposes. Yet such information must be supplemented by and placed within an economic framework of costs and returns; tests of economic rationality and feasibility must be applied. Here too policy makers are likely to receive conflicting advice. Chapters 4 and 5 apply contrasting economic analyses—neoclassical and institutional approaches—to the issues of resource pricing and scarcity. Resource scarcity is (or should be if markets are working effectively) reflected in resource prices. Economic analyses provide a way of investigating scarcity through price relationships resulting from demands as well as from supplies, and when the price of a particular resource commodity increases relative to others, it may stimulate exploration for and development of other sources or substitutes. On the other hand, prices cannot always provide appropriate signals when uncertainties, risks, and externalities exist. Neoclassical economics does provide powerful tools when markets are reasonably competitive, but some key problems are not encompassed in its analyses when competitive forces are absent or controlled, or when price determination is politically motivated. Imperfections in natural resource markets result from government intervention and control and from the economic power wielded by some private organizations such as transnational corporations. A major issue concerns the distribution of benefits between nations owning resources and private corporations possessing the technology to exploit and market those resources.

There is of course keen interest in the more efficient use of energy resources, especially petroleum. Efficiency in use, if it can be significantly increased, will stretch supplies and provide more time for finding and developing additional and alternative sources of energy. Chapter 6, which is concerned in some ways with the physical concepts discussed in Chapter 2, deals mainly with the concepts of efficiency in the use of energy as defined in economic terms. Efficiency in using energy, Chapter 6 suggests, is consistent with the first law of thermodynamics, but from the perspective of the second law of thermodynamics economic definitions allow major inefficiencies. If the source and the quality of energy were chosen to fit more nearly the task to be performed, and if such matching could become an integral part of the concept of efficiency for various production processes, major energy savings would result. As currently constituted, markets and pricing policies do not provide the appropriate signals and incentives for adopting so inclusive a concept of efficiency.

Much of the concern over resource scarcity, pricing, and trade has centered around petroleum and the changes in petroleum markets within the past half-dozen years. Chapter 7 is an illustrative case study of a specific natural resource—petroleum. It provides substantive demonstration of the concepts and concerns of Chapters 2 and 3 (physical availability, scarcity, limits), as well as those of Chapters 4 and 5 (economic dimensions of pricing, markets, and market imperfections). Since the natural characteristics of this particular resource, with its wide range of end uses, have in large part shaped the structural features of the current petroleum industry as well as its technology, Chapter 7 also deals with the specific problems of economic development of the oil economies and anticipates some of the issues of international trade and negotiation treated in later chapters.

Economic development, especially within the developing countries, with recognition of the intricate ties and linkages between development in those countries and development in the industrial countries, provides one of the major themes around which this volume is organized. Chapters 8, 9, and 10 are devoted to aspects of history, theory, and current performance of economic development in relation to natural resource issues and policies. Chapter 8 provides an overview of the evolution of development theories and the general views and concepts of natural resources embodied in these theories. That chapter also focuses on several requisites for development, including natural and human resources, international trade, and systematic and comprehensive planning, and discusses the role, current and potential, of transnational corporations in the development process. Chapter 9 analyzes the importance of structural-institutional variables in development and provides a review of food and population trends and resource potentials and constraints. It also summarizes progress in trade diversification and recent developments in international financial flows and mechanisms. Chapter 10, elaborating concepts of technology and its role in development, especially in relation to natural resources and resource policies, touches on an issue central to the problems addressed in this volume: the role of technology in enlarging and stretching resource supplies. The transfer of and the terms of accessibility to technology by the developing countries is a critical variable and one that is frequently at the center of debate over international trade.

The relations among nation-states and the ways in which these relations or modifications in them may either intensify conflict over natural resources or provide the setting for greater international cooperation are issues considered in Chapters 11, 12, and 13. The current international order and its evolution and the outline of a new world order as well as an agenda for policy to make it possible are discussed in Chapter 11. Chapter 12 discusses the concept of interdependence among nations and the varied meanings and consequent acts associated with that concept by some analysts of, on the one hand, the industrial countries, and on the other, of the developing countries; the author provides a Third World view on these issues. Chapter 13 reviews international law as it relates to natural resource policy issues, discussing national and international ownership and control over selected resources, the search for equity, and the role of law in this search. The subjects encompassed by these three chapters are, perhaps to an even greater degree than the subjects of the preceding chapters, in a state of flux. Very few of the questions can be considered settled matters.

The environment constitutes a system (with many subsystems); nations represent going concerns or systems (or subsystems within the larger international order); resources are scarce relative to human wants and needs for current and future development; policy makers search for reliable projections of the consequences of alternative courses of action. The intricate interconnectedness of all the elements involved can scarcely be comprehended by the human mind unaided. Chapter 14 examines mathematical modeling of socioeconomic-resource systems. The continued evolution of models that incorporate more variables, as well as the complex relationships among them, should prove increasingly useful in the policy-making process, provided of course that reliable data become available and that interaction and feedback within the model are appropriately conceptualized. Chapter 14 attempts to show how some of the key variables treated in previous chapters could be incorporated into more complex models. The author proposes some new elements and some approaches for exploration in future modeling efforts in an attempt to make models more useful to policy making in the areas of resources and development at both national and international levels.

The final chapter of the volume is devoted to discussing policies and the issues in policy formulation at the national, regional, and international levels. In actual practice, efforts must be repeatedly made to achieve, or to try to achieve, a functional or workable integration of policies related to natural resources and development within the international setting and its constraints, and Chapter 15 views policy in this pragmatic sense. Since most policy decisions continue to be made at the level of the nation-state, the emphasis is chiefly on opportunities and responsibilities of nations. Some possible moves toward joint action and greater international cooperation are suggested, however. In addition, the chapter highlights the importance of the human resource and its development. It concludes with a methodological note on public policy formulation and on the roles of public participation and research in designing more rational policies.

For a number of reasons—because appropriate data are often lacking, because assumptions about future adjustments and adaptations differ, and because historical and political perspective and interpretation vary—issues of natural resource policies in relation to economic development and international cooperation generate quite different opinions. Nevertheless, substantial agreement does exist that there is a need for more balanced development which will conserve resources and also a need for increased transfer of resources from rich to poor, and that structural changes in present configurations of economic and political power—both within and among countries—will be required to meet these needs. Diverging views arise, however, when concrete proposals for action to adjust to these generally recognized conditions are put forward.

The existence of more than 150 independent, sovereign nation-states in the world increases the complexity of these problems. The nations of the world are extremely diverse with respect to population size and density, technological development, per capita income, natural resources under national control, economic, political, and military power, and social, cultural, economic, and political organization. This tremendous diversity notwithstanding, a greater unity of purpose and a more balanced global development *are* essential if the people of this world are to avoid ever more destructive confrontations and are instead to move toward a system where tensions are reduced and conflicts resolved through joint deliberation and negotiation.

# I. NATURAL RESOURCES

# 1 *Peter Dorner & Mahmoud A. El-Shafie*

# Natural Resource Issues in Economic Development: The International Setting

A sense of uneasiness permeates current thought on issues of world development. Massive poverty and rapidly growing populations, increasing debts and food shortages, political turmoil and a feeling of general instability in the world persist despite more than 30 years of concerted efforts in development planning, capital transfer and technical assistance, and design of new international institutions—both political and economic—to deal with these problems. Awareness of scarcity is pervasive—scarcity of capital, scarcity of skills, scarcity of ideas and solutions to pressing national and international problems, and scarcity of natural resources.

Resource scarcities, especially for minerals and fossil fuels, have arisen in the past, but they were generally wartime shortages brought by demands for military hardware and the severance of prewar supply channels. These shortages did inspire special policies for resource conservation and rationing, and heavy demand during the Korean War and the post-World War II reconstructions elevated prices for some raw materials, but all such shortages were seen as temporary aberrations. Fundamental faith in a return to "normal" conditions following short-term "sacrifices" in the interests of national security was unshaken.

There were, of course, warnings about future resource scarcities from some scholars and public officials. At least throughout the 1950s, however, optimism prevailed—the reconstruction of Europe and Japan from

17

the devastation of war supported prevailing views that economic development in the Third World could be achieved by transferring capital, technology, and "know-how." That the development of agriculture and industry in the Third World along lines similar to those in the industrial world might place unsustainable demands on natural resources was not a central issue of concern in the literature on economic development.

But beginning in the 1960s, early warning that this sort of development might be unsustainable because of eventual resource limits was strengthened by mounting evidence of environmental deterioration. Increasingly intense resource use and exploitation could threaten the provision of such basics as air and water of the quality needed to sustain renewable life systems.

Uneasiness mounted in the 1970s. From early 1972 to mid-1974 the UN index of export prices of all primary commodities increased by more than 150 percent (three times the advance that occurred during the Korean War). No period within the past 100 years has seen a rise in commodity prices as rapid as that of 1972-73 (63 percent), or any 3-year period in which they rose as rapidly as in 1971-74 (159 percent) (Cooper and Laurence 1975, cited by Fried 1976, p. 641).

Those years, of course, witnessed abrupt increases in food prices because of the simultaneous crop production shortfalls in several world regions as well as the sharp increases in crude oil prices resulting from concerted action by the Organization of the Petroleum Exporting Countries (OPEC). High rates of inflation, unprecedented instability in exchange rates among leading world currencies, and phenomenal speculative movements in commodity markets during and following these years accentuated the problems posed by food and oil price increases and heightened anxiety about the future. OPEC's successes were interpreted by some as a potential pattern for widespread organization and price increases in other commodity markets. And the gloomy predictions of *The Limits to Growth* (Meadows et al. 1972) gave support to the view that these commodity price rises were not a cyclical phenomenon but were early manifestations of a new and disquieting secular trend.

A nagging question remains: Were these price upswings a "mere" cyclical phenomenon, or is the world indeed facing new conditions for natural resources and primary commodities?

Human memories tend to be short. True, petroleum prices have not fallen, but general price inflation since 1973-74 has eroded the initial economic impact of the price increases. As of this writing, there is a short-term glut in the petroleum market, in part because of conservation measures, slow economic recovery from the mid-1970s' recession, new sources of supply (North Sea, Mexico, and Alaska), and increased production of energy from other sources (UNITAR 1978).

Yet, so it seems to us, the world is indeed facing new conditions. With petroleum, for instance, it is not the mere rise in price but the prospect of eventual physical limits to its supply that is worrisome. All oil producers will in time repeat the experience of the United States, where production peaked in 1970 and has since declined. Economies based on oil must inevitably change to other energy sources, and such changes are likely to have effects on the industrial and social character of the countries involved that are much more profound and far-reaching than the effects of the shift from wood to coal or from coal to oil and natural gas (Abelson and Hammond 1976).

## The Historical Setting

In *The Great Frontier,* Walter Prescott Webb (1952) suggested that the discovery of the "new world"\* of the Americas marked the beginning of a 400-year boom in modern history.

"What was the essential character of the frontier? It was inherently a vast body of wealth without proprietors . . . ," says Webb. "When this great area was made available to the crowded and impoverished people of the Metropolis [i.e., Western Europe], they swarmed out like bees to suck up the nectar of wealth, much of which they brought home to the mother hive. This sudden, continuing, and ever-increasing flood of wealth precipitated on the Metropolis a business boom such as the world had never known before and probably can never know again . . . " (quoted in Kelso 1977).

Webb further contends, as did Frederick Jackson Turner (1893) almost a century ago, that this enormous potential wealth nurtured a distinct set of economic, political, and social institutions geared to its exploitation and development. In short, says Webb, the present superstructure of Western civilization remains grounded in these boom conditions. And in North America, more so than in Europe, there has been an underlying assumption of nearly inexhaustible natural resources and a reliance, rarely questioned before the end of World War II, on individual initiative for their exploitation. Only a few of the great conservationists and naturalists voiced apprehensions. Wisconsin's Aldo Leopold (1949, p. ix) raised an issue that has only lately become popular: " . . . this much is crystal

---

\*The "new world" was itself a European concept. For the native Americans, both North and South, who had inhabited these lands for thousands of years, this was not a new world nor did they, generally, share in the boom conditions.

clear: our bigger-and-better society is now like a hypochondriac, so obsessed with its own economic health as to have lost the capacity to remain healthy. The whole world is so greedy for more bathtubs that it has lost the stability necessary to build them, or even to turn off the tap. Nothing could be more salutary at this stage than a little healthy contempt for a plethora of material blessings." It is more and more obvious that beyond a certain point human happiness is not so directly correlated with increased consumption of material goods as the general economic rationale underlying a high consumption society would lead one to believe.

In the first 200–250 years after permanent European colonization of the "new world," the boom conditions were manifest in horizontal expansion, population movements and settlement, new discoveries and exploitation of precious metals, and adoption and increased cultivation of the "new" plant varieties domesticated by native Americans as well as the plants and livestock introduced by the colonists from Europe. But increasingly throughout the eighteenth century, and with added momentum in the nineteenth and especially in the twentieth centuries, the boom's primary expression was modern industrialism.

The gradual shift from agrarian to industrial societies along with the development and progressive sophistication of experimental science were certainly key factors in Europe's political and economic dominance of the world. The very significant developments and achievements in human culture and philosophy, in engineering works and mathematics in some of the world's oldest civilizations were no match for the highly integrated knowledge, power, and control over physical nature which are grounded in experimental science. Whether the motive force undergirding the colonial policies of Great Britain and the states of Western Europe was economic or political in nature remains debatable. In the Marx-Hobson-Lenin interpretation, it was entirely an economic phenomenon, especially the great push and competition for colonies among the European powers after 1870. Others believe, however, that the rapid extension of formal control over the independent areas of Africa and the East was specifically political in origin, the result of fears and rivalries within Europe. Hobson himself believed that the gains from imperialism were a delusion. In fact the abandonment of empire after World War II was often followed by substantial increases in the former colonialists' rates of economic growth (Boulding and Mukerjie 1972). In any case, the developments in science, technology, and engineering and the industrial processes to which they gave rise did split the developmental paths of Europe apart from the paths of those other nations which are today's developing countries.

In that transition from an agrarian to an industrially based system, societies' dependence on renewable (flow) resources (plants, animals, water, air, sunshine, and land—renewable in the sense that appropriate improvement and conservation measures can maintain and increase their productive capacity) gave way to reliance on nonrenewable (stock) resources. Even beyond the first half of the nineteenth century, most of the power needed to run an economy was supplied by wind, water, animals and people—all renewable resources. In the United States, as late as 1850, coal (a stock resource) supplied only 10 percent as much fuel as was provided by firewood (a flow resource). Annual production of fuel wood rose until 1870, after which it declined as fuel wood's uses were increasingly replaced by coal (Berg 1978). Although its beginnings were somewhat earlier, the transition from coal to petroleum (substituting for one stock resource another which has a greater diversity of end uses and several other desirable qualities as an energy source) is primarily a twentieth-century phenomenon.

Along with this transition from flow to stock energy resources came other changes that increased reliance on stock resources in all areas of human life, including agriculture: from oxen and horses to trucks, tractors, and automobiles; from green and animal manure to chemically manufactured fertilizers; from wooden tools and implements to those of steel; from wood and other renewable resources in building construction to steel, glass, concrete, aluminum, and others which are in themselves stock resources or rely on intensive use of fossil fuels in their manufacture; from natural fibers and rubber to petroleum-derived synthetics and plastics; etc.

The economic value of these finite, stock resources could not really be appreciated and determined outside of the industrialization process. The "owners" of these stock resources in countries beyond the immediate sphere of European industrialism were much more conscious of and attuned to the value of their renewable resources. Because many of these countries, with their focus on renewable resources, were also under the colonial rule of industrializing nations, it is not surprising that the latter nations, the chief users of stock resources, could maintain the prices of stock resources at relatively low levels advantageous to their own development. This ability was undoubtedly a central factor in the rapid shift from renewable to stock resources in the transition from agrarian to industrial production.

Perhaps the most striking example of the way in which industrialization and economic growth came increasingly to depend on the use of finite stock resources is once again the growth in world production and the use of crude oil (although the case of many metals is not too different). Since 1890, on the average, world production of crude oil has increased at a rate of about 7 percent per year. Production doubled about every 10 years, so that the amount of oil produced during each decade was equal to all the oil ever produced up to that time. By the end of 1963, for example, cumulative world crude oil production amounted to 150 billion barrels; by the end of 1973, it reached 299 billion barrels (Hubbert 1978). Because the amount of crude oil remaining in the earth is limited and finite, such doubling cannot continue for many more decades.

## Some Current Comparisons

A highly disproportionate share of stock resources of fossil fuels and hard minerals has been and continues to be consumed by the industrial countries. These countries, however, have fewer than one-third of the world's people. The other two-thirds live in the economically less developed countries. The low level of labor productivity and the high rate of population growth in those developing countries keep average per capita incomes and consumption very low relative to incomes and consumption in the industrial countries. The people in the developing countries are naturally anxious to expand their economies and increase their level of living, and accelerated development in these countries along the same resource-intensive paths followed by the industrial countries will intensify greatly the demand for natural resources of all kinds.

If we look at total energy consumption per capita (in tons of coal equivalent) as a proxy for total resource consumption, each individual in the industrial countries consumed in 1970 about six times as much, on the average, as his counterpart in the developing countries (Batisse 1974, citing Ward and Dubos 1972). This ratio is substantially greater if only commercial sources of energy are considered (petroleum, electric power, coal, and natural gas). For example, in 1975 the industrial countries consumed 10 times as much commercial energy per capita as the middle income countries and almost 100 times as much as the very low income countries of the Third World (World Bank 1978, pp. 76–78). In developing countries, 50 percent or more of the total energy used may be obtained from noncommercial sources—wood, dung, and crop residues. The usual techniques with which such fuels are utilized normally make them less efficient in the net usable energy yield than commercial fuels. Increased use of noncommercial fuels also creates serious problems in some areas— deforestation, soil depletion and erosion, lower crop yields, etc. (Makhijani and Poole 1975).

The much larger populations and the more rapid rate of population growth in the developing countries, continued or intensified consumption patterns in the industrial world, and a "catching up" or "closing the gap" by populations of other countries can suggest projections of materials exhaustion that could bring civilization tumbling down. Furthermore, even without materials exhaustion, environmental consequences could be catastrophic. Something short of ecological chaos can still mean disaster for " . . . stress can fundamentally change an ecological system so that while it may act in some 'stable' manner, the basic laws which govern it may have changed so radically that previous data about system behavior are no longer relevant" (Matthews 1977).

Several caveats and clarifications must be introduced at this point. Population growth rates of the industrial countries now average about one percent per year or less. In the United States, per capita consumption of nonenergy minerals, forest products, and fibers has leveled off in recent years, although energy consumption per capita has continued to rise. Price increases for materials (including energy) should lead to conservation measures; there is tremendous slack and waste in current industrial systems. On the other hand, per capita use of materials in developing countries has been growing, starting, of course, from a much lower base. A good illustration is the more than doubled per capita steel consumption in India between 1950 and 1970 (Landsberg 1976).

## Some Definitional and Conceptual Problems

An important issue in the debate over resource scarcity is the very concept of "resources." Accepted definitions of a "resource" do vary substantially among disciplines. The concept of natural resources used in this chapter—although not necessarily in other chapters—is the one generally used by economists. We can identify specific physical substances— mineral-bearing ores, standing timber, crude oil, and so forth, and call them natural resources. However, the concept of natural resources need not refer to a fixed or finite quantity or quality. It is instead " . . . a dynamic concept because what is considered useless at one time (say, uranium ore or steep mountain slopes) may become a major resource through a change in technology (nuclear power) or a change in ways of life (winter sports). It is mainly an economic concept, since a potentiality of the natural world becomes a resource only when its utilization is profitable. But it is a useful concept since it reminds us that man is neither angel nor demigod and entirely depends for his survival on the resources he can draw from his environment" (Batisse 1974).

The word "profitable" is poorly chosen, as we shall discuss later, but Batisse's basic point is well taken. What constitutes a natural resource from the human perspective depends on the kind of knowledge and technology acquired by a society and upon human tastes, values, and lifestyles. For instance " . . . in the nearly 19th century, crude oil encountered at the earth's surface or in salt wells was viewed as an obnoxious nuisance or, at best, was bottled and sold as patent medicines" (Hueckel 1975). Resources ". . . originate as useless or neutral 'stuff' existing on or in the earth and are transformed into useful substances through human knowledge. . . . Conversely, human activity can also 'destroy' certain resources either directly or physically as in the use of fossil minerals for fuels and in the 'working out' of individual metallic ore deposits, or indirectly through technological obsolescence, such as in advances that provide an alternative resource that is more economic than or that overcomes the physical limitations of an existing resource, or both. Indirect destruction of a specific resource by reduction of usefulness also may be complete in that the resource is returned once again to being neutral 'stuff'" (Radcliffe 1976).

The major implication in these statements is that the future availability and accessibility of natural resources is very difficult to determine because we may not try to measure or to estimate that which is not currently considered a resource. What will be considered a resource is essentially a function of the technical, managerial, and professional skills acquired by the human population. Although the concept of finiteness or exhaustibility of a particular resource is meaningful and subject to measurement, it is unlikely to be applied to materials that are considered "neutral stuff" until the time these materials can be transformed into resources (or substitutes for current resources). Even more difficult to estimate are the future demands that will be placed on resources. Tastes do change, and increasing costs do lead to lower demands. Technology has allowed more efficient use of resources as well as cheaper and more abundant substitutes for more costly and less abundant resources. Increased recycling of materials holds promise in some areas.

On the other hand, technological and engineering breakthroughs required to shift, for example, to a major new energy source (nuclear fusion or solar) either have not yet occurred or are not yet economically competitive with current sources. Nor is the adoption of such technology, once it becomes available, a matter like switching to hybrid seed corn or nylon stockings. A shift in energy technologies will have profound effects on society, will probably require vast capital investments in new processes and in the reconstruction of production, transportation, housing, and other facilities, and will likely take 25–50 years or more for adjustments. If such adjustments are attempted in too short a time they will be highly disruptive. The concern over future supplies of petroleum and some key minerals is certainly justified in terms of the long lead times and transitions that will be needed as these resources become scarcer.

We are faced with a dilemma noted by Batisse. Many of the quantitative predictions made in the last 30 years have been grossly in error. In a period of unprecedented change, it is in fact impossible to picture the world one generation ahead. Yet anxiety about the future, as well as the need for economic and social planning and forecasting imposed by modern technology itself, compels us to make some estimates, even if we shall constantly have to revise them (Batisse 1974).

Environmental limits also impose uncertainty. There are no clear methodologies for measurement and assessment—certainly not on a global scale. Apart from basic food and shelter requirements, any long-term assumption about human behavior is nothing more than guesswork. The gradual perception that the earth and its resources are limited and that the environment can tolerate only so much modification will eventually create unpredictable social and cultural feedbacks. ". . . We do perceive some absolute limitations, such as available space and global heat balance, but these limitations are still too far ahead to give us clear guidance for today's courses of action, except to tell us to be more cautious and less wasteful" (Batisse 1974).

Questions are now being raised whether it is possible to meet the basic human needs of growing populations without transgressing resource and environmental "outer limits." These "outer limits," as noted, are not clearly definable at this time. Is it therefore justifiable to use this elusive concept as the major criterion of resource use and conservation policies? Certainly other positive goals, objectives, values, and priorities held by individuals and societies may well be considered even more important than the negative one of not transgressing such ill-defined "outer limits"; the fulfillment of the basic human needs of the world's people, for instance, is certainly a widely held objective. At national levels higher priority may be given to objectives such as national security, individual liberty, full employment, and others. Even as the concept of "outer limits" is given more concrete expression in scientific, measurable terms, it is not likely that the nontransgression of such limits will be considered the only goal, to which all others must be subordinated.

## The Public Interest in Natural Resources

Natural resources, then, may include anything in the material universe that someone considers useful or beneficial or potentially beneficial. Consequently there is continuous tension and conflict among those who evaluate potentialities differently and set priorities accordingly. This is why Batisse's "profitability" criterion is too imprecise. The question is: Profitable for whom? Profitability may mean the creation of surplus value above the production costs of an enterprise, or value in use to an individual or to a society, or intrinsic value in exchange for other things.

Whaling may be profitable for the Japanese and the Soviet fleets, yet others value whales not in monetary profit but in terms of the whales' very existence. The "misplacement" of materials in the environment (water, air, and land pollution) may be profitable for some but costly for others or for society as a whole. The values associated with preservation of wilderness areas and of endangered biological species can hardly be quantified in conventional benefit/cost analyses.

Natural resources are in varying degrees owned, exploited, and transformed by individuals or groups of individuals, by corporations, and by governments. But in all cases natural resources are invested with an inherent public interest. The public character associated with natural resources arises from differences in evaluation and the frequent divergence between private and public benefits and costs of resource use and exploitation. Furthermore, the interests and needs of future generations (as viewed by the present generation) may conflict with prospects of stock resource exhaustion and flow resource irreversibilities.

The identification of particular publics will depend on the resource(s) in question—it may be a local public, or a public corresponding to a nation-state, or publics with international concerns and organization. The constant tension and conflict between various private and public purposes, and between the purposes of different publics, are likely to intensify with accelerated economic growth, increasing populations, certain developments in technology, and the expanding power of some groups to exploit resources in a way that may be interpreted by the less powerful as contrary to their own or a larger public (and future publics') interests. Disagreements are especially likely in the light of a growing consciousness of some physical and environmental limits. Thus there is heightened concern about natural resource availabilities, estimates of future supplies, accessibility to these resources, issues of ownership and sovereignty over specific types of resources, conservation, rates of exploitation, etc. Especially for resource materials moving in international trade, there are major differences and frequent disputes about pricing practices and policies.

The need and the desire for accelerated development in the developing countries raise issues that are far from simple. Some of the developing countries are resource-rich, although the resources may not be commercially exploited, or the wealth may be of such recent origin that populations remain poor. Other countries are, of course, resource-poor, even in the basic resources for meeting food needs. Land and water are widely distributed, but population densities vary tremendously, and there are great differences in land quality. In terms of land per capita available for agricultural production (or potentially convertible to such uses in the future) Latin America and Africa with a few nations excepted have the greatest potential while most of Asia has far more limited prospects. However, water available for agricultural use is often lacking—especially in North Africa and the Middle East. Despite opportunities for increasing the cultivated and irrigated land area and for boosting production through yield increases, the world food problem—producing enough food for growing populations *and* devising production and distribution systems to serve all the people including the desperately poor—is far from resolution.

## Natural Resources in International Trade

The pattern of world trade in food has changed considerably since World War II. Latin America, Africa, Asia, and the USSR, net prewar exporters of cereal grains, are now major importers (except for a few countries such as Argentina and Thailand). Western Europe has remained a deficit region, although with lower grain imports now than 40 years ago, while the major exporters, the United States and Canada, have multiplied their exports 19-fold (from an average of 5 million tons yearly in 1934–38 to 94 million tons in 1975); Australia and New Zealand have almost tripled their annual exports (from 3 to 8 million tons) over this period (Wortman and Cummings 1978, p. 22).

In contrast to cereals, most of the tropical crops, such as cocoa, rubber, tea, coffee, sugar, bananas, pineapple, coconut, and oil palm, and fiber crops, such as jute and substantial quantities of cotton, are produced in the developing countries. Many countries depend heavily on these crops for their export earnings. Except for the major petroleum exporting countries, most other developing nations rely on export earnings from non-energy-producing ores and minerals. Mining activity too is very unevenly distributed in the world. Among the developing countries as a whole, those producing the bulk of the mining and mineral exports have only 5 percent of the Third World population; 55 percent of the Third World population lives in countries whose production of minerals is negligible (Tinbergen 1976, p. 255).

Production shares of nonenergy ores have been highly stable since 1950, with one-half of total world production coming from the developed market economies and the other half split between Third World countries and the centrally planned economies. The developed market economies depend heavily on imports for their energy producing substances, metals, and ores (primarily from the Third World countries) while the centrally planned economies are virtually self-sufficient, the USSR offsetting deficits of the Eastern European countries (Tinbergen 1976, pp. 255–56).*

Third World commodity trade amounts to one-fifth of total world trade in commodities. Excluding petroleum, twelve commodities account for 80 percent of Third World commodity export earnings. Manufactured goods exported from Third World countries are still only a small percentage of total world manufactured goods exports. However, exports of manufactures have been rising at a fairly high rate (with, of course, some major differences among countries). From 1960 to 1975, exports of manufactures from the developing countries taken as a group grew in real terms at the rate of 12.3 percent per year, while total merchandise exports grew at the lower rate of 5.9 percent per year. By 1975, manufactures accounted for 26 percent of all merchandise exports from the developing countries, and they represented 36 percent of the increase in exports over the period 1960–75 (World Bank 1978, p. 28).

There is need for perspective on these overall averages. The fact that commodity trade of Third World countries is only one-fifth of total world trade in commodities does not make the conditions and terms of trade in primary commodities less important for these countries. On the contrary, these commodities *are* the major source of export earnings for many of them. Furthermore, while the developed market economies are major producers of nonenergy ores (some of them are, of course, also major producers of oil and gas), they nevertheless depend on imports for several key minerals (table 1.1).

There is a wide divergence of incomes among and within countries. According to one classification (Leontief 1977, pp. 71–72), 30 percent of the 1970 world population lived in the developed regions where 1970 average GNP per capita ranged from $4625 in North America to $698 in medium income European countries. On the other hand, the 55 percent of the 1970 world population living in Asia and tropical Africa had an average GNP per capita in 1970 of less than $200. According to the World Bank, the average GNP per capita in 1976 for its classification of countries was as follows: low income countries, $150; middle income countries, $750; industrial countries, $6200; capital surplus oil exporters, $6310; and centrally planned economies, $2280 (World Bank 1978, pp. 76–77). Within poor countries, the income share of the top 20 percent is generally greater and the income share of the bottom 20 percent lower than the corresponding shares in the wealthier countries (Ahluwalia 1978; Jain 1975).

This wide gulf in levels of income (and consumption) frequently leads to wasteful use of natural resources and to lower-valued end-product uses

---

*The United States and Canada are only 25 percent dependent on imports. Corresponding figures for Western Europe and Japan are 75 and 94 percent, respectively.

TABLE 1.1

Dependence on Selected Imported Industrial Raw Materials, 1975
(Imports as a percentage of consumption)

|  | United States | European Community | Japan |
|---|---|---|---|
| Aluminum (ore and metal) | 84 | 75 | 100 |
| Chromium | 91 | 98 | 98 |
| Cobalt | 98 | 98 | 98 |
| Copper | a | 98 | 90 |
| Iron (ore and metal) | 29 | 55 | 99 |
| Lead | 11 | 85 | 73 |
| Manganese | 98 | 99 | 88 |
| Natural rubber | 100 | 100 | 100 |
| Nickel | 72 | 100 | 100 |
| Phosphates | a | 100 | 100 |
| Tin | 84 | 93 | 97 |
| Tungsten | 55 | 100 | 100 |
| Zinc | 61 | 70 | 53 |

Source: *International Economic Report* 1977, Table 78, p. 187.
[a]Net exporter in 1975.

than the resources' scarcity might warrant. When commodity trade and pricing issues are treated within a private (or even national) accounting framework of profit and/or utility maximization (*within* current patterns of income distribution and the current framework of national and corporate economic leverage and power), their resolution is likely to differ considerably from that which would result if the distribution of income and power were substantially changed.

## The Call for a New International Economic Order

In view of the needs and—most would agree—the desirability of increasing opportunities, raising productivity, and thereby improving incomes of the poorer people in all countries and especially in the poorest countries, natural resource policies and the appropriate paths for future development are central and heated issues of international debate. Many Third World countries have little more at present than certain natural resources as the vehicles around which to build their development programs. Resource requirements and access, terms of trade, appropriate technology, structural changes, population densities and growth rates, the role of agriculture, and the financing of development needs through both internal savings and international capital transfers are seen with a new sense of urgency.

This new urgency is being brought to the attention of national leaders everywhere by proposals of Third World countries for a New International Economic Order. These countries insist that the current or "old" order discriminates against them, that they have merely traded domination under colonialism for a new economic dependence inherent in the trading relationships between and among themselves, the industrial countries, and the large and powerful transnational corporations. Many of the issues relate specifically to the pricing of commodity exports and the costs of imported technology and manufactured goods.

It is obvious that many Third World countries export commodities required by industrial as well as by other developing countries. All Third World countries need and are anxious to obtain additional capital and the technology appropriate for accelerating their development efforts. They seek to establish a sustainable base for future development if and when some of their natural resource exports decline. Establishing such a base implies (and it is indeed the goal of many of these countries) that more of the productive activities of materials processing and manufacturing be relocated in the developing countries, nearer to the natural resource base. This concern is especially evident in cases where petroleum (a clearly exhaustible resource) is the only or the major source of export earnings.

Producers of primary commodities maintain, with justification, that the present tariff structures discriminate against the location of processing industries within their countries. "Among the OECD countries generally, duties are either zero or small on most ores and concentrates and substantial on semi-finished and finished products manufactured from these primary materials. Japan is the worst offender, but the tariff structure of other industrial countries also discriminates in favor of their processing industries. This practice penalizes the primary producers in efforts to sell processed products in OECD markets" (Fried 1976, p. 646, note 15).

Great emphasis is also being placed on improving the terms of trade for Third World exports vis-à-vis major imports, but there are complications here because many developing countries (and some of the poorest among them) are also importers of at least some natural resource and agricultural commodities. First, it is well to keep in mind that the bulk of world trade is generated by the developed market economies. In 1976, 71 percent of the merchandise exports from the industrial economies went to (i.e., were imported by) other industrial nations. In that same year, 21 percent of their exports went to the developing countries. For the developing countries (low and middle income, respectively) in 1976, 65 and 72 percent of the merchandise exports went to the industrial countries while 30 and 24 percent went to other developing countries (World Bank 1978, pp. 90–91). A substantial part of the flow from the developed to the developing market economies is in the form of capital equipment, food grains, and manufactures, whereas the reverse flow includes petroleum, tropical agricultural commodities, minerals and ores, and lesser quantities of other goods.

In terms of the trade flows from the developing to the developed market economies, oil is in a unique class. It makes up a substantial proportion of the value of world exports (5 percent in 1973 and 12 percent after the oil price increases of 1973-74). In 1974 oil exports, valued at about $115 billion, were somewhat larger than exports of cereals, oil seeds, and all other foodstuffs combined; net copper exports, greatest among the minerals and ores, probably were no more than $5 billion in that year even with the high 1974 prices (Fried 1976). Oil exports are concentrated among a few countries, and demand and supply are price inelastic as are supplies of close substitutes. The exporters (and indeed several of the world's large producers) are basically all Third World countries except for the Soviet Union, whose exports go primarily to Eastern Europe.

Cereal grains, especially wheat, are a somewhat similar case except that export production is concentrated in several of the developed market economies (also, of course, control over supply is much weaker because production is affected importantly by the weather). Some of the tropical agricultural commodities are produced primarily in developing countries, but there is wide variation within this class of products, and substitutes are available for many of them.

Especially in the case of a number of important minerals, exports are not concentrated among developing countries only. For example, of the major U.S. mineral imports in 1976, there were five in which imports from developing countries accounted for more than 50 percent of U.S. consumption: columbium, manganese, aluminum, tin, and flourine. For seven mineral imports, the proportion coming from other developed countries exceeded that from developing countries: cobalt, platinum, chromium, nickel, mercury, zinc, and titanium (*International Economic Report* 1977, p. 12).

Commodity agreements have proven difficult even for products concentrated in a relatively small number of exporting countries, and the diverse production and trade patterns for many of these products will preclude comprehensive agreements involving a substantial number of them. A main point is that many developing countries are themselves importers of the commodities in question. Here again petroleum is an important case. The 1973-74 price increases did sharply raise most countries' expenditures for petroleum and the multitude of products with a petroleum input. In addition, the mid-1970s recession in the industrial world lowered the demand for many commodities which are major exports of some developing countries. Lower volume and lower prices cut export earnings and aggravated balance of payments problems. The external debt of the developing countries (excluding the capital-surplus oil exporting countries) almost doubled between 1973 and 1975, reaching $135 billion in the latter year (*International Economic Report* 1977, pp. 29–30). That doubling, of course, was not totally the result of higher petroleum prices. Nevertheless, it is true that many poor countries must import petroleum, fertilizers, food, and minerals. Gains for some developing (and industrial) countries could come at the expense of other and often much poorer countries. The OPEC countries have established special funds to provide assistance to the poorer countries. Bilateral and multilateral assistance programs are also attempting to allocate more funds to the poorest countries and to the poorest segments of the populations within countries.

However, as will be shown in later chapters, appropriate rearrangements in commodity trade, pricing, and processing are needed and do hold promise for accelerating development and reducing the potential for conflict among nations. Such policies will need to be diverse and flexible to accommodate the variety of conditions in different countries and for different commodities.

It is suggested by some that the "rich" countries should slow down their growth and consumption, especially in view of possible resource scarcities and environmental degradation. Yet if the Third World countries are to accelerate their development, they do need export markets and export proceeds with which to pay for necessary imports. There must be changes in current economic structures in order to achieve a major slowdown of industrial nations' economic growth and a simultaneous speedup in Third World rates of growth. As their economies develop and diversify, more trade among the developing countries will certainly present new opportunities for restructuring the current world system and for achieving greater self-reliance within the Third World.

The economic problems alone, and their interrelations and interdependencies, are extremely complex. Indeed, words like *complex* begin to sound glib in the face of the world's intricately bound economic, social, political, and environmental problems. The unaided human mind cannot really grasp the almost countless implications and reverberations of alternative courses of action. New concepts in the mathematical theory of systems and the enlarged capacities of electronic computers have enhanced our ability to deal with complex relationships more quickly, but even these powerful tools are useful only to the extent that reasonably accurate raw data are available and that the linkages of the real world are appreciated and simulated with reasonable fidelity.

Mathematical modeling and computer simulation may have much to offer in understanding world, regional, and other large systems, and in examining the possible effects of policy. Both with and aside from advances in modeling efforts, however, goes the tremendous mental job of envisioning and designing the new practical arrangements—nationally, regionally, and internationally—that must be developed if mankind is to survive on this "spaceship earth."

We must rethink and redefine the evolving interdependence and interconnectedness among nations. We need to review, extend, and possibly reformulate the roles of international and regional organizations and institutions. New procedural arrangements must be devised and negotiated. The key issues of equity (perhaps not realizable outside the process of negotiation) in international trade and the other relations among the world's nations and peoples must be addressed. Income distribution within nations must be changed so that the poorer segments of the population get a fairer and more productive share of the benefits of economic growth. Imaginative development of international law is needed to encourage cooperation and reduce the possibility of confrontation. If expenditures on armaments continue to divert energies and to dissipate resources, the nations of the world may find it impossible to move much beyond the level of continuing crisis and a constant flirting with catastrophe.

## References

Abelson, Philip H., and Allen L. Hammond. 1976. "The New World of Materials," *Science* 191: 633-36.

Ahluwalia, Montek S. 1978. "Inequality, Poverty and Development," *Development Digest* 16: 102-24. Excerpted from *Journal of Development Economics* 3: 307-41 (1976).

Batisse, Michel. 1974. "Global Prospects for Natural Resources," *Nature and Resources* 10: 2-7.

Berg, Charles A. 1978. "Process Innovation and Changes in Industrial Energy Use," *Science* 199: 608-14.

Boulding, Kenneth E., and Tapan Mukerjie, eds. 1972. *Economic Imperialism.* Ann Arbor: University of Michigan Press.

Cooper, R. N., and R. Z. Laurence. 1975. "The 1972-77 Commodity Boom," Brookings Panel on Economic Activity, December 4-5 (cited in Edward R. Fried, "International Trade in Raw Materials: Myths and Realities," *Science* 191 (1976): 641-46).

Fried, Edward R. 1976. "International Trade in Raw Materials: Myths and Realities," *Science* 191: 641-46.

Hubbert, M. King. 1978. "World Energy Resources." In *Proceedings of the Wisconsin Seminar on Natural Resource Policies in Relation to Economic Development and International Cooperation*, vol. 1. Madison: Institute for Environmental Studies, University of Wisconsin.

Hueckel, Glenn. 1975. "A Historical Approach to Future Economic Growth," *Science* 187: 925–31.
*International Economic Report of the President.* 1977. Washington, D.C.: U.S. Government Printing Office.
Jain, Shail. 1975. *Size Distribution of Income.* Washington, D.C.: World Bank.
Kelso, M. M. 1977. "Natural Resource Economics: The Upsetting Discipline," *American Journal of Agricultural Economics* 59: 815–23.
Landsberg, Hans H. 1976. "Materials: Some Recent Trends and Issues," *Science* 191: 637–41.
Leontief, Wassily W. 1977. *The Future of the World Economy.* New York: Oxford University Press.
Leopold, Aldo. 1949. *A Sand County Almanac.* New York: Oxford University Press.
Makhijani, Arjun, with collaboration of Alan Poole. 1975. *Energy and Agriculture in the Third World.* Cambridge, Massachusetts: Ballinger.
Matthews, William H. 1977. "Where Are the Outer Limits?" *Mazingira* 1: 55–65.
Meadows, Donella H., Dennis L. Meadows, Jørgen Randers, and William W. Behrens III. 1972. *The Limits to Growth.* New York: Universe Books.
Radcliffe, S. Victor. 1976. "World Changes and Chances: Some New Perspectives for Materials," *Science* 191: 700–707.
Tinbergen, Jan, coord. 1976. *RIO—Reshaping the International Order: A Report to the Club of Rome.* New York: Dutton.
Turner, Frederick Jackson. 1893. "The Significance of the Frontier in American History." Written for the American Historical Association and republished in his *The Frontier in American History.* New York, 1920.
UNITAR (United Nations Institute for Training and Research). 1978. *Important For the Future* 3(2): 1–15.
Ward, Barbara, and René Dubos. 1972. *Only One Earth.* New York: Norton.
Webb, Walter Prescott. 1952. *The Great Frontier.* Boston: Houghton Mifflin.
World Bank. 1978. *World Development Report, 1978.* New York: Oxford University Press.
Wortman, Sterling, and Ralph W. Cummings, Jr. 1978. *To Feed This World: The Challenge and the Strategy.* Baltimore: Johns Hopkins University Press.

# 2 *John Steinhart*

# Availability of Mineral Resources

Everything we touch or use in the modern world consists of, or is manufactured from, natural resources. Even the most exotic "synthetics" are made from natural resources. All of the naturally occurring chemical elements are used to some degree. It is seldom noticed, however, that almost every mineral, rock, and organic compound is occasionally used in a state little modified from that in which it is found, often for mundane purposes as fill or building materials. For most rocks and minerals, the amounts used are so small in comparison to the quantities available that the material is not accounted as a natural resource. In this sense, most natural resources are not scarce, but it does appear that the proportions in which humanity uses resources differ considerably from the proportions in which natural materials are available.

Economists usually attach some economic condition to the definition of natural resources, qualifying the definition in terms of profitability, widespread use, or some similar criterion. These qualifications lead to the often repeated statement that economic conditions (or technological advances) "create" resources. Although understandable as a metaphor, the statement has provoked some misunderstanding because nothing is actually created in the earth—however much conditions have changed. Governments, to judge by their laws and actions, seem to subscribe to yet another definition. Laws for subsurface minerals, at least, are written to

36 NATURAL RESOURCES

include what may yet become accessible or economically exploitable as well as resources economically important at present.

When physical scientists and engineers speak of the *resource base** of a particular substance, they usually mean the finite, total quantity that is present (whether that quantity is accurately known or not). They use the term *reserves* for that fraction of the total resource that has been measured and is producible under present economic conditions. The U.S. Geological Survey and the U.S. Bureau of Mines further divide reserves into "measured," "indicated," and "inferred" reserves, qualitative measures of the degree of certainty with which quantities are known. Figure 2.1 displays the graphical resource classification which the National Academy of Sciences recommends be used as "a common frame of reference for all resource discussions" (NAS 1975, p. 4). Note that the classification considers economic viability as only one of two dimensions.

Variety in usage of the term "resources" has produced, among economists and policy makers, serious misunderstandings of the meaning of resource estimates produced by scientists and engineers. It should not be thought, however, that the estimates of mineral resources provided to policy makers by physical scientists have been estimates of *terrestrial abundance*, that is, of the total resource base. The reasons for this apparent contradiction are easy to understand. First, many resource estimates made by prestigious groups of scientists have had conditions imposed upon the exercise, either by the authority requesting the estimate or by agreement among the participants. These *conditional estimates* (as de Jouvenel [1967] calls them) will differ, depending upon the constraints. The National Materials Policy Act of 1970, for example, imposed seven specific conditions on the commission it established, and general language in the act provides further guidance to the kinds of forecasts wanted. Most national and international resource estimates have been made as conditional estimates, but the conditions and assumptions are often very different from one group to another. Conditions and assumptions of past forecasts are seldom mentioned later when resource estimates from various sources are compared on the assumption that the estimates ought to be similar.

There is a second, more uncontrollable, reason for differences in resource estimates. Each scientist and engineer, when making quantitative assessments of resources, makes assumptions about the amounts that might be recoverable. This series of assumptions about future technology, physical barriers, and general economic conditions, and about the distribution and concentrations of the actual mineral materials, is usually

*Terms used in a technical sense at this point are in italics.

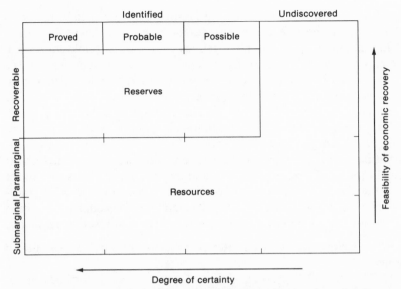

Fig. 2.1. Classification of mineral reserves and resources (degree of certainty increases from right to left and feasibility of economic recovery increases from bottom to top).

specified incompletely or sometimes not even mentioned. One of the most serious shortcomings of the resource classification shown in figure 2.1 is the lack of agreed upon rules for the limits of "submarginal" economic viability and for "speculative" undiscovered resources. Comparable quantitative resource estimates cannot be made for categories divided by qualitative boundaries, yet that is what figure 2.1 implies.

None of the foregoing suggests agreement among scientists and engineers about the actual distribution or accessibility of resources. Published estimates vary considerably, as do the time scales and assumptions that the estimates represent. Responsible cornucopians* like Feinberg or Weinberg appeal strongly to theory and gross averages, but do state their assumptions (Feinberg 1977; Weinberg 1967; Goeller and Weinberg 1976). They explicitly postulate successful planning in contrast to continual failure of such planning in the past, autocratic government controls, and a moderately priced "inexhaustible, nonpolluting source of energy." These issues are ones that can be discussed, and both Feinberg and Weinberg are explicit in their understanding that mineral resources are finite and that real shortages could occur, although both seem to think that fail-

*I use the term *responsible* to indicate a willingness to examine the assumptions and consequences of their estimates. Cornucopians who argue that we have not had trouble in the past or who appeal to magical technological fixes are irresponsible.

ure of human institutions rather than resource limits would be the probable cause. At the other extreme are resource estimates that seem to imply rigid amounts of perfectly homogenous commodities (Goldsmith et al. 1972; Meadows et al. 1972). Even these resource estimates did state assumptions and conditions that were rarely mentioned in the storm of criticism occasioned by their rather gloomy conclusions.

Within the community of physical and biological scientists and engineers, practically every shade of opinion on resource availability is represented. It is possible, although difficult, to reconcile these views and the resulting estimates of the conditional availability of resources through the usual process of scientific research and disputation. It is less easy to see how the disagreements with economists are to be reconciled. With prices and markets at the center of their paradigm and an economic definition of resources, economists have a different concept of resource estimates.

What follows, then, is an attempt to assess resource availability in terms of:
1. The strengths and weaknesses of some common methods of resource estimation.
2. The onset of difficulties for geochemically scarce elements.
3. Technological prospects and limitations for resource production, including substitution.
4. The time course of resource production;
5. Some national and international issues in resource production, with some special attention to developing nations.

The current state of knowledge does not permit all these issues to be resolved; differing views can be discussed and an opinion offered, but some directions for useful research will also be suggested.

## Methods of Resource Estimation

No single method has achieved dominance in those resource estimates which include both known and undiscovered resources. The methods discussed here illustrate the principal techniques used. There is much reference to copper and petroleum as well-studied examples, but each commodity has some special features which may require variations in method. Elements that commonly occur together, for example, add the complication of co-producing or wasting one of the components.

Despite the fact that resource estimates do not usually pertain to total terrestrial abundance, such estimates do exist (see Erikson 1973, for a summary), and there is closer agreement on these totals than on "available" resources. Such terrestrial abundance estimates can be used to provide some insights into resource availability.

## Resource Estimates from Elemental Abundances

Elemental abundances together with the finite mass of the earth provide absolute bounds on the amount of any material present on the earth. If an estimate of the deepest depths from which minerals will ultimately be extracted is also specified, these boundaries are reduced by several orders of magnitude. Such limits on accessible depths depend upon technological capabilities, of course, but there are good physical reasons for supposing any technology will be sharply limited in depth; rising temperature and pressure and the diminished strength of rocks under these conditions will limit both mining and drilling depths. What is equally limiting for the rare elements is that concentrations characteristic of the surface decrease in both number and variety with depth or disappear altogether. Within these confines costs of access measured against prices for retrieved minerals will determine what depths will be attempted for commercial production. Because of sharply nonlinear cost increases with increasing depth, even substantial price increases are not likely to induce much additional production from great depths.

The National Academy of Sciences' Committee on Mineral Resources and the Environment (COMRATE [NAS 1975]) used an average copper content for the earth's crust of 58 parts per million (ppm) to calculate $4.6 \times 10^{15}$ metric tons (MT) as the copper content of the entire crust. It assumed 4.5 km as the limit of mining and so reduced the available tonnage to $1.4 \times 10^{14}$ MT—even if the entire continental crust to this depth were mined and processed. If a society were willing to mine and process 1 percent of the crust, $1.4 \times 10^{12}$ MT could theoretically be recovered.*

But some of the crust is richer, and much of it leaner, than 58 ppm. Considering the well-studied and copper-rich southwestern United States, COMRATE noted that no more than 0.01 percent of the area is underlain by deposits richer than 0.1 percent copper.** Copper mineralized areas of the southwestern United States are considerably less than 10 percent of the entire (and well explored) United States but generously assume 10 percent of the earth's crust to be that richly endowed with copper (and retain 4.5 km as accessible depth). Maximum resource amounts would then be

---

*This also seems a large allowance. It would be equivalent to the United States mining the state of Indiana to a depth of 4.5 km or the continent of Africa mining an area larger than Upper Volta.

**A deposit of 0.1 percent is below present economic ore grade. Producing deposits are, at present, 3 to 30 times richer in copper.

$1.4 \times 10^9$ MT, about seven times the known reserves of $2 \times 10^8$ MT. Erikson (1973) and Cloud (1975) reach similar estimates beginning from crustal abundances for copper.

This example illustrates one way to relate measured reserves to total crustal quantities. For many important minerals, however, the data are more sparse than for copper. Erikson (1973) and Skinner (1976) present estimates of this type for other mineral commodities.

### Resource Estimates from Geological Similarity

Each mineral deposit is unique in some way. Nevertheless, most current fuel and mineral production comes from a rather small number of deposit types. A number of other types of mineral occurrence are recognized and have been studied in some detail even though they are not now in production (usually for economic reasons). At coarser scales geologic mapping is available for most of the world. Thus large quantities of empirical data are available about the physical and chemical state, structural features, large and small scale geological associations, and a host of other geological variables for most types of mineral deposits.

There is no present method for combining this store of information into resource estimates, and perhaps even more important, no agreement about the weights that quantifiable factors of occurrence should have relative to one another. Many clear geological relations are not even quantifiable and inference about poorly explored areas is a matter of experience and judgment.

More effort has been expended on resource estimates from geological analogy, to try to extend knowledge from well-explored to poorly explored areas, than on all other methods combined. Although estimates have been put forward by government agencies, professional groups, industry associations, and international organizations as well as individuals, the most ambitious and detailed work has been accomplished by private companies engaged in the search for and production of minerals. For example, Hubbert (1974) discusses the otherwise unpublished estimates for world oil and gas done under the auspices of the Sun Oil Company by C. L. Jodry. Jodry wrote Hubbert that

A study was made of all the (sedimentary) basins of the world, explored and unexplored, based on a 90 parameter geologic data set. These data were used with every published prediction that I could find and with much private unpublished material that has been made available to me. . . . Various curve-fitting methods were also used to check the reasonableness of the conclusions. Total ultimate reserves for all of the basins in each geographic unit listed were summed up, and these totals again checked for consistency against published data.

Such estimates represent a formidable effort and must be taken seriously.

However, not much more than a broad comment like Jodry's and the aggregated total estimate is usually known of such proprietary estimates for at least two reasons: time, effort, and private data represent expenditures by companies to enhance their information and competitive position; and the data, methods, and judgments are too extensive to publish in the established scientific literature. One is reduced to accepting or rejecting such estimates without examining detailed calculations and assumptions or having any way to determine sensitivity of the results to methods, data, and assumptions. This situation is unfortunate when one considers the undeniable concentrations of talent employed by resource companies and their stores of private data.

Mineral resource estimates originating in industry associations, professional scientific bodies, ad hoc government committees, or international organizations are sometimes given great weight because of the eminence of the scientists involved. Yet these activities are most often part-time public service by the scientists, and most of the actual work is done by anonymous staff members with whatever data and methods are at hand. Data and methods are sometimes published but often too sketchily for independent analysis. As a measure of lowest common denominator opinion among some leading scientists, such reports are valuable, but the lack of consistent results from study to study is not reassuring. Such resource studies suffer further from a lack of continuity in effort. To start anew each time a study is begun surely suggests much wasted effort and a limited ability to advance the art of resource estimation. Personal experience suggests that there is no obvious relationship between the length of time such studies take and the amount of effort actually expended on them.

Public agencies could apply to estimates the continuity of effort that ad hoc committees lack, but that potential has not always made their estimates more reliable. Hubbert (1974) discusses past U.S. Geological Survey (USGS) estimates of recoverable oil and gas and shows that the wide variability of the official estimates resulted from changing assumptions and methods and not from new data (see also Menard 1978). Whether professional and personal conflicts or political considerations in some way biased these or other government agencies' estimates is impossible to say, but one should remember that all government agencies exist in an inherently political matrix. The case of the official USGS estimates is especially important, because they have tended to be the basis for much past U.S. policy. The Ford Foundation Energy Policy Project seems also to have depended largely upon USGS estimates.

### Resource Cycle Analysis

Behind the notion of resource cycle analysis lies the beguilingly simple observation that, for any finite mineral resource, as for any single deposit, production must begin from zero, rise to one or more peaks, and ultimately decline again toward zero. Hubbert assumes that cumulative production will approximate a logistic growth curve.*

The logistic curve approximates an astonishing variety of growth phenomena in biological and human settings (Thompson 1952; deSolla Price 1963). A logistic curve for growth should be expected when conditions (often impossible to specify in detail) external to the growth being observed do not change drastically. However, among the external changes that might be expected to alter resource production cycles' fit to a logistic curve are rapid technological changes in either producing or consuming industries, arrival of cheaper alternative resources, and rapid demand changes consequent upon general levels of economic activity. We will return to disrupted resource cycles later. For now it is sufficient to note that the general form of the logistic curve offers a comparative ideal against which to measure resource production: a rapidly expanding first phase, followed by a mature phase with slower growth and often declining rates of growth, succeeded in turn by slowly declining production and, ultimately, by low levels or cessation of production.

In any case, the logistic form was hypothesized, and Hubbert showed that it fit the history of U.S. oil and gas production quite well (1956; 1969; 1974). Venezuela and Bahrain, already in an advanced stage on the oil depletion cycle, fit the same model rather well. Lieberman (1976) found that the logistic model also fit production of high grade uranium ore, despite the history of government intervention in this market. Figure 2.2 shows the logistic growth curves for discovery, cumulative production, and accumulation of proven reserves. Figure 2.3 shows the rates (formally the first derivatives) for these three series. As it happens, data for discovery, reserves, and production of oil are available for the U.S. past. Oil production data are independent of discovery data, but reserve data are derived from the same information as the discovery series. Thus there are two data sets, and both series are consistent with curves such as those of figure 2.3. Because the discovery series leads the production series in time (10–11 years in U.S. experience), the predictive value of the logistic curve model can be tested by using the discovery curve to project the production history. Hubbert did this in 1956 for U.S. oil production (when less than half of cumulative 1970 production had been produced), and in 1956 he accurately predicted the 1970 peak of U.S. production. He did the same for natural gas. His estimate of $Q_\infty$ for oil (see figure 2.2) of $165 \times 10^9$ barrels is near the mean of current estimates for total recoverable U.S.

---

*The logistic curve (also known as the sigmoid curve) is formally $Y_t = (1 + e^{-x})^{-1}$, where $x = c(t - t_i)$, $t$ is time, and $c$ is a constant. Hubbert's own description of his methods differs somewhat from that given here (see Hubbert 1969; 1974).

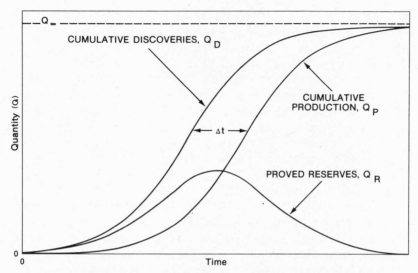

Fig. 2.2. The logistic curve as a representation of cumulative resource production. $Q_\infty$ is the amount of the resource ultimately to be produced, and $\Delta t$ is the time lag between discovery and production. Source: Hubbert (1974).

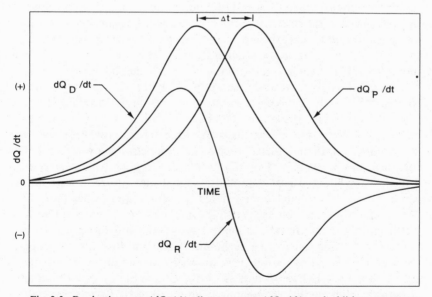

Fig. 2.3. Production rates ($dQ_P/dt$), discovery rates ($dQ_D/dt$), and additions to reserves ($dQ_R/dt$) as a function of time. These curves are formally the first derivatives of the curves in figure 2.2. Source: Hubbert (1974).

oil. Hubbert's work seems to have attracted little attention except among earth science professionals. Some oil companies were showing curves like those in figure 2.3 for projecting domestic oil production well before the 1973 oil embargo but without specific mention of the logistic curve.

As a predictive series, however, the discovery data exhibit fairly large fluctuations because annual exploration effort is strongly affected by general economic conditions and several other factors. In addition, the discovery of an oil field is credited to the year of discovery, but the amount ultimately recoverable from that field is not known for many years until its full extent is measured and production is "proved out." Hubbert (1967) used data from older fields to show that final production averages 5.8 times the amounts identified at the time of discovery (all oil fields were contained in the range 4.5 to 6.1). Although this multiplier could conceivably change in the future, it is unchallenged as a characterization of the past. It was used to increase estimates of ultimate production of known fields; for older fields the multiplier declines exponentially from the value of 5.8, and the corrections are large only for the newest discoveries. Because the empirical data used to extrapolate final production from initial discovery estimates pertain to a period when the recovered fraction of oil in place was continually increasing with improved technology and technique (e.g., secondary recovery methods and the like), use of a larger multiplier for future recovery would require that technique and technology advance at a rate faster than that of the past. It seems likely that increasing difficulties and expenses in improving total recovery percentages, together with more accurate initial estimates of field size, will make this multiplier smaller, not larger, even though much higher oil prices will press for increased recovery. It was apparently a lack of understanding of how to predict ultimate field recovery that caused resource economists Lovejoy and Homan (1965) to dismiss Hubbert's work in a few paragraphs.

To make better use of the discovery time series, Hubbert drew on Zapp's (1962) work and treated discovery as a function of exploratory effort measured as barrels of oil discovered per foot of exploratory hole drilled. Zapp lumped past data and assumed that future finding rates would be the same, but Hubbert noted that finding rates per foot had been declining as one would expect if the search effort was directed by the intelligent choice of always drilling the most promising prospects. Hubbert shows finding rate to be a declining exponential function of exploratory effort. By fitting such a curve another estimate of $Q_\infty$ (see figure 2.2) is obtained—172 × 10⁹ barrels for the United States. After reserves are subtracted from that estimate, only about 30 × 10⁹ barrels remain to be discovered (excluding Alaska; Hubbert 1974). As in the case of projecting ultimate field production, this time series has the technological improvements of the past imbedded in it. The increase in finding rates in the 1920s, for example, is probably due to the first widespread use of geophysical methods. Even a projection of declining success in discovery assumes that technological improvement will continue at past rates; improved success ratios would imply quantitatively more rapid technological advance or wholly new environments, rich in oil, in which to look. This last possibility cannot be ruled out (for example, buried deltas, continental rises, and Third World nations previously not open to exploration), but almost certainly that possibility implies higher costs.

Menard (1978) and Menard and Sharman (1975) confirmed Hubbert's results with a random drilling model. Modeling a number of random searches and comparing them with the actual history of discovery, Menard concluded that if amounts of oil in excess of Hubbert's estimates did remain undiscovered in the U.S., then the past search for oil had been worse than a random process. In other words, Menard showed that optimistic views about large undiscovered U.S. fields imply that geological and geophysical exploration, instead of improving the chances of finding oil, systematically directed the drilling effort to the wrong places. This conclusion is demonstrably false.

Menard (1976) also draws attention to the discovery history as a function of field size (fig. 2.4).* After the peak in rate of discovery of class 8 and larger fields in the 1930s, progressively smaller fields have been the main finds in the United States. As Menard points out, histories and projections of oil production assume (usually implicitly) that the mixture of field sizes remaining to be found is the same as that already found. But figure 2.4 suggests a limit as one progresses to smaller fields. Data from the Denver-Julesberg Basin for size classes 4–7 suggests that finding and producing costs double for each stepdown in size class. For classes less than 4, costs could rise even more steeply because exploration is seeking ever smaller targets. To see the size problem at a clear extreme, suppose that the $30 \times 10^9$ barrels of U.S. oil remaining to be discovered exist in 3 billion randomly distributed fields of 10 barrels each.

This line of evidence suggests that some oil industry estimates may be much too optimistic. Menard combines the random drilling model with the discovery history for giant oil fields to show that one widely quoted industry estimate (Moody et al. 1970) of 25–28 undiscovered giant fields in the United States in 1968 implies that exploratory drilling would have been 50 times more successful if industry had drilled randomly instead of employing scientific search.

---

*Here I use Menard's classification of field size as exponents of 10 barrels ultimately recovered. Thus a class 6 field will yield between $10^6$ and $10^7$ bbls.

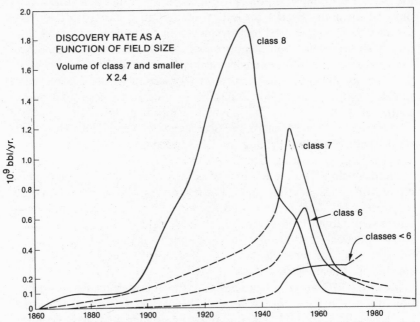

Fig. 2.4. Discovery history of U.S. oil fields by field size. For smaller fields, estimated reserves have been increased by a factor of 2.4 to allow for extension of fields. Source: Menard (1976).

## The Abundant and the Scarce: Two Classes of Raw Materials

Almost three-fourths of the earth's crust is composed of silicon and oxygen. If another eight elements are added to these two—aluminum, iron, calcium, magnesium, sodium, potassium, titanium, and hydrogen—slightly more than 99 percent of the earth's crust has been accounted for. These elements may be taken as the *abundant elements*. The other naturally occurring elements together constitute almost 1 percent of the earth's crust and are subsequently referred to as the *geochemically scarce elements*. Choice of the boundary between the two classes is to some extent arbitrary. Manganese and phosphorus, for example, at crustal abundances near 0.1 percent are only slightly less common than hydrogen.

The abundant elements pose no problem of absolute scarcity for the foreseeable future even in expanded use, although energy and environmental side effects may increase their prices considerably. They also constitute the most important substitution possibilities for scarcer materials.

The geochemically scarce elements are not only uncommon in an absolute sense, but their enrichment to a grade at which exploitation is possible occurs under very special sets of geologic circumstances, and their geographic distribution is very limited. These scarce elements have played a crucial technological role. As technology has grown more complex and sophisticated, most of the scarce elements have been employed in larger and larger quantities. Substitution will be discussed in a later section, but increased difficulties are to be expected with growing demand for the scarce elements.

## Energy, Material, and Technological Problems in Production of Scarce Resources

There are only two physical inputs to any society—energy and raw materials. The stock of energy is not depleted, but its availability is continually reduced as *low entropy* stocks are converted to unavailable *high entropy* stocks in the form of heat. Neither are minerals really "consumed"; they are degraded or disseminated in use so that even incomplete recycling requires expenditure of still more materials and energy. Some materials are lost or degraded beyond recovery. Against these inevitable processes we have the ingenuity of technology and technique.

Consider the availability of geochemically scarce minerals in terms of the energy and materials required to produce lower grade and more inaccessible deposits. Escalation in these requirements implies upward price pressures on the metals and minerals that are the products of the process. Many of the difficulties that technology is called upon to overcome can be specified.

Too often discussions of mineral commodities begin and end with a discussion of past trends. The real resource production process begins in the refractory, heterogeneous, and nonlinear earth and ends with both valued products and unwanted residuals. At every stage, materials and low entropy energy are degraded. For convenience, resource production can be divided into the following six steps:

1. Prospecting techniques, which range from a person on foot to sophisticated geological, geophysical, and geochemical methods.
2. Reserve evaluation, which usually involves drilling, assisted at times by increasingly sophisticated analytical methods. Steps (1) and (2) are usually considered together as exploration.
3. Preproduction development, which is here considered separately from actual production because energy, materials, and money are expended with no returns, often for periods of several years.
4. Mining and beneficiation of ores, which usually result in some enrichment in the substance sought.

5. Smelting and refining, which chemically and/or physically alter enriched ores to produce the desired substance in sufficient purity for the applications in which it is a "raw material."
6. Other requirements, which include but are not limited to environmental costs, waste disposal costs, water requirements, and settlement costs (for personnel).

### Prospecting

Most of the minerals found before 1950 were discovered from surface outcrops of the mineral (oil and gas are exceptions, although a surprising number of these were found from oil seeps in earlier days). These deposits, which still provide a large portion of world output, were found by explorers, prospectors, and geologists and had little or no cost associated with discovery. Other deposits that do not show producible grades of ore at the surface were found at low cost by geologists by mapping and inference from structures and mineral associations. For this class of mineral exploration, costs are sufficiently low, compared to subsequent operations, to be properly neglected when considering the future.

On a surface prospecting basis, much of the earth's land area has been well explored. The principal areas whose surfaces have not been closely examined lie under ice (e.g., Greenland or Antarctica) or under water, or perhaps within tropical rain forests or high-latitude tundra (parts of the Amazon basin or Siberia, for example). Nearly all of these areas require remote methods of exploration and/or expensive remote sampling methods. Although surface geological exploratory work will still be useful, it too has become more costly.

At issue here are future costs which depend upon both the success ratio (quantity found per unit effort) and upon the unit cost of the methods employed. The many sophisticated methods of mineral exploration in use today do depend upon some common physical laws which are unlikely to change. The sensitivity of most exploration methods declines in proportion to the square of the distance from detectors to deposit (e.g., gravitational, magnetic, and electrical). For any exploration method there is a continual struggle against the fall of sensitivity with depth, against the ever-increasing "noise" added to the signal by longer paths through the heterogeneous earth, and against the requirements for more closely spaced and precise measurements in the search for smaller deposits or more subtle geochemical gradients. As prospecting pushes into more remote and hostile environments, costs in materials and energy increase dramatically.

In response to these and other problems, prospecting techniques and instruments have continually changed and expanded. One need only consider the search for oil in 1920, 1945, and 1970 to obtain some feel for the extent of change. From a truck and a few men interpreting results in the field, prospecting has evolved to complex and expensive searches involving teams with sophisticated instruments and carefully orchestrated agendas backed by highly skilled laboratory analysts and an ever-growing array of expensive equipment. COMRATE (NAS 1975) cites Canadian data on copper to show that between 1951 and 1970 exploration costs increased from 0.6 percent to 2.0 percent of the gross value of the metal found; in highly mineralized areas of the southwestern United States, exploration costs increased between 1955 and 1969 from 0.1 percent to 2.2 percent of the gross value of the metal discovered. Note that these measures correct for inflation by comparing exploration expense with values of minerals found at the time. COMRATE concludes that "over the last 20 years, the efficiency of the exploration dollar has decreased by about two-thirds. It appears that this decrease will continue." The search for massive sulfide deposits in Canada has been even less rewarding, with exploration costs reaching 10 percent of the value of the discovered mineral (NAS 1975). These costs are discouraging because massive sulfides constitute one of the least costly production possibilities for copper, nickel, and several associated metals.

Future search efforts for geochemically scarce minerals will undoubtedly be aided by technological advances. But such advances must first overcome increasing difficulties posed by the earth. A sum of these difficulties includes a term inversely proportional to the square of the depth to the deposit; a term inversely proportional to the grade of the ore; and a term inversely proportional to the area underlain by the deposit. As figure 2.4 shows, a history of discovery of oil demonstrates that large deposits were found before small ones. Small ore deposits at great depth can be found and produced only at vastly increased relative prices—if at all.

For developing countries, pursuit of these directions in mineral prospecting increases reliance on imported technology and raises demands on the pool of highly trained scientists and engineers. For those areas of the world where civilizations have flourished for thousands of years, the first and cheapest phase of mineral prospecting, at least for the metals used in those earlier civilizations, has already gone by. High grade deposits of gold, silver, lead, copper, and other materials discovered by lone prospectors could and did contribute to the modern industrial growth of the United States and Canada. It is unlikely that any such era will aid industrial growth in the Middle East, North Africa, or much of Asia.

## Reserve Evaluation

The end of the prospecting phase provides no more than clues to possible mineral deposits. In the case of buried deposits, prospecting yields only a geophysical, geochemical, or geological anomaly which may not even indicate concentrations of useful minerals. To find out what and how much is actually present requires the drill.

Drilling costs per meter increase rapidly as depth increases. Drilling the shallow portion of an eventual deep hole is often more expensive than drilling shallow holes because of the special provisions necessary to accommodate later deep drilling. Small deposits require more evaluative drilling per ton of ore ultimately produced than do large deposits, because the perimeter to be defined grows longer in direct proportion to the horizontal dimensions of the ore body, while the volume of ore is proportional to the product of the horizontal and the vertical dimensions. Thus an idealized cubical ore body 500 meters on a side would present a perimeter of 2000 meters and yield $125 \times 10^6$ cubic meters of ore. A cubical ore body 1000 meters on a side would merely double the perimeter to 4000 meters but ore amounts would increase eightfold to $10^9$ cubic meters. Because the actual amount of the desired substance is obtained from the product of grade times ore quantity, it follows that reserve evaluation expenses are also inversely proportional to the grade of ore.

### Preproduction Development of Mineral Deposits

There was a time, less than a century ago, when the finder of a mineral deposit simply bought or registered a claim in the morning and, with simple tools, began mining in the afternoon. Indeed, two Scottish surveyors, setting up transits on a tiny reef in Lake Superior in 1868, found a vein of native silver continuing from the reef into shallow, chilly water. By nightfall they had mined more than 200 kilograms of pure silver with nothing but a crowbar (Murdoch 1964).* Compare this effort with the expensive and time-consuming preparations required to open a low grade copper deposit or to begin offshore oil production. Writing in the 1960s, Lovering (1969) gave five years or more as the average time between discovery and first production of a mineral deposit (with another five years consumed in previous exploration). These development times are highly variable but generally are longer for large deposits, deep deposits, deposits in hostile or remote environments, and deposits in densely settled areas. Because direct environmental degradation is proportional to the total tonnage of rock that must be processed, low grade deposits generally mean longer preproduction time for permits and special control arrangements.

*This find, the Silver Islet Mine, is interesting for another reason. It produced more than 5 percent of the silver output for the United States in the early 1870s on a surface area of less than 350 square meters. This type of very rich find will not occur in those developing countries where surface expressions of traditionally valuable metals have long since been worked by preceding civilizations.

"Up-front" investment without income is also increased by larger, more complex, technology required for low grade ores and for difficult environments.

Some idea of how these preproduction costs can change may be seen from the North Sea oil platforms. In 1970–71, in water depths of 100–200 feet, platforms typically cost $5 to $8 million. In 1975–76, in water 450–500 feet deep, platforms cost more than $120 million. If all the cost increase were due solely to increased water depth, the cost increase would be proportional to the square of the water depth (with some increase left to assign to inflationary effects), but this case is undoubtedly far more complex than that.

For another example consider the problems of a remote environment in oil production on the North Slope of Alaska. Pipeline costs of nearly $7 billion will add 20 to 50 cents to the cost of each barrel delivered to South Alaska (depending upon the choice of optimistic or pessimistic estimates of the amount of oil to be produced on the North Slope). Alaska also illustrates the increasing time lag, in recent years, for large projects in remote and difficult environments—ten years elapsed between proving of the field and the first oil deliveries. Natural gas from the same fields will apparently not be delivered until 15 years or more after discovery.

It is difficult, perhaps impossible, to assess the magnitude of capital costs in the next 25 years as resource supply difficulties escalate and still more difficult to estimate energy and material requirements without knowing the specific technology to be employed. Nevertheless, an example of potential financial problems is provided by Gaines (1973) for the United States:

The total estimated capital spending by the energy, communications and metals industries alone in the 15 years 1971 through 1985, in constant 1971 dollars, adds to approximately $1.1 trillion. It should be stressed that all of the estimates included in this total are very crude projections and could be significantly off target; if they are, it is more likely that they understate rather than overstate the level of capital spending. In the five years 1967 through 1971, capital spending by this group of industries equalled approximately 40 per cent of total plant and equipment spending by American industry, with the proportion steadily increasing from 36 per cent in 1967 to 45 per cent in 1971. In view of the extent of the need for new capacity, it is likely that this proportion will continue to increase, perhaps averaging about 50 per cent over the 15 years 1971 through 1985. If this should prove to be the case, total capital spending in fixed 1971 dollars would amount to $2.2 trillion over the period, or $147 billion annually. Total spending on plant and equipment in 1971 was $81 billion, and by 1973 had climbed to $92 billion in 1971 prices. . . .

Even on all of the very conservative assumptions, that have been employed in this analysis, it is quite clear that the urgent need to improve our supply capability in energy and other basic industries will impose very considerable demands upon the financial system. Of the total capital spending projected here, perhaps as much as one-half will be covered from internal cash flow sources—an assumption which in turn assumes a liberal government policy toward price increases that will permit these industries to generate the profits necessary to encourage the needed investment and to develop the needed cash flow. This would still leave $65–$70 billion per year to be raised from external sources. In the three years 1970–1972, which were record years for capital financing by industry, U.S. corporations raised an annual average of $26 billion in the bond and equity markets. On the most optimistic assumptions with respect to growth in savings flows available to the longer-term capital markets, it would not seem possible that industry will be able to meet its external requirements for long-term capital in the domestic bond and equity markets.

In making these estimates Gaines further assumed some relaxation in air pollution standards. Developing countries that have many demands for capital and limited access to it will face correspondingly worse problems, with or without environmental controls.

## Mining and Beneficiation of Ores

Only the very richest ores can be simply dug and transported to the smelters. For some of the abundant elements this is still possible, as in the richest bauxites. Most mineral production, however, requires removal of surface or shaft material followed by mining which often excavates a great deal of unwanted material. Low grade copper ores now in U.S. production require processing 500 tons of rock for each ton of copper produced (Cook 1976). Typical procedures involve mining of the ore (and often some barren rock with the ore), crushing and grinding it to a degree of fineness dictated by the grain sizes of the desired mineral, and enriching it by flotation, gravity sorting, or some other process dependent on the physical or chemical properties of the specific ore. The enriched ore concentrate is then ready for the smelter.

For most past and present production of minerals, mining and beneficiation of ores have required only a fraction of the energy needed in the smelting step (2 to 10 percent is typical for common minerals today—Bravard et al. 1972). But as ore grades decline, energy demands in mining and beneficiation rise rapidly. Copper ores now mined at 0.3 percent copper content demand about 4 times as much energy per ton in mining and beneficiation as 1.0 percent copper ores (Bravard et al. 1972). This increase in energy requirements is inversely proportional to grade, and the amount of material that must be disposed of is also inversely proportional to grade. In the search for economies of scale to counteract some of the effects of the decline of ore grade, surface mining of copper has increasingly displaced underground mining. Deposits beyond the modest burial depths permitting open pit mining may not be exploitable at all if the grade is low, no matter how extensive the deposit. Copper production costs for Kennecott in the United States are between 61 and 74 cents per pound of copper—at or above 1978 market prices for copper and far higher than production costs for the richer ores in production in Peru, Chile, Zaire, and Zambia (*Business Week* 7 August 1978, pp. 54–60). One result has been pressures on the U.S. government for import quotas, tariffs, and government stockpile purchases.

*In situ* mining of very low grade ores has often been suggested as a way to avoid this class of problems, but despite many years of work in this direction, little progress has been made in finding low cost methods for in-place rock fracturing and solution leaching (NAS 1975). Even if such methods are found, "provision must then be made to avoid the loss of leaching solutions and the consequent contamination of groundwater and surface water" and for the inherently lower efficiency of extraction (Lovering 1969). COMRATE concludes that even if such methods were eventually developed they would not affect production for 20 years or more (NAS 1975), and one would still need to find large deposits of even lower grade ores.

For copper and a number of other geochemically scarce elements, such large lower grade deposits have not been found despite considerable search. The reasons lie in the chemistry of low concentration deposits of scarce elements. Ore concentration prior to smelting can occur only to the extent that the particular chemical compound (mineral) containing the wanted substance can be selectively concentrated and barren material rejected. But many scarce elements do not form separate compounds at very low concentrations. Whatever amounts of scarce elements are present are often locked in solid silicate solutions of common minerals. In crystal lattices, scarce elements occasionally substitute for abundant elements of the same ionic diameter (see Mason 1958). Many such substitutions are known: lithium and nickel for magnesium; vanadium, cobalt, scandium, and, at times, chromium for iron; lead and rubidium for potassium; and so forth. Not only are these replacements occasional (hence the low concentrations of the scarce elements), but enrichment is no longer as effective because the minerals in which the scarce element substitutes often constitute a large portion of the total rock mined. Instead of sending a few tons of highly enriched concentrate to the smelter, vastly larger amounts of low concentration must be dealt with. Skinner (1976) suggests that most quantities of geochemically scarce elements are locked up in this way in common rock-forming minerals. Resource optimists like

Feinberg (1977) seem unaware of these fundamental chemical differences at low concentrations and extrapolate data from present ores to the much lower grades without regard for changed chemical conditions.

We should expect to find, as the grade in any particular source of metal decreases, that "the total energy to recover the metal increases at first gradually until the energy for mining and milling approaches that for smelting and refining, after which the total energy required increases rapidly" (Page and Creasy 1975).

## Smelting and Refining

This step in the production of mineral raw materials has, in the past, been the most energy consumptive step and often the most capital intensive per unit of output. In addition, smelting and refining have generated large quantities of solid, liquid, and gaseous residuals that have brought increased regulation in the effort to maintain satisfactory air and water quality.

Pursuit of enlarged output from lower grade or otherwise less available mineral deposits suggests three important issues for the future. First, so long as ores or concentrates achieve the same richness, lower grade deposits occasion no particular change in smelting requirements, but if different types of ores with stronger chemical bonds are used energy requirements will escalate. This sort of change can be anticipated for some geochemically abundant elements. Indeed, in the shift from magnesium oxides to seawater as a source of magnesium and in the grade reduction in bauxite ores for aluminum, such changes have occurred in the past. Although these changes can and do exert upward pressures on prices (and on capital costs as well), the adjustments pose no insurmountable problem. They do, however, mean that developing nations will face raw material costs higher (in real terms) than those formerly faced by today's developed nations.

Second, depletion of the geochemically scarce elements is proceeding faster than it is for abundant elements because scarce elements are used at much higher rates in comparison to their terrestrial abundance (Skinner 1976). As production shifts to lower grade ores and to ores with more difficult chemical bonds, the amount of "ore" smelted and refined per unit output rises dramatically, and each unit of ore processed will take still more energy to disrupt more stable chemical bonds. Because direct costs for energy in smelting and refining typically represent 5 to 20 percent of market price (Bravard et al. 1972), factors of ore quality could lead to abrupt price changes.

Third, pollution control measures for smelters are likely to increase capital costs, especially in industrial countries and anywhere a dramatic increase in fossil fuel use occurs. Rising energy requirements and lower grade of ore concentrates both worsen this problem. Many developing countries could claim some relative advantage if they have substantial undeveloped water power or are not now threatened with existing industrial and vehicular pollution.

## Technology and Mineral Production

The standard remedy for the difficulties discussed above has been an appeal to technological innovation to provide new methods and devices to offset increased costs. Before speculation on the prospects for a technical solution to the problems, some consideration of past technological change is in order. Adoption of new technology has undeniably transformed mineral production in the past. Were it not for these changes, much productive mining of today would be impossible. There is no way copper ores containing less than 1 percent copper could be produced at present prices with the mining methods of 1900.

How well has technological innovation of the past kept up with the increasing difficulties in mineral production? The conventional view usually begins with the conclusion of Barnett and Morse (1963) that unit costs must have been declining because their analysis showed stable or slowly declining resource prices. Especially for the last few decades, this point is debatable. Lovering (1969), for example, examines the case of copper and concludes: "Contrary to Barnett and Morse (1963), and to Barnett (1967), *unit costs are not declining*, nor have they been for a decade" (Lovering's emphasis). One is tempted to conclude that changes in the mineral industries, including technological advance and organizational and scale economies, have just barely kept abreast of the increasing difficulties of resource production.

But how much have the difficulties discussed in previous sections actually beset mineral production? Strangely enough, no one knows very clearly on an average basis. Typically one assumes that the highest grade and most accessible resources will be produced first and that higher cost and lower grade resources will be reserved until the cheapest are exhausted, but the accidents of exploration, political goals (like resource independence), and world industrial development have often caused this rational assumption to be violated. Expensive offshore production was undertaken long before Middle Eastern oil resources had more than a tiny fraction of their total amount produced.

To return once again to copper as an example, average U.S. ore grades declined from 4 percent copper in 1900 to about 1 percent in 1945 and about 0.5 percent in 1974. In the rest of the world, however, rich new deposits came into production throughout this period: Chile between 1910 and 1920; Zaire in the 1920s; Zambia in the 1930s; Peru, the Philippines, the USSR, Canada, and Australia (and substantial new production in Chile and Zaire) in the 1950s and 1960s; Iran, Indonesia, New Guinea, and others in the 1970s. All of these deposits (except some in Canada) are of higher grade than typical U.S. ores. It is not clear whether average ore grade has been going up or down. It is worth noting that few of these deposits were recently discovered; many have been known for decades but exploited only recently. Throughout this century (until 1970) real unit energy costs have been declining. It seems likely that technology has not yet been asked to contribute much in mitigating the problems posed by more difficult access to resources. In the last decade, however, many mineral prices have increased dramatically. Copper prices have doubled since the mid-1960s, far outstripping increases in the wholesale price index for the United States (U.S. Department of Commerce 1978). These increases may well be driven largely by increases in real energy prices.

All commodities have their own unique situations and their own production histories. All have had technological change (the special case of oil is discussed in chapter 7), but in only a few has production yet had to compensate for lower grade and more difficult sources. Mercury production may be an exception. Mercury prices have quadrupled in the past 30 years while prices for other metal and mineral commodities were only doubling.

For a few of the geochemically scarce elements, then, difficulties of the kind discussed above have increased, but this group is a small fraction of the raw materials supply. For most mineral commodities, average grade of ore has not yet changed much, and technology has been used mainly to expand total output. Improved productivity of labor over the past five or six decades shows that technological advance has, in industrial countries at least, provided higher wages as well as expanded output. The main elements of technological change in mineral production in the twentieth century are well known: replacement of human and animal power with diesel engines and electric motors; improved materials and design, permitting scale enlargement for mining equipment; advances in low cost bulk transport, reducing but not eliminating locational advantages; and increased efficiency in the production of electric power. For specific minerals, mining and processing innovations (catalytic cracking in refineries, new enrichment processes, and the like) have permitted lower prices or use of lower grade resources or both. Thus there seem to be two main categories of technological change of interest in mineral production:

1. Industry-specific advances that increased resource availability or lowered costs or both.
2. Application to mineral production of general technological advances.

This distinction is useful—even if oversimplified—because only the first kind of technological change might be stimulated by increased market prices for mineral raw materials. Unless (or until) raw materials and energy constitute a much larger fraction of total cost of final products, it is wishful thinking to suppose that increased difficulties in mineral production will by themselves bring about broad front technological change of the second type.

Technological change has not come quickly to the mineral industries. The techniques which made possible the substitution of taconite ores for hematite ores in production of iron and steel required nearly 50 years of work; even the assembly of land for this change began 60 years ago (Burgess 1975). The time lag between technology understood in the laboratory and technology in widespread industrial use is much greater than generally supposed.

Lovering (1969) concluded that, for the past 20 years, "technology is barely keeping pace with increased costs of extraction," and his observation agrees with the input/output analysis of energy use by Reardon (1972), who showed that technological changes just barely reduced energy use in mineral industries between 1948 and 1963.

Long-time mineral industry observer Cook (1976) is not optimistic about the next few decades:

It appears that further increases in the efficiency of extracting geologic resources will be difficult to achieve. There is in view no more efficient transport device than the diesel-electric locomotive or the diesel-powered truck. Draglines, power shovels, grinders, crushers, flotation machines, and air compressors are best powered by electricity; there is in view no economic way of increasing efficiency of electricity generation in a thermal power plant much above the present 40 percent. Economies of scale in mining are still being achieved in surface operations, but will be limited ultimately by the size of individual deposits or by the lack of flexibility of enormous machines.

Note than an answer to Cook's pessimism requires just the sort of broad front technological change that resource difficulties alone may not be able to stimulate. Shifts from coal-fired to nuclear-generated electricity reduce the overall efficiency of new power plants from the 40 percent cited by Cook to 30–33 percent. The combination of rising electric rates and declining conversion efficiencies for those who choose the nuclear

58 NATURAL RESOURCES

route portends a considerable challenge to technological innovation merely to offset these effects.

Previous sections drew attention to rapidly rising energy requirements for mining and beneficiation of minerals as grade of ore declines. The problems posed for technology by this class of problems were discussed by COMRATE:

The very low energy efficiency for fine grinding of ores in conventional tumbling mills is well known and is responsible for 60–75 percent of the energy used for beneficiation. The possibilities of novel grinding processes that use significantly less energy are not promising, but the potential savings from such developments are so important as to warrant thorough investigation (NAS 1975).

There is a haunting contrast in the mineral literature between the sober and sometimes pessimistic technological estimates of the scientists and engineers who must devise the new technology and the complacent optimism of many social scientists and government officials. Even experienced resource economists treat technology as an exogenous variable and by extrapolating from the past conclude on an optimistic note. Netschert (1958) provides an instructive example. His comfortable conclusion—that U.S. oil and gas would not be limited by availability of the resource base because of projected technological advance—has been shown by events to be false. Meanwhile, Hubbert's conclusions of about the same date—that U.S. oil and gas production would peak and begin to decline in the early 1970s—have proven to be nearly correct.

None of the foregoing should be taken as evidence of a total absence of technological opportunities in mineral production. Rapid improvement in communications, especially in computing and control technology based on microprocessors, suggests directions that have not yet been tapped. For new resource production, whole new classes of machinery that optimize operations step by step could both improve productivity and lower certain costs. These innovations will take time, however. In developing countries, with large, underemployed labor pools, such methods might employ more skilled and semiskilled labor aided by sensors and microprocessors and machinery of moderate scale to produce minerals at competitive costs but employ little unskilled labor. This approach depends upon technology transfer or development of national capabilities in these technological directions.

For the distant future other technological improvements are possible, if unpredictable, but in the near term (10–20 years) there are no dramatic technical shifts identified that will mitigate upward pressures on production costs from increased energy prices and less congenial environments of production. Because lead times in mineral industries are substantial, new discoveries will not affect the industry much in the next 20 years. For the long term, all of the difficulties outlined above will beset the geochemically scarce elements. Some of the difficulties (especially environmental and energy ones) will intensify problems for abundant elements. If technology is to balance these difficulties, acceleration of technological advance far beyond the historical rate is required because problems escalate in such a strongly nonlinear fashion at every step in the process.

## The Dimensions of Scarcity

Ingots of metal, barrels of oil, or tiers of cut building stone are enough alike that it is easy to forget how varied are their origins. Perhaps for this reason, discussions of difficulties associated with resource depletion often have a unidimensional feel about them. As present deposits are worked out, it is expected that production will move on to sources that pose the fewest additional difficulties or add the least cost. As we have already seen, there is more than one choice of direction.

Consider an idealized and oversimplified case: Production of a mineral commodity has come from a particular type of deposit of a constant grade; as these deposits are depleted or additional production is desired, one could choose to move to lower grades, more distant ores, deeper ores, ores with more recalcitrant chemistry, or smaller deposits. So long as these options are available, the choice among them depends upon existing technology, relative availability of capital and labor, and a number of other technical, political, and economic issues. The problem is no longer one of simple optimization or cost minimization. Nations and corporations may well choose different directions.

The actual world of mineral production is more complicated than this idealized case. At any one time, a single mineral product may come from deposits of a range of grades, several different chemistries, and a wide variety of deposit sizes, depths, and locations. It seems clear that the expansion of mineral production in the past hundred years has been based on finding new deposits in new geographical regions. This very strategy and the accompanying exploration have confirmed how unevenly the richest mineral deposits are distributed throughout the world.

In Europe, the United States, and some other areas, production has indeed moved toward lower grades, greater depths, and more difficult chemistries. It is not enough, then, to speak of mineral amounts as homogenous material. It is important to know how the quantities of mineral present near the surface of the earth are distributed when measured along the dimensions of scarcity.

### Grade-Tonnage Relationships

Most discussions of resource availability assume, either explicitly or implicitly, that ore tonnages increase exponentially as the grade of ore deposits declines arithmetically. In a recent review, for example, Brooks (1976) not only assumes the exponential increase of ore quantities with declining grade but also postulates that "tonnage of contained metal [in the ore] also increases with decreases in grade, though not so fast as ore." Some analysts from centrally planned economies make the same general assumptions (Dobozi 1977).

The work of Lasky and Blondel after World War II tested some data available at the time and suggested that the exponential-arithmetic relationship might be the general case (Lasky 1950; Blondel and Lasky 1956). The idea was tentatively accepted, and even today one can find references to Lasky's Law and Lasky's Rule. At about the same time Ahrens (1954) showed that distribution of the elements in several common rock types was approximately lognormal (that is, a plot of logarithms of amount against concentration approximated a normal distribution—see figure 2.5b). Each of the rock types examined had a lognormal distribution, but the distributions had different statistical measures. In particular, both mean and median grades may be quite different from one rock type to another for the same element. Examination of ore deposits shows, for each specific type of deposit, that grade and tonnage are also distributed lognormally (Singer 1977; Phillips 1977), but the same studies show that grade is independent of tonnage. It is ironic that one of the specific deposit types demonstrating independence of tonnage and grade, porphyry copper deposits, was used 30 years ago by Lasky in support of the proposed rule relating decline in grade to exponentially increasing amounts of ore (Singer et al. 1975). COMRATE reexamined this issue and concluded: "It is evident that Lasky's principle, while useful in a restricted, practical range of values for some individual mines and mining districts, the geological evidence permitting, must be rejected as a universal tool for the statistical evaluation of mineral production over larger areas. In particular, the use of Lasky's rule to predict future giant-sized, still lower-grade, resources is erroneous, overly optimistic, and unrealistic" (NAS 1975).

One feature of the lognormal distribution is that dispersion in the distribution displaces the median grade to lower values than the mean grade. The effect of this is to permit extrapolation in Lasky's fashion from the richest grades of a particular type of deposit until grades approach the median. Below median grade Lasky's rule fails and tonnages decline sharply; the contained metal declines still more rapidly.

If we accept that each type of ore deposit can be described lognormally, what is the likelihood that the ensemble of all rock types, from richest to leanest, also will be distributed lognormally? There appears no reason to expect this result on theoretical grounds, and empirical evidence about grades between ores presently mined and common rocks is insufficient to resolve the question.

Skinner (1976) has proposed that the overall distribution of many geochemically scarce elements is bimodal (fig. 2.5c) and that in these cases exhaustion of the high grade peak will result in vastly increased difficulties as an abrupt shift to much lower grade deposits is required.

Figure 2.5 illustrates schematically four grade-tonnage relationships. Lasky's Rule might be an approximation for some restricted range, as in either figure 2.5b or 2.5c, but leads to unrealistic values at low concentrations and cannot accommodate bimodal (2.5c) or multimodal (2.5d) distributions. Figure 2.5b probably is a suitable model for the abundant elements. While there is no assurance that the sum of a group of lognormal distributions is itself lognormal, the median concentration of the abundant elements is not much less than the mean concentration, and the modes of concentrations for individual rock types cover a rather narrow range. Thus actual values would probably look much like figure 2.5b, even if the curve were not strictly lognormal. For the geochemically scarce elements, a bimodal or multimodal distribution seems quite possible. Certain enormous enrichments of scarce elements and the special geological circumstances that produce them each have lognormal distributions whose peaks are spread over a large range of grades. Copper concentrations in present ore deposits are 10,000 times richer than copper concentrations in common rocks. To expect that actual physical and chemical conditions in the earth result in the precise amounts of copper-containing rocks—each with its own lognormal distribution—to sum to a smooth overall distribution from the rare high concentrations now mined to a single peak below average crustal abundance is to expect the unlikely. Especially at high levels of enrichment, multimodal peaks may be rather common among scarce elements.

For practical affairs, two more dimensions of the grade-tonnage relationship must be added. First, knowing how much tonnage is available at a particular grade is useful for estimates of mineral availability only if the distribution of deposit size is also known. We have, so far, depended heavily on the largest deposits for much production. Menard has shown this dependence for U.S. oil production (fig. 2.4). Worldwide the four largest oil fields of the 22,000 known fields supply 21 percent of present

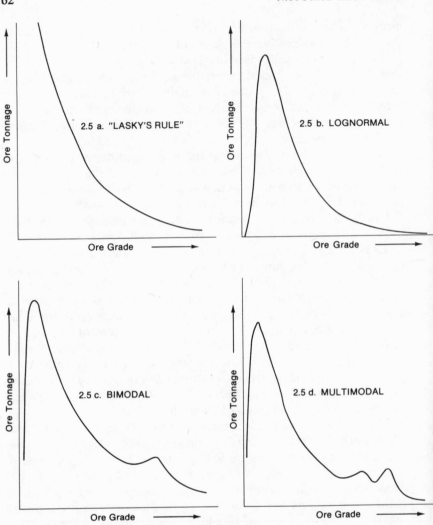

Fig. 2.5. Grade/tonnage distributions.

production (WAES 1977), and 491 giant fields (more than $5 \times 10^7$ barrels per field) account for about 80 percent of known reserves (Meyerhoff 1976).

Second, chemical barriers occur at various places in the grade-tonnage relationship. Temperatures and pressures in the real earth during the enrichment process, as well as the chemical bonds that are possible, all tend to produce multimodal grade-tonnage relations whenever a range of grades is represented by only a few deposit types. While such a multidimensional relationship is not easily drawn, the progress of mining has followed different paths for various scarce elements. The search for oil, for example, has gone to smaller but "rich" deposits and more slowly toward lower oil concentrations found in tar sands and oil shales. By contrast, copper production (in the United States at least) has proceeded to large deposits of lower ore grades while neglecting some small deposits of higher grade.

Present knowledge of mineral distribution is best for the highest enrichments and for concentrations in common rocks. Work is needed to outline the distribution of grades and tonnages of geochemically scarce elements in the enormous range of concentrations between grades now mined and grades in average crustal rocks. Such a survey should pay close attention to both the size distribution of deposits and the chemical barriers that must be overcome in exploitation.

### Resources at Greater Depth

The general lack of success in finding ore bodies at more than modest depth is often assumed to result solely from the lack of suitable methods of exploration, but there are good reasons for supposing that geochemically scarce elements in greatly enriched concentrations become less common as depth increases. First, one must note that many ore bodies grow leaner or more restricted in extent as depth increases (Cook 1976). Second, conditions for deposition of greatly enriched ores, such as open pores and fracture zones and the low temperatures and pressures that cause migrating fluids to deposit materials, are all found only near the surface.

There are sedimentary deposits (placers and laterite soils, for example) which form only at the surface and are not often preserved when material is deeply buried. Deposits that occur in sedimentary rocks by enrichment obviously cannot occur below the depths where sediments are available. Sediment thickness varies from zero to (rarely) 15 km, in most areas 5 km or less. Below 5 km, minerals begin to be reorganized and recrystalized. This metamorphism, which becomes more complete with increasing depth, rarely results in the extreme differentiation that produces ore bodies of the richness currently exploited.

The ocean floors are often cited as a vast untapped source of minerals. But as more is learned about the ocean floors, this abundance appears unlikely. Present land-based mineral production exploits deposits that have been enriched during the last billion years or so. The average age of the ocean floors is about 100 million years; even if all the same processes operated, we would still expect only about 10 percent of the mineral supply per unit area that has been found on land. But all the same mechanisms do not operate. Erosion and shallow reworking is nearly absent on the ocean floors. The common rocks beneath the thin muds of the ocean floors are themselves poorly endowed with many of the geochemically scarce elements and provide little supply for enrichment. The manganese nodules, first found over 100 years ago, are a special ocean resource. They may augment available manganese, nickel, and copper resources— at a price. In addition to the formidable difficulties of large scale mining in the open sea, present methods for processing the nodules require several times as much energy as current copper production (NAS 1975). Improved procedures may well better this picture, but typical development times are rather long and suggest that these resources are still in the future.

### Recycling

The stock of materials in use becomes available, in principle, for reuse as present goods are discarded. Reprocessing scrap takes far less energy than production of virgin materials. This is not a new observation, and recycling has provided a significant source of mineral materials for many years. Scrap material recovery typically represents 10 to 50 percent of discarded material, and the recovery percentage has improved somewhat in the past two decades. Yet for many materials, present uses make vastly improved recycling difficult or impossible. Phosphorus and helium, for example, are dissipated and not recoverable. For materials used in plating, cladding, and alloying, high recovery rates are also difficult to achieve. Such materials include zinc, silver, gold, chromium, cobalt, and others. In some cases present institutional arrangements favor virgin materials, and changes (including incentives) could improve recycling. Technological changes which use more composite materials and more exotic alloys, on the other hand, reduce recycling possibilities. In developing countries, recycling is probably less complete than in developed countries as a source for new manufacture, but reuse of material scrap of all kinds is very high, so less may be lost from in-stock inventories of depletable resources.

Complete recycling is impossible, and practical engineering problems, together with use patterns, make recycling beyond about two-thirds a considerable achievement. Thus recycling cannot even support a steady-state society. Although improved recycling should be sought, growth in materials use continues, and any development route will require a considerable increase in depletable resource use in developing countries.

### Substitution

The abundant minerals—especially iron, aluminum, magnesium, and titanium—offer the main possibilities of substituting for scarcer or more expensive elements. Except for iron, these substitutions carry implications of greatly increased energy use. Substitution of aluminum for copper, for example, triples the energy requirement per ton of metal; titanium for copper multiplies the energy requirement per ton by a factor of seven. Substitution of iron or steel for scarcer materials might reduce energy requirements somewhat, but if exotic alloys are wanted, the energy requirements might increase. When the demand for common metals leads to the use of less concentrated and/or more refractory ores, energy requirements for their production will also increase. These increases have already started in the shift from rich hematite ores to taconite and in the shift to lower grade bauxites for aluminum. Anticipated increments in energy needs range from about 20 percent (for iron) to nearly 100 percent (for titanium) to reach deposits abundant enough for the next century or two (Bravard et al. 1972).

Many future substitutions will surely have to be made for the geochemically scarce elements. Present world use of these scarce elements is profligate in terms of their relative abundance in the earth's crust. Even if we were to mine common rock, as some cornucopians have suggested, the mix of elements would provide proportionately much less of the geochemically scarce elements than the mix presently produced. Thus the common metals plus glass and ceramics and stone and other local building materials offer the long-term substitution possibilities.

Technological possibilities for substitution for scarce materials no doubt can ease the difficulties of transition to more common materials. Often, however, present technological directions lead to substitution of one scarce element for another (see, for example, Chynoweth 1976). Other new materials surveyed by Gabor (1970) are mainly composites involving plastics or ceramics with small amounts of scarce elements. Such materials are promising but do make recycling more difficult. A more dramatic suggestion by Cameron (1975) begins by noting that "there is no natural law that requires that [mineral] demand be technology-controlled." Cameron goes on to suggest that selection among technological options "be controlled primarily by the availability of minerals." Now that the principle of technology assessment is generally accepted, such an idea might be worth more attention. At least the necessity for substitutions serves notice that present resource demands are not well suited to future availability.

### Resource Availability and Development

Development, even of a kind somewhat different from that of present industrial countries, will require expanded resource production. Growing difficulties with resource production have come and will continue to come upon us step by step. Only a few resources appear to be in danger of absolute scarcity in the next few decades, but the more quickly poor nations develop along industrial routes, the sooner resource scarcity will be encountered. A developed globe at resource use levels equal to present per capita use in the United States would multiply resource needs by a factor of ten or more. Such a hypothetical outcome means both scarcity and dramatically higher raw materials prices. If Mesarovic and Pestel's (1974, p. 138) suggestion that early stages of development require still higher levels of resource use is accurate, the case looks threatening, especially if rising energy costs are added.

Yet the industrial nations continue to increase per capita resource use (although less rapidly than in the past). Will these amounts level off at twice present values or at some other foreseeable level? Developing countries will face higher and higher resource costs for development the longer development is delayed.

### The Time Course of Resource Production

Development will not come suddenly, and difficulties and cost increases *are* mostly incremental. The cycles of resource production from inception to exhaustion are important for individual deposits and for national resource production, and too little attention has been paid to the features of these cycles.

Too much attention has instead focussed on ultimately available amounts, important as that question may be. The arrival of a peak in production, and the subsequent decline, is of much more immediate interest. We have no experience on the backside of resource curves on a worldwide basis, but if present oil estimates are correct, we will encounter that downslope for oil in the 1980s or 1990s. Nevertheless, there are many examples of mineral production in decline or at an end for individual ore deposits, mining districts, and nations. These examples suggest the situation that must eventually face any nation that bases a development plan on returns from mineral production. Anecdotal examples from the United States are not encouraging. In the "richest country in the world," districts with shrinking resource production are some of the most persistent poverty areas in the country: Look at anthracite coal districts, the Michigan copper region, or the Mississippi Valley lead and zinc districts. Not all of these are actual depletion cases, but they do illustrate the desirability of exploring social impacts associated with declining resource curves. Among the features often observed in areas of shrinking resource production are persistent unemployment, uneven economic response (even to sharply increased prices), frequent year to year instability in production, and technological stagnation. Cause and effect for these cases are not yet clear, nor can any general conclusions be verified, but if some or all of these difficulties do result from declining resource production, developing nations must control the production cycle, plan to cope with the difficulties, or count on *only* the rising portion of resource production, not on the wealth implied by ultimately recoverable resource quantities.

The matter of instability in resource production on the declining side of the curve may be the most serious. DeSolla Price (1963) identifies U.S. production of copper, zinc, and bituminous coal as examples of interrupted logistic curves and points to the ensuing oscillation in production. Hotelling (1931), in his pioneer economic study of resources, notes that this sort of rapid variation is undesirable and that it "involves forces of a different sort from those with which economic theory is ordinarily concerned." The social history of zinc, copper, and coal mining districts in the United States testifies to the risks of fluctuating mineral production.

I hypothesize that the onset of instability in resource production begins as peak production is near but that it can occur sooner. At that onset problems would be quantitatively worst for a developing nation because the resource sector would be at its maximum size. Present "overcapacity" for several mineral commodities and projected further excess capacity as other nations bring mineral production on line must increase the probability of disruption in planned growth of mineral production. Instability may be the result. Boom and bust commodity markets have been especially difficult for developing nations in which a mineral commodity is the principal source of foreign exchange earnings.

More immediate problems arise from the asymmetry of costs in resource production cycles. As resource production progresses, problems and costs escalate. As Ayres (1978, pp. 46–47) puts it: "The classical economic theory of exhaustible resources, as developed by Hotelling, Herfindahl, and others, does predict the exploitation of the highest quality (i.e., lowest cost) reserves first, *but has not, so far, allowed for the positive feedback between decreasing quality of the remaining resources and the rate of extraction*. Nor have the increasing environmental costs of this entropic buildup been incorporated in models of optimum extraction" (Ayres' own emphasis). Barnett and Morse (1963) argue that average resource prices have remained stable or declined and conclude that technological advance, substitution, and imports account for this apparent violation of physical expectations as ore grade declines. An explanation at least as plausible as theirs could be constructed in terms of the expansion of the frontiers of resource exploitation since the middle of the nineteenth century. Augmentation or replacement of first European and later American mineral sources with colonial or developing country sources often meant higher grades of ore and lower labor costs. Meanwhile, real energy

68                                                    NATURAL RESOURCES

prices were declining, and ocean transport added little cost. When Middle
Eastern oil entered the market it was (and is) produced at lower costs than
oil for many other districts in production. The newly opened copper
mines at Toquepala, Peru possess copper ores three times richer than
those of some large copper-producing districts in the southwestern United
States, and are 20 percent richer than the average of all U.S. deposits
(Page and Creasy 1975). For some mineral commodities, the average
grade of resources in production may actually have been increasing.

In any case, the future is not automatically a projection of the past.
Steeply increasing difficulties on the production end appear at every turn.
Energy will grow relatively more expensive in the next few decades. It is
often overlooked that U.S. electricity costs ended a 60-year relative decline in the middle 1960s and began increasing a full eight years before the
oil embargo. The United States, a mature industrial nation with well-
advanced resource production, uses 16 percent of all its energy for mining, extraction, and beneficiation of ores to produce metals which fall 25
percent short of fulfilling U.S. demand (Cloud 1977). Meanwhile, unexplored areas in moderate climates are vanishing, and the search for and
production of minerals is being pursued into harsher and more costly environments. Capital, energy, and labor costs of exploration and production all increase under these conditions.

Substitution of capital for resource inputs appears quite limited according to Humphrey and Moroney (1975). Berndt and Wood (1975) find
some substitution possible but show capital and energy to be complementary and so imply that such substitution comes at the expense of increased
energy requirements. In this area there is, as yet, no agreement on analytical procedures.

Long and Schipper (1976) in their study of many of these matters conclude:

The crucial issues regarding resource scarcities concern the rates and prices at
which resources will be available and the political constraints to using them in
ever-increasing amounts. Increasing world-wide demand for resources may create
supply-demand disequilibria. Although these will eventually be resolved by market forces, the additional costs during the periods of disequilibrium may be large
and are to be avoided. While market and policy mechanisms may well be sufficient
tools with which to achieve an optimal rate of resource ultilization, *we know too
little about how this optimal rate should be defined and evaluated* (emphasis
added).

Elsewhere they emphasize "the need for careful assessment of the income-
distribution impacts of policies that affect resource allocation. Economic
efficiency does not guarantee the fairness of the resulting distribution."

The foregoing discussion assumes increased world demand for resources. A discussion of such projections is beyond the scope of this paper, but a recent review of mineral demand forecasting models by Wright (1977) shows increasing rates of material consumption with rising income for all forecasts and identifies serious problems in the process. Rates of economic growth and intensity of resource use are often treated as stable variables (or constants). Wright says that "none of [the models] as constructed can deliver a comprehensive view of resource futures, since they cannot take into account supply or institutional factors endogenously." I cannot help but add that most present world models include little or no closing of the gap between rich and poor nations. Even the optimized Bariloche model (Herrera et al. 1976) still leaves Africa and Asia with per capita annual incomes of less than $600 (1960 dollars) well into the next century.

## Resource Development Strategies

This concluding section draws some speculative inferences for development from the previous discussion. It assumes only that a government does attempt to steer development whether by planning, by taxes, or by other incentives.

Mustafa (1977) points out the early need for an understanding of how much and what kinds of resources are available. Some recent suggestions for an improved inventory of U.S. mineral resources (Menard 1978) show how little attention has been paid to the best methods for obtaining such an inventory. The needs of development planners are not likely to be served by the priorities that determine the exploration plans of transnational corporations. For one thing, development plans have considerably longer duration than corporate discount rates allow. Long range development plans would be helped if total deposit size is proved before production begins. An inventory of resources in support of development plans should especially seek high grade mineral deposits, including those of moderate and small size, for several reasons.

Strategy for production or extension of existing production should be chosen with some attention to "oversupply" of some commodities. Excess capacity has meaning only in terms of world growth rates. Projections of growth rates seem very uncertain and quite variable. For a nation wishing a stable income, maximum flexibility should be sought. For this reason alone, mineral deposits of small and medium size might be developed first. But there are other advantages to such a strategy:

1. The time lag between plan and production is ordinarily shorter for smaller deposits, so quicker and more flexible response to world conditions is usually possible.

2. The largest mineral operations typically need some of the most so-phisticated technology to take advantage of economies of scale. If technology transfer is the answer, it must be noted that it isn't work-ing very well. Too often, the result is need for more foreign corpora-tions and a larger proportion of expensive imported machinery.

3. Capital needs arise in smaller increments, and access to financing should thus be easier.

4. For mineral developments of moderate size, the choice of foreign corporations is greatly enlarged, if one is to be included in the proj-ect, and negotiations with potential contractors become more com-petitive.*

5. Population dislocation and ensuing development problems are likely to take a scale more easily managed.

6. Downstream industries could be fitted more smoothly to develop-ment plans over time and in location.

7. The needs of a number of mineral developments of small or moder-ate size offer the chance for a developing country to begin manufac-ture of mining equipment based on internal demand.

8. As a purely statistical matter, several smaller projects have a better chance of some success than one large one. A large development project that fails is automatically a national problem.

Some may object that this strategy might mean higher unit production costs and thus lower income, but developing countries often have depos-its of grades higher than world averages to overcome such disadvantages. The opportunity costs of the strategy are what seem relevant to develop-ment, however, and these seem to favor the suggested strategy (Jamali 1978). Longer range plans could be made for the largest mineral deposits, with the incidental benefit of allowing more time for the costly process of assessing their full extent.

In the light of discussion of the time course of resource production, I would suggest that production be restrained, if possible, well short of the theoretical peak. Managing a shrinking industry in a growing or a stag-nant economy can never be an easy task. If the logistic curve has any value as a model, one conclusion would be that the declining side of a re-source production curve presents problems. A stable production level should be chosen such that production can last a minimum of several gen-erations to reduce and spread out future social costs. Resources in the ground seem likely to appreciate in value at or above the interest rate. If

*For those who hold that large corporations are just as competitive as smaller ones, it must be admitted that the largest corporations do wield political and market power, some-times in several countries (Lindblom 1977; Barnet and Muller 1974).

greater total production is required, it might be better to put additional mineral districts in production (assuming the national inventory shows this to be possible). Downstream industries should be sought with careful attention to the choice of technology.*

The choice of price strategy seems less clear and subject to much controversy. The absolute levels of prices of depletable resources are referred to costs or are free or are indeterminate in both Marxist and non-Marxist economics (Papp 1977; Hotelling 1931).** Support has been advanced for marginal cost, average cost, opportunity cost, and replacement cost, among others, as appropriate price references. With marginal cost as a minimum, I would suggest pricing strategies that move to estimated replacement cost well in advance of the rapid price rises occasioned by a shift to poorer grade resources. This strategy should increase total return at the same time consumers are receiving timely advance warnings at a stage when technological shifts can be painful and slow.

International commodity agreements or other arrangements among producers and consumers could diminish or eliminate many of the above problems, and such possible measures are discussed in other chapters. So long as natural resource production is viewed primarily in national security terms, agreements may be limited in scope, but the full extent of actual resource interdependence of the world economy is not yet clear. Nothing in the foregoing strategy should prevent such agreements. The flexibility of the strategy suggested might, in practice, give a nation more latitude in seeking agreements.

## References

Ahrens, L. H. 1954. "The Lognormal Distribution of the Elements," *Geochimica et Cosmochimica Acta* 5: 49–73.

Ayres, Robert U. 1978. *Resources, Environment, and Economics: Applications of the Materials/Energy Balance Principle*. New York: Wiley.

Barnet, R. J., and R. E. Muller. 1974. *Global Reach: The Power of the Multinational Corporations*. New York: Simon & Schuster.

Barnett, H. J. 1967. "The Myth of Our Vanishing Resources," *Transactions* [of Social Sciences and Modern Society] 4: 7–10.

*Stimulating discussions by Schumacher (1973) and Lovins (1977), as well as the example of China and the vulnerability of the highly industrial countries as demonstrated by the 1973 oil embargo, challenge some of the cherished notions of industrial development.

**Hotelling's absolute price level depends upon the initial price, which in turn depends "upon demand and upon total supply of the substance." But at the time the former is determined the latter is unknown. In actual cases for commodities, the initial price seems to have been the result of historical accident.

72                                                        NATURAL RESOURCES

Barnett, Harold J., and Chandler Morse. 1953. *Scarcity and Growth: The Economics of Natural Resource Availability*. Baltimore: Johns Hopkins University Press.
Berndt, E. R., and D. O. Wood. 1975. "Technology, Prices, and the Derived Demand for Energy," *Review of Economics and Statistics* 57: 259–68.
Blondel, F., and S. G. Lasky. 1956. "Mineral Reserves and Mineral Resources," *Economic Geology* 51: 686–97.
Bravard, J. C., H. B. Flora, and C. Portal. 1972. "Energy Expenditures Associated With the Production and Recycling of Metals," ORNL-NSF-EP-24. Oakridge, Tennessee: Oakridge National Laboratories.
Brooks, D. B. 1976. "Mineral Supply as a Stock." In W. A. Vogely, ed., *Economics of the Mineral Industries*. 3rd ed. New York: American Institute of Mining, Metallurgical, and Petroleum Engineers, pp. 127–207.
Brooks, D. B., and P. W. Andrews. 1974. "Mineral Resources, Economic Growth, and World Population," *Science* 185: 13–19.
Burgess, C. H. 1975. "Mineral Resources, Productive Capacity, and Related Problems: An Industry Point of View." In R. W. Marsden, ed., *Politics, Minerals, and Survival*. Madison: University of Wisconsin Press, pp. 55–66.
Cameron, Eugene. 1975. "Alternatives for Survival." In R. W. Marsden, ed., *Politics, Minerals, and Survival*. Madison: University of Wisconsin Press, pp. 67–80.
Chynoweth, A. G. 1976. "Electronic Materials: Functional Substitutions," *Science* 191: 725–32.
Cloud, Preston. 1975. "Mineral Resources Today and Tomorrow." In W. W. Murdoch, ed., *Environment: Resources, Pollution and Society*. Sunderland, Massachusetts: Sinauer Associates, pp. 97–120.
Cloud, Preston. 1977. "Entropy, Materials, and Posterity," *Geologische Rundschau* 66: 678–96.
Cook, E. 1976. *Man, Energy, Society*. San Francisco: Freeman.
de Jouvenel, Bertrand. 1967. *The Art of Conjecture*. New York: Basic Books.
deSolla Price, D. J. 1963. *Little Science, Big Science*. New York: Columbia University Press.
Dobozi, I. 1977. "Forecasting Structural Changes in the International Raw Materials Industries and Markets," Report no. 22. Budapest: Hungarian Scientific Council for World Economy.
Erickson, R. L. 1973. "Crustal Abundances of Elements, and Mineral Reserves and Resources." In D. A. Brobst and W. P. Pratt, eds., *United States Mineral Resources*. USGS Professional Paper 820. Washington, D.C: U.S. Geological Survey, pp. 21–26.
Feinberg, Gerald. 1977. "Material Needs and Technological Innovation: Some Hopes—and Some Doubts." In G. Garvey and L. A. Gravey, eds., *International Resource Flows*. Lexington, Massachusetts: Heath, pp. 149–72.
Gabor, Dennis. 1970. *Innovations: Scientific, Technological, and Social*. New York: Oxford University Press.
Gaines, Tilford. 1973. "Financial Implications of Material Shortages," *Economic Report of Manufacturers' Hanover Trust*. New York: MHT.

Goeller, H. E., and A. M. Weinberg. 1976. "The Age of Substitutability," *Science* 191: 683-89.

Goldsmith, Edward, Robert Allen, Michael Allaby, John Davoll, and Sam Lawrence. 1972. *Blueprint for Survival*. Boston: Houghton Mifflin.

Herrera, A. O., H. D. Skolnik, G. Chichilnisky, G. C. Gallopin, J. E. Hardoy, D. Mosovich, E. Oteiza, G. Brest, C. E. Suarez, and L. Talavera. 1976. *Catastrophe or New Society? A Latin American World Model*. Ottawa: International Research Center.

Hotelling, Harold. 1931. "The Economics of Exhaustible Resources," *Journal of Political Economy* 39: 137-75.

Hubbert, M. King. 1956. "Nuclear Energy and the Fossil Fuels." In *Drilling Production and Practice*. New York: American Petroleum Institute, pp. 7-25.

Hubbert, M. King. 1967. "Degree of Advancement of Petroleum Exploration in the United States," *American Association of Petroleum Geologists Bulletin* 51: 2207-27.

Hubbert, M. King. 1969. "Energy Resources." In P. Cloud, *Resources and Man*. San Francisco: Freeman, pp. 157-242.

Hubbert, M. King. 1974. "US Energy Resources, A Review as of 1972." In *U.S. Senate Committee on Interior and Insular Affairs, A National Fuels and Energy Policy Study*. Washington, D.C.: U.S. Government Printing Office.

Humphrey David Burras, and J. R. Moroney. 1975. "Substitution Among Capital, Labor, and Natural Resource Products in American Manufacturing," *Journal of Political Economy* 83: 57-82.

Jamali, Usameh. 1978. "The Opportunity Cost of Producing and Selling Oil as Crude." In *Proceedings of the Wisconsin Seminar on Natural Resource Policies in Relation to Economic Development and International Cooperation*, vol. 2. Madison: Institute for Environmental Studies, University of Wisconsin.

Lasky, S. G. 1950. "How Tonnage and Grade Relationships Help Predict Ore Reserves," *Engineering and Mining Journal* 151: 81-85.

Lieberman, M. A. 1976. "United States Uranium Resources—An Analysis of Historical Data," *Science* 192: 431-36.

Lindblom, C. E. 1977. *Politics and Markets*. New York: Basic Books.

Long, Thomas Veach II, and Lee Schipper. 1976. "Resource and Energy Substitution." In U.S. Congress Joint Economic Committee, *U.S. Economic Growth from 1976 to 1986: Prospects, Problems, and Patterns, Volume 4—Resources and Energy*. Washington, D.C: U.S. Government Printing Office, pp. 94-121.

Lovejoy, W. F., and P. T. Homan. 1965. *Methods of Estimating Reserves of Crude Oil, Natural Gas, and Natural Gas Liquids*. Washington, D.C.: Resources for the Future.

Lovering, T. S. 1969. "Mineral Resources From the Land." In P. Cloud, *Resources and Man*. San Francisco: Freeman, pp. 109-34.

Lovins, A. B. 1977. *Soft Energy Paths: Toward a Durable Peace*. Cambridge, Massachusetts: Ballinger.

Mason, B. 1958. *Principles of Geochemistry*. 2nd ed. New York: Wiley.

74                                                      NATURAL RESOURCES

Meadows, Donella H., Dennis L. Meadows, Jørgen Randers, and William W.
    Behrens III. 1972. *The Limits to Growth.* New York: Universe Books.
Menard, H. W. 1976. "Exploration History and Random Drilling Models." In
    *Proceedings of the Annual Meeting of the Association of Indonesian
    Petroleum Geologists.* Djakarta: AIPG, pp. 1–12.
Menard, H. W. 1978. "Random Drilling Models and the Information Base for
    National Oil Policy," [in press].
Menard, H. W., and G. Sharman. 1975. "Scientific Uses of Random Drilling
    Models," *Science* 190: 337–43.
Mesarovic, Mihajlo, and Edvard Pestel. 1974. *Mankind at the Turning Point:
    The Second Report to the Club of Rome.* New York: Dutton.
Meyerhoff, A. A. 1976. "Economic and Geopolitical Implications of Giant Pet-
    roleum Fields," *American Scientist* 64: 536–41.
Moody, J. D., J. W. Mooney, and J. Spivak. 1970. "Giant Oil Fields in North
    America." In M. T. Halbouty, ed., *Geology of Giant Petroleum Fields.* Tulsa,
    Oklahoma: American Association of Petroleum Geologists, pp. 8–17.
Murdoch, Angus. 1964. *Boom Copper.* Calumet, Michigan: Drier and Koepel.
Mustafa, Adnan. 1977. "Impediments to the Technological Development of the
    Petroleum and Mineral Resources Sector in Western Asia Countries." United
    Nations Economic and Social Council, Economic Commission for Western
    Asia, E/ECWA/NR/SEM., 1/15.
NAS (National Academy of Sciences), Committee on Mineral Resources and the
    Environment (COMRATE). 1975. *Mineral Resources and the Environment.*
    Washington, D.C.: NAS.
Netschert, Bruce. 1958. *The Future Supply of Oil and Gas.* Baltimore: Johns
    Hopkins University Press.
Page, N. J., and S. C. Creasy. 1975. "Ore Grade, Metal Production and
    Energy," *Journal of Research of the U.S. Geological Survey* 3(1): 9–13.
Papp, D. S. 1977. "Marxism-Leninism and Natural Resources," *Resources Pol-
    icy* 3: 134–48.
Phillips, W. G. B. 1977. "Statistical Estimation of Global Mineral Resources,"
    *Resources Policy* 3: 268–80.
Reardon, W. A. 1972. "An Input/Output Analysis of Energy Changes from 1947
    to 1958 and 1958 to 1963." Northwest Pacific Laboratory Report. Richland,
    Washington: Battelle Memorial Institute.
Schumacher, E. F. 1973. *Small is Beautiful: Economics as if People Mattered.*
    New York: Harper & Row.
Singer, D. A. 1977. "Long-term Adequacy of Metal Resources," *Resources Pol-
    icy* 3: 127–33.
Singer, D. A., P. P. Cox, and L. J. Drew. 1975. *Grade and Tonnage Relation-
    ships Among Copper Deposits.* USGS Professional Paper 907A. Washington,
    D.C.: U.S. Geological Survey.
Skinner, B. F. 1976. "A Second Iron Age Ahead?" *American Scientist* 64: 258–
    69.
Thompson, D'Arcy. 1952. *On Growth and Form.* New York: Cambridge Univer-
    sity Press.

U.S. Department of Commerce. 1978. *Statistical Abstract of the United States.* Washington, D.C.: U.S. Government Printing Office.

WAES (Workshop on Alternative Energy Strategies, Massachusetts Institute of Technology). 1977. *Energy: Global Prospects 1985–2000.* New York: McGraw-Hill.

Weinberg, A. M. 1967. *Reflections on Big Science.* Cambridge, Massachusetts: MIT Press.

Wright, S. 1977. "Long-term Resource Demand," *Resources Policy* 3: 261–67.

Zapp, A. D. 1962. *Future Petroleum Producing Capacity of the United States.* USGS Bulletin 1142-H. Washington, D.C.: U.S. Geological Survey.

# 3 *John E. Ross*

# Natural Limits to Natural Resources

There is continuing worldwide debate over the rates and the methods we are now using to develop natural resources. One general point of view warns that environmental breakdown is inevitable should the world continue on its present course in resource use and pollution. This point of view also sees a looming crisis in energy supplies and a steady erosion in our ability to expand food supplies at a rate sufficient to meet growing food demands. In sum, this view says we are moving toward general scarcity, which at the worst would mean a rapid decline from present rates of resource consumption or at best an orderly retreat.

Another general point of view says that environmental pessimists overreact, that new technological alternatives based in research will ease the problems of resource exploitation, that man's history is one of continual reconstruction of the world, that the real and overriding problem is to provide some general relief from the subsistence lives (or worse) suffered by so many of the world's people.

This chapter tries to back off a step from these contrasting views and to draw out the grains of rationality that may prevail in the arguments put forth by those who warn of environmental decline, but also to describe some general concepts that can be used to assess these warnings. It does not embrace environmental determinism, which would say we are still very much at the mercy of environmental conditions, nor does it embrace

77

technological determinism, which would say that environmental limits are of little concern.

I do believe that natural limits to natural resources are imposed by both the quantity and quality of resources. Whether these limits can be recognized, assessed, and dealt with in the course of world development is the issue. To examine this broad question this chapter uses two environmental frameworks:

1. Carrying capacity of the environment, involving the capacity for continuing production of both renewable and nonrenewable resources and the capacity of the environment to absorb and recycle the wastes of industrial processes.
2. Environmental limits (irreversibilities, outer limits, and environmental change), involving the capacity to live within certain eventual limits.

It is clear that the issues cannot be resolved using only these concepts, nor fully resolved at this time even with additional concepts. The real world of natural resource use and resource limits involves values, judgments, and the current state of technology. Data on resource reserves are far from precise. Consumption forecasts use judgments and a host of assumptions which may not prove correct. Technology is open-ended and may hold in store some quantum surprises.

Nevertheless, the concepts of carrying capacity and environmental limits still demand attention. World population moves upward; per capita demand increases; growth is an integral of both. There is a self-propelling momentum in economic expansion. Institutional forces, including employment demands, capital commitments, profits, welfare systems, and national sovereignty over resources often dominate decision making. Is there room for and need for environmental considerations among these pressures?

The concepts of carrying capacity and environmental limits can, at a minimum, provide some descriptive idea of what is happening or what might likely happen. They could also be used as standards against which we could evaluate and reshape developmental schemes. There also appear to be contemporary socio-environmental forces, emerging from and responding to the rates and means of resource use, that have not traditionally been incorporated into economic and engineering assessments. The latter part of this chapter examines some of these phenomena.

Finally, there is an outline of an approach to assessment derived from the concepts of carrying capacity and environmental limits.

## The Rise of Issues

The issues of natural limits, although much older, pushed into greater public and world attention about 10 years ago. In April 1968, a group of citizens meeting in Rome set up a study titled "A Project on the Predicament of Mankind." The project was concerned with "the five basic factors that determine, and therefore ultimately limit growth on this planet— population, agricultural production, natural resources, industrial production, and pollution" (Meadows et al. 1972, p. 11).

The report of the project, titled *The Limits to Growth*, presented a provocative conclusion: "We have seen that positive feedback loops operating without any constraints generate exponential growth. In the world system two positive feedback loops are dominant now, producing exponential growth of population and of industrial capital. . . . Negative feedback loops become stronger and stronger as growth approaches the ultimate limit, or carrying capacity, of the system's environment. . . . Finally the negative loops balance or dominate the positive ones, and growth comes to an end. . . . In the world system the negative feedback loops involve such processes as pollution of the environment, depletion of nonrenewable resources, and famine. . . . The delays inherent in the action of these negative loops tend to allow population and capital to overshoot their ultimately sustainable levels" (Meadows et al. 1972, pp. 156–57).

This prediction of fundamental change drew criticisms of the quality of the Club of Rome model, the quality of its data, the clarity of the definitions implied in some of its central concepts, the nature of market response to resource shortages, and the viability of technology.

The report was also challenged on its basic premise—that there are limits to growth. The report did, however, reaffirm that human population, agricultural and industrial production, natural resources, and pollution are linked together and are rapidly becoming more closely linked, at the global level, by increasing flows of people, resources, currencies, and technology. Furthermore, and just as important, the report did cast another shadow over a once almost unquestioned potential for continued economic growth.

From the controversy stirred by *The Limits to Growth* and other works like it, a set of questions has emerged:

1. Under what combination of conditions would economic growth be naturally limited by depletion of resources or by scarcity of critical resources?
2. Under what combination of conditions would economic growth be

naturally limited by inability to bring together the array of renewable and nonrenewable resources, particularly as a result of changing supplies of and requirements for energy?
3. Are natural limits such that adjustments will be catastrophic or orderly and manageable?
4. If there is catastrophe, will it be geographically local or regional or will it spread in a global pattern?
5. How would a "warning system" anticipate limits and responses to limits, and how could these be dealt with in terms of policies and institutions?

## Carrying Capacity

The Club of Rome report and many other contemporary studies that deal with resource limits have global carrying capacity as a central concept, although they may not use the term. Carrying capacity is relatively easy to define in a local environment, more elusive in an expanding setting. Heilbroner (1974, p. 47) agrees with others that there "*is* an absolute limit to the ability of the earth to support or tolerate the process of industrial activity." He implies two aspects of carrying capacity with the words "support" and "tolerate." The first suggests continuing productivity of resources. The second implies capacity of the environment to absorb and recycle wastes of production processes.

When Heilbroner examines possible timetables of environmental disruption, he finds a baffling set of considerations: Despite the certainty that a limit impends, we have only an imprecise capability to predict the time span within which we will have to adjust. The initial problem is the availability of resources necessary to sustain industrial output.

For example, world production of crude oil—probably the preeminent nonrenewable resource of current societies—has doubled every 10 years, on the average, since 1890. By the end of 1973 cumulative world crude oil production had reached 299 billion barrels (Hubbert 1978). At past growth rates cumulative production would reach about 600 billion barrels by 1983 and about 1200 billion barrels by 1993. World reserves of petroleum look quite limited against that kind of projection, but circumstances could change. The rate of consumption might change. Human values related to patterns of petroleum consumption might change. Substitutions for petroleum might come into play. Much of the projected annual growth in production stems from consumption in the industrial countries; it does not yet depend much upon worldwide population growth, nor upon future resource distribution between those who are now rich and those who are poor. Presumably the continuance of such a rate of growth in the industrial countries would involve, at least, consumption of some of the products in other parts of the world, if not a major readjustment in use of future production.

One issue is whether we have the resources to permit us to sustain increases in output. But a considerable proportion of the resources we extract today does not become output; it ends up as waste, and the question must be asked whether the environment can absorb the waste.

The global problem is complicated because we do not have accurate knowledge on most of the world's resources. Amounts and concentrations of resources; physical limits, if any, to extraction; technology to increase amounts recovered; substitutability for resources in short supply; resource costs in energy, materials, and money as development proceeds; and features of the resource production cycle are all in question, but that does not diminish our need to know. Not only are world resources still inadequately evaluated, but the very definition of a resource changes as the ability to "extract" substances improves. This might imply that no insurmountable barrier need arise from resource exhaustion for millenia, given appropriate technology and availability of sufficient energy. That implication assumes we will develop the necessary technology to ultimately, if not immediately, refine such basic materials as granite and seawater. It assumes that the side effects of extracting and processing the necessary vast quantities of rock and water will not be so deleterious as to rule out the new technologies. It assumes the availability of vast new amounts of energy. It assumes that the globe can physically support and tolerate such a human society.

The carrying capacity concept emerged in somewhat more mundane circumstances as a measure in applied biology at a local level. Leopold (1933, p. 51) offered one of the earliest references to the concept. He talked of a saturation point where the numbers of a particular species of grazing animals approached the point where grasslands (the environment) could support no more individuals without a general and continuing decline in the quality of the pastureland. Carrying capacity meant a unit of land's ability to support a species or some optimum mix of species. It is interesting that the concept referred initially to management of "wildlife" as an exploitable resource.

Carrying capacity was also used by government range management specialists responsible for allocating animal grazing rights on public domain lands in the western United States as early as the 1930s. Technically, carrying capacity was defined as the number of cows or sheep that could be pastured per month per acre. For example, the capacity might be 20 cows for one month or 2 cows for ten months. It has been a highly usable concept for almost half a century in a system where one knows the annual production of a renewable resource like grass, where one knows how much a cow will eat, and where there is a high degree of authority or control over the resource. In the western United States that authority is expressed in line fences, allotments, fees, and laws.

Of course, the amount and quality of forage will vary from year to year depending on annual rainfall and previous management. It is possible to reserve certain portions of the land from all grazing for a period to allow recovery. There is a known optimum production, based on the physical characteristics of the land, and a balance between production and consumption—an environmental homeostasis of sorts, if not a steady state. Consumption is constrained by the environment in a very meaningful way. Conceptual physical limits of the environment are integrated with biological resources.

The case in the western United States is relatively simple because there is a homogeneous demand (cattle and sheep pasturage) competing for a homogeneous resource (forage on the public domain). Problems of allocating the resource among competing priorities can be handled within this setting. The resource in question is an allocatable commons. Biology and economics play a balanced role in allocating a resource that is at least potentially renewable on an annual cycle. It is also quite clear that the maximum level of grazing can exceed carrying capacity and cause a decline from which there would be no recovery, at least in a meaningful time span. Not all grazing land systems in the world are as tightly controlled. In other systems, after several consecutive years of drought, there are the alternatives of selling off the herd, importing feed, or letting the herd starve. It is also possible that the human population dependent on the herd for livelihood can migrate from the drought area or can itself starve.

### "Overgrazing"

Hardin (1968) wrote a well-known essay on the "tragedy of the commons," the abuse of a shared grazing ground as each individual herdsman, whether motivated by market opportunities or other social forces, concludes that the only sensible course in his private calculus is to add more animals in order to take advantage of a common resource. Of course, Hardin saw a larger problem than degradation of a community pasture. His "tragedy" applied to any setting where resource exploitation exceeds the ability of the environment to sustain a level of production—groundwater supplies, forests, ocean fisheries, water and air quality, soils, or, in Hardin's own preoccupation, the numbers of people occupying the "pastures" of the world.

On the surface, it would appear that carrying capacity is applicable primarily to renewable resources, but distinctions between renewable and nonrenewable resources do blur. Forage relies on water. When productivity is a function of annual rainfall only, that rainfall meets the classic definition of a renewable resource. Technology may intervene and produce water from the ground by pumping. Pumping rates may exceed by many times the annual recharge rate and lead to unintentional aquifer subsidence or to intentional river channelization, which in turn can reduce or eliminate recharge, the basis of renewability. This exploitation of water moves closer to consumptive use of a stock resource, which in this case is the capability of natural reservoirs to hold water.

The question of carrying capacity, for specific resources or more appropriately for an array of interactive and supportive resources, asks if rate of withdrawal exceeds rate of recharge. A first subsidiary question is whether a resource, especially a limiting resource, has a substitute. Substitution cannot be judged on economic criteria alone; it must also be judged in environmental terms. For example, a switch from petroleum to coal is not without widespread environmental and carrying capacity implications.

Giarini (1978) puts the relation between economic behavior and carrying capacity in terms of the law of diminishing returns. The classical case of diminishing returns involves a fixed amount of land for which adding units of labor (and/or capital) will increase total yield but in decreasing amount for each additional unit, until no increase at all becomes possible. (Of course, a breakthrough in the supply of the fixed or scarce factor would erase the constraint.) Giarini calls the law of diminishing returns the economists' version of a more general law. A system tends to an equilibrium via the mechanism of negative feedback loops, which bring a system to a more or less steady condition or cause a net decline. The system may fail to respond positively to additional increments of a factor or the additional increments may, in themselves, cause a negative reaction. The law of diminishing returns and carrying capacity deal with inputs and response to inputs. They are both concerned with the idea of production over time and with eventual scarcity of one or more production factors, whether these factors occur naturally or are technologically introduced.

A scarce factor in the case of food production might be a long-term natural variable, such as the amount or status of arable land. It might be a short-run natural variable, such as one year's rainfall, or it might be a synthetic input such as nitrogen fertilizer. Technology intervenes as the coefficient which steadily pushes back limits by introducing an uninterrupted flow of new applied inventions. It is in this sense that the Malthusian problem has been pushed into the future. Adding up available land and known agricultural production on the one side, and increasing populations on the other, Malthus concluded that the two were incompatible and that the world was condemned to starvation. At about the same time, the potato arrived in Europe from the New World and vastly increased food production capacity. The potato was a classic innovation, making possible a quantum change in capacity to produce and "a new energy level" that contravened the law of diminishing returns and changed carrying capacity, at least at the time of introduction and for an ensuing period. Later, population grew to the level of support permitted by some optimum production of potatoes, and/or constraints came into play in potato production. Famine and population migration resulted. The introduction of the potato was different, however, from adding more of the factors required to produce traditional food crops before its introduction.

## Carrying Capacity and Food

We cannot banish the problem of carrying capacity by searching the hinterlands of the world for latter-day potatoes. There is a tendency to forget that only energy makes things happen. It has been largely the growth of energy use that has permitted other kinds of growth—food production, steel or aluminum production, transportation, communication, population, or pollution (Steinhart and Steinhart 1974, p. 60). The discovery and introduction of petroleum certainly produced a quantum change in ability to bring forth resources and greatly changed the world's carrying capacity for human population and per capita consumption. The dilemma, of course, is that the "carrying capacity" of the world to create petroleum has not been changed. For all practical purposes it is a nonrenewable resource. To maintain anything approaching present rates of growth in population or consumption will require a substitute, a quantum change in nonrenewable energy resources, or a quantum shift to a renewable energy source.

In primitive cultures 5 to 50 calories of food were obtained for each calorie invested; some highly civilized cultures have done as well and occasionally better, but industrialized food production requires an input of 5 to 10 calories of fuel to obtain 1 calorie of food (Steinhart and Steinhart 1974, p. 85). It can be taken for granted that world food production has increased in fairly close proportion to the increase in population. Although all of this increase in much of the world does not follow the methods of industrialized food production, the yield of food is certainly not unrelated to the availability of energy. The crucial question is whether the increase in food production relies fundamentally on nonrenewable energy sources that have a predictable timetable for their decline and whether substitutions or true innovations can be brought on line in some orderly fashion.

Pimentel et al. (1973) summarize the problem: "Both the U.S. type of agriculture and 'green revolution' agriculture have been eminently successful in increasing crop yields through improved technology. However, one non-renewable resource, fossil fuel, is at this time the most important element in the impressive yields and quality of agriculture in the United States. Energy is used in mechanized agricultural production for machinery, transport, irrigation, fertilizers, pesticides, and other management. Fossil fuel inputs (oil and gas, primarily) have, in fact, become so indispensable to modern agriculture that the anticipated energy crisis will have a significant impact upon food production in all parts of the world which have adopted or are adopting the Western system."

Pimentel et al. (1973) also point out that from 1945 to 1970, mean U.S. corn yields increased from 34 bushels to 81 bushels per acre. This seems a quantum change in carrying capacity. However, mean energy inputs simultaneously increased from 0.9 million kcal to 2.9 million kcal per acre. Hence the yield in corn calories decreased from 3.7 kcal per kcal of energy input in 1945 to 2.8 kcal per kcal of energy input in 1970, a drop of 24 percent. Crop production costs in U.S. and similar kinds of agriculture will closely reflect changes in energy costs, and if conventional energy sources become scarce and their costs change, the impact on agriculture as an industry and a way of life will be very significant. Technological adjustments could use renewable sources of energy (solar, wind, biologically generated methane) to replace some of the current energy sources. Functions of locomotion in agriculture will require more innovation. And it is, of course, possible that labor/energy ratios will shift. It is not correct to say that depletion of petroleum and natural gas prescribes a decline in agriculture, but it does prescribe change.

The costs to the natural environment in current technological systems have been great—depleted soils, pollution, and disruption of natural plant and animal populations. In a sense, we have increased production but not changed carrying capacity. The problem is to back away from the fossil energy–food energy ratio, and to substitute alternative energy in a rational way. Recent evidence indicates that per capita food production in most developing countries declined in 1977 (UN 1978, p. 20). The decline extends a trend of eroding agricultural production that has continued for several years. During the 1970s, food production in both developed and developing countries increased at a slower rate—2.4 percent per year—than during the 1960s, when it rose 2.8 percent per year. The report of the World Food Council (UN 1978) attributes the slowdown in developing countries to bad weather, wars, disarray in government agricultural programs, and declining levels of aid from developing countries, a combination of environmental and social causes for the problem. The main environmental "limit" is weather. What is not clear is the extent to which the world food system faces diminishing returns that require a series of quantum changes in technology, whether there are some very real qualitative or quantitative limits in land, water, and energy, or whether the limits lie with our social and economic inability to apply ourselves to food production. There is a theoretical limit in the relationship of available water, land, and food production. The number of people that a unit of arable land will feed is in large part a function of the optimum amount of water in the climatic environment where the arable land is located. Throughout most of history available water has been determined by annual rainfall within the watershed. Perhaps some "normal" or modal level of carrying capacity in this dimension can be specified by research. It is clear that we must understand the interrelationships among resources, renewable and nonrenewable, and food production; we must try to anticipate limiting factors. But further, we must understand the relationships between natural resources and institutional handling of resources. Then the concept of carrying capacity has a more useful meaning. It has limited use defined only in biological and physical terms, but it can have considerable value if it can be expressed as a part of a system of evaluation in development.

## Environmental Limits

Environmental limits can be expressed in terms of irreversible changes (existing in nature but also affected by man), outer limits (boundary conditions for development), and environmental fluctuations (also natural but again under man's influence). Environmental limits are based in the natural environment. If intelligent beings and technological man did not exist, limits would still exist. The point is that man is involved in accelerating or decelerating these natural processes. That is obvious; the issue is whether, where, and when these limits and man's part in them will also limit development or even enforce a decline from present levels of development.

### Irreversibilities

The concept of irreversibilities involves related thermodynamic perspectives. Although nothing is destroyed (the First Law of Thermodynamics), everything is scattered to the four winds (the Second Law of Thermodynamics). The second law, stated another way, says that free and available energy degrades to latent and unavailable energy over time. To put the second law in still another useful way, there is a constant tendency in nature for order to turn into disorder.

Mankind manages to dip into these processes and catch the breaking wave for a ride, but he does not change them. It is not possible to reverse the basic processes, to run them backwards. It is possible, however, without violating these laws, for a process to return matter to a previously attained phase, on a local and temporary scale, when there is a relatively abundant supply of available energy. Although order becomes disorder, it is possible to reorganize matter into an orderly pattern for a time.

The stock of fossil fuels is an example. A combination of solar energy and living systems under a particular set of environmental conditions, over a very long period of time, produced petroleum, coal, and natural gas. That is fortunate for those of us living in the twentieth century. While that energy is "trapped in time," the sun that provided it continues slowly and ponderously to fizzle out on a time scale of billions of years. Long before the sun exhausts itself, however, the fossil fuels will be degraded to heat.

Another example is the oak tree, which on an annual cycle produces leaves and stores energy for its own use next season. It produces acorns which produce other oak trees through genetic organization. The individual tree may live over 100 years, but eventually all oak trees and all acorns will degrade to randomness, even though oak trees belong to one of the most widespread and adaptable of currently living botanical families.

We may now be approaching a period in which evolution of some living creatures will be directly dominated by man, at least in the short run. As science unravels both the structure of the atom and the structure of the living molecule, it appears possible we will manipulate the environment much more intensively than in the past, either through the release of energy now locked in the atom or through the manipulation of the basic order of the living molecule. This is not totally safe terrain. It is possible that the manipulation of the atom with consequent radioactive release will destroy order in the DNA molecule for individuals, species, and life. Mankind will have fallen off its wave—civilizations will have fallen or intelligence as we know it will have faltered. It is also possible that manipulation of the DNA molecule will release exotic pathogens into the environment and overcome the built-in survival factors that evolution has given us through the long fight for survival in a competitive and resource-scarce world.

Both the ideas of life cycles and the manipulation of those cycles do not, however, change the fact that the entropic degradation of the universe, as conceived by classical thermodynamics, is an irrevocable process. Free energy, once transformed into latent energy, cannot be recuperated (Georgescu-Roegen 1971, p. 196). Irreversibility is a process independent of mankind when cast in an economic framework—*our* well-being and survival.

## Finding Outer Limits

We are using up the richest mineral ores. These, just as fossil energy, were concentrated in some earlier time. Can we muster the organization to exploit the more dispersed minerals or even the ones that aren't concentrated at all but are randomly dispersed in the environment?

We are using up reservoirs of fuels, ranging from the fossil ones like coal and petroleum to the more contemporary ones like wood. Can we expect a "recovery of order" via the storing of solar energy in any meaningful time span?

As we colonize natural ecosystems to provide food and shelter, we are eliminating some species and restructuring ecosystems. Does loss of species and complicated ecosystems imply irreversibilities that are of any consequence to resource productivity or to our own survival?

Will accelerated use of energy or restructuring of ecosystems set in motion irreversible changes in the physical environment, most specifically basic change in global carbon and nitrogen cycles and the evolving pattern of climate?

To specify these questions of irreversibility, however, is to state only half the problem. The other half asks, where *are* the outer limits? When the phrase *outer limits* arose a few years ago, it was generally used in a global context to suggest the fragility of major planetary life support systems and processes (Matthews 1977). The mental image, and one at least implied in *The Limits to Growth*, is a sharp boundary across which lies steep decline. The concept is much more complex and requires full consideration of the role man plays in setting limits because these are determined not only by the quantity of existing resources and the laws of nature, but also by the way man conducts his activities with respect to this natural situation. It is possible to change man's activities and thus influence the limits themselves or the speed with which limits are reached.

Elemental abundances, together with the finite mass of the earth, of course provide absolute limits to the amount of any material present on the earth. Practical limits of exploiting resources are a function of physical conditions but also a function of man's activities. Conversion of a theoretical resource into a usable reserve depends in part on scientific knowledge, technological capability, and economic and social priorities.

One can at least foresee a process by which the outer limits of specific nonrenewable resources can be assessed in a process of forecasting reserves and production. This is a process in which we should be gaining skill, although the outlook for "outlooking" is not that encouraging. In a similar way, outer limits for specific renewable resources—the point at which they can no longer renew themselves or can no longer be "grown" by man because of a changing environment—might be assessable.

Environmental systems and their components are much more complex and difficult to define and analyze. One must understand the relationships of resources in an "ecosystem" sense, including the process of exploitation. It is necessary to try to know how these relationships operate and how individuals and human organizations will respond. While we are bound to the natural limits and "riding the wave" we are also participating in the process. A series of examples may help to see how this process now appears to be working. (The amount and quality of arable and irrigable land may well be the most significant example; it is discussed in chapter 9 of this volume.)

## Copper

Copper production in the United States offers one example (Leonardo Scholars 1975, pp. 102–4). The average copper ore mined in the United States in 1970 contained about 0.6 percent copper. Some ores with as little as 0.3 percent copper were being mined, and far richer ores were formerly mined; rich ore bodies undoubtedly remain to be discovered and exploited, but generally we will need to exploit lower and lower grades of ores.

In 1970, along with 2.27 million tons of pure copper, the industry produced 607 million tons of overburden (surface materials) and 258 million tons of tailings (processing residue). As the grade of the ore declines, the amount of overburden and tailings obviously increases. There are clear implications of increase in the amount of energy required to process the lower grade ore and in the amounts of pollutants (waste) "activated" in the environment.

Mined copper is not necessarily lost. In 1968, the United States consumed just over 3.25 million short tons of copper, of which domestic ores accounted for 45 percent and scrap constituted 42 percent. Imports accounted for the balance. Old and new copper scrap actually recycled amounted to 61 percent of the scrap available for recycling. Some 966 thousand tons of scrap copper were not recycled, and were "lost" because of disposal (although some may be recoverable at a later date).

From the standpoint of copper users, it may not have been important to dissipate a million tons of copper in 1969. For one thing, the price of copper was relatively low that year; supplies were apparently ample in that particular economic setting. Plastics and aluminum were still making inroads on copper as substitutes for plumbing and electrical wiring. However, the energy that was used in processing the new lower-grade virgin copper ore was irreversibly lost.

## Phosphorus

Phosphorus may be of more critical importance than copper because it is more closely linked to our biological support system and may be of more limited supply. Phosphorus exists in the biosphere almost exclusively as phosphate (Smith 1971), mostly immobilized in rock, soil, or sediments as phosphate salts with very low solubilities in water. Phosphorus is absolutely essential to living plants and therefore to crop production. Man mines phosphate rock for fertilizer, and in 1968, fertilizer application resulted in more than 50 percent of the estimated total global phosphorus runoff to the oceans (Smith 1971). Also, phosphorus is rapidly immobilized in the soil, even before plants can make optimum use of it.

Known phosphate reserves are variously estimated at 3,000 to 6,000 million tons, enough to last *at present rates of consumption* in fertilizers for 410 years. However, 39 percent of the world's population now uses 86 percent of the world's fertilizer. Bringing the rest of the world's people to the consumption rates now characteristic of that 39 percent would increase the use of fertilizers by a factor of 2.6. If this should happen quickly (which is highly unlikely), the lifetime of known supplies would be 158 years. Recently the human population has grown at an annual rate of 1.9 percent and the use of phosphate fertilizers at 5.2 percent. If these growth rates were projected into the future, known reserves would be used in 60 years.

New reserves of phosphorus certainly will be found. It has been theoretically estimated that the upper limit may be 600,000 million tons in materials, but physical and environmental difficulties, at the least, are bound to accompany any production and use on that scale. Such problems of recovery are described in chapter 2 of this volume.

## Water

Water may well provide a future example of irreversibility and outer limits. That seems quite impossible considering the staggering amount stored in the oceans, but therein is the problem. The oceans represent 97.2 percent of the total water of the earth (Harte and Socolow 1971, p. 262). Ocean water is potentially available for direct or indirect human use but not without a huge energy commitment. The great majority of the globe's nonsaline water is stored in glaciers and icecaps or as deep lying groundwater and is not generally available. Annual rainfall on the land is transpired by plant life, evaporated directly from the land, or carried as runoff to the sea in about equal shares. Man is very limited in his ability to alter this distribution. With current technology, we cannot alter evapotranspiration rates to any extent without affecting rainfall.

World geography sets the relative distribution of rainfall, and fresh water is much more precious in some parts of the world than others. Moreover, the amount in the annual water cycle varies from year to year.

There are short-run variations in water deposition in cycles of apparently 11 to 22 to 100 years and much longer ones associated with world glacial eras. The impact of droughts on man in any part of the world indicates how exceedingly close many people still live to the margin set by annual rainfall.

It is quite possible to remove from surface and shallow ground reservoirs, year after year, more water than falls as rain. Reservoirs will decline, and to the extent that we tap bodies of groundwater too, we move toward an outer limit. Water is a nonrenewable resource to the extent that its use is consumptive. Groundwater overdrafts in arid regions of the United States (and elsewhere) are a troubling case in point. Mined groundwater is the basis for expanded economic activities that face an uncertain future. In the U.S. high plains, extending from Texas to Nebraska, the annual overdraft is now about 14 million acre-feet, an amount equalling the natural flow of the Colorado River.

Rainfall, not the size of groundwater reservoirs, is the most likely determinant of the maximum amount of water that will be available for human use. In the United States, the quantity of fresh water continuously available depends on an average precipitation of 30 inches per year, but obviously not all that is available as a resource. Some 70 percent of average annual precipitation evaporates or transpires. The result is a net annual runoff of 8.6 inches (Greenwood and Edwards 1973, p. 163). Because only about one-fourth of this amount is currently being used in the United States, it might seem adequate for the time being. Uneven distribution and poor catchments, however, cause much slippage, and much of what is captured becomes useless through pollution. The United States, or at least major parts of the United States, has traditionally been considered water abundant to the point that the water itself is a free resource. The Second U.S. National Water Assessment (USWRC 1978, p. 35) suggested otherwise: "With ever increasing demands being placed upon limited water resources, it has become evident that in most of the U.S. water has become a scarce resource; scarce in the sense that one use will affect other uses. Competition for water is a fact. Tradeoffs must be considered seriously. In some cases there will be restrictions on use and therefore development, and water is no longer a free good." A strategy of conservation, reuse, recycling, and weather modification was recommended.

If and as water becomes limiting in a particular geographic area, one would expect a shift toward development in water surplus regions. Up to now human population distribution in the United States has not paralleled geographic water supply. There will be increasing pressures to transport water in the United States and/or to move people. Similar problems of transporting resources and/or moving people exist around the world. The pressure can be expected to extend beyond the borders of a given country, even on a continental scale. Only if we can take care to return used water to reservoirs as clean as when it was borrowed can we exceed the limit set by rainfall. If we increase the rate of runoff by interfering with the aquifer deposition system or accelerate inland salinization of water, we will set another outer limit for growth and development.

## Extinction

Perhaps the clearest case of an irreversibility is the extinction of a living species. It is inevitable that all living matter will become "extinct" in the very long run. Species extinction is a natural process. All organisms are replaced sooner or later by better adapted, newly evolved forms. A species may vanish and be supplanted, in part, by other species, or it may gradually evolve into one or more new species as the progenitor becomes "extinct." Australopithecus, an early but near cousin of ours, most likely disappeared forever. But Homo habilis and Homo erectus, probably direct progenitors of ours, are extinct in the sense that the configuration of their genes no longer survives.

Technological man has speeded up the natural process of species extinctions to abrupt extinctions which have left gaps in the fabric of living communities (Wagner 1971, p. 301). Species that normally would have undergone a long and natural decline because of inability to cope with some change in the environment have quite suddenly become eliminated. It would appear that humans have in modern times participated directly in the elimination of about 150 birds and mammals (Wagner 1971, p. 316), undoubtedly some plants, and quite likely some insects and microscopic forms of life.

Some species have been extinguished because they have been eaten by humans, others in attempts to increase the yields of specific resources by eliminating or introducing competitors. Still others have been eliminated by pollutants or through patterns of land use which have changed entire environments.

There is a clear-cut economic issue if a species is itself a prominent resource, as for some ocean fishes and mammals under heavy exploitive pressure. Another important case has to do with food species and their remaining wild variants. An example is the common tomato. In the United States' diet the tomato now ranks first among fruits and vegetables in providing ten critical vitamins and minerals. In 1977 commercial production of tomatoes occupied 491,000 acres, and yields have jumped from about 13.5 metric tons to around 51.5 tons per hectare in California within the last 20 years (Rick 1978).

Tomatoes originated in the Andean region of the New World, where they reached a fairly advanced stage of domestication before being taken to Europe and eventually returned to the Americas. The cultivated tomato is one of nine species recognized in the genus. The fruits of the related species are far less attractive, but they have potential value because of their genetic diversity. From them genes for resistance to disease and for improved quality of fruit have been bred into cultivated forms. The diversity of the genes promises many more advances. A case in point is the high tolerance to salt discovered in a type that thrives on the shores of the Galapagos Islands. Another species flourishes in exceedingly dry habitats in western Peru. Wild species may be eliminated by the pressure to bring uncultivated lands in the Andes into farm production. If so, some of the tomatoes' genetic potential will be lost. Perhaps it will become possible to create desirable traits in plants by laboratory manipulation, but perhaps not. This economic threat in extinctions almost surely applies in other current food crops (potatoes) and to species not currently recognized as food resources.

The problem of extinction is no simple matter of single species' disappearance here or there, however. Tropical rain forests, especially in the Amazon basin, illustrate the complexity of the problem. There is evidence that under increasingly intensive use of the land in rain forest regions, tropical ecosystems are in danger of losing many of their exceedingly numerous species (Gomez-Pompa et al. 1972). Many tropical nations and peoples are looking for ways to use great tracts of land in permanent agricultural cropping, not in temporary and shifting cultivation by the old slash and burn methods. There are native species on site adapted to this kind of change, but they appear to be some of the existing "secondary" species.

Wholesale planting of alien species and typical farm crops, if major and sustained, can lead to "savannization" and "desertification." The pattern and productivity of biotic communities, soil structure, and even climatic conditions is an interrelated mix of cause and effect in all ecosystems, but disruption of these relations can be particularly evident and rapid in tropical forests. Not only tropical biotic communities are susceptible to extinction and irreversibilities; possibly susceptible to irreversible degradation too are tropical lateritic soils. As yet we know little about the technological structure needed to maintain agricultural productivity in the humid tropics, and this is, to put it bluntly, a sad state of affairs. This is not to say that sustained production is impossible, but the technology of development in relatively arid parts of the tropics or temperate zones will almost certainly not prove directly transferrable to the wet tropics.

*Ecosystems*

The environment covers over the sudden death of an individual, and even the disappearance of a species, but not without reverberations. The ecosystem, a conceptual unit of biological organization, is all the organisms in a given area and all their interactions with each other and with the physical environment, including energy, so that a flow of energy leads to trophic structures (nutritional pyramids among species) and to material flows within the system.

An ecosystem can vary in size and range. It might be a small, rather uniform, local system; it might be a regional basin; it might be a particular geographic zone circling the globe (subtropical deserts or tundra), or it might be a global ecosystem.

Ecosystem development and maintenance are, in theory, part of an orderly process that is directional and therefore predictable. The process involves modification of the physical environment by the biological components of the system itself even though the physical environment sets boundary conditions for the pattern and rate of change, and often sets limits on how far ecosystem development can go. Ecosystems tend toward a stability in which maximum attainable biomass and functional interactions among organisms are maintained. Odum (1970) has classified trends in ecosystem development into system energetics, system structure, life history, nutrient cycling, natural selection pressures, and overall homeostasis. Natural forces according to Odum's theory lead to a maximum interactive support of complex biomass structure. He concludes that a system which is readjusting after some major disturbance, with population and species declines, will move from monotony toward diversity and from simplicity toward complexity. Diversity and complexity are supposedly more stable states.

Odum's view that diversity and complexity tend to produce and maintain stability is not universally accepted. May (1973) defines stability in an ecosystem as the tendency for population size perturbations to dampen out in time and as return of the system to some persistent configuration. His models suggest that when a "prey" population has a growth rate large relative to that of its "predator," an increase in environmental carrying capacity may move the predator-prey population system from a stable equilibrium point to a cycle in which their populations oscillate in a regular manner between defined limits. As prey habitat conditions improve, population numbers of both prey and predator will increasingly fluctuate. However, May's models also suggest that if a population system has a potentially stabilizing negative feedback which is applied with a time delay that is longer than the natural time scale of the system (generation length), the result will be instability rather than stability. A vegetation-herbivore system with no predators may thus be unstable. May's work suggests that systems with many species or with complex trophic interconnections may be less stable than those with few species; complexity begets instability rather than stability. The number of links in the web simply increases the probability of instability.

In nature, systems do vary along a scale of diversity, from simple to complex, and have varying systems of checks and balances. Ecosystem food chains tend to grow into complex webs. In a mature forest less than 10 percent of annual net production is consumed in the living state. Most of the production finds its way into detritus through delayed and complex pathways involving little understood microorganismic processes. Biotic control of population density and nutrient cycling provide the feedback mechanisms to prevent overshoots and oscillations.

Schultz (1974) has described systemic interrelationships in as natural an ecosystem (and as "simple," by relative standards) as one is likely to encounter in the world today, the Alaskan tundra. Legend has it that lemmings (small tundra rodents) propagate wildly whereupon most of the masses of the population rush psychotically to an icy suicide in the Arctic oceans. Legends are popularly believed stories, often attempts to account for phenomena, in this case the unmistakable, periodic rise and fall in lemming numbers. (There seem to be marked dispersals at high population densities, but lemmings do not rush to the sea.) Schultz' research shows a series of synchronous cycles in the tundra ecosystem. Early in summer of a high lemming year, the forage is calcium and phosphorus rich. The soil has thawed deep into the mineral layer because grazing, burrowing, and nest building by the lemmings has altered the insulation of the surface and absorption of sun energy.

But in the next year, forage production is low and the percentage of calcium and phosphorus in the lemming diet is below that required for milk production. Nutrients in organic matter have not yet been released by decomposition. Predators in the form of jaegers (sea birds) have been hungry and busy in preceding months. In the third year, plants are recovering from the severe grazing two years earlier, but dead herbs still insulate the soil surface. In the fourth year plants have recovered. The forage accumulates minerals. Decomposition of the dead grass is high, and there is enough food to support a large population of lemmings. Not until a nutritional threshold has been reached can the lemming population build up. No grazing at all would be disastrous to the vegetation and to the soil as well.

While human beings are not lemmings (or jaegers) the example makes a point: the whole notion of causality is under question in an ecosystem framework. In this case it is not possible to say the lemmings are the driving force, any more than the vegetation, the soil, or the microflora, in maintaining the synchronous cycles. Nor is it even possible to attribute the cycles wholly to nutritional factors. Theories of genetic and/or physiological change in accord with population densities have also been propounded and may well be partly or equally valid. Feedback loops are both positive and negative; there is no reason why a control system should have but one governor.

There is another point: severe stress or rapid changes brought by outside forces can rob an ecosystem of such interactive functions and allow uncontrolled growth of certain species to occur. Elimination of predators vastly changes the structure. Elimination of some of the lower animals in the food chain may lead to a collapse of the complex pyramid and a return to a simpler biological structure.

In the case of the human being, and in the ecosystem context, technology can be considered the intervention designed to control or eliminate negative feedback but also to reinforce positive feedback. Thus the viability of technology must be assessed in terms of a sophisticated understanding of ecosystems.

The goal of agriculture or forestry, as now generally practiced, is to achieve high rates of production of readily harvestable products with little standing crop left to accumulate on the landscape. We strive for the maximum share in the edible or other usable proportion of the crop. But, of course, man does not live by food and fiber alone. We also need a balance of carbon dioxide and oxygen in the atmosphere and the climatic buffer provided by masses of water and vegetation. These integrating forces emerge from the so-called nonproductive landscapes as well as the productive. Complex technological systems must therefore be assessed within the ecosystem framework, not just in terms of a single desired output.

There is a more global example of this kind of assessment. Over the past decade several reviews of the world carbon budget have confirmed an annual increase in the carbon dioxide content of air worldwide. It is almost certainly man-caused (Woodwell et al. 1978). The source of the carbon has been commonly assumed to be combustion of fossil fuels. Because the amount of $CO_2$ accumulating in the atmosphere is less than half the total released from fossil fuels, other sinks for $CO_2$ have been sought. The major potential sink is the oceans, but mixing rates appear too low for the oceans to accommodate all the $CO_2$ thought to be released in excess of that accumulating in the atmosphere. Researchers have generally assumed that living plants on the land might be a sink, especially in view of the stimulation of photosynthesis by enhanced concentrations of $CO_2$.

More recent work has indicated that vegetation is not a sink but in the net an additional source of $CO_2$ because of one important factor. The world's forests have been reduced appreciably as human population has increased. The forests of western Europe were reduced from more than 90 percent of the land area to around 20 percent in the last 1000 years. A parallel reduction occurred earlier in parts of the Mediterranean Basin, the Levant, and Asia. These changes released significant quantities of carbon, perhaps as much as 25 percent of that currently within the atmosphere. What has happened to the standing crop of forest and humus in the world over the last 100 years, more specifically the tropical rain forests? Woodwell et al. (1978) report an estimate of humid forest clearance per year of 0.6 to 1.5 percent of the extant area. If a rate of clearing of 1 to 2 percent per year were applied to the forests of the earth, the amount of carbon released in this manner annually would be one to two times the amount currently released from fossil fuels. The cropping of forest soils (and wetland peats) also leads to decay of humus and carbon release. Human activities in the near future could release additional amounts of $CO_2$ into the atmosphere with results that are substantially unpredictable. The issue is important because changes in $CO_2$ content of air have potential for changing worldwide climate. The supposition to date has been that increased carbon dioxide would bring atmospheric warming and consequent significant shifts—some favorable, some unfavorable—in agricultural carrying capacity in major agricultural regions. The global carbon budget is still very much unknown, but the consequences of possible changes could be described.

### Environmental Change

As we survey our environment, we rationally assume that the conditions we see are normal, whether in tropic, temperate, or subarctic zones. The climate, the land forms, the other living creatures are seen as normal. Normal becomes what we know, but current environmental conditions are not the same as past ones.

Latest estimates suggest that the earth as a planet is around 5000 million years old and that man has been evident (as a toolmaker) for only the last 2 to 3 million years (Goudie 1977, p. 1). The environmental changes which have occurred during the time that man, the toolmaker, has inhabited the earth have been huge, however. Changes, whether in climate, vegetation belts, animal populations, or soil and landforms have been massive. Changes are obviously still taking place, at various speeds and at various scales.

For example, glaciers covered much of the northern temperate zones just 10,000 years ago. Those glaciers had lain there for up to 50,000 years; men existed and presumably prospered in those times right up to the edge of the glaciers. Since this glacial episode the area of the earth covered by frozen water has been reduced to one-third of what it was at the most recent glacial maximum. The waters released have raised ocean levels by more than 100 meters. Vegetation belts have swung through tens of degrees of latitude; inland lakes have been born, have expanded and contracted, and disappeared; desert sand fields have advanced and retreated (Goudie 1977, p. 2). The impact on the numbers and living conditions of man has been enormous.

Five or ten thousand years may seem a scale irrelevant to the immediate problems of the world, but the point is that we are not done with environmental change in these long-run terms or in smaller and shorter yet still influential terms. Lakes or glaciers or deserts do not appear or disappear overnight, but the gradual and cumulative nature of the effects of environmental change make them no less significant. Moreover, there are substantial, and so far not very predictable, shifts in the process of change.

Nearly one thousand years ago the Vikings were moving into Iceland and Greenland. Drift ice had rarely appeared in these seas in the 900s and was apparently unknown between 1020 and 1194. Settlements reached a reasonable size but then declined in late medieval times; by about the year 1400, there was no regular communication between Europe and any part of Greenland. Deteriorating climatic conditions limited communication and restricted fishing. Starting about 1220, records from Iceland show a 200-year trough of lower temperatures, also a time of distress in European agriculture, with too much humidity, mild temperatures, and an outbreak of ergot blight of grain.

Another cold period started about 1600 and lasted to the beginning of this century. It is called the "Little Ice Age" and brought agricultural changes all over the northern hemisphere. Early in the present century, however, the average temperature of the higher latitudes started to rise, especially in the far North Atlantic. Indian monsoons became more reliable; European winters were less severe; midsummer frosts in the north central United States ceased. This amelioration of the climate ended about 1945, and since then a return to cooler climates has been proceeding. It would seem that the first part of the twentieth century was a uniquely benign period, climatically, for agricultural production the world over. Since 1950 the world has apparently entered a time of greater variability of climate from year to year and perhaps decade to decade in the middle latitudes. Less rain has fallen in the poleward portions of the monsoon regions, and monsoons have been less reliable in general. Cooler summers have prevailed, in general, in northern Europe, the USSR, and northern Japan, with shortened growing seasons and awkward springs in the central United States and Europe (Bryson 1974, p. 12).

While we can generalize to some extent about how climate changes, we know much less about why it changes. Unstable and unpredictable weather cannot be taken lightly at a time when the world must strive to increase food production at rates of 3 percent per year or more. Man himself may well be a significant contributor to climatic change on regional and global scales. Fossil fuel combustion and deforestation might release enough $CO_2$ to raise temperatures, perhaps stimulate the oceans' release of further $CO_2$, and possibly raise ambient atmospheric temperatures as much as 2°C over the next 25 years. Opposing cooling effects of a higher atmospheric reflectivity brought by the "dust" generated in industry and agriculture are not, however, independent of deforestation and energy use, nor are stratospheric introduction of nitrous oxides with possible effects on the ozone layer, species extinctions, or soil deterioration. No environmental change of irreversibility proceeds in isolation from other changes, or from man, and the reverberations of seemingly minor or incremental change may be substantial and surprising indeed.

## Socio-Environmental Forces

The anxieties about the future which have seemed so prominent in the last 20 years are at least partly based in uncertainty about our ability either to keep up with human demands on resources or to contain and control these demands—uncertainty about the maintenance of those local and global ecosystems which include humanity as a prominent component.

All societies, and industrial societies in particular, have relied heavily on diffusion of technology through economic systems and the rational adoption of alternative technologies while recognizing that there are regional, social, economic, and environmental differences among societies.

Technology, by definition, is man-created and man-centered. Technology gives abundant evidence that we modify natural processes in the environment, processes which by themselves are inherently indifferent to the technological successes or failures of man. Specific technological developments may be quantum breakthroughs or they may be gains in efficiency of already established processes, but there are also various systemic environmental constraints among societies, and technologically based development is not automatically open-ended. Natural limits may very well conflict with ambitions for and realities of national and global development. I will not argue that pessimism is a required consequence, but rather that our situation is far more complex than we had imagined 10 or 20 years ago.

Decision making in market economies implies multitudes of individual decisions at the moments of exchange, even in the case of decisions made in futures markets. It is almost an instantaneous process. The framework for most other institutional policy and political decisions in any economy is also relatively short, on the order of days, months, and years.

However, if the process of making policy decisions relies on consensus and resolution of conflict among competing interests, there may be advantage in postponing decisions as long as possible. Moreover, to the extent that we can peer even dimly into the future, environmental and social constraints argue for a margin of error; if limits appear, even on the horizon, it seems rational to be conservative about resource use. Under circumstances in which demands for early action are not matched by adequate information, logic calls for caution and a tolerance for uncertainty, for margins of safety between human needs and their sources of supply. Strategies and institutional arrangements must be flexible enough to adapt to unforeseen and sudden changes. Maneuverability avoids the risk often inherent in some technological solutions and irreversible processes.

Market, institutional, social, and environmental forces seem to work together, although by no means in parallel or simple ways, to preclude confident long-term commitments and solutions.

The conventional approach to resource policy making has been to separate problems and to deal with them one at a time. One can see the same approach in reductionist and specialized science and technology. Until very recently administration of natural resources and environmental policies have proceeded on this commonsense philosophy (Caldwell 1978). This process is incremental. Policy evolves over time in relatively small steps on specific problems or conflicts, through market decisions or adjudication among competing parties or decree of the powerful. Courts or markets or resource decrees, however, do not exist or work on the scale of global resource scarcities, deterioration in world or regional ecosystems, unsustainable rates and kinds of growth, or trade-offs among present and future generations (Ross 1977). In these cases the consequences of discrete decisions penetrate throughout society and change the character of other problems. Problems are linked, convoluted, and conditional; "solutions" to one problem may be contingent upon solutions to others, and attempts to isolate answers to some problems may worsen others or generate new ones.

A short-term policy framework may bear little relationship to the kinds and rates of environmental change or the time needed to make involved and complex substitutions in major resource categories. Issues of carrying capacity and environmental limits do tend to be relatively slow-moving in terms of becoming socially obvious, but the time required for the reproductive cycles of renewable resources, and certainly for the deposition of nonrenewable resources, does not automatically correspond to changes in the timing of technology, social worries, or rates of growth. Even those options that are made available by technological innovation may be subverted by the increasing amounts of time required to find resources and to produce and distribute them. In an ecosystemic sense and in the sense of complex technological processes, renewable and nonrenewable resources become interrelated and interdependent.

There is a tendency in technologically oriented societies to set goals and to deal with the "engineering time" required to achieve them. What may be missed are the relationships between engineering requirements and rates of growth and change in other systems aiming at other goals, including "systems" of national or global economic development.

In fact we are trying to establish integrative processes, patterns, and rates of growth which bring together resources, technology, and information in a systemic environment. The need for systemic analysis is changing and increasing. More specifically:

1. The need for technological integration could be growing about as fast as resource consumption. Under current rates of growth, systemic organizational requirements could be four times as strong a force at the end of the century as they are now. These requirements involve not only engineering systems and hardware but also institutional structure.
2. The need for specialized information and the volume of information itself could be growing as fast as resource consumption. Complexity of structure and the volume of information processed may change exponentially in time.

It seems likely that more and more time will be required, in terms of advance planning, to maintain a given rate of growth.

The problem of time in resource exploitation and development is related to the problem of scale. Increasing size of economic unit—"economy of scale"—in resource exploitation has some inherent advantages. Economy of scale is in part related to the dispersement of a resource, its physical characteristics, and the nature of the market. But a scale, in industrial or social or ecological processes, implies variability in economy from one end of the spectrum to the other with an "optimum" location along that scale dependent on an array of criteria. It is plain, for instance, that a food production system relying heavily on fossil energy may "optimize" at a different scale than a food system based more extensively on renewable energy or labor intensity.

The trend in industrial countries is toward increasingly larger geographic scales in assembling, processing, and distributing resources. A different pattern of resource use might well counteract this integrative resource momentum, but for now industrial economies often seem to depend on aggregation and integration of materials from scattered sites and sources in complex manufacturing processes. Supply lines get longer in both physical and organizational terms. Information for control of complex processes becomes increasingly necessary and increasingly abundant. Uncertainty, both natural and man-related, must be reduced in order to maintain established kinds and rates of growth.

Planning at national or international levels must recognize the increasing volume of different resources required in economic growth and change. This drawing together of the material of development is cast against the natural condition of uneven distribution and uneven quality of resources and technology and knowledge around the world. Planning must develop the engineering and informational networks needed to manage the integration of resources. Planning must develop markets, money systems, and other social institutions to maintain integrated systems. We would expect, and are seeing, new networks of institutions with a mounting requirement of stability and reliability. Is it possible that the need to foresee the future may be increasing at the rate of growth? Were this absolutely true, with each doubling of resource use, we would need to double lead planning time. Assessment of carrying capacities, irreversibilities, and environmental change must be able to react to quick rates of change.

In social systems that make no provision beyond the short term, social trauma and instability threaten these increasingly complex integrated networks. Stability in natural ecosystems bears both definite analogical and definite functional relations to stability in evolving social systems. There are social forces at work that derive from the issues of carrying capacity, environmental limits, and the current state of exploitation of natural resources. One might expect these inconsistencies to become more troublesome until they are dealt with quite specifically in development strategies.

## Assessment Implications

The idea of natural limits to natural resources cannot be treated in isolation as some physical or biological imposition; rather it must be viewed in the systemic context of development and social organization, including cooperation among nations. Development implies at the least a new arrangement in the use of natural resources, almost surely an increase in the use of resources, and possibly an increasing rate of increase. Cooperation among nations means regional and global perspectives, even though not all limits and decisions will operate at regional or global levels.

Holdgate (1978) has summarized the kinds of problems which appear to require international scientific attention and governmental evaluation. His categories use essentially a geographic scale:

1. Changes in global atmospheric and oceanic and terrestrial systems that might affect the global environment—for example, the world carbon cycle.

2. Changes in regional water, air, or biotic systems that might affect a number of nations—for example, the elimination of a major tropical forest, desert expansion in a certain zone, or soil erosion and depletion in a major grain belt.
3. Changes affecting two nations—for example, a major change in the flow of a river that arises in one country and enters another.
4. Environmental changes which, while of local scale for the time being, are also of wide human concern for many nations—for example, resistance of disease vectors to pesticides or spread of toxic substances from a plethora of sources into ecosystems.

The first class (changes in global systems) is the hardest to analyze and the most intractable if corrective action is needed. Such problems develop over decades and demand a consensus among a substantial part of the world community. Implied trade-offs may be so great as to paralyze concerted action. The second and third kinds of problems are at least theoretically easier to treat because fewer people and nations are involved. The fourth category may be the easiest to analyze, but the resolution of these potentially pandemic kinds of problems is obviously not easy.

Holdgate also divides the potential for response into two categories. First is the scientific assessment of an environmental change. The issue is to derive the probability of occurrence of various events and situations and the margin of uncertainty about such predictions. Second is socioeconomic evaluation of the costs and benefits of possible changes, the costs of corrective action, and the costs of overreaction (including false alarms), all on various time scales. This all seems quite rational and orderly, but it is an expensive and demanding undertaking.

Even so, such assessments seem necessary and overdue. Yet there is still a fundamental difficulty in responding if assessments are available. Many of the predictions will have a fairly high degree of uncertainty: not only margins of error in prediction per se but also long response times and the possibility that social, economic, and technological changes will invalidate evaluations of costs and benefits in the interim. The alerts and warnings of global assessment would likely tend to focus on specific pollutants, specific chemical cycles, or specific criteria such as ambient air or water quality. They would probably tend not to deal with broad issues of carrying capacity or environmental limits or resource supplies because the margin of error (and perception) is still so great on these issues. A more systemic scheme of analysis is needed on these wider issues.

Such a systemic assessment might be applied in regional settings—for instance the Middle East. The natural geography itself is taken as the dependent variable, at least for purposes of defining the issues. The variable of attention is not, initially or only, the standard of living of nations or the economy of the region. The exercise first focuses attention on the environment and its carrying capacity. After this initial consideration, it is then, of course, necessary to backtrack to reconsider trade-offs and interrelationships between the environment and development.

Because the regional ecosystem is the dependent variable, we can put aside, again initially, national boundaries. For this case then, the area of interest is the eastern Mediterranean region, the Nile River drainage basin, the Red Sea, the Arabian peninsula, and the Tigris/Euphrates drainage basin. (Obviously, the region is neither self-sufficient nor in a steady state in terms of identified resources, but that is not the question at the moment.) We are interested in the relationships of land systems and water systems, both fresh and marine. In the widest perspective of regional assessment we are interested in:

1.  Regional sufficiency of resources over time—that is, sustained carrying capacity for development and the regional system's ability to absorb certain levels of stress while maintaining productive capacity.
2.  Changes in the resource base because of depletion or pollution— both specific irreversible changes (resource depletion, interruption of resource renewal, loss of system components) and more general environmental changes likely to "tax" the productivity of the entire region in predictable ways.

Issues in either category might be treated in terms of environmental scale (local versus generic, primary versus secondary impacts) and in terms of developmental needs (rates and kinds of development vis-à-vis uncertainties in predicting impacts and demands on institutional structure, change, and flexibility).

More detailed perspectives need not confine their focus to particular resources. It is possible, for instance, to apply a framework of ecosystem assessment to regional subsystems such as food production—the interrelations among arable land, water supply, nutrients including fertilizers, and alternative energy strategies in agriculture. Questions of interest in the further subcategory of water supply might include:

1.  Variation in rainfall in drainage basins over time.
2.  Water quality standards in agriculture and in competing economic functions.
3.  Regional water management and allocation standards and procedures.
4.  Access to and depletion of groundwater.
5.  Agricultural practices and control of water-related erosion and salinization.

It is possible to assess, for another example, that broad effect of resource use and economic development called pollution. Pollutants of various sorts in one segment of development (industry, agriculture, fisheries) can preclude some kinds of development in other segments, accelerate resource depletion or diminish renewal capacity, and impose costs in public health. Pollution issues of immediate impact might include:

1. Intrusion of heavy metals, toxic chemicals, nutrient loadings, oil spills or dumpings, and other pollutants in land, air, and water systems.
2. Physical and biological transport of pollutants in river channels, deltas, coastal and littoral zones, deep waters, airsheds, etc.
3. Effects of pollution on land and marine organisms, including trophic structures supporting economic species and the economic species themselves.

Pollution issues of more generic impact on system quality, stability, and productivity over time might include:

1. Salinity, acidity, and albedo effects.
2. Relationships between contaminants and human health, either directly or indirectly through food chains or water and air systems.
3. Irreversible impacts or changes in carrying capacity for specific resources (for example, a change in salinity that reduces sardine stocks).
4. Origins of pollutants, point or nonpoint, their persistence and the potential for eliminating them by substitutions in industrial and agricultural production.
5. Future nonlinear and threshold responses not necessarily predictable from current trends.
6. Synergisms among contaminants.

The kinds of analyses posed above, while complicated, are rather tidy in themselves or in a more complex model which integrates assessments of specific resources, production subsystems, and environmental issues. A look at the realities of this regional example, however, will show national governments with sovereign control of resources, different approaches to the way government is organized, conflicting territorial interests, and different levels of development. In addition, there is a nonuniform division of ownership and control of resources between the private and the public sectors and a not necessarily matching division of sources of capital. Some resources are in the commons, that is, without ownership. In addition, there are geopolitical interests outside the region because of the value of its resources or because of military and strategic aspects. Finally, and of vast importance, the region has one of the longest histories of social and cultural development of any area in the world. All these forces, blended together, are reflected in political policy, which is superimposed upon environmental, economic, and developmental policy.

Many nations are fairly well along in developing pollution standards and enforcements within their boundaries. There are only limited policy structures to date in developing antipollution programs between and among nations. Some nations are also beginning to develop more general policies for evaluating developmental proposals against general environmental standards. Under the U.S. National Environmental Protection Act of 1970, environmental impact reviews have been used mostly for specific sites or projects and have not tended to be generic or systemic in nature. There is not much evidence that environmental questions have as yet had a significant role in evaluating general policies of growth and development. However, this more general review is very much a part of discussions now emerging on national or international energy policies, water policies, and regional growth policies—those policies which assess the supply and quality of resources as part of strategic planning.

The issues of natural limits and carrying capacity are now having some effect on general management of common international resources of the oceans, the atmosphere, and the Antarctic continent. Issues of sovereignty loom, however, as technology opens the way to economic exploitation of resources in these areas. The reports of the UN Conference on the Human Environment in Stockholm in 1972 came closest to defining a general set of global environmental standards and objectives. So far, with minor exceptions, there has been little progress in working out more specific environmental criteria.

It seems clear that most of the concerns about natural limits of natural resources fall somewhat below the encompassing global change implied in the world carbon cycle, for instance, and should therefore be more tractable problems. But that does not mean that these issues are of minor importance in local, regional, and international development schemes.

Natural systems do not inherently match the pace of man's economic ambitions or necessarily allow easy reversal of man's mistakes, but to look at environmental considerations as somehow threatening to development doesn't make sense, because the issues are real and cannot be brushed aside. We cannot even partly disengage from complex global resource interdependencies without major changes in world social structure, and we cannot "disengage" from ecosystems at all. There is no alternative context for life.

In considering natural limits, we need to do two cardinal things as we attempt to resolve the problems of development and cooperation detailed

in other chapters of this book: first, develop a much deeper understanding of the demands we place on earth's resource systems over time and
second, find and incorporate developmental standards which describe
and evaluate short and long-term environmental risks involved in particular paths of development.

## References

Bryson, Reid A. 1974. *Climate and World Food Systems III: The Lessons of Cli-
matic History*, IES Report 27. Madison: Institute for Environmental Studies,
University of Wisconsin.
Caldwell, Lynton K. 1978. "Strategies and Alternatives: The Ethics and Politics
of Survival." Aldo Leopold Memorial Colloquium, University of Wisconsin,
Madison, Wisconsin.
Georgescu-Roegen, Nicholas. 1971. *The Entropy Law and the Economic Pro-
cess*. Cambridge, Massachusetts: Harvard University Press.
Giarini, Orio. 1978. "The Internal Limits to Growth," *The Ecologist Quarterly* 1:
6–20.
Gomez-Pompa, A., C. Vázquez-Yanes, and S. Guevara. 1972. "The Tropical
Rain Forest: A Nonrenewable Resource," *Science* 177: 762–65.
Goudie, Andrew. 1977. *Environmental Change*. Oxford: Clarendon Press.
Greenwood, Ned, and J. M. B. Edwards. 1973. *Human Environments and Natu-
ral Systems: A Conflict of Dominion*. North Scituate, Massachusetts: Dux-
bury.
Hardin, Garrett. 1968. "The Tragedy of the Commons," *Science* 162: 1243–48.
Harte, John, and Robert H. Socolow. 1971. *Patient Earth*. New York: Holt,
Rinehart and Winston.
Heilbroner, Robert L. 1974. *An Inquiry Into the Human Prospect*. New York:
Norton.
Holdgate, Martin. 1978. "Conclusions." Aspen Institute Workshop on the As-
sessment and Alert of Major Environmental Hazards, Aspen Institute, Aspen,
Colorado.
Hubbert, M. King. 1978. "World Energy Resources." In *Proceedings of the Wis-
consin Seminar on Natural Resource Policies in Relation to Economic Devel-
opment and International Cooperation*, vol. 1. Madison: Institute for Environ-
mental Studies, University of Wisconsin.
Leonardo Scholars. 1975. *Resources and Decisions*. North Scituate, Massachu-
setts: Duxbury.
Leopold, Aldo. 1933. *Game Management*. New York: Charles Scribner's Sons.
Matthews, William H. 1977. "Where Are the Outer Limits?" *Mazingira* 1: 55–65.
May, Robert M. 1973. *Stability and Complexity in Model Ecosystems. Mono-
graph in Population Biology No. 6*. Princeton, New Jersey: Princeton Univer-
sity Press.
Meadows, Donella H., Dennis L. Meadows, Jørgen Randers, and William W.
Behrens III. 1972. *The Limits to Growth*. New York: Universe Books.

Odum, Eugene P. 1970. "The Strategy of Ecosystem Development." In Eugene P. Odum, ed., *The Crisis of Survival.* Glenview, Illinois: Scott, Foresman, pp. 49–72.

Pimentel, David, L. E. Hurd, A. C. Bellotti, M. J. Forster, I. N. Oka, O. D. Sholes, and R. J. Whitman. 1973. "Food Production and the Energy Crisis," *Science* 182: 443–49.

Rick, Charles M. 1978. "The Tomato," *Scientific American* 239(2): 76–87.

Ross, John E. 1977. "From This Valley They Say We Are Going." *Biological Science* 27(4): 254–58.

Schultz, Arnold M. 1974. "A Study of an Ecosystem: The Arctic Tundra." In Douglas Daetz and Richard H. Pantell, eds., *Environmental Modeling: Analysis and Management.* Stroudsburg, Pennsylvania: Dowden, Hutchinson and Ross.

Smith, Frederick. 1971. "Cycles of Elements." In *Man in the Living Environment, The Institute of Ecology Report of the Workshop on Global Ecological Problems.* Indianapolis, Indiana: The Institute of Ecology, Bradley University, pp. 41–84.

Steinhart, Carol, and John Steinhart. 1974. *Energy: Sources, Use and Role in Human Affairs.* North Scituate, Massachusetts: Duxbury.

UN (United Nations). 1978. "Report of the World Food Council on the Work of Its Fourth Session," Official Records of the 33rd Session of the General Assembly, A/33/Supp. 19. New York: UN.

USWRC (U.S. Water Resources Council). 1978. *The Nation's Water Resources, The Second National Water Assessment: Summary Report.* Washington, D.C.: U.S. Government Printing Office.

Wagner, Richard H. 1971. *Environment and Man.* New York: Norton.

Woodwell, G. M., R. H. Whittaker, W. A. Reiners, G. E. Likens, C. C. Delwiche, and D. B. Botkin. 1978. "The Biota and the World Carbon Budget," *Science* 199: 141–46.

# 4  *Edgar L. Feige & David M. Blau*

# The Economics of Natural Resource Scarcity and Implications for Development Policy and International Cooperation

Of course it is useless to think of substituting any other kinds of fuel for coal. . . . To extend the use of petroleum then is only a new way of pushing the consumption of coal. It is more likely to be an aggravation than a remedy.—Jevons (1906, pp. 183–84)

The entire issue of resource scarcity has been dramatically brought to world attention as a result of two events that occurred quite by coincidence at the same time: the formation of the effective OPEC cartel which forced a rapid fourfold increase in the price of oil and the doomsday forecasts emanating from the world modeling systems associated with the Club of Rome report. This is not the first time in history that there have been natural resource crises and predictions of impending doom, nor is it likely to be the last. So far, however, doom has not arrived. Why, then, have the predictions proved so wrong? They have certainly been made by men of learning and distinction—Malthus, Mill, and Jevons among them.

We do not intend to argue from history that current concerns about scarcity, population growth, and pollution are frivolous. It is certainly not unfounded pessimism to point out that severe problems loom on the horizon if present rates of population growth continue. The dangers of unchecked environmental pollution are also certainly very real. And we recognize that considering natural resource use as completely separate and distinct from environmental considerations misses an essential element of the problem.

While recognizing the validity of some of the issues raised by the doomsday models, however, we consider them quite inadequate as a tool for appraising the likelihood and impact of the crises they predict (Kay and Mirrlees 1975).

It is our view that the application of neoclassical economic theory to the natural resource area provides a much more powerful and illuminating framework for considering these issues and allows consideration of factors that will be powerful determinants of future resource use but which have been consistently underestimated in the forecasts of doom throughout the years. The most significant of these factors are surely the extraordinary substitution possibilities (in both consumption and production) induced by changes in the relative prices of resources and the often unpredictable and dramatic technological innovations which provide alternative means of satisfying human needs (Rosenberg 1973).

Economic theory focuses attention on the role of prices in allocating resources both spatially and intertemporally. It provides a rigorous conceptual framework for an understanding of the behavior of resource markets and makes explicit those assumptions required to deduce necessary and sufficient conditions for predicting particular outcomes. When such outcomes are deemed socially desirable, the theory provides explicit guidelines for implementing policy designed to achieve those desirable ends. On the other hand, when the assumptions of the theory are violated in practice, the theory can serve as a tool both for predicting alternative sets of outcomes and for evaluating the relative merits of proposed changes in the institutional organization of the economy.

Economic theory demonstrates that under certain sets of conditions markets do what we want them to do. We are, therefore, better off analyzing the conditions that are violated in practice and formulating policies to correct these conditions than simply ignoring the theory because of real world departures from some of the simplifying assumptions.

This chapter, therefore, is written in the spirit of allowing economic theory to alert us to the respects in which natural resource markets do not achieve the desired goals and to serve as a guide to how policy intervention can help markets to function more effectively.

The first section makes the point that physical resource scarcity as such has no necessary economic meaning. It presents an economic definition of scarcity, suggests how it can best be measured, and analyzes what implications, if any, it has for economic growth. The second section then examines, within the context of a highly simplified economic framework, the conditions that must hold for efficient use of exhaustible natural resources. It points out that there are innumerable efficient paths for resource use, but to take the next step and decide which efficient path is optimal involves value judgments. Only when these value judgments are made explicit can appropriate policies be designed to achieve the desired ends.

A third section discusses how various complicating factors inherent in economic life—uncertainty, risk, externalities, disequilibrium, and institutional constraints—alter the ability of markets to achieve an efficient path. The fourth section contains our policy recommendations for achieving efficient and optimal resource use within a context of international cooperation. The final section concludes the paper with a statement of our own values—that, in our judgment, the ultimate aim of development should be to raise the living standard of the poor everywhere—and of our strongly held view that the issue of efficient resource use is conceptually different from the issue of the optimal distribution of income and power, a distribution which should be pursued through active use of domestic tax policy.

## Natural Resource Scarcity

Exhaustible natural resources such as petroleum, coal, copper, or iron cannot help but become scarcer in a purely physical sense if they are being used by man to satisfy economic wants. Also, the ability of natural environments to recover from harm done to them by by-products of the economic system is surely not limitless.

What is at issue, however, is whether the seemingly straightforward conclusion that if such resources are not consciously conserved we will face inevitable economic decline is, in fact, warranted. Much attention has been recently given to this question. One answer—provided by the so-called doomsday models of Meadows, Forrester, and others—is that the exhaustion of natural resources together with population growth and increasing environmental contamination will indeed lead inexorably to declining standards of living unless drastic conservation measures are taken. Another answer—provided by neoclassical economists—is that physical resource scarcity as such has no obvious economic meaning or necessary economic consequences.

History alone tells us that the consequences of increasing physical scarcity are hard to predict and often turn out to be completely outside the widest range of theorizing by technological experts of any given era. Malthus, Jevons, Ricardo, Mill, and others predicted a steady decline in the quantity of natural resources as a result of economic growth and, in turn, a declining potential for income growth as more labor and capital would have to be used per unit of constant quality resource extracted. All have proved wrong so far. We take the position that such predictions are no more likely to prove right than they have been to date and that assessing the economic consequences of physical resource scarcity is, indeed, a complicated matter. This section, therefore, discusses the question of what economic meaning can be attached to resource scarcity and how such scarcity can fruitfully be measured.

## The Economic Meaning and Measurement of Resource Scarcity

There are two main ways in which scarcity of natural resources may have economic significance: (1) they are in some sense essential inputs into the production of goods which satisfy economic wants; and (2) they or perhaps the natural environment around them satisfy economic wants directly *in situ*, without being extracted and processed. In both cases, how economically significant the scarcity is depends on the extent to which the resources in question can be replaced by others. To quote Smith (1978), "... scarcity must be treated in relative terms. ... Any scarcity index must take account of the process by which the resource is supplied, as well as the nature of all demands for it." As Solow (1974b) has observed, "If it is very easy to substitute other factors for natural resources, then there is in principle no 'problem.' The world can, in effect, get along without natural resources, so exhaustion is just an event, not a catastrophe."

A common way of measuring resource scarcity—by taking the estimated physical quantity of reserves of a given resource and dividing it by annual demand (current or projected at current growth rates) to produce a concept called "number of years worth of consumption still available" (Albers et al. 1976)—is both conceptually and empirically an inadequate measure of scarcity.

First, it is well known that reserve estimates are often very unreliable because it is simply not worth the expenditure to map out more than a few years' worth of reserves at a time, and price increases often render known but previously uneconomic reserves worth extracting and induce exploration for new deposits. Some physical resource measures may give a better indication of quantities than others (Brobst and Pratt 1973), but this does not change their lack of economic significance. In essence, measured reserves themselves are outcomes of economic decision making and so cannot be treated as if they will not respond to changing economic conditions (Pindyck 1978b).

Second, projecting levels or rates of growth of demand more than a few years into the future is an uncertain exercise at best and potentially quite misleading. Price changes, shifts in demand patterns, environmental regulations, technological changes, and other forces have often turned yesterday's growth into today's decline. Examples of natural resources for which this has occurred are easy to find: tin, lead, and mercury come immediately to mind.

The only significant redeeming feature of such an exercise would be its use in the case of natural resources for which no markets exist, that is, those which are basically public goods.* In these cases, while the measure would still suffer from the drawbacks cited above, there would be no alternative because there is no market in which the social valuation of the resource can be measured. However, it does not seem to be used for these types of natural resources, perhaps because of the inherent difficulty in measuring quantities of clean air, clean water, etc.

Economists have devoted much effort in recent years to devising and evaluating alternative measures of economically relevent natural resource scarcity. The most widely considered measures are the real price of natural resource products, the unit cost of natural resource products, and the scarcity rental rate of natural resources *in situ* (Barnett and Morse 1963; Barnett 1976).

Real price is defined as the market price of a natural resource product relative to a benchmark price such as a GNP deflator. As can be shown formally (Fisher 1976, for example), market price is conceptually the sum of marginal extraction cost (equivalent to unit cost) plus the scarcity rental. The real price measure thus incorporates the other two scarcity measures. It is considered by most analysts as probably the most appropriate measure of the three because it has the essential property, at least in principle, of summarizing "the sacrifices, direct and indirect, made to obtain a unit of the resource"—that is, "the labor and capital (and other resource) inputs required to extract and convert it, and an indirect cost, the value of future consumption foregone" (Fisher 1976).

The unit cost measure suffers because (1) if the quality of the resource is declining, the unit costs of extraction will increase irrespective of the magnitude of future scarcity; (2) it deals only with the supply side of a resource market whereas demand considerations are also important in assessing economic scarcity; (3) it is difficult to quantify because even for a single resource, data must be aggregated across firms with different technologies, different factors, and different factor costs for the same factor; and (4) in the presence of certain types of technological change, it can move in a direction opposite to that of the real price (see Brown and Field 1976; Fisher 1976; Smith 1978; Heal 1976; Solow and Wan 1976).

The main drawbacks to the scarcity rental rate are that (1) it may fall as depletion proceeds if lower quality deposits become more economical to market, whether or not other indicators give evidence of economic scarcity;** (2) in situations of high elasticity of substitution (indicating that

---

*A "pure" public good has the property that one individual's consumption does not subtract from the amount available for consumption by other individuals. Classic examples are bridges and natural beauty. It is well known that markets cannot allocate public goods efficiently.

**Fisher (1976). The same idea was expressed by Ricardo and Mill.

increasing physical scarcity will not pose a serious economic problem) the rental rate could still rise at the rate of interest (Brown and Field 1976); and (3) it is difficult to observe empirically both because it involves data on ore quantity and quality that companies exploiting the deposits may not want to release and because tax laws may constitute an incentive to underestimate (or at least understate) it.

Market measures of scarcity do have their own drawbacks, however. First, the common property or public good aspect of some natural resources means that in those cases such a measure may not exist because the resources are not traded on markets or are free for the taking. The problem of measuring and evaluating the seriousness of scarcity of exhaustible common property resources is recognized as one of the major cases in which a market system will fail to give society the proper signals. Second, the absence of sufficiently comprehensive futures and forward markets for resources means that the methods by which people form expectations about the future course of prices can influence the actual price path thus limiting the usefulness of prices as scarcity indicators. Heal's work (1978) on this subject shows explicitly that prices need not accurately indicate relative scarcity under these circumstances. Third, changes in the institutional environment such as tax laws or property rights and in market structure may significantly affect the course of prices while real economic scarcity is unchanged. However, even though these effects can be significant, it is also possible to estimate them in practice.*

Although these drawbacks limit the confidence that can be placed in conclusions drawn from market measures of scarcity, their usefulness is not entirely impaired. Much of the current theoretical work on the economics of exhaustible resources concerns the nature of the modifications to standard results caused by deviation from "ideal" conditions. That is, attempts are made to characterize the price path that would result under the conditions of uncertainty, oligopoly, etc., so that empirically these types of effects could be recognized. This work bears directly on scarcity measurement because it enables modification of the usual measures to account for common real world conditions.

*In an ideal world of perfect competitive markets, real price would be close to an ideal measure of relative scarcity. In any realistic setting it may have its own drawbacks, of course, in that market prices can reflect changes in market structure and institutional arrangements and may have volatile speculative components, none of which are necessarily related to increasing scarcity. The real price will also, in general, be sensitive to the choice of a benchmark price. However, this may not necessarily be a drawback: "A consumer probably should be interested in the price of resource products relative to other products he purchases and would therefore use a retail price index or the equivalent. A firm using a resource product as an input should be interested in the price of other inputs such as labor or capital, or an index of other factor prices" (Brown and Field 1976).

Scarcity measurement is a useful exercise which, if done carefully, can yield valuable information about changes in relative scarcity that otherwise can only be guessed at. The essential point is that prices do convey information on scarcity values which otherwise could be obtained, at perhaps substantial cost, only by sifting through enormous amounts of geologic, demographic, legal, and technical data. Prices monitor the informed judgments of market participants and industry experts as to the likely future course of demand, supply, and the institutional environment and thus can give advance warning of impending scarcity.

## Scarcity and Growth

If we have defined scarcity in an economically meaningful sense and devised ways of measuring it, let us now see whether anything can be said about its potential impact on economic growth. The obvious first question to ask here (Stiglitz 1976) is why should the scarcity of natural resources impose a greater burden than scarcity of other factors of production or commodities? When other factors or commodities are scarce their prices tend to be bid up and producers or consumers turn to substitutes. The economic impact of scarcity of a natural resource could thus be alleviated by substituting labor, capital, or another factor for the resource in the production process of a given good or by substituting other goods that use less of the resource. Alternative ways out of an otherwise binding resource constraint could be provided by technical progress which economizes on the use of natural resources or by increasing returns to scale (Rosenberg 1973).

Dasgupta and Heal (1974), Solow (1974b), and Stiglitz (1974) have analyzed the conditions under which it is possible for an economy to sustain a constant per capita level of consumption with an exhaustible resource as an input to production. Although the results vary depending upon the particular assumptions made, a common thread in these studies is the crucial nature of the elasticity of substitution between natural resources and capital in the limit as the stock of the natural resource declines.* If that elasticity is greater than one, then natural resources will not prove to be a

---

*The elasticity of substitution between two factors of production is defined as the percentage change in the ratio of the amounts used of the two factors induced by a given percentage change in their price ratio. If $K$ and $N$ represent quantities of capital and natural resources, respectively, and $P_K$ and $P_N$ their prices, then the elasticity of substitution between $K$ and $N$,

$$\sigma = \frac{\dfrac{d(K/N)}{K/N}}{\dfrac{d(P_N/P_K)}{P_N/P_K}}$$

constraint on the consumption standard. If it is equal to one but the share of capital in national income is greater than the share of natural resources, or if there is resource-augmenting technical change, again no resource constraint will appear. In short, as depletion of the resource drives up its price relative to the price of capital, it is possible to substitute capital for the resource at a rate "faster" than the rate of the resource's price increase. As the resource's price increases, the demands made on it decline along with its supply, and the reduced supply, therefore, does not constrain output. This can be true even if resources are necessary for production in the sense that output would fall to zero without at least some resource input. In the words of Peterson and Fisher (1977), "The simple fact that resources are finite, and are necessary for production, does not imply that the resource-using economy must eventually stagnate and decline."

So the question of the potential effect of resource scarcity on growth is essentially empirical—how large is the elasticity of substitution between natural resources and capital? Humphrey and Moroney (1975) estimated that in only two out of six U.S. manufacturing sectors studied was the elasticity of substitution between reproducible capital and an index of natural resource products greater than one, and in two other sectors the elasticity was negative, indicating complementarity rather than substitutability. These estimates are not, however, especially reliable (and elasticities could, in any case, change significantly as the resource gets nearer to depletion). Berndt and Wood (1975) discuss elasticity of substitution in some detail.

## Efficiency and Optimality in Economies
## with Exhaustible Natural Resources

In the previous section we discussed ways of detecting economically significant scarcity of exhaustible resources and concluded that real price was probably the most appropriate measure with an increasing trend of real price indicating increasing economic scarcity. This section discusses the policy implications of finding increasing economic scarcity in this sense.

We submit that increasing scarcity of an exhaustible resource has no obvious economic implications until more is known about the underlying forces giving rise to the indication of scarcity. If the resource is being used efficiently, in a sense to be made precise below, then government policy can only improve welfare by causing a shift to another efficient path of resource use preferred to the initial path. If resources are not being used efficiently, then welfare can be increased by a shift to an efficient path. But that we may be wasting our resources on an inefficient path does not automatically imply that they are growing economically scarcer.

The truly important questions from a policy perspective thus become: are we using our exhaustible resources efficiently and are we using them optimally? The first part of this section characterizes efficiency in the use of natural resources and discusses the ability of markets to achieve efficiency. The second part characterizes the optimal use of exhaustible resources under various conditions and discusses appropriate policy measures to ensure an optimal use of resources.

### Efficient Use of Exhaustible Resources

Economists have an explicit definition of economic efficiency: A resource is being allocated efficiently if a unit of the resource has the same value in all of its uses.* (Note that "value" as yet has nothing necessarily to do with observed prices—it could just as easily reflect shadow prices from an economic plan.) The rationale behind this concept is straightforward. If a resource had higher value in one use than in another, the total value of the resource to society could be increased by shifting some of the resource from the lower value use to the higher value use. Other things equal, transferring the resource to its higher value use will improve the economic welfare of society.**

The concept of economic efficiency if often used in static situations. At a given moment in time, if the marginal social product of a resource differs in two uses (both current), then this is said to be evidence of inefficiency. Such evidence is usually searched for by examining market structure and government regulations, or by looking for externalities and public good aspects of resource use. The efficiency concept generalizes easily to a dynamic context: Alternative uses of a resource include uses at different rates, so efficiency is achieved if the value of the resource is the same whenever it is consumed as well as in the varying ways in which it may be used (Stiglitz 1976). As Dasgupta and Heal (1978, chapter 7) have emphasized, dynamic or intertemporal efficiency refers to an entire path of resource use through time, so judging whether or not a current pattern of resource use is efficient requires not only looking at current rates of use but "peering into the distant future" as well.

The main issues of interest here are the conditions characterizing an in-

*Hertzmark (1978) and Berry et al. (undated) explore the relationship between thermodynamic and economic efficiency concepts. It turns out that under certain circumstances thermodynamic efficiency requires price paths similar to those required for economic efficiency.

**In this discussion we abstract from real world problems such as transactions costs which can limit the degree to which reallocating resources toward an efficient configuration will actually increase welfare. Welfare here refers strictly to economic welfare. In general, we will be dealing with the utility of consumption of goods and services rather than more general quality-of-life indicators.

tertemporally efficient resource use path and whether a market system can guarantee efficiency.

Assume for simplicity that we are concerned only with aggregate output, produced without externalities, so that we needn't worry for the moment about allocations of the resource among different uses at any given moment of time—static efficiency is not of concern. Suppose that social welfare is measured by some increasing function of aggregate consumption of output in a given period.* Consider any two adjacent periods of time. If there is a positive rate of return to capital, evidenced by a market interest rate or a social discount rate used by planners, then this should be incorporated in the measurement of value for the following reason: If a unit of the resource is extracted and used in the first period, it has a certain value measured by its marginal productivity in the production of aggregate output. It is worth expending an amount of output equal to the marginal product (MP) of the resource (valued in terms of aggregate output) in the first period in order to have the use of the resource in that first period. If this amount of output were instead invested in capital formation, however, its value in the next period would have increased by a factor of 1 + $r$, where $r$ is the marginal productivity of capital. Suppose that the marginal product of the resource grew by *less* than this factor from the first period to the next. Then the value to a private owner or to the state of a unit of the resource in the ground would be lower in the second period than in the first, in comparison with the alternative use of the output needed to obtain the use of the resource. This would induce the holder to use up his stocks of the resource in the first period. If, in contrast, the marginal product of the resource grew by *more* than the discount factor, then the resource would be more valuable in the second period, and this would cause its use to be delayed until then.

Using the yardstick of the rate of return on capital—because investment in new capital formation is the alternative productive use of the output needed to obtain a unit of the resource—we have established that the marginal product of the resource must grow from one period to the next at the rate $r$ in order for the resource to be used efficiently. If not, welfare could be increased by shifting the use of some of the resource from one period to another, until its value was the same in both periods.** Because this applies to any two adjacent periods, a necessary condition for efficient use of an exhaustible resource is that the percentage rate of change

*This in effect ignores distribution problems within generations. This issue is irrelevant to the discussion here, but see our comments in the introduction and conclusion.

**By shifting resource use appropriately among periods, the value will be equated in different periods because of diminishing return to the resource, holding quantities of other factors of production fixed.

of its marginal product must always equal the rate of return on capital. In a competitive economy in which firms maximize the present discounted value of profits, the marginal product of a resource equals its real price, and the rate of return on capital equals the interest rate. This casts the efficiency criterion in the familiar form of the Hotelling rule (1931): real price must rise at a rate equal to the rate of interest.

So far it has been assumed that the marginal extraction cost is constant and that the real price of the resource depends only on its use. If technology is not constant, then the Hotelling rule for efficiency must be modified to account for the fact that at different points of time it costs different amounts of aggregate output to extract a unit of the resource. For efficiency to hold, therefore, the real price should rise at a rate which is a weighted average of the interest rate and the rate of change of the marginal extraction costs, where the weights are the share of scarcity rental and cost in price.

But even this modified version of the Hotelling rule does not guarantee efficiency: although it is a necessary condition, it is not sufficient. It is entirely possible for it to be met and for the stock of the resource still never to be entirely depleted, because an exponentially rising real price may eventually choke off all demand before the point of total depletion is reached. It is clearly inefficient to leave some of the resource in the ground forever when its value (marginal product) has not fallen to zero (in fact, as the resource nears depletion, its value is likely to be quite high if substitutes do not become available).* Adding to the Hotelling rule the stipulation that in the limit the entire stock of the resource should be depleted gives us both necessary and sufficient conditions for an intertemporally efficient pattern of natural resource use. The depletion condition guarantees "global efficiency" and also points up the importance of someone taking the long view where natural resources are concerned. This is one of the main insights of dynamic natural resource economics. The intuitive condition for efficiency, derived by generalizing the familiar static condition, is not sufficient in this case. The price may rise with the interest rate, but if it starts from the "wrong" level then the resource could be depleted too quickly or too slowly for efficiency.

The question now becomes, can a market system guarantee an efficient use of exhaustible resources? That is, will the modified Hotelling rule be met? This question is important because, other things equal, markets are more efficient than alternative resource allocation systems. Working

---

*This applies to natural resources which have no use other than as factors of production. For resources which also have value as "natural amenities," efficiency may well require leaving some of the resource permanently unextracted. We focus on issues related to this subject in the next section.

within a market framework is, again other things being equal, preferable to nonmarket policies.

If we again simplify matters by assuming the absence of externalities, uncertainty, or disequilibrium, then it is a well-established result that perfectly competitive markets will indeed allocate exhaustible resources efficiently. Under these conditions the economy will necessarily be in intertemporal competitive equilibrium, which is characterized by the existence of a complete set of forward markets extending into the indefinite future. Given that these forward markets exist, the Hotelling rule is also the condition for the existence of an intertemporal competitive equilibrium, and because it also guarantees efficiency under these conditions (having ruled out disequilibrium), the market will support an intertemporally efficient allocation of exhaustible resources (Dasgupta and Heal 1978, chapter 8).

It is important to note that this result is contingent on a set of conditions which are quite severe. Dasgupta and Heal (1978, p. 22), who originated many of the findings discussed here, state that " . . . the claim that a decentralized competitive environment will ensure an efficient utilization of natural resources is a very tenuous one." It is, nevertheless, a useful claim, for we now have a benchmark against which to compare actual market performance. This we do in the following section where we review recent research results on how well a market allocates exhaustible resources when the stringent assumptions used above are relaxed. Before leaving this issue, one potential source of inefficiency will be briefly examined here: imperfect competition. It is relatively easy to analyze; it is widely prevalent in exhaustible resource markets; and in some cases it has quite straightforward policy implications.

Beginning with the case of a single firm controlling all deposits of a given resource, we can easily show that whether or not the efficiency conditions are violated depends upon how the elasticity of demand for the resource changes over time. This is familiar from static monopoly theory: the monopolist takes account of the downward sloping demand curve facing him while competitive producers are so small relative to total demand that they perceive an infinitely elastic demand at the market price. A private or public monopolist who wants to maximize the present discounted value of profits can be shown to extract at a rate which causes his marginal revenue—rather than price—to rise at the rate of interest; he produces so as to set the discounted value of marginal revenue equal in all periods. If the elasticity of demand does not change over time, then marginal revenue is proportional to price, and having marginal revenue rise at the rate of interest means price will do so as well.* In this case monopoly

---

*Marginal revenue $MR = P(1 + \frac{1}{\varepsilon})$, where $P$ is price and $\varepsilon$ is the elasticity of demand. If $\varepsilon$ remains constant then it is easy to see by logarithmic differentiation that marginal revenue and price rise at the same rate.

causes no inefficiency because it results in a price path identical to the competitive price path. The type of resource for which this might hold would be one which is an inexpensive but essential input into a product for which no substitutes exist within its price range. Chromite as an input into stainless steel is a good example.

If, instead, the demand elasticity for the resource increases over time (that is, demand becomes more elastic) due, say, to the development of substitutes for the resource in response to its increasing price, then the monopolist would like to cause price to rise at a rate lower than the rate of interest. It can be demonstrated that this will lead to a price path which is above the competitive path initially and then below it after a certain point, provided that the entire stock of the resource is eventually extracted in both cases. This leads to excessive conservation by the monopolist in the initial period with that excess made up for by too rapid depletion later in a clearly inefficient allocation (Heal 1978).

If the market is characterized not by a pure monopolist but by one large supplier (or a cartel) and a group of smaller competing producers, then matters become more complex. Depending upon the particular assumptions made about extraction costs for the cartel and for the "competitive fringe," complex price paths can result. In general, they follow the pattern of the monopolist facing an increasing demand elasticity and produce a market that does not support an efficient allocation. The direction of the bias is toward excessive conservation. Because oligopoly and restrictive cartel practices are obviously prevalent in such markets as oil, for example, scarcity is less likely to be a problem than it would be in a more competitive situation.

Dasgupta and Heal (1978) and Pindyck (1978a) have simulated the petroleum market in an attempt to check the predictions of this theory against an actual market that seems to conform to the oligopoly with competitive fringe pattern. Both sets of results confirm that the current price is now above the competitive price but is likely not to rise much at all in real terms over the next two decades whereas the price in a competitive market would be lower now but rising faster in the future. Pindyck also reports that the formation of the OPEC cartel raised the present value of the discounted stream of future profits to OPEC countries by 55 percent —a substantial inducement for the cartel to stay together.

Another form of oliogopolistic behavior which has received attention in the literature is the case in which there exists a "backstop technology" which, at a relatively high price, makes available an essentially unlimited supply of a substitute for the resource in question. Nordhaus (1973), who coined the phrase, gave the example of the breeder reactor providing an unlimited energy source as a substitute for fossil fuels, although at a substantially higher price per BTU.

The equilibrium outcome in this situation would be for the cartel to price the resource in such a way that there is no incentive to develop the backstop technology. This involves a period during which price rises at a rate that allows the cartel's marginal revenue to rise at the rate of interest, followed by a period during which the price is slightly below the price at which the backstop technology becomes economical. As Heal (1978) points out, the private return to lowering the price of the backstop technology via technical improvement is zero, because the cartel will find it rational to lower its price until it is again just below the backstop price. However, because the social return in terms of increased consumer surplus may be substantial (because the resource price will fall), government intervention may be called for.

Before moving to a discussion of optimal resource use, we should note that many critics question the appropriateness of the concepts and techniques of neoclassical economics in the context of natural resources. The question has been posed "whether there are unique features of the processes by which the extractive services of natural resources are used, that make the conventional neoclassical production analysis ill equipped to deal with the problem for which it is being employed" (Smith and Krutilla 1976). One frequent criticism is that the conventional analysis, as described above, ignores the "common property" aspects of natural resource uses and that comparisons between two alternative uses (*in situ* common property final consumption services versus extractive intermediate goods) are inappropriate "in deriving the demand for the services of natural resource" (Smith and Krutilla 1976). Other critics point to the extreme lack of realism involved in assuming perfect foresight or the existence of a complete set of forward and risk markets; to the lack of a theory describing behavior out of equilibrium when expectations are not fulfilled; and to the absence of descriptions of behavior in the presence of uncertain property rights, stock size, and future technological conditions.

Those familiar with contemporary theoretical economics will recognize these points as the focus of much ongoing work—often in a more general context than natural resource economics per se because the criticisms apply to many different areas of economic theory. We shall explore some of this work in the next section, in which we flesh out the simplified theory presented here by incorporating more realistic but also more complicating factors into our analysis.

## Optimal Use of Exhaustible Resources

The issue of efficiency in the use of exhaustible resources is concerned with waste. If we are not using our resources efficiently, then we are wasting them, and it is possible in principle to make all generations from the present onward better off by switching to an efficient path of resource use. Such a switch would allow more output to be produced from the fixed available stock of exhaustible resources which could then be distributed among generations in such a way as to make any or all future generations better off.

Optimality, in contrast, is concerned with a different question: Given that efficient use is being made of available resources, which efficient path should we be on? That is, how should the maximum producible output be distributed through time? There is an unlimited number of efficient paths; an optimal path picks one of these and declares it the "best." It is obvious that we are now out of the realm of descriptive or "positive" economics and into the realm of ethical or "normative" economics. Choosing an optimal path means choosing who is to be made better off at the expense of whom because, given the efficiency, there is no way to make one individual or generation better off without making another worse off. This is clearly an ethical choice and necessarily involves value judgments.

Although the market can be used as a tool for achieving an optimal path already decided upon, it cannot without intervention guarantee that the optimal path will indeed be followed. This results from the fact that previous market allocations have determined, at least in part, the current and future distribution of wealth and income which in turn heavily influences the particular efficient outcome the market comes up with (assuming that the market does indeed allocate efficiently). We thus recognize that the market can achieve the efficient resource allocation decided upon as optimal only if income and wealth are distributed in an appropriate way. Page (1977, p. 163) describes this well-known fact: "For each distribution of market power in the present and implied intertemporal allocation of resource usage, there exists a social welfare function and discount rate such that maximization of the present value of this social welfare function under this discount rate leads to the same allocation of resource usage as given under the efficiency criterion."* The first section of this chapter notes the normative views we bring to the subject of the optimal depletion of exhaustible resources and the accompanying optimal distribution of wealth and income through time and within the present generation. Here we discuss the characteristics of optimal depletion paths generated by different broad classes of ethical norms.

The first point to be made is that when considering optimal depletion of exhaustible resources, we generally are trying to maximize economic welfare through time. This has two interrelated implications.

*Page uses the phrase *efficiency criterion* to denote the outcome of a set of perfect markets.

One is that the welfare of a given generation is not derived directly from the availability to that generation of a given stock of natural resources (again leaving natural amenities aside for the moment) but from the consumption possibilities per capita as a whole. A larger stock of natural resources will, other things equal, imply higher potential welfare but so also will a larger capital stock, improved technology, and lower population. In the words of Stiglitz (1976), "One should not look at equity in a narrow sense of simply looking at the division of natural resources between the present and future generations; the present generation may give future generations fewer natural resources (this is inevitable in the case of exhaustible natural resources), but it will give future generations a higher level of technology and more capital."

The second implication is that we must put weights on the welfare of different generations. This is where ethical norms come in. Should the standard practice of discounting of future utilities be employed? If so, at what rate? Should the objective be to equalize the welfare of different generations as much as possible? Why should the present generation save and invest a portion of its output in order to improve the welfare of succeeding generations? How does one deal with the fact that population growth increases the size of future generations?

The standard application of optimal economic growth theory to an economy with exhaustible resources goes as follows. The objective is to maximize, for either a finite or infinite horizon, the present discounted value of the utility of consumption. In order to focus on intergenerational equity it is usually assumed that the intragenerational distribution of welfare will follow the same pattern for each generation; for example, each individual has identical tastes and receives an equal share of current output. This assumption simply allows us to focus on the essential aspects of the problem without needless complications. We can concentrate on the utility of a typical individual and simply multiply by the number of individuals to obtain a generation's "total welfare" which is then weighted by the discount factor applied to this generation. This discount factor is selected by society to reflect both ethical criteria and economic conditions. For example, it has been argued that there is no ethical justification for weighting the utility of future generations less than that of the current generation. A positive discount factor would, however, still be appropriate if there is a positive rate of return on capital because in this case the current generation sacrifices some of its output in order to accumulate capital which increases the output available to future generations. Thus it is frequently asserted that the social rate of return to capital is the appropriate discount rate, and it is known that under certain circumstances the market rate of interest will equal the social rate of return to capital.

The maximization is subject to three sorts of constraints. First, the size of the resource stock (assumed to be known) naturally constrains output and, therefore, welfare if the resource is essential in the sense made precise in the previous section. Second, not all the currently produced output can be used for consumption: some must be invested in order to maintain or increase the size of the capital stock (the optimal rate of growth of the capital stock is an outcome of the maximization). And third, consumption levels cannot fall below survival minimums, and resource use and capital stock cannot be negative.

The results of exercises along these lines can be classified according to three criteria: whether population growth is included, whether an infinite horizon is used, and whether a positive discount rate is used. With respect to the first criterion, it is argued by Dasgupta and Heal (1974) that because this problem is concerned with the implications of finite resource stocks for intertemporal planning, it is inappropriate simply to assume a constant exogenous rate of population growth; in the long run such a constant rate of growth will be impossible. Ideally, therefore, an optimum population policy should be part of the model, but because this is such a complex problem, they instead consider only a constant population through time and rationalize that decision by suggesting that "the objective of zero population growth has been accepted and achieved" (Dasgupta and Heal 1974). Other analyses have used the standard assumption of exogenous exponential population growth. With respect to the second criterion, although infinite horizon planning models are rarely used in practice, both types of models have been explored in the literature. An infinite horizon is often justified theoretically by noting that a finite horizon arbitrarily leaves out of account all future generations beyond a certain point in time. The third criterion has already been commented on. Models have been developed with and without a positive discount rate, and the special case of Rawls' "max-min" criterion has received attention as well.

Dasgupta and Heal (1974), assuming constant population, show that with a positive discount rate and an infinite horizon, per capita consumption will generally rise over time at first and then fall continuously. Furthermore, they find that if the resource is essential, it is optimal to deplete an approximately constant percentage of the resource stock each period and so imply that it is not optimal to exhaust the resource stock.* The

---

*These and other authors in the field generally use rather special functional forms, such as Cobb-Douglas or Constant Elasticity of Substitution production functions and iso-elastic utility functions. The latter have the property of constant elasticity of marginal utility at all levels of consumption.

higher the discount rate (that is, the less weight we put on the welfare of more distant future generations), the larger is this percentage. If, instead, the discount rate is zero, they find that the influence of the productivity of capital causes per capita consumption to rise continuously. (It should be noted that this particular result was derived under the assumption that the elasticity of substitution is equal to one and that the elasticity of output with respect to capital is greater than the elasticity of output with respect to the resource.)

Stiglitz (1974) analyzes another case in which per capita consumption grows through time along an optimal path. He uses a model in which population grows exponentially, utility is discounted, and the production function is of the Cobb-Douglas type. Optimizing over an infinite horizon, Stiglitz demonstrates how the choice of the discount rate affects the optimal path. For example, if the discount rate is high relative to the rate of technical progress, then the more elastic is marginal utility and the lower is the optimal rate of depletion. This runs counter to the intuitive result from simpler models that a higher discount rate necessarily implies more rapid depletion (Stiglitz 1974).

In an interesting model analyzed by Solow (1974a), the ethical criterion used is Rawls' max-min standard applied intertemporally. This amounts to maximizing the welfare of the poorest generation. The Rawlsian criterion, in a model with an infinite horizon, no population growth, no technological change, and a Cobb-Douglas production function, implies that the per capita consumption of each generation is the same and that the largest constant consumption level possible depends directly on the size of the initial capital stock. Each generation invests enough of its output in creating new capital to replace the resources it has used up. This suffices to maintain output constant through time because, under the Cobb-Douglas assumption, the elasticity of substitution between capital and natural resources is one. This result contrasts sharply with the results of the almost identical model analyzed by Dasgupta and Heal (1974) in which a discount rate of zero allows consumption to grow without bound. Depletion of natural resources proceeds more slowly in their model because capital accumulation is not constrained by the requirement that earlier generations not be made worse off by investing a lot so that later generations can enjoy a higher standard of living. Solow summarizes the implications of the max-min criterion by noting its main difficulty: "It requires an initial capital stock big enough to support a decent standard of living, else it perpetrates poverty, but it cannot tell us why the initial capital stock should ever have been accumulated" (Solow 1974a).

It is important to point out that actually implementing this sort of optimality analysis faces many obstacles, not the least of which is the inability of the present generation to dictate policies to future generations, even assuming they have identical preferences. Discussions of second best alternatives note that forced conservation of natural resources, although inefficient, could at least guarantee that future generations will have some production possibilities. Forced saving plans could achieve the same purpose. Peterson and Fisher (1977) provide a useful summary of this literature.

The discussion of this section has revealed certain points worth reemphasizing. First, it is crucial to be very explicit about the ethical norms one uses when planning intertemporal consumption. Second, we have explicit conditions under which the resource constraint does not inevitably cause the economy to stagnate and decline; thus empirical work can provide extremely useful guidance as to whether we are in fact likely to face a binding resource constraint. And, third, the analysis of imperfect competition reveals some areas in which government policy could clearly eliminate inefficiency. We return to these points in later sections when we discuss policy implications and recommendations.

## Uncertainty, Externalities, and Other Complicating Factors

The discussion so far has been of natural resources in a rather pristine economic world. Perfectly operating markets have been our context, except in the discussion of imperfect competition; externalities associated with depletion of natural resources have been absent; perfect certainty with respect to the future course of prices, demand, technology, and stock size have all been assumed; markets have always been in equilibrium; and institutions other than markets have not been incorporated.

This section incorporates certain factors that, although they complicate the analysis, are important considerations in the real world in which policy decisions must be made—uncertainty and risk, externalities, disequilibrium, and institutional constraints. In some cases, the complications result in intuitively plausible modifications to conditions derived in the simpler framework. In others, however, the results are complex modifications difficult to interpret—the price one must pay for moving closer to reality.

### Uncertainty and Risk

Uncertainty and risk permeate most aspects of natural resource industries to a greater degree than in many other areas. The total stock of a resource is invariably unknown, and although increasing the effort devoted to exploration may result in increasing known reserves, the timing and size of discoveries are to a large degree unknown in advance. Also, future demand for a resource is in general unknown. Substitutes may be developed which render a resource uneconomic to use, but when such a substitute will be found cannot be known with certainty even though, again, increasing the research and development effort increases the probability of discovering such a substitute sooner. The more likely the discovery of a substitute which reduces the value of the resource stock, the riskier it is to hold stocks of the resource.

We are not completely in the dark about the course of future discoveries and technological developments, however, and we can proceed by describing as much as we know about the relationships between exploration and research and development effort and the likelihood of discovery and development of substitutes. We can then examine the implications of the remaining uncertainty for efficiency and optimality.

Suppose that an exhaustible resource is an essential input into the production of aggregate output in an economy. Research is underway on a product which is a perfect substitute for the resource in production and which would, when fully developed, be available in essentially unlimited supply at a constant cost. This scenario is not too farfetched a representation of the energy industry with, for example, solar energy as the substitute for fossil fuels. It is assumed that the characteristics of the substitute technology are known with certainty and that the only unknown is the date at which it becomes feasible to use it. For now we assume that the timing of the innovation cannot be influenced by increased research and development expenditures (an assumption we later relax).

In this framework it has been shown that if there is a positive probability of the substitute being developed at any time, and if risk-neutrality* prevails, then an intertemporal competitive equilibrium will be characterized by the following inequality at each moment of time: $r_t \leq \dot{p}_t/p_t \leq r_t + \theta_t$ where $r_t$ and $p_t$ are interest rate and price of the resource at time $t$; $\dot{p}_t/p_t$ the instantaneous rate of change of price at time $t$; and $\theta_t$ is the probability that the substitute will be available at time $t$, given that it has not become available previously.** Because $\theta_t > 0$ for all $t$, the Hotelling rule is modified in a simple manner: price rises at a rate at least as fast as the interest rate and at most as fast as the interest rate plus a factor representing the conditional probability of discovery of the substitute. The interpretation of this result is straightforward: once the substitute is in use, the remaining resource stocks will lose some or all of their economic value. Therefore, in equilibrium, in order for there to be sufficient inducement

---

*An individual is said to be risk-neutral when he is indifferent between any two outcomes with the same expected value and different variances.

**Note that $\theta_t$ is time-variant; for example, given that a substantial research effort is directed toward development of the substitute, $\theta_t$ probably increases over time.

to hold stocks of the resource and run the risk of a capital loss, the price must rise at a higher rate than otherwise to compensate the holders for bearing this risk. This could imply either a lower or a higher extraction rate than would prevail without uncertainty because two counteracting forces are at work.

On the one hand, the resource will be worth less at the date of availability of the substitute; there is an inducement to deplete the resource more rapidly than otherwise. On the other hand, the consequences of running out of the resource before the substitute is available are drastic under the assumption that the resource is essential for production until that time. If the initial stock is relatively large, the latter factor will dominate and the extraction rate will be lower than with perfect certainty. If the stock is small enough, then the former motive will dominate and the extraction path will be more rapid (Dasgupta and Stiglitz 1976).

In another analysis with a model of this type, Dasgupta and Heal (1974) found that when a monopolist owns either the resource stock or the right to produce the substitute or both, then the resulting extraction rate is definitely biased downward. In each case the resource is extracted too slowly for intertemporal efficiency. In a special case in which a planner is attempting to find the optimal depletion path in a model of this type with the added stipulation that once the substitute becomes available the existing resource stock *and* the existing capital stock become valueless (their prices fall to zero), the Hotelling rule becomes exact again: $\dot{p}_t/p_t = r_t + \theta_t$. This demonstrates the restrictive assumptions required in order to account for uncertainty by increasing the discount rate by a determinate amount (Dasgupta and Heal 1974).

The simple modification to the Hotelling rule brought about by incorporating this particular form of uncertainty is due mainly to the exogenous and costless nature of the technological change. In models which explicitly allow for incremental research and development effort—which reduces output available for consumption or capital formation and increases the probability of successful development of the substitute—the optimal depletion rate can no longer be characterized by a simple variant of the Hotelling rule. Several conditions characterize the optimal depletion rate, including one which states that if part of aggregate output is used for research and development, then the marginal expected value of using output for research and development must equal its marginal value in its alternative productive use, namely capital formation. But the research and development effort need not begin immediately along the optimal path and also does not necessarily increase until the substitute is developed. Again, the size of the initial resource stock plays a key role in determining when research begins and when the effort peaks and starts declining (assuming the effort has not reached fruition already). Eventually, as the resource stock declines, it will be found worthwhile to begin the research and development effort which will entail declining per capita consumption until the effort pays off. The important point is that it is optimal to delay work on the substitute until the growing size of the capital stock and the declining size of the resource stock make the marginal expected value of the research and development effort comparable to the marginal value of other uses of aggregate output (Kamien and Schwartz 1978).*

Another type of uncertainty, peculiar to natural resources, concerns the size of the stock, the extraction costs of different deposits, and the value of exploration (Petersen 1975). The results of models designed to examine these issues hinge on whether it is possible (at a cost) to generate information about various resource deposits in the process of exploring without actually drilling the deposits. If it is assumed that this is not possible, that the only way to gain information about a particular deposit is by drilling it, then it has been shown that the optimal exploration and extraction policy will be characterized by a "reservation cost" strategy (Gilbert 1976a). This strategy means that if a deposit is drilled and it is found that the extraction cost is above a certain cutoff level, then the resource should not be extracted immediately but saved for later. If the extraction cost is below this level, the deposit should be worked right away. The optimal cutoff level of extraction costs is endogenous to the model and naturally varies through time as lower cost deposits are depleted. A key result in this area is that competitive, profit maximizing firms will follow the socially efficient exploration and extraction path (Gilbert 1976b).

When it is possible to generate information concerning deposits without actually drilling them, the latter result is reversed. It is common in models of imperfect information to find that when information has value in determining the appropriate rate of extraction but can be produced only at some cost, competitive firms will, in general, not efficiently allocate investment in this type of information. This is a consequence of the inevitable externalities associated with the production of information. The reasons why externalities cause market allocations to be inefficient are discussed below. In general, the efficient extraction rate under this type of uncertainty is slower than the efficient rate for the mean value of the resource stock (Gilbert 1976b).

A third type of uncertainty concerns future demand for the services of the resource. The results for this type of model indicate that if all produc-

*These models, of course, neglect technological developments the characteristics of which cannot be anticipated in advance and also the general benefits to society of basic research and learning by doing.

ers of the resource agree on the nature of the uncertainty facing them, and if they are risk-neutral, then the market allocation will be efficient, given that the expected value of utility is maximized. If, however, producers are risk-averse while society is risk-neutral, then depletion would be too rapid —because in order to minimize the variance of their expected profits, producers find it worthwhile to extract the resource quickly and forego some potential future profits rather than leave it in the ground and face the possibility, however remote, of a sharp decline in future demand (Weinstein and Zeckhauser 1975).

## Externalities

An externality (positive or negative) is said to exist whenever the actions of one producer or consumer affect the welfare or production possibilities of another agent in a way not accounted for by flows of commodities on markets. In general, an externality occurs when a decentralized economy has, for whatever reason, insufficient incentive to create a market for commodities that are actually changing hands. Three main types of externalities are recognized in the literature (the terminology follows Bator 1958):

1. Ownership externalities which reflect an inability actually to appropriate the full value from a factor of production which has a positive marginal product. An example is the case in which information generated by one producer about a resource deposit cannot be kept from other producers so that the producer who made the effort to collect the information does not receive the full benefit from it.
2. Technical externalities in which, for example, a production process generates an unwanted by-product or reduces the value of adjoining locations.
3. Public goods externalities, cases in which one individual's consumption of a good does not subtract from the amount available to other consumers. Clean air is an example of a public good, as are bridges, national defense, and national historical monuments. The recent cancellation of the $450 million Pyramid Oasis project in Cairo points up the increasing sensitivity to such externality issues in all parts of the world.

The problem of externalities has come up frequently in our discussion because of the widely held belief that externalities often occur in connection with the extraction of exhaustible resources. Exploration activities, pools of oil under adjoining parcels of land, environmental degradation caused by mining, and even overcrowding of national parks exemplify externalities involving natural resources (see Dasgupta and Heal 1978, chapter 15, for discussion of these examples). In general, one cannot expect markets to allocate resources efficiently when externalities are present. The reason is simply that the complete set of markets required for an efficient allocation does not exist. For example, there is no market for pollution in which individuals can purchase the right to emit pollutants or the right to avoid pollution. In some cases where markets for information do exist, they are generally not as extensive as would be required for efficiency.

The presence of externalities clearly warrants consideration of policy intervention to lead to an efficient resource allocation. A natural question to ask is whether an appropriate policy would establish markets for those commodities for which the private incentive to do so is apparently insufficient. This type of policy has been studied extensively, particularly with respect to establishing the "optimum" level of pollution. However, there are a number of reasons why this may not be the most feasible approach to the externality problem (Dasgupta and Heal 1978, chapter 3). First, for a market to exist, it must be possible to exclude those who do not purchase a good from enjoying the benefits of it. This is clearly next to impossible for goods such as clean air, national defense, and even a pool of oil under adjoining parcels of land. Second, the existence of a market does not automatically guarantee that its outcome will be a competitive equilibrium. For externalities specific to a certain locale, the number of people who might be involved in a market would be quite small and the market structure might be more of a bilateral oligopoly than a competitive one. Third, in the case of technical externalities, a market may not guarantee even the existence of a competitive equilibrium. For example, when pollution is a joint product of a production process, it may be impossible for technical reasons to establish equilibrium simultaneously in the market for the produced good and for the pollution (there is the possibility of a nonconvex production possibility set).

If the establishment of a complete set of competitive markets is infeasible, what other ways exist for dealing with external effects? Borrowing from the large body of literature on the subject, especially the useful survey by Mishan (1971), one can identify several. One solution, and probably the best one from a theoretical viewpoint, is to impose optimal excise or "Pigouvian" taxes and subsidies in such a way as to induce the market toward an efficient allocation. Although this can be a relatively simple theoretical exercise, it is extremely difficult in practice to obtain the information needed for the calculation of such taxes and subsidies. One does not frequently observe Pigouvian taxes being imposed in practice.

Another commonly proposed solution, particularly in cases in which there are common property aspects involved, is regulation of access or property rights. This regulation may involve political restrictions and standards which implicitly determine the extent of externalities present.* Most of the remedies suggested involve modifying legal rights, market structure, or prices and incomes facing the participants and then allowing the market to follow its course. In many cases this will be the best way of eliminating an externality without undue disruption of other activities.

## Disequilibrium

One of the assumptions underlying most of the previous analysis is that markets are always in equilibrium or, at least, that they tend to move quickly to their new equilibrium positions after a shock. This assumption is very likely to be valid when futures markets and risk markets exist because these institutions enable people to form accurate expectations about the future. Such markets mean that an unexpected shock such as a large new discovery, or a change in the degree of market power exercised by a cartel, even though unpredictable, will not lead to an unstable trend or spiral away from its new equilibrium position. In the absence of futures and risk markets, individuals must find another way of forming their expectations about future prices. One possible method is simply to extrapolate past price trends into the future with a model relating the rate of change of price to excess demand. Another way is to use a forecast based on all available relevant information including likely trends in demand, discoveries, government regulations, business cycles, and so forth. The former method may be characterized as "adaptive expectations" and the latter as "rational expectations."

It turns out that the method of expectation formation assumed is a crucial determinant of whether or not a market for an exhaustible resource will exhibit short-run stability. Stiglitz (1975) argues the matter in the following way. First, suppose that expectations are formed by the adaptive method and that the market is initially in intertemporal equilibrium. Suppose that an exogenous shock leads producers to expect that the rate of price increase will exceed the interest rate for the next few periods. This leads them to view holding their stocks in anticipation of capital gains as a more profitable activity than extracting and selling the resource, so production ceases (or slows down if there are fixed costs). The reduced rate of output relative to demand causes the current price to be bid up and reinforces the expectation of a rate of price increase in excess of the interest rate. This reinforces owners of the resource stock in their belief that holding the resource off the market will be profitable and causes the price actually to rise at a rate greater than the interest rate, whereas the new

---

*It can be argued that the profit motive itself determines the nature of the environment in which it operates. This view is undoubtedly true to a degree but ignores the evolution of legal restrictions on economic behavior.

long-run equilibrium would be characterized only by a shift in the level of the price with no change in the rate of price increase.

Heal (1978) and Stiglitz (1974) consider the same situation but suppose that expectations are formed rationally. Now an exogenous shock which leads to the expectation of higher prices in the future will lead to an immediate increase in the price level with no change in the rate of price increase. The market attains its new long-run equilibrium quickly and directly because individuals expect the resource stocks to be a better asset than others in the economy, so they immediately purchase it, bidding up its price to the point at which the expectation of a future price increase no longer is warranted.

The role of expectations formation is thus very important for the short-run stability of natural resource markets when futures and risk markets do not exist. Evidence about which expectations hypothesis seems to conform to empirical behavior is an important research aim in economic theory, and it is now possible to construct tests which distinguish alternative expectations hypotheses on the basis of empirical data. One can readily see that natural resource markets are often characterized by short-run instability leading to violent price fluctuations which may indicate the presence of adaptive expectations formation. But the implications for government policy are not clear because often the shocks to the market are caused by governments themselves. Two recommendations that do emerge from a study of this problem are the desirability of establishing long-term risk and futures markets and of promoting stable government regulations. We elaborate on this in our policy discussion in the next section. First, however, we discuss how government actions may adversely affect natural resource markets.

## Institutional Considerations

Markets do not function in a vacuum. Rather, as we are painfully aware, a complex array of private and, primarily, government institutions form the environment in which natural resources are allocated. Government policies in the form of general taxes, subsidies, regulations, and similar interventions directed specifically toward natural resources have a strong influence on the efficiency with which markets allocate natural resources. This large and complex area has been surveyed in detail by Brannon (1975) and Stiglitz (1975); here we restrict discussion to some of the government interventions which have fairly obvious impacts on natural resource markets.

Taxes of various kinds affect natural resource industries. Income taxes generally are not distortional, but special provisions that apply to natural resource industries are a different matter. These include the depletion allowance which makes the petroleum industry, for instance, a more attractive investment prospect than it might otherwise be. The allowance's effects lead to a faster depletion rate, particularly under monopoly, and could induce more exploration than is optimal. It is also argued that special treatment of some natural resource industries penalizes others which are generally the more risky and capital-intensive ones (Stiglitz 1974).

Government leasing policy can have a significant impact on whether lowest cost deposits are extracted before higher cost deposits as required for efficiency. The so-called "diligence clause" requiring some development of a tract within five years of leasing it, for instance, could cause firms to extract deposits which they would otherwise hold off the market while waiting for the price to rise (Stiglitz 1975).

Price regulations also have strong observable effects on natural resource markets. Holding the price fixed results in obvious inefficiencies because efficiency requires an increasing price unless technical change offsets the rising scarcity rental. Fixed prices can induce excessive depletion as firms observe that there is no return to holding stocks off the market.

General economy-wide taxes create a wedge between rates of return available to private investors and the social discount rate which reflects the actual productivity of capital. That wedge can result in significant departures from efficiency if the social discount rate is considered the appropriate figure by which to discount future utility and profits.

Finally, the recent tendency to substitute political motivations for economic considerations in determining production rates for key energy resources obviously reduces the ability of any economic theory to predict adequately the future course of extraction patterns, prices of energy, or impacts in either developing or developed nations.

### Implications for Development Policy and International Cooperation

We have devoted considerable space to a review of the economic theory of exhaustible resources. We turn now to the all-important policy implications of the theory. What are appropriate policies with respect to natural resources for national, regional, and international bodies interested in promoting economic development and international cooperation?

The importance of natural resources to the great majority of developing countries is incontestable. A perusal of data for 83 developing nations which belong to the International Monetary Fund reveals that 27 of them get over half of their export earnings from exhaustible resources; when agricultural, fishery, and forestry products are included, most developing countries get nearly 100 percent of their export earnings from natural resources. The significance of these numbers lies in the fact that most developing countries do not have large indigenous capital goods sectors and so are forced to rely on imports of capital goods in order to achieve desired levels of investment.* Earnings from natural resource exports thus provide crucial foreign exchange and relieve bottlenecks that would arise if developing countries were forced to build up their capital stocks from scratch. A number of familiar issues related to this reliance on natural resource exports are relevant here.

First, the sharp short-run price fluctuations characteristic of many markets for natural resource products have subjected development efforts to sudden severe shocks which can undermine the best planning efforts and leave an economy reeling. These price fluctuations result from the generally price-inelastic nature of the derived demand for many natural resource products on the one hand, and from the considerable lags involved in increasing extractive and processing capacity on the other. It is not uncommon to find new capacity appearing in response to previous high levels of demand just at a time when demand in industrial countries is falling because of a downturn in the business cycle and bringing a sharp drop in the resource price. Numerous proposals for stabilizing resource prices have been made and some, such as commodity agreements, have been tried in practice.

Second, the long-run trend in the terms of international trade of developing countries has been a subject of controversy for many years. It has been claimed that these terms of trade have undergone a secular deterioration throughout the present century. The counterclaim that the developing countries have, in fact, experienced an upward trend in their terms of trade has been made with equal forcefulness. One of the main reasons for cartel formation by developing nations has been the perception that without some kind of action, their terms of trade would continue to deteriorate.

Third, in an effort to overcome dependence on export earnings from natural resource products, many developing countries favor import substitution in an attempt to develop a diversified industrial structure. International trade policy thus becomes a policy instrument with profound effects on resource allocation and development efforts both within and between industrial countries and developing countries.

Another issue closely allied to trade policy is factor mobility and policies relating to it. This point arises in connection with issues such as the recycling of "petro-dollars" and foreign investment in the resource sectors of developing countries.

Before we discuss each of these issues in more detail, a caveat is in or-

---

*Imports of necessities such as food are also important but do not contribute directly to development.

der. Many of the policies we recommend are based on the assumption that governments are capable of imposing an optimal tax and tariff structure. For example, a common result from the theory of optimal taxation is that it is generally more efficient, in the sense of reducing total welfare by less, to raise a given amount of revenue by lump-sum or income taxes than by excise or trade taxes. This view ignores the obvious fact that most governments are severely constrained by various political factors and are unable or unwilling to carry out certain types of policies. The problem is discussed cogently by Sen (1972) and by Dasgupta and Stiglitz (1974), who evaluate the optimality of various tax structures under different types of constraints. We note that many of the policies suggested here may have to be modified in the light of particular constraints which exist in different countries. In the spirit of optimism, however, we consider it important to spell out optimal policies—that is, those which have the biggest potential impact on welfare—in the hope that understanding what should be done will help overcome narrow political vision in the effort to hasten the development process.

## Price Fluctuations

The economic theory of natural resources is mainly concerned with long-run trends and as such has little to say about short-run phenomena such as price fluctuations caused by the business cycle and the lags involved in expanding capacity. Nevertheless, some insights can be gained from natural resource theory and some aspects of general price theory in analyzing this important problem.

Multilateral arrangements such as international commodity agreements are commonly proposed as a means of stabilizing the export prices faced by developing countries. Bilateral long-term contracts are also suggested frequently, but can arrangements of either breadth be effective? The Hotelling rule tells us that in the long run exhaustible resource prices will follow an exponentially increasing trend, once cost reducing technological improvements are no longer significantly affecting the market. Attempts to fix a resource price within fairly narrow bounds will sooner or later face the pressure of an increasing long-run trend in the price.

A more reasonable solution may be to attempt to limit price fluctuations around an increasing trend. In principle, a commodity agreement could be designed to do this. However, the benefits of successful price stabilization must be balanced against the costs of achieving it. The common tools employed in commodity agreements are buffer stocks and export controls. Buffer stocks can tie up an immense amount of resources if they are to be successful. Desai's study (1966) of the international agreement on tin, the only exhaustible resource for which one exists, showed that the buffer stock required in order to meet the stabilization goal of the agreement would need to be inordinately large. The actual size of the buffer stock has been considerably smaller, and as a result the agreement has not been notably successful in dampening price fluctuations.

Although export controls are a powerful tool for preventing a price from falling, they too have a cost—in terms of lost sales. Inelastic demand may dictate a high price and low sales as a profit-maximizing strategy for a commodity agreement acting as a monopolist, of course, in which case the cost (to consumers) is the consumer surplus lost as a result of monopolistic actions.

Are alternative means for stabilizing export prices of developing countries available? The answer is probably no, but there are methods by which the harmful effects of sharp price fluctuations on developing nations' economies may be ameliorated. These methods stem from the well-known principle of welfare economics mentioned earlier: Under general conditions, an income tax is a less costly way (in terms of welfare) of raising a given amount of revenue than a commodity tax or some other form of price distortion, of which buffer stocks and export controls are examples.

An efficient method of alleviating temporary revenue shortfalls in developing countries because of price shifts would be loans from a fund set up for this purpose and managed by an international development agency such as the World Bank. The cost of maintaining such a fund would be less than the cost of stabilizing the price via the usual tools of commodity agreements, especially because repayments to the fund would be made during periods of high prices. This proposal recognizes the need for industrial countries to aid in offsetting temporary blows to economies which cannot easily absorb such shocks but provides that aid in a way which minimizes the cost and avoids distorting market price signals. It would be necessary in practice to determine when a price change is a signal of temporary disequilibrium and when it betokens a "real" change in underlying demand or supply conditions. Although this could be a difficult task, it should not be insurmountable and could aid market participants by providing additional information about future trends.

## Terms of Trade

Prebisch (1950) and Singer (1950) popularized the notion that the terms of trade between primary products and manufactures, a relation not necessarily equivalent to the terms of trade between developing and developed countries but with some major exceptions approximately the same, had been declining for some time and would likely continue to do so. Singer argued that this decline did not reflect a trend in real costs; he held that, in fact, technological progress was reducing costs in manufacturing at a faster rate than in primary industries so that one would have expected an improvement in terms of trade of primary products. The actual decline occurred, it was asserted, because of monopoly power in the developed countries used against the developing nations. Strong labor unions in the industrial countries were supposed to have appropriated the benefits of lower manufacturing costs and improved members' incomes so that prices of manufactured goods did not fall while the benefits of technological progress in primary industries in developing countries were appropriated by the industrial nations as a result of monopsonistic buying power.

Kindleberger (1956; 1964) has shown that the general pattern of trends in the terms of trade supported the Prebisch-Singer hypothesis through the early 1960s with some exceptions. The reasons emphasized by Kindleberger and others for the appearance of this trend differ somewhat from those of Singer and Prebisch. Differences in the capacities of developing versus industrial nations to shift resources and expand or contract supply of primary products in response to incipient price changes, along with differences in the relative ease of entry and exit and income inelastic demand for primary products, combined to give the result. The damaging effects of the observed decline in the terms of trade for developing countries are called into question, however, when it is remembered that lower relative prices can stimulate demand and thus increase the volume of trade and that the quality of manufactured goods has increased significantly over the relevant period, offsetting to some degree their higher relative prices. Other factors also working to mitigate the effects of declining terms of trade for developing countries include the declining relative price of internationally traded services, provided mainly by advanced nations, and the improved share of profits from foreign investments received by developing nations' governments.

What can we expect the trend in the terms of trade to look like in the future for developing country exporters of primary products? Natural resource theory provides some guidance. This century has witnessed sharp advances in the technology of extracting primary products, particularly nonrenewable resources, and the resulting declines in extraction cost have prevented scarcity rental increases from consistently forcing market prices up, although the cost declines experienced in manufacturing have been even greater. If, as some claim, the pace of technological progress has been slowing in recent years, and if this trend continues, the force of an exponentially increasing scarcity rental will begin to make itself felt in the form of rising market prices for nonrenewable resources relative to manufactured goods' prices. At the same time, demand for these resources may decline as cheaper substitutes are developed, a trend which has already affected tin and lead. Furthermore, raw material price increases may well be passed along in the prices of manufactured goods imported by developing countries, and some of the benefits to exporters of higher natural resource prices may be offset. The petroleum price increases of the mid-1970s provide a case in point.

The above results may be difficult to disentangle, but no obvious case emerges for an effort to keep primary product prices artificially high over the coming years. Unexpected events such as major new discoveries, technological advances, and development of substitutes may offset the force of a rising scarcity rental, but the negative effects of such events on development prospects are best countered by nondistorting policy actions rather than by manipulated prices. The maintenance of artificially high prices (whether through government controls or cartel pricing arrangements) for primary products is likely to hasten the development of substitutes and increase the reluctance of industrial nations to cooperate in other ways with developing countries.

The formation of cartels has been chosen by a number of exporters as a means of ensuring a high relative price for their natural resource exports. The petroleum cartel, OPEC, has succeeded in maintaining the price structure imposed in late 1973 and early 1974, although the terms of trade of the OPEC countries appear to have declined since then, from their initial sharply improved level, as a result of induced inflation in the industrial countries. The worldwide recession of 1974–75, which many economists believe was caused in part by the oil shock, reinforced a decline, already induced by the price increases, in the demand for oil. This has naturally contributed to a slower relative rate of extraction. Although this means that scarcity is less likely to be a problem than otherwise, there is no presumption that the current extraction rate is efficient.

From the point of view of world welfare, the magnitude and rapidity of the OPEC price increases have seriously contributed to economic and political instability throughout the world. The industrial countries have suffered from the dual maladies of higher inflation and higher unemployment and have, tragically, resorted to higher levels of arms sales to highly unstable regimes in order to offset the balance of payments implications of the higher cost of oil. Oil-importing developing countries have had to curtail development programs in order to offset the increased constraint on foreign exchange reserves. It is ironic that the huge windfall profits to oil-exporting nations have themselves been a mixed blessing. In order to sustain artificially higher oil prices, production rates have been reduced well below actual production capacity, and higher real costs of unit output have resulted. Moreover, the scramble to modernize and to acquire western technologies has led to considerable economic waste as well as to political instability as the recent events in Iran serve to illustrate.

Defenders of the cartel's actions point out that the OPEC countries have provided aid to some other developing nations and that the Eurocurrency market has fostered the "recycling" of excess OPEC liquid capital to other countries with profitable investment opportunities. This amounts to an involuntary transfer payment from industrial oil importers to developing countries. Although we favor resource transfer in this direction, we note that this particular way of achieving it imposes a burden of efficiency on both the donors and the recipients—the latter because of the generally higher interest rate charged by private banks compared to official international agencies. Given the limited ability of OPEC countries to absorb and productively use more capital, this may be an opportune time for negotiation of a halt to further price increases in exchange for increased nonmilitary aid and technical assistance channelled through international agencies to their most productive uses.

## *Trade Policy*

Import substitution and export promotion for manufactures are two policies favored by many developing countries as a way to overcome their dependence on export earnings from natural resource products. The former policy involves the imposition of high tariffs on, or outright prohibition of imports of, goods that the country would like to produce domestically. The latter policy aims at shifting resources into those manufacturing sectors the products of which can successfully compete with their higher-labor-cost counterparts in industrial countries. Textiles, electronic components, and steel are examples of the industries in which some developing countries find themselves with a comparative advantage. However, they face barriers to the markets of industrial countries in the form of tariffs which, even though not prohibitive, can still limit the revenue received by developing country exporters.

A well-known result from the theory of international trade is that under fairly general conditions potential world welfare is maximized under a free trade regime (Samuelson 1939). Every country could be made better off by an appropriate redistribution of the increased income available as a result of switching to a free trade regime. The inefficiencies associated with import substitution efforts since World War II are well known, as are those currently associated with the tariffs and other barriers to the exports of manufactures from developing to industrial countries. The benefits to developing nations of adopting a free trade policy, along with the adoption of such a policy by the industrial countries, could be quite significant—especially if one of the explicit aims of the policy is the promotion of development so that any substantial increase in revenue accruing to advanced countries would be contributed to a development fund.

142                                          NATURAL RESOURCES

South Korea and Taiwan provide encouraging examples of how the export of manufactures can spur development that benefits the majority of people in the country, while a recent episode in the Philippines demonstrates the impact on growth of removing various types of distortions (Williamson 1971; Williamson 1976). Although many developing countries may not be in a position to develop successfully manufacturing industries for export purposes, the more efficient resource allocation that would result from liberalized trade policies would be likely to offset any potential harm from relying on export earnings from primary products, provided the recommendations made above as an alternative to price stabilization efforts are implemented.

### Foreign Investment

As part of the overall trade policy of many developing countries, it is common to find restrictions of various kinds placed on foreign direct investment. These restrictions are often specifically applied to natural resource industries which provide the country with a large part of its foreign exchange earnings. Foreign investment in the natural resource sector of a developing country is typically made by firms attempting to integrate vertically in order to assure themselves sources of supply of raw materials and perhaps even to erect barriers to entry by potential competitors needing the same raw material in their home country. These firms often have specialized technical knowledge to which they have exclusive rights, having developed and implemented extraction processes in other locations.

One of the main reasons forwarded for restrictions on foreign investment in the natural resource sector is that the foreign firms in this sector extract the resource at a rate more rapid than desired by a nation and repatriate too high a portion of their profits. This view induces developing country governments to nationalize existing foreign investments and prohibit further investment by foreign firms. However, this policy has a cost as well, because it may take a long time before the government can run extraction enterprises with the same degree of efficiency as the foreign firms.

Consider the reasons why a foreign firm would extract the resource at a rate considered too rapid by the developing country. If the firm and the country use the same discount rate in their calculations and have the same information, their desired extraction rates may still differ if their objectives differ. (That is, the firm is maximizing the present value of its stream of profits while the country presumably has a variety of social objectives involving growth, employment, inflation, income distribution, etc.) But this does not necessarily explain the divergence in desired extraction rates. It is entirely possible that in a period of declining demand for its product, the firm would like to extract at a slower rate than that desired by the country. In this case differing discount rates are likely to be the cause. Private and social discount rates may differ for a number of reasons; the relevant one here is uncertainty over future property rights. If the firm attaches a high probability to expropriation or other restrictions, then it will tend to increase its discount factor and in turn move to more rapid extraction because a unit of the resource extracted becomes worth relatively more the sooner it is available. Firms are not likely to pursue a socially optimal exploration program if they believe they will get no benefit by doing so.

This is a case in which the effects of uncertainty have an obvious cure—creation of a relatively stable political environment with respect to foreign investment. This does not mean relinquishing all control of the natural resource sector to foreign firms; rather it means developing policies that allow foreign firms to operate in such a way as to maximize the gains to the developing country from their activities. Such a policy could involve, for example, a high tax on profits along with guarantees of security of investments. This type of policy may also have the beneficial effect of inducing a more nearly optimal exploration program. The best discovery prospects are currently located in the developing countries, and an increased exploration could be of considerable benefit to them.

## Conclusions

Natural resource theory provides a conceptual framework which can aid in understanding the complex choices facing decision makers with responsibility for natural resource policy. The preceding sections have spelled out the contributions of the theory in some detail and pointed to the implications of the theory for policies relating to economic development and international cooperation. Although such theory is an invaluable aid to decision making, it cannot, as we have noted, provide the moral guidance which ultimately determines the program of action chosen. A crucial part of the decision making process is the values of the decision maker because these play an important role in the choice of goals. Too commonly these values remain implicit, and examination of the policy recommendations themselves is required in order to infer the nature of the goals behind them.

The single most important institutional factor likely to affect the future of the economies of both developing and developed nations is the trend toward cartelization of natural resource industries. It is in this area that economic theory is least likely to produce useful predictions because the rapidly emerging network of international resource cartels displays a disturbing tendency to use political rather than economic motivations as the basis for resource production and distribution decisions. The major OPEC producers of the Middle East have come to view their natural resource endowment not simply as an economic resource to be optimally allocated over time, but rather as a political "weapon" to be wielded through the use of production quotas which in turn lead to an escalation of the prices of energy resources. The Arab oil embargo of 1973 and the subsequent quadrupling of oil prices was the first dramatic event symbolizing the "politicalization" of decision making in energy resources. As the disparity between outcomes of the market mechanism and outcomes of political decisions grows, we can predict only a growth in uncertainty and instability affecting both developing and developed nations.

The policies we advocate in this chapter tend to emphasize the value of the market mechanism in allocating resources efficiently. We note, however, that an optimal resource allocation will result from market forces only if the distribution of wealth and purchasing power conforms with the goals of the society's social welfare function. We do not propose that a market solution to natural resource allocation problems be carried out in a vacuum. Rather, explicit development goals and policies to implement them must precede any use of the market mechanism to achieve an optimal resource allocation.

An example of the importance of this is the overwhelming emphasis in development policy placed on growth of GNP to the exclusion of other aims until fairly recently. Only in this decade has it been widely realized that maximizing the growth of GNP does not automatically result in gradual improvement of the standard of living of the poor who, in our judgment, should be the ultimate target of development policy.

A redistribution of wealth from the advanced nations to the developing countries is crucial but cannot succeed in improving the lot of the poor unless significant and sometimes drastic changes occur in the social structure and government policies of many developing nations. We do not favor the imposition of Western values on non-Western nations, but the distribution of income and power in many developing countries is highly skewed. It is, therefore, largely up to the developing nation to assure a more equitable distribution of income. International policies, such as the ones described in the previous section, can make a substantial contribution to the achievement of development goals but cannot offset the effects of the ongoing and increasing concentration of wealth in the hands of elites. Rhetoric cannot hide the reality of poverty faced by the majority of developing countries' citizens.

The blame for this must fall in part on the advanced industrial nations of the West and East. Many corrupt, autocratic governments with little will to pursue broad development goals are propped up by either the

Western bloc or the Communist bloc. The arms race fostered by the advanced nations diverts an astounding amount of resources away from productive uses. Each side puts heavy emphasis on maintaining political and ideological bonds with its client countries while the economic and social development of the developing countries becomes an afterthought. Instead of allocating aid on the basis of strategic importance or political alliance, it behooves the advanced nations to channel assistance so as to maximize its impact on the development of the poor in all countries and to make aid contingent on its use for constructive purposes. The most significant mechanism for both improved efficiency and a more equitable redistribution of resources remains the free market. Increasing the possibilities of labor and capital mobility between nations can go a long way toward the establishment of an equitable world order, and it is our conjecture that long after the rhetoric of "North-South" dialogs is forgotten, market mechanisms will survive as the most compelling force in the production of both equity and efficiency.

## References

Albers, J. P., W. C. Bawiec, and L. F. Rooney. 1976. *Demand for Nonfuel Minerals and Materials by the United States Energy Industry, 1975–90*. USGS Professional Paper 1006-A. Washington, D.C.: U.S. Geological Survey.

Barnett, Harold. 1976. "Scarcity and Growth: Revisited." Forum on the Economics of Natural Resource Scarcity, Resources for the Future, Washington, D.C.

Barnett, Harold J., and Chandler Morse. 1963. *Scarcity and Growth: The Economics of Natural Resource Availability*. Baltimore: Johns Hopkins University Press.

Bator, F. 1958. "The Anatomy of Market Failure," *Quarterly Journal of Economics* 72: 351–79.

Berndt, E. R., and D. O. Wood. 1975. "Technology, Prices, and the Derived Demand for Energy," *Review of Economics and Statistics* 57: 259–68.

Berry, R. Stephan, Geoffrey Heal, and Peter Salamon. Undated. "On a Relation Between Economic and Thermodynamic Optima: A Working Paper." Department of Chemistry, University of Chicago, Chicago, Illinois and Department of Economics, University of Sussex, England.

Brannon, G. M. ed. 1975. *Studies in Energy Tax Policy*. Cambridge, Massachusetts: Ballinger.

Brobst, D. A., and W. P. Pratt, eds. 1973. *United States Mineral Resources*. USGS Professional Paper 820. Washington, D.C.: U.S. Geological Survey.

Brown, G. M., and B. C. Field. 1976. "The Adequacy of Measures for Signalling the Scarcity of Natural Resources." Forum on the Economics of Natural Resource Scarcity, Resources for the Future, Washington, D.C.

Dasgupta, P., and G. Heal. 1974. "The Optimal Depletion of Exhaustible Resources." In *Symposium on the Economics of Exhaustible Resources, Review of Economic Studies* 42: 3-28.

Dasgupta, P., and G. Heal. 1978. *Economics of Exhaustible Resources.* Cambridge Economic Handbooks (forthcoming).

Dasgupta, P., and J. Stiglitz. 1974. "Benefit-Cost Analysis and Trade Policies," *Journal of Political Economy* 82: 1-33.

Dasgupta, P., and J. Stiglitz. 1976. "Uncertainty and the Rate of Extraction Under Alternative Institutional Arrangements," Technical Report no. 179. Economic Series, Institute for Mathematical Studies in the Social Sciences, Stanford University, Stanford, California.

Desai, M. 1966. "An Econometric Model of the World Tin Economy, 1948-1961," *Econometrica* 34: 105-34.

Fisher, A. 1976. "On Measures of Natural Resource Scarcity." Forum on the Economics of Natural Resource Scarcity, Resources for the Future, Washington, D.C.

Gilbert, R. J. 1976a. "Search Strategies for Non-Renewable Resource Deposits," Technical Report no. 196. Economic Series, Institute for Mathematical Studies in the Social Sciences, Stanford University, Stanford, California.

Gilbert, R. J. 1976b. "Optimal Depletion of an Uncertain Stock," Technical Report no. 207. Economic Series, Institute for Mathematical Studies in the Social Sciences, Stanford University, Stanford, California.

Heal, G. 1976. "The Relationship Between Price and Extraction Cost for a Resource with a Backstop Technology," *Bell Journal of Economics* 7: 371-78.

Heal, G. 1978. "Resource Prices and Resource Scarcity." In *Proceedings of the Wisconsin Seminar on Natural Resource Policies in Relation to Economic Development and International Cooperation*, vol. 1. Madison: Institute for Environmental Studies, University of Wisconsin.

Hertzmark, D. I. 1978. "Economics, Thermodynamics, and the Allocation of Energy." Ph. D. thesis, University of Wisconsin-Madison.

Hotelling, Harold. 1931. "The Economics of Exhaustible Resources," *Journal of Political Economy* 39: 137-73.

Humphrey, David Burras, and J. R. Moroney. 1975. "Substitution Among Capital, Labor, and Natural Resource Products in American Manufacturing," *Journal of Political Economy* 83: 57-82.

Jevons, S. 1906. *The Coal Question.* New York: A. M. Kelley.

Kamien, N. I., and N. L. Schwartz. 1978. "Optimal Exhaustible Resource Depletion with Endogenous Technical Change," *Review of Economic Studies* 45: 179-96.

Kay, J., and J. Mirrlees. 1975. "The Desirability of Natural Resource Depletion." In J. Pearce, ed., *The Economics of Natural Resource Depletion.* New York: Wiley, pp. 140-76.

Kindleberger, Charles P. 1956. *The Terms of Trade: A European Case Study.* New York: Wiley.

Kindleberger, Charles P. 1964. "Terms of Trade for Primary Products." In Marion Clawson, ed., *Natural Resources and International Development.* Baltimore: Johns Hopkins University Press, pp. 339-65.

Mishan, E. 1971. "The Postwar Literature on Externalities: A Survey," *Journal of Economic Literature* 9: 1–28.

Nordhaus, W. 1973. "The Allocation of Energy Resources," *Brookings Papers on Economic Activity*, no. 3, 529–70.

Page, R. T. 1977. *Conservation and Economic Efficiency: An Approach to Materials Policy.* Baltimore: Johns Hopkins University Press.

Petersen, F. M. 1975. "Two Externalities in Petroleum Exploration." In G. M. Brannon, ed., *Studies in Energy Tax Policy.* Cambridge, Massachusetts: Ballinger, pp. 101–13.

Peterson, F., and A. Fisher. 1977. "The Exploitation of Extractive Resources: A Survey," *Economic Journal* 87: 681–721.

Pindyck, Robert S. 1978a. "Gains to Producers from the Cartelization of Exhaustible Resources," *Review of Economics and Statistics* 60: 238–51.

Pindyck, Robert S. 1978b. "The Optimal Exploration and Production of Nonrenewable Resources," *Journal of Political Economy* 86: 841–61.

Prebisch, Raul. 1950. *The Economic Development of Latin America and its Principal Problems.* New York: UN Department of Economic Affairs.

Rosenberg, N. 1973. "Innovative Responses to Materials Shortages." Papers and Proceedings of the 85th Annual Meeting of the American Economic Association, *American Economic Review* 63(2): 111–18.

Samuelson, Paul. 1939. "The Gains from International Trade," *Canadian Journal of Economics and Political Science* 5: 195–205.

Sen, A. K. 1972. "Control Areas and Accounting Prices: An Approach to Economic Evaluation," *Economic Journal* 82: 486–501.

Singer, Hans. 1950. "The Distribution of Gains Between Investing and Borrowing Countries." Papers and Proceedings of the 62nd Annual Meeting of the American Economic Association, *American Economic Review* 40(2): 473–85.

Smith, V. Kerry. 1978. "Measuring Natural Resource Scarcity: Theory and Practice." *Journal of Environmental Economics and Management* 5: 150–71.

Smith, V. K., and J. Krutilla. 1976. "The Economics of Natural Resource Scarcity." Forum on the Economics of Natural Resource Scarcity, Resources for the Future, Washington, D.C.

Solow, R. M. 1974a. "Intergenerational Equity and Exhaustible Resources." In *Symposium on the Economics of Exhaustible Resources, Review of Economic Studies* 42: 29–45.

Solow, R. M. 1974b. "The Economics of Resources or the Resources of Economics." Papers and Proceedings of the 86th Annual Meeting of the American Economic Association, *American Economic Review* 64(2): 1–14.

Solow, R. M., and F. Y. Wan. 1976. "Extraction Costs in the Theory of Exhaustible Resources," *Bell Journal of Economics* 7: 359–70.

Stiglitz, J. 1974. "Growth with Exhaustible Natural Resources: Efficient and Optimal Growth Paths." In *Symposium on the Economics of Exhaustible Resources, Review of Economic Studies* 42: 123–37.

Stiglitz, J. 1975. "The Efficiency of Market Prices in Long-Run Allocations in the Oil Industry." In G. M. Brannon, ed., *Studies in Energy Tax Policy.* Cambridge, Massachusetts: Ballinger, pp. 55–99.

Stiglitz, J. 1976. "A Neoclassical Analysis of the Economics of Natural Resources." Forum on the Economics of Natural Resource Scarcity, Resources for the Future, Washington, D.C.

Weinstein, M. C., and R. J. Zeckhauser. 1975. "The Optimal Consumption of Depletable Natural Resources," *Quarterly Journal of Economics* 89: 371-92.

Williamson, J. G. 1971. "Capital Accumulation, Labor Saving, and Labor Absorption Once More," *Quarterly Journal of Economics* 85: 40-65.

Williamson, J. G. 1976. "Private Domestic Savings in Korea: Can a Pessimistic Past be Reconciled with an Optimistic Plan?" Department of Economics, University of Wisconsin-Madison.

# 5 *Mahmoud A. El-Shafie and Raymond J. Penn*

# Market Imperfections, Market Structures, and Resource Pricing

Most resource commodities produced in the developing countries are exported to the industrial countries of Europe and North America and to Japan, the main consuming centers for mineral ores, fossil fuels, natural fibers, beverage crops, and other industrial raw materials moving in international trade. A relatively small share of the primary products of developing countries is destined for export to the centrally planned economies and a still smaller percentage is traded among the developing countries themselves.

Most commodity trade with centrally planned economies is carried out through bilateral negotiations between official agencies of each side. These bilateral arrangements are concluded through collective bargaining between buyers and sellers on prices, quantities, qualities, deliveries, payments, and other conditions involved in the exchange. Many of the resource commodities traded between developing and developed economies are exchanges in spot markets for immediate delivery or in stock exchanges for future delivery under laws, regulations, customs, and practices designed and applied by governments, business enterprises, and other human associations.

Whatever the political systems of trading partners, world markets for natural resource commodities are characterized by the dominance of man-made institutions and human actors with diverse interests and unequal economic powers that do affect supply availabilities, demand levels, and market performance in pricing resources and allocating them among various uses. Dominant institutions—nation-states, large corporations, producers' and consumers' associations, and others—all play decisive roles as owners, controllers, administrators, and/or users of natural resources, and all of them establish criteria for action based on private or limited interests not including social costs and benefits equitably shared among nations and peoples. The extent of their influence in domestic and international resource markets depends on the relative economic and political strength of participating agents and on the range of opportunities for manipulating resource supplies, market conditions, and product pricing.

The outcome, especially in terms of development of developing countries, is fluctuating resource prices and export earnings, deteriorating terms of trade, and nominal prices whose real purchasing power is decreasing—in short, a return for export of depletable resources insufficient to replace them in the future with productive assets needed in development.

## Market Imperfection and Market Structure

It should be remembered that "market," in this chapter, should nearly always be read to mean conditions in the marketplace. Traditional market theory does not recognize property rights, but in the marketplace it is those rights which are really exchanged. Economic resources, whether privately or publicly owned, command a price not only because they have utility but also because they are scarce and can be held by owners for their own use or withheld from others until a price is agreed upon by willing buyers and sellers through a process of bargaining and negotiation in the absence of oppression, confiscation, or exploitation and on a basis of equality, liberty, and the protection of law. Ownership is always a present right to a future use or sale of materials as well as intangible property. Evaluation in the bargaining process looks to future expectations of income, power, and utility, all of which are affected by rights of ownership and control.

Central problems and heated issues of international trade in resource commodities find expression in the persistent instability in world markets —the wide fluctuations of raw material prices from one moment to the next and the ensuing swings of export earnings in resource-producing countries, especially developing countries. The problems brought by instability are aggravated by periodic declines in the purchasing power of foreign exchange receipts from developing country exports as inflationary pressures in western economies and the sporadic disturbances in currency exchange rates drive down that purchasing power.

Spot markets for a wide variety of nonperishable agricultural commodities and for certain minerals have been created mainly in industrial western economies to provide immediate price quotations for offerings and deliveries based on supply-demand conditions and established specifications of products. Parallel futures markets also operate for some commodities to provide information, however imperfect, on future availabilities, future deliveries, and future prices—advice of a sort in making decisions about production and marketing and in reducing risk and uncertainty. Futures markets have not, however, been established for important mining products such as crude petroleum, bauxite, iron ores, and other ores or concentrates. Supply and marketing of these commodities have typically been controlled by a few big producers while consumption demand has been more widely dispersed. Long-term futures markets, if they did exist, would presumably provide producers as well as buyers with alternative opportunities for selecting and switching reciprocal partners and would damp the rigid, nonreciprocal imperfections resulting from monopolistic and oligopsonistic practices of a relatively few and powerful agents which can manipulate supply sources and demand levels.

High degrees of market instability are exemplified by the price fluctuations for copper, lead, tungsten, zinc, and phosphate (see, for instance, World Bank 1978, p. 20). Short-lived rises in prices of these metals stimulate larger production which in turn depresses market prices. The prices of some other metals may be fixed by a dominant producer or group of producers, in the cases of aluminum and nickel, or regulated by a market agreement, in the case of tin. For some minerals, producing nations can effectively set prices or taxes, as for OPEC oil and Moroccan phosphate.

Third World commodity trade amounts to only one-fifth of total world trade in commodities and, excluding petroleum, twelve of these commodities account for 80 percent of the export earnings of Third World countries. It has been estimated (Tinbergen 1976, p. 34) that final consumers in industrial countries pay over $200 billion for these commodities and the products derived directly from them while exporting nations receive only $30 billion, or about 15 percent of the consumers' costs because the vast share of raw material processing is done outside the producing/exporting nations.

Samuels (1977) noted the nature of imperfection in the market: "Institutions, such as the market, are not neutral" but the "market is formed by and gives effect to the institutions (power structure) which operate through it." Samuels contends that " 'efficiency' is a function of power

and the valuational process (governing whose interests count) which operates through the power structure. . . . The specification of the rights and
interests which are to count is a function of institutions, power structure
and power play." Efficiency criteria, in other words, pertain to some presumption as to whose interests (or rights) do count, and such criteria thus
require a specification of rights and interests in effect within a specific
power structure, that is, specific institutions.

Boulding (1977) notes that "the concept of the market can be generalized to that of the opportunities open for selecting and switching reciprocity partners." He adds that "imperfection in the market is related to the
lack of alternative reciprocity partners, up to the point of monopoly
where only one partner is possible. Imperfections may arise out of ignorance of alternatives or out of diversity of reciprocity offerings," or from
the unevenness of alternative opportunities open to the sellers and buyers.
Boulding also points out that the relative price structure "is an important
element in determining the structure of overall terms of reciprocity which
are a function of the 'terms of trade', that is, the ratio of the quantities of
economic goods given up to economic goods received. And this, of
course, is a direct function of the relative price structure."

Boulding (1977) furthermore recognizes that the equilibrium model
based on the competitive structure of relative prices does not sufficiently
anticipate future resource scarcity. Recent alarms about future scarcities
of depletable mineral and energy resources have been both unnecessarily
exaggerated and unjustifiably ridiculed. There is, nevertheless, a growing
consciousness of possible future scarcities which may, says Boulding,
warrant raising relative prices now to economize on current rates of exploitation and cut down wastage in present use. The world surely faces a
long-term trend of highly noticeable increases in relative prices of many
raw materials as the easily available sources are exhausted and as deeper
mines, deeper wells, Arctic, offshore, seabed, and other high cost alternatives become necessary. The competitive market mechanism does not adequately anticipate and incorporate changes of this sort, especially those
that are fairly far in the future (Boulding 1977).

### Transnational Corporations

Transnational corporations need special attention when considering resource market imperfection and pricing. By definition they are large and
can acquire the assets necessary for exploration, production, transport,
processing, and/or marketing of most natural resources. They operate in
more than one nation, and their allocations and resource pricing within
any one nation can be made in the ways that yield the most profit for the
company's entire operations. Some, such as major oil companies, are

horizontally and/or vertically integrated within a single industry; others have a horizontal dimension in the sense of diversification across industries. Some control the patents and knowledge to build the intricate facilities needed to exploit natural resources. Transnationals control and operate international communications systems and the world movement of cereal food products.

It is easy to oversimplify the image of transnationals, to begin to suppose that each company is equally powerful and quite single-minded in pursuit of uncomplicated interests. Each one is, in fact, unique in kind and degree of multinational operations and in the way it perceives its interests. Nevertheless, it seems clearly necessary to consider the role of transnationals—and the people in them—in the development of natural resources. It is necessary to understand, in a general way, how they make their resource allocations and determine their prices; their interests in improving the corporation and increasing profit may not always correspond to a nation's development interests.

Transnational corporations have often held an economic and market power that allows them to separate prices paid for primary output from those charged for selling final products to ultimate users or consumers. Low prices set by these giant enterprises at the production end where resources are grown or extracted have been used to determine royalties and rental payments to the governments of developing countries as well as to calculate income taxes. Transference or accounting prices at various points in the downstream operations controlled and integrated by corporations are then set to realize maximum profits for these "forward" activities in transport, processing, manufacturing, and marketing. This kind of integration and pricing persists among transnationals and their affiliated enterprises in a variety of hard minerals and a number of tropical products including coffee, tea, cocoa, and natural rubber. Of more than 600 transnationals having their headquarters in North America, Western Europe, or Japan, the largest 300 U.S. enterprises and their foreign subsidiaries alone account for 28 percent of total world exports, including 47 percent of exports of primary products and 20 percent of exports of manufactured goods; it has been estimated that without change in present trends, transnational enterprises could control more than 40 percent of world production (outside the centrally planned nations) before the end of the 1980s (Tinbergen 1976, p. 39).

The market has not been a satisfactory mechanism for resource pricing when it is observed that the price of grain increased by nearly 250 percent in one year, following a 3 percent decline in world grain production in 1973–74. The price of sugar, for another example, quadrupled during 1974–75 in spite of a rise in world output of 4.7 percent over 1973 output.

One transnational corporation marketing and processing cocoa managed to corner the world market and raise the price to consumers multifold in 1974–75. The international market in nickel had been dominated for several decades, until the end of the 1950s, by a single transnational company which supplied over 80 percent of the nickel requirements of western countries; its published price was long recognized as *the* representative price of the metal (its market share has since been reduced to 35 percent and its monopoly price undercut by competitive processors or producers in the United States, Australia, and elsewhere [IMF 1978a]).

Seven giant corporations pumping and marketing crude oil managed to keep prices paid to Middle Eastern producing countries at less than one dollar per barrel for nearly two decades between 1952 and 1971 until OPEC took unilateral control of the price of crude oil in 1973. Concerted action by the major producers of staple foods for export, coupled with crop failures in many developing countries in 1972–73 and the depletion of reserve stocks of food in 1972, set the stage for powerful actors to raise the world market prices for grains, sugar, coffee, and soybeans in 1974 to a level some three to four times higher than in 1970 (Tinbergen 1976, p. 13).

Transnational corporations have the economic and political power to confront and bargain with raw material producing and exporting countries. Through vertical integration—ownership or control of downstream operations from shipping through processing and manufacturing to selling to final consumers—and sometimes through horizontal integration as well, transnationals maintain their power. They are often aided by powerful financing institutions in their parent countries and sometimes have the economic as well as political backing of their home governments. In some respects large banks are also transnationals. They mobilize—at their own discretion—funds for other transnationals which control production, marketing, processing, and consumption of resource products. Producing nations have little access to world markets except through giant transnational enterprises, brokerage houses, and organized trade dealers in the few international commodity exchanges located mainly in industrial countries. "Independent" brokers and dealers may well represent business firms which exert powerful influence in determining prices of important resource products worldwide.

Nominal prices of resource commodities may reflect their real values to corporations but not necessarily to developing countries that are more interested in the exchange values of these resources in terms of other goods and services needed for domestic consumption and national economic development. Real prices for resources in terms of what they can buy back in other resources or products, rather than stability of nominal (money) prices, is a central issue in resource pricing for developing country exporters of agricultural and mineral raw materials. According to the United Nations the terms of trade for primary products exported from developing countries (versus commodity imports from industrial countries) declined by more than 10 percent between 1950 and 1960 with a further deterioration of nearly 8 percent between 1961 and 1970. (UNDESA 1962; UNDESA 1968; UNDESA 1972; see also World Bank 1978, p. 10).

## Trade Agreements

International trade in many metal ores and certain agricultural commodities has shown regional flows between major exporting and nearby importing countries. For example, exports of iron ore from Venezuela and Canada cover the deficit in U.S. domestic output while Sweden is the major exporter to Western Europe. Bauxite imports into Western Europe come from other European countries including Yugoslavia, Hungary, and Greece, while the United States and Canada import most of their bauxite from Caribbean and West African countries as well as Australia. Japan meets its import needs for iron ore and bauxite from Australia and other nearby sources in Southeast Asia. The USSR is the main supplier of petroleum and a wide range of minerals to other Eastern European members of the Council of Mutual Economic Assistance (CMEA). Canada, the United States, Australia, and New Zealand tend to divide the market for wheat exports on a regional basis. A sizable portion of the sugar moving in world trade is administered by a number of regional and bilateral agreements (and an international sugar agreement) which regulate its imports and exports between member countries.

Prices are commonly a central bargaining issue in trade transactions, and price agreements between trading partners usually determine the benefits accruing to the partners. However, the ownership structure in some integrated mining industries and the artificial nature of some price quotations, whether accounting and transference prices or posted prices by the more powerful among the partners, suggest that prices can tip the scale of benefits in favor of those with bargaining strength. Relative bargaining powers under concessionary arrangements between companies and governments, for instance, will influence the fiscal conditions on which investors are permitted to exploit resources.

The pricing mechanism for mineral resources fails to account for the full economic costs of resource extraction and depletion. Rent, royalties, or the purchase of land may demonstrate the use-value of a site for farm production, building construction, or recreational purposes as long as the indestructable quality of land itself remains intact. But in mining this quality is destroyed by ore extraction and depletion of a deposit which may thus be gotten free of charge unless an appropriate cost of replacement is paid. Whenever the cost of replacement is not paid, distortions will inevitably be carried through as underpricing of the raw materials payment per unit of output to resource owners and as underpricing for end-uses to consumers. As Breimyer (1978) observed, many contemporary economists have not been in the habit of allowing for differential rent payment for better oil fields or low cost mines over and above marginal oil fields or mineral deposits. They have not addressed the problem of a reservation price on crude oil, coal, or mineral ores, nor have they calculated the anticipated price effect of progressive exhaustion of a stock material when successive depletions result in higher extraction costs and yield progressively smaller physical output and declining returns to resource owners. He suggests that these economists may have to recognize, in the pricing of extractive products, an implicit temporal reservation price to which is added any monopolization element plus the rent some suppliers get by virtue of locational advantages and relative superiority in the quality of minerals in their possession.

Trade policies of governments in major resource exporting and importing countries, more so than competitive market forces, have shaped international trade in primary commodities and commodity pricing. Between the end of World War II and the mid-1960s, bilateral agreements dominated international resource trade. Multilateral bargaining and international commodity agreements were confined to a few commodities—wheat (since 1949), sugar (since 1937), tin (since 1953), and coffee (since 1963)—for which stablization of supply and prices was paramount in both importing and exporting countries.

Multilateral trade negotiations in the 1960s did reduce import tariffs among developed Western countries by nearly one-half and did set in motion other trade liberalization among European and North American nations. However, developed nation imports from the developing countries continued to suffer trade obstacles including quantitative or qualitative restrictions and high tariffs imposed to isolate industrial countries' domestic agricultural and manufacturing sectors from international competition. Furthermore, the General Agreement on Tariffs and Trade (GATT) had favored the promotion of trade among advanced countries and failed to safeguard the interests of developing countries in bilateral trade negotiations between the two counterparts. The principle of reciprocity in trade negotiation and the "most favored nation" principle are two elements in GATT that serve the interests of major partners whose strong bargaining position is further strengthened by a prevailing international division of labor historically established on the basis of nonreciprocity and dependence rather than reciprocity and interdependence (Tinbergen 1976, p. 237).

## Commodity Agreements

A few international commodity agreements concluded between the late 1960s and the mid-1970s were largely designed to prevent excessive short-term price fluctuations of individual commodities. They established zones within which prices could fluctuate and relied on export quotas and buffer stocks to regulate the flow of commodities between member countries. A system of information exchange was usually incorporated to provide producing and consuming countries with an early warning device about production shortfalls, anticipated oversupplies, and changes in demand. Such agreements, however, did not tackle exporting countries' lack of access to world markets nor address importing countries' problem of securing adequate supplies. These agreements confined themselves to price stabilization within a predetermined zone of price variability; they gave little or no attention to improving the marketing and distribution system or to effecting closer cooperation among raw material producers to counterbalance oligopolistic purchasing practices of transnational corporations in particular commodity markets (IMF 1977b).

Agreements to stabilize prices are not, except by specific quota, agreements to higher prices, let alone increasing prices. Commodity price stabilizations, as desirable as they may be, will not automatically better the income positions of developing countries. Even with stable *and* higher prices for primary products, the developing countries will still face the difficult fundamental task of turning income from trade to investment in development—investment in knowledge, organization, technology, and capital. One would expect, however, that exporting and importing countries which join a price stabilization agreement will adhere to its provisions on price ceiling and floor as well as quotas. The lack of well-defined measures to enforce such provisions has often led to collapse of agreements under pressure of supply shortages, sudden price rises, or lack of stockpiling arrangements to equate supply and demand within a stipulated price range.

The first International Wheat Agreement ratified in 1949, for example, specified that consuming and producing countries agreed to carry out a given percentage of the trade at prices within the target zone, but the current agreement (renewed in June 1974) has no provisions for establishing a price range or for regulating supplies and thus has no direct effect on world trade in wheat (IMF 1977c).

Two International Coffee Agreements were ratified for the periods 1963–68 and 1968–72, but the latter fell apart with a fundamentally changed supply position in Brazil and steeply rising prices. A third Agreement of October 1976 introduced a system of export quotas; quotas could be suspended in the case of continued price increases. Greater emphasis was put on prompt reporting of production shortfalls by exporting countries and the efficient assumption of those shortfalls by surplus producers, in addition to the abolition of procedures to establish long-term output goals to avoid overproduction. Some provisions of the 1968 agreement were retained, including sanctions against exports in excess of quotas, limits on imports from nonmember countries, and the possibility of introducing a stockpiling policy.

The first International Cocoa Agreement of 1973–76 was followed by a second agreement for 1976–79. Both relied on a joint system of export quotas and on a buffer stock to be financed by a levy on cocoa trade. However, the price stabilization mechanism has yet to be applied even though (i.e., because) market prices have remained substantially above the specified price ceiling. All major exporters of cocoa and most importers (except the United States, which is the leading importer) have been members of the two agreements.

An international tea agreement has been discussed by FAO, UNCTAD, and the producing countries of which India, Sri Lanka, China, and Kenya are the world's major exporters; the United Kingdom and the United States are the world's leading importers. UNCTAD considers tea one of its ten "core" commodities to be covered by "common fund" price support agreements and one of the most depressed agricultural commodities in international trade. However, it is unlikely that an agreement will materialize until the leading importers of tea, especially the United States and United Kingdom, show interest in joining with leading exporters to ratify such an agreement.

UNCTAD has recently explored with developing country exporters of iron ore and copper the possibility of commodity agreements similar to the long-standing International Tin Agreement, renewed for the fifth time in 1976. However, difficulties for any copper agreement include the lack of consensus among exporting and importing countries about any international buffer stock or even about an international copper council to serve as a forum for collecting and exchanging information on copper (IMF 1978a). Iron ore's heterogeneity provides obstacles to establishing price ranges, export quotas, or buffer stocks.

International trade in sugar since 1937 has come under partial control of several agreements among exporting and importing countries. Before 1978 nearly half of the world's sugar was traded under the International Sugar Agreement of 1968; the Commonwealth Sugar Agreement of the Lomé Convention between the European Economic Community and a group of West African, Caribbean, and Pacific countries; and Cuba's sugar contract with the USSR and other CMEA countries. Price fluctuations were very wide in sugar exports not traded under these agreements: in 1968 the price was 1.4 cents per pound, in 1974 it reached 56.6 cents per pound, but in October 1977 it was back to 7.1 cents per pound. The recent International Sugar Agreement, worked out with the assistance of UNCTAD, stipulates export quotas, national buffer stocks, and a per pound price zone between an 11-cent floor and a 21-cent ceiling. Stockpiling under the agreement is to be financed by a fund to which exporters and importers pay a processing tax of one-fourth to one-third cent per pound, and to which the IMF Buffer Stock Facility makes loans available in amounts not exceeding 50 percent of the country's currency quota with the IMF (Penn 1978).

Since the first session of UNCTAD in Geneva in 1964, the developing countries have continued to insist that the stabilization of commodity markets ought to be approached on a multiproduct basis, not commodity by commodity. The multiproduct approach was recommended by the UN General Assembly in Resolution 3202 (S-VI) of May 1974 which called for "an overall integrated plan for ensuring just and stable markets for a comprehensive range of commodities of export interest to developing countries." The UNCTAD Secretariat in 1974 and 1975 defined the principal objectives and techniques of such an Integrated Program of Commodities and proposed implementation measures for discussion by the Trade and Development Board and the UNCTAD Committee on Commodities. An Integrated Program would create a "Common Fund" to finance a network of internationally held commodity stocks, a system of multilateral purchase and supply commitments in commodity trade, an improved compensatory financing facility for export shortfalls, and a scheme of international assistance for export diversification. It would also set up a comprehensive network of individual commodity agreements which would rely on international buffer stock mechanisms to stabilize commodity prices with support from supply-management measures in order to maintain a reasonable relationship between the prices of commodities and the prices of the products exchanged for them in international trade (El-Naggar 1978).

## Producers' Associations

Other organizational arrangements for cooperation among countries exporting certain minerals or agricultural products have been established in recent years, but their respective roles and bargaining strengths differ. The Intergovernmental Council for Copper Exporting Countries (CIPEC) was created in 1967 by Chile, Peru, Zaire, and Zambia. Indonesia in 1975 and Mauritania in 1976 joined as full members; Australia and Papua New Guinea have become associate members. Member countries account for nearly 45 percent of world copper exports, if the centrally planned economies are excluded, but CIPEC has not been able thus far to take advantage of its relatively prominent supply position and influence market price because most members depend heavily on copper exports for foreign exchange earnings. Other important exporters of copper—Canada, Poland, Mexico, Uganda, and Iran—are not CIPEC members or supporters. Furthermore, CIPEC producers continue to accept London Metal Exchange prices as a basis for negotiation with copper buyers while neglecting to coordinate their production and marketing activities and so reducing CIPEC effectiveness as a market power.

The International Bauxite Association (IBA) includes Jamaica, Haiti, Surinam, the Dominican Republic, Guyana, Ghana, Sierra Leone, Guinea, Yugoslavia, and Australia, which together account for more than 80 percent of bauxite production (again excluding the centrally planned economies). IBA has enhanced the bargaining position of its members in extracting higher taxes and resource rents from the transnational companies involved in bauxite production and downstream operations in the aluminum industry. The boost in producer revenues seems to have been practically possible because bauxite costs amount to only 3–5 percent of fabricated aluminum rod or sheet prices. Manufacturing companies can easily pass an increase in ore prices to the consumer of the fabricated products (World Bank 1974).

The association of Iron Ore Exporting Countries was formed in 1975 with 11 members—Australia, Algeria, Chile, India, Liberia, Mauritania, Peru, Sierra Leone, Sweden, Tunisia, and Venezuela—whose total exports account for 75 percent of world exports (once more excluding the centrally planned economies). The association's declared objectives include the orderly and healthy growth of export trade; fair and remunerative returns from iron ore exploitation, processing, and marketing; and the promotion of close cooperation among member countries for economic and social development. Because the price of iron ore accounts for about 10 percent of iron ingot prices, a moderate rise in the price of ore could be easily absorbed in the price of steel or cast iron (UNCTAD 1976).

The now familiar Organization of the Petroleum Exporting Countries (OPEC) was formed in 1960 to enhance the bargaining position of developing country crude oil exporters vis-à-vis the transnational enterprises, which until 1971 controlled not only marketing but also production of oil in OPEC nations. For a decade OPEC had little influence on oil prices.

Whenever the world market for a given resource is regulated by an international commodity agreement—as for tin, wheat, sugar, coffee, and cocoa—an international commodity council is formed to administer the agreement among its members. Tin-producing and tin-consuming countries, for example, are equally represented on the International Tin Council which fixes the scale of prices, manages the buffer stock, regulates tin flow into the market, and reviews the scale of prices periodically.

The tin agreement and its periodic price reviews have been successful in imparting, along a rising trend, a price "stability" satisfactory to both exporters and importers; price floors and ceilings have held. In constant-value dollars, London tin prices have risen by an average of 2.6 percent per year during 1950–75 versus 1.6 percent for all metal and other ores (Tinbergen 1976, p. 256). The average deviation of annual tin prices from the five-year moving average for 1955–76—long- rather than short-term fluctuation—has been only 5–10 percent, below the average deviations of 10–15 percent for lead and phosphate rock and well below the 15 + percent for copper and zinc (World Bank 1978, p. 20). Other international commodity councils, however, have been less effective in stabilizing markets and prices in the short term or along a long-term upward trend.

### Stockpiling and Domestic Protection

Policies of national governments in major resource exporting and importing countries have exercised great influence on market conditions, price behaviors, and direction of trade. Industrial countries such as the United States, Japan, the Federal Republic of Germany, and others have instituted stockpiling programs for strategic raw materials. Open market purchases and sales to replenish or diminish stockpiles have also been used to stabilize market supplies and prices for domestic consumption or for export. National governments in growing numbers actively engage in devising scarcity-induced controls on resource use rates to conserve or preserve resources or to establish terms of concession for exploitation. Expanding public intervention is also seen in quantitative or qualitative controls over exports and imports of commodities under marketing boards, state trading agencies, buffer stock facilities, import-export licenses, quotas, and even nationalization of supply sources previously held by private companies. From the early 1960s to the mid-1970s, state-owned mining capacity in developing market economies rose from nearly nil to nearly 35 percent for copper and to about 45 percent for tin; it proceeded, however, at a much slower rate in other minerals (Labys 1978).

Governments in the four major wheat-exporting countries have acquired relatively large stocks as a result of their domestic price support programs and have taken measures to regulate wheat exports to deficit countries. Meanwhile, importing governments in Europe and Japan have tried to insulate their domestic markets from the world market to hold domestic prices constant. Such insulating trade policy often involves decreasing the protection for domestic producers when the world price rises and raising protective tariffs when the world price falls (Grennes et al. 1978). Sizable portions of surplus production are exported under concessional terms or direct government-to-government contracts, amounting to one-third of international trade in rice (Timmer and Falcon 1975) and to even higher portions in wheat, sugar, and some tropical products.

Producers of farm commodities are often protected by their national governments against high degrees of uncertainty and numerous risks which cannot be averted without government intervention. Governments in many developing and industrial countries have adopted complicated systems of public action in granting production subsidies, creating stockpiles, regulating stock flows to the markets, and setting administered prices for domestic output and sometimes exports too. Government intervention is often intended to stabilize production and the income from it, to reduce frequent irregularities in demand-supply situations, or to provide some security of expectations to domestic producers of strategic commodities intended for home or foreign markets.

### Substitution and Resource Pricing

Because world demand for primary commodities is generally inelastic, attempts by the developing countries to expand production for export tend to put intense downward pressure on export prices. Moreover, any persistent curtailment of production to raise prices and export earnings in the short run tends to stimulate the development of close substitutes or to shift demand to other more accessible products. Output cuts can actually bring declines in prices and earnings from a resource threatened by substitution.

Although simple concepts of substitution rates and price elasticities of substitution are in use among economists and technologists, no comprehensive theory of substitution has been worked out to explain how replacement of one resource input or product for another takes place or how close substitutes are priced under costly technological adaptation, with time lags, to produce a cheaper substitute for a resource in any or all end-uses. Economists usually take the price of the substitute as given and overlook the fact that the product to be replaced in theory may be controlled in practice by powerful producers who can hold its price below the price of a substitute. Economists may also forget that quality differentials can outweigh price differentials for buyers.

A certain degree of complementarity often exists in the consumption of primary products and their substitutes. World consumption is rising for both natural and synthetic rubbers, but because output of natural rubber has lagged behind demand, the output of synthetic rubber has expanded at a faster pace to fill the gap. Although the two products are partial substitutes for one another in specific uses, they appear to complement each other in the totality of uses. Natural fibers and synthetic fibers, as inputs in textile manufacturing, seem to be a similar case. Production and consumption of man-made fibers increased at annual rates of 10 percent between the 1930s and the mid-1950s, 8 percent from the late 1950s until 1974, and lower percentages since then. Cotton consumption increased 2 percent per annum on the average during 1960–73, 2.7 percent in 1974, and nearly 4 percent in 1975 (IMF 1977a). Consumption of other natural fibers including wool, flax, and silk has been more or less stationary in absolute terms, but their shares as a percentage of the consumption of all fibers (synthetic and natural combined) have declined.

World production of cotton fluctuated in the 1960s and 1970s but displayed on the average a rising trend. Cotton exports of 3.6 to 3.9 million tons per year in the early 1960s grew to a record volume of 4.6 million tons in 1972–73. World output of man-made fibers also increased, but more steadily and rapidly, from about 5.5 million tons per year in the early 1960s to 10.9 million tons by 1973. Output did slow thereafter because of rising costs of petrochemicals—the basic input for production of noncellulosic fibers including polyester, nylon, acrylics, and modacrylics. The 30-year expansion in output of cellulosic fibers such as rayon and acetate came to a standstill in the 1960s with rising costs of wood pulp and competition from noncellulosic fibers. Displacement of cotton by polyester and other petrochemical fibers in textile production had been partly induced by the sustained decline in the prices of man-made fibers between the 1950s and the early 1970s as real prices of petroleum edged downward, especially in comparison to cotton prices, which were creeping upward. Consumer fashions and the superior qualities of natural cotton and wool have lately been effective in protecting the demand for both in mill consumption, especially in developing countries where production of textiles from cotton continues to rise (IMF 1977a). Production of natural rubber is concentrated in four developing countries—Malaysia, Indonesia, Thailand, and Sri Lanka—which yielded in 1971–75 about 85 percent of world exports. The industrial countries, of course, produce the bulk of world output of synthetic rubber from petrochemicals. By 1974 the total apparent consumption of rubber amounted to 7.45 million tons of which 4.76 million, nearly 64 percent, were synthetic (UN 1977, pp. 145, 181, 273). The wholesale price of natural rubber in Malaysia, the world's biggest producer, was nearly the same in 1960 and 1974, at 34.8 cents per pound, but substantially below that figure in many intervening years. At that same time, nevertheless, production of synthetic rubber was steadily increasing to meet rising demand in the industrial countries. Between

1966 and 1973, synthetic output increased by 76 percent while that of natural rubber increased by 46 percent. The increase in consumption of natural rubber—13 percent between 1970 and 1973—compares to a 27 percent increase for synthetic rubber. Complementarity of the two products has been more apparent than substitutability. This trend is likely to continue, even though the price of petrochemicals increased more than fivefold between 1973 and 1977 when the price of natural rubber increased only 30 percent (IMF 1978b).

The output of plastics from petrochemicals grew about 15 percent annually between 1952 and 1973, from 2.5 million tons to 41.1 million tons. This trend is expected to continue in the coming decade as plastics substitute for paper, wood, cardboard, and other crating or packaging materials and for wood, glass, cement, and certain metals in building construction, furnitures, fixtures, machinery, transport equipment, household appliances, etc. Little information is available on the price of plastics in the above uses. It would be very interesting to learn the effect of the steep rise in petroleum and gas prices on production costs and selling prices for plastics and such other petrochemical-based products as fertilizers and synthetic fibers. The possible effects on future rates of substitution deserve to be thoroughly investigated.

Among minerals—aluminum and copper, for instance—different rates of substitution have taken place in specific uses. The rates and ranges of substitution differ from metal to metal, as between aluminum and copper versus steel and other metals versus tin and its few substitutes. Producers of certain metals (e.g., copper) may refrain from attempting to raise prices for fear of drastic shifts of demand in favor of substitutes (e.g., aluminum), but such efforts to forestall substitution cannot necessarily be confined to a few metals or a few uses.

Oil, gas, and coal are substitutes as sources of fuel for generation of electric power but not as inputs in the wide spectrum of petrochemical industries, the products of which represent higher-valued uses. Changes in the relative prices of substitutes have impact on the intermediate demand for resource commodities and resource pricing while price differentials continue to prevail, but lead time is usually needed to change input mixes and to create new productive installations. Adequate lead time is often necessary to persuade final users of the relative advantage in shifting consumption from a long established resource to a newly introduced one.

The complicated process of creating, adopting, and effectively replacing one resource with another is a long-term one. High prices for a resource tend to guide its allocation into high priority uses and high-valued consumption as low cost substitutes become available for low-valued uses. Keeping prices of stock resources at low levels is conducive to waste of scarce resources in low-valued uses and to imbalanced rates of depletion between valuable resources such as petroleum and more abundant materials such as coal. The continuing search for new sources of energy to replace oil and gas as fuels for generating heat or electricity does not conflict with the medium and longer interests of both developed and developing countries in confining oil and gas to higher-valued uses and thus prolonging their utility for the welfare of present and future generations.

## Resource Pricing

Primary producers have been rightfully concerned about real prices for commodities they sell to industrial countries versus goods and services they buy from those same countries. Real exchange values are more important than the nominal prices for which purchasing power has periodically deteriorated because of instabilities of the international currencies used as media of exchange. Even the short-lived boom periods in prices of primary commodities—the Korean War years or the 1973–74 upsurge in prices of certain commodities—have been characterized by feverish speculative movements in internationally traded commodities and inflationary price rises that reached exorbitant rates during the 1970s. Unit value of exports of developing countries divided by unit value of their imports has shown a long-term downtrend since the early 1950s. This indication of the unfavorable terms of trade for these countries, which depend on export earnings to finance economic development, emphasized the significance of the divergence between exchange values (or real prices) and nominal (money) prices.

Large industrial countries such as the United States and the USSR enjoy economic powers as well as political influence by which they are able to separate prices paid for domestic output of resources from prices they pay to international suppliers of identical commodities and from prices they charge for exports of such resources to the rest of the world. Increased output of depletable stock resources in developing countries cannot be expected to continue indefinitely without higher export prices that adequately compensate resource owners for the loss of the original resource through accelerated depletion—that is, adequate replacement of the extracted resources by other income-generating productive assets. Such replacement will not materialize without deliberate efforts on the part of developing countries to expand their national productive capacities through industrialization and diversification of domestic output on available resource bases. These efforts, however, have been hampered by the relatively low level of earnings from export prices which include no allowances for depreciation, depletion, or obsolescence of the finite resources being extracted. Pricing of manufactured products exported from industrial countries, by contrast, does allow for depreciation, depletion, and obsolescence based on costs of production or reproduction.

The emerging producers' and exporters' associations among developing countries make it reasonable to expect that strengthened bargaining positions and collective action will be geared to attaining higher exchange values for primary exports. These countries are economically justified in asking for higher export prices which incorporate resource depletion allowances and in seeking an equitable share of the contribution of primary resource inputs to high-value uses, rather than low-value uses, on the basis of opportunity cost concepts. Of course, the opportunity cost in pricing finite resources would relate the price of their outputs to the cost of substitutes, which in most cases would be substantially more expensive than finite stock resources now are (El-Shafie 1978).

Problems of market imperfection are not purely technical or economic in nature and origin. They can be traced to socio-political and institutional considerations, all of which affect resource management decisions on the supply side and influence product flows and pricing on the demand side. Resource allocation cannot be left entirely to uncorrected market mechanisms and to the profit-oriented rationales of private interests which heavily discount future values in favor of present consumption and short-run gains at the cost of long-term security and the legitimate interests of future generations. The capitalization and discounting principles appropriate in evaluating man-made capital assets cannot be regarded as suitable in the valuation and pricing of stock natural resources, which have social values over and above their utility values to present generations or to the individual. Unlike man-made capital assets, stock natural resources when exhausted through use cannot be renewed or reproduced at any cost or price. The foregone benefits to society in resource depletion cannot be calculated by commercial rates of discount which omit the preferences and value systems of future generations facing scarcities of stock resources because of present consumption patterns.

Trade and pricing policies for natural resources are greatly complicated by distributional questions in real political economies where resource exploitation and distribution of value added cannot be isolated from the production/pricing process in which property rights, industrial concentration, market power, and other institutional controls are prominent. Developing countries, dependent on a narrow resource base for generating national production, employment opportunities, and higher incomes, want fair access to export markets in advanced countries and equitable pricing for the products they must export in exchange for imported industrial goods, production technologies, and food supplies. "Fairness" is an aspect of distribution accepted and more or less practiced within industrial countries but neglected or institutionally nonexistent in the international trade between countries. Resource-based developing countries have been squeezed between the low-employment content of the extractive mining sector, the low productivity of congested labor in the agricultural sector, and the meagerness of technological resources for manufacturing development (except at exorbitant costs, not all of which are monetary).

Dealers and buyers in international markets exercise greater influence on the determination of primary commodity prices when domestic demand for those commodities is weak and the bulk of output is destined for export. In spite of their comparative advantage in natural resource availabilities, developing countries find it very difficult to counter that influence by establishing resource-based industries at home. The development of such industries depends on technologies, skills, and markets which are largely controlled by industrial countries or transnational corporations.

The world is a big place in which to make improvements in market allocation of natural resources, but there is much more room than is often recognized for mutual action in relocating manufacturing industries in developing countries. Joint ventures with industrial countries or with transnational corporations interested in continued resource and product flows at reasonable prices are particularly attractive whenever existing capacity in advanced countries must shoulder social externalities, the costs of avoiding environmental hazards, and rising labor expenses in addition to the mounting costs of raw material imports. Transnational enterprises can play a major role in helping to relocate resource-based industries. In joint enterprise arrangements these corporations can provide technological, managerial, and financial requisites while developing countries can provide stable supplies of raw materials and sizable labor pools at reasonable costs, subject to the sharing of accrued gains from industrial relocation on an equitable basis.

The interests of resource consuming countries and those of producing countries could be mutually served also if public policies in both groups of nations were to attend to principles of public cost and public benefit in the allocation and pricing of resources. It is reasonable to expect that public policies at national, regional, or international levels should aim at a drastic shift in resource consumption from lower-valued uses to higher-valued uses, whether finite resources come from domestic sources or imports. Such policies also need to be oriented toward allocation of resources in production of useful goods and services on the basis of maximization of benefits (output, value-added, and profits) and minimization of inputs of finite resources (in quantity and real value). These policies, furthermore, need to guide the valuation of finite resources and resource units

168 NATURAL RESOURCES

(or price) on the basis of opportunity costs in higher-valued uses and/or replacement; both cost measures would approach the social cost of such resources to their producers and consumers. Nation-states, rich and poor, can face up to the existing limits on growth of production and consumption to stock resources by mutual cooperation for mutual benefit. Nations must share the cost of resource depletion through use and must divide the accrued benefits from use on an equitable basis.

## References

Breimyer, H. F. 1978. "Agriculture's Three Economies in a Changing Resource Environment," *American Journal of Agricultural Economics* 60: 37–47.

Boulding, K. E. 1977. "Prices and Other Institutions," *Journal of Economic Issues* 11: 809–21.

El-Naggar, S. 1978. "Natural Resources, Economic Development, and the New International Economic Order." In *Proceedings of the Wisconsin Seminar on Natural Resource Policies in Relation to Economic Development and International Cooperation*, vol. 1. Madison: Institute for Environmental Studies, University of Wisconsin.

El-Shafie, M. A. 1978. "Inadequacies of the Price System in Allocating Depletable Resources." In *Proceedings of the Wisconsin Seminar on Natural Resource Policies in Relation to Economic Development and International Cooperation*, vol. 2. Madison: Institute for Environmental Studies, University of Wisconsin.

Grennes, T., P. R. Johnson, and M. Thursby. 1978. "Insulating Trade Policies, Inventories, and Wheat Price Stability," *American Journal of Agricultural Economics* 60: 132–34.

IMF (International Monetary Fund). 1977a. "Cotton Prices Show Upward Trend as Market Becomes More Volatile," *IMF Survey* 6: 72–74.

IMF (International Monetary Fund). 1977b. "Focus Returns to UNCTAD as CIEC Agrees in Principle to Establish a Common Fund," *IMF Survey* 6: 220–23.

IMF (International Monetary Fund). 1977c. "Status of International Agreements for Some Major Commodities," *IMF Survey* 6: 223.

IMF (International Monetary Fund). 1978a. "Outlook for Metal Markets Brighter in 1978 With Benefits for Producers and Exporters," *IMF Survey* 7: 33–37.

IMF (International Monetary Fund). 1978b. *International Financial Statistics* vol. 31, no. 5, p. 55.

Labys, W. C. 1978. "Market Structure, Power, and Performance in Resource Price Formation." In *Proceedings of the Wisconsin Seminar on Natural Resource Policies in Relation to Economic Development and International Cooperation*, vol.1. Madison: Institute for Environmental Studies, University of Wisconsin.

Penn, R. J. 1978. "The 1978 International Sugar Agreement." In *Proceedings of the Wisconsin Seminar on Natural Resource Policies in Relation to Economic Development and International Cooperation*, vol. 2. Madison: Institute for Environmental Studies, University of Wisconsin.

Samuels, W. J. 1977. "Technology vis-à-vis Institutions in the JEI: A Suggested Interpretation," *Journal of Economic Issues* 11: 871-95.

Timmer, C. P., and W. P. Falcon. 1975. "The Impact of Price on Rice Trade in Asia." In G. S. Tolley and P. A. Zadrozny, eds., *Trade, Agriculture, and Development*. Cambridge, Massachusetts: Ballinger, pp. 57-89.

Tinbergen, Jan coord. 1976. *RIO—Reshaping the International Order: A Report to the Club of Rome*. New York: Dutton.

UN (United Nations). 1977. *Statistical Yearbook 1976*. New York: UN.

UNCTAD (United Nations Conference on Trade and Development). 1976. "Proportion Between Export Prices and Consumer Prices of Selected Commodities Exported by Developing Countries," TD/184/Supp. 3. UNCTAD IV, Nairobi, Kenya.

UNDESA (United Nations Department of Economic and Social Affairs). 1962. *World Economic Survey 1961*. New York: UN.

UNDESA (United Nations Department of Economic and Social Affairs). 1968. *World Economic Survey 1967*. New York: UN.

UNDESA (United Nations Department of Economic and Social Affairs). 1972. *World Economic Survey 1971*. New York: UN.

World Bank. 1974. *Prospects for Exports of Bauxite/Alumina/Aluminum from Developing Countries*. Commodity Paper no. 12 Washington, D.C.: World Bank.

World Bank. 1978. *World Development Report, 1978*. New York: Oxford University Press.

*Abdulaziz Al-Wattari,*
*John Steinhart, & Donald Hertzmark*

# Efficiency, Conservation, and Development

Like many other authors we see before us a rapidly changing world with problems. To put it as optimistically as possible, there is such a bewildering variety of challenges and opportunities, each with its own advocates and detractors, that mere description is difficult and comprehensive visions of the future all too rare. As much as anything, it is complexity that threatens to defeat us, and the search for basic principles and understanding of the limits and opportunities of the earth takes on a new urgency. We will examine the familiar notions of conservation and efficiency and show that promising directions for resource use and development—directions different from some of those prescribed by conventional wisdom in either industrial or developing nations—are indicated.

World models and scenarios for the future proliferate, and those that are not downright disastrous tend to be amplified projections of the past with a fervent but nonspecific faith in future technologies' ability to remedy unsolved problems. Even the optimistic projections that presume constant raw material and energy prices (Leontief 1977; Herrera et al. 1976) show at best scant narrowing of the gap between the rich and poor of the world.

Scientists and engineers, who are called upon to generate the technology for the future, have begun to assess the systematic properties of the earth to determine just what is needed. It is not that technological possi-

171

bilities have disappeared. On the contrary, there are a number of technological options in both developing and industrial nations, and criteria are
needed to provide ways of choosing among these options. To this task scientists and engineers bring the apparatus of systems analysis and thermodynamics as descriptors and bounds of anything that happens. As Cloud
(1977) puts it: "Materials and energy are the interdependent feedstocks of
economic systems, and thermodynamics is their moderator." Biological
scientists have added their experience in assessing natural systems at various levels of aggregation. Because most natural systems do not exchange
money, biologists have developed a powerful array of methods using energy and material flows to derive valuable insights about such matters as
stability and resilience in the face of change. Clark's (1976) elegant demonstration that both "renewable" and "stock" resources are always depleted too fast in real economic systems if the discount rate exceeds the
renewal rate for the resource need not be a dismal theorem if the lesson is
used to seek a fully renewable future. Certainly, efficient and conservative strategies are indicated for everyone with the aim of both present and
future equity.

What we suggest in the following sections is that choice of better efficiency measures coupled with conservation of raw materials that grow
more inaccessible and expensive with time offer better possibilities for developing countries, different objectives for industrial nations, slowing of
environmental degradation, and, because of the foregoing, a concrete set
of real interdependencies upon which a basis for international cooperation may be sought.

## Tasks and Production

We define a task as the process of design, specification, and provision
of means to achieve a desired goal. In the most general sense of planning
the goals are the basic necessities of food, clothing, shelter, and health
and the desirables of education, leisure, entertainment, and perhaps
many others. The tasks are to design, specify, and provide the commodities and services that will achieve these goals from the resources that are
or can be made available. These resources are labor, raw materials, fuels,
land, and the current level of understanding of design and engineering.
As an intermediate step, some of these resources may have to be converted to capital equipment, equipment whose services over time assist in
the accomplishment of tasks.

This formulation would adequately describe the problem before us if
we could begin anew in the world with a clean slate. The world or a nation
begins, however, with an existing system of commodity production, an

existing population, and whatever capital equipment is already in place. Thus tasks must be viewed at a more detailed level and must include the question of how to pursue goals from our present position without losing sight of the goals themselves.

Any economic production activity involves a sequence of physical tasks or functions in which production inputs—raw materials, energy, labor, and capital equipment—are made to undergo predetermined transformations into a finished good or service. Any energy applications involved in these tasks are presumed to be economically efficient although not market valued. This presumption is derived from a previous assumption, made at the state of designing the process and its capital equipment, that the resources, energy, and other required factor inputs have been chosen from a set of the most efficient available designs (sometimes called "the book of blueprints") to minimize output costs for a given set of factor prices.

At this interface of engineering, design, and economics the set of possibilities that represents the maximum output obtainable from any combination of inputs is known as the production function. "The production function is price-independent, by definition: It is supposed to represent strictly technological relationships. A profit-maximizing firm (presumably) 'knows' this function and uses it to determine the optimum output (quantity and quality) in relation to its markets and in relation to input requirements" (Ayres 1978, p. 39). Thus specified, a production function applies only to the commodities produced rather than the tasks to be performed. For production to be undertaken for the first time, or in a new place, such a function cannot be known in any empirical sense under different conditions of resource supply, labor availability and costs, and so forth. Such production functions for any real world case are only estimates until some particular combination is tried. For incremental changes in an existing industrial society, information gleaned from similar cases may ease these difficulties, but for production of a new type or in a new setting such estimates may bear little relation to past or future experience, as in the case of nuclear power (Bupp and Derain 1978).

"Underlying the basic concept of a production function—and absolutely essential to it, is the notion of *substitutability,*" says Ayres (1978, p. 39); he goes on to discuss the physical constraints to free substitution among inputs. For present purposes it is sufficient to note two constraints for raw materials and energy:

1. Raw materials embodied in the output of the production are required in proportion to the desired output; thus substitution of raw materials for other factors of production can only increase or reduce wastage of these materials. Less obvious, but equally con-

straining, is that the energy captured as work and embodied in the physical changes in the materials is also required in proportion to the output.

2. Energy cannot be segregated as an input and compared to capital and labor in simple fashion because real capital equipment requires energy for its manufacture, and labor entails an energy expenditure (although not often one of direct concern to a single firm) that depends upon the matrix of the society from which the labor is drawn. Such inputs are said to be complementary in the sense that more capital input requires more energy. Even though energy may be saved overall in this sort of substitution, it need not be. We will return to some of these issues later.

These ideas have been introduced in order to emphasize the conclusion that tasks as here defined are not the same thing as production of specific products to perform the tasks. To discuss efficient paths of development and their relation to the allocation of depletable resources is more than a problem in conventional economics because economic efficiency can be discussed only *after* some agreement has been reached about what commodities are to be produced.

What remains is to inquire into the efficient achievement of these tasks in the presence of limited resources. In most general terms, efficiency can be evaluated in two ways derived from the first and second laws of thermodynamics. First law efficiency, comparing input and output of a specific process, provides useful tests for the functioning of current processes but few clues about what other processes are possible. This efficiency measure is suitable for incremental improvement of task performance but fails as a guide for optimum allocation of scarce resources over time, as Georgescu-Roegen (1971) has shown. Second law efficiency takes account of the task to be performed and the best present or proposed methods of accomplishing the task with minimum inputs. In what follows we propose to show the linear independence of these efficiency measures and to show that economic theory's claim to efficient allocation rests on a first law measure which neglects the second law.

For technological directions, second law efficiency measures lead to resource-conservative strategies neglected by standard economic measures. In part this neglect occurs because capital services are regarded as independent factors of production whereas any engineer knows that expenditures of fuels and raw materials for capital goods were specified by the choice of the technology.

From a physical standpoint, the problem of economic development is to accomplish necessary and desirable tasks via the production of commodities. The features that distinguish one society from another cause the tasks to be satisfied in varied ways throughout the world, and the availability of resources plays a major role in determining how the given tasks are to be accomplished. In a region with abundant forests and little sunshine the task of providing heat might be accomplished by burning wood and subsequently capturing some of the energy liberated in combustion. On the other hand, a region with little wood and much sunshine might provide heat by "capturing" sunlight in the massive earthen walls of local housing. In both cases the task is the same—to provide heat at 15°–20°C. What differs are the commodities required to perform these tasks. In the former case, the commodities needed to provide heat are the fuel itself, a stove, and some facilities for disposal of waste products. In the latter case, the required commodity is a large amount of building material.

This example can obviously be extended to other tasks to reinforce the point that from the view of an individual or a society, it is the performance of the task, relative to the commodities available for satisfying the task, that is important. But if the task can be met in a number of ways, then it is the role of designers and engineers to determine the nature of the task so that design sciences can provide suitable commodities. Determining the requirements of a task in physical units is an often tedious but relatively straightforward exercise in applied physics, chemistry, and biology. Once the requirements given by a task are properly specified, it is the job of engineers, planners, and business people to design and provide the necessary commodities. In fact, only if the description of a task unnecessarily includes commodity requirements does the performance of a task impose certain patterns of commodity production. Even a complete specification of tasks by an economic planning agency does not impose any particular requirements in terms of commodity production. The patterns of commodity production come from relating tasks to available resources.

### Efficiency, Conservation, and Thermodynamics

The search for an efficient and conservative strategy for development demands first a measure for efficiency that will allow one strategy to be compared with another. The concepts of economic efficiency have been used for this purpose, and chapter 4 discusses the implications for resources that arise from this measure. We suggest that measures associated with energy flows provide other insights into efficiency and lead to strategies different from those of economics.

Advantages to the use of energy measures accrue from the fundamental role of energy transfer and degradation in all activity and from the practical importance of energy supplies in present world politics. Before outlining these advantages more specifically, it is necessary to explore briefly the indices of efficiency that derive from the laws of thermodynamics.

## First Law Efficiency

The first law of thermodynamics is often called the mass conservation law because it states that the quantity of matter-energy in the universe (or inside any closed system) is constant. From this we may deduce immediately the commonsense postulate that there does not exist any device which is capable of producing more energy than it consumes. If the total outputs of energy from a given system or device must be strictly less than or equal to the energy inputs to that system or device then it must be that the ratio of useful energy outputs to total energy inputs gives a measure of the effectiveness of the system in providing the useful energy outputs. That relation is the first law efficiency ratio:

$$e = \frac{\text{useful energy outputs}}{\text{total energy inputs}} \qquad (6.1)$$

If we measure both the numerator and the denominator of equation (6.1) in the same units (joules or calories, for example), the equation gives a means of comparing the effectiveness of alternative methods for obtaining a certain quantity of joules for the performance of some task or simply for the production of energy resources for input into other processes. For example, if we define a task as the provision of a given quantity of joules for heating water in a house, then the most convenient way to pose the question is in terms of temperature differentials between the heat source and the end use. In the case of heating water, assume that the temperature of the end use is 333 °K (about 140 °F or 60 °C). Assume that the temperature of the source is the temperature at the power plant, in the case of electric resistance heating, or the flame temperature, in the case of gas heating. These figures are, respectively, 825°K and 960°K. These uses then have a first law efficiency of 0.59 for an electric resistance heater and 0.65 for a standard gas water heater. From these figures it would appear that there is little room for dramatic improvements in the efficiency of using energy to heat water, at least for improvements of the sort experienced during the past 50 years. And in the sense conveyed by equation (6.1), this impression is a correct one. This impression leads quite directly and naturally to the policy conclusion that the benefits of improved efficiency are meager relative to increased production for the supply of necessary quantities of energy.

This notion of efficiency is captured by equation (6.1) in which useful energy outputs include both outputs of fuels and energy per se and that quantity of energy and raw materials embodied in the output itself. In the case of energy converters like electric power generating stations, the comparison is simply between energy output and total energy input, including a prorated share of the energy involved in plant construction. Yet the first law of thermodynamics tells us that energy is never created or destroyed; thus in the power plant case some energy inputs emerge, not as electric power output, but as relatively low temperature hot water from the cooling cycle of the power plant and, ultimately, as fully exhausted capital equipment. In the case of physical products emerging from a process, one must determine the energy actually captured in useful work in the manufacturing process and seek the lost energy in the waste materials, waste heat, frictional processes, and so on accompanying a productive process. Yet work, besides having an intuitive meaning, has a very definite physical meaning measured in the same units as energy. This standard of available work used in the process serves as a convenient measure to compare productive processes and is used in engineering and design studies to choose the most economical way of achieving a desired output.

We do not actually consume energy or raw materials but merely rearrange them or change them chemically or physically in ways that are useful to us. In the process, we consume available work of both the intuitive and the specific physical kind. The first law measure of efficiency in equation (6.1) falls short of the kind of efficiency index we would like to have, however. For one thing, burning natural gas in a furnace to heat a house delivers 60 percent of the energy in the fuel to the plenum of the furnace as heat and gives the impression of a moderately efficient process for which no enormous multiple of efficiency could be expected. Yet if we were to use the same energy in the form of electricity to drive a heat pump, it could supply more heat to the house than the electric energy supplied to the heat pump. This circumstance leads to an efficiency index greater than 1 and clearly violates our expectation of an index of 1 (or 100 percent) as a theoretical maximum. Air conditioners and heat pumps do typically exhibit first law efficiencies (usually called coefficients of performance) greater than 1; for commercial units available at present, the coefficients are often around 2. There is no physical paradox because a heat pump supplies to the interior of a building heat that is extracted from the heat external to the building (where the ambient temperature is already lower than inside). The heat is pumped "uphill" in a thermodynamic sense to provide the low temperature heat required.

First law efficiency also provides an inadequate measure in the case of heat engines, such as a steam power plant. The maximum first law efficiency for an ideal heat engine is given by:

$$e = (T_1 - T_2)/T_1 \qquad (6.2)$$

where $T_1$ and $T_2$ are the initial and final temperatures expressed in degrees Kelvin. Thus for an upper temperature of 811°K. (1000°F) and a low temperature cooling reservoir of 311°K (100°F), efficiencies of 60 percent might be possible from equation (6.2). Results from equation (6.1) would indicate efficiencies of 40 percent by the best modern steam power plant, but such results do not show that those plants have actually achieved two-thirds of maximum actual theoretical efficiency. To arrive at a more useful definition of efficiency, we need to take the second law of thermodynamics into account as well and to calculate a different sort of efficiency measure.

We shall leave this argument for the moment, however, and extend the insights of net energy analysis by complicating the situation somewhat. In the water heater example it was assumed that the energy source for the electric heater was the output of the electric generating station; in the case of the gas heater it was assumed that the pipe leading into the heater was the energy source. Both assumptions are, of course, untrue. Electricity is produced in steam power stations (ignore hydroelectric power for the moment) or in gas or oil turbines from raw fuels at something other than perfect thermal efficiency. That is, a substantial portion of the total energy contained in the fuel is not transformed into electricity at the power station. For modern, well-designed steam power stations, the usual figures cited for first law efficiency in producing electricity are on the order of 0.33 to 0.40 (APS 1975, pp. 47–59). Losses during transmission of the electricity further reduce this figure to the range of 0.25 to 0.30 as the net energy efficiency of delivering electricity to a dwelling. This calculation ignores the energy costs of constructing the power station as well as the energy costs of mining and transporting the fuel. If these energy "costs" are significant relative to the energy costs of the entire process, they must be included, but at present there are no generally accepted protocols for deciding where to bound the analysis. As in other fields, such as economics, one rough and ready measure is sensitivity testing to see whether final values of efficiency respond dramatically to changes in the boundaries of the analysis. In the case of gas, we get a range of figures which depend on the source of the gas and the conditions of production. For example, if the gas is obtained from a high quality large reservoir, then the net energy efficiency of its production is about 0.77. Alternatively, the same fuel coming from a small reservoir can be produced at an efficiency of about 0.66 (both figures are from the Institute of Gas Technology 1976). Consider, however, the proposals to mine coal and gasify it according to one of several available technologies. Again using data supplied by the Institute of Gas Technology, the net energy efficiency of producing gas from subbituminous coal (5.8 × 10⁶ joules/kg) may be calculated at about 0.37. Other proposed gasification schemes have estimated efficiencies from 0.20 to 0.60.

We now have the figures necessary to compare alternative energy processes on the basis of their net energy efficiencies. To get the final figures we simply multiply the relevant intermediate numbers: the overall first law efficiency of heating water with electricity from a power station whose efficiency is 0.33 when the efficiency of transmission is 0.75 and the efficiency of the household heater itself is 0.59 is: $e = (0.33)(0.75)(0.59) = 0.15$. Similar calculations for other alternatives yield the following figures:

| | |
|---|---|
| electricity—high | $e = 0.17$ |
| low | $e = 0.15$ |
| gas—large reservoir | $e = 0.50$ |
| small reservoir | $e = 0.43$ |
| synthetic gas | $e = 0.24$ |

It is not surprising that the natural gas methods are superior to the electric alternatives in terms of the proportion of fuel that sees actual use at the final stage. What is noteworthy about these figures is the implication that gasification of coal is no better from a material balance standpoint than electricity from coal because two-thirds of the coal is still wasted in the process. This is one way of stating the second major insight of the first law-material balance approach: The more completely a process utilizes its energy source, the less will be the negative externalities (pollution) generated by that process. In simple physical terms, a process which converts 0.40 of its fuel source to a useful form must dispose of the remaining 0.60 as an undesired effluent. A look at the stages in which low efficiencies occur is a useful guide to the location and magnitude of the pollution potentials of a given process or project. In the previous example, the relatively low efficiency of electric generation indicates that the major externality is at the power plant. The low efficiency of coal gasification points out that the major pollution problem occurs at the point of gasification, usually near the mine.

Some ecologists have proposed that tracing the energy flows of a system provides the proper perspective from which to understand the working of the system (see, for instance, Odum 1971, pp. 58–103). It should be sufficient for present purposes to note that information of different types is required in modern societies simply because the interests, time horizons, and responsibilities of decision makers will vary among institutions and over time. A perfectly functioning neoclassical market will yield much of the same information as first law efficiency. In an imperfect world, however, reliance solely on price information would surely disregard some of the insights developed above.

## Second Law Efficiency

The first law efficiency measure has several shortcomings which prevent it from being a complete measure of the effectiveness with which energy is used and produced. The first and most serious of these problems is that heterogeneity of available work is disregarded by the first law measure. That is, there exist quality differentials among energy sources with respect to the work that can be done by a given quantity of energy. As a simple example, consider a particular quantity of energy, say, $10^6$ joules. If this energy is available at 150 °C, it can perform a variety of useful tasks provided that they do not require a temperature of more than 150°C. In contrast, consider the same quantity of energy available at 75°C; the range of possible tasks has obviously constricted. Simply measuring available energy in terms of joules is incomplete. The other coordinate required to provide a complete thermodynamic description of an energy source is a qualitative one. In the thermodynamic sense, the first energy source is of higher quality than the second one because it has more available work.

If we suppose that mechanical work is to be done or electricity to be generated by way of a heat engine, equation (6.2) can be used to display the theoretical limit of available work from these two identical amounts of energy at different original temperatures. Using 10°C as the temperature of the environment, equation (6.2) gives 0.35 and 0.19 as the theoretical limit with which the 150°C and the 75°C energy, respectively, could be converted to mechanical work. In this case, then, the 150°C reservoir could produce almost twice the available work that the 75°C source could. Actual heat engines would, of course, have proportionately lower efficiencies. That is, more tasks can be accomplished with the first source than with the second.

In figure 6.1 the vertical axis represents the temperature at which a given energy source becomes available, and the horizontal axis gives an index of the increase in *una*vailable work of the system as a result of declines in the temperature (quality) coordinate. The area under the curve represents the total available work from a given source and, in that sense, is the thermodynamic ideal. The continuous decrease in the quantity of the available work from a particular source as seen in the figure represents the second major defect of the first law measure. Under that measure, there are no data available on the continuous and irreversible decrease in the total quantity of available work (because time and entropy

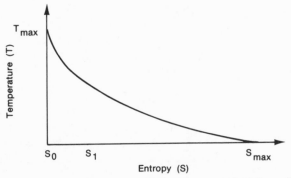

Fig. 6.1. Idealized temperature-entropy diagram for energy initially available at $T_{max}$.

both occur only in one direction) in the system. Using the temperature-entropy diagram, however, it is clear that the total available work from $S_0$ to $S_{max}$ is greater than that from $S_1$ to $S_{max}$. That is, the area under the curve starting at $S_0$ is greater than the area under the curve starting at $S_1$. With these issues in mind we can now define the second law efficiency measure as the ratio of the minimum quantity of available work needed to perform a task to the actual amount of available work used for the task:

$$\eta = \frac{B_{min}}{B} \qquad (6.3)$$

This ratio measures the degree to which the minimum known energy need (numerator) is matched to the actual use of energy (denominator). It is thus a physicist's measure of the thermodynamic economy of the source-use combinations that exist. In this case the denominator sets the opportunity cost of the energy source because once the energy is used for a particular task it cannot be reused for another task which requires a higher quality than the initial task. The energy remaining can, however, be used for a lower quality task than the initial one. The lower uses must occur after the higher ones in time as a consequence of irreversibility.

The measures of efficiency given by the first and second laws are independent of one another. Figure 6.2 shows a number of first law efficiencies ($e$) plotted against second law efficiencies ($\eta$) for the same processes. No evidence of functional dependence appears,* and a policy or program which attempts to maximize first law efficiency will have no systematic relation to second law efficiency.

---

*Linear independence of $\eta$ and $e$ is easily shown: Let $\varphi$ be the useful energy in output (which includes energy embodied in output goods) and $B_a$ be the actual energy input. Then

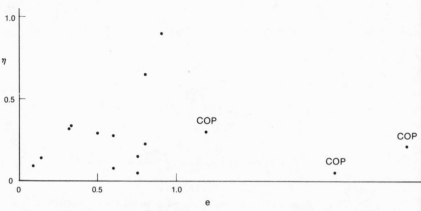

Fig. 6.2. First law efficiencies ($e$) as a function of second law efficiencies ($\eta$) [COP = coefficient of performance for first law efficiencies > 1.0]. Source: Data from Ayres (1978) and Ross and Williams (1977).

Thus far the discussion of efficiency has been set in terms of thermodynamics alone. In what follows we shall compare this notion of efficiency with the one used in neoclassical economic theory. It is important to note at the outset that these two notions of efficiency are not congruent. That is, economic efficiency is not a special case of thermodynamic efficiency, nor is the converse true. What is of interest are the interrelations among the two modes of analysis in terms of the different information that is given about existing or planned allocations of resources. The discussion below has been limited to competitive economies because imperfect competition theories are indeterminate with respect to prices and quantities as long as

1. firms can influence prices and quantities on both the supply and demand sides;

---

linear dependence between $\eta$ and $e$ requires that constants $\alpha$ and $\beta$ exist such that, using equations (6.1) and (6.3),

$$\frac{B_{min}}{B_a} = \alpha \frac{\varphi}{B_a} + \beta$$

*or*                                $B_{min} = \alpha \varphi + \beta B_a$

Differentiating with respect to energy in output ($\varphi$) gives

$$\frac{d B_{min}}{d \varphi} = \alpha$$

This result is false on physical grounds because it would require, among many other things, that the constants of chemical reactions change in proportion to the efficiencies of industrial processes using those reactions.

2. firms can influence the demand curves for their products;
3. firms have goals other than profit maximization/cost minimization such as maximizing growth, revenue, or nonoptimum policies (satisficing).

The concept of efficiency in economics is really quite simple. An allocation of goods is said to be efficient if an increase in the production of some commodity must necessarily cause a decrease in the production of some other commodity or commodities. The only additional assumption that is needed to describe the neoclassical efficiency conditions is one which states that producers obey simple optimization rules of cost minimization or profit maximization in determining the optimal combinations of inputs and outputs. We can now state two propositions concerning efficient allocations of energy from an economic standpoint:

1. A competitive firm will choose only technically (first law) efficient combinations of inputs to produce a particular level of output. Of these technically efficient input combinations it will choose the minimum cost one.
2. A competitive economy tends to maximize first law efficiency in the employment of energy.

If two energy resources are used interchangeably although their purchase prices and use costs vary, proposition 1 requires that their first law efficiencies vary inversely with their prices. The intuitive rationale for proposition 2 comes from the idea that the important measure of the efficiency of an economic system is the ratio of net output to total inputs. The policy implications of these propositions are several. The first is that low efficiency technologies (or worse, industries for which $e$ is less than 0) will lower the overall efficiency of the energy economy and require a greater flow of resources to maintain a given level of final (net) output. Other implications concern the rationale for price differentials among alternative energy sources based not only on the price of the resource but also on the expenses necessary to utilize the resource. And while this last aspect of energy pricing admits to qualitative differences among alternative energy sources as regards pollution-abatement expenses and the like, the first law measure from which the basic ranking is derived neglects the essential feature of the quality of the energy itself—a feature crucial to proper allocation according to second law principles.

In order to have a proper allocation according to second law efficiency, it would be necessary to reorient the basic unit around which price is set from the joule alone to the joule of a particular quality. In the case where qualitative distinctions are made by temperature differentials, we would need to define a continuum of energy commodities from the highest conceivable temperature to the ambient or sink temperature. Defining this continuum is impossible, and the procedure adopted in actuality would need to be a far simpler one probably based on discrete differentials of a few degrees. Even this "practical" step confronts a large number of energy resources of different qualities, and allowing for other types of qualitative differences which affect the cost of using the resource as well as its productivity raises the number of energy resources enormously. Unfortunately, we would indeed need to define these many many commodities if the price system were to allocate energy properly. (The reader should note that all comments about the perfectly competitive neoclassical economy apply with equal force to perfect planning models because the same assumptions concerning tastes, technology, and criteria are made for the two systems in their pure forms.) Perhaps the most important of the implications of the second law measure for policy is that the need to consider energy as qualitatively heterogeneous had to be imposed on the model from the outside.

The temperature-entropy curve of figure 6.1 represents a thermodynamic ideal. In reality, entropy will always increase at a more rapid rate than this minimum. There are two primary reasons for this. The first is that any process will take some finite nonzero amount of time to be completed.* The second is that achievement of perfect matching is not really achievable in practicable processes; there must be discrete differentials from one process to the next. Cascading, or using thermal effluent from one process as the energy source of a successive one, is depicted in figure 6.3. This figure shows three distinct processes arranged in order of descending quality of energy used. Process 2 uses the thermal effluent of process 1 as its energy source. The practical problem that must be solved, of course, is how to array processes and technologies in order to utilize the greatest feasible proportion of the available work of the energy source.

One procedure for programming such a sequence of activities is to set a goal for thermodynamic efficiency and then to minimize the cost of the technologies that would perform the requisite tasks. A model of such an allocation method is a dynamic programming or optimal control type of model in which the objective is to minimize costs of energy inputs (state variables) and associated capital equipment (control variables) while obeying a transition equation governing the decrease in available work through time for the energy source under consideration. (A model of this

*Note that in neoclassical economics efficiency conditions are usually given for instantaneous production whereas in physics the highest efficiency is achieved for infinitely slow processes.

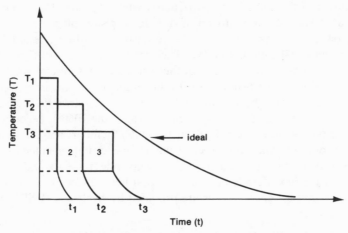

1—single source-use combination expels waste heat at $T_2$ and exhausts available work at time $t_1$

2—process uses waste heat at $T_2$ from process 1 and extends extraction of available work to $t_2 > t_1$

3—process uses waste heat at $T_3$ from process 2 and again extends extraction of available work to $t_3 > t_2 > t_1$

If total work extracted from a given energy source is denoted by the boxed areas, then clearly $1 < 1 + 2 < 1 + 2 + 3$. If so, the waste heat from a high temperature process such as 1 should have a positive price (ignoring for a moment pollution). The whole spectrum of available work, rather than a single level of quality, is the proper domain of concern for efficiency.

Fig. 6.3. Graphical example of cascading of several successively lower temperature processes to achieve higher second law efficiencies.

type is displayed fully in Hertzmark 1978, chapter 4.) Sensitivity testing of the model is accomplished by varying the target levels of thermodynamic efficiency and then comparing the total costs of accomplishing given tasks. Because energy and capital are complementary in the short run (Berndt and Wood 1975) and may be both substitutes and complements in the longer run, the a priori assumption that improved thermodynamic efficiency increases costs (Berry et al. undated) cannot be justified.

We have been at some pains to outline the distinctions that arise in the efficiency measures derived from the first and second laws of thermodynamics and to relate these measures to the concept of economic efficiency. More extensive discussions of the thermodynamics are available in recent literature (APS 1975; Ross and Williams 1977). Neither efficiency measure can be used exclusively.

First law efficiency still provides a useful performance comparison for operations of the same kind, particularly when capital costs are already sunk. For example, comparison of one steam power plant with another on a first law basis assesses their relative conversion efficiencies, and consideration of past gains in first law efficiency of conversion of fuel to electricity shows the source of many of the cost reductions in final goods that use electricity in their production. In the United States the improvement in first law efficiency by a factor of 4 or 5 in the years since 1910, together with the slowly declining real cost of fuel (until the 1960s), accounts for much of the increase in labor productivity (C. Steinhart and J. Steinhart 1974). From the same data it is clear that efficiency improvements of this kind constitute a unique and unrepeatable episode (fig. 6.4). Indeed, estimates for the next decade or two show first law efficiencies declining as more of societies' energy needs are provided by electricity (USDI 1975).

### Energy Analysis and Complementarity

In much of what follows we discuss energy flows and quantities in conjunction with economic parameters. The description of productive activities of society used in policy making has been dominated by economic analyses for many years, but in the past decade analyses of energy flows have occupied a small but growing number of scientists. Energy analysis itself is not new. Energy budgets have played an important role in biology, physics, chemistry, and the earth sciences for many years. Even the

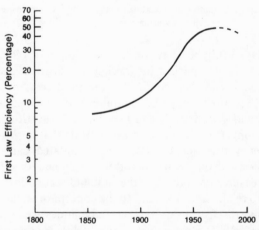

Fig. 6.4. Historical trends in U.S. first law efficiencies. Source: Data for 1800–1950 from Putnam (1953, p. 90), for 1950–60 from Cook (1976, p. 116), for 1960–85 from USDI (1975, p. 67).

conception of energy costs and benefits as fundamental measures of civilizations has old roots. In 1912 Nobel Laureate Frederick Soddy wrote:

Civilization as it is at present, even on the purely physical side, is not a continuous self-supporting movement. . . . It becomes possible only after an age-long accumulation of energy, by the supplementing of income out of capital. Its appetite increases by what it feeds on. It reaps what it has not sown and exhausts, so far, without replenishing. Its raw material is energy and its product is knowledge. The only knowledge which will justify its existence and postpone the day of reckoning is the knowledge that will replenish rather than diminish its limited resources (Soddy 1912, quoted in Thomas 1977).

The proliferation of research under the name "energy analysis" has produced a false impression of a unified activity or even a new discipline. Although the name may be here to stay, such impressions of uniformity are erroneous, and the notion of a new discipline is at least premature and probably wrong. At the simplest level, energy analysis is simply energy accounting derived from previous experience in studying energy flows and budgets in ecosystems and nonmarket societies. At the other side of the spectrum are those who propose an energy theory of value and energy analysis as a comprehensive framework of theory within which economic theory is a special case (Odum and Odum 1976). Both the procedures and the claims for various schemes of energy analysis have been discussed at length in recent summaries (Gilliland 1978; Thomas 1977). Some economists have objected to energy analysis while other economists have emphasized energy's fundamental importance for economic theory (Georgescu-Roegen 1971; Webb and Pearce 1977; Common 1977).

Without attempting a classification of energy analysis, we wish to explore implications for resource flows and Third World development. It must be pointed out that energy, as a quantitative descriptor of societies' activities, has two unchallenged advantages over monetary flows used for the same purpose:

1. Invariability of energy measures. A 1978 joule is the same as a 1910 joule. Joules eliminate the vagaries of choosing appropriate price deflators to compare different times and places. Introduction of available work or other thermodynamic quality measures complicates matters but in no way alters the invariability of the units of measurement.
2. Universality of energy flows. Anything that happens anytime and anywhere is accompanied by an irreversible flow of energy and a resulting increase in entropy. For those societies (including many of the developing countries) where much of societal activity is not re-

corded in national accounts or takes place outside any markets, energy accounts could provide quantitative assessment of the activity.

If, as some have suggested, energy analysis provides no information not already included in more complete form in economic analysis, then these two advantages would make energy analysis worthwhile simply as an independent verification of some analytical results. The linear independence of first law and second law efficiencies implies, however, that energy analysis does contain information not contained in traditional economic analysis.

In short, energy analysis in some of its varied forms appears to promise a complement to typical economic analysis in the search for more efficient paths to development. Much more research is needed to ascertain just how insightful this approach may be. For the present, energy analyses' results appear to be complementary to those of economic analyses in the sense that Bohr (1958) uses the term: Both sets of results represent valid descriptions of the same set of phenomena (in this case, the productive process), but one cannot be simply transformed into the other.* Georgescu-Roegen (1971, p. 101) also concludes (on different grounds) that thermodynamic measures cannot easily be transformed to economic measurements.

It remains to be seen how completely energy analysis can provide an alternative quantification of the productive processes of society. It was shown in chapter 2 that resource production from lower grade, less accessible, and less available ores is accompanied by nonlinear increases in energy requirements. Larger and more complex capital goods generally require larger energy inputs. Berndt and Wood (1975) show from economic analysis that attempts to substitute capital for resource inputs lead to increased energy requirements. In addition, the focus of thermodynamics on irreversibility of energy flows corresponds with the commonplace observation that execution of one program generally excludes a number of others, besides irrevocably expending some resources on the chosen program. Finally, the inclusion of real time with its one way flow permits discussion of the relation between rate of development and resources needed for development. At present, energy analysis seems to be the only promising direction in the search for a quantitative link between the functioning of "natural" ecosystems and "man-made" subsystems. But much more work is required on the energy flows in man's subsystems even to reach the degree of sophistication already achieved in thermodynamic discussion of ecosystems (see Gallucci 1973).

*The classical paradox of electrons' behavior as waves in one set of observations and particles in another is often cited as an example of such complementarity.

## Conservation and Efficiency in Industrial Countries

First law energy efficiencies in the United States, averaging nearly 50 percent in the 1960s (see figure 6.4), are projected to decline in the future. Efficiencies calculated from the second law indicate a very different picture of the U.S. economy (table 6.1). Although considerable improvement in efficiency in industry is still possible, the opportunities for dramatic reductions in fuel use are seen to be in space heating, hot water heating, refrigeration, and transportation. Dumas (1976, p. 264), in an engineering study, calculates that changes in technology for improvement of second law efficiencies and other conservative measures could lead to 30–50 percent reductions in energy use and concludes that such a strategy "will at minimum stretch existing supplies to the limit, reduce the pressure for expansion of energy resources sufficiently to allow more reasoned and complete evaluation of the monetary, ecological, and safety costs of such expansion, and contribute importantly to a major reduction in air, water, and solid waste pollution. And it will do so without significantly reducing the standard of living. It is hard to ask more than that." Other studies show similar reductions possible with slight changes in life style but considerable change in technological directions (Ross and Williams 1977; Steinhart et al. 1977; Lovins 1977).

Similar strategies have been proposed for Canada (Lovins 1976), Sweden (Johansson and Steen 1977), and by no less than four separate studies

TABLE 6.1
Second Law Efficiencies for Some Energy Uses in the United States

| Energy-consuming activities (Current technology) | Second law efficiency (percentage) |
|---|---|
| **Residential and commercial** | |
| Space heating | |
| Fossil-fuel-fired furnace | 5 |
| Electric resistive | 2.5 |
| Air conditioning | 4.5 |
| Water heating | |
| Gas | 3 |
| Electric | 1.5 |
| Refrigeration | 4 |
| **Transportation** | |
| Automobile | 9 |
| **Industrial** | |
| Electric power generation | 33 |
| Process-steam production | 33 |
| Steel production | 23 |
| Aluminum production | 13 |

Source: Ross and Williams 1977.

for France (*Soft Energy Notes* 1978). All these proposals and studies imply changes in technological direction and project overall economic savings in the process. Furthermore, despite some increases in particular raw materials requirements, the overall effect is to reduce materials demand. In the U.S. case alone, for example, smaller and more efficient automobiles would cut total steel demand by as much as 10 percent.

If these strategies are so promising, why then are they not promptly adopted? One reason is pure momentum. Present technological directions, from autos and steel to nuclear power and highways, are backed by strong vested interests in industrial countries. In addition, as Schon (1971, p. 189) shows in his study of technological change, the central government's "inherently limited informational capacity restricts the scope of adaptation." Faced with powerful vested interests, large sunk costs in present technological directions, and the limited adaptability of centralized government, change may come slowly in most industrial countries.

Yet the message seeps through. Most industrial nations have conservation at the center of their announced strategies to deal with energy problems, and these strategies include efforts at better thermodynamic matching of source to use. We find, for example, U.S. Energy Secretary Schlesinger saying: "My judgment is that solar energy can be increasingly useful for industrial process heat and that it has been neglected in that area. . . . We should put a great deal of emphasis behind an industrial process heat program" (*Business Week* 9 October 1978, pp. 90–91). He recommends, in fact, better second law matching, just the kind of technological change difficult to incorporate into present industrial plant processes.

In industrial nations the possibilities for conservation and second law efficiency improvements are beginning to affect domestic policy directions. One result is increased efforts to export to the Third World the complex, high energy technologies characteristic of the traditional paths of industrial growth. Consider, for example, the intense efforts to sell nuclear power plants in the Third World. Most of the technical elites in the Third World were trained in industrial countries, and as Sardar and Rosser-Owen (1977, p. 538) put it: "One of the public effects of having an occidentalized elite taking the political decisions involved in science policy . . . is conspicuous technology. This is a sort of international 'keeping up with the Joneses' or 'gamesmanship.' It clearly illustrates the problem of who is taking what decisions about science policy, and whether they are really appropriate for the domestic needs of the country."

The industrial nations themselves are vigorously seeking new directions for technological innovation. Even while squabbling among themselves about the terms of trade and export quantities of finished goods, most have clearly targeted developing countries as potential markets for high technology goods.

Growth in labor productivity slowed (or even stopped) in most developed countries in the years since 1973. Nordhaus (1972) argued, before the 1973 oil price increases, that the decreases in 1967–71 contain a long-term component that is not automatically reversible. The timing, which corresponds with the end of real price decreases in electricity in 1966–67 and modest oil price increases from 1969 onward, suggests that energy costs may play a role here. Could it be that the sources of labor productivity have been mainly the result of substitution, by way of technology, of cheap energy (in real terms growing ever cheaper from 1920 to 1965) for labor?

Evidence has been presented showing that farm productivity, which had grown concurrently with energy inputs to the U.S. food system from 1920 to 1970, began to level off in the late 1960s (J. S. Steinhart and C. E. Steinhart 1974). Such improvements in labor productivity are usually attributed to technological advance. Yet Boretsky (1975) states bluntly that "the essence of most innovations in civilian technology has been the substitution, usually in all kinds of equipment and mechanical implements, of BTUs for human and animal energy." His thesis is supported by a review of 61 important technological innovations of modern times (Jewkes et al. 1969). More than three-fourths of them implied substantial escalation in energy use, and 7 of the 61 required oil or natural gas feedstocks as well. Although the future may be unpredictable, attempts to project recent directions led Gabor (1970) to compile 79 possible physical and biological innovations deemed likely by experts. Of these, 67 would require substantially increased energy use. Careful studies of productivity of all factors of production, including energy and raw materials, might go a long way toward resolving this matter. Griliches and Jorgenson (1967) consider a time profile of capital and labor inputs and conclude that "if real product and real factor input are accurately accounted for, the observed growth in total factor productivity is negligible."

The real world is always complex, and many studies emphasize the heterogeneous origins of technological innovation, but Renshaw (1976, p. 40) comes close to our conclusion about productivity increase: "Though it would be an oversimplification to attribute all increases in productivity to mere substitution of inanimate energy for human beings and other resources, there is a sense in which it is more enlightening to speak in terms of factors affecting the speed, scale, and technical efficiency of converting heat into work than to simply measure that portion of total output which cannot be explained by an increase in labor and capital and, for want of more rational understanding, call it all 'technical progress.'"

## Implications for Developing Countries

The income gap between rich and poor nations, growing since World

War II, shows as dramatically in energy consumption as it does in dollar incomes. Brown (1976) found that in 1950 the nations of the world were distributed continuously, if irregularly, across a range of per capita energy consumption from 32 kce (kg coal equivalent) to 8000 kce. By 1970 this distribution had become distinctly bimodal. Nations holding three-fourths of the world's population used energy at per capita rates of 64 kce to 500 kce; the rich countries' per capita rates ranged from 1000 to 16,000 kce; almost no nations filled the gap from 500 to 1000 kce. By itself this bit of information is scarcely more than interesting. After all, much of both real economic activity and energy use take place outside national accountings. The difference is that attempts to make inclusive calculations for economic accounts are very difficult and necessarily dependent on assumptions and indirect evidence but that energy flows can be measured directly although not necessarily with ease. It should be an early priority to estimate these energy flows.

But what have conservation and efficiency to do with the needs of developing countries? Traditional living and production methods have evolved to fit local conditions. But, as Eckholm (1976) points out, increased population densities and migration have placed new strains on food production and fuel supply, and traditional adaptations may be quite inappropriate. Goldemberg (1978), for example, notes that a shift from open fires to simple stoves for cooking could reduce the time required for fuelwood search substantially and, more than incidentally, could reduce pressure on fuel supplies. Such strategy is conservative and improves second law efficiency but would not be easily identified by available economic indicators.

Present discussions of development talk of technology transfer and industrial development in a way that suggests that developing countries can repeat, in a much shorter time, the industrial development of the rich countries. There are at least five problems with a "strategy" so simple:

1. Most of the technology available for transfer is powered by oil or natural gas.
2. Much of the "downstream" technology for commodity processing is large scale technology; its use implies exports for the developing countries. There is some evidence that industrial countries will raise trade barriers if present capacity is adequate for industrial nations' own needs.
3. New technology to exploit the technological directions indicated by second law efficiency, as with all new technology, may be difficult to obtain from the nations that develop it. Because of the great differences in existing technology between rich and poor, devices de-

veloped to fit into industrial settings may not even be useful in the developing nations.

4. The development path taken by industrial countries demanded sharply rising energy inputs per dollar of GNP for several decades in the early stages of industrialization. To undertake such a commitment in the form of long-lived capital equipment at the very time industrial nations are forced to change their technical direction may actually worsen the relative position of developing countries.

5. The strategy itself may involve a misreading of history.

The patterns of energy use in developed countries make it no surprise to find that most equipment is fired with oil and gas or, to a lesser extent, with coal. The remaining technology is based almost entirely on electrical energy. In most developing countries, electrical energy serves mainly the urban areas and, for many uses, yields a very poor second law efficiency (in space and water heating or process heat generation, for instance). Those nations with abundant hydroelectric power may elect this route, but distribution networks will be hard to justify until commercial and residential loads are larger. In this case, the newest technology is nuclear generating stations. Besides requiring large jumps in electric demand (because of the scale of economical plants), a nuclear route imposes considerable dependence on (or even controls from) vendor nations. Problems of development abound in rural and village areas, but it is hard to think of one of those problems to which nuclear power is a solution. Developing countries might note that few orders for nuclear plants have been placed in the last two years in industrial nations. Two long-time consultants of the U.S. and French nuclear programs have recently concluded that the technology is not economically competitive (Bupp and Derain 1978).

Technology based on fossil fuel energy is now the principle kind for farm, industrial, and residential equipment. Most of the technology exported to (and increasingly manufactured in) developing countries is oil and gas fired. Rapid expansion of this kind of technology carries with it escalation in oil and possibly in gas imports. For countries without domestic oil and gas production, balance of payments deficits from fuel imports are already a problem. These technologies exhibit moderate to low second law efficiencies even in the industrial settings where they were developed. Exported to poorer nations, such equipment of course retains its low second law efficiencies; the equipment itself is often inappropriate. Papanek (1973) concludes that better exploitation of design opportunities could improve the match to developing countries' needs at smaller costs. Many of his suggestions lead to reduced fuel and resource use as well.

Mamdani (1972), studying Indian villagers, noted that the smallest available tractors were 35 horsepower models but that average land holdings were less than nine acres scattered among several small plots. His consequent recommendation—consolidation of land holdings—glosses over the mismatch of equipment to *present* problems and needs.

At a larger scale, many raw material producing nations have indicated interest in entering "downstream" activities based on domestic resource production (Attiga 1977; Tomeh 1977; Moran 1974). Downstream technology, at least in its most recent forms, is very sophisticated in energy and raw material use: "In a well designed process plant a unit of energy may be used five times or more before rejection to the environment" (Whiting 1978). This is one kind of second law efficiency gain discussed above, and its cascading of energy use is the practical realization of the scheme illustrated in figure 6.3. These recent developments, however, are often held as proprietary technology by corporations, and they are among the most difficult to transfer to other nations. In the United States and most European countries such proprietary interests are protected by law, and governments are left with little latitude to bring about transfer. Newly improved technologies of this sort are represented in large scale chemical plants, refineries, and raw materials finishing, among other activities. They constitute one of the two main classes of second law efficiency gains seen by Ross and Williams (1977) as promising but "highly engineered devices designed for specialized tasks." If transfer of technology of this class can be arranged, it may well be a good investment from a technical point of view, but it is not without problems.

First, such sophisticated technology is capital intensive and generates only modest amounts of employment among unskilled and semiskilled laborers. At the same time it can strain the limited pools of skilled technical talent in developing nations. It offers the risk of establishing new "enclaves" of activity in poor nations, and it remains to be seen if such enclaves are easier to incorporate into domestic economies when owned domestically.

Second and more serious is the large scale of these new efficient plants. Most developing countries lack the domestic markets to utilize their output fully, and the industrial countries, theoretical importers, have been reluctant to admit new producers into what has been their own preserve. Etienne Davignon, EEC trade commissioner, was blunt in his warning to developing countries "to stop getting into manufacturing facilities, primarily steel, that provide competition for the rich world" (*Manchester Guardian* 11 June 1978, quoted in Barraclough 1978). In the aftermath of 1973, some Western intellectuals pushed this line of argument still further: "Manufacturing entails labor, skill and intelligence. That technological innovation reduces the presence of labor in no way affects the central issue: It takes very little production to obtain petroleum. Oil is simply pumped from the ground, and that is accomplished by western technology. Those now garnering enormous riches from this activity in fact neither sow nor reap" (Seabury 1975). As mentioned, domestic law may be cited to protect proprietary industry ownership of technology, and the United States has also been willing to intervene to prohibit certain technological transfers on political grounds, as in the case of advanced oil drilling technology wanted by the Soviet Union in the summer of 1978. In an odd way, technology is now a private property matter while resources are declared to be the "common heritage of mankind."

The purpose of raising these cautions is not to foster despair but to recognize the issues surrounding transfer of large-scale efficient technology for what they are: neither technical nor economic, but political.

Development patterns based on heavy industry may carry serious penalties, especially if the most efficient technology is not available. The economic growth of the United States from 1880 to 1920 was accompanied by a continuous decline in the number of GNP dollars generated per unit of energy expended (fig. 6.5). Such falling energy efficiencies in income production have been observed in other countries at times, and some consider them a regular feature of industrialization (Mesarovic and Pestel 1974, p. 138). Darmstadter et al. (1971, p. 36) concluded that "the scope for industrial growth that implies a large expansion in energy requirements relative to national output growth is a function of the country's stage and pattern of development." We suggest that one of the patterns of development responsible for this escalation of energy use is the construction of inefficient capital equipment, perhaps already obsolescent but with a long life in production. This view is supported by the high energy/GNP ratios of Eastern European countries with heavy industries based on older technology.

New interests in developed countries focus on efficiency gains from fluidized bed combustion, cogeneration, efficient appliances, cascading production equipment, and distributed systems (Whiting 1978; Lovins 1977; USDOE 1978). To apply some of these possibilities in developing countries may be easier than it is in industrial nations with extensive sunk costs in present capital equipment and very different domestic markets. Meanwhile, these developments are sufficiently new that many of the "turnkey" industrial plants could be on the way to obsolescence even before the plant is completed.

In a broader historical context, even industrialization may be misread. The supposed sequence of science and technology—research, development, and commercialization—is so firmly ingrained in much present

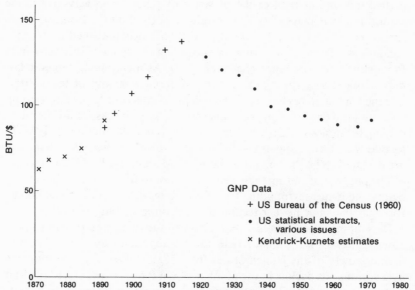

Fig. 6.5. Energy intensity of U.S. economic growth 1870–1975 (thousands of BTUs/ dollar GNP, five-year averages). Sources: Schurr and Netschert (1960) on energy use; U.S. Bureau of the Census (1960) and U.S. Bureau of the Census, *Statistical Abstract of the United States* (various issues) on energy use and GNP.

thinking that the history of industry is often obscured. No scientific understanding of the steam engine was accomplished until more than 40 years after it had been put in service. Useful innovation upon which the industrial revolution rests was devised by local people in response to needs. The focus of such innovation was problems needing solutions; the innovators were seldom formally trained in science and engineering. Speaking of the Erie Canal, Morison (1974, p. 44) observes that the builders "opened the first—and quite possibly the best—school of general engineering in this country. . . . From this experience these scores of men went out to build with ingenuity and confidence many different kinds of things in many different parts of the country." John Jervis, for example, entered this school as an untutored woodcutter and went on to build the New York water system and the first locomotive in America. Although such efforts no doubt made use of whatever scientific and technical information was at hand, the importance of the focus on immediate problems should not be underestimated. To defer action for basic research may sometimes be a mistake. Utterback (1974), in a survey of innovation and diffusion of industrial technology, concludes that "basic research does not seem to be significant as a direct source of innovations." The Chinese reliance on internally generated technology has produced some notable successes as well as some failures (no one need prove again that backyard steel production is not a viable choice). The overall results, however, compare favorably with what has been accomplished by other countries with far more outside aid (Stavrianos 1976).

Other differences in setting between the rich countries and developing countries serve to suggest that attempts to apply past formulas for industrialization are inappropriate. Population densities and land availability, labor force, competition, and a host of other contrasts between developed and developing countries suggest that successful development paths for today are unlikely to be those of the past.

### Developing Efficient and Conservational Technology

Technology alone is never sufficient to guarantee solutions to the problems discussed above. Little or none of present industrial technology was designed to be appropriate for developing nations. Acceptance of currently available technology, and the conditions under which is it offered by industrial countries, seems a recipe for what Amin (1974) has described as "the modernization of poverty."

Natural resource supplies and prices have precipitated a change of technical direction in the developed countries, and poor nations might do well to seek a path of development that not only suits their own special domestic conditions but also anticipates changes of direction (fig. 6.6). Such a development may involve "appropriate technology" (Eckaus 1977), but, as a prescription, such a choice is not very helpful. No one is likely to favor inappropriate technology. "Intermediate technology" (Schumacher 1973) may be a more descriptive term, but it is hardly quantitative.

Changed directions for developing countries have elicited a variety of suggestions for incremental technological improvement along intermediate technology routes. From some engineers come direct calls to reassess what is needed rather than to build still more complex equipment (Morgan 1977). Housing needs could bring labor intensive solutions that fit central aid to local needs and local materials (Stokes 1978). The more traditional, aid-oriented Overseas Development Council is seriously investigating village needs and appropriately scaled energy assists to tasks (Howe 1977). And from some Third World scientists comes a range of suggestions for cogeneration, mini-hydroelectric installations, improved stoves, biogas generators, biomass fuels, and other efforts that exhibit task matching and good second law efficiencies at modest scale (Goldemberg 1978). Projects of this kind are numerous in China and their contribution to rural and urban development impressive (Smil 1977; Stavrianos 1976). Although no detailed data are available, some of the small scale ef-

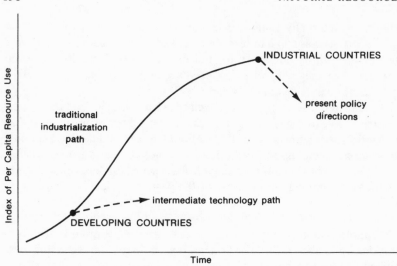

Fig. 6.6. Graphical representation of traditional development/resource use path and policy options (no scale).

forts which failed in China ("backyard" steelmaking) had low second law efficiencies.*

Second law efficiencies can provide a practical and quantitative measure with which to choose, or to choose among, intermediate technologies in planning for development. Not every high second law efficiency arises in intermediate technology, and there are certainly other features of intermediate technology to be considered. Good second law efficiencies, in short, are a necessary but not sufficient criterion for evaluating technology for development.

There is a more abstract side to developing more effective technological directions. Papanek (1973), among industrial designers, makes a strong case that design for tasks is the only way to arrive at an economy of means and lowest cost. The design process, guided by focus on the specific task or problem, then meshes well with the second law criterion. Yet, however much this attitude might bring design closer to an art rather than a science, it is still the fundamental goal of all engineering. Simon (1969, pp. 55–65, 58–59) says it well:

Historically and traditionally, it has been the task of the science disciplines to teach about natural things: how things are and how they work. It has been the task

---

*This conclusion can be estimated by using actual large-scale steel mill requirements for $B_{min}$ in equation (6.3). The actual values for any conceivable "backyard" process ($B_{actual}$) would give low values for $\eta$.

of engineering schools to teach about artificial things: how to make artifacts that have desired properties and how to design. . . . Design is the core of all professional training; it is the principal mark that distinguishes the professions from the sciences. . . . The natural sciences are concerned with how things are. Design, on the other hand, is concerned with how things ought to be, with devising artifacts to attain goals.

Thus the connection is complete. Planning for tasks leads to a second law efficiency measure as a criterion, and such a focus on tasks raises choices for design and "how things ought to be done." Because markets, even where they function well in developing countries, will not maximize second law efficiencies, both the practical and abstract arguments indicate that second law evaluation is a tool properly part of the development planning process. Efficiency and appropriate design can be fostered. If markets also function in the area of a task, they will help to select high first law efficiencies and will further improve choice.

## Conclusions

We began by showing in a formal way the functional independence of the efficiency measures that derive from first and second law thermodynamic considerations. Economic efficiency in allocation of resources was shown to move toward higher first law efficiencies but, in general, not to optimize second law efficiencies. This arises, in commonsense terms, because economic efficiency is concerned with the production and exchange of commodities while the second law treats tasks and objectives.

Issues of design and how things ought to be connect second law measures with the planning for development. This universality of energy flows permits consideration of the large nonmarket sectors in developing nations. Because these nonmarket activities most often involve the poorest persons with the fewest advantages, plans may be evaluated rationally "to the greatest benefit of the least advantaged" (Rawls 1971, p. 302).

We conclude, then, that:

1. Second law efficiency measures provide one rational, quantitative way of evaluating projects and technological choices for resource allocation. Such measures are necessary but almost certainly not sufficient.
2. Good thermodynamic matching in a heterogeneous environment often means decentralization of choices and smaller scale enterprises. Certainly, the larger the unit scale of projects, the more of a compromise that must be made for any specific task or goal. This conclusion does not necessarily imply decentralized information flows or assistance.

3. Some highly complex, large-scale technologies do exhibit good second law efficiencies; here too, rational choice among large projects can be aided by second law tests of efficiency.
4. A strategy of conservation and thermodynamic matching anticipates the changing directions of industrial nations and takes advantage, as an asset, of the early stage of development in many countries. Some existing options for developing countries are closed to developed countries both by the immense capital investment in present directions and by political coalitions supporting present directions.

## Research Recommendations

To follow up these conclusions and to test their utility in practical affairs, several kinds of information are needed of which the following seem to be the most urgent:

1. End-use thermodynamic profiles of developing countries are badly needed. Even for industrial countries such information is spotty and incomplete. Only when such data are in hand can tasks and matching be quantitatively considered.
2. End-use energy data need to be collected in such a way that they can be disaggregated in accordance with the tasks associated with basic human needs (food, clothing, shelter, and the like). Pleas for such a functional classification have been made before and the work is well underway in industrial nations. With such data the ongoing efforts to create an index of basic human needs or quality of life might be better linked to development choices.
3. Energy analysis of human societies should continue as a complement to economic analysis. No doubt many of the early claims for energy analysis will prove wrong and overly optimistic, but energy analysis is already playing a role in policy formulation, at least in the United States (Williamson 1978). The universality and invariability of quantitative energy measures, if nothing else, make efforts in this direction promising for developing nations. In particular, the relation of energy analysis to resource allocation needs further study.

## References

Amin, Galal. 1974. *The Modernization of Poverty*. Leiden, The Netherlands: E. J. Brill.
APS (American Physical Society). 1975. "Efficient Use of Energy," *AIP Conference Proceedings 25*. New York: American Institute of Physics.
Attiga, A. A. 1977. "Regional Cooperation in Downstream Investments—the

Case of OAPEC." OPEC Seminar on the Present and Future Role of National Oil Companies, Vienna, Austria.

Ayres, Robert U. 1978. *Resources, Environment, and Economics: Applications of the Materials/Energy Balance Principle.* New York: Wiley.

Barraclough, Geoffrey. 1978. "Waiting for the New Order," *New York Review of Books* 25 (16): 45–53.

Berndt, E. R., and D. O. Wood. 1975. "Technology, Prices and the Derived Demand for Energy," *Review of Economics and Statistics* 57: 259–68.

Berry, R. S., G. Heal, and P. Salamon. Undated. "On a Relation Between Economic and Thermodynamic Optima: A Working Paper." Department of Chemistry, University of Chicago, Chicago, Illinois, and Department of Economics, University of Sussex, England.

Bohr, Niels. 1958. *Atomic Physics and Human Knowledge.* New York: Wiley.

Boretsky, M. 1975. "Trends in U.S. Technology: A Political Economist's View," *American Scientist* 63: 70–82.

Brown, H. 1976. "Energy in Our Future," *Annual Review of Energy* 1: 1–36.

Bupp, I. C., and J. C. Derain. 1978. *Light Water: How the Nuclear Dream Dissolved.* New York: Basic Books.

Clark, Colin W. 1976. *Mathematical Bioeconomics: The Optimal Management of Renewable Resources.* New York: Wiley.

Cloud, Preston. 1977. "Entropy, Materials, and Posterity," *Geologische Rundschau* 66: 678–96.

Common, M. 1977. "The Economics of Energy Analysis Reconsidered." In J. A. G. Thomas, ed., *Energy Analysis.* Boulder, Colorado: Westview, pp. 140–47.

Cook. E. 1976. *Man, Energy, and Society.* San Francisco: Freeman.

Darmstadter, J., with P. D. Teitelbaum and J. G. Polach. 1971. *Energy in the World Economy: A Statistical Review of Trends in Output, Trade, and Consumption Since 1925.* Baltimore: Johns Hopkins University Press.

Dumas, L. J. 1976. *The Conservation Response: Strategies for the Design and Operation of Energy-Using Systems.* Lexington, Massachusetts: Lexington Books.

Eckaus, R. S. 1977. *Appropriate Technologies for Developing Countries.* Washington, D.C.: National Academy of Sciences.

Eckholm, E. 1976. *Losing Ground: Environmental Stress and World Food Prospects.* New York: Norton.

Gabor, Dennis. 1970. *Innovations: Scientific, Technological, and Social.* New York: Oxford University Press.

Gallucci, V. F. 1973. "On the Principles of Thermodynamics in Ecology," *Annual Review of Ecology and Systematics* 4: 329–57.

Georgescu-Roegen, Nicholas. 1971. *The Entropy Law and the Economic Process.* Cambridge, Massachusetts: Harvard University Press.

Gilliland, Martha, ed. 1978. *Energy Analysis: A New Public Policy Tool.* Boulder, Colorado: Westview.

Goldemberg, José. 1978. "Energy Strategy for Developed and Less Developed Countries," Report PU/CES 70. Princeton University, Princeton, New Jersey.

Griliches, A., and D. W. Jorgenson. 1967. "The Explanation of Productivity Change," *Review of Economic Studies* 34: 249–83.

Herrera, A. O., H. D. Scolnik, G. Chichilnisky, G. C. Gallopin, J. E. Hardoy, D. Mosovich, E. Oteiza, G. Brest, C. E. Suarez, and L. Talavera. 1976. *Catastrophe or New Society? A Latin American World Model*. Ottawa: International Research Center.

Hertzmark, D. I. 1978. "Economics, Thermodynamics, and the Allocation of Energy." Ph.D. thesis, University of Wisconsin-Madison.

Howe, J. W. 1977. *Energy for the Villages of Africa*. Washington, D.C.: Overseas Development Council.

Institute of Gas Technology. 1976. *A Comparison of the Net Energy Production Ratios of Integrated Systems Supplying Natural Gas, and SNG from Coal*. Chicago, Illinois.

Jewkes, J., D. Sawers, and R. Stillerman, 1969. *The Sources of Invention*. 2nd ed. New York: Norton.

Johansson, T. B., and P. Steen. 1977. *Solar Sweden*. Stockholm: Secretariat for Future Studies.

Kendrick, John W. 1961. *Productivity Trends in the United States*. New York: National Bureau of Economic Research.

Leontief, Wassily W. 1977. *The Future of the World Economy*. New York: Oxford University Press.

Lovins, A. B. 1976. "Energy Strategy: The Industry, Small Business and Public Stakes." In L. C. Ruedisili and M. W. Firebaugh, eds., *Perspectives on Energy: Issues, Ideas, and Environmental Dilemmas*. 2nd ed. New York: Oxford University Press, pp. 539–52.

Lovins, A. B. 1977. *Soft Energy Paths: Toward a Durable Peace*. Cambridge, Massachusetts: Ballinger.

Mamdani, M. 1972. *The Myth of Population Control*. New York: Monthly Review Press.

Mesarovic, Mihajlo, and Edvard Pestel. 1974. *Mankind at the Turning Point: The Second Report to the Club of Rome*. New York: Dutton.

Moran, T. H. 1974. *Multinational Corporations and the Politics of Dependence: Copper in Chile*. Princeton, New Jersey: Princeton University Press.

Morgan, R. P. 1977. "Technology and International Development: New Directions Needed," *Chemical and Engineering News* 55 (46): 31–39.

Morison, E. 1974. *From Know-How to Nowhere: The Development of American Technology*. New York: Basic Books.

Nordhaus, W. D. 1972. "The Recent Productivity Slowdown," *Brookings Papers on Economic Activity*, no. 3, 493–536.

Odum, H. T. 1971. *Environment, Power, and Society*. New York, Wiley.

Odum, H. T., and E. C. Odum. 1976. *Energy Basis for Man and Nature*. New York: McGraw-Hill.

Papanek, V. 1973. *Design for the Real World: Human Ecology and Social Change*. New York: Bantam Books.

Pauli, W. 1973. *Lectures on Physics*. Cambridge, Massachusetts: MIT Press.

Putnam, P. C. 1953. *Energy in the Future*. New York: Van Nostrand.

Rawls, John. 1971. *A Theory of Justice.* Cambridge, Massachusetts: Harvard University Press.

Renshaw, E. F. 1976. *The End of Progress: Adjusting to a No-growth Economy.* North Scituate, Massachusetts: Duxbury.

Ross, M. H., and R. H. Williams. 1977. "The Potential for Fuel Conservation," *Technology Review* 79(4): 49–57.

Sardar, Ziauddim, and Darwud Rosser-Owen. 1977. "Science Policy in Developing Countries." In I. Spiegel-Rosing and D. deSolla Price, eds., *Science, Technology and Society.* London: Sage pp. 535–75.

Schon, D. 1971. *Beyond the Stable State.* New York: Norton.

Schumacher, E. F. 1973. *Small is Beautiful: Economics as if People Mattered.* New York: Harper & Row.

Schurr, S. H., and B. C. Netschert. 1960. *Energy in the American Economy, 1850–1975.* Baltimore: Johns Hopkins University Press.

Seabury, P. 1975. "The Moral Issue," *The New Leader* (February 17), pp. 11–13.

Simon, Herbert A. 1969. *The Sciences of the Artificial.* Cambridge, Massachusetts: MIT Press.

Smil, Vaclav. 1977. "Intermediate Energy Technology in China," *Bulletin of the Atomic Scientists* 33(2): 25–31.

Soddy, F. 1912. *Matter and Energy.* London: Williams and Norgate.

*Soft Energy Notes.* 1978. "Four New Studies Address a Soft Energy Path for France," *Soft Energy Notes* 1: 37–40.

Stavrianos, L. S. 1976. *The Promise of the Coming Dark Age.* San Francisco: Freeman.

Steinhart, Carol, and John Steinhart. 1974. *Energy: Sources, Use and Role in Human Affairs.* North Scituate, Massachusetts: Duxbury.

Steinhart, J. S., and C. E. Steinhart. 1974. "Energy Use in the U.S. Food System," *Science* 184: 307–16.

Steinhart, J. S., M. E. Hanson, R. W. Gates, C. C. DeWinkel, K. Briody, M. Thornsjo, and S. Kabala. 1977. "A Low Energy Scenario for the United States: 1975–2050." In L. C. Ruedisili and M. W. Firebaugh, eds., *Perspectives on Energy: Issues, Ideas, and Environmental Dilemmas.* 2nd ed. New York: Oxford University Press, pp. 553–80.

Stokes, Bruce. 1978. "Do-it-Yourself Housing: A Chance for Shelter in Tomorrow's Crowded World," *The Futurist* 12: 233–37.

Thomas, J. A. G., ed. 1977. *Energy Analysis.* Boulder, Colorado: Westview.

Tomeh, George J. 1977. "OAPEC: Its Growing Role in Arab and World Affairs," *Journal of Energy and Development* 3(1): 26–36.

U.S. Bureau of the Census. 1960. *Historical Statistics of the United States, Colonial Times to 1957.* Washington, D.C.: U.S. Government Printing Office.

USDI (U.S. Department of the Interior). 1975. *Energy Perspectives.* Washington, D.C.: U.S. Government Printing Office.

USDOE (U.S. Department of Energy). 1978. *Distributed Energy Systems.* Washington, D.C.: USDOE.

Utterback, J. M. 1974. "Innovation in Industry and the Diffusion of Technology," *Science* 183: 620–26.

Webb, M., and D. Pearce. 1977. "The Economics of Energy Analysis." In J. A. G. Thomas, ed., *Energy Analysis.* Boulder, Colorado: Westview, pp. 126–39.

Whiting, M. 1978. "Industry Saves Energy: Progress Report, 1977," *Annual Review of Energy* 3: 181–99.

Williamson, R. H. 1978. "Energy Analysis in Energy Research and Development: Planning and Decisionmaking." In Martha Gilliland, ed., *Energy Analysis: A New Public Policy Tool.* Boulder, Colorado: Westview, pp. 89–96.

# 7 *Abdulaziz Al-Wattari*

# The Case of Petroleum

Petroleum—the Latin root means "rock oil"—was known and used in ancient civilizations of Mesopotamia (contemporary Iraq) some 4000 years ago. As an industry, however, catering to modern requirements of energy and lubricants, it is young—a little over a century old. The technology created and developed to service this industry is also new in the sense that it has not, principally, evolved from older handicraft techniques or any prior state of the arts.

The specific industrial activities that constitute modern oil industry technologies—the economically and technologically definable functions of exploration, drilling, production, transportation by pipeline and tanker, refining, and distribution of petroleum products—are derived from the principles of physics and chemistry and brought about predominantly through the medium of professional research, experimental development, and demonstration.

## Natural Characteristics

The natural physical-chemical properties of oil and the nature of its geological occurrences are of fundamental importance for all discovery, transport, and processing of petroleum as well as for using all its major "economic" products. DeChazeau and Khan (1959, p. 61) provide a succinct summary of oil's natural characteristics:

The oil industry is what it is very largely because of the peculiarities of its raw material. First and foremost, petroleum is a fluid both as "captured" from the hidden recesses of the earth and as it passes through processing into final uses. Second, it is concealed in the earth: all the advances of modern science have been incapable of eliminating the high element of gamble in its quest. Third, it is a raw material of almost infinite potentialities—some will be lost forever if care is not taken, some can be secured simply, others only with costly special equipment—from which a varying pattern of final products can be procured at a price. And finally, oil is an exhaustible resource, dissipated as used, of which the quantity of ultiate supply is not known. No one of these characteristics is unique to oil; but their combination is truly unique and it imparts an unmatched potentially explosive vehemence to competitive forces in the industry.

The ways in which these fundamental characteristics have influenced, indeed largely determined, the economics and organizational structure of the industry are detailed below.

## Fluidity

Petroleum occurs in nature as a liquid associated with natural gas, which causes the oil to move across pressure gradients within the reservoir.* All the commercial petroleum derivatives are also fluids. The property of fluidity allows continuous movement in pipelines and processing equipment from reservoir through producing well to field production plant, then through pipeline, tanker, or tank truck transport networks to refineries, depots, and final distribution outlets. Mass transfer takes place by pump and compressor where the fluids, often combustible, are not handled by man.

The "convenience" of this natural liquidity of petroleum and its products is one major reason for its favorable economics compared to solid fuels, particularly coal. Also, the high hydrogen-to-carbon ratio of petroleum makes its calorific value the highest among natural chemical fuels;** it does not suffer from some of coal's well-known environmental disadvantages in production and use. It is noteworthy that most of the research associated with coal and oil shales has centered on imparting fluidity or converting to gas (by costly energy-intensive methods).

Transport's key role in petroleum economics—from field to storage to refineries to market—often blurs the demarcation lines among petroleum

---

*The terms *petroleum*, *oil*, and *crude oil* are often used interchangeably. In the context of this chapter, reference to crude oil is intended to mean the typical Middle Eastern crudes coming from the several giant fields which provide the core of production to world markets. The range of their gravities is between 28° and 36° API.

**The heat value, for example, of fuel oil is about 19,000 BTU/lb, whereas that of coal ranges between 12,000 (for lignite) and 15,000 (for anthracite).

activities and suggests an obvious advantage in linking them for optimization of the system. In this, oil is not unique among industries, but as Frankel (1969, pp. 38–39) points out, the material amount of oil moved is essentially the same in volume into and out of the refinery. With steel, by contrast, the amount of raw material that enters a blast furnace is many times the weight and bulk of the iron produced. In a modern refinery the volume of crude input is roughly equal to that of total product volume minus any fuel used for processing. Frankel further notes that pipelines save the cost of transporting "empties."

### Economies of Scale and Flow

Because of its combustible nature, petroleum as both raw material and products must unavoidably move in a closed system of pipes, vessels, etc., from source to final consumer. The simple geometry of three-dimensional space permits large internal economies of scale* in moving and processing media. In general, for such types of equipment, investment cost is proportional to surface area while output, at full capacity use, is a function of the volume of the tanks, tubes, vessels, etc. For such equipment investment cost per unit output does not increase proportionately with increase in capacity (provided that no constraints exist elsewhere in the production system or its auxiliary infrastructural complements). For refineries and petrochemical plants, which are processing systems made essentially from tubular and other similar equipment, a simple empirical rule relates cost of plant to its capacity:

$$\frac{C2}{C1} = \left[\frac{Q2}{Q1}\right]^f$$

where $Q1$ and $Q2$ are two capacities, and $C1$ and $C2$ are the respective costs. The exponent $f$ for refinery plants is about 0.6 and gives the rule its name—the Point Six Rule (Nelson 1958, p. 879). Using this rule and 1956 cost figures, an atmospheric distillation plant of 20,000 barrels per day (bpd), for example, cost about $1.2 million, while a similar plant with five times the capacity cost about $3.6 million. That is, investment cost increased only three times, while capacity gained five times. Table 7.1 shows values of the $f$ exponent for a number of petrochemical plants.

Fluid flow also makes possible the continuous transfer of petroleum and its products in transport and processing. Hydrocarbon processing systems or their subsystems can be kept on production stream for a year or even more, continuously. Stable demand growth rates requiring pro-

---

*Other economies of scale external to the individual plant but internal to a firm are touched upon in the discussion of petroleum industry organization and integration.

TABLE 7.1.
Capacity Ratio Exponents for Complete Process Plants

| Process plant | Exponent ($f$) |
|---|---|
| Acetylene | 0.75 |
| Ammonia | 0.74 |
| Ammonium nitrate | 0.54 |
| Benzene | 0.61 |
| Chlorine/caustic soda | 0.45 |
| Ethanol | 0.60 |
| Ethylene | 0.58 |
| Ethylene oxide | 0.79 |
| Formaldehyde | 0.55 |
| Methanol | 0.83 |
| Nitric acid | 0.56 |
| Oxygen | 0.64 |
| Phosphoric acid | 0.58 |
| Polyethylene (low pressure) | 0.67 |
| Polyethylene (high pressure) | 0.70 |
| Styrene | 0.68 |
| Sulfuric acid (contact) | 0.62 |
| Urea | 0.59 |

Source: Unpublished data of the Organization of Arab Petroleum Exporting Countries (OAPEC), 1977.

duction of a large volume of supplies have made continuous processing feasible in refining, in contrast to the "batch" methods used in the early refining days of this century. Continuous processing has in fact resulted in additional economies, particularly in linked production operations.

### Derived Economic Features—Downstream Activities

"Downstream" economic activities in the petroleum industry are here considered to begin with a "developed" petroleum field after exploration, an activity quite distinct in its peculiarities and implications. Downstream activities are the extraction of petroleum, its transport by pipeline and/or tanker, its refining, and distribution of its products. All these activities are founded on those natural characteristics of the petroleum resource which allow continuous flow through fixed pipes and vessels to the separation and modification stages at which crude oil becomes a commercial product mix to meet changing demand. At each stage, activities are carried out with little direct human "handling." This generalization does not entirely fit the distribution phase, of course, but that exception does not upset the main thesis: The system is predominantly made up of fixed capital assets, incorporates complex technology, and allows a fine degree of control within each stage and among stages. With rising demand the system can grow larger and larger while deriving increasing benefits from economies of scale. The system is highly capital intensive (in terms of the capital/labor ratio), perhaps the most intensive in the industrial sector and much higher, for example, than the analogous coal system. Variable labor cost is small. Therefore, to keep the system continuously running at the highest practical level of activity would seem the rational decision for a cost-minimizing decision maker, everything else being equal. The rule would seem to be "the more you produce and sell, the lower are your per unit fixed costs and the quicker you can recover heavy capital commitments." The behavioral implications for those in charge of refining (indeed of any industry with a high fixed-to-variable cost ratio) is to push for maximum saleable output because the extra barrel passed through processing—the marginal barrel above average refinery capacity utilization—needs essentially to bear only the low variable cost component. It follows that it even pays sometimes to sell at prices below opportunity cost before one is compelled to reduce output. There is an inherent tendency to overproduce to attain maximum capacity utilization. Competition follows, and for some major refining markets in the United States and Northern Europe, this competitiveness is analytically and empirically well established (Griffen 1972; Deam 1974).

The other behavioral implication flowing from size and capital intensity is a tendency to minimize any uncertainty that threatens continuous operation; hence the economic necessity to secure supplies of raw material on the one hand and to exercise certain discipline in markets on the other.

The foregoing dictates and "explains" in some measure the industry's structure as it evolved from the days of the Standard Oil cartel until the early 1970s and even later. One must add, with regard to downstream activities, that capital intensity brings enormous investment requirements which do much to discourage new firms' entry and to reinforce concentration in the industry.

## Finding Oil

The methods of prospecting for oil involve geology and geophysics followed by exploratory drilling. Geologic crews are first dispatched to study the outcrops. Sedimentology work and geochemistry follow. In the absence of surface geologic features indicating prospective drilling areas, geophysical methods are relied upon to investigate subsurface structures where petroleum accumulations are perceived to be possible and to determine where to drill. The sequence begins with the less expensive techniques and moves to the more costly when necessary. Magnetic, gravimetric, and seismic techniques run in this order in most cases. Drilling in search of oil starts with the more promising structures thus located.

If petroleum is in fact discovered and recovery found to be economically feasible, a plan is prepared for developing an oil field. The functions carried out before development constitute exploration. This process is quite distinct technically and economically. Its basic features resemble those of research and development—a probe into the unknown as regards both quantity and quality of petroleum sought.

The activities involved in "proving-up" or developing discovered reserves and bringing oil to the surface for sale and use take on the features of normal investment in physical assets to produce value-added. The amount of development investment depends not only on the true (but unknown) size of the reservoir but also on the desired amount of oil to be "proved"—made available for initial extraction. This development process for a reserve or a discovery is an industrial investment in the sense that it does not involve the kind of risks inherent in exploration. In terms of finance, if borrowing and lending are involved, "proving" is considered essentially a normal business transaction. A discovered reserve may be proved in one investment or in stages. The giant Ghawar field in Saudi Arabia is a remarkable instance of the latter type of investment. A number of what were thought to be independent fields were discovered and developed, but many years of investigation of reservoir behavior showed them to be one huge field. In the United States, field development is subject to many regulations on number of wells, well spacing, and rate of production in relation to the technically determined "maximum efficient rate" (MER) of extraction.

Exploration and development are commonly recognized as quite distinct because of their entirely different levels of risk and uncertainty; however, any perceived relation between them, whether stable or unstable, gives rise to outstanding differences of opinion on whether a rationale exists for controlling and regulating the oil industry. The prevailing view among most producing nations, one shared by many scholars, is that production and hence price have always been administered (it is immaterial how or by whom) because of the uncertainties in finding oil, the unevenness of petroleum reservoirs in size and geographic distribution, and the relative importance of oil to producers and consumers (WAES 1977). These features have held true for the industry since its inception in 1859, despite all technological advances. Exploration still requires heavy expenditure of risk money in view of the low rate of success in discovering new oil. Many dry holes must be financed out of the gains from successful ones, and all such costs are part of the operator's fixed overhead.

Wildcat well success rates average only about 5 percent and are declining. It is the successful few, however, who attract new venture money to exploration and keep the hunt going in hope of more lucky strikes. The ease of sinking a well in a common pool and the "law of capture" prompted regulation in the United States, as operators tried to outdo each other in producing and selling oil for quick recovery of their heavy "overhead" or finding cost. With excess production leading to lower prices and waste of resource, major producing states within the United States universally introduced regulatory conservation measures and some form of price administration in 1930 and 1931.

In the same way, but much later, concern over depletion in view of their own expected needs led Middle Eastern producing countries to limit their output and to use their weight (that is, power) in the market to set a base price for exported oil.

Although Adelman (1972, p. 25) recognizes the distinct character of exploration and development, he nevertheless describes the two as "linked because they are imperfect substitutes for each other. . . . " He explains this to mean that by investing more in the certain activity of development, one increases one's proved reserves and so avoids, for a time, the risk of looking for new oil, a task which can be postponed. But how can one determine the validity of this view under a basically uncertain situation for all new finds? Besides, for large operators the range of reserve expansion to ultimate recovery can be estimated (within limits) only when averaged over several fields. Do not the regulation and conservation of what certainly exists in giant fields seem more rational than depleting these reserves according to marginal cost criteria? Adelman (1972, pp. 34–38) further waters down the certainty of reserves in giant Middle Eastern fields by calling the phenomenon of giant oil fields "random shocks" so that they fit his marginalization model of a world petroleum market. Accordingly he decides that output from these fields represents an overcapacity that constitutes a sort of hydraulic pressure on an "artificial price dam" which keeps prices from falling to their natural floor of marginal cost. Concepts of depletion and the producing state's time preferences of production are noninformation to Adelman's market model. Neither does he pay attention to the specific nature of the resource.

In actual practice, expectations based on optimism or pessimism about oil reserves do influence the actions of big buyers and big sellers, and because there is no futures market in oil (it can be kept without cost in its natural habitat), major producers and consumers may have to find a form of agreement governing future relations.

Marginal cost pricing concepts derived from production theory, when applied to petroleum production, run against the snag of discontinuity, both conceptual and empirical, between the finding stage and the field development stage for new oil. Investment at the finding stage is not based on a predetermined set of information about a desired product because both quantity and quality are in fact unknown. Investment in the "proving up" or development stage is based on such information, but these two activities are not, a priori, additive and therefore cannot analytically be treated as one production function.

The actual discontinuity is created by the nature of petroleum, alluded to earlier, which for the foreseeable future limits substitution in certain petroleum-specific uses; petroleum's depletion as a finite stock resource; and the different time preference rates of petroleum's various owners and users. Only the creation of a "backstop technology" that makes continuous substitution at the margin possible and feasible may validate the assumptions of production theory. In the meantime, regulation and price administration, as have been the case in the history of the industry, seem unavoidable.

### Growth

Supply economics, as advanced above, is largely dictated by the nature of the oil resource and the facts of three-dimensional space. The technology developed to meet exponentially growing demand has, among other advances, pushed back the limits of structural material strength to build increasingly large capital equipment in the production system, and so to lower cost per unit output of value added and bring forward ever-increasing amounts of petroleum derivatives, old and new.

The demand for oil, really a derived demand for its derivatives, has been changing not only in terms of quantities produced and used but also in terms of the derivatives' quality and variety. In the beginning crude oil was produced primarily to distill from it hydrocarbons of the kerosene boiling range. Kerosene then was the "economic" product widely used as an illuminant and as a source of household cooking heat (it is still widely used for these two purposes in most developing countries).

Gasoline, on the other hand, was a byproduct of little use, a hazardous material which brought mostly disposal problems. It was only after the mass production of the private auto that gasoline gained substantial production value (in the United States around 1923) and that oil production began to be geared to rising demand for gasoline. Kerosene, other middle distillates, and fuel oil became the byproducts and were marketed in competition with other available fuel substitutes. The superior quality of fuel oil as a boiler fuel quickly established it as a growth leader in central power generation plants and in ships' and railroads' power plants. From 1929 to 1955 its annual sales for heating purposes rose from 37 to 426 million tons in the United States (DeChazeau and Khan 1959, p. 4). World-wide consumption of fuel oil, including ships' bunker oil, rose from 770 thousand bpd in 1938 to 13.5 million bpd in 1973 (BP 1959; BP 1967; BP 1977) at an annually compounded rate of growth of 8.5 percent.

Middle distillates developed their foothold in the domestic heating markets of the United States and in the diesel power plants of railroad locomotives, trucks, ships, and small industries. Last but not least is commercial aviation, in which demand for middle distillates (jet fuel) rose from 170 thousand bpd in 1930 to 14.59 million bpd in 1977 at a compound growth rate of more than 12 percent annually.

Refined fuels, apart from gasoline and some middle distillates with their captive markets, were sold in price competition with substitutes and not on the basis of production costs. Gasoline, but not these other fuels, has always borne the major proportion of total refining costs. Although some middle distillates, notably diesel and jet fuel, did evolve their own cost/price market orientation along with gasoline's, fuel oil remained in price competition with solid fuels and sold at about crude acquisition cost or a little below. With the 1973 price jump for crude oil, fuel oil now represents a cost penalty, at going product prices, for most refiners. Consequently there has for some time been an increasing effort on the part of major refining centers to convert as much fuel oil as possible to lighter products to improve refining economics. This shift away from fuel oil can be clearly seen in Table 7.2.

Growth of demand for products has led to an equivalent rise in demand for crude oil and to astounding growth rates in the production of crude. Total world production according to Frankel (1969, p. 1) rose from about 1 million metric tons annually (mta) in 1870 to 21 million mta in 1900 to about 300 million mta in 1939 and then, according to British Petroleum (1977), to 1990 million mta in 1968 and 3040 million mta in 1977. The rule of thumb in the international petroleum industry had been, until recently, that oil production would double every ten years in a 7.1 percent annual growth rate. When supplies keep coming with only minor interruptions, a sort of stable expectation develops among both producers and consumers. Such expectations about a stock natural resource have not been conducive to gradual changes on the demand side to allow for diminishing reserves or to prepare for their ultimate exhaustion. On the supply side the responsibility to induce appropriate expectations—whether by pricing, taxing, or other political or regulatory means—lies with a few decision makers in private and public institutions. That responsibility can hardly be judged, in retrospect, to have been adequately discharged during most of the cheap energy era.

TABLE 7.2
Refinery Production: Percent Yield of Products
(Excluding refinery fuel)

| Year | LPG | Mogas naphtha | Middle distillates | Fuel oil | Other products | Total production |
|------|-----|---------------|--------------------|----------|----------------|------------------|
| | | | FRANCE | | | |
| 1972 | 2.3 | 18.0 | 41.8 | 33.0 | 4.9 | 100.0 |
| 1973 | 2.2 | 18.5 | 40.4 | 33.0 | 5.9 | 100.0 |
| 1977 | 2.5 | 19.8 | 39.2 | 31.9 | 6.6 | 100.0 |
| | | | GERMANY | | | |
| 1972 | 2.2 | 18.0 | 42.0 | 28.5 | 9.3 | 100.0 |
| 1973 | 2.3 | 19.4 | 41.8 | 27.0 | 9.5 | 100.0 |
| 1977 | 2.8 | 22.3 | 42.3 | 22.2 | 10.4 | 100.0 |
| | | | ITALY | | | |
| 1972 | 2.1 | 19.3 | 27.6 | 48.4 | 2.6 | 100.0 |
| 1973 | 2.2 | 19.1 | 29.1 | 47.1 | 2.5 | 100.0 |
| 1977[a] | 2.4 | 19.4 | 30.3 | 45.1 | 2.8 | 100.0 |
| | | | THE NETHERLANDS | | | |
| 1972 | 1.3 | 17.2 | 36.5 | 40.2 | 4.8 | 100.0 |
| 1973 | 1.4 | 17.8 | 36.6 | 39.1 | 5.1 | 100.0 |
| 1977 | 1.8 | 19.2 | 37.8 | 34.5 | 6.7 | 100.0 |
| | | | UNITED KINGDOM | | | |
| 1972 | 1.5 | 19.5 | 32.6 | 41.2 | 5.2 | 100.0 |
| 1973 | 1.6 | 20.2 | 33.1 | 39.7 | 5.4 | 100.0 |
| 1977 | 1.8 | 22.3 | 34.7 | 35.3 | 5.9 | 100.0 |
| | | AVERAGE OF 5 EUROPEAN COUNTRIES | | | | |
| 1972 | 1.9 | 18.5 | 36.0 | 38.3 | 5.3 | 100.0 |
| 1973 | 2.0 | 19.1 | 36.2 | 37.0 | 5.7 | 100.0 |
| 1977 | 2.3 | 20.7 | 37.0 | 33.4 | 6.6 | 100.0 |
| | | | CANADA | | | |
| 1973 | 1.3 | 32.7 | 15.0 | 40.5 | 10.5 | 100.0 |
| 1976 | 2.0 | 35.4 | 16.3 | 36.0 | 10.3 | 100.0 |
| 1977 | 1.9 | 33.8 | 16.4 | 35.8 | 12.1 | 100.0 |
| | | UNITED STATES OF AMERICA | | | | |
| 1972 | 2.5 | 49.9 | 28.6 | 6.1 | 12.9 | 100.0 |
| 1973 | 2.5 | 48.9 | 28.5 | 7.0 | 13.1 | 100.0 |
| 1976 | 2.2 | 48.7 | 27.4 | 9.4 | 12.3 | 100.0 |
| 1977[b] | 2.1 | 46.1 | 28.1 | 11.0 | 12.7 | 100.0 |
| | | | JAPAN | | | |
| 1972 | 6.8 | 23.3 | 15.7 | 50.9 | 3.3 | 100.0 |
| 1973 | 6.2 | 22.5 | 17.3 | 50.8 | 3.2 | 100.0 |
| 1977 | 6.2 | 23.7 | 18.9 | 48.4 | 2.8 | 100.0 |

Source: *Oil & Energy Trends Supplement,* 21 July 1978, p. 2.
[a]January–November 1977.
[b]January–October 1977.

214

Proved reserves have also been rising—from 34 billion barrels in 1938 to 77 billion barrels in 1949, 290 billion barrels in 1959, and 654 billion barrels in 1977 (BP 1959; BP 1977)—but at a lower rate than net additions to reserves.

Petroleum as a source of energy has meanwhile accounted for ever-larger shares of total energy consumption; the 15 percent share of 1925 grew to 60 percent in 1975. Coal production, simultaneously, has either stayed stable or risen slightly (it is subsidized in many countries) relative to total energy demand growth.

The phenomenal increases in petroleum extraction and consumption relative to the total available resource base of fossil hydrocarbons (proved petroleum and coal reserves) are rather disturbing. Much more oil than coal has been and is being extracted relative to their respective availabilities. That is to say, production of each is inversely proportional to the size of its known reserves. Disproportionate growth allowed cumulative production of oil in 1968 to match that of coal, at roughly 20 billion tons each, according to unpublished OAPEC figures. By 1975 cumulative production figures were 36 and 46 billion tons for coal and oil, respectively. With current proven reserves at 87 billion tons for oil and 700 billion tons for coal (WAES 1977, p. 28), it seems quite clear that oil prices, however determined, have not performed a rational allocative function, if rationality means that one ought to use more of one's most plentiful stock materials. Most oil products (more than half of 1977 U.S. crude consumption) have essentially no physical substitutes now or in the near future. These unsubstitutable products supply vital land, sea, and air transport, or raw materials to the chemical industry, which adds the highest value to petroleum hydrocarbons in the form of nonfuel products. Some petrochemical products, such as agricultural chemicals or photosensitive materials, command 100 times the value of naphtha, their raw material.

Crude prices have allowed overconsumption of oil, scarce relative to coal in physical terms, and a resulting imbalance in the world's resource base of fossil hydrocarbons. It is paradoxical that the highest value uses consume the least oil; the petrochemical industry in the United States consumes just 7 percent of crude production, in the form of naphtha (*Business Week*, 31 July 1978, p. 68).

Large and growing economies, geared to demand, make the most use of petroleum and take advantage of its unique qualities in both production and use. Supply of petroleum has for a relatively long time been highly elastic, and the system somehow did not register operationally effective signals for gradually bringing on the production of substitutes. Demand, on the other hand, was inelastic to price changes at the price level prevailing prior to 1973.

## The Industry

A basic premise in this chapter is that the oil industry's size and techno-economic characteristics are determined largely by the natural physical characteristics of the petroleum raw material and by the very high rates of growth in its production and consumption accompanying major technological developments in the transport industry. It is now worthwhile to look at the structure of the industry, apart from the resource, in particular at its organization and technology and briefly at its finance.

The most important features of the international petroleum industry are its huge size, its dominance by a few highly intergrated transnational corporations, its markets, its complex rather decentralized technological system in which many firms participate (with the reins of control in transnational corporate hands), and its enormous financial power based largely on self-financing.

By concentration or horizontal integration is meant the geographic extension and absolute size of markets in which one firm carries on economic activities.* In 1976 the nine largest oil firms provided 60 percent of world production, directly or through purchases from OPEC nations. These same companies refined 50 percent of this crude and distributed more than 55 percent of world petroleum products. Of the 15 largest transnational corporations involved in the production, refining, and distribution of petroleum, 10 are of U.S. registry. The two largest, Exxon and Royal Dutch Shell, attained and held the top position right from the industry's beginning; most others have also retained their early positions.

The industry's size in financial terms is colossal. According to the Chase Manhattan Bank (1976), at the end of 1975 the industry's fixed assets were $334 billion, 40 percent of which were in the United States. Capital expenditures (including exploration expenditures) were $52 billion in 1975, 36 percent of which were in the United States. (Notice should be taken of the large share of exploration and crude production assets, 40 percent of the total, as risk capital requirements.) *Fortune* magazine's 1976 annual ranking of the 500 largest corporations shows that 15 oil firms are among the largest 50 companies in the world and that 7 among the top 10 are oil firms, each of which has assets of $10 billion or more. Total sales for the 15 biggest oil firms were $263 billion in 1976. The oil companies are largely self-financing; U.S. oil firms provided 67 percent of their capital needs internally in 1976, with a ratio of long-term debt to total capital employed of 26.7 percent. Estimates by the Chase Manhattan Bank (1976) of capital needs among oil firms during 1976–85 are $900

---

*Horizontal integration as defined here does not include diversification—entry into non-petroleum activities.

billion worldwide, 50 percent of which will be spent in the United States. Vertical integration means undertaking all phases of petroleum industry activities in a process that can be traced from finding and developing petroleum reserves to selling products and derivatives to final consumers. The magnitude of involvement in each segment may not be equal to that of succeeding or preceding segments in terms of the physical amount of products handled; the integrated company may not necessarily balance crude and products at the interphases. For example, adjustments of quantities of various crude inputs at a refinery to obtain an optimum product mix is a continuing management process. Furthermore, the industry focus differs from one company to another. Some run extensive natural gas production and processing activities for markets entirely different from those for crude and its products. Others are engaged in one kind or another of petrochemical production activity run in conjunction with their refineries, the latter supplying certain inputs to the former, notably feedstocks of refinery gases or naphtha. There are a great many other inputs of technological goods and services of a highly specialized nature fed from external sources to all segments of a vertically integrated oil company. A precise definition of vertical integration is, in fact, not possible. It follows that legal definitions are arbitrary when the functional ones are blurred. The point is that countless economically separable activities are involved, among which only the major conventional segments—exploration, production, refining, and distribution—can be clearly identified. The technology and management scheme that links them as one secure whole for the day-to-day purposes of meeting market requirements is what distinguishes integration as an operational concept. It is in this way that an integrated company differs from a holding company, which primarily exercises financial control over diverse activities. As a scheme of technology and management, vertical integration in petroleum has become even more systematized by the use of large computers. Refineries and petrochemical plants have optimizers and on-line computer controls which keep processing rates tuned to predetermined optima. Linear programming is extensively used by large firms in both refinery and transport, and operational research methods are applied in product distribution networks.

All the large or "major" oil companies are integrated, and most integrated firms must be "majors" because integration without the necessary concentration may be economically useless—think of one small oil field tied to one small refinery.

Integration in the public image, of course, relates not so much to this "technological" definition as to implied power, especially in conjunction with horizontal integration, and to financial power bearing on market competition and barriers to market entry. Integration is not unique to the oil industry; petroleum, however, does provide a well-known and controversial example of the conflicts arising from size and market dominance associated with integration, both in the United States where it began and in the rest of the world with all its international implications. Integration has been used as a tool of monopoly in individual countries and in the world today is still used as a tool in an international oligopoly which operated for many decades with collusive practices, direct and indirect.

The question of economic efficiency of an integrated structure versus a nonintegrated one remains a largely unsettled issue in the petroleum case. Although there are observable operating and managerial gains from the integrated form of organization, these do not flow completely from the physical or functional linking of individual processes with gains realized at the interfaces (energy saving, reduction of storage requirements, etc.). They come more from better overall planning and coordination of production and investment. That is to say, better knowledge of final markets and management control of sequential levels of operation have potentially significant economies. By contrast, nonintegrated firms must operate under a higher level of uncertainty, one which often leads to losses brought by overestimates of demand without the assurance of markets that integrated firms are able to secure. The losses come from underutilization of the large fixed assets typical of a capital intensive industry.

One can of course argue the opposite: that in the likelihood of interruption the integrated system will stand to lose more. Reckoning benefits of integration relative to actual performance of nonintegrated companies is not possible without a reference standard because some advantages of integration may be secured at the expense of others (DeChazeau and Khan 1959, pp. 263–268). Of course, integration does allow the firm to distribute the financial risks of exploration and research and development over the rest of its activities. DeChazeau and Khan conclude (1959, p. 268), after examining the issue, that "the lower costs thus achieved (from integration) are strategic, not social advantages; they reflect less the efficiency of this form of business organization than the disadvantages of nonintegration imposed by the preemptions of the integrated companies."

The international oil industry is dominated by seven or eight majors. This concentration—greater, for instance, than that in the United States —has even more significance than concentration within a country because international implications arise in the absence of an international regulatory authority. The power that integration confers, given the volume and importance of the oil resource and its products, can and most often has been used to distribute costs and benefits to suit corporate optima —to maximize profits and growth or both—rather than producing countries' welfare preferences. The companies optimize the whole integrated system toward their objectives. Welfare suboptima for some segmental activities carried out in individual nations are of little or no concern to the companies. This process indeed took place for decades in the concessionary era, when countries' petroleum resources were geared to demand-based oil consuming economies. "A high degree of integration inevitably introduces an important element of arbitrariness in the allocation of overhead costs to different operations and the setting of the prices at which goods and services are transferred between the subsidiary entities of the firms" (Penrose 1968, p. 43). This scope for decision has been used, for example, in managing corporate tax liabilities to various nations in order to maximize after tax earnings.

Size also confers power. The management of an oil company controls the use of great amounts of resources, commands large markets, and spends enormous funds as a buyer and employer. These features imply economic power or a significant ability to influence resource use and distribution of goods, prices, and income (Penrose 1968, p. 51). The larger the firm the greater is such power.

The extent of power in the early days of the oil industry was such that the Standard Oil cartel could apply it ruthlessly to crush competition in the U.S. oil industry. The majors' early strategy in dominating Middle East oil needs no elaboration here. Their power of integration still persists despite loss of production control over Middle East oil. It is now being used more carefully in allocating investment, transferring tradable know-how and technology, and expending venture capital in exploration. Corporate profits from the production of OPEC nations, or from buying OPEC oil directly, are not as great as they were in the concession era, but they are still very significant and can be used, as in the past, in attempts to find oil elsewhere or to finance real investments. Table 7.3 provides some figures on the distribution of exploration expenditure.

*Technology*

The petroleum industry is a research intensive industry. Expenditures on research and development, applied and fundamental, are large in absolute terms and as a proportion of companies' incomes. Research and experimental development expenditures in 1976 within the 15 principal oil transnationals, as calculated from their annual reports (Heigel 1978), was between 0.3 percent and 0.7 percent of corporate sales. At $263 billion in total sales for these 15 companies in 1976, a figure of 0.5 percent for research and development means a $1.3 billion outlay. Because of the nature of the petroleum resource and the great advances in physical sciences, particularly chemistry, technological opportunities for research

TABLE 7.3
Exploration Expenditure
($ million)

|               | 1961 | 1962 | 1963 | 1964 | 1965 | 1966 | 1967 | 1968 | 1969 | 1970 |
|---------------|------|------|------|------|------|------|------|------|------|------|
| Middle East   | 30   | 25   | 30   | 30   | 35   | 50   | 50   | 50   | 50   | 50   |
| Europe        | 40   | 25   | 75   | 90   | 150  | 75   | 100  | 125  | 125  | 100  |
| United States | 600  | 575  | 600  | 650  | 610  | 650  | 615  | 715  | 715  | 665  |

Source: Chase Manhattan Bank (1976).

and development in oil have been vast. Professional research and development have yielded a constant stream of improved or completely new production techniques in all phases of the industry and new or substitute products in petrochemicals. Some of this work was performed directly by the companies themselves, some of it, especially in recent years, by a variety of firms and institutions that serve the industry's demand for new or improved techniques, materials, equipment, and products. Estimates from production functions for refining and petrochemical industries, or from rates of return on research and development expenditure, suggest that the industry's research and development have given a rate of technological progress among the highest in the manufacturing sector, perhaps second only to that of the electronics industry.

As technologies and know-how have grown in number and complexity, so has the diversity of firms and institutions that own them, beyond that major portion owned or controlled by the oil transnationals themselves. Only a few technologies, such as oil-well logging, are monopolized by single owners.

What constitutes a crucial "technology," however, to the oil transnational is management know-how, a hard-to-define or quantify accumulation of specific skills and experience in management. It is this sort of nontradable entity that maintains technological control over integrated operations. Coupled with their technological base, it has helped entry and expansion of the transnationals in petrochemical manufacture as well as their diversification into nuclear energy, coal and mineral mining, seabed nodule recovery, and very recently, by Exxon, computer technology.

The survey by Heigel (1978) on the diversity of ownership of petroleum technology shows that the oil transnationals do perform necessary research and development, usually to develop a technique or piece of equipment in collaboration with specialized partners (contractors, equipment manufacturers, or suppliers) or with independent research and development institutes. Only for certain types of equipment-drilling gear and oil tankers have manufacturers evolved complete and independent responsibility for research and development.

The petroleum transnational is generally not the sole owner of technologies. Ownership is divided among contractors, equipment manufacturers, and engineering and construction companies. This split holds true even for the few decisive techniques, those highly specific ones embodying the results of large research efforts. But ownership may not be the key issue because the oil transnational acquires detailed know-how on all production, refining, and distribution operations that it considers of vital interest. In the services sectors of geophysics, drilling, and transport, they share control with others. However, control over know-how is still considered decisive in other industry segments which they share with no one. It is this know-how which forms the basis of power in the petroleum industry.

The exploration and production sectors especially involve numerous technologies. Table 7.4 illustrates, in a quick but comprehensive way, the oil companies' technological strategy. They perform research and development alone, with varying degrees of success, or with others; program the development of specific techniques or equipment; turn over results to equipment makers; or incorporate the technique in the services of contractors. The thorough utilization of all facilities and equipment gives them "virtual monopoly" of know-how at all integrated levels.

The implication of the transnationals' technological strategy for the national oil companies of the oil countries is isolation from the knowledge centers that supply most of the sophisticated inputs. Pressed by lost time, national oil companies currently seek to develop a degree of technological independence while in the meantime importing whole "package" technologies—an entire refinery, LNG plant, ethylene cracker, etc.—whose component technologies, developed over decades by the transnationals, are little known outside the majors. The cost of those imports is high because suppliers, including the transnationals, charge for proprietary technology and know-how plus some "rent," even for some nonproprietary knowledge. In view of the size of the effort required, only a joint and carefully considered plan on a regional basis might possibly meet the oil countries' costs of direct and accelerated transfer *and* provide a learning opportunity under current and planned investment. The transnationals, on the other hand, do have an interest as long-term crude buyers in making such a task succeed by agreeing to a new and more equitable kind of relation with petroleum producers and providing them a real opportunity to acquire a real part of cumulative industry experience.

## Developing Producers' Own Oil Resources

Producers' steps to control their own national oil resources have so far taken the form of nationalization, negotiated takeovers with term-sale

TABLE 7.4
Breakdown of Decisive Technologies and Know-how in the Petroleum Industry

| Petroleum sector | Type of company involved in research and development | Technology | | Know-how | |
|---|---|---|---|---|---|
| | | Main holder | Decisive characteristic | Control | Decisive characteristic |
| Geology—Geophysics | C/OC | C | yes | C/OC | yes |
| Drilling | | | | | |
| Onshore | M | M | no | OC/C | yes |
| Offshore | M | M | yes | OC/C | yes |
| • equipment | M | M | yes | OC/C | yes |
| • services | C/M | C/M | yes | C | yes |
| Field development | | | | | |
| Onshore | M/OC | M | no | OC/C | yes |
| Offshore | EC/OC/M | M/EC | yes | C/OC | yes |
| Production | | | | | |
| Onshore | M | M | no | OC/C | yes |
| Offshore | M/OC | M/OC | yes | OC/C | yes |
| Enhanced recovery | M/OC | M | no | OC | yes |
| Transportation | | | | | |
| Tankers | M | M | no | C/OC | no |
| LNG carriers | EC/M | M | no | C/OC | no |
| Pipelines | M | M | no | C/OC | no |
| Refining—Petrochemicals | L/OC | EC | no | OC | yes |
| Distribution | OC | M | no | OC | yes |

Source: Heigel 1978.

M = Manufacturer  
C = Contractor  
L = Licensor  
OC = International oil company  
EC = Engineering constructor

222

contracts with former concessionaires, or an equity participation in company assets which allows the producing nation to market a share of the oil and to participate in decisions on corporate plans and investments.

Having attained direct national control over production and pricing of their petroleum resources in the 1970s, the major oil producing countries (members of OAPEC, in the focus of this chapter)* face choices and decisions beyond the petroleum price issue. An area of greater immediate and long-term importance to their own countries is the management of current and future development of their oil industry in a period of changing conditions and trends. Technology is an example of such change; producing nations are now investing billions of dollars in what is considered a relatively mature oil industry technology. This investment is proceeding at a time when the industrial nations are preparing for what has been called the revolution of the microprocessor, the microminiaturized computer around which new control systems for almost every kind of process and product may well be designed in the next decade or two. Knowing how important such control systems are, particularly in the petroleum processing industry, might not producers fear premature obsolescence of a good part of their newly acquired plant and equipment? The technological opportunities that microprocessors offer the petroleum industry are no doubt great. However, the technological underdevelopment of the national oil companies and their lack of adequate research and development systems cast much doubt on their ability to take full advantage of such opportunities.

Past conflicts with concessionaire companies over a host of issues on national territory are now giving way to other conflicts over prices and markets, not just about petroleum and its products, but also about the conditions governing producing countries' imports of technological goods and services from the transnationals. While such issues are actually being confronted in the markets, they are also being debated elsewhere, at the UN and in such forums as the North-South dialogs.

### Priorities

The choices and decisions facing the oil producers, whether governments or national oil companies, are immensely important to the future of the international oil industry (both exploration and production) and to their own economies. The most difficult immediate decisions for the oil industry's development in OAPEC nations are those of setting investment priorities and allocating resources, including financial resources,

*OAPEC, the Organization of Arab Petroleum Exporting Countries, is comprised of ten member states: Algeria, Libya, Egypt, Syria, Iraq, Saudi Arabia, Kuwait, Bahrain, Qatar, and the United Arab Emirates.

over the industry's chain of downstream activities. Although financial requirements present no constraint for the time being to some oil nations, the problems of developing other necessary inputs involve manpower and technology. Here, national oil companies must try to provide specialized skills and training for national manpower and to lessen technological dependence by developing an indigenous technological base to serve their oil industry efficiently and economically. Despite notable strides by some national oil companies in manpower and technology, there remain real constraints of a long-term nature. Those constraints exist outside the oil sector but directly influence its development as governments seek to integrate the oil sector with the rest of the economy, to end oil's former hegemony, and to do away with dualistic economies imposed by the old concession system. Problems of training and manpower development will get more attention later.

## Plans and Projects

Between 1975 and 1982 the major oil producers of OAPEC are planning or currently carrying out investment schemes worth some $70 billion in 1976 dollars. Most of this investment effort will go to downstream petroleum projects. The largest proportion—about 38 percent or some $27 billion—is allocated to natural gas schemes. Next is $22 billion for transportation facilities—tankers, pipelines, shipping terminals, and so on. Another $21 billion will go to refineries and petrochemical plants including nitrogenous fertilizer plants. (An additional $12 billion will go for ancillary and infrastructural facilities connected with the oil projects.)

## Natural Gas

Natural gas projects, planned primarily to conserve and utilize associated gas, get priority consideration. Contemplated investments equal one-half of Chase Manhattan Bank's estimate (1976) of the world petroleum industry's capital expenditure for 1976. Although a significant part will go to liquid natural gas (LNG) projects in OAPEC member states, notably Algeria and the United Arab Emirates, the majority of these investments will be devoted to the conservation and use of associated natural gas (ANG). Saudi Arabia alone will spend some $14 billion to gather, process, reinject, or use the ANG formerly flared by Aramco on grounds of "commercial infeasibility." Similar projects on smaller scales are underway in all the Arab oil states, primarily to put an end to gas waste. Flaring of ANG has so far meant the accumulated destruction of the equivalent of roughly seven billion barrels of oil within the OAPEC area alone. That is a striking figure when one realizes that U.S. oil reserves in 1977 were only 35 billion barrels.

ANG flaring is one of the strongest pieces of evidence of the conflict between public and private interests. The priority given to ending the flares, immediately after direct national control was attained, manifests national convictions about the senselessness of a waste once justified by discounted cash flow analysis of net benefits of gas conservation projects. True, commercial benefits from these gas projects will accrue to the countries undertaking them. Cash benefits will flow from sale of liquid petroleum gas (LPG), condensed from ANG and from ethane, as a petrochemical feedstock. But there will also be longer term benefits of stock resource savings, not in gas alone but also in the extended life of oil reserves replaced by gas in domestic Arab uses. These ANG investments, in other words, have worldwide implications for energy conservation.

Another point of division between oil countries and transnationals lies in the ordering of domestic investments. Oil concessionaires never treated ANG as a basis for domestic industry in OAPEC nations (apart from minor use as a boiler fuel). They claimed, as subsidiaries of parent transnationals, to be confined to the oil production business. Others among the parent companies' affiliates and subsidiaries, however, were and are among the largest chemical producers in the world.

OAPEC nations' gas projects, by contrast, emphasize petrochemical production, a significant proportion of which will find itself growing domestic and/or regional markets. In eight of ten OAPEC countries, ethylene plants are or will soon be under construction. Many countries will go farther downstream to synthesize other chemicals from ethylene. Furthermore, all OAPEC countries are or will be producing more ammonia and urea fertilizers from ANG. The new economic parameters for ANG utilization show that the highest value in the short term lies in extensive domestic use, replacing whenever possible some liquid fuels. Reinjection is next; it improves oil recovery and saves equivalent amounts of crude for future production. Indirect export is third; when an energy intensive industry's fuel needs are a crucial element in total production costs, as in aluminum smelting, oil refining, or iron ore reduction, it might be feasible to set up such facilities on the coasts of some major ANG producers. Export of ANG as LNG ranks at the bottom of the set in view of the new economic parameters. Liquefaction and LNG shipping technology are highly capital intensive, even more so than petroleum refining, and they are new and as yet unstable technologies with no linkage to domestic sectors' technological requirements. The result is a high cost product (LNG) with almost all costs going to fixed capital rigidly tied to captive export market centers which must be far away (5000 miles at least) to make expensive transport by special LNG tankers economically feasible. In short, crude oil production cost is 15–25 cents per barrel in the major OAPEC producing states, but the equivalent LNG barrel costs $10-12 before it can be put in the gas pipeline system of the final consumer.

Table 7.5 shows production, utilization, and flaring of ANG in OAPEC nations, 1969-76. A great deal of room for conservation obviously remains, but despite the urgency to conserve ANG, OAPEC projects will face delays. Beyond the typically long lead times of such projects are the tough conditions and terms under which ANG technology is being acquired. Unless a sense of urgency is shared by the suppliers of technology, large quantities of gas will continue to be destroyed at the current rate of 60 percent of the ANG which must be extracted along with the crude oil that satisfies the present import needs of major oil consumers.* It is nevertheless hoped that flaring can cease by 1985.

TABLE 7.5
Production and Utilization of Natural Gas in OAPEC States, 1969-76
(Million cubic meters)

|  | 1969 | 1970 | 1971 | 1972 | 1973 | 1974 | 1975 | 1976 |
|---|---|---|---|---|---|---|---|---|
| ALGERIA | | | | | | | | |
| Produced | 8733 | 9912 | 13375 | 15529 | 17679[a] | 19829 | 20951 | 20639 |
| Reinjected | 1553 | 1553[a] | 2002 | 1877 | 318 | 2208[a] | 10856 | 2208 |
| Utilized | 3768[a] | 3768 | 8563 | 5027 | 6916 | 5621 | | 8271 |
| Flared | 3413 | 3413 | 2810 | 8625 | 10455[a] | 12000[a] | 10095 | 10160 |
| % flared to produced | 39.1% | 34.4% | 21% | 55.5% | 59.1% | 60.5% | 48.2% | 49.2% |
| IRAQ | | | | | | | | |
| Produced | 6162 | 6130 | 8010 | 7422[x] | 8732[x] | 9255[x] | 10451[x] | 13149[x] |
| Utilized | 762 | 784 | 925 | 935[x] | 1210[x] | 1162[x] | 1654[x] | 1985 |
| Flared | 5400 | 5346 | 7085 | 6487[x] | 7522[x] | 8093[x] | 8796[x] | 11164[x] |
| % flared to produced | 87.6% | 87.2% | 88.4% | 87.4% | 87.1% | 87.4% | 84.2% | 84.9% |
| KUWAIT | | | | | | | | |
| Produced | 14529 | 16132 | 18209 | 18343 | 16450 | 13222 | 10829 | 11211 |
| Reinjected | 1398 | | | 1866 | 2238 | | 1196 | |
| Utilized | 3728 | 5770 | 6230 | 5126 | 5267 | 7120 | 5205 | 6906 |
| Flared | 9404 | 10362 | 11979 | 11351 | 8945 | 6102 | 4428 | 4245 |
| % flared to produced | 64.7% | 64.2% | 65.7% | 61.8% | 54.3% | 46.1% | 40.8% | 37.8% |

*Norway has recently postponed crude production to prevent wasting ANG through flaring.

TABLE 7.5 (*continued*)
Production and Utilization of Natural Gas in OAPEC States, 1969–76
(Million cubic meters)

| | 1969 | 1970 | 1971 | 1972 | 1973 | 1974 | 1975 | 1976 |
|---|---|---|---|---|---|---|---|---|
| | | | | LIBYA | | | | |
| Produced | 18874 | 19366 | 15759 | 14047 | 16283 | 12045 | 13848 | 17952 |
| Utilized | 6874[a] | 6366[a] | 5905 | 7813 | 10909 | 9775 | 10835 | 14320 |
| Flared | 12000[a] | 13000[a] | 9854 | 6234 | 5374 | 2270 | 3012 | 3632 |
| % flared to produced | 63.5% | 67.1% | 62.5% | 44.3% | 33% | 18.8% | 21.7% | 20.2% |
| | | | | QATAR | | | | |
| Produced | 3557 | 3710 | 4514 | 5380 | 6213 | 5151 | 5437 | 4732 |
| Utilized | 850 | 1002 | 1005 | 1103 | 1580 | 1300 | 2209 | 1476 |
| Flared | 2707 | 2708 | 3509 | 4277 | 4633 | 3851 | 3228 | 3256 |
| % flared to produced | 72.9% | 72.9% | 77.7% | 79.4% | 74.5% | 74.7% | 59.3% | 68.8% |
| | | | | SAUDI ARABIA | | | | |
| Produced | 16875 | 20625 | 25481 | 32568 | 44292 | 47310 | 37812 | 47873 |
| Reinjected | 2866 | 3532 | 2933 | 2703 | | | | |
| Utilized | 1744 | 2261 | 2625 | 2806 | 6299 | 8223 | 8644 | 10006 |
| Flared | 12265 | 14832 | 19896 | 27059 | 37993 | 39087 | 29168 | 37867 |
| % flared to produced | 72.6% | 71.9% | 78.1% | 83.1% | 85.7% | 82.6% | 77.1% | 79.1% |
| | | | | UNITED ARAB EMIRATES | | | | |
| Produced | 6742 | 7536 | 10430 | 11215 | 13690 | 13054 | 12233 | 15410 |
| Utilized | 569 | 663 | 1045 | 1038 | 1251 | 1200 | 1090 | 1070 |
| Flared | 6173 | 6873 | 9385 | 10177 | 12439 | 11854 | 11143 | 14340 |
| % flared to produced | 91.5% | 91.2% | 89.9% | 90.7% | 90.8% | 90.8% | 91.1% | 93.1% |
| | | | | EGYPT | | | | |
| Produced | | | | | | | 50[x] | 239 |
| | | | | BAHRAIN | | | | |
| Produced | | | 1838 | 2343 | 2834 | 2876 | 3044 | |
| Utilized | | | 1838 | 2343 | 2834 | 2876 | 3044 | |
| | | | | SYRIA | | | | |
| Produced | | | | | | | | 476 |
| Utilized | | | | | | | | 116 |
| Flared | | | | | | | | 360 |
| % flared to produced | | | | | | | | 75.6% |

Sources: OPEC 1976; OPEC 1977; OAPEC 1977; Petroconsultants S.A. 1977.
[a]Estimates.                    [x]Official information.

Refining

Crude oil must be refined into products before it can be used even as a boiler fuel, although there are some very minor exceptions. Refining operations involve first primary distillation, the initial physical separation of oil into main products according to boiling point. Raw products are then directed to further finishing, or to conversion into lighter fuels and lubes by secondary refining which usually involves catalysis and/or hydrogenation.

Conversion refining uses complex chemical/physical means and equipment, relatively recent technology, to improve quality and tailor the output mix to market needs. Catalytic cracking, one such process of secondary refining, was developed in the United States at a time of rising demand for gasoline; natural constitutent hydrocarbons (about 20–30 percent) could not meet such demand except in refining greater quantities of crude oil and thus creating a surplus co-product. Cracking and other conversion processes of secondary refining made it possible to convert heavy middle distillates into higher proportions of gasoline. There were economic limitations, but higher prices for crude oil and the diseconomy of producing fuel oils have prompted refiners in many major markets to resort increasingly to conversion refining, an energy intensive and more complex activity with an even higher capital intensity than primary refining.

Refinery location, once considered to be a market determined decision, has had a varied history. Big modern plants are expensive; some now cost more than one billion dollars, as do the ones under construction in Saudi Arabia. Their productive life can exceed 20 years, and location with a view to markets can be a crucial factor on purely economic grounds. In 1949, for example, more than 50 percent of total world refining capacity was located in crude producing areas; the figure held true both for the United States and the rest of the world (BP 1959). In 1959 the same percentage still held for the United States, but the figure was declining elsewhere. In that year, Middle East refining capacity represented 5.7% of the world's total while Western Europe and Japan—considered to be the Middle East's natural markets—had 19.5 percent of world capacity. By 1977 the relative share of the Middle East had declined further to 4.1 percent while that of Western Europe and Japan rose to 34.1 percent.

(There has also been another kind of location shift. During the 1950s, when the move of refining out of the Middle East gathered momentum following Iran's oil nationalization of 1951, coastal areas were favored for new refineries. In the 1960s many refineries "moved" to inland consumption centers with crude supplied to them by pipeline. Since then a counter trend has returned many refineries to coastal areas accessible to the very large crude carriers.)

Refining is a link in an integrated chain for transnational corporations, but it is seen as the raw material processing stage for developing nations that want to process their own raw materials before export in an effort to initiate industrialization. The UN-sponsored Lima declaration of 1976 set a target of 35 percent of world industrial output within developing countries by the year 2000, up from the present 5 percent. Current thinking within UNIDO is that refining and petrochemical production in developing countries may be the only hope of getting anywhere near this target. For OAPEC nations, refining and petrochemical manufacture represent the leading industries of energy and material production and should play the role that the coal and steel industries did in the industrialization of the West.

As with the case of ANG industries, domestic refining was resisted by concessionaire transnationals. Their monopoly power over oil production and pricing was used even to delay domestic efforts to attain self-sufficiency in fuels and lubricants. The consequence for many OAPEC countries, of course, was lost time to "learn" by investing in complex industry, and this lost time in part explains the rush to massive refining investment after direct national control was obtained in the early 1970s. The conflict of interest, again, was between the transnationals' objectives of optimizing their worldwide integrated networks and the producers' objectives of optimizing domestic welfare functions—unacceptable suboptima for the transnationals. It is worth noting here that the refineries erected by transnationals in Bahrain, Kuwait, and Saudi Arabia since the 1930s were essentially of the primary sort; they produced heavy products for Far Eastern and (to a lesser extent) European markets and for ship bunkering.

After the 1973 price increase, refinery economics shifted in favor of increased capacity at the Middle East crude source and product export to the natural markets of Europe and the Far East. The favorable cost shift was influenced by the following factors:

1. A significant increase in refining energy costs—something like 40 percent of total running cost. A modern refinery uses on average the equivalent of 10 percent of its crude as fuel. If that energy is supplied from natural gas which would otherwise be flared, a net cost saving for local Middle East refiners could result, but there is cost penalty for competitors refining near consumption markets. Other cost penalties are those of transporting the fuel energy (10 percent of crude) and the investment in extra refinery capacity to be used in refining fuel for the refineries' own use.
2. For Middle Eastern nations, financing refinery investment became cheaper—in terms of opportunity cost—than holding oil revenues in deposits or financial paper.

3. Land sites are still, as before, cheaper in the Middle East.
4. Pollution control remains less rigid in the Middle East.
5. Labor cost was and remains lower in the Middle East.

There are cost penalties for the producer states as well. Most significant is the higher cost of transporting products rather than crude. Another is the cost of capital and technology imports. Finally, refinery maintenance costs in harsh desert climates are marginally higher. However, these are not binding constraints. Larger product tankers and improved logistics can reduce the crude/product freight differential. A greater degree of technological autonomy is possible and can lead to lower costs all around.

What is really missing is willingness on the part of major oil consuming nations and transnational companies to agree to the principle of industrial relocation by allowing a certain percentage of consumers' oil requirements to be imported in the form of products. It is not in the major producers' own interests to refine all their crude output. It is, however, in their interest to set up a viable refining industry at the currently optimum unit size established for this industry. The aim is to use a refining industry of efficient size as a heavy industry focal point for further industrialization. Because refining is a marginal industry, in the sense of generating only a small value-added, efficient capacity stands above domestic requirements in many oil nations; hence the need to export the surplus in the medium term (about five years).

Surplus refining capacity, however, is exactly what European refiners are suffering now and will continue to suffer for some time. Capacity utilization, which used to average 90 percent, declined to 75 percent worldwide and to 60 percent in Europe in 1975. This idle capacity, compounded by problems of recent economic recessions, set a rather unfavorable atmosphere for the "Euro-Arab dialog," the attempt between the European Economic Community and the countries of the Arab League to agree on future refinery and petrochemical investments and market sharing. It is now conceded on both sides that Europe cannot expect to run near capacity until 1982 and that only marginal European imports of refined products can be expected by 1985.

These developments did not discourage most OAPEC nations from going ahead with their investments, albeit at a less ambitious level. The Arab region's internal demand for refinery products is rising fast; economic growth rates for most countries are expected to be 4 to 8 percent per annum until 2000, according to a joint OAPEC/Arab Fund estimate. At present, total Arab refinery capacity is 2.2 million bpd. Capacity is expected to rise to 3.1 million bpd by 1982 and to 4.0 million bpd by 1985. Arab consumption is expected to grow, from its current 1.7 million bpd, to 2.3 by 1982 and to 3.2 million bpd by 1985. If inter-Arab trade in refined products develops as expected, the exportable surplus from the region may therefore be less than one million bpd. Long-term regional requirements have been estimated to be as high as 14 million bpd by the year 2000, but a figure of 10 million bpd seems more reasonable.

Even if the economics were completely in favor of export-oriented OAPEC refining, international political factors would remain a stumbling block. These same factors were indeed behind the refining industry's initial move, in the 1950s, from the Middle East to consumption centers in Europe and Japan. According to a 1978 report in the *Petroleum Intelligence Weekly*, "The governmental takeover of most Middle East refining capacity could well be encouraging oil companies to expand their own refining capacity closer to markets. This seems illustrated by the 'substantial accord' reached by British Petroleum, Caltex and Singapore Petroleum Group last week on the underlying principles of joining forces in Singapore to create a shared 170,000 bpd refinery . . . A major motivation for BP to move into a shared venture is understood to be the loss of its former positions in the big export refineries in Iran, Kuwait and Aden." If products from this Singapore refinery are aimed at Japan's growing market, for example, it could mean a dimishing opportunity for OAPEC nations in the Japanese market, considered to be more amenable to bilateral agreements on refining than Europe's markets, which are more fragmented and largely under the hold of a few transnational corporations. Here again the attitude of the transnationals can be decisive in international economic relationships, particularly for industrial relocation.

In the refining case, agreement between oil producers and consumers is essential. Accords can, if allowed to work, help to plan investment in both areas to fit the desired product pattern, minimize waste, and optimize capacity use. Such agreements may confer a long-term advantage in stabilizing markets, an aim traditionally served by the transnational oligopoly through its integrated networks and implicit and explicit market sharing.

Established product marketing networks and heavy demands for investment to penetrate them on the one hand, and the need for management know-how on the other, are partly behind the tendency of some OAPEC countries to opt for joint ventures with transnationals in refining and petrochemical investment. The huge development in Saudi Arabia's two oil industrial centers of Jubail and Yanbu are examples. Kuwait, which already has the largest national refining complex among OAPEC states at 450,000 bpd, has no plans to expand at home but is considering joint investment in refining and petrochemicals in Rumania, Indonesia, Yugoslavia, Spain, and some other countries. By doing so Kuwait will in fact be exporting capital—that is, investing directly in foreign markets to secure sales of its own petroleum there in the future.

## Petrochemicals

The position of OAPEC nations for entry into petrochemicals is potentially even stronger than their refining stance because of ANG feedstock availability and the technological options for using it for this purpose. Ethylene, the most important petrochemicals commodity, can be produced by cracking the ethane component of ANG, which is ethane rich (10 percent plus) in most OAPEC oil fields. Ethylene can therefore be produced in economically feasible units (400,000 tons/year) at half the cost or less of producing it by naptha cracking, as is done in Europe and Japan (Al-Wattari 1975; Borham 1978).

There are, however, complicating factors on the marketing side because of the large range in quality specifications among petrochemical commodities such as polyethylene. The market is highly specialized and likely to become more so as the variety of valuable chemicals derived from ethylene is enlarged. Overseas trading in ethylene is limited. It requires an LNG technology which would not make much economic sense given the marginal value added in its production. The only feasible route is to polymerize it into polyethylene or derive liquid and solid chemicals from it such as ethylene glycol, ethylene dichloride, etc. The attitude of the European Economic Community toward entry of polyethylene in its markets has thus far not been encouraging. There currently exists so much surplus capacity in the chemical industry in Europe that it has even discouraged the British from building ethane cracking facilities for their own North Sea gas. Agreement seems essential to avoid resource-wasting competition, but prospects for agreement in the near future are not good.

Potential regional petrochemical demand must be developed in view of the current and planned capacity buildup taking place in many OAPEC countries, often in units of less than optimally efficient size for export markets. Those countries with joint venture arrangements do not seem unduly worried about markets. The petrochemicals referred to above will all be produced according to current plans. The total polyethylene capacity expected in 1985 will be 5.5 million tons or 4.9 percent of world capacity. The hold of oil transnationals on petrochemical production is great and again suggests a need for OAPEC producers to coordinate activities in meeting market conditions.

The conclusion of this review of plans and projects to which investment has been committed is that a regional approach to refining and petrochemical development can help to remove some bottlenecks facing individual OAPEC nations and can give them the necessary concentration to compete with the transnationals. The overall object of the huge investment is to provide wider opportunities for industrialization in order to stimulate development in other sectors which are too small, in many individual OAPEC countries, to enjoy the full benefits of the multiplier effect. In the past, the transnationals' behavior and the petroleum industry's structure meant that the multiplier effect of investment for industrializing and using petroleum worked to the benefit of those countries which could make the best of the opportunities petroleum offers as an industry, as a raw material, and as a fuel—that is, to the benefit of the industrially advanced oil consumers. Only a well-balanced economy of the size and orientation of a typical industrial state now stands a chance of doing likewise, if that chance is at all warranted under changing technology. Regional economic integration opens up some such opportunities by rendering them economically feasible. It seems inescapable to conclude that OAPEC countries, through their national oil companies, may have little option in the foreseeable future but to emulate the oil transnationals in horizontal and vertical integration.

## The Industry's State of Development

Much has been written about the very large oil companies' quest to cartelize and control the oil industry since its inception in the last century. Little has been said, however, about the less interesting side of the consequences of their behavior on technological and manpower development in the regions which gave them their real power and wealth—the resource owners, the oil producing nations. One Arab scholar who studies the problems of science and technology in developing countries and the Arab world in particular writes, "One of the striking examples [of failure to acquire scientific and technological knowledge] in the modern history of the Middle East is that despite the existence of oil companies for dozens of years, very little science and technology have been transferred to it" (Zahlan 1974). He goes on to explain why that has been so in terms of the Arabs' inadequate understanding of what is involved in the process of technological transfer. Even though that "understanding" is certainly an important factor in terms of broad social and institutional (especially governmental) attitude, it can hardly be denied that the transnationals have done little to transfer basic oil technology and not much to change prevailing local attitudes on what is involved in technology transfer.

Before the petroleum industry takeover by most OAPEC nations, the transnationals were uninterested in creating indigenous technological and engineering research and training capabilities, even when the countries involved had an adequate human resource base. The transnationals typically established no more than the absolute minimum technological support base required for operations which were essentially routine in nature. All their research and training functions were carried out at their home base. Furthermore, these companies, through their operating affiliates, did little to encourage career development in oil for potential job seekers among local citizens. In their early years they confined employment of nationals to the lowest echelon. Much later, during the 1960s under determined pressure from some OAPEC governments, notably Iraq, the companies' employment methods were modified to give better chances for qualified national manpower to penetrate the various employment barriers. Even then responsible company functions, whether in management, technology, or finance, were essentially confined to expatriates brought in through the parent companies' network of worldwide personnel movement. They took most if not all key analytical tasks in geology, geophysics, engineering, processing, and finance "outside" the producing country.

The transnationals also kept the size of their assets in producing countries —capital equipment and industrial plant—to a bare minimum. Accurate figures here are difficult to obtain. To get some idea, the annual investment figures in identical petroleum activities for the Middle East and the United States, respectively, have been aggregated for 1966–76 as a surrogate measure (Chase Manhattan Bank 1976). Middle Eastern crude and natural gas production assets totalled $6,550 million vis-à-vis total petroleum industry assets in the Middle East of $14,730 million. The corresponding figures in the United States were $20,290 million and $122,900 million. The relative gap in these financial figures for oil and gas capital assets in the two areas might be explained by the size and productivity of Middle East oil fields, but aggregates also imply the very small relative size of downstream investment—refining and petrochemical activities—in the producing states. Even domestic needs for these products in some OAPEC nations were, until recently, being imported.

The observable consequences and their implications of underinvestment and lack of indigenous technological development over many decades have been and indeed remain in many OAPEC states:

1. There is a small and inadequate amount of technological and scientific manpower whether for research and training centers or in-house, short-term research (the technological support base of all major engineering and technological departments).
2. It follows that little know-how (cumulative experience) and information, especially in research and training, have been allowed to accumulate.
3. Research and training infrastructure or hardware such as labs and

other technological research facilities are underdeveloped, sometimes completely absent.

4. With no petroleum sector demand for university graduates or research in the basic sciences and engineering because of the local petroleum industry's links to its established technological home in the transnationals' home countries, a great opportunity to contribute to the development of national scientific and technological institutions has been lost.

5. Confining the producers to the production of crude oil and gas in the upstream and to some simple refinery processing has, in effect, denied this major and vital raw material and energy industry the leading sector role it could have played in these countries' development.

### Technological Priorities

In setting national technological priorities there are variations among OAPEC member nations. These differences derive from inter-country variety in resource endowments, including climate, in demographic conditions, and in geographic orientation to markets. More directly relevant are differences in the size and natural conditions of petroleum reservoirs. Differences in these two important parameters are partly reflected in prevailing rates of production and in philosophy about long-term management of reserves. But such differences often are more a matter of degree than of substance in considering requisite technological activity because all national oil companies do carry out all basic petroleum industry functions. It is also reasonable to assume that all national oil companies are currently engaged in programs to improve their technological capabilities, although some have a clearer order of priorities than others.

If one must single out a first priority for all the national oil companies, that priority must take its precedence from the nature of responsibility of the national oil company. As a specialized national entity with direct responsibilities for the technical and economic aspects of the oil sector, the national oil company must first develop its own management team. It must provide itself with the necessary information network to keep abreast of all major oil activities inside and outside its own country. The management team must include a staff which can act as advisor and counsellor on all major petroleum issues and work out and present policy options for the oil sectors' higher authorities. In other words, what the transnational corporation used to do with the help of its knowledge centers abroad must now be done within the autonomy of the individual OAPEC state. With continued changes in the economic and technological conditions of the industry, management development at all levels becomes an ongoing activity. The first technological requirement to be "transferred" and learned, and the most difficult one at that, is petroleum industry management technology and know-how. It is difficult because it involves learning an untradable and untransferrable accumulation of long experience of people and organizations. Mastering the science and technology of optimization is only a portion.

Another priority in the area of technology and engineering is creating or strengthening problem-solving capabilities to support all the functioning departments of the various petroleum activities. Short-term research work and high level manpower training form the basic tasks for such a technological support system. It will be impossible to achieve any reasonable level of autonomy without an adequate technological and engineering base. The extent and level of sophistication of such capabilities is the most important measure of the degree of technological development of any national oil company. Such capabilities can grow over time with the growing complexity of petroleum functions that national oil companies take on. However, capabilities to handle, more directly, fundamental technological tasks can grow only gradually. For example, any country with a large exploration program requires a geophysical data processing center of its own. Data processing and interpretation are indispensible for building expertise and teaching it, through in-house training or research institutes, to inexperienced new graduates. Individual country research and training emphasis will differ depending on how decisive the particular activity is within the spectrum of all other activities. A country with extensive LNG commitments surely requires a stronger research and training capability in cryogenics than, say, in catalysis, if it has got only a small refining potential.

### Technological Transfer

Technological dependence of OAPEC oil sectors on imported knowhow as well as hardware, a legacy of the transnationals, remains the basic feature of their current state of technology. Practically every major project undertaken in any part of the petroleum sector requires investigations or research performed wholly or partly through import of foreign knowhow, even though many steps do not involve any proprietary knowledge. Feasibility studies, engineering designs, material procurement, construction, and even operation are sometimes performed by outside contractors, usually on the basis of a completed "turnkey" project. There are some important exceptions in Iraq and Algeria, which have developed limited capabilities for direct project execution (the direct transfer of technology approach) in pipeline design and construction and in some refinery process construction from individually procured machinery and equipment. But the majority of planned projects (including the $70 billion worth of oil sector projects referred to earlier) are destined to go "turnkey." This approach has been termed "indirect"; others call it the "black box" approach to imply that technological know-how is embodied in component parts and skills of specialists who thought out and put together the package. That kind of nonconcern with components, of course, loses the countries a learning opportunity. Had they been organized to take advantage of it, they might have combined such freshly acquired know-how and other training aids to create a new technological base capable of further development. It may be optimal for a profit-maximizing firm to follow the "turnkey" method of project construction to realize, for example, early production to meet expected demand, but for a developing country such an approach can lead only to continued dependence, at least throughout the life of the oil cycle. In broad terms, consultants and contractors are asked to perform the following tasks:

1. Feasibility studies
2. Mapping technological options
3. Project design and engineering
4. Procurement and construction
5. Manpower training (for operational staff)
6. Production organization and management
7. Logistics and market information

It is clear enough that the indirect approach might be the surest way to get the job done on time, perhaps avoiding costly delays, but this approach is nevertheless inconsistent with the long-term objectives of technological autonomy and invariably contributes to high capital cost of production plants. The direct approach, which essentially avoids buying "free" knowledge, can be less expensive and at the same time can allow know-how to accumulate by developing specialized skills along with complementary hardware such as laboratories, computers, information and documentation centers, and training aids.

The direct approach uses the following sources and procedures in an organized effort to "unpackage" the finished plant and involves indigenous manpower as an increasingly larger proportion of the total effort (cost) in all bits of specific techniques and know-how incorporated in the full "package":

1. Flow of publications
2. Movement of persons between countries
3. Education and training
4. Exchange program for personnel

5. Employment of foreign experts as teachers or consultants
6. Import of pieces of equipment and their relevant literature
7. License agreements for patented technology

Depending on the state of development of the various technological and engineering departments of the oil sector of OAPEC nations, increasingly higher degrees of self-dependence can be attained by using more and more of the first five facilities above and less and less of the last two.

On a more practical level, design and engineering bodies capable of undertaking a large refining project, for example, are not economically feasible for any one single country in the OAPEC group. For the OAPEC regional market, however, a design and engineering capability would seem quite feasible on purely economic grounds, given the size of planned and expected construction in member nations. It is highly desirable to form a nucleus from existing minor capabilities and work upward toward a major organization able to take an increasing share of the total OAPEC market. Scale economy, rate of capacity use, and learning by project replication all contribute to cost reduction in projects undertaken by such a large entity.

Because of the current basic role of the transnationals in the execution of large projects, a new approach is required to involve national institutions and foreign firms in new relationships. Such relationships must be based on participation in the sense of deep involvement; national institutions must be properly provided with information and other capabilities to develop concepts and designs and during later stages to participate in project execution. This approach might at first remain dependent on foreign consulting and contracting firms. That is acceptable but conditional upon realizing the active and conscious development of indigenous manpower, institutions, and facilities.

### Manpower and Employment

The petroleum industry is a capital-intensive industry. It employs a very small proportion of the total labor force in any oil region, whether Iraq or Texas. In practice, these characteristics imply two distinct sets of problems for a developing country.

The first is that many of those whom it does employ must be of the highest caliber in specific fields of technology and management and must be entrusted with tremendous concentrations of wealth and productive capital. This imposes fundamental and practical training problems on an already inadequate science and technology base.

The second set of problems is brought on by the very high capital intensity of the oil industry, especially of downstream petroleum activities,

and by the huge size of unit investment in individual refineries and petrochemical plants: Developing countries, such as some OAPEC nations,
must face long-term skewness in investment allocation. Because the petroleum sector claims a large proportion of available investment capital
but provides so little employment, other sectors of the economy receive
inadequate investment and the petroleum sector reinforces the very problem it had originally created by inappropriateness of its technology. That
is to say, the nonoil sector which must be counted on to restore employment balance might not grow fast enough, for lack of investment resources, to do so.

The aggregate employment of the oil sector in OAPEC countries is
about 200,000, only 1 percent of an estimated actively working population of 20 million, roughly equally divided between farm and nonfarm
workers. The petroleum industry thus employs only 2 percent of the nonfarm work force, a tiny share, but the oil sector in most OAPEC countries leads all other sectors in size of assets and asset growth rate. Total
planned investment in downstream developments alone (refining, petrochemicals, natural gas, transport facilities) is estimated at $70 billion for
the period from 1975 to 1982.* An OAPEC preliminary survey of manpower requirements of the oil sector in member states, conducted in 1975,
shows a need for training and developing some 101,000 more people in
various skills (not including office workers). The ensuing incremental
capital/labor intensity is $700,000 for each additional worker to be trained
for employment in the planning period.

The petroleum industry, in summary, imposes technological and natural limits to employment. Jobs must be provided by measures in other
sectors—the investment resources problem notwithstanding—and by
more intensive downstream oil industrialization. Paradoxically, the Arab
world, and particularly its oil states, employs foreign labor on a large
scale, in part because of the unavailability of indigenous skilled manpower in many activities. In financial terms the cost of employing foreign
skills is very high. Some estimate the annual bill for highly skilled labor
alone at $5 billion for the Arab world as a whole. Management and tech-
nical staff from Europe or America cost on an average something like
$200,000 per annum per employee.

There is now general awareness among Arab government leaders, economic planners, and intelligentsia that sound development will never be
attained without satisfactory development of human resources and manpower. They feel that, for too long, national development of the Arab

*The size of aggregate planned investment for the Arab world according to Arab devel-
opment programs is reckoned at about $277 billion for the same period.

world has run far ahead of the process of preparing and training and re-
taining new and sophisticated skills essential for filling the job opportunities created. They are aware also that this problem constitutes for the
Arab world and its individual nations a real barrier on the path to development. Unless overcome, it can cause postponement or elimination of
many current projects. In the long run, as Arab depletable wealth approaches exhaustion, it means failure to attain industrialization.

It is now widely recognized that the basic problems of developing manpower resources and supply in the developing Arab world, put at their
simplest, are the low literacy rate among the population, the very little
emphasis on vocational training in the educational system, and the low
social status of manual and directly productive labor. Before skillful labor is developed on a large scale, trainees must first learn to read and
write. Vocational training puts them one step closer to employment. And
finally, social attitudes hold the process together as a working and stable
mechanism.

There is, of course, no short and easy answer to this complex of problems. They are by nature numerous and interrelated, involving the condition of Arab society at this crossroad of its history. Society itself must
participate in the process of reshaping itself according to modern knowledge, its resource endowment, and its outlook and aspirations. But its
history and culture must never be lost. Individual countries' efforts are
crucial; an overall Arab regional direction is equally essential to identify
common problems in education and elsewhere and to create new joint institutions of learning to meet common national priorities. A new kind of
university educational system, research and information centers to deal
with common problems of technology analysis and evaluation, and so on
all the way down to primary and kindergarten education must be consistent with creative technological development and industrialization objectives. Regional training and information centers for certain highly specialized and complex technological and management skills are in many
cases the urgent economic answer to the continuous demand for those
skills.

## The Oil Economies

There had been, until recently, relatively little outside academic interest
in the problems of economic development in the oil-producing nations of
the Middle East; oil and its export were instead the chief concerns. The oil
transnationals may have discouraged other sorts of attention, but academic apathy is hard to explain. Perhaps it existed because the oil states
of the Middle East were few in number and poor despite "their" oil wealth.

Even petroleum production began recently in the Middle East. Before World War II, only Iraq among Arab nations produced any substantial amount of crude oil—4.32 million long tons in 1938, part of a world output of 270 million tons (Longrigg 1968, p. 478). Royalty payments were insignificant—for Iraq, about 17 cents per barrel.

The introduction of the "profit sharing" arrangement in the Middle East in 1951 brought some increase in government revenue, to about 75–88 cents per barrel during 1957–70 in the typical case of Saudi Arabia (Adelman 1972, p. 208). Payments to governments were used for governmental expenditure in the ordinary fiscal budget or, when at the disposal of a ruler, dispensed at his discretion before organized government bureaucracies existed in some countries.

Apart from those cash payments, there was no attempt on the part of concessionaire companies to use petroleum as an energy source or as a raw material for industry to stimulate internal economic development, even in countries such as Iraq endowed with a broad and viable natural resource base. Beyond limited employment opportunities in some oil activities and small purchases from local merchants, little was done on the domestic economic front. Transnationals completely avoided, as a matter of policy, the domestic social environment; the policy seems also to have suited most Middle Eastern governments of the time.

Economic and social isolation helped to create "oil enclaves" within the oil nations. The nature of the resource and the industry's capital intensity provided a rationale for this dualism, but they can hardly serve as an excuse for discouraging oil-based domestic development, especially where real opportunities already existed. Gas was flared rather than utilized, and the international prices for petroleum products applied in domestic markets helped to distort development incentives and to discourage local refining or petrochemical production. This is not to mention indirect meddling in domestic politics. These are behavioral factors having nothing to do with either the nature of the product or the industry. Rather they formed a part of a strategy to keep oil nations away from oil, to make sure that the integrated chain from oil field to ultimate consumer was controlled and optimized around transnational corporate objectives. The "local" partners in the 50–50 "profit" division—the governments of oil states—were "sleeping" partners by design. Objectives of a petroleum industry organized to interact with domestic economies would have given different outcomes. The U.S. petroleum industry's role in the American economy bears some elements of an example but not an analog. The Mexican oil industry, nationalized in 1938, has been fairly well integrated within the Mexican economy, to name perhaps a more relevant example.

Iraq was the first Middle East oil producer, in 1951, to introduce the practice of using oil income for development. Promulgated legislation specifically allocated 70 percent of the government's oil revenues for use in a separate development budget.

The events of the 1970s brought with them three important changes of developmental implication for the region. First, a substantial increase was attained in oil income from the regular export of oil. Second, a sudden increase in awareness of oil depletion stimulated a drive to accelerate economic development by infusion of funds from increasing oil revenues. Third, an increased measure of autonomy was conferred by direct national control over oil production and pricing.

Apathy from the outside has given way in late years to heightened interest in the oil countries and their problems. The rise in oil income, for a few oil states, beyond their ability to spend it created the phenomenon of surplus petro-dollars (and all the imagery surrounding them); hence the interest of the international financial community. The rush of most oil nations into big expenditures created opportunities for businesses in unprecedented number and variety, particularly from the West and Japan, to reinforce or establish "positions" in the area. All this, of course, stands aside from the concern about future petroleum supplies and availabilities. Pessimism brought by sudden awareness of oil depletion followed the production cutbacks and the oil embargo of 1973, although the facts on reserves and production rates had been public knowledge for years. The same awareness also gave the Middle East a new prominence in the international public information media, usually not a very flattering prominence.

The oil nations remain few in number. Five OAPEC states—Saudi Arabia, Kuwait, Iraq, the United Arab Emirates, and Libya—produce nearly 90 percent of Arab oil, and OAPEC as a whole produced 62 percent of OPEC oil in 1976, but academic and research interest in the kind of problems these states have still remains relatively slight, even within the countries concerned.

### Characteristics of Petroleum Economies

Income from petroleum exports in the major exporting countries of OAPEC represents a large proportion of their gross domestic products, most of their export earnings (see table 7.6), and the largest source of budgeted fiscal revenues. In Saudi Arabia, for example, petroleum production (including petroleum refining) was 81.7 percent of GDP, 90 percent of government budget revenues, and 96 percent of total receipts on current accounts for the Islamic year 1974–75 (Economist Intelligence Unit 1977). In Iraq, a country endowed with a much wider resource base, oil in 1973 accounted for 44.6 percent of GDP, 83 percent of total govern-

TABLE 7.6
Ratios of Petroleum Exports to Total Exports, Total Imports, and GDP
in Some OAPEC Member Countries

|  | 1971 | 1972 | 1973 | 1974 | 1975 | 1976 | 1977 |
|---|---|---|---|---|---|---|---|
|  |  |  | ALGERIA |  |  |  |  |
| Total exports | 71.4 | 78.0 | 82.7 | 91.1 | 91.4 | 87.4 |  |
| Total imports | 50.0 | 68.7 | 69.7 | 103.6 | 69.3 | 85.1 |  |
| GDP | 12.8 | 16.8 | 19.3 | 36.1 | 29.7 | 29.1 |  |
|  |  |  | IRAQ |  |  |  |  |
| Total exports | 94.3 | 92.2 | 94.5 | 98.6 | 98.5 | 98.3 |  |
| Total imports | 153.0 | 145.1 | 205.4 | 274.4 | 194.0 | 262.7 |  |
| GDP | 25.9 | 23.1 | 34.1 | 56.9 | 60.0 | — |  |
|  |  |  | KUWAIT |  |  |  |  |
| Total exports | 94.4 | 92.7 | 91.2 | 94.3 | 91.2 | 91.1 |  |
| Total imports | 328.5 | 297.3 | 288.0 | 598.7 | 329.9 | 269.3 |  |
| GDP | 56.7 | 51.2 | 41.5 | 77.6 | 70.9 | 71.3 |  |
|  |  |  | SAUDI ARABIA |  |  |  |  |
| Total exports | 99.8 | 99.7 | 99.6 | 99.9 | 99.8 | 99.9 | 99.9 |
| Total imports | 420.4 | 396.2 | 384.8 | 1082.7 | 657.4 | 414.9 | — |
| GDP | 67.4 | 65.9 | 69.3 | — | 72.6 | 82.2 | 74.7 |
|  |  |  | LIBYA |  |  |  |  |
| Total exports | 99.8 | 99.8 | 99.9 | 99.9 | 99.9 | 99.9 | 99.9 |
| Total imports | 402.6 | 231.9 | 191.1 | 257.9 | 169.8 | 262.6 | — |
| GDP | 62.0 | 44.4 | 45.9 | 53.1 | 46.3 | 49.6 | 49.9 |
|  |  |  | QATAR |  |  |  |  |
| Total exports | 96.3 | 96.2 | 97.3 | 78.2 | 97.2 | 96.7 | 99.1 |
| Total imports | 274.6 | 271.5 | 308.3 | 730.3 | 425.9 | 257.3 | 165.6 |
|  |  |  | BAHRAIN |  |  |  |  |
| Total exports | 76.4 | 69.9 | 69.1 | 85.7 | 82.4 | 77.2 | 78.1 |
| Total imports | 65.8 | 64.5 | 64.2 | 96.7 | 82.7 | 70.3 | 70.1 |
|  |  | UNITED ARAB EMIRATES |  |  |  |  |  |
| Total exports | 95.9 | 95.9 | 96.6 | 98.7 | 97.8 | 96.4 | 96.0 |
| Total imports | 258.9 | 214.9 | 212.0 | 369.9 | 250.1 | 247.7 | 202.6 |

Source: IMF 1978.

ment revenues, and 98 percent of total export earnings (Economist Intelligence Unit 1977). The predominance of petroleum is clearly overwhelming in both of these rather different oil nations.

Few will doubt the benefits of large money incomes. They raise per capita GNP, provide a source of investment, and hence permit higher income growth. Relatively high rates of growth, between 6 and 8 percent against 4 percent or less for other Arab states, have been recorded by all the oil economies. Oil also provides foreign exchange earnings, usually a constraint to economic development in most developing countries. High incomes have also enhanced the international credit standing of the oil countries by expanding the flow of their foreign exchange earnings to billions of dollars. In other words, the sheer financial weight of some Middle East oil nations has become a considerable "asset."

But what, one may ask, does this financial strength mean in real terms? Although a source of finance, the oil industry is only a small employer and represented, until recently, a relatively small capital accumulation concentrated at the crude oil production stage. Petroleum income registers a high per capita GNP but does not accrue as payments to factors of production, labor and capital, actually engaged in the generation of gross national product. It is rather, to a large extent, the return on the privilege of national ownership of a natural resource.

The mechanism implied by the economic concept of GNP—the process of creating domestic output, not the statistic—is almost absent. The concept of uniform flow of labor and capital services organized in a network of myriad microeconomic activities does not apply to the oil nations with their high GNP statistics. These economies in fact display a structural imbalance between a large financial sector and small, underdeveloped real sectors. Consumption does not take place, for the most part, from earned incomes but through a distribution process provided, essentially, by the nations' bureaucracies. This structural imbalance between real efforts of production and the privilege of consumption does not augur well for the future for the simple reason that petroleum is a depletable resource which cannot be relied on for too long to provide the rent element built into the mechanism of government financial receipts.

Awareness of this structural weakness is revealed in the oil states' sense of urgency. They want to develop quickly before the petroleum runs out. Such feelings are strongest in those oil countries poorly endowed with other natural resources, including population or hospitable climate.

The concept of absorptive capacity only partly conveys the problem. Because of constraints and bottlenecks, a developing country acquiring large financial resources cannot take full advantage of them by investing domestically in the short and medium term. Other available resources, with strong financial backing, can solve the problem of infrastructure, but for long-term, steady, and stable growth, other conditions, essentially social, must be met.

A sudden influx of money, coming in the midst of poverty and underdevelopment, brings to the surface pent up demands and expectations in the form of urgent social wants that poverty had suppressed for generations. These rising expectations are powerful in all the oil economies and are exerting mounting pressure for government action to de-emphasize investment in favor of consumption. Governments may resist such pressures at first but, for obvious political considerations, ultimately give in. A torrent of consumption expenditures follows. The consequences are too well known to elaborate. The low supply elasticity for goods and services typical of developing countries brings inflation and a flood of imports which carry with them additional imported inflation. An OAPEC study of patterns of foreign trade of member states concluded that all indicators show rising import rates, high trade ratios, and a stagnant Hirshman's commodity export concentration implying no change in the composition of exports and rising import absorption.

The experience of great income growth is disassociated from economic development. Development projects have long lead times; many years will elapse before they contribute significantly to the process of income generation. In the meantime, petroleum income growth is earned mainly through the actions of governments on oil markets. The accumulated wealth is largely independent of the acts of economic agents and factors of production in the economy. This independence further complicates the problem of income distribution inherent in economic organizations using inappropriate production technologies and a distorted system of valuation of inputs and outputs under unequal power of economic actors. The state further loosens the ties as it receives income and redistributes it through channels of public expenditure. The whole structure is conducive neither to developing economic incentives nor to developing aspirations and attitudes toward work. The danger is that economic agents will come to think that they have a claim, independent from any reward for real effort, to a share of the oil revenues. Such an expectation in fact existed in some producing states in the early days of petroleum production. Many still harbor the feeling that pressure groups will form to push claims in order to divert part of the revenues to their private use (Mabro 1976).

In summary, oil provides an opportunity to look to distant horizons, to plan and organize the economy, and to allow for a logical sequence of investment which could make up for lost time. The need for that longer view runs high now as oil production heads toward a peak and ultimately toward exhaustion. Simultaneously, however, petroleum wealth shortens the view and tips the balance of social time preferences in favor of the present—consumption now. This contradiction will prove difficult to reconcile.

Current development efforts, prompted by considerations of depletion and the use of financial incomes to accelerate growth, are meeting the bottlenecks of inadequate infrastructure and other social obstacles inherent in underdevelopment itself, especially those scarce untradable factors of management and organization which are usually presumed to exist or to evolve rapidly within the development process. Although bottlenecks of physical infrastructure can be removed in the medium term by conventional approaches, developing the manpower, skilled and specialized and properly structured to balance all sectoral needs, will continue to be the most formidable task facing the oil states.

Current bottlenecks and shortages will take their toll in resource waste of one kind or another—delays, foreign substitutes of needed skills, unemployment of the unskilled or those with unusable skills, etc. In the long run, development will be determined by what society believes development to be. The danger now is a persistent view that somehow everyone is "rightly" entitled to share in an oil wealth and that governments should fulfill all social wants from the state coffers. This view misses the point if it thinks that development is some sort of purchasable transfer of hardware that can be left to governments alone. Development is in the end a locally produced "social technology" built by the people themselves from small mechanisms into larger processes that cohere only in the presence of appropriate social attitudes and incentives.

### Petroleum and International Cooperation

The petroleum resource is unique in its combination of natural characteristics; it is hard to find, depletable, and unevenly distributed geographically. These characteristics create a weak and directionless link at the interface with the downstream structures that turn oil into final consumer products. This weakness makes the entire system highly vulnerable to and hence in need of control. That is to say, discovery and extraction of the resource and its allocation to present and future users require some administration and a degree of control. It is not a self-adjusting system in the same way industrial processes, with value added downstream, are whole systemic processes in which cost of production acts on price in the long run. Because of steady exponential growth of demand for its products, petroleum will eventually run up against the uncertainty of new discovery. The resource is finite. There are only so many years before depletion, and the question of petroleum production and allocation becomes fundamentally a decision of controlling agents and not of a self-adjusting market mechanism. The controlling agents may change over time—a cartel at one point, a regulatory agency and an oligopoly at another, or an association of sovereign governments at present, but the basic mechanism persists. The facts of control and administration of production and pricing have been features of the petroleum industry throughout its history.

An energy supply system could, perhaps, manifest the economic theorist's ideal of a self-adjusting competitive market if the uncertainty in the discovery process were somehow removed, if an inexhaustible supply could predictably be found, or if some technology based on a renewable source were commercially developed. Those possibilities are not in sight now. Major producers/exporters of petroleum and its major consumers/ importers will have to cooperate to avoid unacceptable developments in the future.

What are those developments, what specific kind of interdependence do they imply, and how can international cooperation provide a practical solution to them? Questions such as these arising from the energy "crisis" have occupied the time of many researchers and policy makers since the early 1970s when energy problems were brought to world attention by a rise in oil price which happened to coincide with production cutbacks and embargo consequent to the Arab-Israeli war of 1973.

One likely development on the world energy scene is a supply/demand imbalance by 1985 even if OPEC nations produce at their maximum efficient rate and use all their current and probable slack capacity to the full.* In such an eventuality, crude oil prices would unavoidably rise beyond the ability of most consumers/importers to pay. This is clearly one unacceptable and potentially explosive situation for the world economy.** The kind of "interdependence" implied by such a development must be avoided in favor of worldwide cooperation, particularly between the major oil exporting nations and the major oil consuming countries of the OECD. Such cooperation would be aimed at achieving a smooth energy transition from current overdependence on petroleum (oil and natural gas) and reducing its current 60 percent share in energy use to approximately 35 percent by 2000 and 25 percent by 2020.*** That transition should allow enough petroleum reserves for use in petroleum-specific applications only—transportation and petrochemical production. It should also permit the major exporters to plan their own energy transition along with the rest of the world and to acquire substitute energy technology on terms and conditions as favorable as those of the technology developers.

*Such forecasts are made by WAES (1977) and by the Conservation Commission of the World Energy Conference (1978), among others.
**The effects on crude oil markets of the probable entry of Mexico and China, in the opinion of this writer, are not likely to be great enough to change expectations of impending energy shortage drastically. In the history of Mexican oil development policy since nationalization in 1938, Mexico's main concern has been and probably will continue to be long-term growing domestic demand. China too may similarly plan production strategy with long-term views of potential domestic demand and industrial modernization as its first priority. Both Mexico and China are likely to link their crude prices to those set by OPEC.
***The figures are offered by the Conservation Commission of the World Energy Conference (1978).

To call on OPEC nations to produce at their maximum efficient rate during the transition period, most likely at a faster rate than domestically warranted, in order to help alleviate an expected energy crunch requires consuming nations to assist the producers in attaining their economic development targets independently from a world optimum price for oil assigned for the transition period. Such assistance would be a return for OPEC's parting with the stock resource which served temporarily as a sort of capital base for member nations.

Such a scope for cooperation is admittedly very broad. The desirability of it has already been declared by OPEC (1975) and subsequently debated during the Paris Conference of 1976–77 without any significant positive results. The need for translating such broad propositions of cooperation into concrete and negotiable proposals remains pending.

The need will become more urgent, but the ways in which events are unfolding at present leave little room for optimism that such a desirable form of international cooperation is drawing any closer to realization. The opposite seems, in fact, to be taking place. International resources and technology are not being pooled to find more oil in areas where it is more likely to be found—the sedimentary basins of the Middle East (Amin 1978). A large portion of exploration resources are instead going to offshore Arctic and other regions where chances of finding oil are lesser ones or, at best, very costly ones. In the meantime OPEC producers must follow domestic development priorities which understate investment in exploration and development of additional reserves in favor of more urgent economic and social development schemes. And, instead of allowing for higher oil and energy prices to bring forth greater investments in the production of substitutes and to induce lower demand and greater conservation, major consumers are instead pressuring OPEC producers to keep the oil price constant or even lower in real terms in the face of a declining value of the U.S. dollar and a rising rate of international inflation, especially for the capital equipment required for economic development of the oil exporting countries.

## Concluding Remarks

In the historic perspective of the concession era, it would seem that the exogenous introduction of a "new" technology to exploit the petroleum resources of a developing country by direct foreign investment for purposes of export has resulted in some financial benefits to the resource's sovereign owners but has brought with it many major problems. This outcome is largely attributable to the nature of the resource, characteristics of the petroleum technology that evolved under the impact of high volume growth of oil supplies and consumption, and the different, often divergent, objectives and behaviors of integrated transnationals and nations owning the resource. Problems ensuing or revealed after attainment of direct national control by petroleum-producing states are:

1.  Transnational oil companies kept their activities dependent on centers of technology abroad and hence left an inadequately developed technological base for the succeeding national oil companies. The time lost during decades of this technological dependence makes the task of acquiring accumulated know-how for the producing countries costly and time consuming because it involves nontradable components. This situation weakens the position of national oil companies vis-à-vis oil and technology transnationals in world markets. The technological sources of productivity of the industry, as developed by the petroleum transnationals and others, are not generally available at competitive prices for the oil states while large scale production and processing as another source of productivity linked to export markets may be inconsistent with producers' national development requirements.
2.  Under an overall strategy of cheap energy policies applied through the transnationals, petroleum—a stock resource—was produced at rates inconsistent with the structure of the world resource base of fossil hydrocarbons in order to meet energy demand growth from a convenient source. Petroleum supplies 60 percent of energy needs but constitutes only 11 percent of available fossil fuel reserves under current technology.
3.  Crude pricing and production rates were determined unilaterally and independently of producing nations' domestic preferences by integrated transnationals which jointly exercised control over Middle East oil resources for decades.
4.  The lack of substitutes for some major petroleum derivatives (in transport and petrochemical needs) created a rigid derived demand for crude oil imports. The resulting international interdependence means that some crude-producing states may have no option but to maintain high levels of crude output beyond their domestic financial requirements for revenues.
5.  The present role of the petroleum sector in typical Middle East oil economies seems anomalous and dualistic. A large financial sector is not linked organically to whole or healthy developing real sectors. These factors have led to overconsumption from rising foreign imports and, in the process, a rather dependent society not earning, in the main, a proper wage. Accelerating development motivated by

depletion considerations runs up against bottlenecks of inadequate infrastructure in the medium term and against constraints of unstructured manpower and incentives.

6. Economic organizations' objectives do matter in the petroleum industry. Some developing countries have successfully evolved policies and organizations for handling their petroleum resources in a manner that conforms and interacts with their economic development requirements while in the meantime creating an autonomous technological capability within and around their national oil companies, attaining a higher degree of self-reliance, providing adequate incentives for engagement of other nonpetroleum domestic resources as inputs to the petroleum sector, and reducing the level of technological imports. By contrast, transnational corporate objectives have led to resource waste in the forms of natural gas flaring, overproduction of crude, and underdevelopment of national petroleum sectors dependent on imported technology.

7. An interdependence, which demands new and extensive kinds of international cooperation, ought to be gradually evolving as an energy crunch develops in the next 10 years. Existing tendencies do not lead in that direction and unstable, potentially dangerous outcomes may follow.

## References

Adelman, M. A. 1972. *The World Petroleum Market*. Baltimore: Johns Hopkins University Press for Resources for the Future.

Al-Wattari, A. 1975. "[Petrochemical developments in OAPEC areas: aims and impact]," *Oil and Arab Cooperation* 1(1):16–34 (English abstract p. 155).

Amin, M. S. 1978. "Petroleum Exploration in the OAPEC Countries and Its Future Prospects." OAPEC, Kuwait.

Borham, M. A. 1978. "[Projects for exploitation of natural gas in Arab countries and the importance of its utilization locally]," *Oil and Arab Cooperation* 4(3):14–56 (English abstract pp. 191–92).

BP (British Petroleum Company Ltd.). 1959. *BP Statistical Review of the World Oil Industry*. London: Britannic House.

BP (British Petroleum Company Ltd.). 1967. *BP Statistical Review of the World Oil Industry*. London: Britannic House.

BP (British Petroleum Company Ltd.). 1977. *BP Statistical Review of the World Oil Industry*. London: Britannic House.

Chase Manhattan Bank. 1976. *Capital Investments of the World Petroleum Industry*. New York: CMB.

Conservation Commission of the World Energy Conference. 1978. "World Energy—Looking Ahead to 2020," *Report of the World Energy Conference*. London: IPC Science and Technology Press.

DeChazeau, Melvin G., and Alfred E. Khan. 1959. *Integration and Competition in the Petroleum Industry.* Petroleum Monograph Series, vol. 3. New Haven: Yale University Press.

Deam, Robert J. 1974. "World Model for Optimum Refining," *Hydrocarbon Processing and Petroleum Refiner* 53:101-10.

Economist Intelligence Unit, Ltd. 1977. *A Study of Middle East Economies.* London: EIU, pp. 113-15.

Energy Research Unit, Queen Mary College. 1974. "World Energy Modelling: Part 2. Preliminary Results from the Petroleum/Natural Gas Model." In Milton Searle, ed., *Energy Modelling.* Guilford, England: IPC Science and Technology Press, pp. 91-117.

Frankel, P. H. 1969. *Essentials of Petroleum: A Key to Oil Economics.* London: Clark, Doble, and Brennon.

Griffen, G. M. 1972. "The Process Analysis Alternative to Statistical Cost Functions: An Application to Petroleum Refining," *American Economic Review* 62:46-56.

Heigel, M. 1978. "Ownership of Petroleum Technologies," ESA/NRET/AG11/BP3. United Nations Interregional Symposium on State Petroleum Enterprises in Developing Countries, Vienna, Austria.

IMF (International Monetary Fund). 1978. *International Financial Statistics,* vol. 31, no. 8.

Longrigg, Stephen. 1968. *Oil in the Middle East: Its Discovery and Development.* London: Royal Institute of International Affairs.

Mabro, Robert. 1976. *Iran 1980-1985: Problems and Challenges of Development.* London: Royal Institute of International Affairs.

Nelson, W. L. 1958. *Petroleum Refinery Engineering.* New York: McGraw-Hill.

OAPEC (Organization of Arab Petroleum Exporting Countries). 1977. *Annual Statistical Report.* Kuwait: OAPEC.

OPEC (Organization of the Petroleum Exporting Countries). 1975. *Solemn Declaration of the Algiers Conference of the Sovereigns and Heads of State of the OPEC Member Countries.* Vienna: OPEC.

OPEC (Organization of the Petroleum Exporting Countries). 1976. *Annual Statistical Bulletin 1975.* Vienna: OPEC.

OPEC (Organization of the Petroleum Exporting Countries). 1977. *Annual Statistical Bulletin 1976.* Vienna: OPEC.

Penrose, Edith. 1968. *The Large International Firm in Developing Countries: The International Petroleum Industry.* Cambridge, Massachusetts: MIT Press.

Petroconsultants S. A. 1977. *Annual Review 1976.* Geneva: Petroconsultants S. A.

WAES (Workshop on Alternative Energy Strategies, Massachusetts Institute of Technology). 1977. *Energy: Global Prospects 1985-2000.* New York: McGraw-Hill.

Zahlan, A. B. 1974. "Investing Oil Revenue in Arab Science & Technology Development." Seminar on Investing Oil Revenues in Arab Development, Beirut, November 22-30.

# II. ECONOMIC DEVELOPMENT

# 8  *Mahmoud A. El-Shafie & I. H. Abdel-Rahman*

# Economic and Social Development

Economic and social development processes and practices in the developing countries have been and will always be closely linked to the prevailing conditions and corresponding developments in the industrial countries. National and international concern about the development of less-developed economies has been mostly a recent phenomenon associated with the political independence of many countries, especially since the end of World War II, and with nationalistic drives in search of social betterment and economic growth to meet the rising expectations of the peoples of the emerging nation-states.

Before World War II the development of developing countries was no major concern in the advanced countries. Europe, North America, and Japan were just emerging from the severe depression of the 1930s and were heading toward a major war; the USSR was politically and economically isolated. Much of Africa, Asia, and Oceania were under the political and economic domination of the colonial powers of Europe. Latin American countries were at the time more or less dependent on the advanced countries of North America and Western Europe which, preoccupied with their own national development, were primarily interested in drawing on the resources of overseas colonies and nations to foster development at home.

Growth efforts in developing countries and colonies concentrated, under these prewar circumstances, on one or two leading sectors. The raw materials from plantations and mining enclaves were exported to pay the bills for import of manufactured goods from the advanced countries. Industrialization of developing countries was largely discouraged; education was slighted and social development almost neglected. First priority in investment went to the development of natural resources destined for export and to the concomitant infrastructure. Second priority was assigned to the welfare of ruling minorities and of the docile bureaucracy necessary for security and internal stability. Health, education, trade, and other services were last on the list of priorities.

It is evident from history that economic development has always been associated with and perhaps has even resulted from political and social changes; it has not been purely economic. The real forces driving change and growth are the political ones of independence, nationalism, and participation of the people and their human associations in mobilizing available resources and establishing new institutions to generate and accelerate national development.

The war years and the immediate postwar events of the 1940s realized, to a large extent, the political objective of independence for many countries, although not without conflict and fragmentation of previously consolidated territories. The industrial countries, after World War II, came to handle their economic relations with the poor countries through concessionary arrangements and agreements with new governments, not directly as before. Nevertheless, the industrial countries had already established for themselves historical advantages. The capacity to process raw materials had been developed and kept within their own boundaries. Their bargaining strength in pricing both raw material imports from and manufactured exports to the developing countries survived independence. The international division of labor thus established continues to give distributional advantages to industrial countries and disadvantages to developing countries producing natural resource commodities for export.

At the end of World War II the Allied powers created the United Nations system (to which most socialist countries adhered) and the Bretton Woods monetary organizations (from which most socialist countries abstained). There was an attempt to establish a World Trade Organization in Havana, but the United States scuttled the attempt, and GATT was formed outside the UN system as a trade club of the prosperous Western countries. These postwar institutions called for eventual liberalization of foreign trade, currency convertibility and reserves, and financing for reconstruction of war-devastated countries, especially in Western Europe and Japan. They also propounded the responsibility of national governments for macroeconomic management to ensure full employment, social welfare, economic stability, and growth and prosperity.

All these arrangements produced beneficial results for the Western market economies but did very little to enhance the development of developing countries. Postwar demobilization accomplished a gradual return to peacetime production (especially in the United States), and reconstruction programs were successful in devising an almost completely new structure of economic activities in West Germany, Japan, Italy, and some other devastated nations. The Marshall Plan was accompanied politically by the OECD and NATO alliances in the West, with corresponding organizations in the Eastern bloc, including the CMEA and Warsaw Pact.

The Korean War manifested clearly "cold war" strategies, increased the demand for raw materials, and set in motion the commodity price fluctuations which would plague the economies of the developing countries. It also stimulated the military demands which have grown unhalted for the succeeding 25 years. Many industrial countries saw high rates of economic growth and began to realize the conditions for currency convertibility, full employment, and a gradual reduction of trade barriers among them. Transnational corporations began to expand and to become an important feature of the economic order.

These successes created confidence, if not exhilaration, about Western economic thought and the "unlimited" possibilities for growth and a "postindustrial state." Management (in the sense of macrostate and corporate management) became the task of a new elite in a thriving society. Liberal capitalism was thought to be here to stay forever, and this optimism was applied in new attention to the problems of development of developing countries. A concept of "linear" growth—a sort of sequential development process—assumed that developing countries could climb, step by step, the same ladder of growth that industrial countries had earlier ascended in the nineteenth century. Agricultural incomes would be developed to provide a market for industrial products; supplies of raw materials for export (in addition to minerals, which were extracted and exported by corporate enclaves) would be stimulated by local demand and import substitution (assuming antecedent growth of consumption and imports) under limited and temporary customs protection.

The development strategy suitable for nineteenth-century frontier economies turned out to be far from appropriate for the second half of the twentieth century when technological capabilities for reaching other planets have been created, giant corporations have captured principal resources and markets, and economic concentration has characterized world and local trade. Solutions to the development problems of developing countries could no longer be solved by schemes which concentrated on infrastructural projects (power, transport, irrigation, and, lately, education) with little capital offered for industrialization, and which left mining and petroleum production almost exclusively to transnational enterprises.

During the 1950s and 1960s the expansion of the economic influence of industrial countries paralleled a mounting resentment of developing countries to the policies of ex-colonial powers which persistently opposed national liberation movements and frequently challenged programs of economic independence. Some developing countries adopted non-Western political systems; others became disenchanted with the outcome of development efforts under "free market" conditions and found it necessary, politically and economically, to expand the role of the state and create a public sector to replace foreign monopolies and enterprises. Development planning measures of this sort, initially seen as political heresy by the Western countries, would eventually become commendable instruments in the view of UN agencies and many political economists.

Following the Treaty of Rome in 1957, and after some initial attempts at coordination of coal, iron, and steel production, the European cooperation movement began to grow. The creation of the European Economic Community (EEC) immediately led to the establishment of free trade areas in Europe (EFTA), in Latin America (LAFTA), and elsewhere. Regional or subregional arrangements also proliferated among groups of developing countries to coordinate national development and trade policies and to widen markets in support of future industrialization. Such regional groupings included the Central American Common Market, the Arab Economic Unity Council, the Association of Southeast Asian Nations, the West African Economic Community, and the East African Common Market. Some of these groups hoped to damp the effects of political and economic fragmentation and to substitute complementarity for competitiveness among members in dealing with external situations. Other regional organizations hoped to harmonize their national development undertakings, to cooperate in the transfer of technology and the movement of capital and labor in joint ventures, and even to achieve full economic and cultural integration (UNDESA 1968).

In short, it became evident to the developing countries in the early 1960s that they needed to pool their resources and work together toward common objectives of development on regional levels and on a worldwide basis. The surge of interest in regionalism demonstrated an increasing awareness of problems of development in relatively small nations with small internal markets and narrow resource bases. It also showed that developing countries were beginning to recognize collective interests separate from those of the industrial countries of the East or the West.

Nevertheless, most developing countries remain aware that they cannot industrialize their economies on a large scale without the cooperation of the advanced countries, which dominate sizable markets, control the transfer of industrial technologies, and have the facilities for training managerial and technical skills, as well as for financing the various needs of comprehensive development. Many developing countries, however, face internal obstacles which restrain national efforts for economic and social development despite the availability of abundant natural resources, ample manpower, locational advantages, and, in many cases, important markets. Their economies have long been organized along traditional lines that could not induce development on a large multidimensional scale, and elements of these traditional difficulties persist in many countries. Traditional economies are usually characterized by human institutions (caste, custom, law, etc.), social organizations such as tenure arrangements, and other modes of human behavior not conducive to shouldering development responsibilities or enlisting effective participation of people in growth and change. The capabilities of developing economies to sustain or accelerate growth and change are limited in the absence of appropriate institutions and innovations to transform human attitudes, group behavior, social structure, and the organizations of production.

The process of economic and social development is basically national. It is all-encompassing; it deals with all components of the social system and their interactions. At the national level, economic and social development is made manifest by dynamic changes in the structure of the economy and its operation, by self-sustaining growth of productive capacities, as well as diversification of production and rising income levels. Growth and change take place also in the structure and composition of manpower skills, in employment opportunities, in occupational distribution of the labor force, in the origin of national income, and in income distribution. This multiplicity of interrelated changes is necessary in national economic development but cannot be effected in any orderly way without a national policy framework and a strategy for development that relates objectives of development to available means to attain them. A development strategy must also seek to remove the constraints which hold back the creativity of people. It must try to involve all people individually or collectively in the processes of growth and change on the basis of stability, security of expectations, and equality of opportunities in employment, production, and distribution of benefits and sacrifices.

## Some Development Theories

Development of any country occurs within a socio-economic framework of resources and institutions. The track of development is greatly influenced by the political system of the country and the degree of positive response of its people and their human organizations to the requirements for growth and change. Various theories of economic development have attempted to explain the process of growth and change in terms of selected economic variables and tried to establish mathematical or logical relationships between independent and dependent parameters of the economic system. There appears to be general agreement in most theories that the growth and change of output, employment, and income depend on independent variables such as savings, investment, technological advance, resource combinations, techniques of production, organizational forms, etc. Economists recognize the importance of increasing the productive capacity of the economy through savings and investment, with technological advances playing a major role in raising productivity, lowering production costs, and realizing operating surpluses for further investment.

Every classical economist—Smith, Mill, Ricardo, Malthus, even Marx —who dealt with the development and growth of economies had also to address problems concerning the distribution of the growing and changing income or product. All of them had in mind some model of economic development of the economy in which they lived, and all focused on technological advance and population growth as related to natural resources (called land) and production therefrom. All of them addressed savings, investments, profit, and wages, and so came to problems of distribution, but all emphasized the role of private entrepreneurs in generating economic development and neglected the leadership of governments and other modern institutions in initiating, sustaining, and accelerating development. They could not foresee the great diversity of present day economies or appreciate the complexity of development problems in such a world. In dealing with distribution, the classical economists focused on conflicting interests within one economy and so reached different conclusions and stances. They denied the authority of government in harmonizing group interests and overlooked forward and backward linkages among technical advance and industrialization and the investment opportunities which industry creates to sustain development.

Recognition has slowly grown that national development includes socio-political and other noneconomic variables—patterns of behavior, social relationships, social and natural environments, regional and international relations and institutions, and more. Wallich (1952), for example, argued that the demonstration effect produced by rapid communication and transportation among nations widens the horizons of people, creates strong desires for higher levels of living, and leads people to pressure governments for public efforts in development and welfare. Hoselitz (1957) emphasized the role of social environment and appropriate institutions in collecting savings and undertaking investment as well as stimulating individuals to become entrepreneurs; he added that industrial changes could be induced through planning by central authority. Nurkse (1967) highlighted the role of government in making large investments in consumer goods industries in developing countries to counteract the tendency toward rising demand for imported goods because of the demonstration effect. He advocated isolationist policy, as in Japan and Eastern Europe in early stages of industrial development, to avoid such problems.

Most of those economists and Hagen (1962) accepted the thesis that economic development is achieved gradually and in stages during which appropriate institutions are created, social environment becomes conducive, and scientific knowledge, as well as technological advances, is introduced to effect growth and change. In addition, Hagen stressed the creativity of individuals, group behavior, and socio-psychological factors in effecting far-reaching changes in political organization, social structure, and human attitudes towards development.

Other economists, however, elaborated on development strategies rather than theories. Rosenstein-Rodan (1943; 1961) advocated strategies of balanced growth for industrialization and emphasized the need for substantial foreign aid to developing countries for investment in transport, power, education, and other social amenities which could help to provide the "big push" for development. He also directed attention to the importance of government action in large-scale training programs to supply needed skills and to the promotion of trade exchanges between developing and developed regions for their mutual benefit. He regarded the creation of common regional markets and regional investment trusts as vehicles for liberalizing international trade and capital mobility and for stimulating exports of new industrial products from developing countries to advanced countries.

Hirschman (1958) noted that scarcity of decision-making abilities, lack of scientific management, and absence of appropriate institutions would make balanced growth strategies in developing countries infeasible. He recommended, instead, a strategy of "unbalanced" growth based on a chain of carefully planned industries with strong backward and forward linkage effects; these would later induce further investment in linked industries. Myrdal (1968) reminded that socio-cultural differences between developed and developing countries demand objective study of the economies, societies, and cultures of developing countries in order to devise strategies suited to their specific needs and conditions.

One rather striking feature of nearly all these development theories and strategies is their unconcern with natural resource policies. For many years most economists looked upon resources, explicitly or not, as a gift of nature and treated the products derived from them as a form of capital. Natural resources were seen, when commonly held, as mere factors of production commanding a rent just as any man-made fixed asset does.

Resources, when privately held, commanded economic rent as a distributive share for owners or as a compensation for productivity differentials in comparison to some marginal situation. Moreover, trade (and in a sense comparative advantage) was assumed to exist among equals; powers of property rights in the marketplace were ignored under standard competitive theorems.

Although they do contribute to explaining growth and change and do help in guiding economic and social policies toward development, none of these theories or strategies have proved readily applicable to development in all countries or under all the variable and complex conditions of economic concentration, differential market power, and dependence on nonrenewable resources irreplaceable at any cost or price. Current theories fail to accommodate the comprehensiveness of development processes because they try to explain them largely in terms of capital/product or capital/labor ratios, propensities to invest, save, import, or export, and other tools of marginal or incremental analysis. At their cores these theories have been built around such factors as the advance and transfer of technology, mobility of capital, labor, and products, and the allocation of resources by market forces rather than by coherent planning. The experience of Eastern European countries with central planning for economic and social development does, however, provide another mold for growth and change. The government acts as the central planning agency, the authority for harmonizing diverse interests, the entrepreneurial functionary in detecting and capturing investment opportunities, and the designer of allocative as well as distributive mechanisms.

## Planning for Development

Experience with planning in developing countries is extremely varied in scope, content, time horizon, and objectives. A notable forerunner was the Indian experience under Nehru, beginning in 1948. This trial stimulated planning approaches in many developing countries and to some extent in the market-oriented industrial economies of France, Japan, the Federal Republic of Germany, and others. Planning as a general approach to macromanagement of national development efforts is now pursued and applied not only by nation-states but also at regional and international levels. The Alliance for Progress as a program of U.S.-Latin American cooperation was one such attempt which stressed the need for social and institutional change through investments in education, health services, potable water, land reform, and the like. The first United Nations development decade in the 1960s appreciated the complexity and extent of development problems of the developing countries. Two better-known annual targets of that first development decade—an average growth rate of 5 percent of GDP in the developing countries and an aggregate aid flow of 1 percent of GNP from the advanced countries—are really less important than the embodied concept of indicative planning at the international level. This conceptual procedure was followed in the second UN development decade of the 1970s under UNCTAD, UNIDO, and the evolving GATT, and in other UN agencies concerned with energy, food, and environment.

The development planning exercises which many countries have attempted in the last two decades are supposedly based on some future outlook for development needs, prospects, and problems. But proper plans for development need to be formulated on the basis of some chosen strategy, some organizational and institutional frame within which available resources will be mobilized and allocated to attain predetermined objectives. Many developing countries have formulated plans but have forgotten about planning as a continuous process of decision making to fulfill plan objectives. Some countries with formal development plans have paid little attention to designing and enacting policies of implementation. Others have assembled long lists of investment projects without any real attempt to fit these projects into national objectives, defined priorities, local environmental conditions, or organizational and administrative schemes. Often plans are not tested for financial and technical or socioeconomic and administrative feasibility.

The development of developing countries must meet the genuine aspirations of people, satisfy their basic needs for better living, and accomplish freedom from want, ill health, illiteracy, idleness, and exploitation. Sustained increases in productive capacities, diversification of the productive economic base and of employment opportunities, and savings for additional development cannot be accomplished without stability and progressive industrialization in the full sense of the concept, not in the narrow sense of establishing industrial facilities based on equipment, hardware, processes, skills, and even raw materials bought from other nations. Development needs to enlist the active participation of individual people, human organizations, and the state. The concept of participatory development built around people and geared to meeting their needs has in some sense been applied in China, which has striven to combine production and income with equity in distribution, full employment, and social as well as institutional change.

## Manpower Requirements

Economic activities cannot be undertaken without human labor equipped with technical skills and human knowledge using natural resources and man-made assets of capital and technology to produce goods and services. Economic development has in the past been accompanied by reductions in the proportion of the labor force employed in agriculture and mining and by increases in the proportion employed in manufacturing and service sectors. In the course of economic development, a growing proportion of total investment is destined to finance intersectoral movements of labor and its training.

The need for more and better education, training, and social services is undoubtedly great in all developing countries, and some appropriate balance must be maintained between economic and social sectors in the total development effort. In a growing number of countries the responsibility for education at all levels and for training labor in strategic skills and specialities has been increasingly assigned to the government. Employment opportunities created by investment programs in developing countries have been captured by migratory labor from exogenous sources more often than is desirable, and educational planning in many developing countries has yet to pay sufficient attention to the problem of appropriate quality and quantity of educated and trained manpower and the occupational mix of employment opportunities.

Technical cooperation programs, whether bilateral or multilateral, cannot be expected to fill the gap between availability and need for skilled manpower except on a partial and temporary basis. Many aid-giving industrial countries have frequently tied their technical assistance to donor delivery and pricing of skills as well as equipment. The "necessary" skills are usually determined unilaterally without adequate thought for the conditions and needs of recipient countries, which often look upon such aid as "extra" resources, the use of which need not be optimized.

Failures in development can often be traced to bad decisions in procuring equipment, errors in engineering design, adoption of unsuitable processes, inadequate plant layout, installation of excess capacity, and/or waste of counterpart resources—in short, to poor advice and inappropriate counsel. Some developing countries have been able to avoid many of these mistakes because they had national cadres of qualified personnel and an institutional framework to evaluate offers of aid in the light of domestic requirements. Some other countries prefer to establish joint ventures with foreign capital through which appropriate technology, including higher skills, can be acquired along with modern management techniques and a share in the export market. Still other developing countries have undertaken major physical developments on a turnkey basis and have later discovered that the shortcomings of such high-cost arrangements could have been avoided had they paid more attention to indigenous manpower skills in accord with domestic requirements of growth and change.

## International Trade

During the first half of the twentieth century, the long-term prices of agricultural and mineral raw materials exported from developing countries have declined vis-à-vis prices of imports of manufactured products from industrial countries (UNDESA 1962; UNDESA 1972). In order to maintain a constant level of foreign exchange earnings from those raw material exports and to finance the wide range of imports of consumer goods, input goods, and capital equipment, the developing countries have had to expand the volume of raw material exports. Lack of diversification of production and the small share of the manufacturing sector in most developing nations' exports have kept their economies heavily dependent on the resource imports of the industrial countries. For instance, petroleum constituted more than 90 percent of the value of exports of all OPEC countries put together for 1975–77, although a few countries such as Gabon, Indonesia, and Ecuador had more diversified exports of which petroleum accounted for about 80, 70, and 55 percent, respectively (IMF 1978). Even in countries such as the Congo and Syria—not major producers —oil exports have exceeded 60 percent of total exports, on the average, for the years since 1974 (IMF 1978).

Copper accounted for more than 80 percent of Chile's and Zambia's total exports, although only about 40 percent of Zaire's exports. Iron ore constituted approximately 72 percent and 86 percent of the exports of Liberia and Mauritania, respectively, while phosphate amounted to 52 percent, 44 percent, and 25 percent of total exports of Togo, Morocco, and Senegal, respectively (IMF 1978). About 30 developing countries in Africa, Asia, and Latin America, other than those already mentioned, still depend on the export of one single primary product to earn more than 40 percent of foreign exchange receipts. Examples include tea in Sri Lanka; cotton in Mali, Chad, and the Sudan; cacao in Ghana; tobacco in Malawi; sugar in Mauritius, Cuba, Guyana, and the Dominican Republic; coffee in Rwanda, Colombia, El Salvador, and Burundi; rice in Burma; bauxite in Jamaica; uranium in Niger; and groundnuts in The Gambia. A relatively few countries with more diversified resource bases have been able to develop domestic production in several commodities for export diversification of raw materials and manufactures. These include Argentina, Brazil, Mexico, Bolivia, Peru, India, Malaysia, the Philippines, and Thailand (IMF 1978).

Table 8.1 shows both the magnitude and shares of exports and imports in advanced countries of the OECD, petroleum exporting countries, and other developing countries over the last 20 years. The pertinent point is that share of world trade for "other" developing countries, those which

TABLE 8.1
Value of World Exports and Imports in Advanced and Developing Countries in 1957, 1967, and 1976 (in Billions of U.S. Dollars) and Shares of World Trade

| | 1957 | 1967 | 1976 | 1957 | 1967 | 1976 |
|---|---|---|---|---|---|---|
| | Value of exports | | | Value of imports | | |
| Advanced countries | 76.4 | 153.7 | 657.9 | 79.3 | 162.1 | 715.4 |
| Petroleum-exporting countries | 6.9 | 12.1 | 133.1 | 5.6 | 6.7 | 62.9 |
| Other developing countries | 18.2 | 26.8 | 115.5 | 23.3 | 34.6 | 144.7 |
| World totals | 101.5 | 192.7 | 906.5 | 108.3 | 203.4 | 923.0 |
| | Percentages of world trade | | | | | |
| Advanced countries | 75.2 | 79.9 | 72.5 | 73.3 | 79.6 | 77.5 |
| Petroleum-exporting countries | 6.8 | 6.2 | 14.6 | 5.2 | 3.3 | 6.8 |
| Other developing countries | 18.0 | 13.9 | 12.9 | 21.5 | 17.1 | 15.7 |
| World totals | 100.0 | 100.0 | 100.0 | 100.0 | 100.0 | 100.0 |

Source: IMF 1978, pp. 44–49

export little or no oil, has continued to decline, despite a fourfold increase in exports and imports for 1967–76, and that trade deficits in these countries have persisted and indeed grown larger for two decades. They have repeatedly had to finance these deficits through foreign loans and foreign aid. Moreover, some petroleum-exporting countries such as Algeria and Iraq have joined other developing nations in borrowing abroad in recent years under the pressure of development requirements and the mounting costs of importing food, capital equipment, and technologies from industrial countries where oligopolistic and inflationary prices of exports continue to prevail.

In view of the persistent balance of trade deficits in many developing countries and the unfavorable terms of trade for their exports, the Secretary General of UNCTAD has recently listed the essentials of a new international economic order as "lessening of the vulnerability of developing countries to the decreasing prices for their primary exports; expanded external markets for the manufactured goods of developing countries; improved conditions for their acquiring, developing and applying technology; a new international monetary system more responsive to the needs of developing countries and the lessening of their dependence on developed countries by encouraging self-reliance and closer cooperation among developing countries themselves" (UNCTAD 1977).

These developing countries are economically justified in bargaining for higher prices for their primary exports and in insisting on price stabilization schemes that can bring higher earnings from increased exports of depletable resources as time goes on. However, price guarantees for primary products without stabilizing the terms of trade between raw materials and manufactured goods will not reduce price and income disparities, nor will they produce an equitable distribution of benefits and sacrifices among primary producers and manufacturers.

Although industrial development based on domestically oriented production of import substitutes has been taking place in more and more developing countries, recent years have also seen attention to the development of export-oriented industries, especially those requiring intensive labor and/or domestically available inputs of raw materials—textiles, footwear, and apparel; electronics, calculators, office equipment, and assembled transport equipment (mostly produced under subcontracts with transnational enterprises); or iron and steel, nonferrous metals, and chemicals.

Exports of manufactures from developing countries in 1975 amounted to U.S. $26 billion, half of which came from 4 countries—Taiwan, Korea, Spain, and Hong Kong—and another third of which came from 12 other countries—Brazil, India, Greece, Mexico, Yugoslavia, Portugal, Turkey, Singapore, Malaysia, the Philippines, Thailand, and Morocco (World Bank 1978, pp. 10, 16). In consequence of the rising exports of manufactured products between 1960 and 1975, the share of primary commodities in total exports of developing countries (*excluding* petroleum and petroleum products) fell from 68 percent to 34 percent while the manufactured exports' share rose from 14 percent to about 26 percent (World Bank 1978, p. 19). Nevertheless, manufactured exports of developing countries formed only 1.2 percent of the total consumption of industrial countries in 1975 (World Bank 1978, p. 28).

By comparison, the developed countries, of course, enjoy a much wider diversity in primary and manufactured production, as well as services including transport, insurance, banking and technological services, all of which command higher values in international trade than the raw material exports from developing countries. The developed countries in 1975 accounted for about 90 percent of total world exports of industrial products and, if fuel is excluded, about 65 percent of total world exports of raw materials (World Bank 1978, p. 19).

## Resources for Development and the Influence of Transnationals

Both developed and developing countries have been affected by the transnational corporations, grown strong in both number and breadth of interest since World War II. Transnationals have captured important natural resources in mining and agriculture through an elaborate network of subsidiaries, affiliates, and collaborators, especially in the developing countries.

The economic power and market strength of some of these corporations have grown in tandem with their ability to integrate processing, transport, marketing, manufacturing, and financing. Their power has been supported by progressive accumulation of industrial technologies protected by patent rights, copyrights, and other arrangments which contribute to market imperfections, noncompetititve pricing, and restrictive practices. These corporations have, perhaps, been extremely effective in management and technical application, but their efficiency in profit maximization sometimes runs against public interests and policies in countries where they operate and in countries where they are chartered. The assets of certain of these corporations are larger than those of many developing countries combined, their influence is great, and their power can represent, in some cases, a danger to host countries and to the international community as a whole.

Partly in reaction to the transnationals' power, some developing countries have organized resource exporters' or producers' associations to enhance their collective bargaining strength in the marketing of crude petroleum, bauxite, copper, iron ore, rubber, coffee, and other primary products moving in world trade, mostly from developing to developed countries. Although OPEC is well known to the world because of its success in pricing oil, associations of copper exporters, iron ore exporters, and others have been less effective in collective bargaining with importing countries or transnational enterprises. Some industrial countries do produce sizable portions of the world output of petroleum, iron ore, bauxite, nickel, copper, and other minerals, but a relatively few developing countries account for almost all the remaining production and export of petroleum and metallic minerals—12 countries in the case of oil and another 12 in the case of metal ores. These developing countries do have the chance to establish corresponding resource-based industries on a large scale with, possibly, the collaboration of transnational enterprises. But there are 50 other developing countries (with nearly 55 percent of the Third World population) whose mineral production is very marginal, about $2 per capita; they have little chance to industrialize along these lines and probably must concentrate on agricultural development and labor-intensive manufacturing industries for which appropriate technological requirements are available at reasonable cost.

However, historical patterns of resource processing and transnational corporate control of technology, marketing, or the resources themselves mean that expanding resource-based industries in developing countries is not merely a technical, financial, or economic matter but also one of politics and market power. Transnational enterprises, labor unions, and governments in the industrial countries will play a decisive role.

Great potential does exist for the development of resource-based industries in developing countries through joint ventures with industrial countries, but realizing that potential will require multidimensional cooperation among members of the international community to shift global industrial structure to the mutual benefit of all countries concerned. Part of the difficulty may stem from the political fact that many industrial countries tend to equate the private interests of big business organizations, particularly transnational enterprises, with national or public interests. If global interdependence is fully understood, if its implications are recognized and its beneficial, long-run effects on increasing labor and capital productivity are appreciated, it will be to the advantage of all countries to support efforts to relocate industries and minimize costs for the international community at large. Potential demand based on development requirements of developing countries can help sustain and expand production and employment in important export-oriented sectors of many industrial economies, provided that both groups of countries move jointly to strengthen lines of development beneficial to both.

There is legitimate worry that the world's demands are beginning to strain the supply of some natural resources, both renewable and nonrenewable. Will increasing consciousness of scarcity of energy, water, grains, and certain minerals induce more conservation and more rational utilization of these valuable resources and lessen depletion rates and waste? Will resource-intensive technologies be supplanted by resource-saving technologies? These questions must concern policy makers and the general publics in both industrial and developing countries. They bear on common interests and world welfare; the answers will help to determine development paths of the future as well as corrective policy measures of the present.

Issues of resource conservation and use are of paramount importance to the development of developing countries because no country can progress without a natural resource base *and* a human resource base properly equipped to use available natural resources for development. Even those developing countries rich in natural resources must face policy decisions about appropriate rates of extraction of finite, stock resources for export markets. Extraction rates commensurate with foreign exchange needs of their domestic economies will not necessarily be the rates wanted by importing countries. Can producers of finite resources expect higher prices that account for the full economic costs of resource extraction and depletion? Can producers expect consuming countries to assist in investment in discovery and development of additional reserves to prolong stock resources' life span? What measures of international cooperation can be expected from industrial countries to help expand the productive capacities of exporting countries through industrialization that compensates resource producers for the income-generating resources they lose through export?

Exponential growth in a finite environment cannot continue indefinitely because of the physical scarcity of depletable resources in the face of population growth and/or the disruption of ecological cycles that account for the production of renewable resources. Limits to growth exist, but their proximity can be exaggerated by assuming that high rates of wasteful exploitation of resources will continue, that rapid population growth cannot be halted, that the frontiers of productive and useful investments are insignificant, and that opportunities to satisfy the needs of the poor are drying up. In looking at the world of poor and rich nations, it will surely be extremely difficult to accept proximate or "nearby" limits to growth of developing nations, or to conclude that economic and social development is, in the final analysis, a "zero-sum game." However, perceptions of scarcity among the publics of developed and developing nations alike may induce nations to shift from material-intensive technologies toward energy-frugal and material-saving devices.

Developing and developed countries in increasing numbers have learned that they need to enforce national regulatory measures for conservation and orderly use of natural resources vulnerable to depletion, exhaustion, and irreversibility. Finite resources that are exhaustible, and irreplaceable at any cost, require public policies for pricing, conservation, and use, even if we do not now know how many new resource stocks will be discovered in the future. It is not unreasonable to expect that there exist unknown economic resources. Advances in technologies and their applications to space, seabed, and tropical or polar regions might produce vast supplies of certain resources. Within the last two decades of human history valuable and astounding advances have taken place in nuclear energy, supersonics, ballistics, computers, electronics, and communication facilities, to mention just a few accomplishments. Such formidable developments materialized amid world tension, agitation, conflict, and political struggle rather than any cooperative utopia.

Expansion of the resource base in both quantity and quality is, of course, an essential ingredient of adequate development in any country. Economy in allocating available resources is another integral part of the development process. Much of the technology required for discovery and economic use of natural resources is in the hands of corporations headquartered in the industrial countries. Cooperative arrangements between these enterprises and the resource-rich developing countries for concerted action in discovering and using additional natural resources could ask transnationals to supply strategic inputs of technology and equipment as well as marketing facilities for the output of national operators. Somewhat similar arrangements between petroleum-producing countries and transnational corporations have been tried in recent years; other countries rich in strategic hard minerals or other resources might try the same approach. The transnationals may well see increased profits from such new forms of relations (Mikdashi 1978). Other possibilities to be explored are "public multinational corporations" (Tinbergen 1976) or expanded multilateral programs of technical cooperation in resource management and development under the auspices of UNDP, other UN agencies, or the World Bank consultative service (World Bank 1977).

## New Approaches to Development

New approaches to world problems—ones which might bring about more balanced development and more rational management of resources with a greater sense of equity and justice, prosperity, and peace—have been much discussed in recent years. Many problems, whether sectoral, national, regional, or global, are amenable to solution in a comprehensive analytical framework based on pragmatism and foresight but appear intractable if treated one by one apart from the intricacies of whole socioeconomic and political systems. "Management by crises" has done little but aggravate problems with the monetary crisis, the foreign trade crisis, the energy crisis, the food crisis, and other problems crippling the steadiness of growth. "Management by objectives" is also in a predicament because objectives are not clearly defined and priorities are not specified; it is all too easy to find programs working at cross-purposes. Objectives must be coherent, consistent, and complementary—not necessarily immediately and in every small detail but over a reasonable time—if development is to be started and sustained on national, regional, or international levels. Of course, agreement on objectives and means to fulfill them is easier to obtain on national and regional levels if decision-making machineries exist to harmonize conflicting interests over time and if these machineries have the ability to mobilize resources and the power to allocate them. Agreement becomes more difficult at the international level because the power of decision rests with individual sovereign states.

One should never expect unanimous or even majority agreement among countries on global strategies of development. It is usually optimistic to hope for much agreement on sectoral strategies to reconcile conflicting interests and divergent policies of two countries or groups of countries. The diversity of labels and overlapping categories—rich and poor; developing, developed and least developed; market-oriented, mixed, and centrally planned; land-locked and island economies—illustrates the unlikely prospects for even a limited consensus.

Regional groupings of countries can complement and strengthen national development efforts if common objectives to be pursued by collective action can be clearly defined. Regional mechanisms and institutions can harmonize national policies in a regional perspective, can pool and mobilize certain national resources, can enhance exchanges of technology and products and maintain a mutually beneficial trade balance among members, and can enable member countries to bargain collectively with the outside world for all those ends. Some regional groups of developing countries formed a decade or more ago, however, had little success because they lacked the diversified resource base to increase the size of the regional market and seldom had the skilled labor, advanced technologies, or surplus capital to share.

Many developing countries have looked outward for development requirements, spending more time in seeking this outside aid than in building their capacity for internal savings and investment, expending great efforts to persuade the industrial countries to do for them what they have not been prepared to do for themselves. They have waited for policies of the industrial countries to adjust in their favor without taking serious steps to formulate appropriate strategies and policies for development that suits local conditions. Some developing countries tried with little success to emulate growth paths followed by the centrally planned economies of Eastern Europe while forgetting that mutual cooperation, commonality of interests, and regional institutions to harmonize national policies and to mobilize resources across national borders are among contributory factors to success. Many more developing countries tried to imitate growth paths of Western industrial countries, also without much success because they failed to recognize that narrow concepts of economic profit and private cost are largely inappropriate guides to social and economic development of the developing countries, which require broadly based concepts of social profitability and social cost (Tinbergen 1976, p. 76).

Experience has indicated that most developing countries need to devise long-term strategies and comprehensive policies suited to objectives, conditions, and problems within their borders. The growth strategies of Eastern Europe or the West are examples of development under specific socio-political and economic circumstances and not models which the developing countries must emulate. Neither is it necessary to accept popular or oversimplified prescriptions. The poor countries do not necessarily aspire to "close the income gap" between themselves and the rich industrial nations; nowhere does such an explicit objective occur in development plans or policies of the developing countries.

Population growth, often seen in the past as a source of productive manpower and a stimulus for demand, has more recently been seen as a reservoir for unemployment and a burden on development, yet it is not necessary to presume that those who urge population control and family planning upon the poor countries as a prerequisite for development have got the entire answer. These advocates appear to miss the significance of people as agents of development and to slight the ultimate objectives of growth and change—human betterment and welfare. They ignore the historical experience that birth rates began to drop sharply only *after* improvements in living standards became reasonably general in consequence of sustained rises in labor productivity and labor's share of national income (Lekachman 1977). This phenomenon is worth studying very closely: after two or three decades of development attempts in poor countries, the share of wages and salaries in national income ranges between 25 and 35 percent versus 50 to 65 percent in advanced countries where rates of population growth are relatively small (UN 1976). Correlations between full employment (especially women's employment) and the rate of population growth also deserve scrutiny (ILO 1977). With spreading education for women in developed economies and expanded work opportunities under sustained economic growth, the participation rates of women in the labor force accelerated, and fertility rates tended to fall. A similar trend might be expected in developing countries where progress in general education is fairly rapid but where women's share of wage employment is still small.

Economic and social development plans in many developing countries often try to meet a variety of long term objectives—to diversify production and employment, to attain higher consumption levels, to expand exports and reduce imports, and to realize higher levels of living for the masses as well as a more equitable distribution of national income. So many important objectives may be difficult to reconcile over a few years and can hardly be achieved simultaneously. Essential prerequisites for economic growth are long term in nature; institutional changes take time, and the creation of needed skills for progressive application of modern technology or the development of other infrastructure can materialize only over many years. Development, therefore, cannot be viewed without reference to its short and long term objectives (national, regional, or international) or without adequate planning. Means to achieve objectives need to be feasible and consistent with the goals of development. It is important to define clearly primary targets, the realization of which would provide the necessary means to achieve secondary or derived objectives, and to recall that policy planning is an integral part of the planning process.

### References

Hagen, Everett. 1962. *On the Theory of Social Change: How Economic Growth Begins*. Homewood, Illinois: The Dorsey Press.
Hirschman, Albert. 1958. *The Strategy of Economic Development*. New Haven: Yale University Press.

274                                                      ECONOMIC DEVELOPMENT

Hoselitz, Bert. 1957. "Non-Economic Factors in Economic Development." Papers and Proceedings of the 69th Annual Meeting of the American Economic Association, *American Economic Review* 47(2): 28–41.
ILO (International Labour Organization). 1977. *Yearbook of Labour Statistics.* Geneva: ILO.
IMF (International Monetary Fund). 1978. *International Financial Statistics*, vol. 31, no. 5.
Lekachman, Robert. 1977. "How the Rich Can Help the Poor," *Challenge* (September–October), pp. 48–52.
Mikdashi, Zuhayr. 1978. "Commodity Agreements and International Economic Cooperation." In *Proceedings of the Wisconsin Seminar on Natural Resource Policies in Relation to Economic Development and International Cooperation*, vol. 1. Madison: Institute for Environmental Studies, University of Wisconsin.
Myrdal, Gunnar. 1968. *Asian Drama: An Inquiry into the Poverty of Nations.* New York: Pantheon.
Nurkse, Ragnar. 1967. *Problems of Capital Formation in the Underdeveloped Countries.* New York: Oxford University Press.
Rosenstein-Rodan, Paul. 1943. "Problems of Industrialization of Eastern and South-Eastern Europe," *The Economic Journal* 53: 202–11.
Rosenstein-Rodan, Paul. 1961. "Notes on the Theory of the 'Big Push'." In Howard S. Ellis and Henry C. Wallich, eds., *Economic Development for Latin America: Proceedings of a Conference Held by the International Economic Association.* London: Macmillan, pp. 57–73.
Tinbergen, Jan, coord. 1976. *RIO—Reshaping the International Order: A Report to the Club of Rome.* New York: Dutton.
UN (United Nations). 1976. *Yearbook of National Accounts.* New York: UN.
UNCTAD (United Nations Conference on Trade and Development). 1977. *New Directions and New Structures for Trade and Development: Report by the Secretary General of UNCTAD.* New York: UN.
UNDESA (United Nations Department of Economic and Social Affairs). 1962. *World Economic Survey 1961.* New York: UN.
UNDESA (United Nations Department of Economic and Social Affairs). 1968. *World Economic Survey 1967.* New York: UN.
UNDESA (United Nations Department of Economic and Social Affairs). 1972. *World Economic Survey 1971.* New York: UN.
Wallich, Henry. 1952. "The Theory of Derived Development." Third Meeting of the Central Bank Technicians of the American Continent, Havana, Cuba.
World Bank. 1977. "The Role and Use of Consultants in Bank Group Projects," Report no. 1824. Washington, D.C.: World Bank.
World Bank. 1978. *World Development Report, 1978.* New York: Oxford University Press.

# 9 *Peter Dorner & Raymond J. Penn*

# Food, Population, Trade Diversification, and Finance

It is difficult to deal with any basic issue of development on a world scale because of the diversity of conditions among countries and, of course, within countries too. There is a tendency to overgeneralize when dealing with issues on a global basis. Furthermore, it is the physical and allegedly measurable aspects that tend to be emphasized in both national and international discussions while underlying political, cultural, and institutional conditions are de-emphasized because it is difficult, if not impossible, to classify and measure these aspects. Even for the supposedly measurable indicators, it is not always clear to what extent the critical variables have in fact been accurately recorded. As pointed out by Kuznets 15 years ago: "It may not be an exaggeration to say that we deal here not with data on the distribution of income by size but with estimates or judgments by courageous and ingenious scholars" (Kuznets 1963, quoted by Morawetz 1977, p. 38). The situation today may be somewhat improved, but basic measurement problems remain.

There is no denying that there are hundreds of millions of poverty-stricken people in the world. Yet the conventional basis of comparing nations, GNP per capita, seems seriously to overstate the real income gap between rich and poor nations. The conventional statistics converted to U.S. dollars at official exchange rates show more than one billion people in the Third World (over 600 million in India alone) with average per capita GNP of $140 or less in 1975. If this is interpreted to mean that these people are consuming each year an amount of goods and services equivalent to those that could be purchased in the United States for $140, most are so poor that they could not survive, let alone increase their numbers. If that is not the interpretation to be given to these figures, it is not clear just what they do mean. The most recent evidence indicates that "purchasing-power parity" estimates of per capita income in the poorest countries are over three times as great as those given by the conventional measures. Accordingly, India's per capita income comes to about $450 instead of $140 (Morawetz 1977, pp. 4–5, citing figures from Kravis et al. 1977; see also World Bank 1978, p. 115).

Consider the following hypothetical example of a country with 50 million people, of whom 20 million live in the cities and 30 million live on farms (a reasonable division for many of the developing countries). Assume that this country imports $1 billion worth of food annually and has a $500 million deficit in its trade balances. Increased commercial production and marketing of agricultural exports to offset this deficit might well be hailed as a great achievement. On the other hand, suppose the production of subsistence food crops increased by an equal amount but instead of entering marketing channels was consumed by the producing farm families. In this case, depending on the extent and accuracy of internal production and marketing estimates, production gains might not be recorded at all, even though 60 percent of the population added substantially to its level of living.

The discussions that follow will deal with physical measures of some strategic variables in food production, population, trade diversification, and development finance. We must, however, be constantly on guard against misinterpretation of these numbers, especially in making international comparisons. It is particularly important to keep in mind that averages tell nothing about distribution, whether these averages pertain to individual nation-states or to groups of states.

## The Structural-Institutional Context

There are structural issues of a social, economic, and political nature that are more difficult to comprehend and resolve than the physical problems. And to attempt to resolve physical problems of production without structural-institutional changes seems only to intensify the social problems inherent in highly skewed patterns of distribution. The "socio-institutional environment" provides the framework within which economic processes function. That environment includes the spectrum of laws, administrative and management rules, and social conventions and customs that set

the limits for individuals and enterprises with respect to "rights and duties," "liberties and exposures," "security of expectations," and, in short,
determine " . . . *who can do what to whom and what defenses 'whom'
has against 'who' . . .* " in relation to resources and to sharing the product derived from the use of those resources (National Research Council
1977, p. 55; see also Commons 1959).

This "socio-institutional environment" is highly specific to individual
countries or even to regions within countries. All societies have rules and
institutions that define property rights in resources. These rights pertain
to individuals, groups, and the state. In some systems, individual private
property in land is prohibited—landed property can be held only by
groups or by the state. There are institutional provisions empowering certain public agencies to administer the laws and rules pertaining to property rights. Such rules change over time as a result of increased pressure
on resources and administrative or judicial interpretation.

The point is that rights of access to and use of land, water, minerals—
natural resources in general—are never issues of strictly private concern
but are always matters of public concern (Penn 1961). Private property is,
in fact, a creation of the nation state. Without a state to protect it and enforce the rules, private property would not exist. (In historical experience
with the absence of nation-states, feudal lords had to have their own army
to protect their "property"). Private property is not an absolute right. All
countries have placed major restrictions on these rights, and in some
countries such rights have been all but eliminated.

There are obviously serious social problems and conflicts when the authority to enforce the public's interest in the private ownership and use of
resources falls into the hands of those who themselves have major interests in private property, interests which would be threatened by enforcement of the public's interest in those same resources. Those empowered
to administer the laws and rules pertaining to private property may indeed
come to identify the public's interest with their own private interests. This
corruption of public office is sometimes called the private ownership of
government.

Those with strong vested interests in the current system of property
may argue (identifying their private interest with the public's) that private
property is the basis of the state and of society (indeed, of civilization itself) and that above all it is the fundamental institution underlying the
market economy. They may also claim that private property is a natural
right, even a God-given one, that an attack on private property is an attack of the basic unit of society—the family. However, if these arguments
were truly valid, an objective observer would have to question whether
the institution of private property can perform all these basic functions

when most people are without it. No. One cannot defend liberty and property on these grounds and then attempt to reserve most of their benefits for the wealthy; the very logic of these arguments would suggest a much wider distribution of property. Such arguments are basically intended to justify and to protect the status quo.

Many revolutions and civil wars have been fought over issues of rights in property and their distribution, but these issues are not confined to the internal affairs of nation-states. Resources and populations are distributed very unevenly among the more than 150 nation-states now in existence. With growing populations, greater desires and efforts for accelerated development, rising world trade in natural resources and their products, mounting inequalities among and within nation-states, and the increasing interdependence of nations, rights to property and its use are also key issues in the international setting.

This concern with the public interest in the rights of access to and use of land, water, minerals, and other natural resources should not be interpreted as an argument against private property. Rather, the concentration of property under private control versus its wider distribution and the inability to enforce the public interest in private property are the real issues. Private property is not an absolute right. These questions of property always involve that dual relation of private and public, whether within or among nation-states: "The question always is, not, *What* is a private purpose over against a public purpose? but, Is the private purpose *also* a public purpose, or *merely* a private purpose? . . . each individual is a 'public utility' to the extent that the public powers are employed in his behalf against others, and a public 'disutility' to the extent that the public powers are employed against him in behalf of others. . . . every private business or job has, in fact, the qualities of both public utility and public disutility, depending on the current economic and human valuations. And it is in restraining the behavior believed to produce public disutility, by imposing new duties, that the opposite behavior of other persons believed to produce public utilities is protected and liberated" (Commons 1957, pp. 326–327.

Commons' points are well illustrated by the following statement on the nature of freedom. "Any freedom enjoyed by any individual consists in a set of securities of expectations concerning the behavior of other individuals and groups. These secure expectations of an individual result from a system of rules—rights, duties, restraints—developed by processes of public action and enforceable at law—which determine what others may and may not do. . . . any individual freedom exists in consequence of the public organization which defines this freedom and secures it for the individual against the adverse action of others. *The slave became a free man, not in virtue of anything new put into him, but in consequence of a set of restraints imposed upon others.* The difference between a free man and a slave is that the free man has security in the knowledge that the forces of public action will be used to limit the activities of those who would do him harm or use him against his will for their purposes" (Long 1953, pp. 318–19).

The world is characterized by scarcity not only of physical resources or "means" to meet certain needs and "ends" but also by a scarcity of opportunities to participate in transforming resources into personal satisfactions and to reap rewards commensurate with such opportunities. Out of these two dimensions of scarcity grow human conflicts within and among nations, but the interdependence of individuals (and states) is such that any conflict that disrupts the mutuality of benefits flowing from interdependence serves only to intensify the scarcities. There is an interest in and a need for maintaining order. The imposition of order by superior physical force is no longer acceptable nor does it seem feasible given the power constellations of the current world. The means of securing order are social and political organization. The major function is to secure rights and opportunities and to impose duties and restraints which in turn secure the expectations of individuals (and nation-states) about the conduct of others. This is a task of devising procedures that will guide conduct in such a way that individuals and groups (and nation-states) can willingly, *and to the mutual advantage of each,* use each other.

We have dwelt on these issues of the "socio-institutional environment" because we believe an understanding of them is fundamental to policy formulation on food, population, trade diversification, and finance. Although we shall not again refer to these socio-institutional matters at such length, what follows must always be seen as no more than a surface reflection of underlying political-social-institutional structures.

## Food and Population

It has taken 8000–10,000 years from the beginning of a settled agriculture until the present to increase knowledge enough to produce food for the more than 4 billion people who now live on earth, and perhaps half a billion or more of these remain undernourished. At the current rate of population growth, the world will have another 4 billion people to feed in about 35 years, and the "technology to produce enough food for 4 billion more people in 25 to 30 years with present diets is not on the books. We may make scientific 'break-throughs'—but if we don't, the darkest days are ahead" (USDA 1975). Malthusian problems have not been banished. Although advances in nutrition have contributed to length of life and thus to rapid growth in populations, problems have been accentuated by triumphs of public health measures in controlling malaria and infectious diseases. It may seem convenient to urge population control upon developing nations as a prerequisite to growth, but it is well to recall that Western birth rates, in the nineteenth century, dropped only after or as economic development proceeded (Lekachman 1977). European nations also had a population outlet in massive migrations to the Americas and elsewhere. Current population-resource problems in the developing countries have another order of magnitude—the absolute numbers of people are much greater—and almost no emigration possibility of consequence.

Human population growth and its restraint are extremely complex phenomena not too well understood even today (Haddad 1978). It may indeed be that significant declines in present population growth rates will not occur until the masses of poor people sense and experience an improvement in their conditions of life, until they have sufficient stake in the "system" so that what they decide and do on their own does make a noticeable difference in those conditions. In an agrarian setting, such a "stake" means access to a secure opportunity on the land. It means redistribution of property rights in land or some other way of providing reasonable security in a remunerative occupation. It means that if ". . . persons are to make their maximum contribution to a society or economy, they need be in a position to make their own life better or worse by acts of their own. As John Stuart Mill observed more than a century ago: The Irish cottier was very poor because 'almost alone amongst mankind . . . he can scarcely be either any better or worse off by any act of his own' "(Parsons 1977). The manner in which increased food production is achieved and the number of people who participate and reap material and educational benefits from this experience may be as important as the production increase itself. One gets a different perspective on the role of land if, in addition to its accepted function of producing food and fiber, it is seen as a vehicle for creating economic opportunities and for upgrading the human skills and capacities required for their exploitation.

If the main problem in the food-population balance is seen as one of increasing food production *and* controlling population growth (and this is the manner in which the issues are frequently cast), policy will likely focus on (1) providing the larger producing units—those with the greatest potential for surplus production—with capital and technology to make them "modern" and highly productive, and (2) family planning. However, if the issue is seen as one of providing employment and secure productive opportunities for the millions who are without them, policy should focus instead on land redistribution, development or selective transfer of technology appropriate to labor surplus conditions, literacy, and human development. The production problem is not ignored with this approach; it is simply resolved in a different manner.

Some may assume that large farm units are more productive and more efficient in the use of resources and that land redistribution is inefficient because small units fail to realize economies of scale. The assumption that the large farm is more efficient has arisen because of the particular measure of productivity or efficiency employed. It is true that labor productivity is consistently higher on larger farms, but this is hardly a measure relevant to policy in a labor surplus economy. Higher labor productivity on large farms comes primarily from mechanization and labor-saving techniques. Land-saving and yield-increasing techniques—improved seed varieties, fertilizers, insecticides, and improved weeding—can be applied efficiently on small farms too. These inputs are divisible. With abundant rural labor and continuous rapid population growth, productivity per unit of land is a more relevant measure, for policy purposes, than labor productivity. There is a considerable body of research showing an inverse relationship in many countries between size of farm and output per unit of land. This inverse relationship holds even among the very highly productive small farms of Japan and Taiwan (Dorner and Kanel 1971).

In farming, those activities where economies of scale do appear are transferred rather early in the modernization process from the farm to the industrial sector—input manufacturing, output processing and marketing, credit financing, etc. On-the-farm tasks allow a wider range of substitutability among factors of production (especially labor and capital) than do many manufacturing processes. The major economies of scale on the farm are associated with labor-displacing mechanization. In countries with surplus labor, such mechanization might be efficient from the private accounting viewpoint of a large farmer, but it is probably very inefficient from the viewpoint of society if the displaced labor is deprived of productive work opportunities. This is, of course, not to argue against all mechanization; machine work, too, can be made divisible through joint ownership, rental, smaller tractors and implements, and so forth. The crucial advantages of some mechanization (better soil preparation, timely planting of second crops where possible, etc.) can be achieved on small as well as large units.

For lowering population growth rates, family planning should not be ignored. Available evidence, however, seems to show that effective family planning and reduced population growth rates are more likely to be achieved under conditions of greater equality in income distribution, a more widespread distribution of productive assets, and basic literacy (Ahluwalia 1978; Haddad 1978). The impressive reduction of the population growth rate in East Asia is heavily influenced by China's massive efforts to curb births; China also has one of the most egalitarian systems of distribution. For the region as a whole, the population growth rate declined from 1.85 percent to 1.18 percent between 1970 and 1975, and the "reduction in the Chinese birth rate from an estimated 32 per thousand to 19 per thousand, or 2.6 points per year, is the most rapid ever recorded for a five year span" (Brown and Stokes 1977).

Ours is not an antigrowth argument. It is well established that the distribution of income worsens in the early stages of development (Ahluwalia 1978), and this seems to occur whether economic growth is proceeding at a slow or a rapid pace (Morawetz 1977, p. 70). Moving through this transitional stage to the point where income inequalities again become narrower may now be much more difficult than it was when the present industrial countries were making that transition. Larger and more rapidly growing populations, capital investment from outside, and a concomitant transfer of technology over a wide spectrum of labor and capital-intensive production methods may make today's transition more difficult than that of the past.

Moreover, when large segments of the population have only tenuous connections to the commercial, monetized sectors of the economy, and when a shortage of administrative capacity stymies large income transfer programs, it becomes very nearly impossible to redistribute incomes to those who are not participating in the production process. The very pattern and organization of production indicates a particular pattern of consumption and distribution. A rapidly growing GNP from the production of luxury houses and automobiles cannot subsequently be converted to low cost housing or bus transport to serve the poor. The very institutions created for promoting faster growth and capital accumulation in Pakistan, says ul Haq, later frustrated all attempts for a better distribution. "I am afraid," he adds, "that the evidence is unmistakable and the conclusion inescapable: divorce between production and distribution policies is false and dangerous. The distribution policies must be built into the very pattern of organization of production" (ul Haq 1971).

Increased production of food without regard for the manner in which production is organized may fail to solve food-population problems. Without employment and participation opportunities and the concomitant ability of people to acquire purchasing power and new skills, food may indeed be available, but at the same time effective demand may be lacking and farm prices may be falling, thus reducing production incentives—all this while people are starving (Barraclough 1977). To concentrate on production without explicitly recognizing the need for better access to productive resources by the excluded masses may yield more output of certain commodities and growing labor productivity for a part of the labor force.

Yet such policies tend to widen income disparities and throw the burden of adjustment on the disadvantaged who swell the ranks of the landless, continue to crowd into existing small farm areas, move out to rapidly shrinking agricultural frontiers, or join the underemployed in the cities.

With all due concern for the constant, serious, and complex problems of producing and distributing enough food for growing populations, one must also credit some achievements. Although many developing countries are increasingly dependent on food imports, especially basic grains (Gaballah 1978), about 90 percent of the world's food is eaten in the countries where it is produced. Only 10 percent moves as food trade or aid —more than 95 percent of this as trade (USDA 1975).

Longer life expectancies certainly imply some improvement in nutrition, even though much of the increase came through the control of infectious and insect borne diseases. In fact, these gains in life expectancy required a century of economic development in the industrial countries but were achieved in the developing world in several decades (Morawetz 1977; Ram and Schultz 1977). Total food production has actually increased at a faster rate in the developing countries than in the developed ones—75 percent and 65 percent, respectively, between 1954 and 1973 (USDA 1975).

In Asia (excluding the centrally planned economies) and North Africa the area of high yielding varieties of wheat and rice increased from practically zero in 1965 to 18 and 16 million hectares of wheat and rice, respectively, in 1972-73 (West 1976). A comparison of the average increase for 1948-52 and 1966-70 shows that the developing countries as a whole increased the area in grain by 36 percent and per hectare grain yields by 32 percent. In the late 1960s both developed and developing countries had roughly equal amounts of land devoted to grain production—close to 300 million hectares each. However, yields were so much higher in the developed countries that they actually accounted for two-thirds of total world grain production.

The real green revolution since 1950 took place in the developed countries, where per hectare grain yields increased by 2.5 percent per year versus 1.4 percent per year in the developing countries. Slower gains in the latter are due at least in part to the many hectares of new land brought into production (West 1976). Although it is difficult to get evidence, some of the new land undoubtedly was of poorer quality and perhaps also more fragile and subject to erosion. However, bringing into cultivation land best left in wetlands or in grass or forest cover is certainly not a new phenomenon nor one confined to the developing countries.

Nevertheless, the major potential for future production gains does seem to lie with increasing yields in the developing countries. Grain yields per hectare in 1971-75 in these countries taken as a whole were only 42 percent of per hectare yields in the developed countries (West 1976), but it is unlikely that yields can continue to rise in the developed countries at the rates of the past 25-30 years. "We have squeezed about all of the grain from an acre of corn that our management technology will permit. It is not at all probable that we could have further quantum increases in yields with refinements in our technology. If we must exact continuing yield increases, it would appear that a complete restructuring of the corn plant will be required in order to more efficiently use light energy" (Pound 1975). The same may be true of several other crops. Increases in soybean production up to now, however, have largely depended on acreage expansion. Failure to get soybeans to respond to heavy fertilization and the absence of hybrids have kept U.S. yields at 25-28 bushels per acre. Overall per acre productivity growth rates for U.S. crops bear out Pound's prognosis. Average annual growth rates for crop production per acre for selected periods were as follows: 1950-65—3.7 percent; 1965-71—2.0 percent; 1971-75—0.4 percent (Schuh 1976).

There is, however, a tremendous gap between what yields are in most developing countries and what they might be. That yield gap represents a tremendous potential food reserve which must be realized in the future. In 1935-39 average grain yields were the same in the industrial and the developing countries, but today there is a difference of 50 percent (Johnson 1976a). It may well be for a variety of reasons that this difference in yields will never be completely eliminated. It is possible, for instance, that the prices of farm inputs having a significant energy component, in particular the price of nitrogen fertilizer, will be substantially higher in the future than in the past. Yet, future costs cannot be easily foreseen: "One important factor is technology and size of plant. Thus, for instance, with a natural gas price of $1.80 per thousand cubic feet [equivalent to oil prices of $11.75 per barrel], the cost of producing nitrogen fertilizer with 1974 technology would be less than the cost with free natural gas and 1960 technology" (Johnson 1976b).

There is a substantial literature critical of the "green revolution" approach to increasing food supplies. Indeed there are many problems—environmental degradation as a result of intensive use (but often correctable misuse) of chemical fertilizers and pesticides, large farm mechanization and displacement of tenants, worsening regional disparities because high yielding varieties thus far developed require reliable irrigation, etc. Some of the physical problems must be altered by additional research. That research is proceeding on nitrogen fixation by nonleguminous plants, biological means of pest control, bred-in resistance to insects and diseases, and other areas. At least some of the problems of regional disparities could be alleviated by new varieties that would increase yields and farmers' net income in rainfed areas "in a poor year" and not only under the most favorable climatic conditions.

Some climatologists are warning that changing weather and climatic patterns might result from a global cooling trend and that in estimating future crop yields we cannot take the "good weather" of the 1930s–60s for granted. Again, not taking it for granted means research with respect to improved forecasting, identification of long-run changes in weather patterns, development of new varieties better adapted to different climatic conditions, and more. Actually, of course, there is very little agreement among climatologists about the likelihood of major climatic changes. There does seem to be a warming effect from increased carbon dioxide in the atmosphere, but this warming may be counterbalanced by the cooling effect of a natural climate cycle (National Defense University 1978, pp. xvii–xviii).

Again, however, we must keep in mind that all the problems are not physical and biological. The social problems are more difficult to resolve because powerful vested interests are involved: "It is not the fault of the green revolution that the credit service does not serve those for whom it was intended, that the extension service is falling behind expectations, that the village . . . councils are essentially political rather than developmental bodies, that security of tenure is not given to the many, that rentals are exorbitant, that ceilings on land ownership are notional. . . . To a considerable extent these are man-made issues of long standing. Modernization of agriculture should include a combination of technical factors geared to higher production *and* improvements in the institutional framework to benefit the rural underprivileged" (Ladejinsky 1970).

Since 1960 a network of ten major international agricultural research and training centers has been established. Each of these is located in a developing region of the world. Most nations now have a center to which they can turn for assistance in solving major technological problems associated with improvement of most commodities and for the training of personnel (Wortman 1976). These centers too have focussed their research primarily on physical and biological problems. Economists and other social scientists are not prominent among the professional staff at these centers.

Several other observations are in order. First, these international centers are not sufficient; individual countries need to build their own research capacities because the work of the centers will never encompass the myriad problems encountered at specific production locations. The research results from these centers need to be adapted, modified, and integrated to local situations. Second, additional crops (and livestock) must be studied; experimental trials should include some of the complex joint-production and intercropping practices frequently found in small farm agriculture. Third, the development of varieties and practices which will provide improved yields and incomes under varying conditions of stress (drought, excess moisture, salinity, cold, etc.) merits much more attention. Fourth, these centers might also be the appropriate vehicles for research into the domestication of new species of plants and, perhaps, animals. Of the tens of thousands of species, only a very small number contributes to the bulk of man's food supply, and practically all of these were domesticated by our ancestors. Modern man has improved upon these but has not made any significant contribution in adding to the stock. Finally, the centers have focussed heavily on the development of biological/chemical technology and, with few exceptions, have done very little to develop a more appropriate mechanical technology for the labor surplus conditions which ordinarily prevail in developing countries.

These International Agricultural Research Centers are relatively new institutions. Several major contributions to increased agricultural productivity have already been made. Many more, of course, are needed. But these centers do hold great promise and are a welcome addition to research efforts that have for many decades concentrated primarily on plantation crops: sugar cane, pineapple, bananas, jute, coffee, tea, cocoa, coconut, oil palm, and rubber, among others. These have been basic export crops for most of the developing world, and there have long been keen interest and influence by foreign companies and governments in their production and productivity. The establishment of these new research centers devoted to the food crops that are the mainstay of human diets—wheat, corn, rice, food legumes, root crops, and vegetables—was overdue.

Substantial gains in food production have been registered, but these gains have not been sufficient. Developing countries as a whole have had to rely on increased food (especially grain) imports. The record is, of course, mixed with some countries showing a much better performance than others. According to FAO estimates, from 1952 to 1972 the rate of increase in food production exceeded the population growth rate for the developing countries taken as a group. However, in about two-thirds of these countries the increase in food production failed to keep up with the growth in total demand for food, and in 34 of them food production did not even match the growth in population (FAO 1975, pp. 93–94). From 1972–1975, food-population imbalances intensified after widespread crop failures and the drawdown of grain reserves in the major exporting countries.

In view of the critical need for more food production and improved distribution, greater per hectare yields in the developing countries certainly seem the quickest way to increase production. But what about the expansion of cultivated land? In the developing countries, over the past 25 years, cropland extensions have been a more important source of increases in food output than increased yields. Available estimates of potentially arable land can furnish a general guide to orders of magnitude but no really precise figures on amounts of land. Roughly 10–11 percent of the ice-free land surface of the world is currently under cultivation. That cropland represents about 41 percent of the total land surface available for cultivation (National Research Council 1977, p. 66; citing Buringh et al. 1975). According to Buringh and associates, 25 percent of the ice-free land surface is potentially arable; a 1967 study estimated this potential at 24 percent (President's Science Advisory Committee 1967, p. 423). A Soviet authority states that land under cultivation could be expanded relatively easily from the current 10–11 percent of ice-free land to 16–17 percent but notes that if marshlands were drained and arid lands irrigated this could be raised to 25–30 percent (National Research Council 1977, p. 66, citing Kovda 1971).

Whether this much land could be brought under cultivation without catastrophic environmental consequences is at least open to question. This course, it would seem to us, is not one to recommend without much more detailed investigation into the complex ecological effects of massive changes in land use. On the other hand, all these estimates agree that it is possible to add substantial amounts of land to the current base of cultivation.

However, distribution of this land does not match distribution of population. Asia has 58 percent of the world's population but only 20 percent of the world's arable land, and three-fourths of that 20 percent is already under cultivation. In contrast, South America has only 5 percent of the world's population but 17 percent of the arable land, and only one-eighth of that 17 percent is now cultivated (National Research Council 1977, p. 67). The two most populous countries in the world, China and India, are already cropping 86 and 85 percent, respectively, of their potential cropland. By way of contrast, corresponding percentages for other regions are: East Africa, 12; Central Africa, 21; North Africa and Middle East, 53; Mexico, 69; Central America, 30; and total all developing market economies, 32 (Crosson and Frederick 1977, pp. 42–43).

Perhaps as significant as these estimates on mere surface areas is the prospect of expanding the irrigated area. It is estimated that the currently irrigated area in the developing world of 85 million hectares can be expanded by another 90 million hectares. Obviously that expansion will take much time, and the investment costs will be high—over $130 billion according to a 1973 estimate (McNamara 1973). FAO objectives for land and water development to 1985 show number of hectares of new irrigation and cost per hectare (in 1974 dollars) as follows: Far East, 15 million hectares at $1467/ha.; Near East, 3 million hectares at $2467/ha.; Africa, 1 million hectares at $2400/ha.; and Latin America, 4 million hectares at $1550/ha. Estimates for development of new (unirrigated) arable hectares and costs are: Far East, 24 million hectares at $396/ha.; Near East, 10 million hectares at $250/ha.; Africa, 34 million hectares at $44/ha.; and Latin America, 85 million hectares at $151/ha. (Crosson and Frederick 1977, p. 51).

It seems evident from these estimates that substantial potential exists for expanding both dryland and irrigated areas (Mohamed 1978). Again, however, the distribution of the land expansion potential does not match the distribution of population. Abundant unused land and water resources of Africa and South America will not solve the problem of food shortages in South Asia, although prospects for new trade among these regions are apparent.

These estimates are crude. Beyond capital, the development of much of the potential land and water resources will require new knowledge of soil management (especially tropical soils) and a better understanding of the ecological consequences of land-use changes. Accumulation of salts under irrigation in arid regions presents another unresolved problem. One estimate contends that half of the previously nonsaline soils in some arid zones have now become saline due to irrigation (National Research Council 1977, p. 71; citing Kovda 1971).

Although the expansion of cultivated area offers opportunities for some countries, it is a more time-consuming and often more costly means of increasing food production than boosting yields on land already in cultivation, especially through better seeds and higher rates of fertilization. For land-scarce countries, attention to yield increases seems the only alternative. Reliance on greater use of inorganic fertilizers and other chemicals does create other problems: increased pressure on finite stocks of raw materials and energy resources (Seif El-Yazal 1978) and accelerated environmental deterioration. In the absence of alternative technologies for producing fixed nitrogen, about 200 million metric tons of nitrogen fertilizer will be required by the end of this century compared to 40 million metric tons used in 1974 (Hardy and Havelka 1975). Without more adequate means than those now available for assessing the environmental impacts of such giant increases in the use of more chemical substances for producing food, we will run major risks. This is why genetic research on atmospheric nitrogen fixation by cereals is so important. Developing better yielding soybeans also offers major opportunities for increasing the production of high quality protein for human diets. Improved crop protection (especially biological and physical measures) is another very significant way to increase available food supplies because pests, according to one estimate, annually destroy 30 percent of the potential worldwide supply of crops, livestock, and forest products (Enis et al. 1975).

It is because of such potentials and in hopes of avoiding the uncertain and hazardous course of overreliance on chemicals that we emphasize science and the need for greater public support of research—both basic and applied—in biological, physical, and social sciences. It is, of course, true that all new knowledge and technology are not of equal worth and importance. There are inescapable valuations to be made. The power of science and technology must be transformed into a public good, not for a particular class nor only for the economically powerful, but for the benefit of mankind.

Food is the most basic need for human survival. Any discussion of development must begin by evaluating the most effective means of providing food for growing populations. All countries need not strive for self-sufficiency. International trade in food (especially grains) has been increasing and can help to avert short-term crises, but ever-greater food imports by developing countries is not a long-term solution. Unless internal food production can be increased substantially, the demands for imports cannot be met in the future, especially when major crop failures occur simultaneously in several regions as in the mid-1970s. With a reliable food supply and a progressive agriculture, countries gain new options in their development efforts. Expansionary fiscal policies and employment creation efforts become feasible without the threat of inflationary pressures from a deficient food supply (Mellor 1976).

Production and employment/distribution aspects cannot be treated separately and in isolation. They must be closely linked within an overall development strategy. The size of farm and the type of organization in farming determine, to a considerable extent, the employment/distribution/incentive/productivity structure of agriculture (Dorner 1972). This structure, perhaps more than any other factor, sets the technological paths of development, as well as the prospects for creating indigenous capacities in adaptive science, and reduces the reliance on capital-intensive foreign technology not suited to the existing factor proportions of many of the developing countries (Dorner 1978). Development based on export of primary commodities (even if stable, higher prices can be achieved through commodity agreements) may well continue to be disappointing if the organizational structure does not build income distribution and employment creation into the very processes of production. Needed skills and entrepreneurial talents are likely to be nurtured as much or more by work opportunities as by formal schooling and/or administrative directions.

## Changing Patterns of Trade

The literature on economic development assumes that development is associated with a structural change—a secular decline of formerly dominant agricultural and extractive production and a rise of secondary and tertiary industries and occupations. Secular decline would not necessarily mean an absolute decline in primary activities, although this might be the case in some instances. The relative share of the population engaged in farm production and the relative share of agricultural production in the gross national product would decline. These relative shares have, in fact, been declining in most countries, even though the absolute number of people in agriculture, as well as the total value of agricultural production, continues to increase.

What the relative decline in the agricultural population means, in effect, is that a smaller proportion of the population is required to produce food, the basic subsistence need, and a larger proportion is available to produce capital and other goods. Increased capital leads to increased labor productivity and thus to higher incomes. However, it is highly unlikely and certainly debatable that such structural transformations will be similar to those which today's industrialized countries underwent during the nineteenth and twentieth centuries. One major reason for doubt is the improbability that similar transformations could be achieved without acute shortages in minerals and energy. The United States now has only about 3 percent of its population engaged in farming, primarily as a result of substituting nonrenewable stock resources—petroleum and minerals—for the renewable resources of land, labor, and animal power. As these stock resources become increasingly scarce and costly, farm production in today's industrial nations will face major readjustments. This stage has not yet been reached, and the problem might continue to be pushed into the future by sustained technological advance, new energy sources, and substitution possibilities, as well as discoveries of new mineral resources. Nevertheless, development planning must give due weight to the prospects that such shortages are likely to develop in the future.

Transformations of the developing countries along paths different from those of the past century have direct bearing on the prospects for "closing the per capita income gap" between developed and developing countries. This "gap" discussion has become popular in recent years, but it is not obvious that many developing countries actually place a "closing of the gap" at the center of their developmental goals. Morawetz (1977), p. 30) points out that "not all of them regard the resource-wasting life style of the developed countries as an end toward which it is worth striving; at least some seem to prefer to create their own development patterns based on their own resources, and needs, and traditions. Second, when thinking of the per capita income that they would like to attain, most people (and governments) tend to think of the income of a close-by reference group." Ul Haq (1976b) also believes that the concept of catching up must be rejected: "Catching up with what? Surely the Third World does not wish to imitate the life styles of the rich nations. It must meet its own basic human needs within the framework of its own cultural values, building development around people rather than people around development" (quoted in Morawetz 1977, p. 30; see also Amin 1978). Lewis (1972) puts it bluntly: " . . . what matters is the absolute progress of LDCs and not the size of the gap" (quoted in Morawetz 1977, p. 30).

One must, of course, be careful not to push this reasoning too far lest it be used by the wealthy as an excuse for inaction. With hundreds of millions of people illiterate, undernourished, and destitute, action by all nations to meet the basic needs of these millions is certainly most urgent. It is, however, highly doubtful that even such basic needs can be met without at least a partial structural transformation, a concomitant growth in manufacturing, and a diversification of exports within the developing countries. Most Third World countries were agrarian exporters of raw materials when they emerged from colonialism to self-rule. Postcolonial patterns of trade and export diversification vary from country to country, but overall there has been some important progress toward economic self-reliance. "Today, in many if not most countries, the growth of industrial exports and the diversification of agricultural exports have reduced significantly the degree of commodity concentration of foreign exchange earnings." There has also been expansion of trade among developing countries, " . . . though such interchange has expanded less than it might have if the participants had followed more liberal trade policies relating to traditional goods" (Morawetz 1977, pp. 60–61.

Beginning in 1976 the United States joined other developed countries in implementing a Generalized System of Preferences (GSP) which provides duty-free entry up to prescribed limits for certain products from eligible developing countries. The original U.S. program covered more than 2,700 items from about 140 developing nations and territories worth in 1974 more than $2.5 billion in U.S. trade. The elimination of duties under GSP gave beneficiary countries an advantage in competing for about 2.5 percent of U.S. imports from all sources (*International Economic Report* 1977, p. 47).

292                                        ECONOMIC DEVELOPMENT

Some developing countries have shown exceptional advances in the export of nontraditional products. For example, in 1950 Brazil still relied on one crop, coffee, for 60 percent of its export earnings; by 1975 coffee provided only 10 percent of those earnings (Morawetz 1977, p. 73). Exports of manufactured goods from Brazil grew from 24 percent of all exports in 1970 to 40 percent in 1977 (*Latin America Economic Report* 1978). Another example is the rapid growth of leather and leather product exports by Colombia, from $24 million to almost $36 million between 1975 and 1977 (*Colombia Today* 13, no. 2 [1978]).

India, with vast resources by virtue of its size and a population of more than 600 million, is commonly thought of as an agricultural country. In terms of population distribution it is, but changes are underway. For example, in 1951 agriculture accounted for 50 percent of the national income and industry for 16 percent; by 1971 the corresponding percentages were 45 and 23. Between 1951 and 1974, total exports from India approximately doubled (in current U.S. dollars) from $1.5 billion to $3 billion. The traditional exports (food, beverages and tobacco, crude materials, mineral fuels, animal and vegetable oils and fats, cotton textiles, and jute manufactures) increased from $1.3 billion to $1.8 billion, accounting for nearly 89 percent of all exports in 1951 but only 60 percent in 1974. Meanwhile, nontraditional exports (chemicals, manufactured goods other than cotton and jute products, machinery and transport equipment, and others) increased from $172 million to $1.2 billion and from 11 percent to 40 percent of total exports (Mellor 1976, p. 194).

Although change never seems rapid enough, such cases illustrate that trade diversification has occurred and that structural transformation is taking place. The problems are immense, but one should not minimize the progress that has been made. As Morawetz (1977, p. 73) notes: "The historical experience illustrates a tendency for rapid interaction to occur between development performance and expectations. 'Upper-limit' projections have been surpassed, 'almost unmeetable challenges' have been met; yet everywhere there is dissatisfaction. It might be useful to bear in mind that first-round success (improvements in health, the Green Revolution) often lead to second-round problems (population explosion, worsening of rural income distribution), and that even in the best of cases, development is a long, slow process measured in generations rather than decades."

## Development Finance

Issues of internal development—food and agriculture, population growth, and export diversification—have so far dominated this discussion, but there is a special international dimension to all development issues because most nations are in some degree open to and affected by economic forces in other nations and in the world market. One particular aspect of strategic importance is the arrangement for international finance and capital transfer. All countries need capital to develop, and most require capital from outside. It is critical to analyze these financial and capital transfer mechanisms in terms of their impact on development conditions and prospects inside nation-states.

Since World War II and the dismantling of colonial empires, a variety of means have been used to channel resources from the wealthier countries to the poorer ones. The vast bulk of the financing for development, however, comes from internal sources. Figures have varied greatly among countries, but external sources of capital have since 1955 averaged no more than 10 percent of the total investment expenditures of the developing market economies. Direct private investments by foreign firms, official grant aid, and public and private loans are all included in that 10 percent (Morawetz 1977, p. 61).

Private foreign investment may add substantially to the productive capacity of a nation's economy, but the private investor is certainly interested in a return on investment equal to or greater than the return which could be made elsewhere. Loans from commercial banks are hard loans with competitive interest rates and relatively short repayment periods. Much of the development assistance provided by the industrial countries (or by the World and Regional Banks) is also in the form of loans— although with various grace periods, interest rate reductions, and generally fairly long repayment periods. Thus the impact in any given year of the various sources of external capital is reduced substantially by interest payments and amortization on past loans and by returns paid to private investors. In addition to loans from various sources, the industrial and OPEC countries do provide some of their assistance to developing countries in the form of grants.

The total net flow of resources to developing countries from all sources reached U.S. $64 billion in 1977, up from $59 billion in 1976, according to the annual estimate of the Development Assistance Committee (DAC) of the Organisation for Economic Cooperation and Development (OECD). Of this total, official development assistance provided by the 17 industrial members of DAC was $14.8 billion in 1977, an 8 percent increase from the $13.7 billion in 1976. Because of inflation, however, there was no increase in real terms. Official development assistance as a percentage of DAC donor countries' GNP has declined over the years: 0.52 in 1960, 0.44 in 1965, 0.34 in 1970, 0.33 in 1976, and 0.31 in 1977. The last is the second lowest percentage since statistics on aid flows were first gathered in the mid-1950s (IMF 1978b; World Bank 1978, p. 99).

The Organization of the Petroleum Exporting Countries (OPEC) has increased its financial assistance to other developing countries. Official development assistance from OPEC (in billions of U.S. dollars) was $1.3 in 1973, $3.4 in 1974, $5.5 in 1975, and $5.2 in 1976. This represents, in each of the last three years, over 2 percent of the donor countries' GNP (World Bank 1978, p. 118).

The most restricted definition of financial transfers to Third World countries is grant or grant-like disbursements. Even these transfers would be reduced if allowance were made for "aid tying" and other restrictive conditions (Singer 1976). Between 1969 and 1975, total public loans to 84 developing countries increased from U.S. $8.9 billion to $32.5 billion while grants and grantlike disbursements increased from U.S. $1.3 billion to $2.6 billion. The grant proportion has plainly declined rather substantially, although there has been some shift in recent years to providing more assistance (and more grants) to the poorest among the developing countries.

Public loans, grants, and grantlike disbursements to those 84 developing countries totalled U.S. $35 billion in 1975. In the same year amortization amounted to $8.8 billion and interest to $5.5 billion so that the net transfer was U.S. $20.8 billion. Total debt outstanding for those 84 countries (including debt to bilateral, multilateral, and private creditors) increased from U.S. $62.5 billion in 1969 to $173.9 billion in 1975 (World Bank 1976).

External *public* debt outstanding as a proportion of GNP has risen rather steadily since 1950 in the developing countries as a whole. In 1976 that proportion was 20.9 percent for the low income countries and 17.0 percent for the middle income countries. Comparable figures for 1970 were 14.2 percent and 13.2 percent for the low and middle income countries, respectively. There is, of course, tremendous variation among individual countries within these broad classes (World Bank 1978, p. 96). The ratio of *total* external debt to GNP is much greater and has been rising more rapidly because private borrowing has represented an increasing share of total debt, at least since 1967. "Debt to private lenders—suppliers' credits, borrowing from private banks, and so forth—rose from less than 30 percent of total foreign debt in 1967 to 50 percent in 1976" (Morawetz 1977, p. 62). During the same time, however, exports from developing countries taken as a group have risen quite rapidly (except for the recession years of the mid-1970s) and have helped to check somewhat the increase in the share of export earnings needed for debt service.

The indebtedness of developing countries is highly concentrated. In 1974, Brazil, India, and Mexico accounted for about 35 percent of the total outstanding public debt. In that year, of 81 countries for which data are available, 18 accounted for 50 percent of the total public debt (Morawetz 1977, p. 65).

The major expansion in international capital flows of recent years has been in loans from private commercial banks. In large part this pool of international lendable funds was created by deposits from the capital surplus oil exporting countries following the abrupt rise in oil prices of 1973–74. The international banks which individually or often jointly underwrite new loans both to private industry and to governments are commonly referred to as Eurobanks, lenders of Eurocurrencies. In 1973 the Eurocurrencies available for lending totalled U.S. $160 billion; that figure nearly doubled to $310 billion by 1976 and will reach an estimated $425 billion by the end of 1978 (*Business Week* 16 October 1978, p. 108).

Although this growth in world liquidity may prove adantageous for some countries, there are also problems inherent in this rapid growth. Continued expansion can be (and some maintain that it has been) inflationary. A major recession could lead to default on national debts to commercial banks with major repercussions on domestic banking systems.

Some of these concerns may be exaggerated. Debt expansion following the rise in oil prices is not too surprising. It was to be expected during a time when nations made major adjustments to new circumstances. There are some indications of a slowdown in the rate of increase in commercial debt of developing countries as these countries begin to adjust their balance of payments positions. The decline in exports from the developing countries during the mid-1970s, because of recession in the industrial countries, has been reversed. Finally, it is important to stress the gains, difficult to measure, for developing countries from a new and global (and, some would maintain, de-politicized) network of financial intermediation (Richardson 1978).

There are, however, other more specific problems and concerns with this large and increasing debt to commercial banks. The ratio of private to official debt for developing countries has risen sharply. More than half of developing country debt is now private debt under hard commercial terms with market interest rates and no grace periods. The burden of this debt is more severe and perhaps less flexible than it was when the bulk of the debt was official debt owed to other governments or international agencies in bilateral or multilateral arrangements.

A second problem is the distribution of this bank credit. About two-thirds of the official debt is owed by the middle income developing countries (and one-third by the low income countries), but almost the entire private debt is owed by the higher income developing countries. Mexico, Brazil, South Korea, and Taiwan accounted for over 60 percent of the publicized Eurocurrency credits extended to developing countries (excluding oil exporters) in 1975 (*International Economic Report* 1977, p. 31). These private loans thus mirror, if not exacerbate, the general distribution problem within the developing world.

Finally, much of the debt owed to commercial banks is used for balance of payments financing. Until about 1972 or 1973 private debt was primarily for project purposes which generated the revenue to pay off the loan. In financing balance of payments deficits, it is not clear whether the loan is financing capital goods that will increase production to pay off the debt or whether it may merely finance consumption and produce no revenues for future debt service.

In view of these problems, and especially the general lack of access to this source of financing for the poorest countries, it has been suggested that more of these surplus funds be channeled through multilateral institutions. OPEC countries have agreed to play a bigger role within the International Monetary Fund (IMF) as partial funders of the "Witteveen Facility," a supplementary credit body which may be the beginning of several kinds of special multilateral aid efforts (Richardson 1978). There was also, " . . . a clever *and financially sound* piece of accountancy" on the part of the IMF in taking a free capital gain from the rise in the value of the gold subscriptions which the IMF has held for some years and in using one-half of that gain in a trust fund designed for special long-maturity loans to developing countries; the other half was returned to nations in proportion to their gold subscriptions (Richardson 1978).

Despite variety in the sources of capital transfer and because of the mounting external debt in many Third World countries, international finance and trading arrangements, it seems to many, must be reorganized and reoriented. According to Ndegwa and Triffin (1976) monetary reforms should include:

(I) The adjustment of world reserve creation to the non-inflationary requirements of potential growth in world trade and production;

(II) A prompter and more symmetrical system of balance-of-payments adjustment among member countries;

(III) A maximum reduction of disequilibrating capital movements and the neutralization of those which could not be effectively prevented.

These and other widely discussed reform measures are reminiscent of the early 1940s before the Bretton Woods agreements which established the IMF and the IBRD (International Bank for Reconstruction and Development/The World Bank). In advance of the Bretton Woods meetings, the United States had tentatively recommended a stabilization fund and a central bank with an international currency. The bank could have made long-term low interest loans to developing countries in addition to carrying out basic central bank functions. It could have accepted deposits and made loans at the rate necessary to maintain desired growth. Additional deposits could have been held as reserves not available for loans and hence not inflationary. The bank could have financed buffer stocks and commodity stabilization programs. These ideas were, however, greatly modified before an official U.S. position was presented at Bretton Woods (Penn 1978).

A second proposal, from the British, had been developed by John Maynard Keynes. He suggested a clearing union which would have had all the authority of a central bank, including creation of an international currency. All international financial accounts would have been cleared through the union. This proposal would also have placed the temporary liquidity of the balance of payments surplus countries at the disposal of the deficit countries and would have set up a commodity bank for the stabilization of primary commodity prices.

Both of these were financial/monetary proposals, but both also contained other features. Most experts evaluating these proposals clearly felt currency stabilization alone would not be adequate. Writing in 1944, Alvin Hansen suggested the need for three international economic institutions: one to take care of monetary stabilization; a second to expand international capital investment; and a third to control and stabilize primary commodity prices (Penn 1978).

It is unfortunate that these very far-reaching and forward-looking proposals did not become part of the international financial mechanisms established at Bretton Woods. However, recent years have seen some modifications in the IMF's Articles of Agreement to incorporate some features of these earlier proposals. The First Amendment to the Fund's Articles of Agreement, in 1969, provided for the issue of Special Drawing Rights (SDR) for use in transactions with the IMF and among consenting countries with the IMF's approval. This provision was based on the assumption that reserve creation through the growth of holding of national currencies would be insufficient to finance desired growth in world trade. "The small expansion coming from this source (SDR) has since been totally overwhelmed by the uncontrolled accumulation of ever-increasing holding of *national* currencies in official and unofficial institutions of other states" (Ndegwa and Triffin 1976).

In April 1978 the Second Amendment to the Fund's Articles of Agreement became operative. This amendment, a complex revision of the Articles, has among its most important features new and flexible provisions dealing with exchange arrangements, a gradual reduction in the role of gold in the international monetary system, changes in SDR characteristics and expansion of SDR uses to enhance its status as an international reserve asset, and simplification and expansion of the Fund's financial operations and transactions (IMF 1978a).

Quota increases approved by the Fund's Board of Governors in March 1976 also went into effect with the Second Amendment, having been approved by the requisite number of member countries. Total Fund quotas will be raised from SDR 29 billion to SDR 39 billion if all members consent to the full increases proposed for them. Each member has the option of paying the entire increase in its own currency or 25 percent of the increase in SDR or the currencies of other members (with their concurrence) specified by the Fund and the balance in the member's own currency. This increase in quotas, along with the various other provisions and the subsequent increase in lendable funds, is certainly an improvement, although even these steps will likely be inadequate, by themselves, to expand and accelerate trade and economic development by the necessary amounts.

In December 1975 the IMF decided to expand and improve substantially its existing Compensatory Financing Facility. This facility is designed to provide financing to Fund members, particularly primary commodity producers, which experience temporary shortfalls in export earnings for reasons largely beyond their own control and which have a balance of payments need for such financing. "The liberalization of the Facility came at an appropriate time, since developing countries faced a major loss in export earnings due to the 1974/75 recession in the industrial countries. Drawings from the expanded IMF Compensatory Financing Facility in the first 7 months of 1976 amounted to $1.7 billion, exceeding the total drawings during its prior 13 years of existence" (*International Economic Report* 1977, p. 35).

Outside of these IMF arrangements but bearing on the stabilization of income from primary commodities is the STABEX Fund. STABEX was originally set up between the European Economic Community and 46 developing countries in Africa, the Caribbean, and the Pacific (ACP). This arrangement is a significant departure from the one-dimensional stabilization of price. Its aim is to stabilize the ACP countries' import capacities (essential to their development potential) through programs of stabilizing their export earnings from primary commodities (Mikdashi 1978).

There have been other concrete measures to modify the mechanisms for international capital flows and technical assistance. However, one of the basic purposes of development is the reduction of poverty, and growth alone, although urgently needed, is insufficient. Poverty must be attacked directly. This recognition grew throughout the 1950s and 1960s and is now widely accepted, yet it did not generally influence official lending and assistance policies until the 1970s. The U.S. Congress in 1973 issued a mandate to the U.S. Agency for International Development to redirect U.S. assistance in order to reach the poor majority in the developing countries and also to concentrate assistance in the very poorest of the developing countries. Also, the President of the World Bank, Robert S. McNamara, has revised its lending policies. In 1967, for example, 54 percent of the Bank's loans were for infrastructure, 20 percent for economic sectors (in which rural development funds were practically nil), 5 percent for social sectors, and 21 percent for "others," including program loans. By 1977, these proportions had shifted to 30 percent for infrastructure, 55 percent for economic sectors (one-third of which was for agriculture with almost two-thirds of that for rural development), 11 percent for social sectors, and 4 percent for others (ul Haq 1978).

"It would be incorrect to suggest that the Bank effort has already made a decisive difference to world proverty," comments ul Haq. "But it would be fair to say that Bank policies have changed rapidly over the course of the last decade to focus on increasing the productivity of the poor. . . . the Bank's role is more to persuade member countries and to give the right policy signals. It cannot coerce national governments into adopting appropriate policies for attacking their poverty problem if they neither have the political will nor the institutional means to do so" (ul Haq 1978).

Ul Haq, in effect, reaffirms that the socio-institutional environment sets the preconditions that influence the economic environment. Where country policies and structures are such that a highly unequal income and resource distribution is supported, many of the benefits of reoriented foreign assistance policies will still "leak" to the upper income groups. Even facilities created for the benefit of the small farmer will turn out to be more fully utilized by the larger farmers and may do positive harm to the small farmers by leading to their displacement and so accentuating rather than alleviating poverty. Official assistance may have to be channelled through local institutions and organizations representing the interests of small farmers and other small producers, and indirect repercussions should be carefully analyzed and controlled in advance (Singer 1976; Dorner 1975).

It seems quite clear that the key issues of natural resource use and policies, economic development, and international cooperation cannot begin to be resolved by action—no matter how well intentioned—at the international level alone. Rather " . . . the developing countries must recognize the intimate link between the reform of the national and international orders. If national economic orders in the poor nations remain unresponsive to the needs of their own poor and if their development strategies continue to benefit only a privileged few, much of the argument for a fundamental reform in the international order will disappear because any benefits flowing from such a reform would go only to a privileged minority in these countries. Moreover, when the international and national orders are dominated by privileged minorities, the possibilities of a tacit collusion between their national interests are quite unlimited. The developing countries have to learn, therefore, that reforms in their own national orders are often the critical bargaining chip they need in pressing for similar reforms at the international level" (ul Haq 1976a, pp. 8–9).

On the other hand, there is little doubt that the industrial nations have gained from their superior economic position. Growth and development on the international level, no less than on the level of the individual nation-state, have strong and inherent tendencies to concentrate benefits among those who, for whatever reason, are able to seize the opportunities offered by growth. At the national level there is a constant need for redistributive measures to offset these tendencies and provide opportunities to those less advantageously situated. Despite developmental assistance and international private investments (some would say even because of them) international mechanisms for such redress have not been adequately developed. The need persists for international mechanisms that will work to reduce the benefits accruing to the rich and the powerful and channel increased resources and support to the poor and the weak.

These issues cannot be resolved only at the international level nor only by individual nation-states acting within the confines of their limited jurisdiction. The aim of new international mechanisms ought to be to structure incentives and sanctions so that nation-states, in furthering their own interests, will serve *not only* those interests but will also serve the wider interests of the international community and will thereby evolve a new order that accommodates the basic needs of people in all nations (Dorner 1978).

Commons (1959, p. 73) defined institutions as collective action in restraint, liberation, and expansion of individual action. That is, in effect, what the world must seek in developing new institutions to define a new international order based on cooperation rather than confrontation. Such arrangements would restrain and curtail certain actions of nation-states, but these very restraints, *if all are subject to them,* would also liberate and expand the possibilities of action by all nations.

### References

Ahluwalia, Montek S. 1978. "Inequality, Poverty and Development," *Development Digest* 16: 102–24. Excerpted from *Journal of Development Economics* 3: 307–41 (December 1976).

Amin, Galal A. 1978. "A Critique of Current Arab Development Policies." In *Proceedings of the Wisconsin Seminar on Natural Resource Policies in Rela-*

*tion to Economic Development and International Cooperation,* vol. 1. Madison: Institute for Environmental Studies, University of Wisconsin.

Barraclough, Solon. 1977. "Agricultural Production Prospects in Latin America," *World Development* 5: 459–76.

Brown, Lester R., and Bruce Stokes. 1977. "World Gains in Family Planning," *Challenge* (November-December), pp. 50–54.

Buringh, P., H. D. J. van Heemst, and G. J. Staring. 1975. "Computation of the Absolute Maximum Food Production of the World." Department of Tropical Soil Science, Agricultural University, Wageningen, The Netherlands.

Commons, John R. 1957. *Legal Foundations of Capitalism.* Madison: University of Wisconsin Press; originally published in 1924 by the Macmillan Company.

Commons, John R. 1959. *Institutional Economics: Its Place in Political Economy.* Madison: University of Wisconsin Press; originally published in 1934 by the Macmillan Company.

Crosson, Pierre R., and Kenneth D. Frederick. 1977. *The World Food Situation.* Research Paper R–6. Washington, D.C.: Resources for the Future.

Dorner, Peter. 1972. *Land Reform and Economic Development.* Middlesex, England: Penguin Books.

Dorner, Peter. 1975. "International Assistance for the Small Farmer," *Challenge* (May-June), pp. 62–64.

Dorner, Peter. 1978. "Economic Development of Agriculture: Issues and Prospects." In *Proceedings of the Wisconsin Seminar on Natural Resource Policies in Relation to Economic Development and International Cooperation,* vol. 2. Madison: Institute for Environmental Studies, University of Wisconson.

Dorner, Peter, and Don Kanel. 1971. "The Economic Case for Land Reform." In Peter Dorner, ed., *Land Reform in Latin America: Issues and Cases. Land Economics Monograph no. 3.* Madison: University of Wisconsin, pp. 39–56.

Enis, W. B. Jr., W. M. Dowler, and W. Klassen. 1975. "Crop Protection to Increase Food Supplies," *Science* 188: 593–98.

FAO (Food and Agricultural Organization of the United Nations). 1975. *The State of Food and Agriculture 1974.* Rome: FAO.

Gaballah, Elsayed. 1978. "Implications of Agricultural Resource Use in the Arab Countries." In *Proceedings of the Wisconsin Seminar on Natural Resource Policies in Relation to Economic Development and International Cooperation,* vol. 1. Madison: Institute for Environmental Studies, University of Wisconsin.

Haddad, Sami. 1978. "A Brief Review of Policies Designed to Reduce Fertility in LDCs." In *Proceedings of the Wisconsin Seminar on Natural Resource Policies in Relation to Economic Development and International Cooperation,* vol. 3. Madison: Institute for Environmental Studies, University of Wisconsin.

Hardy, R. W. F., and U. D. Havelka. 1975. "Nitrogen Fixation Research: A Key to World Food?" *Science* 188: 633–43.

IMF (International Monetary Fund). 1978a. *IMF Survey* 7: 97–107.

IMF (International Monetary Fund). 1978b. *IMF Survey* 7: 193–200.

*International Economic Report of the President.* 1977. Washington, D.C.: U.S. Government Printing Office.

Johnson, D. Gale. 1976a. "Food for the Future: A Perspective," *Population and Development Review* 2: 1–19.

Johnson, D. Gale. 1976b. "Objectives of International Training in Agricultural Economics." In L. P. Schertz. A. R. Stevenson, and A. M. Weisblat, eds., *International Training in Agricultural Economic Development.* New York: Agricultural Development Council, Inc.

Kovda, V. A. 1971. "The Problem of Biological and Economic Productivity of the Earth's Land Areas," *Soviet Geographic* (revised and translated) 12: 6–23.

Kravis. Irving B., Alan Heston, and Robert Summers. 1977. "Real GNP per Capita for 116 Countries, 1970 and 1974." Department of Economics Discussion Paper no. 391, University of Pennsylvania, Philadelphia, Pennsylvania.

Kuznets, Simon. 1963. "Quantitative Aspects of Economic Growth of Nations: VIII. Distribution of Income by Size," *Economic Development and Cultural Change* 2(2): 1–37.

Ladejinsky, Wolf. 1970. "Ironies of India's Green Revolution," *Foreign Affairs* 38: 758–68.

*Latin America Economic Report.* 1978. "United States Attacks Brazil's Trade Policy," 7(21): 166.

Lekachman, Robert. 1977. "How the Rich Can Help the Poor," *Challenge* (September-October), pp. 48–52.

Lewis, W. Arthur. 1972. "Objectives and Prognostications." In Gustav Ranis, ed., *The Gap Between Rich and Poor Nations: Proceedings of a Conference Held by the International Economic Association at Bled, Yugoslavia.* London: Macmillan, pp. 411–20.

Long, Erven J. 1953. "Freedom and Security as Policy Objectives," *Journal of Farm Economics* 35: 317–22.

McNamara, Robert S. 1973. Address to the Board of Governors of the World Bank. Washington, D.C.: World Bank.

Mellor, John W. 1976. *The New Economics of Growth.* Ithaca, New York: Cornell University Press.

Mikdashi, Zuhayr. 1978. "Commodity Agreements and International Economic Cooperation." In *Proceedings of the Wisconsin Seminar on Natural Resource Policies in Relation to Economic Development and International Cooperation,* vol. 1. Madison: Institute for Environmental Studies, University of Wisconsin.

Mohamed, El Saudi A. 1978. "Resource Requirements to Meet World Food Needs: A Review." In *Proceedings of the Wisconsin Seminar on Natural Resource Policies in Relation to Economic Development and International Cooperation,* vol. 3. Madison: Institute for Environmental Studies, University of Wisconsin.

Morawetz, David. 1977. *Twenty-five Years of Economic Development 1950 to 1975.* Washington, D.C.: World Bank.

National Defense University. 1978. *Climatic Change to the Year 2000.* Washington, D.C.: National Defense University.

National Research Council, 1977. *Supporting Papers: World Food and Nutrition Study II.* Washington, D.C.: National Academy of Sciences.

Ndegwa, Duncan, and Robert Triffin. 1976. "The International Monetary Order." In Jan Tinbergen, coord., *RIO—Reshaping the International Order: A Report to the Club of Rome.* New York: Dutton.

Parsons, K. H. 1977. "The Political Economy of Agricultural Development." Sixth National Congress of Colombian Economists, Cali, Colombia.

Penn, Raymond J. 1961. "Public Interest in Private Property (Land)," *Land Economics* 37: 99–104.

Penn, Raymond J. 1978. "Lend Lease: An Experiment in Foreign Exchange." In *Proceedings of the Wisconsin Seminar on Natural Resource Policies in Relation to Economic Development and International Cooperation,* vol. 2. Madison: Institute for Environmental Studies, University of Wisconsin.

Pound, Glenn S. 1975. "The Crucial Role of Agricultural Research." U.S. Congress, House of Representatives, *Hearings before the Subcommittee on Science, Research, and Technology and the Subcommittee on Domestic and International Scientific Planning and Analysis, Committee on Science and Technology,* 94th Cong., 1st sess., no. 51.

President's Science Advisory Committee. 1967. *The World Food Problem,* vol. 2. Washington, D.C.: U.S. Government Printing Office.

Ram, Rati, and Theodore W. Schultz. 1977. "Some Economic Implications of Increases in Life Span with Special Reference to India." Human Capital Paper no. 77:4, University of Chicago, Chicago, Illinois.

Richardson, J. David. 1978. "Some Observations on Recycling Petrodollars, 'Sovereign Debt,' Euro-Banking, and the IMF." In *Proceedings of the Wisconsin Seminar on Natural Resource Policies in Relation to Economic Development and International Cooperation,* vol. 2. Madison: Institute for Environmental Studies, University of Wisconsin.

Schuh, G. Edward. 1976. "The New Macroeconomics of Agriculture," *American Journal of Agricultural Economics* 58: 802–11.

Seif El-Yazal, Said. 1978. "Energy and Agriculture: Issues and Prospects." In *Proceedings of the Wisconsin Seminar on Natural Resource Policies in Relation to Economic Development and International Cooperation,* vol. 3. Madison: Institute for Environmental Studies, University of Wisconsin.

Singer, Hans. 1976. "An Elusive Concept," *CERES* 9(4): 22–26.

ul Haq, Mahbub. 1971. "Employment in the 1970s: A New Perspective," *International Development Review* 4: 9–13.

ul Haq, Mahbub. 1976a. *The Third World and the International Economic Order.* Development Paper no. 22. Washington, D.C.: Overseas Development Council.

ul Haq, Mahbub. 1976b. "Concessions on Structural Change." Paper presented to a Special Meeting of the Club of Rome on the New International Order.

ul Haq, Mahbub. 1978. "Changing Emphasis of the Bank's Lending Policies," *Finance and Development* 15(2): 12–14.

USDA (United States Department of Agriculture). 1975. "Is the World Facing Starvation?" (unnumbered, April).

West, Quentin M. 1976. "The Gap Between Agricultural Technology and the Demand for Food," ERS-628. Washington, D.C.: U.S. Department of Agriculture, Economic Research Service.

World Bank, 1976. *World Bank and IDA Annual Report.* Washington, D.C.: World Bank.

World Bank. 1978; *World Development Report, 1978.* New York: Oxford University Press.

Wortman, Sterling. 1976. "Strategy for the Alleviation of World Hunger." Paper presented at the University of Rochester, Rochester, New York.

# 10 *M. Sarwat Montassir*

# Technology, Development, and Natural Resources

This chapter will examine the status of the scientific and technological bases of developing countries, compare them to the technological "systems" of industrial countries, and attempt to identify developing nations' opportunities for formulating their own strategies of technological development in accord with their own societies' needs. It will not try to recommend specific technologies or technological policies for developing countries.

Elaborate definitions of technology have been composed, but in most usages the original meanings of its Greek root still adhere to the word: art, science, craft, or skill. Connotations of practical, industrial, or applied skills are there too. Technology is mechanical and physical, but beyond that it is part of a process and, in its most serviceable form, part of an evolutionary process in which "technology" is fitted to and created by the requirements of a society.

## Technological "Systems"

Intellectual and scientific innovations may arise independently from individual human inspiration and innovation or pure accident, but in the next instant, as insight becomes information, knowledge in even the most minimal application must be joined with a technological "system" and also with the social, economic, and political structure of society. Technology and society inevitably interact, but they do not necessarily work harmoniously or successfully from the standpoint of the objectives and values of the society. "Technological system" or "scientific and technological system" will often be used here as a shorthand reference to the network of possible interactions among basic research, applied science, engineering, production of goods and services, and other sectors of knowledge, skill, and society. That shorthand does not, however, imply that any technological "system" is a well-understood, smoothly functioning, or easily delineable apparatus, much less a blueprint that can somehow be adapted or designed by a nation. A technological "system" may be whole or disjointed, responsive or inchoate. Its strengths or its weaknesses are characterizations of the adequacy with which technology has come to be linked, in an evolutionary process, with the conditions and needs of a society.

A strong technological system exhibits stimulation by and interaction with monetary sectors, productive sectors, service sectors of transport, education, health, housing, and information, and cultural sectors. Technological systems, although interacting from day to day at the microlevel with government, business, and social institutions, are themselves situated at a macrolevel, and their major features are closely linked with the objectives of society as a whole, within the frame of social needs and insofar as available resources permit.

Through many years of experience and successive adjustment, the scientific and technological capabilities of the industrial countries have evolved as a distinctive yet integral component of the overall social and economic structure of those nations. This is not to say that the "strong" technological systems of the developed countries have reached perfection or stasis. On the contrary, difficulties, limitations, criticisms, and failures do persist; the social, economic, and political matrix of technology is continuously changing. These systems are in varying degree effective and operational because they are dynamic.

Abundant natural resources, labor scarcities, and high levels of motivation had their influence on the technological directions and capacities of the United States, Canada, and Western Europe. Japan, on the other hand, is poor in natural resources and has had to depend upon human skills, organization, and innovation to realize and sustain its fast industrial expansion within an extremely competitive situation. The centrally planned economies of the USSR and Eastern Europe, under a different socio-political system, made technological development a priority in comprehensive national planning. The USSR in particular is also rich in natural resources, although it does have recurrent problems in agriculture. Other technological variants among the developed nations can be noted in the Nordic countries, Southern Europe, or Australia, for example. Technological development is not mere national resolve; it both shapes and is shaped by resource endowments and individual and collective behaviors, attitudes, and values. Technological capacities, problems, and strategies in Spain or Bulgaria differ from those in the United States or the USSR, as do those in Somalia or Bolivia or Saudi Arabia or Mexico or China.

Nevertheless, and despite some variation, the technological systems of the developed nations do have revealing common features. Both basic and applied sciences proceed within the universities, governmental and private industrial laboratories, learned societies, and the communication networks of research and technical journals. Applied science and technology rest upon a network of research and development centers, public and private financing institutions, relations with industry and business, patent registries, and the many institutions for training, testing, designing, monitoring, and disseminating "technology." There are channels for communication, for the flow of funds, for ideas, and eventually for full application of technological innovation, often by productive units which were not the site where the technology was first created. There are, moreover, reverse flows as shortcomings and new objectives are recognized and as problems are sent back to the technological system to solve.

All these arteries of a technological system need not exist in the binding forms of statute and contract. They emerge as working rules of a social, economic, and political reality through interaction with the system of values and the structure of decision making. Such systems have gradually built a technological body of institutions, procedures, codes of conduct, expectations, sectoral relationships, scientific infrastructure, human resources, diffusion channels, engineering and data processing services, and more— the network of dynamic, innovative, "technologically minded" societies.

Technology must inevitably play an important role in the development of developing countries too. In planning for development, the specific technological patterns selected (or newly designed) for use in agricultural, industrial, mining, and other sectors and subsectors and the efficiency of their use are among the essential factors in balancing the relative weights of these sectors and in deciding upon national development plans and strategies.

In countries suffering the social and economic effects of overpopulation of limited agricultural lands, technologies of reclamation, cultivation, irrigation, and settlement can help to expand arable lands, assure more productive use of agricultural resources (including labor), and lessen the ills of concentrated population.

Other technologies stimulated by the demands of small industry, farm-

ers, and handicrafts workers in developing countries (as in the initial
stages of development of the now highly industrial countries) are also socially and economically significant. Look, for example, at the role of the
blacksmith in the early settlers' communities in the United States and at
how his simple "technology" served the developmental objectives of time
and place.

Time-honored designs of farming and irrigation equipment in many
developing countries, or manual looms for cotton and silk weaving in India and Egypt, are other examples worth looking into. India has recently
succeeded, too, in developing a small-scale, economic technology for
manufacturing crystal sugar without resort to the large-scale vacuum pan
technology prevalent elsewhere but unsuited to the nation's agricultural
pattern (Garg 1976). Such simple technologies—especially those which
tend to rely on renewable rather than stock resources—may prove to be,
with improvements, still "appropriate" for many developing countries.

For many decades, however, industry and modern agriculture have
become more and more dependent on nonrenewable (stock) resources
and less dependent on renewable (flow) resources. Both industry and agriculture have tended to emphasize resource-intensive production and
consumption technologies rather than resource-saving and resource-
substituting ones. Dependable estimates of natural resource supplies, in
the physical sense, and the extent of their economic availability are critical to resource policy planning and consequently to economic development in general. Technologies for this purpose have already made vital
contributions, but much remains to be done, especially for those resource
problems—utilization, conservation, distribution, and pricing—which
are critical in the economies of most developing nations. As global
development—particularly accelerated development of the developing
countries—continues on a path of intensive use of stock resources, technologies of resource conservation may well become imperative. Technology must contribute to the effort of formulating policies that can assist in
establishing common grounds between resource exporters (mostly developing countries) and resource importers (mostly developed countries).

The process of development of any country, although planned indige-
nously according to its own strategies and policies, can be neither self-
contained nor based on self-sufficiency. By necessity, development sooner
or later involves a complex regional and international network of trade in
natural resource commodities; pricing of these resource commodities
(and problems of balances of trade and payments); costs and conditions
of technology transfer; costs and conditions of capital transfers, investment, and financing; technical assistance and training of personnel; and a
series of social artifacts which may not mirror those in the technologically

developed countries but will be different than those that had existed within the developing countries.

Many developing countries export raw materials to industrial countries, and import technology, industrial machinery, and consumer goods needed to provide a sustainable base for future development or to satisfy consumer expectations. In the complexities of these transactions, conflicting interests of developed and developing countries often expose handicaps for the latter, a lack of equity persisting since the time of colonialism. Strengthening the bargaining and negotiating capacities of developing countries, both as producers of resources and as markets, is mandatory in all areas related to their national (and regional) economic and social interests, in general, and in the areas of science and technology in particular.

It should be obvious from these quick sketches that "technology" is a main actor in the process of national and regional socio-economic development. Scientific and technological capability of developing countries is indeed a vital factor not only in enabling them to establish sound development policies and strategies congruent with their own development needs but also in formulating suitable policies for their natural resources, in fostering their bargaining capacity in conflicts with economically and politically powerful industrial countries, and in stimulating their indigenous productive capacity.

Developing countries, nationally and regionally, must hope to reach an eventual stage in which they will have their own scientific and technological systems stimulated by and responding to the demands of their own socio-economic and development plans in harmony with their established development strategies.

### National and Collective Technological Self-Reliance

Since the declarations of the UN General Assembly in 1974 on a "New International Economic Order," the phrase "self-reliance" ("national" or "collective") has become a common one in development literature, particularly in discussions of technology. Self-reliance and self-reliance as a "strategy" in national development have been declared in several international forums, and elsewhere, as valid and necessary concepts applicable to developed as well as developing countries (Patel 1975; Montassir 1978; Pugwash Symposium 1975). Without prejudice to such declarations, it should be realized that "self-reliance" is, in fact, a product of an operative, indigenous scientific and technological system or at least of a system on its way to operative status. (It might be pointed out, however, that a country which operates primarily on a subsistence level is in fact self-reliant and, in a certain sense, technologically self-reliant.)

A technological system with its many components evolves gradually in conjunction with economic development, industrialization, socio-political structures, and scientific advances. In this sense, national or collective self-reliance, technologically or economically, is a status of a country (or group of countries) which has built up its capabilities to exercise its own will for policy and decision making in the development process.

The concept of self-reliance does not imply isolation. On the contrary, it calls for cooperation not only among developing countries but also with developed countries. This was well expressed in the Pugwash monograph (1975) of the Dar-es-Salaam symposium: "However self-reliant we try to be, in our economies and our development, we are up against the fact that progress out of poverty has everywhere, throughout history, required some outside induction of capital and expertise. . . . Self-reliance does not mean autarky. It implies mutural benefits from trade and cooperation, and a fairer redistribution of resources satisfying the basic needs."

The cooperation advocated, in whichever form it may take, constitutes a means to an end. A country or a region or an international group of countries should become capable of eliminating excessive dependence and employing its own capacity to promote its own development. This status could be called "self-reliance" or any other name, but what should concern the developing countries at this stage is how to reach that status. In other words, again without prejudice to the concept of self-reliance, the means to reach this status, and not self-reliance per se, is the immediate problem. Although dependence on other countries may operate to the disadvantage of a developing economy, competition among innovative ideas may be a necessary driving force in stimulating development of technology and as a quality control mechanism.

To reach this status and to enhance the evolution of balanced technological institutions, components, and linkages, developing countries need assistance and cooperation among themselves and from the developed nations. To this end, UNCTAD has recommended that regional and subregional centers be established to link and assist national efforts in technological development and transfer and has drafted an "International Code of Conduct on Technology Transfer" with proposed revisions of the legal and juridical environment in which transfer occurs. The UN regional economic commissions are preparing feasibility studies for four regional centers of this type suggested by UNCTAD, and UNESCO has organized biennial "Conferences on the Application of Science and Technology to Development" in Asia, Africa, Latin America, and Arab regions.

There will always be a gap between recommendations and actions, between what should and what can be done, within any developing country or any regional group of countries. Aiding the evolution and consolidation of technological "systems" is no simple job, and it should be realized that formulating technological plans in national, regional, or international forums is only an initial stage to be followed by long work back home in the stages of implementation. The time needed for a technological system to mesh with economic, educational, cultural, and sociopolitical systems must be measured in decades. During all that time there must be continuous effort to keep technology and society developing in concert, not at cross-purposes. Whatever resolutions or plans of action are reached cannot be fully tailored systems "granted" to developing countries. The extent of benefits to be gained will depend on what nations can do in the near and far future to assist the normal evolution of appropriate scientific and technological systems, utilizing plans of action and resolutions as guidelines.

## Technology for Development

The technological systems of developed countries are complex and dynamic structures with effective links to government, science, and education. They have means of internal quality control maintained at the research stage by competition for research funds and by peer review of research plans and results and maintained in production phases by standards, licensing, and public interest criteria. Some countries are also developing regulations and reviews to eliminate or ameliorate the negative effects of one technology upon another or upon the environment. The technological systems of developed countries, lastly, have the capacity to finance and support long lead times in technological adjustment and training.

In this sense, a technological system is not only technological information, nor is it simply qualified and knowledgeable personnel, nor merely a network of research and development centers. A strong technological system must include all those components and relations which stimulate the innovative and imaginative faculties of individuals and groups to find and apply knowledge to the processes of production of goods and services. This two-way interaction between society as a whole and the technological system calls for social and financial support from the society to the technology and a flow of innovations into the economic and social streams. Two-way interactions take place at a multitude of points and through a variety of mechanisms.

Technology may be generated as an idea or a tested procedure in one place, but in general it must be acquired and applied somewhere else. Technology within the industrially advanced societies is thus a continuous process of generation, transfer, adoption, and application. Rules and codes of ownership for protection of technology have been developed to regulate these stages of the technological system.

One important feature of a strong technological system is the "programming" of technology, the stimulation of the system to attain certain objectives. Many innovations are certainly achieved in almost a random manner and cannot be planned or programmed in advance. This comes about in part because of a "climate" of invention or of "pure" research for the sake of knowledge. Other important practical innovations emerge from individuals who are not normally considered to be within the technological sphere. Yet in recent decades, and especially after the two world wars, an organized technological establishment has appeared within the developed countries, and it does seem amenable to "programming."

Technological feats are stimulated or directed by programmed objectives and goals, especially through the infusion of public funds. The approach so far appears to be most effective for programs such as military hardware, space technology, water development in hydroelectric production, flood control, or irrigation, and exploitation of particular categories of minerals. There technological programs appear to have certain characteristics, such as attainment of a specific goal on a certain time schedule and the aggregation of a series of subsystems in phase to achieve the overall goal. They tend not to be open-ended or to provide for alternative strategies. They may have a certain psychology of attainment which is an integrative political force. They may, in part, be successful because they are superimposed on a general technological base.

Technology, as well as labor, capital, raw materials, and management, is an important but rather elusive factor of production. From the engineering point of view, technology is represented in production by the choice and design of the process and hence the equipment, the specification of material inputs, and the quality of the product. It exists, no doubt, in the skill of workers, the capacity of management, the planning and control of operations, and in the economic aspect of substitutability among factors of production. Labor-intensive technologies producing the same or almost the same products can be economically acceptable alternatives under different social conditions and in different locations. In this case one can speak about "alternative technologies" or "choice of technologies." If the possibility of substitution does not exist or exists at high private or social costs, choice of technology is not practicable. Indeed, in the dynamic sense, uneconomic or unacceptable combinations of changing factors of production are the reason—in many cases—for new technology which permits a more economic combination of the available factors of production. In a society where prices, wages, taxes, raw materials, energy, competition, consumer preferences, and market shares are continuously changing, economic management cannot afford to neglect the technological system in maintaining its operations and realizing further security and development.

The growth of technology has been supported by and has contributed to a path of specialization within the structure. This specialization has occurred horizontally, in terms of substantive specialization in economic sectors, and vertically, in terms of segments of a production process. Highly detailed and precise information can be brought to bear on specific questions within the specialty, but information must flow across the boundaries of specialization for technological integration. Specialization has led to professionalization which has led to internal quality control. This whole configuration has led to a dispersal of the power to make decisions on the best development strategy. These circumstances allow socioeconomic development to be described as "technologically led" in the sense that major economic activities are often initiated and maintained by technological ideas, although these ideas, in their turn, may have been motivated or directly programmed by social, ethical, economic, or political forces in the society.

### Technological Systems in Developing Countries

Technological systems in developing countries are weak. Some components may exist: there may be universities, research institutes, qualified graduates, and some sources of finance. Industry, agriculture, transport, health, and other economic and social sectors need "technology" which is "appropriate" to them (we may leave for a while the definition of "appropriateness"). Yet the technological systems, because of fragmented structures which have not co-evolved with agriculture, mining, transport, and other sectors of application, are found almost incapable of helping to solve problems or to speed development. The systems are not harmonious. Some components are weak or even completely absent. The systems, such as they are, get but the barest stimulation from productive and social sectors and do not in turn feed back the necessary innovations and solutions to problems.

Furthermore, the financing of technological systems in developing countries does not seem closely related to general strategies of technological development, nor to the need for links with science on the one hand and economic production on the other. Many governments and other agencies in the developing countries, with the ambition of technological progress, continue to allocate funds in support of "science," "research," and "technology" in a variety of forms. Yet these efforts do not seem to lead to a vigorous technology tied to production, nor do they aid the evolution of balanced technological systems. They too often lead, at best, to more research workers working on foreign technologies, too often technologies "inappropriate" to most problems at home.

Technological circumstances in developing countries are really as varied as the countries themselves. Some nations barely have the nucleus of a potential technological system even though they are resource-rich. Other nations, of course, are poor in almost every sense, yet they too have their sovereign ambitions for a better life. These of course are extreme cases, but the point is that there are varying perspectives on both technology and the hope for development. The "appropriate" technologies which can provide, under local social and economic conditions, a path—not *the* path—to development are not the same in all cases, yet there are perhaps some common concerns.

### *"Appropriate" Technology*

Criteria of "appropriateness" of technology depend on the purposes for which developing countries want technology. The expected purpose is development. But what kind of development? I do not propose to go into detail about the subject of appropriate development patterns for developing countries, but it is useful to put here an obvious yet sometimes forgotten point—technology must be in harmony with the objectives and patterns of development, whether these are explicitly stated or implicitly assumed. To say that technology must be in harmony with the objectives and patterns of development does not mean, however, that there may not be an intense competition of ideas on alternative patterns.

"Appropriate" technology for a developing country, at a certain stage of its development, depends on its strategy of development. This is easy to say, but many developing countries find it difficult to establish a development strategy substantially different from patterns and strategies suggested by the experience of industrially advanced countries. In many cases, they may even have no desire to do so.

A better question, perhaps, than the nature of appropriate development, is what pattern of development is feasible for a developing country under existing circumstances? The aim is, not to cast about for an appropriate pattern of development, but rather to identify the constraints under which a developing country will face the future and to inquire about what is attainable within those constraints. Much depends on the will and capacity of the developing countries to decide upon and implement a certain course of action, although it is only fair to expect that industrial countries will also give attention to this question. The variation between what is appropriate and what is feasible need not be a serious problem in all technological policies, but it is a possibility to keep in mind in posing technological plans.

Nevertheless, the "appropriateness" of technology for a developing country at a certain phase of its development might generally be judged by the extent to which technology meets the following conditions:

- relevance to the factor endowments of the nation
- optimum utilization of natural and human resources
- maximization of output, of fundamental consumption of goods and services, and of the rate of growth
- reduction of balance of payments deficits and unemployment
- greater equity in distribution of income
- improvement of the quality of life (especially in rural areas)
- promotion of political development and stability
- participation in regional development
- ability to solve or avoid environmental problems
- relevance to the cultural environment and to social traditions

In economic terms the choice of technology in any specific activity, or more broadly in the development policy of a sector or a country, should conserve scarce resources and attain higher economic efficiency in their use. It is understood that there must be some real opportunity for choice; the range of choices usually involves the intensity of use of capital, labor, and raw materials, the scale of organization implied in a certain strategy, and the choice of the mix of stock and renewable resources necessary for the strategy, provided that there exist engineering and organizational options to substitute one factor for another. Choice of technology in this sense will, of course, have complex repercussions which must be examined in detail before decisions are made.

## Transfer of Technology

A basic assumption of this analysis is that developing countries should be able to benefit from the technology already existing in the advanced countries instead of trying on their own to reinvent it. If properly done, such transfer of technology can be a great help to economic and social development of the developing countries. The means, institutions, and conditions necessary for the proper selection, acquisition, adaptation, application, and evolution of technology from the industrially advanced countries deserve scrutiny.

Technology is usually generated at specific points within the technological system of the developed countries and then transmitted to other points for application within the same or other developed countries. The process of transferring technology is a continuous one among the advanced countries; it has had failures, but successful transfers have been made for many decades. Transfers of this sort are, once again, an imbedded activity, part of a system evolved through practical experience and closely linked to economic, social, and political attributes of industrial societies.

The developing countries, however—the potential beneficiaries of transfer of the available stock of technological experience and know-how of the advanced countries—are not part of that system of technology generation and application. The problem of transferring technology from advanced to developing countries demands a perspective which cannot be quite the same as a view of technology's transfer within advanced countries. In other words, the problem is how to link a well-developed technological system within advanced countries to a new or potential system in the developing countries. The problem raises all the aspects inherent in the total "technological system" of the developed countries, points of wider economic and social development, and international cooperation.

Agents or components of the technological systems of the advanced countries, when they come into contact with developing countries, may find a lack of experience, knowledge, and capacity, at least by comparison to the situations in which they normally work within advanced countries. This imbalance, a historical fact, can elicit reluctant, cautious, or exploitative attitudes in the agents of the developed countries. Many of them prefer to work, not with the weak technological system of the developing countries, but with the relatively better endowed and more influential investment and productive sector in those countries. That preference in effect bypasses the indigenous technological system and perpetuates its difficulties. Attitudes of reluctance, caution, or exploitation can be combined with a sometimes predatory desire to expand operation, secure footholds for markets, and exploit the natural resources of the developing countries.

Development authorities within the developing countries have often preferred to handle technology as part of an investment agreement with economically active enterprises, especially transnational corporations. National authorities too can be reluctant to deal directly with the unfamiliar and complex technological systems of the advanced countries or with the indigenous technological system, admittedly inefficient and incomplete. Transnational subsidiaries in the developing countries can become technological and economic enclaves separated from the stream of national development and national policies.

The technology of the transnationals tends to be applied to a specific resource of interest and to be highly specialized in the extraction and use of that resource. (The same patterns can, in fact, be seen within the industrial countries when a particularly large stock reserve exists in a relatively remote region that does not have much industrial and urban infrastructure. With the exhaustion of the stock resource the region is left behind as an internal "pocket of poverty.") In many cases, potential resources of developing countries are bypassed and, in effect, wasted because the technology of the transnationals is not part of a technological system tuned by an evolutionary process to the real needs of national societies.

One could pinpoint other weaknesses in the present modes of transferring technology from industrial to developing countries. These include the disparate bargaining strengths of buyers and sellers of technology, unfair price structures for technology, the prevalence of "package deal" and "turnkey" sales of technology, restrictive practices in commercial clauses of contracts, outdated patent systems that do not take sufficient account of the need for innovation, and the frequent inappropriateness of imported technologies to the factor endowments of resource-poor countries.

To limit scope, two major problems of this wide possible spectrum of consideration may be selected for analysis of ways to improve the transfer of technology:

1. How can developing countries increase their capacity to learn about the technology available in the advanced countries, select from that total stock what is likely to be most appropriate to them, and initiate and conduct the necessary procedures for acquiring it under the best conditions with the least harm to their interests?
2. How can the developing countries build their system of technological adaptation, application, and generation, not as a mere replica of the system of the advanced countries, but as an indigenous system harmoniously linked to public policies, research, industrialization, economic growth, and, not least, environmental impact?

If these two problems are evaluated by a developing country in the light of its own institutions, resource endowments, and incentives, the conclusions and the measures consequently devised to deal with the problems might be said to constitute the technological policy of the country. That policy should embody the major objectives, mechanisms, institutions, and guiding principles for public and private action.

Many developing countries have already established such policies, in part, but there have also been recent attempts to identify the elements and the substance of such policies on a more comprehensive basis. The term "plan" may not always be appropriate because in many cases the "plan" does not contain resources for or power of implementation. Other terms such as *policies, objectives, programs,* or *procedures* might better be used. With this understanding, however, the word "plan" will be used to represent the measures related to technological development and application at the national level.

Technology is not something that exists by itself, something which can be moved, transplanted, or traded like a barrel of oil, a sack of wheat, or an ounce of gold. Technological information and know-how may exist in written form, in an industrial process, or in the capacity and dexterity of people. When this information and experience is applied in a process which produces goods and services, the outputs may perhaps be recognized as products of an advanced, an adapted, an intermediate, an appropriate, or an indigenous technology. The production process may require equipment, intermediary products, and other inputs which may themselves deserve one of those adjectives of technology.

Technology, then, is not simply a set of technological information, nor simply a set of equipment and tools, nor simply a set of products, whether goods or services. It is rather a complex "system" which links the information, the know-how, the equipment, and the products, as well as the institutions, personnel, and the process of innovation and application to the economic, social, and political objectives of a society. Technological capacity and technological development must be understood in this comprehensive manner. Each developing country must endeavor to establish for itself a strategy of technological development which will:

1. Establish priorities for policies and resource allocations that can help to evolve and shape a selective but coherent "system" of technology and not simply some uncoordinated components of such a system.
2. Identify national objectives of development, both current and long-run, and establish technological policies, institutions, and activities in conformity with these objectives, especially in science, research, and human resources development.
3. Increase national capacity to select, acquire, and adapt external technologies for national development without incurring excessive costs, losing control over the national economy, or neglecting the evolution of local technological capacity.
4. Recognize that the country itself must determine its own appropriate technological directions yet maintain common and harmonious technological relations with advanced countries, among developing countries as a whole, and among regional groups of developing countries.

### National and Regional Attempts in Technological Development

Several attempts have been made to establish technological plans to regulate the transfer of technology and to stimulate the evolution of national technological capacity. Among these are Mexico's on a national level and that of the Arab countries on a regional level. Brief review of the

Mexican technological plan and the evolving Arab strategy may reveal some practical problems of fostering scientific and technological "systems" in socio-economic development.

## The Case of Mexico

In July 1974 the Mexican National Council for Science and Technology was empowered to prepare a national plan for science and technology. The Council issued in 1976 the "National Indicative Plan for Science and Technology."

The Plan tried to map a strategy for Mexico's move from almost complete dependence on foreign technology to a "technological self-reliance" which did not reject imported technology but regulated and controlled it, adapted it to national aims and needs, and gradually drew from it the experience to evolve indigenous technology.

After a short outline of the social function of science and technology and the need for technological policy at the national level, the Plan illustrated the financial and social costs of Mexican dependence on foreign technology:

1. In 1971 more than 2 billion pesos went abroad in technological payments for royalties, licensing, etc.
2. Patent applications were overwhelmingly dominated by foreign applicants, but few of the patents saw actual use in production in Mexico because market protection was the chief intent; the patents were shelved.
3. Protective policies of import substitution isolated Mexican industry from international competition, encouraged acquisition of proven foreign technologies whose cost could be passed to local consumers, and discouraged innovative indigenous technological development.
4. Technological research and development, guided by the perspectives of industrial countries, tended to concentrate on nonrenewable resources and high cost industrial inputs, not, for instance, the simple and inexpensive inputs needed by small farm agriculture.

Internal demand for technology in Mexico, said the Plan, was weak because "adequate links have not been forged between research institutions and the productive apparatus." Entrepreneurs had no clear view of the importance of research and development and were unwilling to run the risks of internal technological development if foreign technologies could be bought. Agrochemical and mechanical technologies, in particular, were exceedingly dependent on foreign sources, and local firms had too little ability to identify or make explicit their technological needs. The socio-economic and ecological conditions of developing countries, said the Plan, are very different from those of the developed countries in which imported technology is designed, and those conditions require technologies which rationally use available national resources, including abundant labor; impede environmental degradation; and employ national resources in productive activities only marginally important, if at all, to research and development in the industrial nations.

Training, research, and financing alone would not suffice within Mexico, said the Plan; the major national users of technology must be "induced to reorient their demands toward national scientific and technological systems, which must overcome the real competition of foreign technology and the market preferences the users show for it." It would be necessary to influence demand toward indigenous technology, although this does not imply abandonment of knowledge generated abroad. National scientific and technological development, according to the Plan, would require a "climate" in which the "value" of the national technological job and its significance for national objectives were appreciated. A country must define its own scientific and technological needs, objectives, and style and focus on scientific excellence in areas of knowledge little emphasized elsewhere but crucial to the nation, said the Plan.

The Mexican Plan's factual assessment of research and development in the nation found that research and development expenditures almost doubled in the 1969–74 period but remained low in comparison to expenditures in other developing countries such as India and very low compared to industrial countries. The source of research and development monies in Mexico was quite predominantly the national government, directly or through state-owned industries and national universities. Although three-fourths or more of financing and personnel were devoted to applied research, the minimal links among research institutions, universities, and the productive sectors made application of scientific and technological knowledge "disarticulated and uncoordinated."

The national technological policy recommended by the Mexican Plan adopted a six-year planning period in order to tie firmly the technological plan to national economic and social planning and set these goals:

1. A doubling of expenditures (in 1975 pesos) on research and development, specialized education, and diffusion mechanisms between 1976 and 1982.
2. An approximate tripling of research and development personnel in the same period.
3. An increase in the share of expenditures borne by the private (nonforeign) sector and some decrease in the share of the public sector.

Equal attention was devoted to priorities in the allocation of those monies and personnel. On the bases of the technological, social, and economic significance of a sector, its present degree of technological dependence, and its present level of technological capability, researchers and expenditures were allocated to basic research, applied research in consumer and capital goods industries and transport and communication, or applied research in renewable resources' inventories (especially soils, water, and vegetation). More specifically, highest absolute increases in applied research and development would go to sectors

vital for the development of the country: petroleum and energy, agriculture, health and medicine and the main structure of intermediate goods. Nevertheless, expenditures growth rates should be highest in those sectors with a relatively low technological capability and with a relatively high dependence on foreign technology (manufacture of non-durable consumer goods, durable consumer and capital goods, transport and communication). This combination of absolute and relative priorities will enable the scientific technological system by 1982 to have a structure more in accordance with the need of the national scientific-technological development and more suited to attaining self-reliance than at present.

The adequacy of scientific-technological infrastructure was evaluated for sectors (food, forestry, fishing, energy sources, etc.) and for subsectors of agriculture and manufacturing, and sectoral objectives, guidelines, and priorities were set accordingly.

This short review can do no more than sketch the systematic methodological approach of the Mexican technological plan. It was the information revealed by such surveys, however, that allowed the essential gearing of the scientific-technological plan to the overall plan for socio-economic development of the nation. Technological strategies, institutions, and priorities, the allocations of money and manpower, and the legal instruments to control investments and regulate transfer of foreign technology were linked to their counterparts in Mexico's development plan. It was recognized that Mexico's objectives of reorientation of technological demand to internal suppliers, rational acquisition of foreign technology, technological assimilation capacity, and finally technological generation capability must proceed in concert with the wider objectives of Mexican development.

### The Case of Arab Countries

The case of the Arab countries differs from that of Mexico, principally because none of the Arab countries has prepared a scientific and technological plan as extensive or as balanced as Mexico's. Among the Arab countries, some may show more immediate activity in science and technology than Mexico does, and the same may also be true of the number of research scientists or engineers and the adequacy of institutions. These activities, however, have not been framed into technological plans or geared to overall national development plans.

Economic and social indicators (see Sewell 1977) reveal marked disparities among the 21 member states of the Arab League (total population about 147 million). At an extreme of one sort are the oil-exporting countries, with per capita GNPs between U.S. $11,770 and $1,660; at the other end of this scale are the poor countries of the region with per capita GNPs of U.S. $250 or less. Social indicators, however, classify all these nations, "rich" and "poor," as developing countries. As in many developing countries, production of primary resource commodities for export dominates the economies of the Arab region.

The economic and social diversity of the region could mean that a corresponding diversity of technological opportunities exists, but the establishment of regional scientific and technological coordination must be preceded by a regional Arab socio-economic development plan within which a regional technological plan could be imbedded, complete with "regional" objectives, policies, priorities, resource allocations, institutions, infrastructure, etc. As a prerequisite for a regional socio-economic plan, thorough plans on the national level for each country should exist. Regional strategies must complement national strategies. National scientific and technological plans linked to national socio-economic plans should be available as a foundation for a regional plan of either kind. One may question the advisability of trying to establish an Arab regional "system" for science and technology, given the current deficiencies in socio-economic planning in several of the Arab countries.

Continuous regional activity arranged or sponsored by the UN and the Arab League nevertheless indicate a strong desire and willingness of the Arab countries to strengthen their scientific and technological capabilities. The UN Economic Commission for Western Asia (ECWA 1977) has surveyed and evaluated the status of science and technology in 12 Arab countries within ECWA's domain. The same evaluations do apply, in large part, to the rest of the Arab countries (except perhaps Egypt, not included in ECWA's survey).

The ECWA studies found that in 1975 machinery and transport equipment accounted for about 35–40 percent of all imports in seven oil-exporting Arab countries and about 20–30 percent of imports in five Arab countries which exported little or no oil. "Other manufactures" accounted for an additional 20–35 percent of imports in most of these countries, and the cumulative percentages demonstrate the heavy dependence of Arab nations on foreign technology. In many of these countries, the management of this technology depends on nonnationals "imported" along with the equipment.

"The value of technology import and related payments for the region as a whole," concluded the ECWA report, "is of such a magnitude that only a marginal improved trading capability would constitute enormous savings in transfer costs. For example, a one percent reduction in transfer cost of machinery and transport equipment would constitute around U.S. $80 million. Improvements in the technology trading capability could be achieved relatively fast by allowing for some investment to train cadres in negotiating contracts, licenses, trade law, conducts, etc. In addition to improve nationally the terms of technology trade, the repeated individual country negotiations could be substituted for a number of countries and products by sub-regional negotiation procedures (e.g. sub-regional tenders). New institutions such as technology trade banks and technology auctions could also be investigated."

The heavy dependence on foreign consultants for feasibility studies and project management and the huge fees for these services, especially in the oil-exporting countries, have begun to be ameliorated by indigenous capacity in some Arab countries with a scientific and engineering manpower base. However, said the ECWA report, similar developments cannot be expected in other countries, and "the building up of engineering consulting capacity has to be initiated and accelerated by promotional measures of governments. Such measures could include steps for the gradual association of local consulting firms or individuals with contracts awarded to foreign consulting engineering firms. This could take the form of policies to promote sub-contracting to nationals and other protective measures. Engineers' unions could also play a decisive role in the building up of a local capacity in this area. Whatever steps governments decide upon, it should be borne in mind that promotional policies should not cause any delay in development."

ECWA also concluded that the region has played a "rather passive" role in developing the channels for transfer of technology. It has left the initiative and thus regional access to technology largely to developed countries, the sources of technology, and "It is believed that the absence of regular flows of scientific and technological information into the region (other than commercial information) is effectively narrowing down all available transfer channels. . . . The abundance of such information in the world as compared to the few developed outlets for such information in the ECWA region demands technological information exchange arrangements." The region also needs, said ECWA, to forge a greater acceptance of information as a "sales product."

ECWA also examined the capabilities of national scientific and technological institutions in survey countries and found marked weaknesses in many of the countries. Because national development plans are unformulated (or unimplemented) in some countries, ECWA doubted the long-term value of trying to compose workable (let alone complementary) scientific and technological plans. Nevertheless, said ECWA, "the resources embodied in national science and technology organizations are . . . substantial and could very well be directed towards more operational aspects of science and technology." The region, according to ECWA, has seen little progress in the generation of indigenous technology during the last decade, and governments might "consider measures to achieve such acceleration by promoting vigorously the adaptation, development and technology generating efforts of industrial enterprises. . . . It is felt that unless the public and/or private industrial sector is involved in technology development, current efforts even at increased levels will have little effect on the technology gap."

ECWA calculated 1973 or 1974 research and development expenditures as a percentage of GNP and, for six countries with available data, found financing short of the 0.5 percent of GNP target set by the declaration (in 1970) on the strategy for the Second UN Development Decade. ECWA concluded that "many countries are in fact so far removed from these targets that even their use as planning tools can be considered totally irrelevant. Moreover, the small size of many ECWA countries which are likely not to develop a full-fledged science and technology base calls for the introduction of sub-regional considerations in science and technology planning requiring sub-regional instead of national targets. Growth targets for science and technology manpower [and] R&D expenditure might be more appropriate planning tools in many countries of the region."

A summary of the problems of scientific and technological planning in individual nations of the Arab region comes essentially to the same set of circumstances faced in the Mexican Plan: Dependence on imported foreign technology is strong, indigenous demand for technology is weak, scientific and technological infrastructure—institutions, personnel, and financing—is inadequate, and linkages between national productive sectors and whatever national research and development does exist are poorly developed. Opportunities for devising technological plans with the essential link to national socio-economic development plans are largely lacking because development planning is inadequate, even absent.

All such constraints on technological planning at the national level compound the difficulty of beginning to establish a regional Arab scientific and technological "system." There is, nevertheless, much work that can be begun on a cooperative regional basis for short-term benefit and perhaps for the mid- and long-term experience required as a foundation for evolving an eventual regional technological system.

The ECWA report (1977) noted that transfer of technology within the Arab region offers a little-used potential for linking national capacities in cooperative or consortium projects. National research and development capacities are limited and "are likely not to increase substantively over the coming years because of many manpower and institutional constraints." National research and development efforts, ECWA points out, "could be confined to pure national interests and priorities only," and cooperative efforts could be devoted to those common matters for which present "ad hoc endeavours . . . may not prove the most appropriate manner to narrow the research gap between developed and developing countries."

These are precisely the sort of fields of study which the "Rabat Declaration" on regional cooperation (CASTARAB 1976) identified as appropriate topics for regional research in the more rational use of natural resources:

1. Water resources and water management
2. Ecology of arid and semiarid lands
3. Geological and geophysical studies
4. Marine environment and development of coastal areas
5. Nonconventional energy sources

The Declaration also recommended that an "Arab Science and Technology Fund," with initial financing of not less than $500 million, be set up to underwrite such studies. It furthermore acted to secure execution of the resolutions adopted by the Conference by forming a continuing joint committee and a full-time technical secretariat and made CASTARAB a standing conference meeting every three years to secure continuity of action and to evaluate progress.

Another cooperative effort now taking shape under the aegis of UN and Arab regional organizations is the "Arab Center for the Transfer and Development of Technology." This facility should allow shared experience and coordinated action on the problems identified by ECWA—negotiation of transfer arrangements and reduction of transfer costs, a format for building indigenous engineering and consultancy capacities, and means of widening transfer channels to include information "products."

The difficulties involved in regional organization, planning, or policy making are many. At minimum, however, the Arab countries seem to have laid a foundation for achieving a certain degree of cooperation in scientific and technological areas of common interest, through bilateral and multilateral agreements, until a more coherent regional science and technology can be established.

### Technology and Natural Resources Policies

The process of technological development is an integral part of the process of socio-economic and political development. Natural resources that exist physically become economically valued with appropriate technologies to meet a certain demand for final goods and services. Natural resource development and technological policies are closely linked on the demand side by the uses of such resources for energy and in manufacturing processes. They are linked on the supply side by the availability of technology for feasible economic extraction and generation. Technology also enters in the intermediate stages of transport, storage, and marketing of resources. Natural resource policies include questions related to costs and prices, to scarcity and depletion, and to intergenerational linkages. Technology—known, restricted, and sought—is also related to those aspects, as well as to the important question of substitutability between factors of production and between different raw material inputs for the same or similar end uses.

Technological impacts and the content of economic activities are continuously changing, and the valuation, demand, and utilization of natural resources will consequently be subject to constant variety, some of which will be of a technological nature. The major policy question for developing countries is how to allocate resources and follow policies which will eventually create a viable (but selective) technological system to assist in their development.

With limited resources, the developing countries must be very selective in choosing a field for technological development. They cannot approach all subjects, even over a matter of years or decades, but they must include enough of the variables of technological change to pass a minimum threshold for development. They must also seek to balance the growth of technological components. Too many highly trained personnel without adequate equipment and opportunities for application are a prelude to brain-drain and frustration; on the other hand, technology probably does imply some flow of trained personnel back and forth across national boundaries. If the programs of research institutions are not closely related to development requirements and opportunities they become sterile. Nationalistic restrictive policies about transfer of foreign capital and technology may stifle the process of development. Open door policies for foreign capital and technology, on the other hand, may lead to unreasonably high costs of technology, leakages of savings and domestic capital, and thwarted attempts to build an indigenous technological base.

There must be a balance between these alternative policies and components, especially if it is noted that they can be combined in different ways for different sectors and problems. One always deals with a technological mix not only within a country but also within a branch of industry. Multiplicity and diversity allow policies of transfer of technology for certain activities and policies of building local capacity for others. They allow the use of labor-intensive technology in certain activities and capital-intensive technology in others. The most essential element in all of these situations seems to be to stimulate two-way flows of technology, from the stage of transfer or generation to the stage of economic production, and simultaneously from production and application stages to laboratory analysis and experimentation. If these two necessary flows are maintained and stimulated, then the chances of building viable technological systems improve considerably. Resources and priorities must be carefully arranged; well-intended policies of disproportionate development of some components of the system will not create the necessary flows.

On further reflection, it might be agreed that these flows have been historically effective in relating science and technology to development and in introducing successful innovations and inventions, even by unsophisticated individuals, into the stream of economic growth. A government or a nation cannot easily centralize and control forward and backward technological flows. It can, however, recognize their importance and seek to maintain them.

## References

CASTARAB (Conference of Ministers of Arab States Responsible for the Application of Science and Technology to Development). 1976. Document SC-76/CASTARAB/1. Rabat, Morocco.

ECWA (United Nations Economic Commission for Western Asia). 1977. "The Status of Science and Technology in the Western Asia Region," E/ECWA/NR./SEM.1/18. Seminar on Technology Transfer and Change in the Arab Middle East, Beirut, Lebanon.

Garg, M. K. 1976. "The Scaling Down of Modern Technology: Crystal Sugar Manufacturing in India." In N. Jequier, ed., *Appropriate Technology: Problems and Promises.* Paris: Organisation for Economic Cooperation and Development.

Montassir, M. S. 1978. "Technological Self-Reliance of Developing Countries." In *Proceedings of the Wisconsin Seminar on Natural Resource Policies in Relation to Economic Development and International Cooperation,* vol. 2. Madison: Institute for Environmental Studies, University of Wisconsin.

Patel, J. Surendra. 1975. "Collective Self-Reliance of Developing Countries," *Journal of Modern African Studies* 4: 569–83.

Pugwash Symposium. 1975. *Pugwash on Self-Reliance.* Monograph from the Pugwash Symposium on The Role of Self-Reliance in Alternative Strategies for Development, Dar-es-Salaam, Tanzania.

Sewell, John W. 1977. *The United States and World Development: Agenda 1977.* New York: Praeger.

# III. INTERNATIONAL COOPERATION

# 11 *I. H. Abdel-Rahman*

## The International Order

Although the nation-state in the modern sense has become the unit of structure of the world community, there has always been an extranational set of rules and relations which help to govern affairs among national units and which mark the interplay of national policies. In this sense, one can speak about a variety of aspects of world order, according to the perspective of interest and the unit of analysis. Falk (1977), for an example meant to be illustrative and not definitive, has identified nine levels for an inquiry about the world order:

| Religion and Culture | Economics | Anthropology |
| History | Psychology | Ecology |
| Politics | Biology | Astrophysics |

World order studies as most recently practiced, however, have given greater weight to political, economic, and sociological aspects. Lately the first and final levels in Falk's list have also attracted much attention. Cultural aspects—beliefs, values, symbols, myths, and consciousness—define civilization and are increasingly recognized as ultimate sources of motivation of individuals and groups. At the same time they are the seat of ultimate satisfaction and harmony among individuals and groups. A diversity of cultures in a future world of increasing communication and interdependence is a goal for careful examination and contemplation.

331

The final two levels of ecology and cosmology encompass the place of man with respect to nature and the universe as a whole. Some environmental studies try to define safe "inner" and "outer" limits for the interaction of man and nature and to suggest economic, social, political, and technological policies to preserve the necessary balance between man and nature. Although man has stepped on the lunar surface and sent projectiles with sensing equipment to the planets of the solar system, his understanding of the cosmological order is still a limited one for both the microcosmos (the ultimate particles) and the macrocosmos (the galaxies and time-space relations).

The political order, across more than forty centuries of recorded history, has been always interrelated with economic, social, and technological factors. However, for certain purposes, one may speak separately about these aspects while not forgetting their interrelations and interactions.

### Landmarks

This chapter has been titled "The International Order" without specific reference to an "economic" order (although economics will be a main concern) and also without reference to "new," in order to highlight the continuous evolution of thinking about, structure of, and reactions to world order. There are, however, some particularly influential events, or landmarks, along this path of continuous evolution in the various forms and arrangements constituting the world order.

Wars are usually some of the most prominent political landmarks. We may recognize major changes in structure and balance of power after World War I and again after World War II. Two "new" world orders did in fact appear after those wars. In the first "new" order, the League of Nations was formed together with a system of war-indemnities, trusteeships, and mandates; stipulations of the Treaty of Versailles divided the Western nations, during the interwar period, into the "haves" and the "have nots." The tension between the two groups, the emergence of certain ideological and political doctrines, and a crushing economic collapse in the 1930s led to conflict that culminated in World War II. After that war, there emerged a United Nations system which paid more attention than the League had to financial, economic, and social matters, and which recognized the objectives of self-determination, human rights, and decolonization.

Cleveland (1977, p. 2) identifies these events as landmark attempts to establish a just and durable world order. He further defines concepts and measures which may constitute, out of current situations and events, a "third try" at a world order.

In the years since 1973, a number of other landmarks in the search for a world order have occurred that might be acknowledged. The most notable of these, perhaps, was the sixth special session of the General Assembly of the United Nations in April-May 1974, following initiatives by Algeria at the behest of the group of nonaligned countries. The session culminated in the adoption of two important resolutions: the first expressed the collective desire of UN member states to work toward the "Establishment of a New International Economic Order," the second concerned the "program of action" required for attaining a new order.

There have been other landmarks. Toward the end of 1973, the oil embargo by exporting Arab countries and the increase of the international price of oil might be identified, especially by oil-importing countries, as a significant landmark in the evolution of the international secene. Others may point to August 15, 1971, when the United States devalued the dollar and relieved itself unilaterally from the dollar's parity with gold. The world monetary system has not stabilized since then.

The point is that these landmark happenings are not born suddenly, do not arise without a series of other events leading to them, and naturally in their turn lead to a subsequent course of events with striking effects in other areas. Most of the detailed subjects included in the General Assembly's "New Economic Order" resolutions of 1974 had been repeatedly discussed in many earlier forums. The resolution itself was not binding, and it was accepted with many reservations and varying interpretations by different countries. Because it had no teeth in an economic or executive sense, its importance is political inasmuch as it incorporates a set of recommendations and objectives agreed to by the world assembly of nation-states. This is a situation very different from oil prices or dollar devaluation. The latter were actions, and not merely recommendations, taken by governments which decided on the basis of their political and economic interests to act. Other political and economic entities were left free to react in their own interests and in what manner they saw fit and feasible.

Noting the difference between events that are directed toward concepts and principles unbacked by executive power (financial or otherwise) and those events that represent *faits accomplis*, would one consider the first type less effective and merely rhetorical, or would one admit that they really condition the attitudes, values, and eventually the policies and actions of nations? It may be appropriate here to quote John Maynard Keynes: " . . . the ideas of economists and political philosophers, both when they are right and when they are wrong, are more powerful than is commonly understood. Indeed the world is ruled by little else. Practical men, who believe themselves to be quite exempt from any intellectual in-

INTERNATIONAL COOPERATION

fluences, are usually the slaves of some defunct economist. Madmen in authority, who hear voices in the air, are distilling their frenzy from some academic scribbler of a few years back. I am sure that the power of vested interests is vastly exaggerated compared with the gradual encroachment of ideas" (Keynes 1936, p. 383).

The difference between the two types of events is not always clearly understood. The impact of ideas and concepts, as shown by history, is in the long run greater than that of limited "practical" actions. Both take place, and both are important, but, because of their different forms and structures, they cannot be judged by the same measuring rods.

In 1955 the developing countries met together in Bandung, apart from the advanced countries, for the first time after World War II and asserted their identity and interest in world affairs. This political assertion was followed by a conspicuous show of solidarity in Geneva in 1964 at the first United Nations Conference on Trade and Development, which gave rise to the "group of 77" developing countries. The Vietnam War, beyond its political and military significance, may be considered an important event in changing social and psychological attitudes inside the United States and other countries.

We can go on identifying landmarks of our choice. The important point, however, is to recognize that these landmarks are only signposts on the road of a complex and continuous unfolding of events. It is more important to identify underlying causes and the interplay of causative forces than to record chronologically these events or to dramatize them unduly.

## Two Currents and the Timidity of Authority

With the advent of an era of greater communication and mobility of ideas and of people, the frame of thinking has expanded in all countries, particularly in the developing countries. The people of the developing countries formed desires, objectives, and expectations based on the advanced states of income and modernization in the rich, industrial countries, and became less satisfied with their traditional cultural and social relations. These aspirations were actually supported, or at least not opposed, by the tacit understanding (until recently) that developing countries could eventually realize the economic growth and materialistic consumption of the advanced countries, if they followed a certain path and had the patience to "catch up" with the advanced countries. The concept of a "gap" arose first in the area of modernization, much before it came to be measured numerically in the area of trade and per capita income.

The same pattern also existed within and among advanced countries. Low income classes aspired to middle income expenditure patterns, and the latter aspired to still higher levels of consumption and material well being.

The steady growth and stability of the economies of the Western countries in the first three decades after the end of World War II, the successful completion of the reconstruction job in war-devastated Europe, the emergence of Japan within a few years as a major industrial power, the quick and steady expansion of world trade and greater specialization of production, the successful launching of a space program which put a man on the moon, and the very optimistic estimates of the benefits of nuclear energy all combined to sustain the poor countries' aspirations of reaching in due course the same "happy" situation.

Simultaneously there was building another current of thinking and action based on identity. Colonies wanted political independence (and got it) to realize national identity. European countries, already independent for many decades, started to feel the need to assert their identity vis-à-vis the two superpowers to the east and west. Within nations, ethnic and geographical regions pressed claims for greater autonomy and decentralization, local governments, and cultural identity and recognition. These movements may have had their origins in the greater maturity of social groups or, which is not so very different, in the weakening of central authority and a growing desire to share power and benefits in wider circles.

National economic systems, especially in the developing countries, were not able to serve the two currents simultaneously. The international system suffered the same difficulties in recognizing national identities and sovereignty and at the same time maintaining increased growth and better distribution of income. It is not difficult to point to a variety of examples from countries at different economic levels under different political systems.

The conflicts aroused by higher expectations and lack of organization (a description which may outline the two currents) may be aggravated by economic limitations of resources and production or by maldistribution of incomes. It is also not inconceivable that economic and financial difficulties may be in part due to those contradictory phenomena. Here one finds a combination and interaction of social, political, economic, and psychological factors at local, national, and international levels.

Tensions, conflicts, shortcomings, and dynamic social forces in general are not new to societies. They are perhaps the genesis of technological development, economic growth, and social and political reorganization. What is new, to a certain extent, is that these conflicts inside practically all societies are now somehow better apprehended by a wider circle of interested participants at all levels within societies and between them. New features appear—for example, the combination of stagnation and inflation, higher levels of unemployment in the advanced countries while high standards of living persist even among some of the unemployed, or greater accumulated debts and chronic balance of payments deficits in some developing countries together with continuous positive growth, sometimes at high levels.

Governments in the advanced countries do not seem to lack the knowledge or the experience to identify and meet problems, yet they seem unable or unwilling to face problems squarely, tending always to follow short-term, partial, "easy" solutions. The governments of the developing countries do not fare any better, but they may be excused by their lack of knowledge or experience, other reasons notwithstanding. This general timidity of authorities in facing problems is in many cases explained away by the need to keep an eye on public opinion and current political expediencies. This cannot be a satisfactory explanation. The problems, if real, will not be made any the less dangerous by averting or ignoring them. Political success in the next election or popularity with the electorate will not avoid the eventual need to face the main issues. The advanced countries have the financial, economic, and intellectual resources to endure crises, to live with them. On the other hand, the complex machinery of modern industrial societies can sustain serious damage if a hitch develops in a small part of it. The developing countries do not have the economic strength to stand against bad crops, falling prices of exports, or increasing prices of imports, but living at a much lower level, they may find in centuries-old traditions and concepts the solace to develop patience to overcome material and economic difficulties.

## Global Problems

The fact that many problems are no longer limited to one country or group of countries but have instead become global problems is in itself evidence of the timidity of authority in handling major questions by direct and unevasive solutions.

Let us take the question of poverty. There have always been poor people, frequently famines. Can one now simply shrug his shoulders and say, "So what—there are poor people even in the rich countries"? This is true, but such neglect is becoming more and more unacceptable to those who are suffering from poverty and to those who for humanistic or political reasons wish to alleviate it. Per capita income in developing countries as a proportion of that in developed countries stayed fairly constant at around 7-8 percent during the last 25 years. The relative gap between the rich and the poor may not have increased much. What is more important, however, is that the absolute gap between average per capita incomes in the two groups more than doubled, in constant dollars, from U.S. $2191 in 1950 to $4839 in 1975 (Morawetz 1977, p. 26). Some developing countries have in those 25 years realized rates of economic growth larger than the rates of the advanced countries. If these rates were assumed to continue in the future, one could calculate how many years it would take those developing countries to "catch up" with the advanced countries. The results are startling. In the case of some oil-exporting countries and some small countries in East Asia that benefitted from Vietnam expenditures and rapid Japanese growth, the period ranges between 14 and 75 years. For many of the developing countries, the period ranges between 200 and 600 years (Morawetz 1977, table 9).

The 1976 average per capita income in the United States, Sweden, or Switzerland was about $8000; the corresponding figures for India and Bangladesh were $150 and $110, respectively (World Bank 1978, Annex table 1). The disparity numerically is about 70:1. The gap between the rich and the poor, a gap that has been increasing for 100 to 150 years, continues to widen even if income figures are corrected to take into account greater purchasing power in the lower income countries. The poor seem to suffer not only because of the rich in other countries but also because of the policies of the rich minority within their countries. Poverty seems to be spreading and may reach considerable proportions, especially in the heavily populated countries of southern Asia. Efforts to solve problems of extreme poverty must be exercised in the first place by the countries concerned, but most likely external assistance and appropriate changes will also be required from the rest of the world. The spread of abject poverty to increasing numbers of people in the developing countries may endanger world peace and security. All of these arguments and others make the question of poverty and related proposals for income transfer a global problem to be discussed and acted upon at the international level as well as national levels. A recent study by the World Bank concludes: "Given the obstacles they face, elimination of absolute poverty in the Low Income countries by the end of this century seems impossible. A more realistic target would be to reduce the proportions of their populations living in poverty to about 15 to 20 percent by the year 2000, which would still leave nearly 400 million people in absolute poverty" (World Bank 1978, pp. 33–34).

The global nature of problems previously considered local or national matters is becoming apparent in areas other than poverty, of course. The most prominent examples include food, energy, raw materials, environment, transnational enterprises, industrialization and the international division of labor, technology transfer, and the wealth of the seabed. In addition, there are inherently international problems such as the monetary system or international trade, transport, and communication.

The global status of problems does not take them completely out of the concern of individual countries—national actions will continue to be the most immediate and effective—but attacks on these problems must be increasingly harmonized and may sometimes need to be guided or controlled through international consultation, agreement, or binding decisions. Appropriate international machinery and institutions and new principles for relations among different countries and peoples will be requisite. In short, the increasingly global aspect of problems manifests increasing interdependence among nations and the consequent emergence of institutions, rules, and value systems appropriate to those changing conditions.

The world must obviously encounter these requirements in a series of changes and modulations by various countries. One cannot expect that all concerned will agree immediately about any proposed solution or plan of action. There will always be conflicts of interest and candid differences in viewpoints and beliefs. The interaction of conflicting opinions and the interplay of power centers, together with the experiences gained from current happenings, may lead eventually to necessary changes.

In the very specific case when power to act is highly concentrated, a few countries or organizations can actually establish the system they desire; creating a new order becomes a relatively simple and straightforward operation, clearly identified and most likely enforced by the powers which gave rise to it. One such case was the "order" established after the second world war. The leading countries among the victorious allies were few in number, and in the economic and financial fields the United States and the United Kingdom predominated. The composite UN system was proposed and negotiated by many countries, including the USSR, but the Bretton Woods organizations and their working rules were, in fact, the result of consultations and agreements among a few countries.

In the current world situation, the successive actions and consultations required to handle global problems are likely to involve many participating countries whose opinions and interests vary considerably. The division of the world into East and West or North and South, a simplification of convenience, does not eliminate the substantial differences among individual countries within the same group or the need for pluralistic negotiations among a large number of participants.

## Concepts, Declarations, and Actions (or Inactions)

Many present activities for testing and changing the world order (in its economic, political, cultural, social, and other aspects) take place within the UN system and the Bretton Woods agencies simply because these were the organizations established when the last major reshaping of the world order took place in 1945. They also offer a meeting place for representatives from all member countries. Furthermore, by the nature of their policies and programs, the UN and its agencies have put together considerable data and experience about global problems. These bodies' open discussions and the type of "resolutions" authorized by their constitutions create an impression that deliberation and declaration are not effective enough. Any such shortcoming is not the fault of the organizations themselves but rather a limitation in the structure drafted and approved by member governments. There is a limited binding commitment in many of these declarations, yet their political and moral values are much greater.

In addition to the regular functioning of the many intergovernmental and nongovernmental agencies, special conferences and meetings discuss specific questions. In recent years the UN has convened many such conferences on food, population, environment, industrialization, trade and development, science and technology, water resources, women, habitat, and cooperation among developing countries.

Uri (1976, pp. 162–63) notes that " . . . nothing ample enough will be achieved as long as in the United Nations the emphasis remains on 'nations' rather than on 'united'; as long as the debates continue in terms of a transfer of power which is unacceptable to some and inaccessible to others; as long as countries will not in their daily dealings prove really aware of their interdependence, even in their relations with the weakest of them." Cleveland (1977, p. 2) believes that "today, the U.N. reflects quite accurately the political turmoil and tensions of a world in deep transition. But as presently organized and used by its members, it is ill-adapted to arrange the new bargains that are urgently needed, or for getting decisions made on a lengthening list of new global issues." Brown (1973, pp. 303–4) considers that "the United Nations was initially conceived as a global community of nations, the first stage of a world government. After twenty-five years, most observers agree the United Nations has not lived up to its expectations. . . . After the specialized agencies were established in the burst of internationalism during the immediate postwar years, the process essentially came to a halt, but the emergence of problems requiring supranational solutions did not. The circumstances in which we now find ourselves demand that we begin working toward creation of a second generation of supranational institutions." These opinions obviously express some doubts about the efficiency of the UN system and other components of the international machinery of consultation and negotiation, but it is hoped that the aim of criticism in all cases is to strengthen and improve efficacy and not to bring down these organs or to go back to bilateral mechanisms: "If the period following the Second World War was largely the world of the rich, today's world is predominantly the world of the poor. . . . We must choose to focus our attention on the UN system: it may be weak and imperfect yet it remains the only machinery with the potential for constructing a fairer world" (Tinbergen 1976, pp. 42–43).

The world of "resolutions and declarations" is not all. In the course of the dialogs or even the series of monologs heard, new concepts are actually contemplated and expressed. To be sure, the specialists are not generally or readily found in agreement about analysis, statistics, or theories, whether related to global strategy of peace, the widening gap of income and prosperity between the rich and the poor of the world, or other issues. Many studies are ideologically or nationally biased; this is not to say they are not serious or honest. Conflicting opinions can nonetheless lead to a minimum of agreement or at least to a shaking of underlying assumptions and beliefs. The international debate about global problems within the UN and elsewhere is indeed useful in clarifying issues, inviting theses and antitheses, and seeking consensus about certain principles (if not always actions).

These debates reveal different readings of past experience, even if the experience is as fresh as a decade or two or a day or two. It becomes obvious that "forecasting" the future is subject to widely diverging conclusions and opinions. Disparities will be further accentuated by biases and interests which consciously or subconsciously select those estimates which fit. It is a feature of recent years that many forecasts are made; some are published, but many more are not widely known. This multiplicity of forecasts is a reflection of the quick pace of change and the increasing interrelations among the parameters and other factors that enter into forecasting. All decision makers in one way or another are constantly reading the past, assaying the present, and judging the future. This is how they decide, on the basis of their study and in line with their preferences, objectives and values. An inevitable uncertainty may discourage a decision maker from proceeding on a certain course of action in hopes that situations may not materialize, but this same decision maker in the meantime will find it foolish to leave himself unprepared for such eventualities. Consequently a double track policy is devised to act in one direction but to stay alert to any change in the other direction.

With the pace of change and complexity on the world scene, events must be anticipated or even, if possible, manipulated. The "field" or the "market" becomes less capable of giving the right signals fast enough; many decision makers are increasingly "surprised" by unanticipated events. According to some opinion, institutions have not been sensitive enough to the trends they were supposed to discover and alert others about. Schmidt (1974) in the wake of the oil price increases wrote: "At this present stage there can hardly be any doubt that, long before the explosive rise in the prices of almost all raw materials, international economic policy was moving toward a critical phase. . . . Whereas, on the one hand, the world economy was experiencing a fantastic boom, there was, on the other hand, growing uneasiness about the institutions, particularly the slowness with which they were adapting to changing conditions, to new tasks and objectives. . . . The crisis toward which the world economy was moving was not so much one of production as a crisis of its institutions in structural respects."

Yet institutions like the UN and IMF are composed of government representatives. Most of the inertia of these bodies is really the result of national governments' failure to act in the face of mounting problems. The blame can be diplomatically and easily transferred to institutions, but it is the timidity referred to above, or at best the double track policy of not believing an undesirable prognosis and acting on the best and most optimistic assumptions while taking halfhearted protective measures against adverse developments, that is really responsible.

A rational sequential approach to global problems might convoke discussions and dialogs, develop new concepts and principles, agree in general to assessments, and make policy declarations. Programs of action to realize desired results would then be devised. In fact, all of these stages and steps do take place but not always in a "logical" order. A crisis shocks, a hasty action is taken. Sometimes it is an overreaction or a superficial and face-saving reaction. Then discussions start, and many ideas, explanations, interpretations, and statistics are advanced. In this confusion, transitory cyclic features are sometimes not easily distinguished from long-term basic trends. Questions of structural change are not distinguished from symptoms of underlying causes. In a situation of crisis, the blame is thrown politically on the easiest scapegoat available. The pressure of time demands action without much deliberation. When the crisis apparently passes, relaxation and complacency may set in; again there will be no need for deliberation. In this manner, the rationale of short-term decisions and short-sighted partisan political objectives may prevail, despite an inevitable divergence of views and uncertainty of forecasts, over rational and careful examination, assessment, and planning.

This is far too often the attitude and the process in many current decisions—or rather indecisions—about building a new economic and social order to meet dire needs of the poor countries and peoples and to avert much more serious consequences likely to arise for all countries, rich and poor.

The origins of the "recent" global energy problem came many years before the subject of energy attracted dramatic attention in 1973. Food shortages, depletion of food reserves, and increases of food demand in the world market because of large purchases by China and the Soviet Union all arose across many years before drought hit the Sahel countries and drew world attention to food problems, especially within the UN system. One can trace similar unfoldings of events that led to "recent crises" in the monetary system.

The scholar in these circumstances has no course but to continue studying and examining problems, without diversion by frantic overreactions in time of crisis or by the jeering and neglect of the complacent when the storm passes.

## The New World Order

"The new world order" is becoming, as usual in many other instances, a catchword thrown here and there and expected to go soon out of fashion. The term may disappear, but the underlying problems are not going to vanish because of that. These problems, if nothing adequate is done about them, will remain, and their consequences will appear in due course.

It seems appropriate here to enumerate briefly the persistent "issues" subsumed under the general term *world order*. Tinbergen (1976) and his international group of co-workers provide a framework both convenient and comprehensive. This sketch of the issues, and of the proposals and prospects for moving toward a "new order," will rely to a considerable degree on the Tinbergen report.

Part I of the report identified the main problem areas for a new international order:

| | |
|---|---|
| the armaments race | natural resources and energy |
| population | science and technology |
| food | industrialization |
| human settlements | transnational enterprises |
| human environments | the oceans |
| international monetary and | outer space |
|    trading systems | planetary interdependencies |
| concessional assistance | |

Part II of the Tinbergen report treats the architecture of a new international order, strategies for initiating a process of planned change, and methods of sustaining and steering that change.

Part III of the Tinbergen report offers proposals for action in ten different areas that correspond rather closely with the set of problem areas listed above and concludes, by way of illustration, with proposals for three "packages" for international discussion and negotiation. It was felt that besides separate and specific treatment of each topic in the international order by appropriate institutions, there were major core questions which combine many topics of interest to all nations rich and poor and which thus demand a global approach. A "bargaining approach" was deemed the most sensible, considering the present state of world affairs—providing that measures can be taken to realize a more equitable power structure between rich and poor nations. Steps toward that equitability (difficult jobs in themselves) include full resource sovereignty and increased processing of raw materials by producing states, establishment of producers' and exporters' associations, and binding codes of conduct for technology transfer and transnational enterprises, among others (see Tinbergen 1976, pp. 179–80).

## Removing Income Inequities

The first of these package proposals for comprehensive negotiation, as identified in the Tinbergen report, is aimed at removing gross inequities in the distribution of world income and economic opportunities by special attention to the problems of the poorest nations left behind in the process of development and by measures to ensure that the poorest 40 percent of the population in the developing countries gets a fair share in whatever development and economic growth do take place. World Bank President Robert McNamara has repeatedly stressed that the benefits from development projects in the developing countries do not "trickle down" to lower income groups and that new projects which directly benefit the poor in the developing countries must be devised. Between 1950 and 1975 the income disparities between the poor and the rich nations increased in terms of real buying power, and disparities between the poorest nations and the rest of the Third World countries have also increased (Morawetz 1977). The essential objective of a compact against poverty should be to provide at least the minimum human needs for those poor millions through their own efforts, as well as through adequate help by the international community. It has been estimated that a flow of U.S. $10–12 billion per year for the next ten years, together with an appropriate set of domestic programs, policies, and institutional changes, will be sufficient to alleviate the worst forms of poverty by the mid-1980s (Tinbergen 1976, p. 182).

## Harmonious Global Growth

The Tinbergen report's second package proposal for international bargaining seeks to avoid a return to the ruinous inflation, interruptions, and stagnations in global economic growth of recent years. Fundamental reforms are required in the monetary system so that liquidity is not created in an unplanned fashion with almost complete disregard for the financial status of Third World countries. Monetary reform is tied to the control of inflation, the strengthening of the international reserve currency, the damping of fluctuations in prices and markets of primary products, and the defense of the world economic system from unilateral and uncoordinated national decisions.

In the longer run, global harmonization would require coordination of growth patterns and development strategies. It might be incidentally noted that the major Western industrial countries have in the last few years held a number of summit meetings to coordinate their chief economic policies and that the OECD secretariat has submitted estimates and targets for the growth of the 24 OECD member states. What is of interest here is that the Western countries have among themselves established a machinery, a series of studies, and a potential program of economic harmonization. Eventually such a procedure, with due modification and adjustment, could become global and could help to ensure the participation of the poor nations in harmonious global growth.

Another example of a possible start of harmonious global growth is the international machinery, institutions, and programs established in the area of food sufficiency and security. An ultimate global balance between food and population is the kind of objective that can form an important core for further international discussions and agreements on an expanding range of subjects.

### Global Planning and Management of Resources

The third package proposal that the Tinbergen report considers suitable for international negotiation involves controversial and relatively remote prospects—global planning and the management of the world's resources.

The first package proposal—to aid the poorest countries—is the most urgent. There is no difference in principle about it, and the total external resources required from the world community are manageable. The second proposal—harmonious global growth—faces many obstacles and a long, complex bargaining process, but beginnings have, perhaps, been made among the advanced countries. When it comes to economic harmonization between Third World and industrial countries, little has yet been done except in detached areas of aid, industrial preferences, debt negotiations, commodity agreements, and technology. Most of these negotiations are conducted through UN multilateral agencies and therefore share in the previously discussed defects of the UN system as a whole. The

North-South Conference in Paris, which met for almost two years and finally stalled, did not encourage the developing countries to work outside the UN system in negotiations with the industrial countries. Developing countries' suspicions extended even to the Independent Commission on International Development Issues headed by Willy Brandt, established on the initiative of the World Bank president, and financed independently. It might be concluded that the world community is building some experience and some partial efforts toward harmonious economic policies, although none of them has yet been effective enough on the global level.

The third proposal, on global planning and management of resources, finds precious little agreement or experience, even on the principle itself. Whatever resource planning was done in the past on a global scale was done under the flag of military domination in the colonial periods and under the economic domination of transnational enterprises, financial centers, and imperfect commodity markets in more recent years. At best, many years will elapse before the nucleus of a global planning and resource management system emerges, especially because such a system demands a gradual transfer of some power from nation-states to suitable world organizations. It entails also the progressive growth of a global taxation system, central banking, and a world treasury. It requires a world food system and expansion of institutions to coordinate world trade and the international division of labor. Similar institutions will be required in the fields of energy, management of sea and space resources, and environmental protection. All of those functions are now generally exercised by national governments. Even within the most advanced countries, such functions raise many problems. They are now tackled nationally and solved partially; real resolution, however, may depend on international agreement and global policies.

## Recapitulation of the Issues and Prospects for Action

A vast number of subjects are touched in the resolutions of the UN General Assembly and other bodies on the "new international order." The issues, if further studied, reach far beyond the conventional frontiers of "development" and international cooperation toward the most abstract reflections of philosophy and metaphysics. However, the United Nations Institute for Training and Research (UNITAR) and the Center for Economic and Social Studies of the Third World (CESSTW) in Mexico (May 1978—unpublished) have jointly established a tentative list of 33 core issues which must be examined in an evaluation of obstacles and opportunities for the new order:

1. Development financing and related issues, including:
   Development assistance—the attainment of global targets
   Special drawing rights' link to development aid, and the reform
     of the monetary system
   IMF and World Bank decision making and voting systems
   Transfer of real resources through the IMF and World Bank and
     through regional banks and international agencies
   Exchange rates and reserve currencies
   Third World debates
   Use of funds from disarmament
   Technical assistance and the brain-drain

2. International trade and related issues, including
   Expansion and diversification of Third World trade
   Tariff and nontariff trade barriers
   Reimbursement of duties and taxes applied to exports of develop-
     ing countries
   Invisible trade—increasing the share of Third World countries
   Indexation of prices
   Integrated programs of commodities
   Primary producers' associations
   Buffer stocks

3. Industrialization, technology, and related issues, including
   Redeployment of productive capacities
   Transfer of technology
   Transnational corporations
   Restrictive business practices
   Nationalization of foreign property

4. Food, natural resources, and related issues, including
   International food program
   Sovereignty over natural resources
   Compensation for damages suffered under external domination,
     occupation, and apartheid
   Ocean and seabed resources
   Competitiveness of natural resources vis-à-vis synthetic
     substances
   Waste of natural resources and food

5. Institutional and organizational policies and related issues including
   Free choice of states of domestic systems and foreign relations
   Landlocked, least-developed, and island countries
   Economic and technical cooperation among developing countries
   System of consultations for promoting industrial development of
     Third World countries

Restructuring of the economic and social sectors of the United
Nations

6. Social issues including health, income, employment, education,
housing, environment, child care, women's issues, cultural standards, and qualifications of the work force.

Anyone can obviously add or delete issues or reorganize this list. It is presented as one compendium of the broad issues being handled at the international level by one or quite frequently more than one organization.
Some or all of these issues are also discussed at the regional level and in
many nongovernmental, technical, and professional meetings. There is
an ever-growing body of literature too.

The real world of day-to-day action by governments, individuals, and
organizations is not waiting for the results of all of these deliberations.
Actions are being taken in the normal way every day by decision makers
great and small. These actions are impregnated to a considerable, although not formal, extent by current discussions and recommendations.
There is continuous policy reappraisal affected, directly or indirectly, by
current thinking and events.

One cannot expect that at one moment or some certain time someone
will announce that the "new world order" has come, that it has been accepted or rejected. In this world of pluralistic decision makers internally
and externally linked to other levels of decision making, Uri's view of the
process (1976, p. 163) applies:

Intentions [concerning world order] are reaffirmed each time like litanies in
which the layman is hard put to perceive progress towards agreement which has required so much diplomatic subtlety. One cheerfully underwrites hundreds of principles without ever taking actual steps to translate them into realities.

Action demands an entirely different approach: change should be focused on a
few decisive points which carry along the rest. Linking production plans and population prospects, setting criteria for aid, reforming transnational enterprises,
managing the monetary system, restructuring production, transcending narrow
national markets: all this means fewer, more closely interrelated goals, as well as
more integrated instruments to achieve them.

The three package proposals of the Tinbergen report, the list of issues
of the UNITAR-CEESTW project, and Uri's selected short list plainly
have much in common, even though they were put forward for different
purposes. The economic and financial power concentrated in a small
number of countries gives these countries the opportunity—and the
responsibility—to be in the forefront of action, which may begin by reor-
ganizing international economic and financial machinery, especially the

monetary matters of liquidity, reserve currency, and fluctuating exchange rates. Persistent inflation, appreciable unemployment, stagnation, emerging protectionism, and increasing instability of markets are all signs of the present unhealthy situation. These leading countries will be working in their own immediate interests if they take the right decisions. They will soon discover that they must widen the circle of negotiation and agreement to other industrial countries and to the developing countries. In negotiating with the latter, the objectives will simply not be to stop inflation, reduce unemployment, and maintain a system of exchange rates within the industrial nations. These are problems of the rich. The problems of the poor call for different objectives. In a rational and equitable agreement, the poor should be happy to see the rich economies stable and thriving, but they want their own economies to be strengthened by capital flow, technology, better terms of trade, accessibility to markets, debt relief, a fair share of liquidity, greater mobility of labor, and readjustment of prices to allow them to build their appropriate development in harmony with the advanced countries.

### Monitoring Progress Toward a New Order

The General Assembly of the UN is not the sole body concerned with proposals for a new international order, but it has been for more than 25 years engaged in discussing the world economy in general and the development of the developing countries in particular. Documents adopted by the General Assembly as the "Strategy for the First Decade of Development" of the 1960s and "Strategy for the United Nations Second Development Decade" of the 1970s, especially the latter, have recently been faulted as guides to development because sufficient support from the industrial countries has been lacking, development situations changed markedly after 1973, and developing countries themselves are dissatisfied with the performance of the strategies (Bos 1978). The Economic and Social Council (ECOSOC) of the UN, with the advice of a group of experts forming the Committee of Development Planning, had prepared these earlier strategies for the approval of the General Assembly.

Now, however, the General Assembly itself is also engaged in monitoring progress in implementing its recommendations and plan of action for a new international economic order. A General Assembly resolution of December 1977 established a committee of all member countries to meet between the regular sessions of the General Assembly until 1980, when a special session of the General Assembly will be convened to assess the progress made within the United Nations system in establishing the New International Economic Order and, on the basis of that assessment, to take appropriate action for promoting the development of developing countries and international economic cooperation, including the adoption of the new international development strategy for the 1980s.

The statement of the representative of the European Economic Community (EEC) at the May 1978 meeting held as a result of this 1977 resolution illustrates the hurdles confronting those who have the task of designing a new development strategy for the 1980s: " . . . in the context of global interdependence and of structural changes, the damaging effect of the present uncertainties on the economic recovery had been pointed out. Those uncertainties were largely due to the fact that investment had been hampered by uncertain conditions, and related to uncertainties in the field of energy and to the problems in the field of production and trade of raw materials, disequilibrium in the balance of payments situation and erratic exchange rate fluctuations. An expanding world economy would facilitate the necessary structural adjustment in national economies. It should also enable the developing countries to increase their share in international trade and in world economy with a view to reducing the gap between rich and poor countries. . . . increased stability in the monetary field would be profitable to all countries" (UN 1978).

Remarks of the EEC spokesman advance a familiar position of the industrial countries, one which simply states that the developing countries will also be hurt by stagnation and other difficulties of the industrial countries; therefore the industrial nations in their own interest and in the interests of helping the developing countries (on the side) must work toward economic stability, growth, and progress at home. This is an expression of the "dependence" of the developing countries on the industrial countries. This thesis, in the opinion of the developing countries, is insufficient. What they ask for and need are structural changes which give them a chance to survive, not at the level of today's industrial countries, nor with the Western style of modernization and comfort, but just at the level of securing the minimum human needs for the mass of their populations and maintaining through cultural identity their social cohesion and balanced life. This may require a broad and bold approach to structural factors which currently generate the concentration of income in favor of the rich countries.

The preparation of a new strategy document for development in the 1980s will amplify, clarify, monitor, assess, and implement aspects and elements of the new order, not by any one decision at a certain moment, but gradually through a multiplicity of actions and interactions. Perhaps the idea of a "development decade" will be discarded for a new formula of shorter-term projections and plans, something on the order of the two to four years now used by the OECD for its member countries. Perspectives for the world economy as a whole and for specific sectors or problems over a longer period of 10–20 years might be meshed with these shorter-term plans. It may also be desirable to establish an annual review and update that could lead to "revolving" indicative planning in a simple and practical form, capable of being disaggregated regionally by major groups of countries. Such a design could accommodate targets and instruments of implementation for the 1980 decade; it is unlikely that the procedure of UN "decades" of development will be completely discarded, yet no one wants the momentum toward a comprehensive and radical set of changes—a new economic order—to be lost.

Changes are going on now, within both the industrial countries and the developing countries, at least at the level of recognizing current difficulties and viewpoints of the "other side." New approaches and new ideas about alternative development patterns, radically different from the Western pattern, are emerging. These concepts are not yet fully articulated as plans of action, but they must not be misunderstood as a desire on the part of developing countries to forego industrialization and economic growth or to leave these fields again to the advanced countries in favor of some return to primitive production technologies and a more "humane" development. Growth, no doubt, is wanted, but the question is "growth for whom and growth for what?" The answers—there are certainly more than one—may depend in part on some new features on the international scene, features that may be accentuated before the 1980s arrive.

First there is globality, meaning that the development of the developing countries is likely to be seen as an integrated part of the total problem of the world as a whole. The advanced industrial countries, which for many years to come will represent economically, financially, and technologically the greatest weight in world affairs, are beginning to see difficulties, especially in the monetary system and elsewhere too. The U.S. deficit, for instance, brings much concern to all dollar holders, including industrial countries with balance of payments surpluses and OPEC countries. As holders of increasing amounts of dollars, these countries become identified with support and maintenance of the dollar as an effective reserve currency, although they have no control on the policies of the United States. Indeed, U.S. purchases of machinery and equipment (from other industrial countries) and oil (from OPEC nations) are sustaining a demand that is a necessary and economically healthy demand for the exporting countries.

This example is but one instance of the interlocking situations in the world today. The advanced countries claim that their prosperity and growth (when it is resumed) will also benefit many of their customers in the developing countries which otherwise may find it hard to maintain prices and earnings from their exports to the advanced countries. This is true but not the whole truth. The advanced countries have prospered for decades and centuries, and the developing countries are still struggling. There have been mechanisms and rules by which capital accumulation and benefits of development were not shared "equitably" between the industrial rich and the resource-exporting poor.

Hence the need now to wish the advanced countries every success in their attempts to overcome their difficulties but to insist in the meantime that the system must change. The strategy for the 1980s must include this point, must look at the development of the developing countries as an integral and crucial part of the world economic scene and not merely as a marginal or peripheral problem to be dealt with separately.

A second feature of the international scene is probably destined for "new" recognition in the 1980s: The policies and internal development efforts of many of the developing countries are not beyond reproach. Irregularities, confused policies, and lack of balance in creating incomes and distributing benefits certainly exist. The developing countries have rightly been keen to protect their newly acquired independence and national sovereignty after many decades of foreign domination and economic stagnation. They are fully aware of and even oversensitive about neo-colonialism and economic dependence on the industrial powers and transnational corporations. But in the meantime, if they are justifiably requesting certain changes in international economic relations, even if they are seeking redress of past situations and not new gains, they must put their case in sound economic terms. That case must also be supported by appropriate domestic policies, programs, and attitudes. There are various ways by which this obligation, necessary to gain public confidence and support, can be realized without jeopardy to national sovereignty. A sense of fear and suspicion lingers from periods of domination, but the increasing interdependence among nations calls for new attitudes and rules of cooperation. Negotiation and objective bargaining may help to resolve those fears and meet those new requirements.

The developing countries, by pressing necessity, have had no choice but to use every occasion to plead their case in a manner which could on the face of it appear to be a listing of demands without corresponding responsibilities. The obligations of the developing countries are obligations toward themselves, possibly through regional and other organizations, not in forms that may lead to less confidence and more suspicion. The development strategy for the 1980s may include some stipulations to this effect; the concepts of self-reliance and cooperation among the developing countries probably illustrate the search for patterns of development that are internally appropriate and responsible.

A third feature of the development strategies of the 1980s may well be a new appreciation of the levels or "systems" of power and decision. Intergovernmental discussion and negotiation are now and will continue to be the primary instrument, the first "system" of international thought and agreement. The transnational corporations might, however, be said to represent a second "system" and concerned individuals, research groups, or people's organizations a third "system."

This book and its authors are part of the third system of individuals, institutions, nongovernmental organizations, and peoples—in the North and in the South—whose voices are not generally heard in official meetings and corporate board rooms but who after all will gain or suffer from the decisions by "formal" establishments. Jan Pronk, Minister of Development in the Netherlands, speaking before the UN General Assembly in October 1976 on the strategy of development for the 1980s, said: "We must assign and distribute these tasks in a coherent and logical manner among international secretariats and institutes of research and learning. We may call on the wisest and most experienced among us, teachers and thinkers of today, to advise the world on the future. More than in the 'sixties, the world community has at its disposal a variety of institutes and centres of excellence in developed and developing countries. . . . They must now be set to work" (Dag Hammarskjold Foundation 1978). The Dutch and Norwegian governments are sponsoring programs to draw forth the participation of the extragovernmental sector (the third system) in elaborating and implementing a United Nations development strategy for the 1980s and beyond.

In recent years, elements of this third system have been extremely effective in informing public opinion and influencing decisions on major problems, at first on the social and humanistic questions to which philanthropic groups, churches, and social movements have spoken for many years, then on political questions, environmental problems, and development issues. Extragovernmental, nonbusiness organizations have also been active in many of the recent UN conferences, and in some cases their meetings were more lively and informative (even to official delegations) than the formal conference debates. The topics and organizational structures and procedures of this third system may in the future bring a fresh look and a new stimulus to the formal deliberations of the UN and other development bodies preparing strategy for the 1980s.

A fourth and final feature of the strategies of the 1980s will, it is hoped, be a new and stronger determination to push forward with contractual arrangements and specific agreements on international development strategies and not to stop at declarations and recommendations. Agreements and contractual relations have so far been restricited mainly to formal binding treaties; some of the labor conventions; regulatory agreements and codes for navigation, communication, and safety; and epidemic control. There have also been, of course, the major contractual agreements embodied in the establishment of economic and financial institutions such as the World Bank, IMF, and GATT. The political climate, especially in the legislative bodies of some industrial countries, now seems unfavorable to further codified commitments to the developing countries. This reluctance to enter new forms of international agreement is believed to be a reaction to internal economic difficulties.

As the interdependence of nations grows more obvious, however, reluctance may be overcome by sensible and practical considerations, and opportunities for contractual aid and development agreements may be recognized and used. The EEC has established programs of aid for less-developed areas within member countries and may be contemplating "Marshall-like" plans for the relatively less-developed countries of southern Europe. Contractual development agreements have been established for many years between the EEC and certain developing countries. The political overtones of these two cases are well known. One might also recall the "Alliance for Progress" as a type of commitment which did not succeed completely but perhaps exemplified forms of understanding, guidelines, programs, and plans which go beyond mere generalities and reiteration of lofty principles.

Some items from these four categories of remarks about possible or probable new directions and new strengths in a strategy of development for the 1980s may indeed appear in the planning documents of the UN and other development agencies. But a fundamental question remains about the value of the whole exercise: Can the long step from declarations to productive implementation be made?

### Evolving a Dynamic International Division of Labor

As a sort of illustrative summary case for the move from declaration to implementation, consider the possibility, advisability, and feasibility of evolving a dynamically changing international division of labor in which the developing countries with their increasing populations become more economically active in the world, gain greater participation in regulating international economic relations, and yet maintain their cultural identities in a pattern of development appropriate to their conditions, not a copy of the historical pattern of the present industrial countries. Gradual change should involve growth of international trade, on a competitive basis, in those "footloose" products for which alternative choices of production location exist. Because of the imperfections of internal and international markets and other factors such as cyclic effects, time lags in production/demand response, and the difficulties of transfer and choice of technology, policy intervention would be necessary to guide the process of locating new productive facilities.

At this point one must introduce the effects and requirements of a deliberate strategy of satisfying basic human needs, a strategy of food security, and a strategy of smooth transition in energy supply from oil to other sources. All of these strategies, if accepted, would need to be implemented in the final analysis through investment and industrialization policies, using instruments of the market whenever feasible, in addition to fiscal, trade, and monetary policies. Most likely a degree of direct intervention and some physical controls would be required in many cases. A good share of production would probably be destined for domestic consumption, even within the producing communities; this effect would amount to an increasing degree of self-sufficiency in the basic commodities at the local and national levels. In addition there would be a second category of goods that are marketable internationally under import/export conditions and prices in conformity with international agreements and internal development and economic policies.

In the heavily populated developing countries, a careful labor employment policy might favor intensive technologies in harmony with priorities in production of goods which meet basic human needs. One might want, transitionally, a dual system of technology (Tinbergen 1976) and a dual system of production. The two systems would work side by side with due balance through policy instruments.

The prices of commodities exported to international markets would need to be carefully examined in relation to labor wages. Primary commodities in international trade have had difficulties that have been the subject of long and intensive study, culminating in the latest proposals for an integrated commodity agreement and a common fund. In a limited number of cases, agreements between consumers and producers have been reached, but in general market forces combined with arbitrary decisions of one form or another have brought much fluctuation in both demand for and prices of primary commodities. Because a very large share of the exports of the developing countries are primary commodities, and because development performance is highly dependent on export receipts, most developing countries have had great difficulties in financing their development efforts. (The economies of those industrial countries which are also major producers and exporters of primary commodities can, by appropriate internal policies, absorb the shock of demand/price fluctuations or pass them through the manufacturing process to consumers or importers, thus distributing the burden.)

In the past, the developing countries were advised to reduce their dependencies on single export items and to diversify their exports, reduce imports, and follow a policy of industrialization as an imperative objective of economic growth and development. Under policies of import substitution and maximum processing of natural resources, a small number of developing countries were able to increase the share of manufactured goods in their exports and to establish a strong integrated base for further industrialization. During the last few years, however, the prices of grain and food products, especially meat, have been increasing, so the developing countries are being advised to grow more food and reduce the priority previously accorded to industry. In fact, the developing countries need both food, for security and basic consumption, and industry for domestic and export markets. Local food production must be protected from extreme external fluctuations without loss of the incentives which ensure higher productivity and adequate remuneration to growers. Manufactured products and semiprocessed natural resources, as well as primary raw materials exports, must receive domestically and internationally adequate prices not only with respect to the costs of production but also with respect to prices of similar goods produced in the advanced countries with the same quality. Adequate depletion compensation is also needed in the case of stock resources produced for export.

Furtado (1977) has appraised the need to raise the value of labor in the developing countries through the higher pricing of commodities produced by low wage labor for international marketing:

The theory of international specialization explains that it is good business for Brazil to produce coffee, but teaches us very little about the price at which coffee should be sold in the international market. The parameters to measure the advantage of producing coffee are the living conditions of the rural worker in the subsistence economy. . . . But nothing prevents adding another parameter to isolate the international price of coffee from the influence of the low standard of living of the Brazilian rural population. . . .

In the price formation of mineral products, the cost of labour directly employed is of little importance. But a nonrenewable resource should not be spent oblivious to the consequences for future generations. The fact that those resources can be exploited on the basis of criteria strictly reflecting the interests of private individuals surely constitutes one of the most serious shortcomings of our civilization.

Furtado concludes that for one and the same product produced in a high wage country and a low wage country, the fair international price charged to the consumer in the high income country denies a fair share to the low wage country, the difference in many cases going to capital accumulation and high profits for transnational enterprises.

Furtado's arguments demonstrate that it is of little avail to establish export development policies in the developing countries, whether on the basis of agriculture, minerals, or manufactured goods, without ensuring that an increasing share of the returns due to labor cost accrues to the producing country, especially in the form of rising wages. In simpler words, if labor is cheap, it can attract capital and technology, provided that enough margins are created to accumulate and attract capital, sustain the process of development, and hence gradually raise incomes and wages. Then, to continue being competitive, productivity must also increase. Through such a complete cycle with a fair share to the low wage workers and countries, a revised dynamic international division of labor can lead gradually to a more just and equitable international economy.

The same thesis can be further demonstrated in the case of migrant labor. If wages received in the host country do not allow savings (returned to the country of origin to finance private and national development), then labor migration has no benefit to a developing country, especially because the social costs of training and skill scarcity are considerable. Social dangers to the host country are not insignificant. In short, we must avoid creating, through industrialization or labor migration, a new form of social oppression. On the contrary, industrialization within and labor migration from the developing countries, if properly priced and managed, can lead to mutual advantages to all nations and to real development and cooperation. The advanced countries themselves must undergo a series of adjustments—not just a few imports of fans and shoes from the developing countries but an increase in the technology content of their products and in the productivity of their relatively scarce labor resources, with much of the necessary raw materials coming from the developing countries.

There have been outlined here the factors which could evolve a new international division of labor, expand trade and specialization, handle the problem of unemployment and shortage of capital in the developing countries, and at the same time create a progressive movement toward development in harmony with the industrial countries. These claims seem too tall, too good to be tried. They are advanced to show the intricacy of the problems of development, even if taken only from the economic side.

However, development is not just an economic process of growth, or even of growth and distribution. It is much more than that. Studies of the new world order must also delve deep into questions of values, concepts, and objectives of justice and equity, participation, identity, and human dignity.

To recognize the difficulties of the past and to seek solutions for the future are always justified. To ask merely for change without ensuring that the change will be for the better is foolish. More foolish still is to refuse to discuss the problems or the proposals of change, to stick simply to the power of acquisition and the false hope of permanence. Even the strongest and the richest cannot afford to do that.

## References

Bos, H. H. 1978. "Lessons from DD2 for a New Development Decade." In Anthony J. Dolman and Jan van Ettinger, eds., *Partners in Tomorrow: Strategies for a New International Order.* New York: Dutton.
Brown, Lester. 1973. *World Without Borders.* New York: Vintage.
Cleveland, Harlan. 1977. *The Third Try at World Order: U.S. Policy for an Interdependent World.* New York: Aspen Institute for Humanistic Studies.
Dag Hammarskjold Foundation. 1978. "A United Nations Development Strategy for the 'Eighties and Beyond: Participation of the 'Third System' in Elaboration and Implementation," *Development Dialogue* 1978/1: 106–17.
Falk, Richard A. 1977. "Contending Approaches to World Order," *Journal of International Affairs* 31: 171-98.
Furtado, Celso. 1977. "The New International Economic Order," *CTC Reporter* 1(3): 17, 30.
Keynes, John Maynard. 1936. *The General Theory of Employment Interest and Money.* New York: Harcourt Brace.
Morawetz, David. 1977. *Twenty-five Years of Economic Development 1950 to 1975.* Washington, D.C.: World Bank.
Schmidt, Helmut. 1974. "The Struggle for the World Product," *Foreign Affairs* 52: 437-51.
Tinbergen, Jan, coord. 1976. *RIO—Reshaping the International Order: A Report to the Club of Rome.* New York: Dutton.
UN (United Nations). 1978. "Preliminary Report of the Work of the Jazairy Committee Under General Assembly Resolution 32/174." New York: UN.
Uri, Pierre. 1976. *Development Without Dependence.* New York: Praeger.
World Bank. 1978. *World Development Report, 1978.* New York: Oxford University Press.

# 12 *George Tomeh*

# Interdependence:
# A View from the Third World

This chapter is written from a Third World perspective. The overwhelming majority of writers on the issue of interdependence are Western. They have delved into every aspect of the meaning, history, perception, and desirability of interdependence—its manifold factors and applications —but they have done so almost exclusively from a Western perspective. It is true that "North-South" economic and political relations are being treated more and more often by Western writers and scholars, yet rarely is this done in the context of interdependence with the technical sense given that term in the West. On the contrary, the developing countries are usually explicitly or implicitly excluded from Western applications of the concept. There are some exceptions, and they will be considered, but it is well to emphasize my perspective from the outset as it constitutes the basis of this treatment of interdependence.

International relations are living issues for Third World writers and scholars because many of their countries have witnessed acute international crises in recent times. Furthermore, the peoples of the Third World have shared the common experience of colonization and can still see in their lands the vestiges of colonialism. A great many developing nations have experienced cataclysmic events and waves of human suffering. The Middle East, from the dawn of recorded human history, has been a meeting place of cultures, of devastating wars, of currents and countercurrents which have made it one of the particularly sensitive areas of the world.

With all of this, however, interdependence has remained a concept that applies primarily to Western international relations; it is a relatively new and little-debated concept for writers and internationalists in the Third World. What then does the subject mean to the Third World? Do priorities of the Third World coincide with those of the West, and how? Does a reference to interdependence in a speech at an international gathering by a Third World spokesman carry the same meaning or have the same content that Western statesmen and scholars give to it? Can interdependence adequately describe "North-South" relations—economic, political, and others? Does it have more meaning for relations among governments and peoples within the Third World? Most important, can interdependence as a policy or as a goal be made relevant to the developing countries?

I am convinced that the only way in which a non-Westerner can contribute to the analysis of this important issue, one already dealt with at length by Western scholars, is to consider these kinds of questions and to interpret the reaction of developing countries to the Western concept of interdependence. A full analysis of such an issue, an analysis which attempts to relate the present status of mankind to the past and future and claims to do so in all corners of the world, is an ambitious objective beyond the scope of any single chapter. In a briefer review, the aspects of interdependence that an author chooses to emphasize and the conclusions that he reaches represent his own inner experience. The value of such personal analysis perhaps owes not so much to content as to a thought process by which an author generalizes the concept to some vital international issues. This does not mean that the subjective element takes the upper hand over the objective but simply that subjectivity cannot be overlooked in the study of any issue involving past, present, and future human relationships.

When "interdependence" is invoked, it cannot generate in the mind of the African, the Asian, or the Middle Easterner, in whose lands colonialism left bitter and abiding memories, the same mental associations it invokes for the North American or the European. Nor can it bring the idea of human solidarity that it brings to the North Atlantic community. Nevertheless, in the world in which we live, the developed countries need to understand the developing countries and vice versa. This chapter may perhaps help the European or North American reader see how an individual from the Third World approaches and understands the issue of interdependence at this time in human history. Working our way to genuine interdependence is, among other things, a moral stand, an intellectual approach, and an act of will generated by the common and simple fact of belonging to the human family.

## World "Crises" and the Perception of Interdependence

Our troubled era has been repeatedly described as a time of continuing crises. The records of the United Nations from its inception 30 years ago until today are full of annual references to various crises by world statesmen. The word is often used to describe any problem confronting modern man, be it cultural, economic, political, or environmental. Such warnings are not new. Thinkers have alternated between imaginary and real senses of crises in almost every epoch of history. Our era has not lacked wars: civil, regional, and international; conventional and nonconventional; declared and nondeclared; sophisticated and brutal; but always with their own logic and sad legacy for mankind.

What then are the specific aspects of Third World crises on which our attention should be focused to lead to an understanding of interdependence? A group of international scholars, including members of the Forum of the Third World, prepared and submitted "The Dag Hammarskjold Report" on the eve of the Seventh Special Session of the UN General Assembly in September of 1975. The session was called to resume debate on the New International Economic Order. Their report dealt with Third World crises:

The crisis of development lies in the poverty of the masses of the Third World, as well as that of others, whose needs, even the most basic—food, habitat, health, education—are not met. . . . The international crisis is that of a system of unequal economic relations between a few dominant countries and the majority of dominated countries. The crisis in institutions results from their maladjustment to a world undergoing rapid change. The situation cannot be properly understood, much less transformed, unless it is seen as a whole: in the final analysis, the crises are the result of a system of exploitation which profits a power structure based largely in the industrialized world, although not without annexes in the Third World; ruling "elites" of most countries are both accomplices and rivals at the same time. (Dag Hammarskjold Foundation 1975)

It seems clear that the basic conditions of life stand out as the crisis. In September 1978, Robert McNamara, the President of the World Bank, reviewed the Bank's 1978 development report, which deals with fundamental problems now facing the developing countries and explores the relations of those difficulties to underlying trends in the international economy. "Many of the conclusions the report reaches" he said, "are sobering. One of them is much more than that; it is shocking. Even if the projected—and optimistic—growth rates in the developing world are achieved, some 600 million individuals at the end of the century will remain trapped in absolute poverty. Absolute poverty" he continued, "is a condition of life so characterized by malnutrition, illiteracy, disease, high infant mortality, and low life expectancy as to be beneath any reasonable definition of human decency" (McNamara 1978, pp. 1-2).

McNamara went on to say that "the projection of 600 million absolute poor in the year 2000 does not assume a lack of progress in the remaining years of the century. The reduction in absolute poverty in any country depends on the growth of its GNP, the extent of improvement in its distribution, and the increase in population. Since the population of the developing countries is projected to increase from 2.1 billion in 1975 to 3.5 billion in 2000, a failure to reduce the proportion living in poverty would result in the number increasing from 770 million in 1975 to 1300 million in 2000. Hence the projected reduction to 600 million does represent improvement. But it remains unacceptably high" (McNamara 1978, p. 21; for elaboration see World Bank 1978, p. 33).

Although the World Bank projects increasing flows of governmental and private capital to the developing countries, there are questions about whether such an increase will be adequate. The report emphasized three impediments—excessive population growth, inadequate food production, and growing protectionism.

Other reports from the United Nations and some of its specialized agencies look equally grim. In 1974, for instance, the UN reported that more than 460 million people were victims of acute hunger, by the most conservative estimate. If we widen the definition of hunger to include those who get enough calories but not enough protein or other essential nutrients, the number of hungry people might reach anywhere from one to two billion, and many of these people are young children.

Food prices have recently quadrupled because of famines in sub-Saharan Africa and across the Indian subcontinent, because of grain shortages and the 1971 drop of per capita food production in developing countries, and because of massive purchases of U.S. grain by the Soviet Union in 1972. In 1974 three-fourths of the grain that entered world export markets flowed from the United States. "We control as much of the world's grain exports," wrote Simon (1975), "as the Arabs do of the world's oil exports."

The phenomenon of hunger can hardly be overemphasized. Recent writings on interdependence in the West have focussed on the energy crisis of 1973 and on the assertive stands of the Third World on natural resources and raw materials, particularly after the Sixth Special Session of the General Assembly and its declaration on a New International Economic Order.

Let me affirm now that that declaration on a New International Economic Order was the culmination of a struggle waged by the developing countries within and without the UN since its inception, a struggle waged for a more equitable international order economically, socially, and politically. However, of all the issues since 1970 that have led to an increased perception of interdependence, hunger remains the first in significance not only in the sequence of problems but also in gravity and dimension. In nations, regions, or continents, hunger is a deep political issue; it brings awareness of resources, of their scarcity, of their distribution, and of the world system which tries to bring relief. Soaring food prices after 1970 brought realization to every individual in the developing countries, and equally in the industrial countries, of the interrelatedness of the world food supply: "This was but one piece of rapidly accumulating evidence in the 1970s that supported the idea of interdependence" (Simon 1975, p. 6).

A second problem parallel to hunger also gained in gravity after 1970—the devaluation of the dollar and ensuing inflation. "In the US case the demand that nations hold excess dollars in payment for US obligations contributed to the informal dollar glut which eventually forced a formal devaluation in 1971-1973. In the case of most other countries, the lack of wage restraint and the political need to maintain full employment eventually required devaluation. But devaluation in its turn brought inflation, and an increase of export prices which could only be remedied by further devaluation. The alternative course—price and wage restraint—appeared to be politically impossible. In the United States, these tendencies were obvious as early as the Kennedy Administration. In Britain they attained dominance between 1964-67, and in France at least by 1968" (Rosecrance et al. 1977).

Forecasts of an impending oil shortage and a growing dependence on imports of Middle Eastern oil existed in the United States in the late 1960s, yet the rise in the price of oil in October 1973—long overdue—brought what came to be referred to as the "energy crisis." Scholars now attribute much of the increasing perception of interdependence to the "energy crisis." As of October 1973, the energy problem with its derivative issues permeated all levels of Western thought—economic, financial, industrial, scientific, political, and others. A flood of books, essays, and articles, as well as an ever-growing number of national and international conferences, dealt with all aspects of the energy problem, including "interdependence."

From a Third World perspective, certain ideas emerged. The success of OPEC—an intergovernmental organization whose members were bent on the economic and social development of their peoples—in raising the price of oil was considered in the Third World a turning point in history. But, like all great events, it has had its positive and negative aspects. On the positive side, it showed that a group of developing countries was able to put a stop to exploitation by international cartels and monopolies, represented by the transnational companies and supported by their powerful governments. It awakened Third World countries dependent on export of natural resources as their main source of income to the possibilities of actively asserting their rights and correcting what to them had been an "unfair" and "unjust" world order. It led to the convening of two special sessions of the UN General Assembly in 1974 and 1975. It led to the "North-South Dialog," although that ended in deadlock, as well as to numerous other conferences of the UN and its agencies, the World Bank, and scores of bodies and special committees. It challenged the international financial structure and world trade system, already shaken by the devaluation of the dollar. On the whole, it generated an intense realization of an unavoidable "interconnectedness" between North and South, and in fact among all peoples of the world, and established the pressing need for reforms of institutions to cope with those interconnections.

On the negative side, OPEC's success brought an unceasing campaign of charges and threats against OPEC and its members. OPEC is now, in the Western perception, the exemplary cartel. Virtually all global ills have at times been laid at OPEC's door: the great rise in inflation in 1974, the recession of the industrial nations of 1973-75, the rise in unemployment, the balance of payments deficits of the developing countries and their huge debts, and the subnormal rate of world economic recovery in 1976-78. In spite of repeated rebuttals by OPEC spokesmen and member governments and by some Western analysts, attacks continued to appear in newspaper columns, especially preceding every OPEC meeting (Amuzegar 1977); the price of oil was invariably seen as the root of global woes.

Among the many issues which involve all actors on the international scene in claims and counterclaims, that of inflation is of cardinal importance. It is a problem of deep and major concern not only to economists and planners but equally and more so to every breadwinner and to the masses of the world. Inflation is usually first among the "global woes" attributed to the rise in oil prices, but the attribution is in error. The legacy of two world wars and several lesser but sizable military conflicts has played havoc with the economies of the victorious and defeated nations. Huge expenditures on war have exceeded the normal revenues of governments. Governments have sometimes resorted to deficit spending to gain supremacy over others and to divert their peoples' attention from internal economic crisis. The start of inflation can even be traced to the eve of World War I: "The relatively high interdependence attained in 1913 was shattered by the Great War. In order to finance arms programs, economic ministries sold their foreign assets, indulged in wholesale borrowing and in the printing of money. The ensuing inflation caused a dramatic depreciation of currencies against gold" (Rosecrance et al. 1977). Scholars need to examine the earlier origins of inflation, its sequential growth, and the specific inputs and crises that added to its gravity. The net inflationary impact of oil price increases should be determined in that manner.

This then is the order of issues: "The increased American awareness of interdependence may have resulted from the dollar devaluations of the early 1970s, the explosion of food and raw material prices in 1973, and the oil embargo and price hike in late 1973. What this suggests is that the perception has heightened not only because sensitivity has increased but also because the magnitude of economic disturbances that may affect many countries has become larger" (Solomon and Gault 1977, p. 7).

### The Dimension of Time

It should be pointed out that all these problems have been raised and discussed at length since the establishment of the UN. That organization was expected to bring the world, in the vision of its founders, to the threshold of a "new world order" founded on justice, equity, and the liberation of impoverished man. The UN Charter, its preamble, and its first chapter dealt with "purposes and principles" that solemnly called for "conditions of stability and wellbeing," "higher standards of living," "solutions of international economic, social, health and related problems," and "equal rights of men and women and of nations large and small." The early years of the UN brought to the foreground the complaints of the developing countries, then referred to as "underdeveloped" nations. There is not one issue among those enumerated here, including inflation, which was not raised and discussed by 1950 or before or on which resolutions have not been adopted by the UN General Assembly, ECOSOC and its various committees, and the UN agencies.

In order to better visualize the reactions of the Third World, let us take Resolution 523 (VI) on "Integrated Economic Development and Commercial Agreements," adopted by the UN General Assembly in 1952 when no Third World "tyrannical majority" existed. The General Assembly recognized in this resolution

that the under-developed countries have the right to determine freely the use of their natural resources and that they must utilize such resources in order to be in a better position to further the realization of their plans of economic development in accordance with their national interests, and to further the expansion of the world economy. . . . that the existing sharp increase in the demand for raw materials, including the demand for stock-piling, has resulted in an increase in the prices of a number of raw materials and in fluctuation in the prices of others, has in many cases been accompanied by increased prices and reduced availability of important items of machinery, equipment, consumer goods and industrial raw materials necessary for the development of under-developed countries, has created inflationary pressures and brought about the regulation of prices at different relative levels for different products and has thereby caused or increased the economic difficulties in many of the under-developed countries.

This resolution is based on and affirms previous ECOSOC Resolution No. 341 (XII) of 1951. These two resolutions adopted by two principal bodies of the UN more than 25 years ago affirm the right of developing countries to determine freely the use of their natural resources. The resolutions also deal with the failings of international trade, severe inflation, price fluctuations of raw materials and subsequent losses suffered by the "underdeveloped" countries, the widening gap between the rich and the poor nations, and international finance. They attack the basic economic and social problems with which we are still dealing and which have led to the ever-widening gap between the "center" and the "periphery" in the world order. Both resolutions could be attributed to the Sixth or Seventh Special Sessions of the General Assembly or UNCTAD IV without seeming out of context. The world has not advanced a great deal in offering effective solutions and remedies to "global woes" that existed 30 years ago when the oil producers were getting no more than a dollar per barrel of oil and when no Third World "tyrannical majority" existed at the UN. On the contrary, there was at that time a well-known U.S. "mechanical majority" prevailing at the UN. Generations born with these problems are still struggling and waiting almost hopelessly for a more constructive system of international relations and a better understanding of man by man. Bergsten (1973) summarizes:

Despite the impressive growth rates of the aggregate Third World in the 1960s, unemployment exceeds 20 percent in many countries. The per capita income of the poorest LDC's, which now contain half of the world population, has been growing by only 1.5 percent annually. The gap between the income of the richest 10 to 20 percent and the poorest 20 to 40 percent within many LDC's has been getting wider. There are 100 million more illiterates in the Third World now than 20 years ago, and two-thirds of all children there suffer from malnutrition.

On the one hand, we have the "shocking" poverty of hundreds of millions in developing countries, to use the description of McNamara; on the other are the developed countries with a large power base and drive. Both look at the future but with different historical memories, different motives and expectations, and certainly different attitudes about each other. An inherent situation of instability is bound to lead to conflict. Relations among nations are predicated on the assumption of the UN Charter that they are "equal sovereign states;" however, in reality they are unequal.

Power, not law, still yields the ultimate sanction of action. In such a "system," "the powerful exact what they can, and the weak grant what they must" (Tucker 1977a, p. 4). The concept of a "balance of power," be it economic, financial, or military is applicable to relations among equals, not unequals.

This irreducible fact can serve as a stepping-stone to analysis of both the present and the future of international cooperation. To focus attention on consensus and mutuality, rather than conflict and divisiveness, is to miss the heart of the crisis of international cooperation and the flow of the present international body politic. A synthesis can be achieved and a positive approach made only when the elements of conflict have been scrutinized, grasped, discussed, and resolved.

Natural resources and raw material policies constitute an issue on which debate accompanied the birth of the UN and its specialized agencies. The scramble for these resources, their scarcity, the depletable nature of some of them, and the struggle to keep their flow continuous have led in the past and indeed may lead in the future to wars. These problems, including the relevance of development policies to a system of international cooperation, will remain the focus of national concern for a long time. The argument made by the developing countries thirty years ago is still valid—long-range deterioration in the terms of trade of raw material producing countries is a central feature of their "peripheral" relationship to the industrial "center." The consequences of this acute problem continue to impede development and to aggravate the still widening gap between the "periphery" and the "center" within the developing countries themselves. It is obvious that we face a conflict which we cannot afford to ignore. It is only through a rational, constructive approach to conflict that we can obtain positive results.

## Some Interpretations of Interdependence

An intense search for identification is now going on because of the world's "crises." Structural changes have occurred, and new international and regional institutions have been proposed or established. The developed and developing nations are reviewing their internal and their mutual relations. A groping for a more rational world order conducive to better solutions for the problems of mankind is underway. A consensus exists that this is a period of transition. An increasingly interdependent world has become the new focus for the assessment of international relations and cooperation. *Interdependence* follows *sovereignty, national security, collective security, new world order, alliances, peaceful co-existence, nonalignment,* and other phraseology into international usage; the emphasis in each case, historical or current, depends on the actor and the trend he wants to stress.

As we study interdependence, and as generalizations give way to stricter definitions of the concept, it is necessary to ask whether leaders and scholars of the Third World mean the same thing by interdependence as their counterparts in the West or in the East. What are the alternative interpretations? Is interdependence a doctrine or an interpretation of facts? Is it a means or an end? What are the interrelationships among interdependence, dependence, independence, and co-dependence? What criteria can be established to determine whether interdependence exists?

In trying to answer these questions a subjective difficulty stands in the way: "Our differing attitudes towards interdependence are formed by the differing ways in which we depend on others and others depend on us. In fact, it seems to mean anything one wants it to mean. Interdependence is invoked by some as a virtue and by others as a besetting sin. Its name is spoken in tones of prophesy, injunction, or mortification, depending on the speaker's subjective picture of reality" (U.S. Department of State 1975, p. 2).

In charting our way out of this difficulty, a first distinction in the use of the term can be made. "When used by analytical scholars interdependence focuses on sensitivities of societies and policies to one another, and on the vulnerabilities that patterns of transactions may create. . . . The use of interdependence rhetoric by policymakers is quite different"—by them it is used as a symbol to influence public attitudes—and "overtones of equality are clear, and the plea is for greater cooperation with other governments and greater openness to the world" (Bergsten et al. 1975). The same distinction is also made by Keohane and Nye (1977, p. 7): "Political leaders often use interdependence rhetoric to portray interdependence as a natural necessity, as a fact to which policy (and domestic interest groups) must adjust, rather than as a situation partially created by policy itself. They usually argue that conflicts of interest are reduced by interdependence, and that cooperation alone holds the answer to world problems. . . . For those who wish the United States to retain world leadership, interdependence has become part of the new rhetoric."

One can find in the word's present extended application by advocates of *interdependence* a recurrent and familiar phenomenon in the history of human thought. Some analysts have traced the origins of interdependence to the Roman Empire: "In security as in economic affairs, there has been, with occasional lapses, a continuous trend toward greater interdependence, at least since the Roman Empire. That empire bound a vast area together in a single defense system, in which Roman and local forces both participated; interdependence reached unprecedented and seemingly enduring proportions" (Solomon and Gault 1977, p. 73). The same authors also find a long economic development leading to the concept; they trace the concept of interdependence to the Mercantilist school: "The mercantilists can be said to have had a view of interdependence: to them an increase in wealth (and therefore power) by one country could be achieved only at the expense of the wealth (and power) of other countries. With the development of the concept of 'gains from trade' by Ricardo and later classical economists, the perception of interdependence took on a different aspect. Foreign trade in particular and international economic relations in general were no longer a zero sum game. All countries that engaged in trade were better off than they would have been in the absence of trade" (Solomon and Gault 1977, p. 7). The historical approach to interdependence as a concept and as a policy takes us into realms both theoretical and applied which seem remote from our immediate concern with natural resources and international cooperation. Yet it should be remembered that recent attention to interdependence is the direct result of the shock which the world felt following its realization of natural resource scarcity.

To be more specific, a number of basic issues have emerged which challenge the decision-making powers of contemporary nations and international institutions. These issues include resources, poverty, hunger, food, population, environment, trade, development, international finance, transnational corporations, technology, national security, collective security, the wealth of the seas and the oceans' floors, the law of the seas, military expenditures, and labor migration, to mention only the basic ones. The above problems are referred to as "global problems," and the international community is called upon collectively to save "spaceship earth" and devise "planetary bargains" or "global solutions" for the billions of human beings and their needs.

An enumeration of institutions concerned with these issues conveys a quantitative assessment of the concerned actors and reveals the present complicated world order. The situation involves 160 UN member states; principal UN organs dealing with economic, social, and security matters; at least 50 regional, interregional, and subregional organizations; a hundred major transnational corporations and dozens of nonprofit multinationals, all meeting in 700 intergovernmental conferences and more than 3,000 international meetings a year (Cleveland 1977, p. 9).

In defining interdependence, writers invariably begin by underlining the vagueness of the issue and the imprecise use of the word. Waltz (1970) wrote that "the myth of interdependence both obscures the realities of international politics and asserts a false belief about the conditions that may promote peace." Several years later we find that interdependence is still hard to define.

It has come to stand for virtually any given set of relationships or interactions—past, present, and future—between and among any given number of God's creatures and man's enterprises (U.S. Department of State 1975, p. 2).

The term "interdependence" has so many and varied meanings that it is no longer fully clear what investigators intend to signify when they use the term (Rosecrance et al. 1977).

The term interdependence has become a cliché in the space of only a few years (Solomon and Gault 1977, p. 7).

. . . it is morally ambiguous. It can, for example, be a threat to security (Western Europe's dependence on Arab oil) or an enhancement of security (Western Europe's dependence on the U.S. nuclear umbrella) (Cleveland 1977, p. 12).

The scholar from the Third World is bound to be discouraged when faced with so many negative descriptions of interdependence: "myth," "cliché," "slogan," "ambiguous," "imprecise," all given by American scholars after serious endeavor to analyze the concept.

Gradually, however, positive aspects have begun to emerge. The first and perhaps simplest of these is that interdependence is an advanced institutional and structural framework of relations among nations. In an era when international, regional, and subregional organizations have grown and multiplied, and when international relations are channelled through them, interdependence seems to run parallel to principles enunciated in the UN Charter. The Charter posits 15 fundamentals of international economic relations which include among them "sovereign territorial integrity and political independence of states," "mutual and equitable benefit," "peaceful co-existence," "remedying the injustices which have been brought about by force and which deprive a nation of the natural means necessary for its normal development," and "international cooperation for development." No one can afford to ignore the web of relationships woven by the UN's work over 30 years.

Global interdependencies raise ambiguities and fundamental questions for both scholars and policy makers. Alker et al (1974, 3:1) have listed some of these questions: "What are the relevant subjective and objective trends in international security, political economy, ecology, and community building relations, including their underlying conditions, causes and determinitive structures? . . . Within the realm of governmental policy making, what strategies of interdependence should be considered or advocated involving what actions, by whom, in what order, with what institutional bases?" What are, as a result, the various options open to governments or institutions?

Among early writers on interdependence, Karl Deutsch and Richard Cooper have charted trends in the study of interdependence in the 1950s and 1960s. Deutsch (1957) took the foreign trade of West European countries as a measure to gauge the rise and decline of interdependence in the Western hemisphere and found it in decline in the twentieth century. Cooper (1968; 1972) devoted his studies to the North Atlantic community and also took increased sensitivity to foreign trade as a way to gauge interdependence. Because other writers on the issue have variously agreed or disagreed on Cooper's definition of interdependence, a summary of it is necessary.

For Cooper, economic interdependence refers to the sensitivity of economic transactions between two or more nations to economic developments within those nations. If the value of trade is not sensitive to price and income developments in the two countries, then interdependence is low or negligible, irrespective of how much mutual trade exists between them. Conversely, two nations would be highly interdependent, even if their mutual trade is low, if their transactions are highly sensitive to domestic economic developments in the other, such as changes in prices, taxation, inflation, interest rates, etc. Interdependence implies a two-way sensitivity; one-way sensitivity implies a dependent economy.

The United States is highly sensitive to Europe and Japan, even though total U.S. exports to those areas are very low compared to total U.S. output. Cooper finds that such interdependence, where it exists, is ever growing. It is enhanced by technological advances, in transportation and communication, that increase the speed and the reliability of moving goods, funds, persons, information, and ideas across national boundaries.

The effect of interdependence on national economic policies, according to Cooper, is dissipation of the effectiveness of national autonomy in the pursuit of economic objectives. This kind of interdependence is most prevalent in money and capital markets where central banks attempt to control borrowing within a nation only to be thwarted by domestic borrowers who seek monetary funds abroad. In another case, international business firms and international funds may seek tax havens overseas. As nations become more interdependent, previously fragmented markets become united, even despite national policies aimed at controlling these movements. Interdependence in the industrial nations is an ongoing process; institutions must be constructed to regulate the new relationships rather than to suppress them or their consequences, says Cooper.

Following Deutsch and Cooper, Young was another early writer on interdependence who focused on sensitivities of societies and policies to one another and on the domestic repercussions that such patterns of transaction might create. For him, isolation is the opposite of interdependence: "In this sense, the level of isolation in a system increases as events taking place in any given part of the system have less impact on events occurring in each of the other parts of the system" (Young 1969).

More recent writings on interdependence by Waltz (1970), Rosecrance and Stein (1973), Rosecrance et al. (1977), Haas (1975), Keohane and Nye (1977), Bergsten (1973), Bergsten et al. (1975), Grundy (1976), and others have tried to correct or add to Cooper's basic definition of sensitivities of societies and policies to one another.

Contradictions and opposing views are still to be found—does the increase in the volume of trade, investments, commodity exchange, flow of managerial personnel, communication, and transportation really contribute to an increase of interdependence or to an increase of dependence? Do such increases strengthen the forces for peace among nations or, on the contrary, bring circumstances more conducive to war? Do they indicate the existence of a crisis or the absence of it? Many arguments for or against either stand are to be found. We have already noted how different definitions of economic interdependence can be contradictory and can, consequently, influence political trends. Such conflicting views were noted by Wright, who comments: "To some the broadening of international trade, evidence of interdependence, means economic vulnerability to be combatted by every variety of artificial barrier—tariffs, quotas, embargoes, exchange controls, etc.—while to others such trade means an economic division of labor, the essential basis for maintaining and increasing the welfare of every people. The economic condition of the world becomes a source of war or of prosperity according as one envisages it through the glasses of totalitarian sovereignty or of an international order" (Wright 1965, pp. 366–67, quoted by Alker et al. 1974, 1:44).

Interdependence does not necessarily mean symmetrical relations. Several writers, including for example Keohane and Nye (1977), have emphasized aspects of asymmetry. Under this notion interdependence need not imply mutual benefit and might imply the opposite. "Conceptually, interdependence is best defined as a two-way dependence between states or enterprises possessing things of value to others and thus able to indulge or threaten each other with those benefits" (Alker et al. 1974, 1:4).

## Relevance of Interdependence to the Third World

Writings on the Third World and North-South relations in the context of economic development and international cooperation seem to fall into four categories. The first includes those which often seem to consider

Third World peoples as belonging to an altogether lower system of culture, the nature of which sets those people apart. They are looked upon as masses on the margin of history, perhaps even an impediment to the progress of Western culture and civilization.

Morgenthau (1975), in a neo-colonialist approach, sees relations among nations exclusively as power relations: "Many of those [oil-exporting] states are states only by way of what you might call semantic courtesy. . . . It is the oil which all of a sudden has made those plots on the map which we call states important and even powerful factors in world politics." In bygone days of gunboat diplomacy, he notes, consumers could keep the price low through colonial arrangements and the control of consumption, but now, he says, "A state which is powerless in all other respects, which is a nonentity in terms of traditional power, can exert enormous and under certain conditions even decisive power over nations which have all the implements of power at their disposal except one— deposits of oil. . . . The inhabitants of many of these so-called nations count in the hundreds of thousands or even below, and their standard of living is extremely low. Thus, we are dealing here with extremely small orders of quantity. . . . the West is morally disarmed when it considers defending its interests through military means against encroachments by so-called developing nations," says Morgenthau, but "I do not exclude the possibility of military action to rectify this asymmetry. . . . "

To others of this school, law seems to be what the powerful can impose on the weak. International law is comprised of only a few fragile covenants. Diaz-Alejandro (1975) notes Irving Kristol's view (*Wall Street Journal* 13 December 1972) that "gunboats are as necessary for international order as police cars are for domestic order. Smaller nations are not really worried about American atom bombs any more than the Mafia is. And smaller nations are not going to behave reasonably—with a decent respect for the interests of others, including the great powers—unless it is costly to them to behave unreasonably."

A few years later, Kristol (*Wall Street Journal* 17 July 1975) asked no gratitude as a result of the "more affluent being charitable to the poor," but, he said, "when the poor start 'mau-mauing' their actual or potential benefactors, when they begin vilifying them, insulting them, demanding as of right what it is not their right to demand—then one's sense of self-respect may properly take precedence over one's self-imposed humanitarian obligations" (quoted in Hansen 1976, p. 42).

Tucker, who has advocated military occupation of Arab oil fields, deplores the OPEC action by "certain peripheral countries" against the "center" (1977b) and, as to interdependence, replies (1977a, p. 53), "in place of a world in which the hierarchical ordering of states seemed natural and inevitable, interdependence holds out the promise—as another sanguine analyst puts it—of 'a world in which nobody is in charge.'"

The list could be lengthened, but the above citations convey their message in a very direct manner. They constitute a sad reflection on the attitude of man toward man in these last decades of the twentieth century.

A second category of writings on the Third World and North-South relations includes those which study interdependence exclusively as it exists and develops among the industrial countries of Western Europe, the United States, and Japan. Cooper (1968) devotes himself to the North Atlantic community and its economic integration. Keohane and Nye (1977) analyze the relations of the United States with Canada and Australia and take the financial and oceanic issues of these countries as case studies in their analysis of complex interdependence. Rosecrance et al. (1977) analyze economic relations of the United States with six OECD countries and conclude by stating clearly that their investigation of interdependence was confined to "developed nations." Here again, examples could be multiplied to include the majority of American writers on interdependence. Interested people from the Third World, in pursuing the study of interdependence, are bound to question how and where the developing countries fit in this analysis, and they are bound to conclude that their role is marginal to the issue.

There are, however, at least two exceptions. Alker et al. (1974) in collaboration with an Arab scholar, devote a chapter in their second volume to interdependence among Arab countries of the Middle East. Solomon and Gault (1977) do include a two-page summary on "North-South Economic Relations," trade and financial, in an agenda for research.

A third category of writings includes those which state clearly that analysis of interdependence conceptually excludes Third World countries because of institutional differences and dissimilarity of objectives. Cooper (1972), for instance, states that " . . . throughout this discussion the less developed countries have been largely excluded" because economic interdependence among the developed countries is moving so rapidly, in his view, that it creates " . . . a common range of problems between those with broadly similar objectives and institutional set-ups and therefore calls for common and often collectively agreed solutions."

Young (1969) argues that interdependence is higher among the industrial countries of the North Atlantic than it is among the nations of the Third World. To him, higher interdependence levels will mean increasing allocation of resources to accomplish foreign policy objectives, system transformation, and functional specialization among units to ensure maintenance of the system. Waltz (1970) affirms that the inequality of nations produces a condition of equilibrium at a low level of interdependence.

Rosecrance and Stein (1973) adopt, among many indicators of interdependence, the similarity of problems which political elites in the West face, including economic (unemployment, inflation, taxes) and governmental (resentful electorates, interest groups, varied political power centers) problems. Communications have rendered ideological guidelines obsolete, according to Rosecrance and Stein, and political elites instead depend on each other to share experiences, problems, and expertise in order to be better able to conduct the affairs of state. Ball's (1974) concept of trilateralism applies to a tripartite stand of Western Europe, North America, and Japan against OPEC. Saddy, a Third World scholar, has in a forthcoming article also advanced an argument about the irrelevance of the Western concept of interdependence to the Third World.

It would be a hasty conclusion and an indulgence in self-deceit if Third World countries thought that the industrial nations' dependence on developing countries' natural resources, including oil, has made all nations interdependent. Western writers on interdependence probably need to explain to others in a more convincing manner how to interpret correctly those analyses of interdependence which seem to propound an exclusively Western concept of a "rich men's club."

A fourth and final category of writings on the Third World and North-South relations includes those which can be said to form a counterweight in American and West European thinking to the three trends described above. Its representatives have argued the case of the South vis-à-vis the North. Within this school two distinctions can be made. The first subcategory involves those authors who have analyzed North-South relations specifically within the context of interdependence. Diaz-Alejandro (1975) presents a framework for viewing North-South economic relations, and his ". . . primary point of departure is the viewpoint of the South as it faces the whole range of its relationships with the North." Although he allows that the basic units of analysis are world financial, commodity, and labor markets, he also believes that international interdependence is a matter of political will and not merely economic determinism; economic factors are made or unmade by social and political systems and do not arise spontaneously and inevitably out of economic necessity. Which markets are encouraged and which are repressed depends on political decisions, both national and international. At the same time, however, certain technical difficulties preclude the creation of an international market without heavy social costs; other mechanisms must be used in order to attain international interdependence. The purpose of his work, says Diaz-Alejandro, is to search for mechanisms to handle international interdependence in a way compatible with the pursuits of national goals by developing countries. He finds that commodity trade, as an example of interdependence, can operate under the conditions of open and competitive markets, rather than under the existing Western protective barriers and hegemony over natural resources. When free trade is realized, economic interaction between developing and developed countries can operate under conditions of economic efficiency while maintaining unintrusiveness, reversibility, and decomposibility of arrangements. This form of interdependence has not yet appeared.

Furtado (1973) also speaks directly to interdependence: "Underdevelopment was originally characteristic of economies in which an increase in productivity was largely the result of reallocation of resources aimed at obtaining static comparative advantages in international trade. Changes in demand, on a global level, opened the way to significant increases." He advocates the reallocation of resources in order to arrive at a new comparative advantage in trade as a prerequisite for adequate development. External dependence arises when developing countries specialize only in those products that the "central" economy requires or those products that satisfy the acquired tastes of developing country elites with Western-oriented consumption patterns.

Brown-John (1976) analyzes North-South relations under the assumption that the inhabitants of the world have equal claims to the earth's resources, which are increasingly becoming the single most important theme in the relationship of states. Economic development cannot be assured in an unstable market system such as the existing one, he says, but only in a hypothetical future condition under an international regulatory system other than pure market factors. Regulatory regimes, he suggests, find their place within the context of international agreements because "the dynamics of resource allocation ultimately are of a political nature." For Brown-John, interdependence involves linked concepts of dependence, sovereignty, ownership, and four individual relationships of coercion, manipulation, persuasion, and cooperation (independent variables associated with absorption capacity). The author's approach is certainly a most constructive one. Brown (1972), Goulet (1976), ul-Haq (1976), Johnson (1977), Hansen (1976), and Erb and Kallab (1975) are others who specifically analyze North-South relations within the context of interdependence.

The second subcategory of the "counterweight" school involves those authors who analyze North-South relations in the context of a global approach and, while doing so, raise issues associated with interdependence. Myrdal (1968; 1971) and Meadows et al. (1972) describe North-South relations in depth and warn of danger to the whole world if imbalances between North and South are not redressed. In the words of Meadows et al. (1972, p. 195), "World equilibrium can become a reality only if the lot of the so-called developing countries is substantially improved, both in absolute terms and relative to the economically developed nations, and we affirm that this improvement can be achieved only through a global strategy. Short of a world effort, today's already explosive gaps and inequalities will continue to grow larger."

The studies by Fishlow et al. (1978) constitute one of the strongest presentations of the case of the South. Fishlow and his co-authors recognize that the assumptions, policies, and institutions dominant in the past 30 years are no longer adequate. They emphasize the conservative nature of the South's economic demands, basically concepts of international economic relations with mutual benefits in trade and foreign investment. Fishlow et al. also recognize, however, that the reforms they propose may raise serious issues of feasibility. The elites now governing some countries of the South are often "conservative reformists" satisfied with the existing world economic system. The North will not readily accept any obligatory international rules governing transnational enterprises or transfer of technology. Many countries of the South will, on the other hand, resist any policy of the North if it does not include large resource transfers.

In a "basic human needs" strategy, for example, the main problem is financial. One estimate put forward contends that absolute poverty could be ended within 10 to 15 years at a cost of $125 billion (in 1973 dollars); the World Bank has estimated that a 2 percent annual transfer from the upper classes to the bottom 40 percent of the populations of the developing countries could finance the goals of this strategy over a 25-year period. The main obstacle for realizing this sort of financing, of course, lies in existing political systems based on power play.

## A Third World Pragmatic Approach to Interdependence

Some Third World views of interdependence as a policy are found in declarations issued through the UN, especially since 1973: the Declarations of the VI and VII Special Sessions of the General Assembly in 1974–75 on the New International Economic Order; the Charter of Economic Rights and Duties of 1974; the nonaligned countries' official declarations at the Algiers, Lima, and Dakar meetings in 1975; and the Declaration of the Foreign Ministers of the "Group of 77" at the UN in New York in 1977. This enumeration is by no means exhaustive. All these declarations have the following in common:

1. They refer to "interdependence" and identify it with the New International Economic Order, which—according to the Group of 77 declaration of 1977—"should be genuinely shared by all countries

and concerned efforts for its achievement should be undertaken through cooperation between developed and developing countries, and on the principles of equity and sovereign equality."

2. They identify seven basic issues of the New International Economic Order, trade of primary commodities being first among them.
3. They stress negotiations with the developed countries through collective bargaining and so imply accommodation by means of negotiation between rich and poor.

However, the CIEC meetings (the "North-South Dialog") ended in failure, and terms such as "negotiation" and "confrontation" must be qualified. These two terms may be inadequate when carefully analyzed against a background of built-in inequalities. Negotiations between North and South, with the latter lacking bargaining power, have led to no tangible results. This absence of meaningful negotiations means that the international crisis that began with the eclipse of colonialism and the emergence of developing nation-states with built-in inequalities is still with us.

In the meantime, any policy option that would go some way toward mitigating inequalities will be welcome. In this respect, the purpose of any effective action on the international level, transnational company issues notwithstanding, would be:

1. To work toward restructuring the character of world trade in order to achieve greater diffusion of some of the dynamic benefits associated with trade in addition to better use and allocation of existing factor endowments including natural resources;
2. To work toward improving industrial nations' capacity to import developing countries' products on a steady basis by devising commodity agreements of various sorts;
3. To work toward enhancing and enlarging the role of multilateral development institutions in the interest of the developing world.

Tinbergen and his international group of co-workers (1976, p. 44) identified four basic kinds of specific interdependencies between North and South. First, there are countries (usually rich) with food surpluses, and there are countries (often poor) with food deficits. Second, there are needs for energy and minerals in a world where supply and demand have different geographical patterns. Third, there is the possibility of disrupting or destroying "spaceship earth's" life-support system, with consequences for all mankind. Fourth, there are basic hopes for reducing the glaring disparities between the world's rich and poor. "Different nations afford different priorities to these different kinds of interdependencies," says Tinbergen, and it " . . . is thus clear that interdependencies can be, have been, and will be interpreted in a number of ways" when viewed from the different perspectives of rich and poor nations (Tinbergen 1976, p. 44). It should be noted, however, that even here interdependence is used in a general sense rather than a technical one.

### Energy Interdependence

At the turn of the century, the industrial countries, the main consumers of commercial fuels, began to shift from coal to oil. The shift accelerated, and increasing shares of the oil were imported in the 1930s and 1940s as a result of plentiful oil discoveries at low capital investment per unit of output in areas with a low demand for commercial fuels. However, the era of abundant oil discovery at low investment is now over. Reconstruction after World War II and rapid growth rates in consumption with higher living standards have brought the world economy closer to the limits of nonrenewable natural resources. No longer is the increase of supply only a function of monetary investment, but rather of the availability of the actual resource base. This consciousness of scarcity is valid with regard to all raw materials entering the modern industrial process but is most dramatic in the case of oil.

A greater say in the destiny of their economic resources came to the oil-exporting countries with political independence. The valuation of oil is the primary interest of oil-exporting countries because oil represents a depletable patrimony, often the most significant national resource in many countries. Oil pricing should reflect the long-term interests of the countries endowed with this nonrenewable natural resource. The main considerations in producing and exporting oil are its exchange as a depletable asset for other productive assets which will offer continued economic return and a value in exchange which reflects the production and availability of substitutes.

Importers of oil should accept its price as a "given" on the above basis. They should also accept the future needs of an exporting country itself and the comparative advantage its own industries could garner from the use of domestic oil, as a fuel and as a feedstock.

These factors have created transient strains between oil producers and consumers. The industrial countries formed the International Energy Agency in 1974 as a countervailing force to the growing effectiveness of OPEC in setting the price of oil. The weight which the industrial countries can bring to bear is overwhelming; they are the main outlets for oil exports, and they are the main economic source of the multitude of items which modern technology has devised to bring about the more productive societies that oil-exporting nations want. The comparative advantage of the industrial states is their greater efficiency.

Confrontation will shift to coordination. From the point of view of the oil exporters, this coordination should include:

1. A gradual movement of the price of oil toward that of its alternatives. This will entail a slow return by the industrial countries to the use of coal and a greater investment by them in developing new sources of energy. The result would be a lengthened life for oil resources.

2. To the extent that the oil exporters produce quantities beyond their immediate needs, the value of the returns on export should be ensured. Because they invest unutilized monetary balances in the industrial countries, a "real" share of the technological fruits of such investment should be transferred via training and participation in the decisions about products to be produced, not just monetary dividends.

The restraint of the oil exporters in the face of these challenges is evidenced by their acceptance of a price increase for oil smaller than that needed to equal the rising prices they pay for imports, to say nothing about the loss in value of the dollar which they accept as payment for their oil.

The foregoing spells out the kind of interdependence involved in the proposed future relationship between the major exporters of oil (or other nonrenewable resources) and the major importers of oil (or other resources). Such interdependence is crucial, for most observers and analysts concede that the world energy transition will accelerate in the next two decades. Markets cannot cope with the kind of imbalance that might arise in the meantime. A broad strategy is necessary—one that is agreed to by the two groups of nations and one based on mutual negotiations that include the process of exchange alluded to above. Cooperation may seem too general to describe what is required. The harmonization of so many flows is so involved as to seem discouraging. That does not mean that the target is not desirable. The target is transition through a most difficult restructuring of the world resource base of energy and other nonrenewable materials.

## Conclusion

Some writers on world order are already raising questions about the validity of the concept of interdependence in international cooperation. Its imprecision, they say, brings doubts whether all nations should or could commit themselves to it as an objective. New, more binding concepts are suggested to replace it. Laszlo (1978) has suggested "interexistence" to replace "interdependence" and "entente" to replace "detente": "If interdependence is a condition and not a goal, mankind must find a goal that it can pursue through interdependence and beyond it. Such a goal, in fact a goal of goals, is interexistence" (Laszlo 1978, p. 362).

The fact that this and similar questions are raised is a testimony to the never-ending search in the mind of man for his present and future. To ask, therefore, "whither interdependence," as some are asking, is ultimately equivalent to the question "whither mankind." No one can responsibly answer this question without a total world view of man—his place in the world, his relation to others, his being and becoming. What are the forces that govern human history and the future of mankind? If he is solely matter, man is nothing but an accident of nature, a speck in the universe, and a vanishing drop in the ocean of eternity. But if there is a transcendental power—call it "reason," the "spirit," the "logos," or any other principle—then man's destiny, regardless of his color, creed, or race, is but a part of the great human drama. Our world view necessarily determines our value system, and the content of interdependence is closely related to our value system. Is man an end in himself, or is he a means for something else, is but one crucial question. On its answer depends the determination of another equally important question that flows from it: is "interdependence" a smokescreen or a reality?

The burden of the answer lies primarily with the West and not with the Third World. In the long legacy of colonialism, the developing nations were seen, and are still sometimes seen, as essentially producers of raw materials and primary commodities for the industrial economies. Although one can understand such a persistent materialistic approach, one cannot accept it. We deal now on the level of "fundamentals" of international cooperation, and it should be recalled that peoples of the Third World have inherited some of the oldest known cultures of mankind. The two rivers of the Nile and the Euphrates witnessed the birth of two of the oldest civilizations. Arab science and learning were among the principal factors that contributed to the Western renaissance. The Middle East with its great religious and cultural traditions has been one of the fountainheads of European culture. Muhammad, the prophet of Islam, described human community as "an edifice, the different parts of which hold each other together" and as similar to the human body—"when one part of it is hurt, all the other parts share its pain."

During the long centuries of colonization, the colonized peoples constituted simply an administrative problem for the powers that dominated them, and, as such, they lived on the margin of history. Their liberation con-

INTERNATIONAL COOPERATION

stitutes one of the landmarks of the second half of the twentieth century. Human thought has continuously oscillated between two poles, idealism and realism. It is an unending process of trial and error, of self-criticism and of self-correction. If we genuinely think that man is an end in himself, that every human being, no matter how humble he is, that every people no matter how lowly they may be, can all contribute their modest best to the making of human society and history, that poverty does not a priori negate culture and civilization, only then can we begin to have a vision of the unity of mankind. The world system of "interdependence" or "interexistence" we want to build can be the product of our own thinking. It is a self-evident truth that everybody stands to benefit from a better and more equitable world system.

## References

Alker, Hayward R., Jr., Lincoln P. Bloomfield, and Nazli Choucri. 1974. *Analyzing Global Interdependence*, vols. 1–4. Cambridge, Massachusetts: Center for International Studies, Massachusetts Institute of Technology.

Amuzegar, Jahangir. 1977. "A Requiem for the North-South Conference," *Foreign Affairs* 56:136–59.

Ball, George. 1974. "Trilateralism and the Oil Crisis," *Pacific Community* 5: 335–47.

Bergsten, Fred C. 1973. "The Threat from the Third World," *Foreign Policy* 11: 102–24.

Bergsten, Fred C., Robert O. Keohane, and Joseph F. Nye. 1975. "International Economics and International Politics: A Framework for Analysis," *International Organization* 29: 3–36.

Brown, Lester. 1972. *The Interdependence of Nations*. Development Paper no. 10. Washington, D.C.: Overseas Development Council.

Brown-John, C. Lloyd. 1976. "The Politics of Regulatory Functions Under Conditions of Commodity and Resource Scarcity." Annual Meeting of the International Political Science Association, Edinburgh, Scotland.

Cleveland, Harlan. 1977. *The Third Try at World Order: U.S. Policy for an Interdependent World*. New York: Aspen Institute for Humanistic Studies.

Cooper, Richard N. 1968. *The Economics of Interdependence: Economic Policy in the Atlantic Community*. New York: McGraw-Hill.

Cooper, Richard N. 1972. "Economic Interdependence and Foreign Policy in the Seventies," *World Politics*, vol. 24 (January), pp. 159–81.

Dag Hammarskjold Foundation. 1975. *What Now? The 1975 Dag Hammarskjold Report*. Uppsala, Sweden: DHF.

Deutsch, K. 1957. *Political Community and the North Atlantic Area: International Organization in the Light of Historical Experience*. Princeton, New Jersey: Princeton University Press.

Diaz-Alejandro, Carlos F. 1975. "North-South Relations: The Economic Component," *International Organization* 29: 213–41.

Erb, Guy, and Valeriana Kallab, eds. 1975. *Beyond Dependency: The Developing World Speaks Out*. Washington, D.C.: Overseas Development Council.

Fishlow, Albert, Carlos Diaz-Alejandro, Richard R. Fagen, and Roger D. Hansen. 1978. *Rich and Poor Nations in the World Economy*. New York: McGraw-Hill.

Furtado, C. 1973. "The Concept of External Dependence in the Study of Underdevelopment." In C. K. Wilber, comp., *The Political Economy of Development and Underdevelopment*. New York: Random House.

Goulet, Denis. 1976. *World Interdependence: Verbal Smokescreen or New Ethic?* Development Paper no. 21. Washington, D.C.: Overseas Development Council.

Grundy, K. W. 1976. "Intermediary Power and Global Dependency: The Case of South Africa," *International Studies Quarterly* 20: 553-80.

Haas, Ernest B. 1975. "Is There a Hole in the Whole? Knowledge, Technology, Interdependence, and the Construction of International Regimes," *International Organization* 29: 827-76.

Hansen, Roger D. 1976. *The U.S. and World Development: Agenda for Action 1976*. New York: Praeger.

Johnson, Robert H. 1977. *Managing Interdependence: Restructuring the U.S. Government*. Development Paper no. 23. Washington, D.C.: Overseas Development Council.

Keohane, Robert O., and Joseph S. Nye. 1977. *Power and Interdependence*. Boston: Little Brown.

Laszlo, Ervin. 1978. *Goals for Mankind: A Report to the Club of Rome on the New Horizons of the Global Community*. New York: New American Library.

McNamara, Robert S. 1978. Address to the Board of Governors of the World Bank. Washington, D.C.: World Bank.

Meadows, Donella H., Dennis L. Meadows, Jørgen Randers, and William W. Behrens III. 1972. *The Limits to Growth*. New York: Universe Books.

Morgenthau, Hans J. 1975. "World Politics and the Politics of Oil." In Gary D. Eppen, ed., *Energy: The Policy Issues*. Chicago: University of Chicago Press, pp. 43-51.

Myrdal, Gunnar. 1968. *Asian Drama: An Inquiry into the Poverty of Nations*. New York: Pantheon.

Myrdal, Gunnar. 1971. *The Challenge of World Poverty: A World Poverty Program in Outline*. New York: Pantheon.

Rosecrance, Richard, and Arthur Stein. 1973. "Interdependence: Myth or Reality?" *World Politics* 26: 1-26.

Rosecrance, R., A. Alexandroff, W. Koehler, J. Kroll, S. Laquer, and J. Stocker. 1977. "Whither Interdependence?" *International Organization* 31: 425-71.

Saddy, Fehmi. Forthcoming. "A New World Economic Order: The Limits of Accommodation."

Simon, Arthur. 1975. *Bread for the World*. New York: Paulist Press.

Solomon, Robert, and Anne Gault. 1977. *The Interdependence of Nations*. Washington, D.C.: Brookings Institution.

Tinbergen, Jan, coord. 1976. *RIO—Reshaping the International Order: A Report to the Club of Rome*. New York: Dutton.

Tucker, Robert W. 1977a. *The Inequality of Nations*. New York: Basic Books.

Tucker, Robert W. 1977b. "Oil and American Power—Three Years Later," *Commentary* 63(1): 29–36.

ul Haq, Mahbub. 1976. *The Third World and the International Economic Order*. Development Paper no. 22. Washington, D.C.: Overseas Development Council.

U.S. Department of State, Bureau of Public Affairs. 1975. "Toward a Strategy of Interdependence," Media Services Special Report no. 17 (July).

Waltz, K. 1970. "The Myth of National Interdependence." In C. Kindleberger, ed., *The International Corporation: A Symposium*. Cambridge, Massachusetts: MIT Press.

World Bank. 1978. *World Development Report, 1978*. New York: Oxford University Press.

Wright, Quincy. 1965. *A Study of War*. 2nd ed. Chicago: University of Chicago Press.

Young, Oran. 1969. "Interdependencies in World Politics," *International Journal* 24: 726–50.

# 13 *Richard B. Bilder*

# International Law and
# Natural Resource Policies

It is difficult to discuss international resource issues without some understanding of the central role played by international law. International law shapes the underlying framework of the international system for allocating resources by establishing basic rules about circumstances under which nations can assert property rights in resources; this framework influences both how nations see resource problems and the kinds of solutions they consider. International rules and agreements are the form in which nations usually express their resource arrangements; they show how nations deal with these issues now. Finally, international law provides a process, a set of techniques and a body of experience which can help nations to forge better solutions to resource problems; the only tools available for cooperative efforts are those provided by international law.

Because the nature and role of international law are not widely understood, a brief introductory comment may be helpful. In a broad sense, international law embraces all of the formal normative structures and processes—including rules, institutions, and techniques—through which the 150 or so nation-states of the present global community seek to manage their interactions and provide order and predictability in their mutual behavior and relations. Without at least some common rules and institutions, it would be difficult for nations to co-exist peacefully on the same planet or to deal usefully with each other on natural resource or any other questions. The international lawyer specializes in the operation of these international rules and processes and in those aspects of the domestic law of individual nations through which international rules and processes are implemented.

International law develops primarily through consensual arrangements. That is, nations establish among themselves certain rules, institutions, and other normative arrangements on a pragmatic basis because they believe that these will be useful. In most cases, nations expressly consent to particular rules or institutions by accepting specific bilateral or multilateral international agreements. However, under certain circumstances, consent may be implied from participation or acquiescence in the development of customary international rules or decisions of international organizations. Rules, institutions, procedures, and techniques will vary in strength depending on the extent and character of the real agreement or consensus they represent.

Because international rules and institutions emerge from the complex interactions among nations, they inevitably reflect the constantly changing problems, tensions, and diversity of claims and aspirations within international society. The international legal system continually evolves in response to the needs and changing power relationships of the international community which it serves. Indeed, international law can be viewed in the broadest sense as "a process of decision" which functions to clarify international objectives and facilitate rational social choices concerning the problems which the international community faces (Schachter 1977, p. viii).

It is apparent that the international legal system is relatively undeveloped compared to most national legal systems, and some observers are skeptical about its "reality" and efficacy. The international system lacks the kind of highly developed legal institutions we are familiar with in national legal systems—formal law-making authorities such as legislatures, dispute settlement agencies such as courts, and law-applying and enforcing agencies such as a recognized executive and a police force—although the international legal system in practice does have close analogies to these domestic legal institutions. It is also evident that international law is sometimes less than clear, that it does not have as effective a system of sanctions as does domestic law, and that international rules can often be violated with impunity—although this is, of course, sometimes the case with domestic rules too. International law is clearly a weaker and less perfect instrument than we might wish.

There is, however, a great deal of evidence indicating that nations do normally take international rules into account in making decisions and determining policies and that these rules are usually complied with. As a practical matter, international law does a reasonably effective job of controlling official behavior—at least in those workaday and undramatic contexts in which rules generally have their primary significance. There are very practical reasons why nations usually choose to observe international rules: a general interest in maintaining an international system in which the rules of international relations are predictable and reliable; a desire for reciprocal observance of rules by other nations; a fear of retaliation or sanction by other nations if rules are not complied with; bureaucratic habit and convenience; and so forth. In practice, much of the day-to-day business of most foreign offices involves working with these international rules and institutions—their formation, interpretation, application and revision, and their use in the adjustment of disputes.

But it is, of course, also obvious that international rules are only one among many factors which may influence national policy making and decisions. There will certainly be situations—such as those where vital national interests appear to be involved—where national officials disregard legal considerations or give them little weight. Thus international law is a necessary element in understanding how nations deal with natural resource issues, but it is scarcely a sufficient element, and political, economic, social, scientific, or technological factors—such as are described and analyzed at length elsewhere in this book—will often also play an equal or more important role.

The discussion in this chapter focuses on international law and institutions relevant to natural resource policies. I have not attempted to explore the equally important questions of human resource policy, which would involve discussion of international rules, institutions, and other arrangements in such diverse fields as population, health, education, the movement of people (including emigration, immigration, migrant labor, and "brain-drains"), and the protection of human rights. It is worth noting, however, that human resource problems, as with natural resource problems, are now important subjects of international discussion and regulation. In particular, the rapidly growing international law of human rights clearly establishes that the ways in which governments treat their own citizens—once regarded as matters solely within each nation's own jurisdiction and discretion—are now matters of legitimate international concern and action. It is evident that a perception that human beings are common voyagers on "spaceship earth" is influencing not only international resource policies but policies in other areas of international relations as well.

It is not practical here to survey all of the international rules, institutions, arrangements, and procedures bearing on natural resource policies and issues.* Indeed, it is only recently that these problems have even been recognized as a distinct and important field of international concern, and the law in this area is still scattered. No single or coherent body of doctrine has yet emerged which can be appropriately described as an "international law of natural resources," and it is still uncertain whether the many different types of natural resources and the diverse problems they encompass can be adequately handled within a single framework of rules. Instead, this chapter will look briefly at three ways in which international law seems important to thinking about international resource policies and problems:

1. the ways in which differing legal concepts of national property rights affect the structure of international resource arrangements;
2. the ways in which disputes about international law reveal underlying differences in views of "equity" or "fairness" in international natural resource arrangements;
3. the ways in which international law can help nations to reach cooperative arrangements for dealing with natural resource problems.

### International Law and Resource Allocation

International law sets a framework for the international natural resource system by laying down certain fundamental rules as to which nation, if any, may initially "own" or control which resources.** These rules affect basic perceptions of international resource issues—what we think the problems are, what we think we need to do about them, and how we think we can do it.

The international society, like most national societies, allocates rights of access to and control of resources through certain rules, broadly analagous to property rules. In international law these property concepts are

*For a broader and exceptionally thoughtful discussion of various legal and normative aspects of natural resources issues, see Schachter 1977.

**The approach in this section—and throughout this chapter—to the functions of international law and its role in allocating resources is one with which some other international lawyers, especially those in developing nations, might differ. They might, in particular, take the view that a nation's sovereignty or "ownership" over natural resources situated within its own territorial limits is not a right bestowed by or dependent upon international law but rather an inherent right created by and exclusively subject to that nation's own internal law; that international law regarding national sovereignty over resources does not establish but simply recognizes this inherent right; and that in exercising this right of permanent sovereignty over its own natural resources, a nation might choose as a matter of policy to act in accordance with any relevant established international norms but would not be legally bound to do so.

typically put in terms of national sovereignty or territorial or jurisdictional rights. International law usually regards a nation as having sovereignty or jurisdiction—the right to prescribe and enforce rules without outside interference—over all conduct within its territory. Thus a nation normally has the right to control every type of conduct, either by its own citizens or by citizens of other nations, involving resources within its own territories. However, a nation's right to exercise jurisdiction outside its territory is more limited, particularly because it must often be balanced against the claims and interests of other nations. Because the concepts of sovereignty or jurisdiction over resources embrace the right to exclude others from access to or use of these resources, they are functionally equivalent to "national ownership."

These are, of course, legal concepts which have evolved from the need of international society to resolve competing claims to limited resources. A particular natural resource is not inherently any nation's "property"; it becomes "property" only when and to the extent that nations decide to treat it as such in their relations.

The fact that rules of sovereignty, jurisdiction, territory, and property are simply social tools, designed to control behavior, has several implications. First, such legal concepts have only that significance and meaning which a particular international society at a particular time chooses to give them; they may change as social attitudes, circumstances, and purposes change. Second, such concepts have meaning only in the context of the broader international legal system, which may condition or limit these rights. Even as international law recognizes the right of a nation to exercise jurisdiction over particular natural resources, it can also provide that such rights must be exercised with due respect for international agreements freely entered, the rights of aliens, or the interests of other nations.

The international community might have adopted—or might still adopt —a variety of rules to allocate resources among the nations of the world. These include the principles of (1) national control over natural resources; (2) common access to natural resources; (3) joint national control of resources; and (4) international ownership and control of resources. Although the principle of national control over resources is currently dominant, other approaches have significance in particular areas. Each represents a very different, and to some extent competing, approach to issues of natural resource allocation and management. These rules are now in flux, and some of the distinctions among them are beginning to blur.

### National Control over Natural Resources

The most widespread and significant of these approaches to international resource allocation is the principle that a particular nation may acquire sovereignty or exclusive jurisdiction over particular resources. The best-known and most important application of this principle is the rule that resources located in a nation's territory, including its territorial waters, are subject to its sovereignty. Indeed, this rule is now so strongly established that territorial sovereignty and sovereignty over resources present within a nation's territory are usually inseparably linked in peoples' minds. Thus the copper present within Chile's territory is considered "Chile's copper," the oil present within Venezuela's territory is regarded as "Venezuela's oil," and the wheat grown in the United States is regarded as "the United States' wheat." Because almost all of the earth's land area is now claimed by one or another nation, almost all of the earth's land and subsurface resources are now "owned" by some nation under this principle.

However, the reach of this principle is no longer limited to resources found on or under land within national territory; it has recently been extended to many of the important mineral and living resources in seas adjacent to but not legally within national territory. Since 1945 there has been a dramatic expansion in coastal states' claims to jurisdiction over the resources—although not the waters themselves—of the continental shelves and fisheries in the seas along their coasts. These claims have sometimes given rise to serious tensions among nations competing for access to these resources—the "cod war," "tuna war," "shrimp war," and so on. The precise rules applicable to such claims are now under negotiation at the Third UN Law of the Sea Conference, but there is already an overwhelming consensus at the Conference favoring recognition of the right of coastal states to exercise resource jurisdiction in an "Exclusive Economic Zone" extending at least 200 miles out from their coasts. Relying on this consensus, the United States, Canada, Japan, the Soviet Union, and other nations, including those of the European Economic Community, have established 200-mile fishery limits. With the coming into effect of these 200-mile exclusive economic zones in the oceans, most of the earth's economically valuable mineral and living resources are now effectively under some nation's control.

The principle of national sovereignty over resources has generally been held to mean that the nation having such sovereignty has the right to deny all or even certain other nations access to or use of such resources. U.S. restrictions on exports of strategic commodities to certain communist countries and the 1973 Arab oil embargo exemplify the exercise of this type of claim. This principle also means that the sovereign nation can permit access and use to other nations on such terms and conditions as it may choose—for example, by entering concessional agreements or trade agreements or by enacting national laws controlling the exploitation of natural resources by aliens. However, despite nations' broad control over their own resources under this principle, they may nevertheless depend on other nations for some of the benefits accruing from control. Other nations, in the exercise of their own sovereignty, also have rights to control the import of foreign resources into their territory and to control any activities by their nationals exploiting or using foreign resources. The United States, for instance, has on various occasions refused to permit imports of sugar from Cuba, has established quotas on imports of foreign oil, and has imposed constraints on trade, investment, and other transactions with communist and other nations. Consequently, nations which can effectively exploit their resources only with foreign assistance or nations which can effectively profit from their resources only by exporting them may find little practical meaning in the right of national sovereignty over the resources themselves unless other nations are prepared to give aid in exploiting these resources and to permit them access to markets.

This allocation of resources to various nations fixes the context for international resource policies and issues. A nation which needs another nation's resources can secure them only by influencing that nation to supply them. A nation which can obtain benefits from its resources only by selling them abroad can do so only by influencing other nations to take them. Thus the nature and extent of the movement of natural resources among nations necessarily depends upon the kinds of influence which nations can bring to bear on each other. For the most part, national foreign policies concerning resources are attempts to exert such influence.

One way to secure access to markets for resources is coercion—the threat of the use of force. This method was typical of the imperialist and colonialist periods of history. Coercion still plays an important role in many aspects of international affairs, but several factors have constrained the present usefulness of coercion as an option in resource policy. Broadly accepted international norms—written into the UN Charter, the UN Declaration on Colonialism, the UN Declaration on Non-Intervention, and an extensive array of other international instruments and precedents—now clearly prohibit a nation from using force to acquire another nation's territory or resources. In a world of power blocs and alliances, practical political concerns and fears of escalation buttress these norms. The fact that developed nations in recent years have rarely attempted to use military force to protect natural resource interests threatened by developing nations' actions—for example, in response to the wave of recent nationalizations of foreign oil, copper, and other concessions or to the 1973 oil embargo—suggests the extent to which overt coercion has been discarded even by powerful countries as a way of implementing natural resource objectives. Although developed nations have sometimes intervened in support of resource interests in Africa, in Chile, and elsewhere, their intervention has usually been indirect or covert rather than direct and overt.

A second way of influencing other nations to supply or accept natural resources is persuasion and appeals to altruism, goodwill, or general self-interest. Developing nations have recently urged, with some success, that developed nations extend substantial amounts of economic assistance to poorer nations. Such help may involve the flow of developed country resources and monies to developing countries as gifts or as loans at concessionary rates—for example, agricultural commodities under the U.S. P.L. 480 program and, of course, financial grants or loans. It may also take the form of favored treatment for developing country products in developed nation markets—for example, the special status accorded by the EEC to such products under the Lomé Convention. International law now recognizes that developed countries are at least broadly obligated to extend economic assistance to developing nations, and an extensive body of rules, agreements, institutions, and procedures has been designed to facilitate and regulate assistance efforts (Schachter 1976). The question has really become not whether developed nations should give but how much.

A final way in which a nation may secure another's resources or access to another's markets is the mechanism of exchange—international trade. Commercial exchanges of this type are currently the most important basis for international flows of resources, and most present issues of national and international resource policies relate to the negotiation, terms, and conditions of such exchange. The vast and diverse network of international rules, agreements, and institutions facilitating and regulating world trade in resources includes bilateral and multilateral commercial agreements providing for specific exchanges of commodities or establishing broad rules to encourage mutual trade and investment: common markets and free trade areas; arrangements such as the General Agreement on Tariffs and Trade (GATT) for mutual reduction or removal of tariffs and other discriminatory barriers to trade; agreements such as the Lomé Convention to foster trade among specific groups of developed and developing countries; organizations of resource-producing nations, such as OPEC, or of resource importing nations, such as the International Energy Agency, to strengthen bargaining powers or to deal with common concerns; commodity agreements among both producers and consumers, such as the International Tin, Coffee, and Wheat Agreements, to rationalize trade and stabilize prices in particular commodities; UN institutions such as the Conference on Trade and Development (UNCTAD), the regional and economic commissions, and the Food and Agriculture Organization

(FAO); and a wide variety of other bodies dealing with natural resources, trade, and economic development issues.

## Common Access to Natural Resources

A second and contrasting approach to the international allocation of natural resources is the principle that resources should *not* be subject to national sovereignty or jurisdiction but should, in effect, be common property, accessible to any individual or nation wishing to use them.

This principle has found only limited application, chiefly within areas regarded as clearly beyond the limits of national claims to jurisdiction. Moreover, the principle has usually been accepted only in circumstances where resources were either unproven, inaccessible, or available in such quantities that no conflict among potential users has arisen. In practice, where resources have had economic value and restrictions on access have been feasible, some type of property claim—either national or international—has typically been made in an attempt to secure or at least regulate access to the resources. Indeed, there are strong arguments that effective resource management and conservation techniques require some type of proprietary rules. It is now generally recognized that the principle of free access tends to produce overexploitation, economic inefficiency, and "external diseconomies" (Hardin 1968).

Historically, the most prominent example of the principle of common access has been the doctrine of the freedom of the high seas. For several centuries the seas were treated as an international commons. Article 2 of the 1958 Geneva Convention on the High Seas provides in part that:

The high seas being open to all nations, no State may validly purport to subject any part of them to its sovereignty. Freedom of the high seas . . . comprises . . . inter alia . . .
  1. Freedom of navigation;
  2. Freedom of fishing. . . .

Under that doctrine, fishing fleets of any nation have traditionally had the right to capture fish anywhere in the seas beyond coastal states' territorial limits, long regarded as only three miles in breadth.

However, this traditional concept of the freedom of the seas is currently undergoing substantial change. Many coastal states now claim at least 12-mile territorial seas plus jurisdiction over both mineral and living resources in ocean zones reaching out 200 miles, as well as over migratory species of fish, such as salmon, which spawn in their rivers. Special international joint management regimes have been established to regulate other species of high seas fish and aquatic mammals such as tuna and whales. New types of international managerial regimes are being contemplated for the manganese nodules and other mineral resources of the deep seabed. In practice, with respect at least to several significant natural resources—in particular, fish, oil and gas, and minerals—the concept of the oceans as an international commons has all but disappeared.

Another example of international rules purporting to exclude national sovereignty over particular territory is contained in the 1967 UN Treaty on Principles Governing the Activities of States in the Exploration and Use of Outer Space. Article I of that Treaty provides in part that:

Outer space, including the moon and other celestial bodies, shall be free for exploitation and use by all states . . . and there shall be free access to all areas of celestial bodies.

Article II provides that:

Outer space, including the moon and other celestial bodies, is not subject to national appropriation by claim of sovereignty, by means of use or occupation, or by any other means.

Whether the principle of common access will survive circumstances in which national uses of outer space conflict—for example, where satellites begin to interfere with each other or in which exclusive rights to lunar or extraterrestrial resources acquire great value—remains to be seen. The Outer Space Treaty does not specifically deal with these resource questions. Since 1972, the UN's Outer Space Committee has been considering a further treaty governing the future uses of the moon and its resources. However, these negotiations have raised issues closely related to those involved in current negotiations at the UN Law of the Sea Conference—developing nations urging international control of such resources as a "common heritage" and technologically advanced, developed nations urging rules which would permit at least some national access and use. While the prospects of exploiting resources on the moon and other extraterrestrial bodies are now limited, new technology could open these resources to exploitation and exert strong pressure on the common access principle.

### Joint National Control of Resources

A third possible approach to the international allocation of natural resources is the principle that resources common to more than one nation or in which more than one nation has an active and substantial interest should be shared by the countries concerned according to equitable standards and procedures. This concept is suggested, for example, in Article III of the 1974 Charter of Economic Rights and Duties of States, which provides that:

In the exploitation of natural resources shared by two or more countries, each state must co-operate on the basis of a system of information and prior consultations in order to achieve optimum use of such resources without causing damage to the legitimate interests of others.

This concept of joint control finds its most important application in the widely approved principle of equitable utilization or apportionment of rivers or lakes which form a common boundary between nations or lie within more than one country. Under this principle, all of the riparian states of an international river or lake or all of the basin states of an international drainage basin have a right to an equitable and reasonable share in the uses of such waters. Conversely, one riparian or basin nation should not use or allow use of these waters in a way that unreasonably interferes with the legitimate interests of other co-riparian or basin states. The principle implies a need for cooperative approaches in the management of these shared resources. This idea of equitable utilization is now embodied in some 300 international agreements dealing with rivers, lakes, and drainage basins throughout the world. Many of these agreements, such as the U.S.-Canadian Boundary Waters Treaty of 1909, have specific provisions to govern the equitable use of the waters concerned. Some establish joint commissions or other common institutions to facilitate cooperation in the development, management, and use of the waters and in the solution of problems and disputes.

A second area in which the principle of joint national control of resources has been applied is the cooperative management of certain fisheries. The principle of freedom of fishing on the high seas has in many cases led to overexploitation and depletion of stocks and to economic inefficiency for some nations' fleets. One response has been pressure to expand fisheries' limits—to bring particular fisheries under one nation's control and management authority. In this case, a nation's own enforcement agencies can compel compliance with conservation and other regulations. But another reponse has been agreement by all nations in the fishery to create joint institutions—such as the International Whaling Commission, the International Halibut Commission, and the Great Lakes Fisheries Commission—for managing and conserving the particular fishery resource. Some of these commissions have been empowered to set (and to some extent enforce) overall quotas and specific national allocations for catches. In this case, the problems of securing compliance have proved more difficult (Koers 1973).

A third area in which nations have employed the principle of joint control involves problems of international pollution. The concept that nations have responsibilities to each other in this regard is stated in Principle 21 of the UN Declaration on the Environment, adopted by the UN Conference on the Human Environment at Stockholm in 1976:

States have, in accordance with the Charter of the United Nations and the principles of international law, the sovereign right to exploit their own resources pursuant to their own environmental policies, and the responsibility to ensure that activities within their jurisdiction or control do not cause damage to the environment of other States or of areas beyond the limits of national jurisdiction.

A more specific statement of the idea that states should work together toward a joint solution of these types of common resource problems is contained, for example, in a recent draft principle agreed to by a group of UNEP experts in 1977:

States have a duty to co-operate in the field of the environment concerning the conservation and harmonious utilization of natural resources shared by two or more States. Accordingly, consistent with the concept of equitable utilization of shared natural resources, States should cooperate with a view to controlling, preventing, reducing and eliminating adverse environmental effects which may result from the utilization of such resources. Such cooperation shall take place on an equal footing and due account shall be taken of the sovereignty and interests of the States concerned.

Efforts to put cooperative management of common environmental problems into practice include such international agreements as the 1972 London Convention on the Prevention of Marine Pollution by Dumping of Wastes and Other Matter, the 1974 Convention on the Protection of the Marine Environment of the Baltic Sea Area, the 1976 Convention on the Protection of the Mediterranean Against Pollution, and the United Nations Environmental Program (UNEP). In contrast with international declarations, resolutions, and statements of principles, international agreements are, of course, legally binding and usually provide procedures for enforcement.

The unique case of Antarctica and its offshore waters presents, temporarily at least, still another example of joint national control of resources. Much of the continent itself is claimed by one or more nations, but none of these sometimes conflicting claims has been generally accepted. The United States and the Soviet Union, which carry on the most extensive programs in Antarctica, have neither made claims themselves nor recognized claims by any other nation. At present, activities on the continent are governed by the Antarctic Treaty of 1959, a treaty in which 20 countries are now participants. The Treaty demilitarizes the continent, reserves it for peaceful and scientific purposes, and prohibits nuclear explosions or the disposal of radioactive wastes. Conflicting national claims to territory are essentially "frozen" for the 30-year life of the treaty; scientists may pursue their work anywhere on the continent without restrictions. Pursuant to the Treaty, the parties meet biennially to exchange information, to consult on matters of common interest, and to formulate, consider, and recommend to their governments measures in furtherance of the principles and objectives of the Treaty. These measures may include the preservation, exploitation, or conservation of resources.

Up to now, no natural resources of great commercial significance have been exploited on the Antarctic continent, and the Antarctic Treaty is silent about the exploration and exploitation of the continent's resources. However, there is recent evidence that the continent and continental shelf may contain minerals and oil and gas, and there is rising interest in possible harvest of the vast quantities of krill and other living resources in the oceans off Antarctica. Concern that states driven by growing energy and resource requirements might seek to reassert national claims of exclusive access to Antarctica's land and marine resources has been voiced at recent consultative meetings of the Antarctic Treaty parties. Certain collaborative measures have been proposed, including a treaty to ensure conservation of offshore fisheries. It seems that the parties to the Treaty will at least try to maintain the unique cooperative regime they have established.

### International Ownership and Control of Resources

A fourth possible approach to international allocation of natural resources contends that resources should be regarded as the property of all mankind and should be exploited only by or under the management of international institutions. The most important example of this approach is the proposed international regime, now under negotiation at the Third UN Law of the Sea Conference, to govern the exploitation of the resources of the deep seabed.

In the 1960s it became apparent that new deep sea technology might permit the mining of manganese nodules which lie scattered over many areas of the deep seabed. These nodules can reach the size of a small ball and are composed of manganese, iron, nickel, copper, cobalt, and various other minerals. Developing countries feared that a few technologically advanced industrial nations, particularly the United States, might attempt to appropriate these resources for themselves. This concern was galvanized by a series of speeches in the UN by Ambassador Arvid Pardo of Malta in 1967, in which he proposed that the resources of the deep seabed beyond the limits of national jurisdiction be treated as a "common heritage of mankind" subject to international authority. Subsequent General Assembly resolutions and declarations asserted that these resources were indeed "the common heritage of all mankind" not subject to national appropriation or claims of sovereignty, called for a collectively established international regime to exploit deep seabed resources "for the benefit of all mankind," and convened in 1973 the Third UN Law of the Sea Conference. The Conference is supposed to revise broadly the Law of the Sea but has as a major purpose the settlement of this question and the establishment of an international regime to govern seabed mining.

The Conference has proved extremely complex, lengthy, and difficult. It has held eight major negotiation sessions from 1973 through September 1978 and by late 1978 appeared to be in agreement on a number of seabed issues. There is general consensus that deep seabed resources should be regarded as a common heritage; that their mining should be controlled by an International Seabed Authority composed of the nations of the world, represented through an assembly of all nations and a smaller Council, and having some sort of secretariat and technical commission; and that a share of the profits arising from nodule mining should be returned to the international community in some way, primarily for the use of the developing nations. Beyond this, however, significant differences of opinion have continued. These disagreements have centered on the question of access by private or national enterprises to seabed deposits, security of tenure for such enterprises, and the manner in which the resources will actually be exploited. In broad outline, the division of opinion has set the United States and a few other technologically advanced states capable of exploiting the nodules commercially in the near future against a much larger group of developing nations which do not have that capability.

The United States and other technologically advanced nations would ideally prefer an international system of a relatively simple type—in effect amounting to an international licensing system—in which primary responsibility for exploitation would rest in private or national companies. Under their proposals, companies would operate under treaty provisions that would provide commercial access to seabed nodules, protection and security of tenure for these companies' investments, and royalties or a share of profits to the international community. The International Seabed Authority would have carefully spelled out and limited regulatory powers—for example, licensing of companies and protection of ocean environments—and would have little power to interfere with actual operations by commercial enterprises.

Developing countries, on the other hand, have urged a "unitary system" under which seabed nodules would be mined only by the International Seabed Authority through an operating agency called The Enterprise. The Enterprise would presumably hire private or national concerns to assist in actual mining but would itself completely control exploitation and commercial development of the mining sites. Moreover, the Authority would have broad rights to limit rates of exploitation and the price of minerals produced in order to protect the interests of land-based mineral producers and to maximize its own profits. An Assembly of the International Seabed Authority, which would be controlled by developing nations, and the Council of the Authority, which under these proposals would also be controlled by the developing nations, would have broad discretionary powers.

Various compromises have been put forward in an attempt to reconcile these very different approaches. One such alternative is a mixed or "parallel" system under which private and national concerns on the one hand, and the International Enterprise on the other, would separately exploit different sites. Developing nations have had some difficulty with the idea of a mixed system. Essentially, they fear that The Enterprise, with less expertise and experience and fewer financial resources, would simply not be able to compete successfully with private or national companies or consortia and that the technologically advanced states would still end up with the lion's share of the resources. In an effort to meet these objections, technologically advanced nations have offered to give financial and technical assistance to The Enterprise and to accept some limits on seabed production to protect land-based producers, but these proposals have not yet bridged the divide. Many developing countries have continued to press for provisions which would either vest virtually full control in the International Authority or delay actual mining of nodules by private or national companies at least until the time when the International Enterprise is fully operational and able to compete.

Success in these negotiations remains in doubt. The United States and certain other developed nations are beginning to reappraise what they see as a possibly unfavorable global Law of the Sea Treaty and are beginning to consider unilateral action or a less-than-global regime among those nations accepting the same limited approach. The United States, for example, has said that it will not accept a Law of the Sea Treaty which bars access and security of tenure for private companies and that, pending some broadly agreed international regime, traditional freedom of the seas will permit companies to exploit deep seabed minerals. As this is written (in late 1978) the U.S. Congress is considering legislation which would lay the foundation for U.S. private companies or consortia to commence commercial mining of nodules on a unilateral basis or within reciprocal agreements among like-minded developed and perhaps developing nations—at least pending the establishment of an acceptable global regime. In response to the threat of such legislation or other action, some developing countries have suggested that any such unilateral action by developed countries will break up the Conference and have said that they will refuse to recognize the legality of any regime not established by the Conference or not conforming to the "common heritage" principle.

Meanwhile, there are rising doubts about the ultimate value of seabed minerals and the practical gains that any single nation is likely to get through a share in this "common heritage." The widely accepted claim of 200-mile exclusive economic zones by coastal nations has drastically shrunk the area remaining in this "common heritage." Estimates of the time until there are net returns, as well as the magnitude of such returns, from seabed production have become more conservative. It is now apparent that up to ten years may pass before commercial exploitation on a substantial basis becomes possible, and the estimated costs of developing sites have multiplied. In effect, the highly optimistic vision of seabed resources as an immense potential source of funds for economic development has had to be considerably downgraded.

Finally, as material issues at stake in the negotiations have diminished, issues of principle and ideology have become relatively more important. The Law of the Sea negotiations are increasingly linked to broader "North-South" debates and the complex of difficult and emotional issues embraced in the concept of the "New International Economic Order." At least some of the states involved have come to see the negotiations in terms of the precedents which might be established rather than in terms of actual ocean issues and resources. Thus one important issue in the negotiations is how decisions should be made in these new international institutions. Developing nations favor the principle of majority control (which means control by themselves); developed nations favor some form of weighted voting or other system which will protect their interests against what they regard as domination by an "automatic" developing nation majority. Developed nations have a more general concern about erosion of the concept of a role for private enterprise, about lack of security of investments, and about a principle of restricting production or controlling prices in ways adverse to the interest of consuming countries. Some countries on each side apparently believe that it is more important to "win" on these ideological issues than to have the Conference succeed.

Whether the Conference ultimately succeeds or fails, the concepts that inspired it clearly embody certain ideas which could have a lasting impact on the shape of cooperative mechanisms concerning natural resources.

The concept that seabed resources are a "common heritage" of all peoples and ought to be administered by international institutions has been accepted as a guiding principle by almost all nations. That principle creates an interesting and important precedent capable of future expansion as the world encounters increasing and ever more perplexing problems of resource scarcity. Moreover, the vision of an international "Authority," which may itself exploit resources for international purposes, is a major innovation with potentially important precedential effects. Finally, the Conference is a major attempt to reach accommodation between developed and developing countries on an important resource issue, and its outcome could positively or adversely affect negotiations and arrangements on future questions of many kinds.

### International Law and the Search for Equity

International law not only shows how the international resource system works but can also suggest certain respects in which it seems not to be working very well. Uncertainty and debate about applicable rules and institutions may signal a lack of consensus or dissatisfaction over existing arrangements and a need for change. The character of such debates can help to define what the basic differences—often differences in values, perceptions, and objectives—really are. Current disputes and uncertainties about international law's applications to natural resource issues indicate a broad and basic disagreement between developed and developing nations concerning the "fairness" or "equity" of the existing international economic and natural resource system, the values which ought to underlie that system, and the structure of the legal order appropriate to these values.

In broad terms, the developing nations take the position that existing gross disparities between standards of living in developed and developing nations are unjust; that a drastic redistribution of wealth, income, and power in favor of the developing nations is needed to establish some degree of equity; and that the international economic system must be restructured to provide more equality of opportunity among nations and better prospects for such redistribution. They argue that an international society in which a few nations and a small fraction of the world's population are very rich, while most nations and the overwhelming majority of the peoples of the earth are very poor, is inherently unjust—particularly because, in the developing nations' view, rich nations have become rich largely through colonial or other forms of exploitation of the developing world. Moreoever, developing nations believe that not only is there clearly a present imbalance of wealth and power but that inequities are increasing rather than diminishing—the rich are getting richer and the poor, poorer. Developing nations maintain that market forces do not work equally well for rich and poor nations and that poor nations have in practice had little effective role in international economic decision making. As developing nations see it, traditional legal arrangements and institutions, which are largely the creation of the Western developed nations, have tended to support and perpetuate this inequitable system. In effect, the poverty of the developing nations is in part the "fault" of the developed nations and of an economic and legal system which serves developed nations' interests. The developing nations consequently call for a new system—a "New International Economic Order"—designed to redress these imbalances and injustices and establish greater equity.

Developed nations have generally agreed that gross disparities in income and wealth among nations are undesirable and that some redistribution should be sought. They have, however, differed with developing nations about both the reasons for these disparities and the means by which greater equity can be achieved. Developed nations, in the main, justify their relative wealth as resulting from their enterprise, organization, skill, and technology operating principally in the free market context and do not accept the argument that their wealth is based on their exploitation of other peoples or their resources. They argue that developing nations, with some assistance, should through similar efforts be able to achieve economic development and to narrow the existing gap in wealth and income. They argue that the remedy for present problems lies not in any drastic change in the present system, but rather in greater efforts by developing nations to organize their societies in ways which promote, not obstruct, development objectives. As developed nations see it, existing international legal arrangements and institutions continue for the most part to be both adequate and necessary to the achievement of these goals, and any substantial change in these arrangements—particularly those which interfere with free market mechanisms—is likely to make things worse rather than better.

This debate obviously raises many labyrinthine issues—the nature and causes of poverty and economic development; the ways of "breaking out" of the cycle of poverty; the possibility—and desirability—of all nations attaining standards of living and material consumption comparable to those now enjoyed by the richest nations; how material welfare should be measured; and so forth. One of the most difficult of these—and one on which law has a bearing—is the concept of "equity." As Schachter (1977) has pointed out, nations have had great difficulty in agreeing on the kinds of arrangements which are "fair," "just," or "equitable." Equity can be defined by various standards—equality, need, historic entitle-

BILDER: *International Law & Resource Policies*

ment, capacity, degree of contribution, and others. It is not surprising that each nation tends to urge a criterion of "fairness" which most accords with its own interests.

It is beyond the scope of this chapter to attempt a comprehensive look at the issue of equity or to suggest any conclusive answers to the pervasive questions of equity. However, it may be useful to illustrate the kinds of legal contexts in which issues of equity have emerged.

### The Scope of National Sovereignty over Natural Resources

Questions inevitably arise about the "fairness" of the principles which govern the international allocation of natural resources—especially the dominant principle of national sovereignty over resources. Why is it "just" that one nation rather than another should "own" or control a particular resource? How equitable or rational are the basic assumptions upon which the international system currently distributes resources?

The most interesting questions involve the concept of national control. Under the generally accepted distributive principle which permits each nation to control resources within its territory and within 200 miles of any coastline it may have, resources are allocated solely on the basis of geographic accident. Sovereignty over territory carries with it sovereignty over resources, and territorial situs is controlling. Other factors which might conceivably be relevant in determining allocational equity in other contexts, such as equality, effort, or need, have no role, in this view. Sparsely populated nations may control vast wealth in natural resources. Heavily populated nations, with a great need for resources, may control few or none. A nation owning resources vital to other nations may, by virtue of its right of control, threaten to deny or really deny these resources as a way of exerting pressure on other nations to act in ways other than those they would prefer. It is not surprising that nations which are poorly endowed with natural resources and gain little from the principle of national control or which desire greater or more assured access to other nations' resources may see this principle as less than "fair" and press for some international limits on its exercise.

For the time being, these questions are largely theoretical. The principle of national sovereignty over territorial resources is firmly entrenched through both tradition and the realities of effective power, and any substantial modification of this doctrine in the near future seems highly unlikely. Nevertheless, several recent developments may indicate international concern about the equity of the principle of national sovereignty over territorial resources, a growing sympathy for some restraints on the exercise of national sovereignty, and the possibility that at least some change in the way nations view this principle is gradually occurring.

First, there appears to be a fairly broad consensus within the international community that very rich nations should share part of this wealth through economic assistance to needy nations. It is interesting that certain wealthy developed nations such as Sweden, Canada, and the Netherlands, and even certain wealthy developing nations such as Kuwait, Venezuela, and Saudi Arabia seem to view assistance to others as a normative obligation. Some developing nations do frequently phrase requests for aid in terms of claims, obligations, and duties.

Second, debate continues at the Third UN Law of the Sea Conference over coastal state control of resources in adjacent 200-mile ocean zones. Landlocked and "geographically disadvantaged" states continue to press for rules which would permit them an "equitable" share in the benefits of these offshore resources; other nations which have traditionally fished such waters have pressed for rules which recognize and preserve their historic use. The Conference discussions also reveal broader sentiment for the view that coastal nations have not only rights but also international custodial duties in the management and conservation of offshore resources and that coastal states ought to permit other nations access to such ocean resources as they are not able to exploit themselves.

Third, questions have been raised—first by developing or socialist nations facing pressures from Western developed nations, more recently by Western developed nations facing pressures from oil-producing developing nations—about the extent to which international law should permit nations to use their control over resources to bring political or economic pressure on other nations. At some point, the use of such pressures (or of any other types of pressures used improperly or for improper purposes) may fall within the scope of established international norms condemning coercion or intervention. Distinctions between direct military coercion and economic embargo of vital food or resource needs are becoming harder to draw. Both Saudi Arabia and the United States have apparently disclaimed an intention to use the "oil weapon" or the "food weapon," respectively, as a foreign policy device.

Fourth, emerging principles of international environmental law suggest some international constraints on a nation's freedom to pursue any resource policy it chooses, at least if those policies degrade the environment of other nations. A nation may not in principle pollute an international river or discharge wastes from resource exploitation into the atmosphere or oceans, if these threaten severe environmental damage to its neighbors or to the global community. Even in its internal resource decisions, a nation must take some account of the impact of these decisions on other nations' interests.

Sovereignty issues may be foremost, but other approaches to the international allocation of resources also raise questions of "fairness." The principle of joint national control over resources does not, on the face of it, say how a river flowing through or between countries should be allocated among those countries. Should respective geographical shares in the basin, population, historic use, or present needs determine water allocations? What should be the allocative priorities accorded such potential uses as drinking water, irrigation, navigation, industrial use, waste disposal, or recreational use? How are shares in a jointly managed fishery to be allocated—by historic use, currently available fishing capacity, or need —and to what extent should "new" fishing nations be allowed to enter a fishery already subject to joint control by other "established" nations? Should nations currently active on the Antarctic continent be entitled to joint shares in whatever resources may be discovered or exploited there, or should other nations also get some share? If so, on what basis should any division be made?

The principle of international control over resources—as in the continuing negotiations at the Third UN Law of the Sea Conference—also raises difficult and thus far unresolved questions of equity. To developing nations, it would be "unfair" for a few developed nations currently capable of mining seabed resources to reap the benefits of this "common heritage." The only "just" result, in their view, is to give control of these resources to the developing countries themselves, which represent the bulk of the world's nations and population and have the greatest need of the benefits of the seabed. To developed countries, on the other hand, it would be "unfair" for their companies—which have invested effort, skill, and capital in developing the technology of seabed mining—to lose control over the fruits of their enterprise, to have both control and rewards fall instead to nations which have invested little or nothing.

Apart from the issues of equity in each of these allocative principles considered separately, there are also questions of fairness, consistency, and justification of these principles when they are considered collectively. For example, international law recognizes that the United States, physically able to control the flow of the Colorado River, cannot deny Mexico, heavily dependent on these waters, an equitable share in this resource. On the other hand, Mexico, physically able to control its oil resources, can presumably deny to the United States any access whatsoever to Mexican oil, even if the United States ultimately becomes heavily dependent on imports of Mexican oil. In similar fashion, the United States may presumably deny exports of its agricultural commodities to particular foreign nations for political or other reasons, even if these nations are heavily dependent on such exports to feed their peoples. Does the fact that the Colorado River flows a short distance through Mexican territory or that the resource is water rather than oil or grain make such a difference in practice as to justify such very different ways of viewing international rights and obligations concerning these different resources? Again, recent developments indicate that manganese nodules on the deep seabed more than 200 miles from nations' coasts are now to be regarded as "the common heritage of mankind," but fish swimming in the oceans within 200 miles are no longer to be regarded as common property but rather as the exclusive property of the adjacent coastal state. Why is it "fair" that all nations should share in one but not the other? Indeed, the recognition of coastal state jurisdiction over immense oil, fish, and other resources of the adjacent seas may in retrospect appear a short-sighted giveaway—accruing largely to a few developed nations—of potential international resources which might have been better allocated for broader global uses. The principal beneficiaries of 200-mile economic zones have, of course, been large nations with long coastlines and broad continental shelves—chiefly developed nations and particularly the United States, the Soviet Union, Canada, and Australia, as well as a few of the developing nations such as India and Brazil. These are controversial issues but ones which the international community may eventually have to face.

In the long run, increasing tension between the dominant principle of national control over resources and the more recently emergent principles of joint and international control may require some type of accommodation. In the broadest sense, all natural resources (and indeed all knowledge) might be called "the common heritage of mankind." One might visualize a future international society which takes the view that all nations depending on a particular resource share an important interest in it and should in fairness have at least some say in its use and management. International commodity organizations expressly recognize that both producers and consumers share interests in particular resources and should collectively share certain kinds of decisions about these resources; these agreements are, perhaps in embryo, a step in the direction of an all-encompassing "common heritage." It is, of course, most unlikely that we will soon see international or joint control of resources located within national territories. But, as global problems of resource scarcity increase in severity, it is conceivable that, over time, pressures to modify the principle of exclusive national sovereignty over resources may mount.

### The Protection of Foreign Investment

Nations also disagree about the "fairness" of rules for protection of foreign investments in natural resources, and in this area the applicable law is now particularly uncertain and in flux.

Under traditional principles of international law—those supported by most capitalist developed nations—every nation has jurisdiction over the activities of aliens and foreign property interests within its territory. It is recognized that a nation may prohibit the entry of foreign businesses or investments, permit such entry only on compliance with certain conditions, and regulate foreign businesses and investments within its jurisdiction. However, according to traditional doctrine, these rights of the host nation are limited in several respects. A nation may, by entering international agreements, specifically obligate itself to permit entry to foreign businesses and investments and to provide them certain levels of treatment; if so, it is bound by those obligations. A nation is in any event bound by customary international law to provide certain minimum levels of "fair treatment" to aliens and their property within its territory.

Traditional international law also recognizes that every nation, unless it has agreed otherwise, may nationalize or expropriate foreign property within its territory so long as that taking is nonretaliatory, nondiscriminatory, and for a public purpose. In order to comply with international standards of fair treatment, the taking must be accompanied by prompt, adequate, and effective compensation, in the full value of the property taken. A failure to provide such compensation may give rise to an international claim by the home state of the affected alien. Developed nations see these rules as "just." In their view, it would clearly be inequitable if a host nation were to renege on a solemn agreement, take a foreigner's property without paying for it, or otherwise treat aliens, their property, or their investments arbitrarily or unfairly.

Developing and socialist nations have attacked certain of these traditional legal principles on the ground that they have been developed, in their view, by the capitalist and colonialist nations without the participation of socialist and recently emerging nations and are designed solely to serve these Western industrial nations' selfish interests. They believe that some of this traditional law cannot be considered binding on non-Western nations. Developing nations accept, of course, the principle that every state has broad jurisdiction over aliens and alien property within its territory, but they would free this right of many of the constraints that traditional international law appears to impose. As developing nations see it, each nation has an inherent right to control its own resources entirely as it sees fit, without restriction or the threat of foreign pressure or interference. Any alien wishing to do business or invest in a host nation does so subject to that nation's right to exercise its sovereign powers; an alien has no right to demand treatment better than that to which the host nations' citizens are entitled or to ask his home country to intervene or espouse his claim if he is dissatisfied with such treatment. Moreover, every nation has the sovereign right to nationalize or expropriate foreign concessions or other property as it sees fit, paying only whatever compensation it believes is "appropriate."

Developing nations view this approach as "fair," among other reasons, because they believe foreign business interests have often obtained and operated resource concessions and other businessess in non-Western countries in an exploitative and dishonest way. In the past, it is said, foreign concessions and investments were sometimes obtained or accompanied by coercion, fraud, or bribery; foreign investors and companies sometimes failed to make fair payments or pay fair taxes to the host country; foreign businesses, particularly transnational companies, made "excessive" profits; and foreign businessmen or their governments sometimes sought by coercion, political and economic pressures, and other means to improperly influence the host country's political system and affairs in order to advance their business interests. Developing countries see foreign-owned transnational corporations in particular as villains. Of course, whether the evidence supports these charges has been the subject of heated debate.

This position of the developing and socialist nations is spelled out in a number of UN and other declarations and resolutions dealing with "permanent sovereignty over natural resources." The most recent and important of these statements is Article 2 of the 1974 UN Charter of Economic Rights and Duties of States, which provides that:

1. Every state has and shall freely exercise full permanent sovereignty including possession, use and disposal, over all its wealth, natural resources and economic activities.
2. Each state has the right:
   (a) To regulate and exercise authority over foreign investment within its natural jurisdiction in accordance with its laws and regulations and in conformity with its national objectives and priorities. No State shall be compelled to grant preferential treatment to foreign investment;
   (b) To regulate and supervise the activities of transnational corporations within its national jurisdiction and take measures to ensure that such activities comply with its laws, rules and regulations and conform with its economic and social policies. Transnational corporations shall not intervene in the internal affairs of a host State. Every State should, with full regard for its sovereign rights, co-operate with other States in the exercise of the right set forth in this sub-paragraph;
   (c) To nationalize, expropriate or transfer ownership of foreign property, in which case appropriate compensation should be paid by the State adopting such measures, taking into account its relevant laws and regulations and all circumstances that the State considers pertinent. In any case where the question of compensation gives rise to a controversy, it shall be settled un-

der the domestic law of the nationalizing State and by its tribunals, unless it is freely and mutually agreed by all States concerned that other peaceful means be sought on the basis of the sovereign equality of States and in accordance with the principle of free choice of means.

Six of the developed nations, including the United States, expressly stated reservations to this article because it could be construed as inconsistent with what they regarded as existing international law. These nations consequently also voted against the Charter as a whole; ten other developed nations abstained.

Developing nations argue that the Charter of Economic Rights and Duties is in effect the currently binding international law in this respect. They contend that General Assembly declarations can, by virtue of their widespread (although not necessarily universal) support, manifest binding international norms—in effect, create "instant" customary international law. Developed nations, on the other hand, argue that the UN Charter defines General Assembly actions as recommendations not binding on the members. In their view, it is unrealistic to claim that a resolution supported only by developing nations constitutes a binding customary rule when it is apparent that the industrial nations, which represent much of the world's wealth, population, and power, do not support it.

Whatever the technical legal analysis, it seems clear that the Charter and related declarations reveal developing nation attitudes which influence all nations' expectations and which developed nations will have to take into account.

This debate remains unresolved. Developing and socialist nations have often succeeded in nationalizing, expropriating, and otherwise imposing stricter regulation on foreign concessions and investments in resources. However, in many cases of nationalization or expropriation, they have also agreed to pay some compensation, often through negotiation of lump-sum settlements of international claims. In practice, despite continuing differences on matters of abstract legal principle, both developed and developing nations have devised techniques which promote and protect foreign investment and give investors some measure of security. These devices include commercial, or "friendship, commerce, and navigation," treaties; clear conditions and specific protections for investments within domestic law; investment guaranty agreements and programs; the World Bank Convention on the Settlement of Investment Disputes, which provides a mechanism for arbitrating contracts between consenting nations and foreign investors; and a variety of participation, divestment, "fadeout," and other measures to increase national participation and benefits in foreign investments.

These are issues in which reasonable arguments can be made on both sides, and the question of "fairness" will often depend on circumstances. As Arab and other developing nation investments in developed nations increase, multilateral stakes in international rules protecting investments against arbitrary expropriations or actions will grow too, and perspectives may begin to converge. Viewpoints often change when one must consider the "mirror" effects of one's own principles and actions. For example, if Arab nations can take U.S. investments in Arab countries, paying only "appropriate" compensation, persumably the United States can take Arab investments in the United States, also paying only the "appropriate" compensation.

In the final analysis, it may be less important to investors what the relevant rules are—how much special protection or treatment such rules actually afford—than that whatever rules do apply are clear and dependable. There is much to suggest that foreign investment will proceed where profit opportunities exist, that it will adjust to whatever conditions are applicable, so long as investors have some certainty about the rules of the game. Effective flows of investment among nations will require some kind of predictable framework, and international rules are the most practical and effective way of meeting this need.

### Pricing International Resources

Nations again disagree about "fairness" when confronting natural resource prices and the kinds of international arrangements appropriate to the achievement of stable and equitable prices.

Developing nations contend that present prices for the raw materials that they export are inequitably low as compared with the prices of the industrial goods that they import. They press for international arrangements which would both raise these commodity prices relative to the prices of industrial goods imported from developed nations and stabilize commodity prices at these higher real levels. They point to the heavy dependence of many developing economies on earnings from primary commodity exports; to substantial price fluctuations for many of these commodities; and to a purported secular decline in these prices relative to prices of industrial and other goods which they import. They argue that developed nations have traditionally kept commodity prices inequitably low through colonial dominance, market control, and superior bargaining power. They believe that the exploitation of non-Western peoples through the maintenance of low resource prices is one basis for the developed nations' wealth. In the developing nations' view, higher commodity prices can serve as a major means for redressing these injustices and redistributing wealth to those properly entitled to a greater share of it.

To achieve stable higher commodity prices, developing nations propose:

1. More legal and moral support for producers' associations, on the OPEC model, to strengthen the bargaining power of producer nations, to secure "fair" commodity prices, and to establish a framework for producers' cooperation on other common problems;
2. An integrated Long-Term Commodity Program covering some 18 commodities and supported by common institutions and a common fund;
3. The negotiation of preferential trading and tariff agreements to strengthen regional trade among developing countries and to ease access of developing nations' products to developed nations' markets; and
4. Indexing or similar devices in international contracts and price arrangements to maintain the real levels of commodity earnings and purchasing power against the pressure of inflation or declining currency values in developed nations.

These approaches are recommended in the 1974 Charter of Economic Rights and Duties and in a number of other international instruments. For example, Articles 5 and 6 of the Charter provide that:

Article 5
All States have the right to associate in organizations of primary commodity producers in order to develop their national economies to achieve stable financing for their development, and in pursuance of their aims, to assist in the promotion of sustained growth of the world economy, in particular accelerating the development of developing countries. Correspondingly all States have the duty to respect that right by refraining from applying economic and political measures that would limit it.
Article 6
It is the duty of States to contribute to the development of international trade of goods, particularly by means of arrangements and by the conclusion of long-term multilateral commodity agreements, where appropriate, and taking into account the interests of producers and consumers. All States share the responsibility to promote the regular flow and access of all commercial goods traded at stable, remunerative and equitable prices, thus contributing to the equitable development of the world economy, taking into account, in particular, the interests of developing countries.

Developed nations, in contrast, have generally been unwilling to concede that commodity prices are inequitably low or to cooperate in designing international arrangements to increase those prices substantially. In broad terms, they maintain that equitable prices and efficient allocation of resources are best furthered through the free and nondiscriminatory operation of market forces, not through devices which restrain these market forces. They view producers' associations, such as OPEC, as cartels designed to impose artificially high rather than equitable prices. They find harm, not benefit, for the international economy in such "cartels" and argue in particular that OPEC's fivefold increase in petroleum prices in 1973–74 has had a traumatic impact on the international economy. In the Law of the Sea negotiations and elsewhere, developed nations have resisted the concept of production limits as a means of increasing resource prices. Although developed nations have on occasion been prepared to support preferences and commodity agreements on a case-by-case basis— for example, in the Lomé Convention and the International Tin, Coffee, and Wheat Agreements—their view of broader proposals such as UNCTAD's Integrated Program for Commodities has been unenthusiastic at best.

It is not easy to envisage the kind of legal arrangements which might eventually emerge from this debate or the likelihood that price agreements will really help to solve problems of economic development and income maldistribution. An internationally agreed definition of "just prices" is certain to remain elusive, and national definitions will tend to reflect national interests. For a variety of reasons, it seems unlikely that nations producing commodities other than petroleum will be able to emulate OPEC's success in forming associations and in raising prices. Indeed, some observers are skeptical of OPEC's long-term viability. Commodity agreements involving both producers and consumers are subject to several theoretical and practical criticisms; they have had a very mixed record of success and have tended to break down under stress. Preferences are but the reverse side of discrimination, and generate their own problems.

If a major aim is the redistribution of income from the richer to the poorer peoples of the world, higher commodity prices may not be a realistic or effective way of accomplishing the objective. In some developing countries where the rich control most of these resources, a principal effect of higher raw material prices is to make the rich still richer with little benefit to the poorer masses. (It is similarly argued that many foreign aid programs have aided primarily those segments of developing societies which need no aid.) At the least, developing nations can make their appeals to equity and justice more persuasive by ensuring that redistribution to poorer people actually occurs. As many observers have suggested, there is little equity in any arrangements which transfer income from the many less-than-wealthy consumers in developed nations to the very few wealthy people who may control resources in developing nations. Certainly developing nations will win more support from more people in developed nations if they can dispel a widely held image that their governments are frequently undemocratic, oppressive, and corrupt; that their income and wealth is highly concentrated in the hands of a very small group and its powerful friends; and that any higher earnings from international trade will be spent mostly by this dominant group for their own frivolous ends, for armaments, or for other purposes that confer few benefits on their peoples. This is not to suggest that problems of oppression, corruption, concentration of wealth, or waste are unique to developing nations or that the governments of some developed nations do not share responsibility for support of some oppressive and corrupt developing nation regimes.

There are, nevertheless, several commodity-pricing aspects on which both developed and developing nations should be able to agree. All nations share an interest in relative market certainty—in commodity prices likely to remain relatively stable and in a supply and demand likely to remain relatively predictable. There is surely a broad need to stabilize markets when goods are in drastic oversupply and prices are collapsing and to provide some allocative mechanism in conditions of extreme scarcity. Even if nations are unable to agree on a "fair" price in the abstract, they may be able to agree that equitable prices are better approximated by negotiations which both sides perceive as balanced than by one party's fiat or by unequal negotiations. Perhaps that sort of agreement, at least, could be realized through appropriate long-term trade or commodity schemes. International law may not be able to define equity in prices, but it may be able to establish equity in the bargaining processes through which prices are arrived at and commodities exchanged.

A major question, of course, is whether nations might be able to devise some kind of commodity arrangement for oil. On balance, the prospects for such arrangements seem poor, even though there are ways in which both producing and consuming nations could gain from such agreement. Oil-consuming nations might gain assurances against another drastic curtailment of supplies or another abrupt leap of prices as in 1973 and 1974. Under some predictability of supply and price, consuming nations and enterprises could make more rational, more efficient, and more effective plans for energy needs. Oil-producing nations might gain explicit consuming nation acceptance of gradually rising oil prices, consumer cooperation in long-range planning of oil production and distribution, and, in particular, a political and economic climate more conducive to their interests and their planning for the future. Oil-producing nations cannot be very comfortable with a situation in which a fivefold increase in oil prices —whether or not justified—has given rise to resentment and a feeling of exploitation among many oil consumers; in which consuming nations desperately seek to reduce energy needs or develop alternative sources of energy, and in which the ability of producer nations to hold on to their gains, over the long run, may sometimes seem fragile. Producer nations might consider it preferable to enter agreements which consolidate and legitimate their present position—perhaps with indexing provisions to protect certain real prices for oil.

At present, however, producer and consumer nations both appear to believe that they will do better without such agreements. They seem to think that the risks of conceding some points in such agreements are simply not worth whatever security and predictability may result. It is difficult to assess accurately the bases for these attitudes. Apparently producing nations believe, given the ultimate exhaustibility of their resources, that they must secure the highest possible rate of return on their exports within existing political and economic constraints. Producing nations which can use their strong bargaining position on oil as leverage in broader issues of political and economic policy—including Middle East problems—are apparently reluctant to give up this leverage through a settlement covering oil questions alone. Consuming nations, for their part, appear reluctant to sanction existing price levels. They seem to hope that political and market forces, conservation, and alternative energy sources will ultimately make their bargaining position better than it is now. Although consuming nations have apparently been willing to yield on some broader economic and political points in order to secure access to oil, they are not as yet prepared to go as far in this respect as some producers wish. At the moment, each group seems content to wait the situation out, to see what develops. If these are, in fact, the perceptions of the nations involved, the chances for useful cooperation in the immediate future seem slim.

## International Law and Cooperation

International law plays an indispensable role in helping nations to cooperate in managing international natural resource problems. Decisions on a "New International Economic Order" or any other international approaches to resource problems will inevitably have to be expressed in and implemented through international agreements, institutions, and procedures. International lawyers will necessarily be involved in the design of cooperative arrangements and in working out solutions to the complex problems of coordination, risk management, collective decision making, and dispute settlement.

International cooperation is one way, although not the only way, in which nations seek to manage their mutual resource interdependence. Interdependence, in this sense, means simply that a nation cannot effectively realize its natural resource policies without taking the actions and reactions of other nations into account. A nation needing resources which others hold cannot acquire these resources unless others are willing to make them available. A nation whose economy depends on foreign exchange earnings from resource exports cannot sell those resources abroad unless others are prepared to buy them. A nation sharing particular resources with others, such as common international drainage basins, or desiring to use particular resources in common areas beyond the limits of national jurisdiction, such as the manganese nodules on the deep seabeds, cannot effectively use or manage such resources if other nations interfere. It is an accepted fact—indeed a cliché—that for most nations in the present world, interdependence in this sense is a fact, not a choice.

Faced with such interdependence, a nation might seek to reduce its dependence on others' behavior by abandoning or modifying its natural resource objectives or by trying to achieve them through "self-reliance" or "go-it-alone" policies less subject to the effects of other nations' actions. A nation might alternatively seek to coerce or persuade other nations to adopt policies which further, or at least do not interfere with, its own objectives. Finally, a nation might seek to establish cooperative arrangements with other nations, exchanges of behavior which permit each party to advance its resource goals in a more efficient way. Cooperative arrangements are frequently more effective and less costly than the alternatives in dealing with problems of interdependence, both for the nations concerned and for international society in general.

This view does not mean that either interdependence or cooperation is necessarily desirable for its own sake or that the benefits of cooperative arrangements will necessarily be equal for all parties. As Holsti (1978) has noted, "dependence" is more of a reality for most states than "interdependence," and consequently attitudes toward cooperation may differ:

The policies required for global cooperation are essential for the major powers and many other states as well, but they may be a luxury that highly dependent states cannot afford. If there is growing interdependence, it is neither universal nor symmetrical. Until more equitable relations between developed and developing states are achieved, we cannot expect the latter to jump enthusiastically on the international cooperation bandwagon, particularly in those issue-areas (e.g. pollution) where they are not major contributors to the problem.

However, in situations where nations *are* mutually dependent on each other's conduct, it is generally more advantageous to seek cooperative solutions which mutually advance their goals and avoid conflict.

It is unfortunate that international cooperation is not always easily achieved. The nations concerned must first recognize that opportunities for effective cooperation exist and communicate to each other their interest in cooperating. They must come to believe that each can potentially gain from cooperation. Finally, they must find some way of dealing with the risks that each nation may perceive—risks that the eventual costs of cooperation may turn out to exceed the benefits; risks that other nations may not actually perform on their promises; risks that alternative and perhaps better ways of achieving policies may be foreclosed. Experience suggests that governments are reluctant to undertake risks. Efforts to reach cooperative arrangements usually demand long and difficult negotiations full of potential pitfalls.

International legal techniques, however, do provide an extensive toolbox of risk management devices—for example, ways of ensuring that performance will occur or have a certain value, withdrawal arrangements, third party guarantees and dispute settlement methods, and many others —through which nations can overcome problems of uncertainty and distrust and allocate and adjust risks among themselves in a manner which makes mutual cooperation possible. International legal techniques— especially formal international norms—buttress expectations that these understandings will be mutually respected and observed.

Nations have in fact already reached a great number of cooperative means for dealing with international resource issues. In adapting these existing international organizations and agreements and in devising new cooperative arrangements, nations and international law will certainly face a bewildering array of issues. Some of the more significant and pervasive of these can be briefly indicated.

## Participation

International arrangements for managing natural resources cannot work unless a significant number of the directly concerned nations participate. Producers' associations, such as OPEC, will be ineffective unless all major exporters of the resource participate or at least tacitly cooperate. Commodity agreements, such as the International Tin Agreement, cannot operate successfully unless almost all important producers and consumers are prepared to join. Capital-exporting nations cannot establish effective arrangements for protecting foreign investment unless capital-importing nations are willing to share in such arrangements. Arrangements must be designed not only to attract participation by all nations whose cooperation is important but also to ensure that their participation will continue.

## Decision Making

International resource arrangements will inevitably raise difficult questions about the scope, procedures, and effect of collective decision making. If an institution has little real power, if its "decisions" are only hortatory, decision-making procedures may occasion little debate. But if institutions can make decisions on natural resource production, allocation, or pricing with binding legal effect, such procedures clearly become very important.

Issues of decision making have continued to occupy center stage in the "North-South" debate. Developing nations have generally insisted that decision-making authority should rest with the majority of nations participating—a procedure which will, of course, permit developing nations effective control over such decisions. Western developed nations have generally been reluctant to accept the principle of such an "automatic" developing nation majority, which they fear is potentially subject to abuse. They have pointed out that the present "one nation-one vote" formula makes it theoretically possible for two-thirds majorities to be reached in international organizations such as the UN General Assembly by votes of nations representing a very small fraction of the world's population, productive capacity, income, or power. In the absence of any spirit of compromise or accommodation, the overwhelming voting power of developing nations could, as developed nations see it, result—in the words of one recent U.S. representative to the United Nations—in a "tyranny of the majority." Developed nations have consequently pressed, as a condition of their cooperation in new resource and other arrangements, for "fairer" types of decision-making procedures—weighted voting, "veto," or "conciliation" devices—more capable of protecting their interests.

This controversy persists in the UN General Assembly, UNCTAD, commodity agreements, negotiations for the proposed International Seabed Authority, and many other "North-South" meetings. Perhaps in time this issue may become less acute as more nations attain development, interests diverge over a wider spectrum, and the groups of developed and developing nations become more heterogeneous and less cohesive. But, at least in the short run, if effective "North-South" cooperation is to be achieved, some mutually acceptable compromises will have to be reached on this question.

### Dispute Settlement and Enforcement

International cooperative arrangements on natural resources will also involve questions of dispute settlement and enforcement. There can be no guarantee that nations will always comply with their obligations, and the international system currently lacks effective means of compelling compliance. One of the best ways of dealing with disputes is a preventive one of adequate consultation and other anticipatory mechanisms for avoiding dispute. The best of these "other mechanisms," of course, is to ensure that cooperative arrangements are fair and balanced, that they serve the needs of all parties so that all parties want to see continued effective operation of the agreement. International legal devices which can help with this job include joint commissions and other consultative techniques, fact-finding, mediation, arbitration, and international courts. In addition, despite the absence of formal law enforcement agencies in the international system, there are in practice many "informal" pressures which can be brought to bear on nations to meet their obligations—international criticism and various economic or political sanctions, including exclusion from such cooperative arrangements. Imaginative techniques of this sort have been successfully employed in GATT and various commodity agreements, and similarly innovative arrangements for dispute settlement have been proposed in the current Law of the Sea negotiations.

## Conclusion

Problems of sharing the world's resources are not about to be whisked away by technological miracles, by moral revolution, or by political brotherhood. Indeed, the prospects are probably for increased international competition, tension, and possibly war as nations each seek a greater share of resources in an effort to maintain or increase the material standards of living for growing populations. Divergent criteria about "fairness" in resource distribution and about appropriate ways of inducing equity will undoubtedly persist. Differing views may be held about the content and scope of the principle of national sovereignty over territorial resources, the "common heritage" principle, or other allocative principles and about the extent to which these are "inherent" principles, within each nation's sole discretion to interpret, or, alternatively, subject to change through the process of development of international law. Each nation will continue to press for definitions of equity and for resource arrangements which further its own interests and increase its own share of resources. Nations will have little hope of successfully meeting problems of resource allocation, especially under predicted resource scarcities, unless they are prepared to work together in an effort to solve them.

International law cannot draw up solutions to resource problems or make nations cooperate. Law cannot dictate approaches or arrangements or transcend whatever levels of accommodation and cooperation nations themselves are ready to choose. Law is simply one of the tools available to nations in seeking collectively to manage their interactions and to order their socio-political environment. It can, however, help nations to reach cooperative arrangements and help to ensure that such arrangements are sensible, workable, and fair.

There is still a great deal about why and how nations cooperate with each other and about the role of law in furthering such cooperation that we do not know. Are confrontation techniques, such as those apparent in some aspects of current "North-South" issues, an effective way of bringing about eventual cooperation, or do they tend instead to increase ideological and other obstacles to useful cooperation? To what extent are perceptions of equity among all participants a necessary or sufficient condition for enduring cooperative arrangements, and what factors are likely to influence perceptions of exploitation and inequity? What are the appropriate criteria for deciding whether arrangements should be bilateral, regional, or global; for determining the extent to which decision-making authority can be usefully delegated to and exercised by collective agencies; for apportioning votes in such collective decisions?

Diplomats and lawyers lack a clear understanding of how uncertainty and risk affect negotiations or of the role of trust and risk management techniques in overcoming such wariness. Can trust be built up through less important agreements leading gradually to more important ones? Are there ways in which nations can effectively cooperate despite distrust? What legal or other devices might allow nations to manage or adjust such risks in order to reach workable agreements, and what are the advantages and disadvantages of such techniques? How can nations satisfy the inherent tensions between wanting flexibility in their own obligations but certainty about other nations' obligations? Is it realistic to expect guarantees against uncertainty and risk as a condition of cooperation; if not, what kinds and levels of risk are tolerable?

Although there is much we have to learn, at least a few broad conditions for more effective international cooperation on natural resource issues can be suggested. First, both developed and developing nations must come to terms with the fact that their interests are inextricably related and that policies of either confrontation or autarky will thus pose serious risks and costs. There is simply no practical alternative to a degree of cooperation.

Second, nations must admit that any quest for a single standard of equity is likely to prove impossible, that cooperation requires constructive efforts by all nations to reach compromises with others' points of view, and that agreements can be effective only when both sides see them as fair. In particular, the bargaining power of developing nations must be strengthened to enable them to participate more fully in the management of international affairs, and developed nations must take seriously the deeply felt conviction of peoples in developing nations that the present international order is unjust, that they are entitled to greater opportunities to share in the world's resources and wealth. On their part, developing nations must recognize that their claims to "equity" may ring hollow unless their governments take steps to become more representative, to protect and promote the human rights of their people, and to reduce internal inequality and poverty. More than rhetoric or token concessions will be necessary if these fundamental differences are to be bridged and system stability maintained.

Third, nations must move away from unresolvable debates on ideology and "matters of principle" to a reasoned dialogue, workmanlike discussions, and good faith bargaining on the very practical questions of specific and pressing resource and other economic problems. Arrangements should be tailored to solve specific problems, be designed to anticipate and avoid rather than simply to resolve disputes, and provide mechanisms for continuing readjustment among the parties as circumstances change. Even when full agreement proves impossible, it may be useful to establish rudimentary arrangements or institutions which bypass unresolvable problems but provide an adaptable and expandable framework for meeting incipient problems.

Finally, all nations must realize that the peaceful co-existence of nations requires international order; that international order necessarily implies some limits on absolute national sovereignty and discretion; and that international law serves in the broadest sense to implement rather than obstruct the achievement of long-run national interests. National sovereignty should be viewed, not as an ideological absolute, but as a functional approach to the achievement of national goals. Possible gains from unilateral national action must always be balanced against the gains that nations can collectively achieve through international approaches. In the long run, nations cannot hope to have the benefits of international order without also accepting some of the constraints which any order necessarily imposes.

Some believe that the existing international system, based on nation-states, is inherently incapable of coping with long-run problems of resource allocation or other challenges. They insist that some radical transformation in global political structure is necessary if these problems are to be met. With more than 150 nations pursuing separate individual objectives in a competitive effort to increase their share of limited world resources, the chances of somehow achieving a rational and equitable global system of allocation of these resources may indeed seem remote. In fact, the complexity of nations' interactions and interdependencies has reached a level which sometimes appears to defy comprehension and control. It may be, as some have suggested, that a system of equitable and efficient allocation of global resources can ultimately be achieved only through global planning and regulatory techniques implemented by international agencies with supranational authority.

However, if this analysis is correct, it offers small help or comfort;

there is little prospect that such a radical transformation can soon occur. In practice we have little choice but to work as best we can within the structure of the existing system and with the various tools at hand to try to forge effective and fair solutions to the very difficult problems we face. There is reason to hope that if nations bring to such efforts common sense, imagination, a respect for others' views, and goodwill, these problems can be successfully met.

## References

Hardin, Garrett. 1968. "The Tragedy of the Commons," *Science* 162: 1243–48.

Holsti, Kal. 1978. "A New International Politics? Diplomacy in Complex Interdependence," *International Organization* 32: 513–30.

Koers, A. W. 1973. *International Regulation of Marine Fisheries: A Study of Regional Fisheries Organizations*. West Byfleet, England: Fishing News.

Schachter, Oscar. 1976. "The Evolving Law of International Development," *Columbia Journal of Transnational Law* 15: 1–16.

Schachter, Oscar. 1977. *Sharing the World's Resources*. New York: Columbia University Press.

# IV. ANALYTICAL AND POLICY REDIRECTIONS

# 14 *Vincent C. Rideout*

# Modeling Studies of
# Socio-Economic-Resource Systems

The concepts and problems of natural resource policies, economic development, and international cooperation involve the entire physical, economic, and political world system. Some subsets, or narrower aspects of the world system, such as the problems of world oil demand and supply, have received special attention. However, such subsystems, although often complex in themselves, are closely related to a large number of other subsystems, including those which describe the dynamics of population, world trade, resource flows, technological development and transfer, monetary systems, and legal systems. The nature of large systems and the methods for analyzing and studying the effects of modification of systems are therefore important.

A system is an assemblage of components, or entities, which function collectively in some manner. Engineering systems, such as an aircraft-plus-autopilot, are designed by man, while those of nature, such as the human cardiovascular system or a colony of bees, appear to have been designed by natural selection over a long period of random and other change. World and national systems, whether economic or political, have originated through both human design and natural selection.

Systems are often classified according to those of their characteristics which seem most important in their analysis. For example, a system may be described as either a static or a dynamic system; the static system may be described by algebraic equations, while the dynamic system will require differential or difference equations for its description. Systems may also be continuous or discrete, deterministic or stochastic, stable or unstable, or subject to limit cycling, etc.

Although the primary concern of anyone studying socio-economic-resource systems is likely to be analysis, policy makers may also be interested in some aspects of synthesis, in the sense that policy may require some structural changes and not mere modification of exogenous variables or the parameters* of existing structure. In any case, the complexity of these systems makes the future trends of their many important variables difficult to determine. Trial and error methods of analysis and design, often adequate in engineering systems, are sometimes used in socio-economic-resource systems too, but the dangers in their use may be likened to those of trial and error design of a jet aircraft or a nuclear reactor. Modeling procedures long employed in basic science, engineering, and medicine are now beginning to have illuminating applications, without the risks of real world trial and error, in systems which include economic and social factors.

## Modeling and the Use of Models

The analysis of any system requires at least some kind of modeling in which partial or approximate representation of the system is used to aid understanding.** As Rosenblueth and Weiner (1945) put it: "Partial models, imperfect as they may be, are the only means developed by science for understanding the universe."

Even though there are many arguments about the range of their applicability, large economic models which require computer simulation have received more and more attention in recent years. Such economic models are necessarily socio-economic because they include behavior equations. Boulding (1966, p. 222) eloquently supports the use of economic models:

The moral of these considerations is that economic models, especially when it comes to the interpretation of a phenomenon as complex as the dynamic fluctuations or growth of the economy as a whole, are aids to thought and not substitutes. We must beware of too great reliance on the too simple model, for the assumptions of such models are always likely to be falsified. Nevertheless, without the aid

---

*The word *parameter* will be used here in its mathematical sense to refer to those factors in equations which, unlike system variables, are unaffected by system dynamics; they may be constants or exogenous variables.

**The word *model* is here used to mean a representation of a system. It has another meaning in which it refers to a representation of an ideal version of a system.

of these models, the complexity of the subject matter always leads to complete bewilderment or to a retreat into the rituals of pure empiricism and the endless recording of data whose meaning escapes us, or it leads us to thinking with the aid of implicit models which we never openly recognize, and which therefore are all the more likely to lead us astray.

This argument, which is echoed by others (Tinbergen 1967; Day and Groves 1975), is not accepted by all economists. It appears that everyone accepts the notion of models as useful, simplified representations of complex systems but that many will not accept mathematical models, or computer simulation of such models, as being either necessary or useful. The unhappiness of some with mathematics in modeling relates to their unwillingness to accept its use in social sciences. Nevertheless, Rapaport (1959) notes that "mathematics is the only language we have which is uncontaminated by bias derived from content. . . . It makes possible the linking of theories of widely different content but with similar logical structures. It is therefore superbly suited to serve as the language of all science."

The range of mathematical techniques which may need to be brought into play in social system and socio-economic modeling (see Simon 1978) may be disconcerting even to physical scientists who become interested in this sort of study. These techniques primarily depend on formulating dynamic system descriptions in terms of large sets of nonlinear difference or differential equations and on devising computer algorithms for their solution. Although many of these techniques were originated by physical scientists, as in the case of the mathematics of "fuzzy systems" (Zadeh 1965) and the methods of Interpretive Structural Modeling or ISM (Sage 1977), most of the more relevant methods are drawn from the field of economics (Tinbergen 1959; Johnston 1963; Koopmans 1957) and include the determination of behavior equations and the use of stochastic methods. Peterson (1975) has warned of the dangers of overusing some of the newer techniques such as those of information theory. Furthermore, Jahoda (1973) cautions that model-based predictions may be turned, by human choice, into self-fulfilling or self-defeating prophecies.

## Modeling Procedures and Techniques

The primary objective of all socio-economic-resource modeling is to help in understanding some important aspects of the world system. The specific uses for which such models may be designed are four in number:

1. Hypothesis testing. Theories of the more important cause-and-effect couplings in a system may be studied by repetitively rerunning

a model of the past as changes in suspected causal factors are made.
2. Prediction and Policy testing. A system model which has been vali-
dated, so that it can successfully depict the past, may be used to try
to predict the future of interesting aspects of the system. These tests
may be made repetitively as different policies are introduced into
the model in various ways and as uncontrollable exogenous inputs
(weather damage, crop failures, foreign tariff changes, etc.) influence the model.
3. Optimization. If a mathematical criterion (or criteria) which should
be maximized by policy procedures can be set up, a model may be
used to find the best policy choices and levels. This use of a model
may require some repetitive computer simulation of the future as
policy changes are made under the guidance of a computer algorithm which automatically finds the maximum value of the chosen
criterion. Optimization studies of a system may lead to the design of
an adaptive system with a mechanism to preserve optimality.
4. Interaction and Gaming. An interactive computer model is one into
which an operator (who may be a policy maker) can introduce policy changes at appropriate points in time as the model runs. If more
than one policy maker can introduce changes (with different objectives), the model serves as a means for gaming as the several policy
makers compete to realize their individual objectives and optimize
criteria.

In addition to these four primary uses of models, other incidental but
important values are always found. One of these is to reveal areas of missing data or missing knowledge about system structure. Another is to serve
as a mechanism to bring together an interdisciplinary group by giving
them a framework for explaining their concepts to one another and for
indicating their areas of agreement or disagreement. It follows that models are useful in teaching and conceivably may be used to instruct those
who must learn the fundamentals of socio-economic system dynamics,
just as models are now used to teach the principles of the circulation of
blood in the body or the operation of nuclear power reactors. The most
important instructional function of modeling, however, is the education
that model building provides for the modelers and users themselves.

### Paradigms, Criteria, Boundaries, Sectors

Kuhn (1962) popularized the term *paradigm* to refer to the way one perceives and values the world. Everyone, including policy makers and
model builders, has some dominant value framework or paradigm which

will surely influence his or her actions. Such paradigms are so ingrained that they are difficult to recognize. For instance, Harman, a futurist, has spoken of the possibility of a societal metamorphosis which might supplant the industrial-era paradigm with a new set of values more concerned with spiritual aspects of life and ecological ethics (Harman 1976).

Modelers, or those who sponsor them, can best overcome the problems of building a model based on only a single narrow paradigm by using a truly multidisciplinary team, one which includes members from the social sciences as well as the physical and mathematical sciences. The modeler's (or policy maker's) paradigm will indicate which values should be considered and give them a ranking.

In order to compare the results of policies, some numerical values must be attached to a human welfare or quality-of-life criterion (House and McLeod 1977, p. 205; Herrera 1974). This notion, unwholesome as it may seem to humanists, is necessary to avoid the uncertainties and misunderstandings of subjective judgments. Too often an overly simple measure of human welfare, such as GNP per capita, has been used. More complex measures involving health, income distribution, and derivative terms can be obtained from a suitable spectrum of a population by Delphi or other techniques and incorporated into policy models (Elmaghraby 1978).

The boundaries of a model are usually the geographic limits within which interaction is considered. For example, an econometric model of the United States may not include a model of the Middle East, despite the significance of the latter as a source of petroleum for the United States. The inflow of this product and the corresponding outflow of payments must be included in the model but may be considered to be exogenous variables, fixed or varying according to some predetermined pattern.

Those sectors or levels of a model which will be individually modeled—ecological, economic, agricultural, monetary, population, and other submodels—must be chosen. Such submodels have some coupling to each other in each region (and on into other regions). The use of distinct levels is well illustrated by the world model of Mesarovic and Pestel (1974a), although their use of the term *hierarchical* in reference to levels does not seem to fit the nature of the interdependence among levels.

The aggregation of a model refers to the combining or averaging of similar model components. Forrester's World-2 model (Forrester 1971) is the ultimate in geographic aggregation because the entire world population is used as one variable and world industrial output as another. Macroeconomic models combine or aggregate many industries in a single region, while microeconomic and input-output models attempt to deal with individual industries in more detail.

## A Model of Modeling

Even the procedures of modeling may be modeled. Figure 14.1 shows a conceptual model, in logical flow-graph form, of a possible sequence of events in modeling. Here two coupled sequences are shown—one for modelers and one for the policy makers who support the model. (Sometimes groups find support from organizations or individuals other than policy makers; supporters may proceed with a view to influencing policy makers later.)

The first decision which must be faced by policy makers or system analysts is whether to use a conceptual (mental) model, described largely in words, or a more formal mathematical model, described by equations. The former may take the shape of a scenario study in which a desirable future socio-economic-resource system state is postulated, and means for achieving this state are sought (Harman 1976; Steinhart et al. 1977). The more mathematically oriented dynamic model, with which this chapter is primarily concerned, may be used in conjunction with scenario studies.

If a decision is made to build a mathematical model, two very important procedures must follow before model building begins. One is recruiting and organizing the modeling group, which will in turn tend to determine the basic paradigm and techniques used in modeling. The second procedure is determining the objectives of the modeling study. It is essential that the modelers and the policy makers who support the model agree on model objectives; failure to do so has led to many problems in model usage.

The next step, the first technical one in model building, should be the collecting and filing of data, and this activity must continue throughout the life of the model.

With data on hand, model building can proceed. The structure of the model is a matter of considerable difficulty and importance and will be discussed separately. Once the model, or at least some important and somewhat independent parts of it, is ready for test, the model makers may proceed with *verification* of the model, which is the checking of its self-consistency. This is followed by *validation*, checking the model against past history in the real world.* These procedures (shown in feedback loops in figure 14.1 to indicate that corrections may be necessary) should be followed by an *evaluation* procedure (Pugh 1977), preferably carried out by a third party. Use of the model to study policy alternatives may then proceed as shown, with modelers, policy makers, and model working in close collaboration.

*The use of *verification* and *validation* follows U.S. terminology (House and McLeod 1977); in the United Kingdom some modelers reverse the meaning of the terms (Clark et al. 1975).

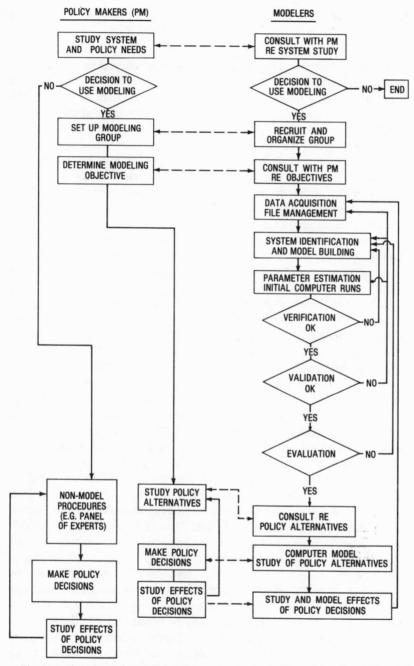

POLICY MAKERS (PM)  MODELERS

STUDY SYSTEM AND POLICY NEEDS

CONSULT WITH PM RE SYSTEM STUDY

DECISION TO USE MODELING — NO

DECISION TO USE MODELING — NO → END

YES  YES

SET UP MODELING GROUP

RECRUIT AND ORGANIZE GROUP

DETERMINE MODELING OBJECTIVE

CONSULT WITH PM RE OBJECTIVES

DATA ACQUISITION FILE MANAGEMENT

SYSTEM IDENTIFICATION AND MODEL BUILDING

PARAMETER ESTIMATION INITIAL COMPUTER RUNS

VERIFICATION OK — NO

YES

VALIDATION OK — NO

YES

EVALUATION — NO

YES

NON-MODEL PROCEDURES (E.G. PANEL OF EXPERTS)

STUDY POLICY ALTERNATIVES

CONSULT RE POLICY ALTERNATIVES

MAKE POLICY DECISIONS

MAKE POLICY DECISIONS

COMPUTER MODEL STUDY OF POLICY ALTERNATIVES

STUDY EFFECTS OF POLICY DECISIONS

STUDY EFFECTS OF POLICY DECISIONS

STUDY AND MODEL EFFECTS OF POLICY DECISIONS

Fig. 14.1 Flow chart of modeling decisions, development, and use by policy makers and modelers.

431

## Model Structure

Decisions about what subsystems to include in a model are critically important in the initial stages of model building. Parsimony in a model is a virtue which must be balanced against the approximations which result from too much aggregation or from omitting geographic areas or sectors of the economy and so increasing the number of exogenous variables.

It has been mentioned that models may be designed with a built-in optimization or goal-seeking mechanism. Such models may be described as prescriptive or normative. They may also be purely descriptive (or positive), with any optimization included only as an add-on feature. Interactive models are designed to permit human intervention during the running of a model through its time frame.

Of more fundamental importance, models may on the one hand be black-box or aprioristic (Tinbergen 1967), based on study of stimulus-response time series of a system and with structure largely ignored. Such models are called "data-rich." On the other hand, a model may be based on system structure and theory-of-process, with one-to-one relationships between terms in equations and details of the system. Such models are said to be "theory-rich." The proper combination of these two extreme approaches may be most desirable (Strongman et al. 1978).

Models may be static or dynamic. However, even static models, if set up at successive intervals, may be used for prediction. Dynamic models, usually expressed mathematically in terms of differential or difference equations, may incorporate various ranges of frequency; monthly data and calculations might be essential in a short-range econometric model, but annual data might be adequate in certain long-range models.

Models may also be deterministic or stochastic (Schweppe 1973). Deterministic models give outputs which are repeated without change if repeated runs are made. Stochastic models (Tintner and Sengupta 1972) will not repeat without change because some randomness of inputs, initial conditions, or parameters is included. Thus in complex nonlinear stochastic systems, many runs may be needed to determine the range of possible outputs—a simulation procedure called the Monte Carlo method.

In the past, socio-economic models have been designed more with the entities (e.g., population size, pollution level) in mind than the flows. The five quite different kinds of flow are those of energy, materials, information, money, and people, and these may be further broken down, in the case of materials, for example. Figure 14.2 shows a diagram of a model of a single region and the interconnections among sectors provided by the various kinds of flow (interconnections to other regions are not shown). Such a model may be regarded as a multiple model and resembles multiple models used in physiological modeling (Beneken and Rideout 1968).

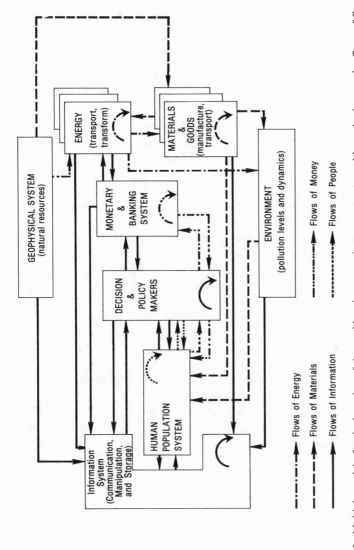

Fig. 14.2. Multiple model of a single region of the world socio-economic-resource system with emphasis on major flows of five variables (flows to and from other regions not indicated).

433

The multiple model in the single-region system of figure 14.2 would consist of five models, one to describe each kind of flow, with required interactions from one model to another. In the analogous model of the mammalian body, information flows in the nervous system, and plasma (akin to money) flows in the cardiovascular system and facilitates the transport of materials and energy throughout the body.

A rather complete description of the modeling procedures used in systems engineering and their application to socio-economic-resource systems has been given by Sage (1977).

*Computer Simulation*

Socio-economic-resource systems, even for a single country, tend to be very complex, and their representation in the form of mathematical models may require nonlinear and stochastic terms. Such simulation studies will tend to require powerful computers with sophisticated software. Repeated runs are necessary if nonlinear stochastic models are used, and still more repetition may be needed if sensitivity studies, parameter estimation, or interactive gaming is of interest. These requirements may easily demand more in the way of computer speed and peripheral output than is obtainable with today's equipment. However, the advent of the microprocessor may soon revolutionize the design of simulation computers by permitting small computers, each devoted to the simulation of a single sector in one disaggregated region, to be interconnected in one large computer (Cyre et al. 1977). Large computers and highly developed software are also required for storing, retrieving, and managing the great amounts of data needed by modelers.

Computer simulation programs may be written in well-known compiler languages such as FORTRAN, so universally used that transferability is not a problem. However, many specially designed modeling languages (see Robinson 1972) are more convenient for dynamic system simulation and are themselves usually written in FORTRAN or some well-known compiler language, so that transfer is easily possible.

## A Review of Socio-Economic-Resource Models

Much early economic theory was related more to ideologies than to mathematical models. The first mathematical models of economic systems were typically linear with simplifications which would permit closed-form analytic solutions. Thus von Neumann's economic growth model (1945), which omitted consideration of both labor input and consumption of goods, was linear and static but allowed the use of powerful matrix algebra methods. These early methods, which include those of Hotelling

(1931), continue to be used by some workers today (Bergstrom 1967), but the advent of computers has now made it possible to use algorithmic procedures to deal with mathematical formulations, including both nonlinearities and stochastic features, and so to give truer descriptions of large socio-economic-resource systems. The answers to questions posed to computer simulations of such systems lack the attractive simplicity of answers given by the simpler closed-form mathematical models, but as Tukey (1962) points out, "Far better an approximate answer to the right question, which is often vague, than an exact answer to the wrong question, which can always be made precise."

## Macroeconomic Models

Both the highly aggregated, large region, macroeconomic models and the more detailed microeconomic models depend upon econometrics, the determination of model structure and parameter values from recorded economic data. Econometric procedures were originated by Tinbergen (1959), who set up a 24-equation macroeconomic model of the Dutch economy in 1936. This model was followed by later models by Tinbergen and by Theil (1966) which led to macroeconomic modeling in other countries. Another early modeler was Frisch (1933). Many theoretical features of these models stem from the work of Keynes (1936).

Macroeconomic models typically consist of behavioral equations (determining variables such as consumption, investment, and wages), together with identities (determining industrial output, prices, and capital stock). These equations interlink endogenous variables (together with some of their values from the past) and exogenous variables such as government expenditures and taxes. A simple linear six-equation example of a macroeconomic model was given by Klein (1950) and is illustrated in diagram form in figure 14.3.

Detail in macroeconomic models may be provided by subsuming models more microeconomic in nature such as the input-output models discussed later or the microeconomic models proposed by Orcutt (1962) and Orcutt et al. (1976). Certain monetary models may also be included (Modigliani 1973).

Models of the U.S. economy have been devised by Klein and others and reviewed by Fromm and Klein (1973) and by Fromm et al. (1975). These include the large Wharton model (originally consisting of 47 behavioral equations and 29 identities) and the still larger Brookings model (originally containing 270 and now 400 equations). Both are being used to study and predict various aspects of the U.S. economy, and both are still being enlarged and improved. The construction, validation, and use of these models has been discussed by Naylor (1971) with the warning that " . . . the

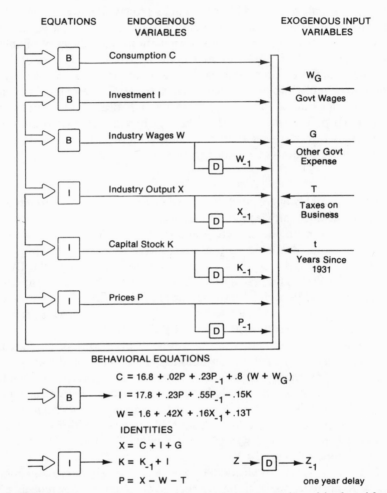

Fig. 14.3. Block diagram of a simple example of an econometric model, adapted from Klein (1950).

formulation of realistic hypotheses concerning the behavior of a dynamic economy requires a considerable knowledge of macroeconomic theory. The analyst who attempts to use simulation techniques as a substitute for a thorough grounding in macroeconomic theory is very likely to find that he has simulated his own ignorance rather than the real world."

These large econometric models are used to attempt prediction of the values of important economic variables, with particular efforts to determine "turning points" as well as sensitivities (or "multipliers") which give relationships between important variables and possible sudden events or policy changes. Some success has been achieved, although for only a few quarters or at best a few years into the future. Problems result from uncertainty about exogenous inputs as well as random or stochastic errors in parameters and in the initial values of variables (Christ 1966; Tinbergen 1967).

Macroeconomic models of regions within a country include the urban models described by Pugh (1977, chapter 3), the OSSIM model of Oregon (Calligan 1976), the San Diego County model (McLeod 1972), and the Susquehanna River Basin model (Hamilton et al. 1969). Models of small countries (Slater and Walsham 1975; Quinn 1977) may not differ too much from such regional models, except that they may include a modeling of government monetary and import duty policies.

Many urban models are weak in their dynamics and do not explicitly contain a modeling of feedback loops but are strongly oriented toward spatial distribution studies of population, industry, etc.; others based on the ideas of system dynamics and urban dynamics introduced by Forrester (1969) do emphasize dynamics and behavioral equations describing feedback effects. The early system dynamics models were not designed to contain much spatial detail and were instead adapted to the study of urban problems of a broad strategic nature (Pugh 1977, chapter 7). However, some attempts have been made to include the suburbs as a separate area in an urban model (Graham 1972) and to apply Forrester's urban dynamics to a specific city and its problems (Porter and Henley 1972).

Beginning in 1968 a number of the large econometric models developed for individual countries and regions were combined in "Project LINK" by Klein and others in order to study world economic problems (Ball 1973; Klein 1976; Glejser 1976). Even the individual models were quite large, and the overall LINK system's complexity is such that the problems of data collecting and of keeping model parameters updated are not easy. Nevertheless, the models have had some success, particularly in predicting turning points where simpler methods such as trend evaluation have failed.

One weakness in macroeconomic models is the failure to include within them submodels of population growth, ecological impact, or resource exhaustion. Where population is needed as an input, for example, it is typically estimated and fed in exogenously. The omission of such submodels was rather natural when econometric models were used only for predictions of a year or two. As attempts are made to predict for longer periods, population and other submodels included within econometric models become more and more necessary.

Because macroeconomic models are dynamic with intrinsic inclusion of positive and negative feedback loops (such loops are described in chapter

3), their utility in explaining and even predicting economic "cycles" has been a long-standing hope (Tinbergen 1967). Despite the use of modern control theory (Runyan 1971), however, the so-called cyclical nature of the U.S. and other economic systems has not been clearly demonstrated in econometric models. In the system dynamics-based model of Mass (1975), business cycles have been demonstrated, but this model has been criticized for its lack of a detailed data base.

The large macroeconomic models of the Tinbergen-Klein type are structural, detailed, nonlinear, dynamic, firmly based on economic data, and simulated with recognition of the stochastic nature of certain variables and parameters. Because of their sound basis on theory and data, they can be and are being steadily improved as well as enlarged. Constant validation efforts have given some indication of their power as well as their problems and have kept modelers from promising too much and from drawing unwarranted conclusions about the distant future.

### Input-Output Models

Although input-output models are among the oldest of economic models (Richardson 1972), their modern development and use have stemmed mostly from the work of Leontief (1966; 1977). The basic construction is simple, linear, and static, consisting of equations of the form:

$$X_j = a_{j1}X_1 + a_{j2}X_2 + \ldots a_{jn}X_n + Y_j$$

Here $X_j$ is the output of the $j$-th firm (or industry or sector, depending on the scale of aggregation), $Y_j$ is the final consumption of this output, and the other terms are the portions of the output $X_j$ required by other firms in the process of manufacture. Once the coefficients $a_{ji}$ of a set of $n$ equations are determined, it is possible by matrix inversion to find the outputs $X_1 \ldots X_n$ to satisfy any set of consumptions $Y$ (provided the $a_{ji}$'s remain constant). Labor, value-added, and import equations may be included, and terms (called "externalities") may be added on to account for taxes and environmental cost (Gutmanis 1975).

However, input-output models do not ordinarily include any consideration of profits, price-setting, or inventory problems, and attempts to introduce dynamic features into these models have not been too satisfactory. The models do provide an important method for making industrial output consistency checks and studying impacts of demand changes and externalities, and they can be used with linear programming methods in certain optimization studies (Richardson 1972). Some rather large input-output models have been set up, including the UN World Model (Leontief 1977).

Input-output models are thought by many to have more value as submodels embedded in macroeconomic models than as stand-alone models for the study of economic systems (Ayres 1978; Glejser 1976; Mesarovic and Pestel 1974a).

## Optimizing Models

Some economic models may include built-in optimizing features, such as a computer algorithm, which will change system inputs or parameters to maximize some criterion (such as GNP or a measure for quality of life).

The use of linear programming for maximizing an objective function in an input-output model has been mentioned. Linear programming was also used by Deam (1974) in optimization studies with a world energy model. Nonlinear programming was used by Manne (1976) to examine effects of cross-price elasticities in a model study of energy technologies.

Westcott (1976), in a study of the U.K. economy, suggested that an optimal control scheme (Tintner and Sengupta 1972, sec. 3.1) might be designed for a simplified model of this system, then tried out on a more detailed nonlinear model, and adjusted as needed. Burmeister and Dobell (1972), on the other hand, suggested that market forces provide a measure of optimal control which has automatically grown or developed as part of the economy and which should be studied by control theorists.

Nonlinear dynamic models cannot easily be optimized by optimal control means. However, hill-climbing optimization* techniques of various kinds can be used in conjunction with rapid rerunning of a simulation model. McCalla (1978) has used such a scheme to study the optimum scheduling of oil and gas production in a model of the economy of a small oil-exporting country under a criterion of maximization of the present value of future worth of investments. Optimization with this model can be repeated for various assumed scenarios for future oil prices as well as rates of interest and inflation.

An ambitious world model, the Bariloche model developed in Argentina (Herrera 1974), contains an optimizing scheme related to satisfaction of basic needs. Optimization was carried out by a sophisticated maximization of criteria at each time step to yield an ideal path for future development policy. This model will be discussed further in a later section on world modeling.

Adaptive control systems differ from optimal control systems in that instead of changing some input variables to optimize some outputs,

---

*Hill-climbing optimization may easily be visualized for the simple case where there are but two variable parameters. If these are thought of as distances in north and south directions and the criterion to be maximized is considered to be the altitude of the terrain, the concept of hill climbing, or steepest ascent maximization, may be visualized as one of constant ascent by the steepest route.

changes are made in parameters or even in structure in order to optimize outputs over a range of expected inputs. Modeling is essential to studies of such systems (Day and Groves 1975; Rajaraman and Rideout 1962).

## Interactive and Gaming Models

The methods used in computer modeling of the behavior of large groups of people are not satisfactory for describing the action of a single person, particularly if that person is a policy maker. The complexity of the mental processes of an individual (or even a small group) may best be included in the model by allowing a real person to interact with the computer-simulated part of the model. A real pilot may be used, for instance, in interactive modeling studies of aircraft designs.

Policy-maker intervention studies are a feature of the Mesarovic-Pestel world models in which the running of a dynamic model on a computer can be halted at any time to introduce policy changes decided by an informed and capable person or team. If two or more persons interact in different regions or sectors of a model, each with an individual set of values and objectives, the interactive model becomes a gaming model. This sort of gaming has been used with rather simple and often static models in connection with studies ranging from real estate development to military problems. It is also possible with large dynamic models such as that of Mesarovic and Pestel.

## Sectoral Modeling

Models may be disaggregated geographically into regions (countries, states, or counties) as well as into sectors or levels. The latter involve submodels of world models or individual sectoral models such as population models (Arthur and McNicoll 1975), energy models (Baughman and Hnyilicza 1975; Deam 1974), agricultural models (Bruckman 1977), resource models (Vousden 1973), environmental models (Daetz and Pantell 1974), commodity models (Labys 1973), and monetary models (Andersen and Carlson 1974) as well as the purely economic models discussed earlier.

Individual model studies of sectors may be valuable in themselves despite the uncertainties which result from treating the rest of the world system as exogenous. Such studies may, of course, lead to more comprehensive models which include two or more sectors in each region if they are multiregion models.

Of all the types of sectoral models mentioned above, the population model has probably received the most attention. Because the behavioral aspects of population growth (particularly birth rate and migration patterns) are not well understood, most demographic models are not too trustworthy. However, the economic models with which demographic models are coupled give rise to more severe difficulties so that errors because of inaccuracies in population growth estimates are often hidden in the stochastic spread of the economic forecasts.

Energy models take many forms, from the scenario and static but regionally detailed types to the system dynamics and optimizing kinds (Koopmans 1978). Unlike population models, which are quite distinct from economic models as to level or sector, an energy model, if part of a large multisector model, is chiefly to be regarded as a segment of the economic sector. Agricultural models, unless dealt with in isolation, are also part of the economic sector. But both energy and agricultural models have a resource aspect which, as with resource models per se, relates them to the sciences of biology, geology, geophysics, oceanography, meteorology, and others.

Only limited attention has been given to stand-alone resource models, and many of these have been of the classical closed-form mathematical type with many of the simplicities this approach requires (Hotelling 1931; Vousden 1973). Nevertheless, important basic notions about optimization of depletable resource usage rates were introduced and will be useful in more detailed resource modeling in the future.

Environmental models, dealing chiefly with the interaction of modern industry and living patterns with ecological systems, have been incorporated into econometric energy models.

Commodity models can give answers of immediate economic value; they have received much attention as econometric models applied to renewable commodities (Labys 1973; 1977; see also figure 14.4) and as system dynamics models applied to depletable commodities (Strongman et al. 1978; Killingsworth 1978). The close relationship of the latter to resource modeling is obvious.

Monetary and fiscal systems are usually considered as part of the economic scene but may be separately modeled as sectors with couplings to the economic model or models of a country.

### Transnational Corporation and Cartel Modeling

Some transnational corporations are larger, in terms of gross product, than any but the larger nations. It would therefore seem important to include explicit modeling of such transnationals in large regional or world models, but this has not been done. Modeling of the transnational corporation as an entity has had some attention from Fourcans and Hindelang (1975), but their modeling was done from the internal viewpoint of the transnationals rather than from that of the world modeler who wants to put models of corporations in a comprehensive model. It may be expected that it will always be difficult to obtain economic data on transnationals,

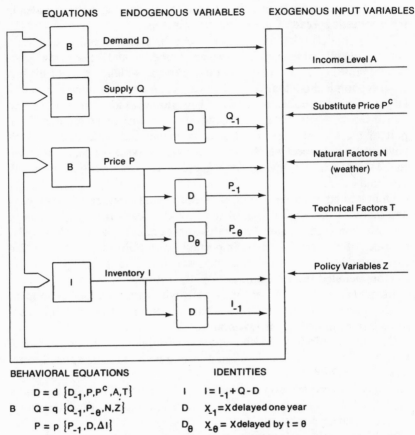

Fig. 14.4 Block diagram of a rudimentary econometric commodity model, adapted from Labys (1977).

and indeed this may be a principal reason for their omission from existing world models.

Neither has the modeling of cartels been explicitly included in large socio-economic models, although effects of their actions have sometimes been introduced as policy changes or exogenous inputs. Again, only a few explicit models of cartels or similar organizations and their interactions with other economic units have appeared (Underwood 1977).

Producers' associations, such as OPEC, have been modeled (Cremer and Weitzman 1976; Marshalla 1977), but once again the amount of attention to modeling producers' (or consumers') organizations has not seemed proportional to the size or importance of some of these units.

## World or Global Models

Several kinds of models have dealt with the entire world in some sense. Some of these, such as Deam's "World Energy Model" (1974), Project LINK (Ball 1973), and the UN Input-Output Model (Leontief 1977), are really limited to a single sector, the Deam model mainly to petroleum and the other two to economics.

The term "World Model" seems to have been largely preempted by Forrester (1968) and others who followed his system dynamics methods. The approach used in his famous World-2 model (Forrester 1971) incorporated many sectors—economics, population, agriculture, pollution, and natural resources (see figure 14.5). But Forrester's World-2 model aggregated the world into a single region, as did its successor, the Meadows' World-3 model (Meadows et al. 1974); furthermore, the use of data in determining the equations of these models, particularly World-2, was quite limited. Because of these factors and because of the small number of equations used in these models, some heroic assumptions had to be made, particularly because the models were used for predictions to the year 2150. Many serious criticisms of these models appeared (Cole et al. 1973; Cuypers and Rademaker 1974; Clark et al. 1975; Richardson 1978), and despite accompanying constructive suggestions as well as rebuttals by

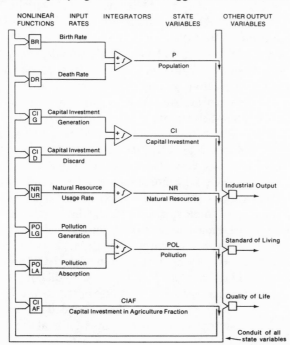

Fig. 14.5. Block diagram of Forrester's World-2 model (1971).

Meadows et al. (1973), these criticisms brought doubts about the value of world and regional modeling generally (Watt 1977).

It is instructive to examine a penetrating critique by Jaeckel (1972) of Forrester's first application of system dynamics modeling (Forrester 1969). Jaeckel, a sociologist, points out that "one of Forrester's main claims is that the behavior of complex systems is counter-intuitive; strictly speaking, however, he has demonstrated this only for models, and as for these, their behavior is perhaps less counter-intuitive as we become accustomed to the particular assumptions defining them." However, Jaeckel does go on to say that "modeling of the type demonstrated by Forrester is obviously highly instructive. It leads to tentative conclusions, insights and questions otherwise not readily obtained. Furthermore, the use of computers allows computational extrapolations, and hence predictions . . . beyond those which the unaided human powers of conception could master."

The world models of Forrester and Meadows were simpler than Forrester's urban models, yet more far-reaching remedies were advocated based on their use. The models were advocative and sensational, and despite their weaknesses they did bring to many minds the need for modeling and indeed the first notions that something of this sort might be attempted. They have been followed by an important geographically disaggregated, multilevel, data-based model—the Mesarovic-Pestel world model (Mesarovic and Pestel 1974b). However, this model too was preceded by a book (Mesarovic and Pestel 1974a) which, like the famous *Limits to Growth* (Meadows et al. 1972), gave model results before model details were published. Strong attempts are now being made to apply the Mesarovic-Pestel model in an interactive manner to important economic problems in various parts of the world. Although in application it is sometimes thought to suffer from being more of a tool of the modeler than of the policy makers, this kind of dynamic data-based model seems an important step forward (Clark et al. 1975; Richardson 1978).

Another ambitious modeling effort resembling that of Mesarovic and Pestel is the Japanese FUGI (Future of Global Interdependence) model of Kaya and his co-workers (Kaya and Suzuki 1974; Kaya 1977; McLeod 1978). This model has three parts linked together: a global macroeconomic model, a global input-output model, and a global metallic resources model. The macroeconomic model is disaggregated into 15 geographic regions, in a manner akin to the organization of the LINK model. In addition to using the FUGI model for short-range prediction of worldwide economic conditions, its designers have attempted to use it to predict what might be expected from various policies intended to improve the lot of the developing countries in a reformed international economic order (Tinbergen 1976).

A somewhat different model, the Bariloche or Latin American World Model (Herrera 1974; Scolnik and Talavera 1974) disaggregates the world into four geographic regions; each is modeled in five sectors. However, no sector is included for natural resources, and criticism of the model for this and for omission of trade among regions has appeared (Clark et al. 1975; Richardson 1978). The model is unique among world models for its normative content and built-in optimization routines, which are called upon at each time step to manipulate the use of capital and labor in order to maximize a quality-of-life criterion. Thus the model output for the future gives both economic conditions (optimized) and the policies necessary to achieve them—all within the limits of the accuracy of the model.

A number of other world modeling efforts have been outlined by Richardson (1978); USSR efforts are referenced by Burkhov (1977).

The world modeling efforts reviewed here may be classified into four groups:

1. World input-output models (the UN model—see Leontief 1977);
2. Macroeconomic or econometric models (of which LINK is the best example);
3. System dynamics world models (ranging from the highly aggregated Forrester models to the more detailed Mesarovic-Pestel and FUGI models);
4. Optimizing world models (Bariloche).

Different though these classes of models may be, future models may include elements from all four. The Mesarovic-Pestel model contains input-output submodels and has some econometric as well as system dynamics features. It is not built for continuous optimizing as the Bariloche model is, but optimizing features could be added.

### The Use of Models in Policy Studies

A dominant paradigm holds that we should be concerned for the welfare of all mankind in a world consisting of mankind on the one hand, and the world's resources on the other, with the two linked by a complex socio-economic environmental system. Although man may change his social values (Harman 1976) and conservation may slow the depletion of resources, the entire system is too complex to expect it will be self-adjusting in even a near-optimal way. The policy maker turns to analysis and modification of the complex socio-economic-resource system in attempting to reduce inequities among people, to raise standards of living, and to reduce threats of local or even global conflict and catastrophe.

Today's world has regions and sectors more closely linked than ever before by modern communication and trade so that the world's problems tend to spill over from one region to another and from one sector to another. New kinds of problems, and indeed of crises, have appeared in which those things once regarded as good (large families, easy transportation into cities) have led to severe difficulties (overpopulation, decay of cities). Remedies may not be effective immediately—there may be a lag of one generation in making any real change in population growth, for example—and there is always the chance that the complexity of the system may defeat a chosen policy or even a group of policies.

The policy maker's problems are very basically those of great responsibility and great difficulty. He or she must attempt to improve the functioning of dynamic systems of awesome complexity whose structures and parameters are largely unknown. The policy maker is urged to adopt various policies by advisors with a variety of theories but often with no direct responsibility for results. Policy makers may escape censure, since it is often difficult to detect errors in policy because socio-economic systems are so complex and because there is no opportunity for applying an experimental approach. Ayres (1978, chapter 1) has spoken feelingly of the problems of economists and policy makers and, among other things, calls for a generalization of the classical economic paradigm and recognition of the need to deal with newer problems of economics which "concern optimal allocation of natural resources among sectors of society, selection of technologies to maximize desired outputs and minimize costly inputs and/or costly wastes, and selection of optimal pollution abatement strategies and investment schedules."

In order to modify a socio-economic-resource system, a number of system inputs or possible structural changes are available to policy makers (with much variation from country to country). These include new or altered taxes, imposition of controls of various kinds, fostering of technological transfer or innovation, import duties, pricing regulations, investments, fiscal and monetary policies, and more. All changes involve practical limitations, and it is desirable to choose permissible policies which may give desired effects while avoiding system oscillations which may be dangerous to the point of catastrophe. It should also be noted that a distinction must be made between long-range planning (or strategy) and shorter-range decision making (tactics).

It may very well be necessary to consider not one or two but a number of policies which to some degree must be implemented simultaneously. There will in general also be a multiplicity—probably a hierarchy—of goals. Some criterion or measurement of the degree of attainment of these goals, weighted according to their importance, is a most difficult part of assessing the results of policy in a model or in a real system.

It is attractive and indeed desirable to look at some simpler decisions, for example in monetary and fiscal matters in the U.S. economy, in a rather uncomplicated fashion (Dornbusch and Fischer 1978, chapter 16). This possibility does not mean that the same decisions should not be looked at with the aid of more complex (and more descriptive) models. When many countries are involved, with combinations of decisions, and when both long and short-range goals must be considered, it may be dangerous to work without some detailed models.

A model of modeling procedures was presented in figure 14.1, but many important modeling decisions are not indicated there. Some of the modeling alternatives include:

> scenario versus econometric modeling
> macroeconomics versus microeconomics
> long-range versus short-range studies
> degree of aggregation.

In many cases it is not a matter of clear-cut choice among alternatives but rather a choice of some useful combination of procedures; for example, scenario and econometric modeling approaches might be combined.

Also, a multiplicity of models may be needed. In particular, a combination of a somewhat simplified long-range planning model and a more detailed short-range decision-making model of the same region may be desirable.

The degree of geographical aggregation in a model and its sectoral detail in various regions are difficult matters which may be affected by available data and computer capability as well as socio-economic considerations. It does not seem that existing models have considered such important entities as transnational corporations, cartels, or producers' and consumers' organizations; a block diagram of a proposed model showing entities which should be considered is given in figure 14.6.

### Conclusions and Thoughts for the Future

In modeling, as in any other enterprise, the costs and risks must be balanced against the probable and possible advantages which may result from the activity. Cost-benefit analyses are particularly difficult in modeling because both costs and benefits include intangibles. But the needs are great, and we have seen an encouraging sequence of successful efforts in large-scale models ranging from the engineering problems of interplanetary probes to the description of DNA. Moreover, as Simon (1978) points out, it is no longer necessary to defend the proposition that mathematics can be used in the social and behavioral sciences. If observations

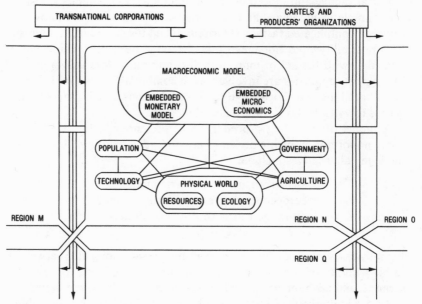

Fig. 14.6. Block diagram of part of a multiregion, multilevel socio-economic-resource model.

of the systems to be modeled provide the data, we have the requisites, need, and theory, as well as men and machines, to proceed with large-scale socio-economic-resource modeling. But ability to proceed does not mean that payoff is even possible, and it is well to enumerate some of the possible costs and benefits.

Measurable costs (which can easily be underestimated) include those of data gathering, for one of the intangible benefits of modeling is that it reveals shortcomings in both theory and data. Costs are proportional to the time spent on a modeling effort, and there is a chance that cost and elapsed time may build beyond expectations before answers are obtained and that in the meantime problems may have to be solved by other means.

One of the dangers in any modeling enterprise is a great gulf between modelers and supporting policy makers (see figure 14.1). Mistrust and lack of useful interaction may be worse if a rift between the two groups appears and grows, possibly as a result of unwarranted expectations of easy success on the part of either or both. Even if policy makers and modelers work well together, forecasts or aid in policy making cannot be better than the model is able to provide. Overconfidence in models more impressive than useful in their mathematical trappings and computer mysteries can be a danger too. Finally, model verification, validation, and evaluation procedures must not be skimped, and they do add significantly to costs and required time.

On the benefit side, there are solid advantages in the possibility of developing a tool which will help interpret the past, predict the future (within limits), and permit alternative policies to be examined. Other gains may result: recognition of gaps in theory, in data collection, or in inclusion of sectors or geographical areas may become apparent, and attention to these points can yield unexpected benefits.

It is often said that the use of modeling procedures by industrial firms becomes necessary because their competitors are using these methods; speed and accuracy of response to problems by the firm may not be adequate unless the methods employed by others are used. Regions and countries may regard themselves as being in competition with other regions and countries and therefore in need of any guidance that models can give. But more important by far is the competition between the future of a country or region and the best future that might be hoped for. Policies based on economic theories cannot effectively be tested or compared, nor can optimum parameter values be determined by extensive experiment with real socio-economic systems. Consideration of the importance of the issues and assessment of dangers, costs, and benefits may lead, not to a question of whether to model, but rather to a question of whether large socio-economic units can afford not to model.

## References

Andersen, Leonall C., and Keith M. Carlson. 1974. "St. Louis Model Revisited," *International Economic Review* 15: 305-27.

Arthur, W. Brian, and Geoffrey McNicoll. 1975. "Large Scale Simulation Models in Population and Development: What Use to Planners?" *Population and Development Review* 1: 251-65.

Ayres, Robert U. 1978. *Resources, Environment, and Economics: Applications of the Materials/Energy Balance Principle*. New York: Wiley.

Ball, Robert J., ed. 1973. *The International Linkage of National Economic Models*. Amsterdam: North Holland.

Baughman, Martin L., and Esteban Hnyilicza. 1975. "Energy Systems: Modeling and Policy Planning," *Proceedings of the IEEE* 63: 475-83.

Beneken, Jan E. W., and Vincent C. Rideout. 1968. "The Use of Multiple Models in Cardiovascular System Studies: Transport and Perturbation Methods," *IEEE Transactions on Bio-Medical Engineering* BME-15: 281-89.

Bergstrom, Abram R. 1967. *The Construction and Use of Economic Models*. London: English University Press.

Boulding, Kenneth E. 1966. *Economic Analysis, Volume II—Macroeconomics*. New York: Harper & Row.

Bruckmann, Gerhart, ed. 1977. *MOIRA: Food and Agriculture Model—*

*Proceedings of the Third IIASA Symposium on Global Modelling.* Laxenburg, Austria: International Institute for Applied Systems Analysis.

Burkhov, V. N. 1977. "Models and Mechanisms of Operation of Hierarchical Systems (Review)," *Automatika i Telemekhanika* 11: 106–31.

Burmeister, Edwin, and A. Rodney Dobell. 1972. "Guidance and Optimal Control of Free-Market Economies: A New Interpretation," *IEEE Transactions on Systems, Man, and Cybernetics* SMC-2: 9–15.

Calligan, C. G. 1976. "The Oregon State Simulation Model: A Laboratory for Policy Makers." In L. Dekker, ed., *Proceedings of the 8th Congress of the International Institute for Analog Computation and the International Association for Mathematics and Computers in Simulation.* Amsterdam: North Holland.

Christ, Carl F. 1966. *Econometric Models and Methods.* New York: Wiley.

Clark, John, and Sam Cole, with Ray Curnow and Mike Hopkins. 1975. *Global Simulation Models: A Comparative Study.* New York: Wiley.

Cole, H. S. D., Christopher Freeman, Marie Johoda, and K. L. R. Pavitt. 1973. *Models of Doom: A Critique of The Limits to Growth.* New York: Universe Books.

Cremer, J., and M. L. Weitzman. 1976. "OPEC and the Monopoly Price of World Oil," MIT-EL-76-015-WP. Massachusetts Institute of Technology Energy Lab, Cambridge, Massachusetts.

Cuypers, J. G. M., and O. Rademaker. 1974. "An Analysis of Forrester's World Dynamics Model," *Automatica* 10: 195–201.

Cyre, W. R., C. J. Davis, A. A. Frank, L. Jedynak, M. J. Redmond, and V. C. Rideout. 1977. "WISPAC: A Parallel Array Computer for Large-Scale System Simulation," *Simulation* 29: 165–72.

Daetz, D., and R. H. Pantell, eds. 1974. *Environmental Modeling: Analysis and Management.* Stroudsburg, Pennsylvania: Dowden, Hutchinson and Ross.

Day, Richard H., and Theodore Groves, eds. 1975. *Adaptive Economic Models.* New York: Academic Press.

Deam, R. J. 1974. "A World Energy Model." In Edward W. Erickson and Leonard Waverman, eds., *The Energy Question, Volume I—The World.* Toronto: University of Toronto Press, pp. 337–49.

Dornbusch, R., and S. Fischer. 1978. *Microeconomics.* New York: McGraw-Hill.

Elmaghraby, A. S. 1978. "Basic Needs Index: Delphi Application." In *Proceedings of the Wisconsin Seminar on Natural Resource Policies in Relation to Economic Development and International Cooperation,* vol. 3. Madison: Institute for Environmental Studies, University of Wisconsin.

Forrester, J. W. 1968. *Principles of Systems.* Cambridge, Massachusetts: Wright-Allen Press.

Forrester, J. W. 1969. *Urban Dynamics.* Cambridge, Massachusetts: MIT Press.

Forrester, J. W. 1971. *World Dynamics.* Cambridge, Massachusetts: Wright-Allen Press.

Fourcans, Andre, and Thomas J. Hindelang. 1975. "Capital Investment Evaluation for the Multinational Firm," *OMEGA* 3: 689–97.

Frisch, Ragnar. 1933. "Propagation Problems and Impulse Problems in Dynamic

Economics." In *Economic Essays in Honor of Gustan Cassel.* London: George Allen and Unwin, pp. 171–205.

Fromm, Gary, and Lawrence R. Klein. 1973. "A Comparison of Eleven Econometric Models of the United States." Papers and Proceedings of the 85th Annual Meeting of the American Economic Association, *American Economic Review* 63(2): 385–93.

Fromm, Gary, William L. Hamilton, and Diane E. Hamilton. 1975. *Federally Supported Mathematical Models: Survey and Analysis.* Washington, D.C.: U.S. Government Printing Office.

Glejser, Herbert, ed. 1976. *Quantitative Study of International Economic Relations.* Amsterdam: North Holland.

Graham, Alan K. 1972. "Modeling City-Suburb Interactions," *Transactions of the IEEE on Systems, Man and Cybernetics* SMC-2: 156–58.

Gutmanis, Ivars. 1975. "Input-Output Models in Economic and Environmental Policy Analyses," *Proceedings of the IEEE* 63: 431–37.

Hamilton, H. R., S. E. Goldstone, J. W. Milliman, A. L. Pugh III, E. B. Roberts, and A. Zellner. 1969. *Systems Simulation for Regional Analysis: An Application to River-Basin Planning.* Cambridge, Massachusetts: MIT Press.

Harman, Willis W. 1976. *An Incomplete Guide to the Future.* San Francisco: San Francisco Book Co.

Herrera, Amilcar. 1974. "Introduction and Basic Assumptions of the Model." In Gerhart Bruckmann, ed., *Latin American World Model: Proceedings of the Second IIASA Symposium on Global Modelling.* Laxenburg, Austria: International Institute for Applied Systems Analysis, pp. 3–8.

Hotelling, Harold. 1931. "The Economics of Exhaustible Resources," *Journal of Political Economy* 39: 137–75.

House, P. W., and John McLeod. 1977. *Large-Scale Models for Policy Evaluation.* New York: Wiley.

Jaeckel, M. T. 1972. "Forrester's Urban Dynamics: A Sociologist's Inductive Critique," *Transactions of the IEEE on Systems, Man, and Cybernetics* SMC-2: 200–216.

Jahoda, M. 1973. "Forecasting: Dilemmas and Assumptions." Science Policy Research Unit, University of Sussex, Sussex, England.

Johnston, John. 1963. *Econometric Methods.* New York: McGraw-Hill.

Kaya, Yoichi. 1977. "Report on Project FUGI—Future of Global Interdependence." Fifth IIASA Global Modelling Conference, International Institute for Applied Systems Analysis, Laxenburg, Austria.

Kaya, Yoichi, and Yutaka Suzuki. 1974. "Global Constraints and a New Vision for Development—II," *Technological Forecasting and Social Change* 6: 371–88.

Keynes, John Maynard. 1936. *The General Theory of Employment Interest and Money.* New York: Harcourt Brace.

Killingsworth, W. R. 1978. "Strategic Planning for Energy, Mining and Natural Resource Industries." In *Proceedings of the Wisconsin Seminar on Natural Resource Policies in Relation to Economic Development and International Cooperation,* vol. 1. Madison: Institute for Environmental Studies, University of Wisconsin.

Klein, Lawrence R. 1950. *Economic Fluctuations in the U.S., 1921–41*. New York: Wiley.

Klein, Lawrence R. 1976. "Five-year experience of linking national econometric models and of forecasting international trade." In Herbert Glejser, ed., *Quantitative Studies of International Economic Relations*. Amsterdam: North Holland, pp. 1–24.

Koopmans, Tjalling C. 1957. *Three Essays on the State of Economic Science*. New York: McGraw-Hill.

Koopmans, Tjalling C. 1978. *Energy Modeling for an Uncertain Future*. Washington, D.C.: National Academy of Sciences.

Kuhn, Thomas S. 1962. *The Structure of Scientific Revolutions*. Chicago: University of Chicago Press.

Labys, Walter C. 1973. *Dynamic Commodity Models: Specification, Estimation, and Simulation*. Lexington, Massachusetts: Lexington Books.

Labys, Walter C. 1977. "Commodity Markets and Models: The Range of Experience." Proceedings of the Conference on Stabilizing World Commodity Markets: Analysis, Practice and Policy, Artie, Virginia.

Leontief, Wassily W. 1966. *Input-Output Economics*. Oxford: Oxford University Press.

Leontief, Wassily W. 1977. *The Future of the World Economy*. New York: Oxford University Press.

Manne, Alan S. 1976. "ETA: A Model for Energy Technology Assessment," *Bell Journal of Economics* 7: 379–406.

Marshalla, Robert A. 1977. "Intertemporal Efficiency and the World Price of Oil —an Empirical Model," *Annals of Economic and Social Measurement* 6: 203–24.

Mass, Nathaniel J. 1975. *Economic Cycles: An Analysis of Underlying Causes*. Cambridge, Massachusetts: Wright-Allen Press.

McCalla, W. M. 1978. "An Optimizing Production Model for a Petroleum Exporting Country." In *Proceedings of the Wisconsin Seminar on Natural Resource Policies in Relation to Economic Development and International Cooperation*, vol. 3. Madison: Institute for Environmental Studies, University of Wisconsin.

McLeod, John. 1972. "Regional Model System—San Diego County," *Simulation* 19(4): v–viii.

McLeod, John. 1978. "FUGI: Another View of the World—and Modeling It," *Simulation* 36(6): vii–x.

Meadows, Dennis L., William W. Behrens III, Donella H. Meadows, Roger F. Naill, Jørgen Randers, and Erich K. O. Zahn. 1974. *Dynamics of Growth in a Finite World*. Cambridge, Massachusetts: Wright-Allen Press.

Meadows, Donella H., Dennis L. Meadows, Jørgen Randers, and William W. Behrens III. 1972. *The Limits to Growth*. New York: Universe Books.

Meadows, Donella H., Dennis L. Meadows, Jørgen Randers, and William W. Behrens III. 1973. "A Response to Sussex." In H. S. D. Cole, Christopher Freeman, Marie Jahoda, and K. L. R. Pavitt, *Models of Doom: A Critique of The Limits to Growth*. New York: Universe Books, pp. 217–40.

Mesarovic, Mihajlo, and Eduard Pestel. 1974a. *Mankind at the Turning Point: The Second Report to the Club of Rome.* New York: Dutton.

Mesarovic, Mihajlo, and Eduard Pestel, eds. 1974b. *Multilevel Computer Model of World Development System.* Laxenburg, Austria: International Institute for Applied Systems Analysis.

Modigliani, Franco. 1973. "The Channels of Monetary Policy in the FMP Econometric Model of the U.S." Massachusetts Institute of Technology, Cambridge, Massachusetts.

Naylor, T. H. 1971. *Computer Simulation Experiments with Models of Economic Systems.* New York: Wiley.

Orcutt, Guy H. 1962. "Microanalytic Models of the United States Economy: Need and Development." Papers and Proceedings of the 74th Annual Meeting of the American Economic Association, *American Economic Review* 52(2): 229–40.

Orcutt, Guy H., S. Caldwell, and R. Werteimer II. 1976. *Policy Exploration through Microanalytic Simulation.* Washington, D.C.: The Urban Institute.

Peterson, David W. 1975. "Transferring Ideas from Engineering to the Social Sciences," *Proceedings of the IEEE* 63: 354–59.

Porter, Howell R., and Ernest J. Henley. 1972. "Application of the Forrester Model to Harris County, Texas," *Transactions of the IEEE on Systems, Man, and Cybernetics* SMC-2: 180–91.

Pugh, R. E. 1977. *Evaluation of Policy Simulation Models: A Conceptual Approach and Case Study.* Washington, D.C.: Information Resources Press.

Quinn, J. E. M. 1977. "The Problems in Building Socio-Economic Mathematical Models for Use in the Developing Countries," *Proceedings of the First International Conference on Mathematical Modeling.* Rolla, Missouri: University of Missouri, pp. 2357–66.

Rajaraman, V., and V. C. Rideout. 1962. "A Survey of Adaptive Control Systems," *Proceedings of the AIEE on Automatic Control* 1(3): 10–27.

Rapaport, Anatol. 1959. "Uses and Limitations of Mathematical Models in Social Science." In Llewellyn Gross, ed., *Symposium on Sociological Theory.* Evanston, Illinois: Row Peterson, pp. 348–72.

Richardson, Harry W. 1972. *Input-Output and Regional Economics.* New York: Wiley.

Richardson, John M., Jr. 1978. "Global Modeling: A Survey and Appraisal." In *Proceedings of the Wisconsin Seminar on Natural Resource Policies in Relation to Economic Development and International Cooperation,* vol. 1. Madison: Institute for Environmental Studies, University of Wisconsin.

Robinson, L. F. 1972. "How GASP, SIMULA, and DYNAMO View a Problem." In I. M. McKay and J. McLeod, eds., *Progress in Simulation.* New York: Gordon and Breach.

Rosenblueth, Arturo, and Norbert Weiner. 1945. "The Role of Models in Science," *Philosophy of Science* 12: 316–21.

Runyan, Harry M. 1971. "Cybernetics of Economic Systems," *IEEE Transactions on Systems, Man, and Cybernetics* SMC-1: 8–18.

Sage, Andrew P. 1977. *Methodology for Large-Scale Systems.* New York: McGraw-Hill.

Schweppe, Fred C. 1973. *Uncertain Dynamic Systems*. Englewood Cliffs, New Jersey: Prentice-Hall.

Scolnik, Hugo, and Luis Talavera. 1974. "The Functioning of the Model and the Demographic Model." In Gerhart Bruckmann, ed., *Latin American World Model: Proceedings of the Second IIASA Symposium on Global Modelling*. Laxenburg, Austria: International Institute for Applied Systems Analysis, pp. 13–31.

Simon, Herbert A. 1978. "The Uses of Mathematics in the Social Sciences," *Mathematics and Computers in Simulation* 20: 159–66.

Slater, Charles C., and Geoffrey Walsham. 1975. "A Systems Simulation Model of the Kenyan Economy," *OMEGA* 3: 557–67.

Steinhart, J. S., M. E. Hanson, R. W. Gates, C. C. DeWinkel, K. Briody, M. Thornsjo, and S. Kabala. 1977. "A Low Energy Scenario for the United States: 1975–2050." In L. C. Ruedisili and M. W. Firebaugh, eds., *Perspectives on Energy: Issues, Ideas, and Environmental Dilemmas*. 2nd ed. New York: Oxford University Press, pp. 553–80.

Strongman, J. E., W. R. Killingsworth, and W. E. Cummings. 1978. "Materials Policy Analysis: A Case Study of Copper." Final Report for the Office of Science and Technology Policy, Pugh-Roberts Associates, Inc., Cambridge, Massachusetts.

Theil, Henri. 1966. *Applied Economic Forecasting*. Amsterdam: North Holland.

Tinbergen, Jan. 1959. "An Economic Policy for 1936." In J. Tinbergen, L. H. Klaassen, L. M. Koyck, and H. J. Witteveen, eds., *Selected Papers*. Amsterdam: North Holland.

Tinbergen, Jan. 1967. *Economic Policy: Principles and Design*. Amsterdam: North Holland.

Tinbergen, Jan, coord. 1976. *RIO—Reshaping the International Order: A Report to the Club of Rome*. New York: Dutton.

Tintner, Gerhard, and Jati K. Sengupta. 1972. *Stochastic Economics: Stochastic Processes, Control, and Programming*. New York: Academic Press.

Tukey, J. W. 1962. "The Future of Data Analysis," *American Mathematical Statistics* 33: 1–67.

Underwood, John. 1977. "Optimal Rules for Cartel Managers with Empirical Applications to the Copper and Tea Markets," *Annals of Economic and Social Measurement* 6: 231–43.

von Neumann, J. [G. Morgenstern, trans.]. 1945. "A Model of General Economic Equilibrium," *Review of Economic Studies* 13: 1–9.

Vousden, Neil. 1973. "Basic Theoretical Issues of Resource Depletion," *Journal of Economic Theory* 6: 126–43.

Watt, Kenneth F. 1977. "Why Won't Anyone Believe Us?" *Simulation* 28: 1–3.

Westcott, J. H. 1976. "Modeling and Control of the U.K. Economy." In V. C. Ho and S. K. Mitter, eds., *Directions in Large-Scale Systems*. New York: Plenum Press, pp. 253–63.

Zadeh, L. A. 1965. "Fuzzy Sets," *Information and Control* 8: 338–53.

# 15 *Peter Dorner & Mahmoud A. El-Shafie*

# Natural Resource and Development Policies

In this final chapter we focus on public policy. We cannot provide specific measures or recommendations on the detailed substantive content of policies. Such content must grow out of the situational context within which policies are developed. Our emphasis is on national policies, although later sections do deal with some of the special problems of policy formulation at the international level among some or all of the many independent nation-states.

The processes—political, intellectual, organizational—by which public policy is formulated may vary widely among nations. Yet the procedures underlying the decision-making process of choosing a development strategy and its policies need to be explicit and institutionally dependable. Neither a broad strategy nor specific substantive policies can be judged only in terms of the internal logical consistency of their elements and components. The final test is the consequences actually produced in the lives of people affected by policy. And requisite in that final test is that men and women affected by policies have a means—a reliable guaranteed procedure—to provide input and feedback in determining and modifying those policies.

We cannot claim that our assumptions in this discussion of natural resource and development policies are universally accepted, nor even that all authors of this volume agree with them. We have stated our views on these matters in a methodological note in the last section of this chapter. The substantive sections of the chapter should be comprehensible without it, yet we believe that a reading of our methodology of policy making will help to clarify our perspective and to provide a basis for understanding some of our policy recommendations. Furthermore, a theoretical conception of how policy judgments are arrived at, whether the one supplied at the end of this chapter or an alternative conception, is necessary. Without it there is a tendency for policy discussions to degenerate into expressions of abstract platitudes of high and noble purpose but purpose completely out of touch with the possibilities and opportunities offered in the real world of affairs.

Although we have made every attempt to be objective in this analysis, we know that our interpretations of events rest on our own evaluations and judgments. We do not, however, apologize for this because we know of no other way to deal with policy questions. To exclude political and social considerations of policy making in an attempt to achieve greater objectivity may result in a greater misrepresentation of the truth than any liberty that authors take in expressing their personal judgments (Amin 1974, p. xiii).

## Changing Perceptions of Natural Resource Supplies

Until quite recently, most nations and national policies seemed to operate on the implicit assumption that resources were, in practice at least, unlimited, that they would always be available as needed, at some price. This simple nationalistic faith failed to recognize the growing economic interdependence among nations. Most nations and policies also assumed that resources were a function of technology (which to a degree, in an economic sense, they are) and that scientists and engineers would always be able to develop new processes and substitutes in the event that some key mineral resource, or land or water for that matter, became scarce.

Europe and Japan have for many years depended on substantial imports of food, petroleum, and minerals. The United States was much more self-sufficient—indeed has been an exporter of many raw materials and remains the largest single exporter of agricultural products—but it too has become increasingly reliant on certain resource imports. Many of the world's resources, especially minerals and petroleum, are of course produced in the developing countries, but the ownership of the economic and technical capabilities for resource exploitation and use is centered in the industrial countries. Until the end of World War II, many of the developing countries were political colonies of the industrial countries; political and economic relations of dependence and the cheap labor in the colonies kept the prices of energy resources and other raw materials low relative to the prices of manufactured products. Because resources seemed unlimited and were cheap, no great need to economize or to conserve them was appreciated.

The assumptions of cheap and plentiful resources meshed well with the predominant and basically nationalistic diagnosis, following the great depression of the 1930s, that the root of the problem of boom and bust economic fluctuations was a recurring deficiency in aggregate demand. Spending, public and private, was the prescription for a high rate of economic growth, and effective management of fiscal and monetary policy was the key instrument for assuring that growth. With sufficient purchasing power, the objectives of full employment of existing manpower, plant, and equipment would be reached and would in turn yield ever-increasing incomes and material well being. That this kind of growth also required an exponential and eventually unsustainable rise in the rates of use of natural resources was not given much thought, and " . . . so it came about that, with this particular and perhaps unintended bent to Keynesianism, a new ethic developed which tended to replace the protestant ethic of frugality in which the industrial world was born" (Castillo 1978).

Rapid rates of population growth in many parts of the world, the dismantling of the colonial system, the drive for political and economic independence by former colonies, the new nations' express desire for more rapid economic growth and development, and the rapid recovery and economic expansion of the industrial nations after World War II have prompted new worries about the availability of enough natural resources to accommodate all these demands. Landscape destruction, soil depletion and erosion, animal and plant extinction, and especially degradation of air and water quality have lately reinforced the postwar perception that ours is a world of limited resources in practice as well as theory.

The old optimism about resource availability has undergone a fundamental change. It is now rather widely recognized that natural resources must be used prudently not only in order to improve the quality of life but also to assure its very preservation.

Concurrently, the developing countries have asserted a greater measure of control over their natural resources, especially petroleum, some minerals, and certain agricultural commodities. The structure of effective ownership and control of these resources has been changing rapidly and pervasively with corresponding repercussions on the conditions of energy and materials supply. These structural changes influence decisions about the quantities of resources that flow into channels of international trade, the rates at which they flow, the forms in which they become available, and the prices at which they can be had. The changes that are taking place are permanent, and " . . . the required adjustments will not be found in the return to any 'normal' conditions of the past; rather, they will give rise to new situations that must be envisaged, designed, and created in actual practice. In addition, the changes that are taking place are pervasive . . . the future will not lead simply to a world of 'expensive' or costly resources. Rather, it will make for a whole new world of politics and economics" (Castillo 1978).

## Natural Resources and Markets

Resource issues have international dimensions quite simply because raw materials and semiprocessed commodities enter the trade among nations. Both exporters and importers have vital interests in that trade, but policy making on resource issues is still confined, by and large, to individual nation-states. Petroleum-exporting countries have organized to achieve greater control over pricing and rates of extraction; whether the same degree of control can be gained by exporters of other resources remains an open question. Up to now, at least, no economically competitive substitutes have been developed for the oil so crucial to current technology. For the present and immediately foreseeable future there is no international authority, and there are few alternatives to the nation-state in making policy on resource use and conservation, taxation, commodity pricing, and market access. Nevertheless, Castillo's "new world of politics and economics" demands that novel policies to deal with all these resource issues and more be envisaged and designed, and "free" markets have simply not done an acceptable job in the view of many of the parties involved.

Markets have not, of course, been free; there have always been interferences with the "free" market. Where there are major disparities in the distribution of income and economic power, the market mechanism ceases to function either efficiently or equitably. It becomes weighted heavily in favor of those with the most purchasing power, and the poor do not have that purchasing power by which market decisions are influenced. Impotence is especially apparent at the international level because there is no world government and few of the usual mechanisms that create pressures for redistribution of income and wealth within countries (ul Haq 1976, p. 3).

Mechanisms for equalizing or offsetting economic power do exist within at least some nations. The industrial countries, for example, have developed specific production and pricing policies for their agricultural commodities and producers. True, such policies "distort" the prices and incomes which would be achieved by unregulated markets and may restrict market entry by other nations wanting to export farm products. Furthermore, in providing a measure of protection to agricultural producers, these policies may raise the price of food to domestic consumers as well as the cost of living for consumers in other nations which must import these farm commodities. Such policies can be carried to extremes justifiable only if the national security of a nation is clearly threatened, but the distortions of moderate and judicious agricultural protection are a matter of degree and nature in which severity is in part a function of the means by which the protection is provided—via the price system, for example, rather than direct income transfer payments.

Agriculture is invariably one of the more competitive sectors, and agricultural producers are price takers for both the inputs they buy from the less-competitive industrial sector and the products they sell to the less-competitive agri-business processing and marketing sector. Through a variety of governmental interventions, the economic power of agricultural producers has been enhanced by allowing them some price-setting power.

The issue is the same for resource commodities moving in international trade. The objectives of gaining some influence over price (and quantity) of exports are more stable prices and earnings and more favorable terms of exchange—both of which are also objectives of internal policies for agricultural producers. There may, however, be one key difference, depending upon the nature of the commodities in question. Agricultural production depends on the use of renewable flow resources (land, water, sunshine, labor) as well as a variety of stock resources, but a nation economically reliant on mining and exporting finite mineral or petroleum resources is, in effect, selling off part of its nonrenewable heritage. (Of course in a larger sense, all natural resources are nonrenewable if appropriate conservation measures are not taken.) The special task for producers of stock resources is to determine a rate of exports and a price for them which will permit improvements in the standard of life of the population as well as the rates of capital accumulation and investment needed to put equivalent income-producing capacity in place as finite resources become depleted and exhausted.

Nothing in this perspective argues against markets or calls for downplaying the role of price in resource use and conservation. A policy designed to regulate and administer *all* prices and quantities of goods is practically impossible at national levels and completely out of reason at the international level. Markets are vital institutions which give the flexibility for registering new conditions of demand and supply. On the other hand, there is a need to achieve greater stability and to avoid wildly fluctuating prices which can be debilitating for the economies of both exporters and importers. Exporters are particularly concerned with the terms of exchange between their raw materials and the finished capital and consumer goods that they import. They want the return on their raw material production to help in transforming their economies, increasing productivity, and diversifying exports.

The point is that there is and has been intervention in current markets but a one-sided intervention. In like manner, before the farm policies of the past 50 years in the industrial countries, market intervention in some sectors—the economic power to influence quantity and price—affected not just those sectors but worked to the disadvantage of the more competitive price-taking sectors. This one-sided intervention was balanced by intervention on the part of government (or in some cases commodity organizations) to countervail the power on the other side of the market. Markets continue to function and to play a most significant role, but the power on both sides of the market is more equal than it was before the countervailing intervention. Power equalization is also the issue in the international markets for raw materials and resource commodities.

The great advantage of markets which function effectively and equitably is that they provide a self-regulating mechanism for adjusting supply and demand through price and for encouraging innovation, improvement, and new production processes. Price trends provide information to consumers and producers whose self-interest induces corrective action to bring supply and demand into balance. When markets do not function equitably, intervention should be restricted to certain strategic points where it has the best chance of success in correcting the grossest inequities. Any attempt to control and administer specific prices at too many points in the entire market chain spawns a growing and cumbersome bureaucracy which eventually loses the ability to make changes. Prices get frozen and lead not only to inefficiencies but also to new inequities. It is important to try to utilize, wherever possible, marketlike mechanisms and incentives to achieve the public purposes desired (Schultze 1977).

All risk and uncertainty cannot and should not be eliminated. Prices need to be free to move within a certain range, perhaps a narrower one with a higher floor than an unregulated market would provide. It is important, however, to preserve the possibility of making mistakes, to allow decision makers to suffer the consequences of their mistaken judgments, and to reward them for good judgments. Comparisons need to be made, *not* between a perfectly functioning market and a rather complex and imperfect regulatory scheme, but between an imperfect market and an imperfect regulatory scheme.

Market interventions may well have side effects on the "innocent bystander." Government intervention in agricultural markets, to return to this example, may raise the short-run price of food, although in the long run the increased level and stability of farm income can actually lead to new investments, increased productivity, and lower food prices. Nevertheless, while farmers' economic condition vis-à-vis industrial suppliers and marketing firms (and urban workers in general) improves, poor consumers and those not a part of the more concentrated and unionized industrial sectors may suffer a loss of purchasing power with higher food prices. Policy must be sensitive to the harmful effects that neutral third parties bear and must include offsetting measures.

Raising the price of some resource commodity in international trade may improve the terms of trade for exports vis-à-vis certain imports. This is what the market intervention is intended to do, but here again there are third-party countries which must pay the higher price for the resource with no offsetting gain. Special provisions may have to be made at the international level to transfer funds and mitigate these disadvantages, especially for the poorer nations. The abrupt increase in petroleum prices in 1973–74, for example, was accompanied by some transfer measures which reduced the burden of these high prices for poor, oil-importing countries. Such compensatory schemes may remain imperfect, but it is important not to lose sight of the need for them. It should be possible to develop measures which assure greater equity for "innocent bystanders" and to incorporate those measures into negotiated marketing agreements for specific commodities.

Higher prices for commodities (especially petroleum, which has a very wide range of end uses) may be intended to shift more of the resource to specific uses. They can indeed achieve some measure of conservation and cause a resource to be rationed, at least roughly, to its highest value uses (Schultze 1977, p. 77), but the question of value depends on who does the valuing under what standards. The process is complicated by major disparities in income distribution both within and among countries. For example, chemicals and synthetics derived from petroleum may be high value uses, but those uses are important mainly to the rich. Kerosene may be a low value use, but kerosene is an important fuel for the poor. If higher prices are used to restrict *low priority* uses of the same product (e.g., gasoline for pleasure boats and automobile racing—and some would not agree with our priorities), the higher price might eliminate uses of much higher priority (auto transport to get to work for those without access to public transportation) before it had any real impact on low priority uses by those well able to afford boating and racing. Price alone can be too blunt and nondiscriminatory an instrument, and it must often be accompanied by subsidies, rationing for particular uses, and other nonmarket distributive mechanisms.

## Opportunities and Responsibilities of Nation-States

Some economic and social problems are strictly domestic; many others have inescapable domestic components and complications which can be resolved only by the people and government of a particular nation. It is illusory to think that countries can do little until external problems of international order and international trade are settled. Self-help *is* important. Charity *must* begin at home. An improved distribution of income *and especially of opportunity* within countries is an obligation of every nation, and that responsibility cannot be delegated without loss of a nation's sovereignty. It is equally defensive and deceptive for industrial countries to contend that they can do little to help until all internal structural reforms have been accomplished by the developing countries. Both faces of this argument are self-serving excuses of the rich and powerful—not the poor and weak—within and among nations.

Inequity within or among nations will not be corrected by economic growth alone. Economic growth has a strong and inherent tendency to skew income distribution and to concentrate its benefits among those able to seize and capitalize, for whatever reason, on the opportunities offered by growth. There is a constant need for redistributive measures to counter this tendency and to provide access to opportunities for those less advantageously situated. The phenomenon also occurs at the international level and so does the same need for redress. The mechanisms of redress at the international level are not adequately developed and this is, of course, one of the primary issues in the debate about the international economic order. However, redistribution at home is not dependent on redistribution at the international level.

It must be reemphasized that *redistribution of opportunity*—rather than a mere redistribution of current income without a change in the opportunity structure—is the core of the problem. The redistribution of current purchasing power to those incapable of working will remain necessary in all societies. But to look upon that sort of redistribution as in any sense approaching a solution to problems of massive poverty, unemployment, and inequality is grossly to misinterpret the functions of government. Even if it is possible to alleviate the worst poverty through postproduction distribution, people cannot simply be placed "on ice" until such time as they are needed. People must be engaged in worthwhile productive activities in order to develop the skills, capacities, and discipline that a productive agriculture and industry require. Output, employment, and distribution objectives must be combined and harmonized within the same policy, and that harmony may be impossible without a redistribution of property and opportunity and related structural changes. National reforms in the internal order are vital " . . . in order to pass on whatever gains are achieved internationally to the masses rather than to a handful of privileged groups. It is also vital in order to gain credibility for the demands for a new international economic order. We cannot very well ask for equality of opportunity internationally if we in the Third World deny the same equality of opportunity to our own people. That is why it is vital that we undertake, in the next phase, major reforms in the internal order" (ul Haq 1976, p. 49).

The extreme case of internal self-help and redistribution is the Peoples' Republic of China. China did not seek outside assistance in its internal transformation; in fact it shunned assistance. Only after several decades of virtual isolation has China begun opening its borders and seeking more trade and scientific interaction with the rest of the world. The Chinese formula, however, would be difficult to follow in smaller nations. China is a continent unto itself, self-sufficient in most of its basic developmental needs and not very dependent on international trade. Many small nations do not have this kind of internal option except as they join their resources, markets, scientific capacity, and investment plans with other nations in some form of regional integration.

Nevertheless, the developing nations can and must see major internal opportunities as well as domestic obligations and responsibilities. A development strategy with a greater balance between agriculture and industry —one standing on two legs, in the Chinese aphorism—and with a greater reliance on renewable resources in both those sectors does offer opportunities for greater self-reliance.

In the understandable urge for rapid development, agriculture has often been slighted and industry pursued along the same lines as in the industrial countries. Those subsectors within agriculture which have gotten some attention have often become more resource and capital intensive than local conditions warrant. The development of both agriculture and industry must shift to paths less dependent on finite stock resources and more reliant on renewable flow resources. In most cases, the developing countries have a better chance to find such paths because they are not yet committed and tied to the resource- and energy-intensive production processes that predominate in the industrial countries. The latter will have to make similar adjustments, but their task will be more difficult.

A more egalitarian opportunity structure which increases earning potential for the poorer segments of a nation's population will help to shift demand in favor of commodities produced with local renewable resources and more labor-intensive methods (Thiesenhusen 1972). The wealthier parts of many developing countries' populations seem to have adopted many of the consumption habits of people in the industrial countries. It is, of course, unlikely that complete income equality is possible or even desirable, but future expansion of personal incomes for those now at the top of the pyramid is unlikely to make demand for goods and services consistent with a balanced development strategy. The expansion of personal incomes for those at the lower levels of the present pyramid might well allow a nation to become more self-reliant in terms of the use and exploitation of locally available resources.

The greatest uncaptured opportunity within most of the developing countries is development of the human resource. Natural resources in the purely physical sense are finite; human intelligence and skills, so far as we know, are not. It is indeed a tragic waste that so many millions of people have had no opportunity to be challenged to develop their human capacities —both the powers of the mind and the skills of physical dexterity. Even the untutored and unsophisticated mind has much to contribute, given the opportunity. All individuals are potentially creative. Human skills and capacities, developed through formal schooling *and* work opportunities, are any nation's true and basic renewable resource. The driving force in the development process is not provided by investment plans and projects of public administrators and private entrepreneurs, important as these are. The informed self-interest and the growing skills of the mass of farmers and urban workers, and their creative human energies, are the real impulse for any long-term progress.

The human resource plays a dual role. Man is a resource as well as the user of resources. Every individual is both user and used, the interested and the object of interest, the reason for development and the means of its realization. Labor is sometimes treated as simply another input in the production process. It is that, and it does represent a cost to be entered in the calculations of planning and project evaluation. But how easy to lose sight of the fact that development must be by and for all the people and that opportunities and incentives and skills are required for its achievement. A society shortchanges itself if it draws upon no more than a small fraction of its potential human creativity, the basic renewable resource. Basic literacy and jobs are requisite if the mass of people now on the fringes of development are to become the valuable national resource they all could in fact be and if they are to improve upon their own condition in the process. There will always be some men and women who do not care to respond to opportunities or test their capacities, but all should be given the chance to develop their potential abilities to the fullest.

Providing opportunities to people is not solely a matter of national interest. The extended human family draws upon the creative genius of its members from all races and all areas of the globe. We of the living generation are the beneficiaries of the human resources, the knowledge and skills, nurtured by past generations. We are apprehensive, and appropriately so, over the welfare of future generations lest our indulgent consumption dissipate some critical resources and jeopardize the future of our children and grandchildren and generations beyond. Yet we do need to retain perspective and include the human resources of the present among our concerns. What is the most valuable of the collective social assets that we pass on to our heirs? We are the future generation of generations past; what were the most valuable assets we inherited? Among them were undoubtedly accumulated and dependable knowledge and skills, institutions, and social organizations. The resources of any society include and indeed are defined by its acquired skills—technological, managerial, professional, and organizational—the intangible capital embodied in the living generation.

Short-term interests may often govern the acts of individuals, but society needs a leadership, a vision, and a strategy that protects and encompasses the interests of future generations. The current generation *must* make long-term economic and social investments for future generations. The present generation is most shortsighted if those who happen to hold advantage (no matter their nation) neglect their responsibility for the investments which will benefit the heirs of the poor. Security is not a need confined to the aged of this generation; it is important to the working population of today so that they may give their children the education and investment that they will need to fully appreciate, utilize, and build upon their inheritance from all past humanity. It is in this way that the security and opportunities of the current generation extend to the future.

Much is heard today about development being a "zero-sum-game"— that whatever one nation gains, another must lose or, in a broader sense, that all the material "progress" made to date by means of science and technology is a delusion based on reckless consumption of "geological capital" in the form of coal, oil, mineral deposits, and the very soil of our sustenance. It is a truism that exponential growth in consumption of resources cannot continue indefinitely, yet many believe that the very recognition of these limits is an important first step, that the problems are not of immediately catastrophic proportions, that it is not too late to deal with them, and that it is possible to find new directions in science and technology and human preferences. Whatever the conclusion with respect to these issues might eventually be, it is a certainty that there is no zero-sum game, in either a narrow or a broad sense, in human knowledge and intelligence. Knowledge grows not in isolation and preservation but in use and distribution.

Most developing countries know that they need greater and more "appropriate" scientific and technological skills—or technological self-reliance. But technological self-reliance means more than having a growing number of people trained in the science and technology of the industrial countries. It means the development of science and technology motivated by indigenous needs and circumstances and organically related to the culture and economy in which they are expected to take root and grow. The basis for evolving a more appropriate science and technology is, in most cases, in place in the practices of local people who have for generations worked with and used their creative talents on the resources available to them. The rising rate of transfer of production techniques from the industrial countries could continue to erode and might eventually destroy the knowledge and the skills which could form the base for a more appropriate science and technology. That transfer is necessary and will, of course, continue, but it should be a highly selective process. The main point, however, is that the evolution of appropriate indigenous science and technology requires basic education for all the people from whose ranks must be drawn the working scientists of the future. People who understand and have actually worked with the existing technological base are, again, that important human resource which needs freedom and the opportunity to nurture indigenous talents. Once this process is underway, highly trained and sophisticated scientific minds can find a greater challenge in working on their country's internal technological needs rather than those of the industrial countries.

The strategic importance of developing the human resource is, of course, not confined to the developing countries. The industrial nations share these opportunities and responsibilities. Here we must think not in terms of categories of nations but in terms of people. People everywhere, in all nations rich and poor, have aspirations and needs and potential creative contributions which cut across conventional political borders. The needs of the poor, especially, are immediate and compelling; the conditions in which they find themselves are not generally of their own making or choosing; their contributions, if they are encouraged to make them, will not be confined to their own welfare but will be shared by humanity in general—by the current generation and generations unborn.

Some responsibilities for adjustment and change are more nearly confined to the industrial nations. For example, it has been estimated that the average individual in the major industrial countries consumes at least six times as much energy as his counterpart in the developing countries. If there is to be a greater effort at conservation of resources, the industrial nations must obviously be answerable for most of the savings. This does not mean halting all growth of national product, but it does mean reducing personal income growth to the point of eventual income stability (Vlerick 1978). That stability will demand simultaneous redistributive measures within the industrial countries because they also have many poor people.

Consumption patterns are only in part a private individual matter. Some individuals may decide of their own volition to cut back on buying and using resource- and energy-intensive products, but their savings will likely be invested in further production of these very products or loaned to others who will buy and use more of the same products. And the judgment (even the sanity) of an individual who asked for a cut in income would certainly be questioned. Even though many people might welcome the opportunity of getting off the treadmill of the mass consumption societies, individuals on their own are relatively helpless to change the system. Basic adjustments can be brought about only by public policy measures— conservation, taxation, rationing, manipulation of the price system, etc.

Whatever form such policies may take, resource conservation through lower growth of personal income and eventual income stability is a basic obligation of the industrial countries. Achieving those objectives will be very difficult because a basic premise of their economic systems is continuous growth in income, investment, production, and consumption. That obstacle notwithstanding, "If we in the West are going to insist that we must have regular increases in our standard of living, no matter who foots the bill, if we continue to rely, as we have relied in the last thirty years, on endless growth and endless consumption as a way out of our self-induced economic problems, disaster will strike us all, rich and poor alike" (Barraclough 1978).

Another fundamental responsibility of the industrial nations is adequate support for research and development in new sources of energy and in modifying production processes to make more effective use of the world's natural resources. They must also work toward an accommodation in the structure of manufacturing so that increased processing of materials and other manufacturing can, over time, take place in the developing countries (Castillo 1978). These too will be difficult adjustments, especially in a slow-growth economy. However, declining rates of population growth and a stabilizing labor force will help to make the adjustments in the industrial countries less painful. Although such fundamental adjustments must be made, they need to be made gradually over several decades to avoid undue disruption.

The industrial countries must also confront their problems of inflation and recession (and in recent times, inflation combined with substantial unemployment). A shift to lower rates of growth, especially in the resource- and energy-intensive commodity and service sectors, and movement toward personal income stability (with more equitable distribution) would probably reduce inflation. These same shifts would, however, tend to foster unemployment. The public policies for dealing with these complex problems have not yet been envisaged. Although there is a great deal of interest in these policy issues on the part of some professionals and some people in public office, much research, public education, and negotiation will be required to arrive at acceptable compromises. There are also no solid data or sound estimates about the impact of reduced economic growth rates in the industrial countries on international trade. If the developing countries can raise their growth rates, and especially if increased trade can be developed among them, the effects of the decline of imports by the industrial countries could be mitigated.

## The Prospects for Joint Action

We assume that a reduction in current inequalities (both within and among nations) is a desirable direction for future world development and that movement in this direction is likely to restrain destructive confrontations and serve as a firmer base for international cooperation. We conclude that the major international issues are those of markets, resources, terms of trade, economic and consumption growth rates, and differentials among parties in economic and political power.

To deal with these issues on a global scale, however, neither a central actor nor a clear mechanism for designing strategy and appropriate policies is available. There are many primary actors—nation-states large and small, rich and poor, and all shades between. There are many gaps in knowledge, and there is no single, internationally accepted institution for designing policies and especially for taking and enforcing action on these issues. The leadership of the UN and its various agencies is vital in providing a forum for debate and in formulating alternative approaches, but thus far at least nation-state members have been unwilling to provide these agencies with much policy-making and enforcement authority.

Most chapters in this volume, including this one, have often lumped nations into two broad and convenient categories—the developing and the industrial countries. This dichotomy is useful for some conceptual purposes examined later, but too frequently it is an oversimplification of real interests and issues. The World Bank (1978) now uses the somewhat more detailed but potentially misleading classification of Low Income Countries; Middle Income Countries; Capital Surplus Oil Exporting Countries; Industrial Countries (all of the OECD member countries except Greece, Portugal, Spain, and Turkey, which are Middle Income Countries); and the Centrally Planned Economies. These classes are still too broad for many purposes. Each includes countries of great variety in size (population, geographic area, or GNP), industrial base, dependence on imports of food and raw materials, etc. For example, both India and Ethiopia are listed among the low income countries, yet India has more than 600 million people, while Ethiopia has fewer than 30 million. Ethiopia is primarily agricultural, but India has an industrial base larger than those of several industrial countries.

The diversity within any such classes is, of course, widely recognized. Less often recognized, at least explicitly, is the diversity within the class of industrial countries. There are differences not only of size but also of dependence on international trade, vulnerability to economic and political maneuvers, and interpretation of threats to national security and sovereignty. The industrial countries, in other words, are not a monolithic entity when it comes to economic and political interests. These interests have perhaps become more divergent since 1974 because of variation in the degree of dependence on future resource (especially petroleum) availability and access.

The problem of economic security—security of supplies—is a real problem. Beyond economic security is national security in general. These dual concerns of economic and general security are especially felt by the European states and Japan because of their greater dependence on resource imports. For them, the idea that accepting or rejecting whatever is offered in terms of foreign investments, especially in the resources field, should be left entirely to the developing countries is not wholly agreeable. "I would agree with this approach," says one European observer, "were it not for this problem of security which is very substantial, especially for us Europeans and for the Japanese" (de Montbrial 1978).

Other lines of divergence in industrial countries' interests are more specific. The dispute among Japan, the United States, and the EEC over Japanese export surpluses and the insistent European and American pressure for restrictions on Japanese exports have turned Japanese attention to alternative outlets, particularly in Southeast Asia. The Common Agricultural Policy of the EEC is a major point of contention between the EEC and the United States, and it was a heavy blow to Australia and New Zealand. After British entry in the EEC, both countries were given five years, until 1978, to cut down if not actually eliminate their traditional exports of relatively cheap farm produce (butter, cheese, meat) to Britain (Barraclough 1978). Australia and New Zealand have since drawn closer to several Southeast Asian nations.

Although no exclusive relationships are anticipated, Barraclough (1978) and others see in these divisions within the industrial world some prospective new alignments and relationships between certain industrial nations and regional groups of developing nations: Europe with Africa and the Middle East; Japan, Australia, and New Zealand with Asia; and the

United States with Latin America. The Lomé convention gives some precedent for such regional ties in terms of trading agreements. Negotiated in 1975, it established a preferential trading arrangement between the EEC and 46 developing countries (four more countries have since been added) of Africa, the Caribbean, and the Pacific, with both reciprocal trade preferences and an aid program operated through the European Development Fund (Barraclough 1978).

Diversity of interests is also prominent within the World Bank's categories of nonindustrial countries, although its income classes can be understood as shorthand descriptions of some of the development assistance needs of low income and middle income nations. Financial and technical assistance for the low income countries must include more grants and "soft" loans to accelerate development of their human and physical resources, to expand employment opportunities, and to enhance distributional equity. Some of these countries, however, have already made substantial progress in developing resources and badly need better market access for their growing diversity of exports.

The middle income countries, although also a most diverse group of nations, are thought to be those which could benefit most by greater access to markets in the industrial countries. These nations can get their needed capital through the regular "hard" loans of the World and Regional Banks, and they are also the principal borrowers from the commercial banking systems of the industrial countries.

Various levels of regional integration and cooperation could provide very significant joint investment and development options for both low and middle income countries and others where economies of size and complementarities in resource pooling offer advantages realizable only in a market larger than that of an individual nation. The same holds for some infrastructural projects in transport and communications systems, for river projects, for scientific and technological coordination, and more.

The final World Bank category of countries, the centrally planned economies, certainly shows much variation too, especially between the USSR and the Peoples' Republic of China, but also among the smaller nations. As a group, these countries are not so closely tied to resource marketing issues as the developing and industrial countries are. Some developing nations, of course, do have strong economic and marketing links to the centrally planned nations, and the industrial countries and the centrally planned economies have expanded trade ties in a variety of commodities and capital goods. It is difficult to envision any really "new" international economic order without cooperation and more participation by the centrally planned economies, which so far have not figured importantly in most issues and proposals of the "North-South debate." Perhaps the most energy and resource intensive kind of production is military hardware, and an end to the armaments race, let alone an absolute reduction in arms, cannot be achieved without this participation.

The World Bank categories and others like them have uses, but in the complex negotiations over commodity marketing and other agreements, the resource policies of the many nation-states involved can hardly be coordinated or harmonized along such simple lines. Some tension and friction and pressure for change are inevitable and, under current circumstances at least, desirable. Nevertheless, in a world dominated by big governments and big businesses, some grouping and pooling of strength is required in order even to attempt to get a fair shake within the international system. The question is—what forms can such grouping take? No two nations have identical or even roughly comparable interests on all issues, and diversity and conflict in any negotiations are likely to be a function not only of the number of countries involved but also of the number of issues on the agenda. For concrete negotiation, bargaining groups (on both sides of the question) will often have to shape themselves in terms of specific issues and specific resources. Some will undoubtedly interpret this practical need as an attempt to weaken resource exporters and to strengthen importers. On most of these issues, however, strength is not to be found in numbers but in control over a strategic commodity or service. This has certainly been well demonstrated by the oil-exporting countries. Furthermore, bringing the big transnational corporations under the more effective control and accountability of a common set of rules is perhaps more likely to be achieved by smaller groups of nations dealing with a specific resource commodity.

This perspective does not deny the possibility of effective linkages among commodity agreements. But the prospect of simultaneously negotiating agreements for 15 or 20 diverse resource commodities by scores of nations with conflicting interests in those resources does not seem promising. In other words, we see severe limits to comprehensive "big package" solutions. Negotiations on many particulars and agreements on specific cooperative measures will probably have to take place at more disaggregate scales, but the more inclusive "North-South" deliberations can help to establish fundamental ideas of common purpose and broad strategy. A concerted stance by many nations may also serve to dramatize certain issues. Even though many of the developing countries which must import oil were adversely affected by OPEC's price increases, as a group they stood behind and supported OPEC's actions. And, judging from events in the past five years, one must count them correct in doing so: They have gotten assistance to offset some of the burden of the higher price for oil, and perhaps more important, they have found new sources of strength and organizational capacity for bringing attention to their problems and for countering the political power of the industrial countries. Agreements on new marketing and pricing practices for a host of raw materials is a very long and difficult job. Perfect solutions are not going to appear. Any resolution of nations' competing interests or world society's problems will be partly satisfactory at best, and it is useless to try to judge the nature and significance of real problems in terms of some abstract utopia. The question is whether proposed resolutions to particular issues are likely to move us along a more promising, more equitable, more sustainable, and less hazardous path than the one on which we now find ourselves.

No complex social organization or technological system springs full-blown from the individual mind or the social process. Systems grow and evolve out of simpler forms; they reach greater size and complexity over time by modifying and restructuring elements of the system, many of them relatively minor elements. That modification and evolution is based on human experience and experiment.

The problem of finding new means and procedures which will improve the terms of trade and the stability of export earnings for exporters and at the same time accommodate the critical needs of importers calls first of all for a mutual willingness to enter discussion and debate and negotiation. "From history we know that such vast changes of purpose have sometimes been achieved by cooperation and dialogue, sometimes by direct and even bloody confrontation, perhaps most often by a confused and uncertain mixture of both confrontation and cooperation. The reason for the uncertainty is obvious. Those who profit by a system become obsessed by their determination to change nothing. . . . Those who suffer can, on the contrary, come to believe that nothing short of total disruption will genuinely affect anything. . . . At this level of polarization, dialogue is impossible and violence inevitable. . . . The task is, therefore, to discover the . . . basic common interests for the whole human species and the workable mixture of dialogue and confrontation that will permit the nations, both the weak and the strong, to discover those interests together . . . " (Ward 1974, quoted in ul Haq 1976, pp. 20–21).

## Toward International Cooperation

Powerful nations were once relatively unrestrained in acting to achieve what they interpreted as their own interests. The weak had to depend on the goodwill and self-imposed forbearance of the strong and powerful; they had to rely on the strong to refrain voluntarily from using power to its limit. For the weak, freedom of action was a privilege granted them by the more powerful. A half-century ago, transnational corporations, too, were more or less able to do as they wished " . . . introducing 'gunboat diplomacy' and 'market forces' and setting royalties. It took challenges— expropriations and other products of evolving 'national unity,' 'strong government,' and 'local experience and expertise'—before multinational operations became a matter of negotiation" (Kanel 1978).

Although none of these manifestations of international power have disappeared, there have been substantial changes in the exercise of such power during the past 30 years. The nation-states of the world have become increasingly interdependent, and even the most powerful actors are restrained in their acts; they must include in the calculation of self-interest the interests of other actors. Even the most powerful are not immune to the adverse consequences of their own acts, and too narrow a view of self-interest in today's interdependent world can prove disastrous.

The problem, of course, is not with power per se. Any system needs power to drive it—physical, economic, political, and moral power. A new world order will not arise from good intentions alone. The problem with power is to prevent its abuses without destroying its necessary functions. It is easy, indeed fashionable, to criticize economically strong states or transnational corporations, and there is much to criticize legitimately. Yet one can hardly imagine a functioning world economy without them. The need is to improve them, to devise ways to make them more accountable, to make them feel more of the adverse consequences of their acts, and so to provide incentives for them to expand their conception of a narrow self-interest to a wider interest. The prerequisite for correcting the abuses of power is identifying not villains and heros but defects in the incentive system that drives ordinary decent people into doing things contrary to the public good (Schultze 1977, p. 18). Powerful organizations are run, after all, by ordinary people, usually quite decent people.

There is an admittedly long way to go if we are to move from a conflictive and potentially destructive present to a more harmonious and cooperative future. New institutional rules and arrangements cannot just restrain but, when applied to all, must serve to liberate the opportunities and make secure the rights of the weak as well as the strong.

There is a need for continuing pressure on the part of the Third World vis-à-vis the industrial world in order to build greater solidarity, bargaining strength, and self-reliance among developing countries. Without these achievements they will continue to depend on the goodwill and forbearance of the industrial nations. Creating such solidarity is not a simple matter—there are real and tremendous cleavages among nations—but it can, we believe, be accomplished. There have already been achievements in trade and international finance, and much more can be done in these areas. There has been a beginning, at least, of a process in which national aims are modified by and jointly determined with those of other states. The process of simultaneous determination of means and ends of national policy has begun to be extended to include international variables and the means and ends of other states.

There are indeed prospects beyond such broad "processes" and piecemeal achievements, but very great obstacles also remain. The international economy or system is not a larger version of a nation state. There is no sovereign authority; there are no accepted procedures for defining the public interest for the world at large. Using power in the public interest—difficult enough at the level of the nation-state—is a function of objective knowledge, of the ability to see with reasonable accuracy the consequences of public action, of established and protected procedures for the participation of people, and of firm leadership with the moral authority to put immediate interests in the perspective of society's long-run interests. These requisites, especially the last, are obviously not met at the international level. Most of the current international negotiations and confrontations involve interest groups trying to work out procedures for achieving parallel power in relation to existing powers.

The president of the World Bank has suggested that the common interests of nations call for a "global compact": a strategy for alleviating poverty within a reasonable time, identifying aid and trade responsibilities of industrial countries, and pressing policy reforms and structural changes in developing countries to improve efficiency of resource use and equity in distribution (Karaosmanoglu 1978). However, many past resolutions and "compacts" have gone unfulfilled. Who would enforce the compact? What recourse would developing countries have if aid goals went unmet, just as the target of 0.7 percent of GNP that industrial nations were to have earmarked for development assistance did? What recourse would industrial nations have if structural reforms meant so little as is evident in the few instituted under past UN resolutions? Recourse is still mostly a matter of goodwill and good intentions rather than constitutionally secured rights and duties.

A "global compact" might work for those resources not yet under dominion of sovereign states—the unclaimed part of the oceans, the atmosphere, other planets, etc. In any event, it is about the only instrument available and so must be tried. Even in these cases, cooperative agreement is no simple matter, as evidenced by the long and tedious deliberations over an acceptable law of the seas.

Another concept of the way in which accord on power is reached is that of stalemate: "An opportunity to set new rules preserving necessary administrative power and eliminating personal abuse of power comes when a stalemate between powers occurs, when for whatever reasons neither the 'weak' nor the 'strong' are able to get all they want under existing rules" (Kanel 1978). Both sides find it advantageous, in this stalemate of power, to change the rules defining rights and duties. This concept of stalemated powers has been demonstrated by labor unions and industrial employers; it has also on occasion been evidenced by individual governments in confrontation with powerful transnational corporations. But a stalemate in power requires defined, focussed, and specific interests. In labor unions' struggles with big business, newly agreed rules provided workers with higher wages, more job security, and better working conditions, while employers were assured a stable work force and uninterrupted use of plant. For people who were not part of a particular bargain, higher prices for the industry's products prompted similar struggles, stalemates, and agreements in other industries and sectors of the economy. Many workers in the service trades, small-scale industry, and agriculture, however, were unable to achieve the same results through organization. There were, in other words, many innocent bystanders who could not on their own recover from the adverse effects of power and organization within the more concentrated economic sectors.

Within nation-states innocent bystanders have recourse to a hierarchy of public powers, with the sovereign national power at the apex, to seek redress of such disadvantages. (The mere fact of nationhood does not assure that redress of grievances will actually be forthcoming. Real redress is a function of established and available public procedures.) The point is, of course, that there is no hierarchical structure of power at the world level. Power at the international level is horizontal or parallel power distributed not among equally powerful but nevertheless among equally sovereign states. Perhaps " . . . current relations among the world's sovereign states might be at a point which parallels the 'estate stage' of 14th century England. . . . Contesting interest groups had no clear powerful sovereign center. The 'estate stage' exhibits contractual, not constitutional, relations and 'peace' by exercise of forbearance" (Parsons 1978).

OPEC, for example, has achieved significant power relative to oil-importing states. And although the capital surplus oil-exporting nations (as well as international agencies) have increased their assistance to poorer oil-importing developing countries, the latter have no constitutional right to such claims, and the former have no constitutional duty to meet them. Procedures for making such rights and duties secure, binding, and enforceable by law do not exist. Other producer groups can organize and seek similar results, but oil is something of a special case among resources. For a variety of reasons, attempts to achieve or expand countervailing power along commodity lines will leave many innocent bystanders still dependent on goodwill and forbearance. New institutional procedures will have to be devised to allow innocent bystander nations redress for injury as a secured right and not merely as a handout at the discretion of the more powerful.

The prospects for reforms of such magnitude, while difficult, confusing, and complex, are not unpromising. Institutions do evolve in response to challenges. Extending and identifying "self-interest" within ever-widening contexts is a basic ingredient of human history. As individuals, we learn to identify with the extended interest of our immediate family at an early age. We have little difficulty in identifying our self-interest with that of the local community. The creation and acceptance of nation-states required people to expand their concept of self-interest beyond the local tribe or community and to give loyalty to a larger social organization.

We do extend sympathy and our concept of self-interest to other nations and at times to all of humanity, at least on some matters. Sympathies, however, ordinarily lack a practical procedural basis. We feel, but we have no means of implementing our feelings. The nations of the world are groping for new institutional means by which national self-interest can be extended and identified with a procedurally secured public interest among nations. Modern communication, trade, and interdependence permit no turning back. A new world order is dependent upon man's ability to extend his concept of community and self-interest in new directions, toward an ethic which " . . . would lead to a saner society, free from the assault of the superfluous, keen to the provision of real needs, prudent in the use of its inherited gifts, just in the relations of its communities, and fully dedicated to the celebration and to the enrichment of life" (Castillo 1978).

## A Methodological Note on Public Policy

Policy must be more than a set of abstractions laid down in a national development plan. Policies consist of concrete objectives, of rules and procedures for developing those objectives, and of substantive acts—implementation—for attaining objectives. Objectives must not only be consistent among themselves, and consistent too in terms of a broader and more comprehensive strategy, but must also be practical and feasible. Policy can be judged only in terms of its consequences—in terms of the difference that it makes in the real world of men and women and their lives.

The designers of policy must remember that it does deal, ultimately, with effects on real people, those living and those yet to be born. The character of natural resource and development policies means that the activating unit will ordinarily be the nation-state. There is much discussion of "old" and "new" international orders, but most policies are time and place specific and are developed by actors at the level of the nation-state. It is within the nation-state as an organizing entity that social judgments and decisions about natural resource use and conservation must be made. Although we have seen attempts to set common international objectives in the UN's declared development decades, such objectives remain empty gestures unless action is taken by nation-states. One cannot discuss policy in a meaningful way without identifying the procedures by which it is formulated and the means and sanctions by which it is implemented and enforced. Actors or activators must be identifiable.

There are, of course, some "international actors" and some international policies. Prime examples are the directorates of major transnational corporations. Their actions may not be considered "public" policy, but the actors are identifiable and their decisions of corporate strategy and policy do integrate, in a coordinated way, variables that cut across national boundaries. There are also some public bodies which formulate and carry out policies on an international level, although not necessarily a worldwide scale—the World Bank, the International Monetary Fund, the UN and its agencies, and others. There are some effective multination commodity organizations which deal with the production, pricing, and marketing of some resources, and there are many bilateral and multilateral agreements. Yet in almost all cases, it is the nation-state as a sovereign governing unit that must concur in such international arrangements or deny its support and oppose such arrangements.

Consequently we emphasize policy making at the national level. Development policies are particularly specific in time and place and must be made at the national level. Policies at regional or international levels, to be effective, must be integrated with or translated into policies at the national level.

## A Framework for National Policy Development

Devising and evaluating public policies involve questions of procedure, strategy, and specific substantive courses of public or government action on some current social or economic problem. In the literature, "policy" discussions usually focus on specific solutions to more or less specific problems. Substantive courses of public action, however, cannot simply be ad hoc responses to current and ever-changing issues and conflicts. A long-term strategy with criteria for selecting specific policies and for judging their relevance and consistency is essential. A national strategy reflects the ideological position (the idealism) of a society with respect to the economic, social, and institutional order that it wishes to create or maintain. Strategy must incorporate those basic structural and institutional changes necessary to achieve and to support the desired national order. A strategy for change might call, for instance, for redistributing land within a system of private property (or conversely, eliminating individual property in land), restructuring the educational system, nationalizing some foreign enterprises (or conversely, inviting some enterprises to work within the country), etc. Strategy catchwords—redistribution with growth, meeting basic human needs, technological self-reliance, and others—can be quite meaningless, nothing more than deceptive diversions, unless they truly embody commitments to public action both feasible and consistent with clear and precise objectives.

Such indistinct concepts as progress, equity, stability, efficiency, security, or rationality have very little value as guides to public action. Progress for whom? Equity for whom? Stability of what? What kind of efficiency under what distributional assumption? Relating clear-cut policy measures to such broad, ill-defined goals is difficult because many policies could be claimed to meet them. They fall in much the same class as appeals to "natural law" in settling disputes; all parties can, and usually do, claim to have God on their side.

What is thought to be progress, even by wide consensus, in the short and medium run may prove disastrous in the longer run. Short-run instability (however measured) may be the only route to long-run stability. Goals, or their more precise expression as objectives, have little meaning except in direct relation to effective and acceptable means for their attainment.

A problem, whether private/individual or public/social, is not a fabrication of the mind. Problems are real phenomena in which objectives as well as means for their achievement are hazy or indeterminate.

The notion of a problem as a "gap" between some ideal value of a variable and its actual value in life is a mechanical concept of society and of little use in formulating policy. Such a concept is obviously useful in evaluating homeostatic systems (significant departures from the "ideal" temperature of the human body do indicate a "problem" to the physician), but there are few if any homeostatic variables in social systems. There is instead constant change and movement. The radical ideas and ideals of one era become the forte of conservative philosophy in another.

In world affairs, consequences of action are neither simple nor unidimensional. Any policy has a multitude of consequences beyond those specifically sought. These "extra" consequences cannot be ignored; they may negate or jeopardize other aims. In this sense the means chosen for trying to attain one objective (eliminating inflation, for example) are also setting (or at least influencing) other objectives (levels of investment and employment). The latter consequences may be unacceptable to the very people anxious to control inflation. Measures toward one objective must be evaluated in terms of their effects on other variables and objectives. It is within this pragmatic effort of evaluation, negotiation, *and experimentation* (because projected consequences are always probabilistic) that ends and means of policy must be simultaneously determined. This holds true to a degree in any nation irrespective of its political form because leaders and policy makers are not totally immune, at least in the longer run, to the consequences of their own acts.

### Policies and Programs

Policies are more flexible than strategies. In the very course of moving toward objectives delineated by a strategy for development, both planned and unanticipated change will require that policies be altered and redirected. More than one policy may be consistent with overall strategy. A more equal distribution of employment and income earning opportunities in the agricultural sector, for instance, might be achieved with a small farm system, a system of production cooperatives, or a mix of both. A free and unregulated market might serve well for some commodities (or at some times), while greater state control might be required for other commodities (or at other times). The means of achieving policy objectives must be determined simultaneously with these objectives, modified when necessary, and kept consistent with strategy. Finally, subcriteria must be developed and research must be carried out to see whether a policy is actually performing as intended.

A level of public action (primarily administrative/managerial) of even greater flexibility than policy is that of program and tactics, which must accommodate the diverse physical, economic, social, and other circumstances where policy is expected to apply. When explicit difficulties and conflicts arise (or when performance is judged inadequate or inconsistent with objectives), the initial response in addressing the problem is modification of programs within the range of action permitted by a policy. If the problem persists, and if enough such instances of poor performance are registered, a particular policy may need to be changed. Alternative policies must be within the range of policies consistent with a particular strategy. If conflicts persist, if measured performance continues to fall short of objectives, the strategy itself comes up for review and eventual change.

### Procedural Issues

"In the long run," according to Meehan (1978), "the constitutional principles adopted for making policies, the policies developed to guide the policy-makers, will have a greater impact on human affairs than any particular policy adopted toward some current social problem." The crucial procedural principles undergirding the substantive matters of strategy, policy, and program do not lend themselves to easy or general description; every nation has its own special political and social organization. The final test of strategy or policy is not internal consistency of means and objectives but the real consequences actually produced. Policies are oriented to the future, of course, and their consequences can be estimated only imperfectly. Policy must be seen as an experimental process in which people are able and willing to learn from failure as well as from success and able to modify policy based on such lessons. Failure and success are not self-evident properties. Controlled and objective research must determine whether consequences—desired ones as well as, inevitably, undesired ones—are on balance favorable.

In addition to constant monitoring of specific policies and their consequences (a condition not met in most countries), there is an urgent need for an unbiased and systematic feedback of information from the people affected (or unaffected) by policy. There are hazards when policy making is controlled by a small, relatively unchanging elite who may become insulated from the real world or get biased reports from a bureaucracy too interested in protecting its own judgments and security. The powers of government and the wisdom of government planning from the top down are limited to the extent that the governed (the people) are not involved in the policy making and implementing processes. People are not only affected by government plans and decisions but *their voluntary acts must be enlisted to bring plans to fruition.*

Can economic development be viable and self-sustaining if most of the people are excluded from effective participation? Participation takes two forms—participation in defining the "public interest" through the political process and participation in producing and distributing the fruits of economic growth. If we define economic development in the broad sense of expanding opportunities and human capacities to exploit them while reducing mass poverty, unemployment, and inequality, we know from casual observation that development can occur without the participation of all the people in either the political or economic spheres. But will development stagnate or even regress if, for example, less than half of the people participate in the processes of policy making? Will development spread and gradually enlist a growing majority if at least half the people share the fruits of growth? Although we have little evidence on these questions, they are matters that must concern those with authority and responsibility for the design of policies.

The procedural issues underlying strategies and policies involve the great questions of keeping people in authority responsive to the needs of the weaker segments (frequently the majority) of society, of fashioning rules to keep policy makers from abusing their power, and of restraining the power of strong private interests to bend public policies for their own benefit. There is no guarantee against the abuse of power except involving more and more people in the policy-making process and creating a climate of freedom so the poor and the weak can organize to bring their needs and demands to the attention of those in power (Brown 1971). The weaker segments of society must share the powers of citizenship and state sovereignty. The potential power of those who have organized themselves in common cause is of four types:

1. Moral and persuasive power brings the plight and the needs of the weak before a wider public and before the powerful and may itself induce officials or others to institute policies of greater benefit to the weak.
2. Self-help through cooperative efforts—the very fact of establishing a common ground and finding common interests—may reveal unrecognized potentials for resource pooling and self-help. Organized groups may in fact (and in cooperation with still others) establish subeconomies within the larger economy and become more self-reliant. Once a greater self-reliance is established, people may find that they can bargain more effectively on policy issues at the national level.
3. Where their circumstances permit, withholding a much-needed service or commodity from the more powerful may provide the weak with leverage for influencing and persuading policy makers.
4. Resistance, if all else fails, may be persuasive to those in power because of the potential threat of violence.

The potential for organizing these kinds of countervailing power and using them effectively depends on many factors (see Galbraith 1952). Powerlessness may be linked to ethnic or other social distinctions. The latitude allowed the weak by the powerful will be an important factor, but it should be clear that those in power at any time are not all of one mind nor always solidly unified. There are diverse positions on issues among factions within any government, and some factions may encourage and identify with some excluded groups in order to enhance and enlarge their own power and popular support. Different groups among the poor may find and identify with different government factions, play off one against the other, and thus obtain some power and concrete advantages in the process.

Finally, the role and the potential power of leadership must not be overlooked. Leaders, people in authority, cannot be effective if they merely respond to the variety of special short-run interests of individuals or groups within society. Policy making demands objective knowledge about alternative courses of action and their consequences. Policy makers must listen to the expressed needs and interests of many people within a society. Effective leadership, however, requires all this and more. Society, unlike an individual, has no fixed life span. It is what it is because of actions taken by generations in the past. Society's current generations must not only provide for the present but must plan and provide for future generations. The leaders of a society, of a nation-state in our terms of reference, must view society as a whole in addition to seeing its individual parts; they must recognize the needs of the future as well as the short-term demands of the present. Leaders must be educators, and to educate effectively they need moral authority and respect acquired through personal integrity, discipline, and uncorruptibility.

A leader must understand the problems and needs of the current generation *and* be able to put them into perspective so that ordinary people can judge their immediate interests vis-à-vis the long-term interests of the society to which they belong. The mark of true leadership is the ability to make unpopular decisions without losing popular support. This comes about as close as possible, in our judgment, to a definition of what is meant by the public interest.

## The Role of Research

The "ends" of government are far from simple. Research on policy questions is vital but also very difficult. To assume that research is simply a matter of working out the means toward an objective set by policy makers is not very helpful. Research itself must deal with the ends of policy—it cannot be avoided—because means are also ends. Conflicting ends, limited resources and capacities, risks and uncertainties, and particular distributions of economic and political power all provide the ingredients of policy. Despite this complexity, policy decisions must frequently be made on issues arising in such urgent forms and such novel contexts that decisions are forced before any research effort can be directed to the matter.

The research enterprise (past, present, and future; biological, physical, and social) is directed toward understanding and verifying how things and events are causally related. Knowledge, the end product of research appropriately conducted, enhances the ability to calculate and project some of the consequences of action and to associate probabilities of occurrence with these projections. Research can help to determine what is possible. Although we are unlikely ever to reduce the possible (the opportunity function) to a single point or do away with all uncertainty about which consequences follow what actions, uncertainty can certainly be narrowed. This is the chief practical contribution of the scientific method. Lessening uncertainty can also reduce divergence in social preferences and evaluations because there will be fewer disagreements over what is possible (Boulding 1958, p. 169).

Knowledge about the possibilities for action and the limits to action is absolutely essential for intelligent decision making. Knowledge *is* power, and it includes the ability to use power intelligently and humanely (Meehan 1978). But if research is to relate more directly to the possibilities and limits of action for particular policy questions, researchers must communicate with policy makers and must be sensitive to the simultaneous determination of means and ends. To be useful in policy making, research must establish the range of possibilities by incorporating into the research design the real world's conflicts and interests *as judged by the researcher* and not solely by official policy positions. This approach demands independence on the part of researchers. It requires courage on the part of the researcher and a willingness to become truly immersed in the contentious problems surrounding major policy questions.

This is a big order, and the scientific and professional disciplines have a long way to go if they are to meet these obligations. It is imperative to protect freedom of speech and of inquiry. The state must support research, though not attempt to curb or control it, even though the conclusions of research may contradict the positions held by the very policy makers who finance it. What are the alternatives? How else can we assure that policy is indeed in the public interest?

Assurances that public action will protect the weak and the powerless (and those yet unborn), and not only the strong and the influential of the current generation, cannot be supplied by any particular policy. Policy, as well as strategy, must change in view of changing circumstances. Nor can such assurances be conferred by absolute power and authority, no matter how benevolent and well intentioned, because power can become corrupted and its vision distorted and outdated without constant feedback and controlled inquiry. Total dependence on a bureaucracy and "in-house" research is likely to go astray because of vested interests in particular policies and bureaucracies' unwarranted belief in their own importance and wisdom. Defining the public interest and instituting policies supportive of that interest are functions of the procedures by which reliable knowledge is obtained and of the corollary public participation by which policies are formulated and conflicts resolved.

Given a climate of free inquiry and open participation of people in the affairs of government, a strong leadership with moral authority can design strategies and policies by which powerful private interests (and public officials too) are induced to act not only in their own interests but in the broader public interest as well. The broad and elusive yet desirable societal goals of justice, equity, and freedom are not substantive ones to be achieved by some specific policy; they (or their opposites) are instead the outcome of the collective procedures by which a society determines its developmental strategies and policies, by which it defines *the public interest*. Criteria for judging any nation or society are more likely to be the collective procedures which that society has created and sustained rather than the material conditions of life of its people.

There are, of course, times of crisis in any nation when certain rights of participation are restricted. There may be external threats to a nation's self-perceived security and integrity as a nation. Sometimes the threats come from within. Too often such threats, real or imagined, lead to repression rather than to a concerted effort to reevaluate and modify the procedures available to the people for joining in the economic and political citizenship of their nation. Modification of these public procedures may be the only way to embark on a new development strategy, with new directions to policies and a more comprehensive participation and utilization of the most fundamental resource—human beings.

## References

Amin, Galal. 1974. *The Modernization of Poverty*. Leiden, The Netherlands: E. J. Brill.

Barraclough, Geoffrey. 1978. "The Struggle for the Third World," *New York Review of Books* 27(17): 47–58.

Boulding, Kenneth E. 1958. *The Skills of the Economist*. Cleveland: Howard Allen, Inc.

Brown, Marion. 1971. "Peasant Organizations as Vehicles of Reform." In Peter Dorner, ed., *Land Reform in Latin America: Issues and Cases. Land Economics Monograph no. 3*. Madison: University of Wisconsin, pp. 187–206.

Castillo, Carlos M. 1978. "The Political Economy of Natural Resources." In *Proceedings of the Wisconsin Seminar on Natural Resource Policies in Relation to Economic Development and International Cooperation*, vol. 1. Madison: Institute for Environmental Studies, University of Wisconsin.

de Montbrial, Thierry. 1978. "Comment." In *From Marshall Plan to Global Interdependence: New Challenges for the Industrialized Nations*. Paris: Organisation for Economic Cooperation and Development.

Galbraith, John Kenneth. 1952. *American Capitalism: The Concept of Countervailing Power*. Boston: Houghton Mifflin.

Kanel, Don. 1978. "Power and Property as Issues in Institutional Economics and Economic Development." In *Proceedings of the Wisconsin Seminar on Natural Resource Policies in Relation to Economic Development and International Cooperation*, vol. 2. Madison: Institute for Environmental Studies, University of Wisconsin.

Karaosmanoglu, Attila. 1978. "Comment." In *From Marshall Plan to Global Interdependence: New Challenges for the Industrialized Nations.* Paris: Organisation for Economic Cooperation and Development.

Meehan, Eugene J. 1978. "Science and Policy-Making: Achieving Mutual Reinforcement." In *Proceedings of the Wisconsin Seminar on Natural Resource Policies in Relation to Economic Development and International Cooperation,* vol. 1. Madison: Institute for Environmental Studies, University of Wisconsin.

Parsons, Kenneth H. 1978. "Public Policy on Natural Resources, Economic Development, and International Cooperation." In *Proceedings of the Wisconsin Seminar on Natural Resource Policies in Relation to Economic Development and International Cooperation,* vol. 2. Madison: Institute for Environmental Studies, University of Wisconsin.

Schultze, Charles L. 1977. *The Public Use of Private Interest.* Washington, D.C.: The Brookings Institution.

Thiesenhusen, W. C. 1972. "A Suggested Policy for Industrial Reinvigoration in Latin America," *Journal of Latin American Studies* 4: 85–104.

ul Haq, Mahbub. 1976. *The Third World and the International Economic Order.* Development Paper no. 22. Washington, D.C.: Overseas Development Council.

Vlerick, André J. 1978. "Comment." In *From Marshall Plan to Global Interdependence: New Challenges for the Industrialized Nations.* Paris: Organisation for Economic Cooperation and Development.

Ward, Barbara. 1974. A statement before the International Symposium on Patterns of Resource Use, Environment, and Development Strategies. United Nations Environment Program and United Nations Conference on Trade and Development, Cocoyoc, Mexico.

World Bank. 1978. *World Development Report, 1978.* New York: Oxford University Press.

# INDEX

# Index

Aden, 231

Africa: per capita GNP in, 28; cost and potential of new land development in, 288; Saharan, 362; and the Lomé convention, 470; mentioned, 255, 265, 298, 310, 391, 469

Agrarian-industrial transition: substitution of stock for flow resources, 20, 21

Agricultural pricing policies, 458, 459

Agricultural research: of needs, 284–85; international centers for, 285–86

Alaska, 19, 51

Alaskan tundra, 95. See also Ecosystems

Algeria: iron ore exporter, 160; and liquid natural gas, 224; natural gas production and utilization, 226; exports and imports, 243; mentioned, 223, 236, 333

Alliance for Progress, 262, 353

Americas: growth of tomatoes in, 93

Andean region: growth of tomatoes in, 92

Antarctic, 405

Antarctica: practices joint national control over resources, 396–97; mentioned, 48

Antarctic Treaty of 1959, 397

Arab Center for the Transfer and Development of Technology, 325

Arab countries, 310, 318, 374

Arab Economic Unity Council, 258

Arab Fund, 230

Arabian Peninsula, 104

Arab-Israeli War of 1973, 247

Arab League, 230, 322

Arab Science and Technology Fund, 325

Aramco, 224

Arctic, 248

Argentina, 27, 265, 439

Armaments: drain on energy and resources by, 33

Asia: changes in grain trade of, 27; and per capita GNP, 28; high-yielding variety acreage in, 283; proportion of world population and land in, 287; mentioned, 49, 97, 255, 265, 310, 337, 469

Association of Southeast Asian Nations, 258

Australia: new copper discoveries in, 56; wheat exporter, 155; iron ore exporter, 160; mentioned, 307, 374, 406, 469

Australopithecus, 92

Bahrain, 42, 223, 226, 229, 243

Balance of power, 367

Bandung, 334

Bangladesh, 337

Bariloche model, 69, 439

Basic human needs strategy: cost estimates of, 377

Bauxite: major exporter of, 265

Biological species: valuation of, endangered, 26

Bolivia, 265, 307

Brandt, Willy, 345

Brazil: and the International Coffee Agreement, 157–58; and export diversification, 265, 267, 292; indebtedness of, 294; and Eurocurrency credits, 295; pricing of coffee in, 355; mentioned, 406

Bretton Woods agreements, 296, 338

Brookings model, 435

Buffer stocks, 137–38, 158. See also Stockpiling

Bulgaria, 307

Burma, 265

Burundi, 265

Cacao: major exporter, 265
Canada: major grain exporter, 27; new
copper discoveries in, 56; wheat exports, 155; copper exporter, 160; technological directions of, 189, 306; oil
refinery production in, 214; fishery
limits, 390; and developmental assistance, 404; mentioned, 49, 374, 406
Capitalism: liberal, 257
Carbon budget: world, 96, 97. *See also*
Ecosystems
Caribbean: and Lomé Convention, 470;
mentioned, 155, 159, 298
Carrying capacity: concepts of, 80–86;
and overgrazing, 82–84; and food, 84–
86
Cartel: formation of, by developing coun-
tries, 136; mentioned, 121, 122, 140,
141, 143, 246
Cartels: international, 363–64; in model-
ing, 441–42, 447
CASTARAB (Conference of Ministers of
Arab States Responsible for the Appli-
cation of Science and Technology to
Development), 325
Center for Economic and Social Studies
of the Third World (CESSTW), 345
Central Africa, 287
Central America, 287
Central American Common Market, 258
Chad, 265
Chile, 53, 56, 159, 160, 265, 391
China, People's Republic of: major tea
exporter, 158; and internally generated
technology, 196–97; and thermody-
namic efficiencies, 197; and backyard
steelmaking, 197–98; and crude oil,
247; and participatory development,
263; and population growth, 281, 282;
proportion of land cropped in, 287;
and food purchases, 342; and self-help,
463; mentioned, 71n, 307, 470
Classical economists: on economic devel-
opment, 260, 369
Classification of nations: used by World
Bank, 468
Climatic change, 98, 99
Club of Rome model, 79, 80
Club of Rome report, 109
Cobb-Douglas function, 125n, 126

Coffee: major exporters of, 265
Colombia, 265, 292
Colonialism, 7, 359–60, 381, 457
Colonial policies: of Britain and West
European nations, 20; economic or
political origins of, 20
Colonies, dependent: and industrial states,
4
Colorado River, 91; U.S.-Mexican inter-
ests in, 405
Committee of Development Planning,
348
Commodity agreements, international:
Tin, 137–38, 158, 392, 412; Wheat,
157, 392, 412; Coffee, 157–58, 392,
412; Cocoa, 158; Commonwealth
Sugar, 158; Lomé Convention, 158;
Sugar, 158; Tea, 158; mentioned, 31
Commodity producers' associations: Inter-
governmental Council for Copper Ex-
porting Countries, 159–60; Interna-
tional Bauxite Association, 160; Iron
Ore Exporting Countries, 160; Organi-
zation of the Petroleum Exporting
Countries, 160; International Tin
Council, 161
Commodity trade: major flows in, 27, 28
Common Agricultural Policy: of the EEC,
469
"Common heritage" principle, 400–401
Common property, 114. *See also* Public
good
Communist bloc, 145
Compensatory Financing Facility, IMF,
298
Congo, 265
Convention on the Protection of the Ma-
rine Environment of the Baltic Sea
Area (1974), 396
Convention on the Protection of the Med-
iterranean Against Pollution (1976),
396
Copper: estimates for the United States,
39, 40; production costs, 53; ore
grades, 53, 55, 56; and energy require-
ments, 89; and environmental burdens,
89; major exporters of, 265
Cotton: major exporters of, 265
Council of Mutual Economic Assistance
(CMEA), 155, 159, 257

COMPOSED BY METRICOMP, GRUNDY CENTER, IOWA
MANUFACTURED BY KINGSPORT PRESS, KINGSPORT, TENNESSEE
TEXT AND DISPLAY LINES ARE SET IN TIMES ROMAN

Library of Congress Cataloging in Publication Data
Wisconsin Seminar on Natural Resource Policies
in Relation to Economic Development and International Cooperation,
University of Wisconsin—Madison, 1977-1978.
    Resources and development.
        Co-sponsored by the
University of Wisconsin—Madison and others.
    Includes bibliographies and index.
    1. Natural resources—Congresses.   2. Economic
development—Congresses.   3. International economic relations—Congresses.
    I. Dorner, Peter, 1925-   II. Shafie, Mahmoud A.
    III. Wisconsin. University-Madison.   IV. Title.
    HC55.W57        1977a        333.7        80-10577
                ISBN 0-299-08250-4